DICTIONARY
OF THEOLOGY

Karl Rahner
Herbert Vorgrimler

DICTIONARY
OF THEOLOGY

SECOND EDITION

CROSSROAD ● NEW YORK

1985
The Crossroad Publishing Company
370 Lexington Avenue, New York, NY 10017

Original edition:
Kleines Theologisches Wörterbuch, 10th edition
by Karl Rahner and Herbert Vorgrimler
with the assistance of Kuno Füssell
Verlag Herder, Freiburg, 1976

First English edition 1965
Published in Great Britain under the title
Concise Theological Dictionary and in the United States
under the title *Theological Dictionary*

Second edition, 1981
Translated by Richard Strachan, David Smith,
Robert Nowell and Sarah O'Brien Twohig
Copyright © Herder KG, 1965, 1976, 1981

Printed in the United States of America

Library of Congress Cataloging in Publication Data

Rahner, Karl, 1904-   Dictionary of theology.

Translation of: Kleines theologisches Wörterbuch.
1. Theology—Dictionaries. 2. Catholic Church—Dictionaries.
I. Vorgrimler, Herbert. II. Strachan, Richard.
III. Title.   BR95.R313 1981   230'.2'0321   81-5492
ISBN 0-8245-0040-7   AACR2
ISBN 0-8245-0691-X (pbk.)

Authors' Preface

The first German edition of this book was published in December 1961. It was so well received that we felt our purpose had been understood and appreciated. This second, thoroughly revised and augmented English edition, is translated from the tenth German edition. Like the first, it is intended to provide brief explanations, in alphabetical order, of the most important concepts of modern Catholic dogmatic theology for readers who are prepared to make a certain intellectual effort. Simply to repeat time-honoured formulae would have been easier, but this has not been done. Concerned though we have been with the unity of theology and its object, no dictionary, of course, can be a substitute for the systematic exposition of Christian truth, and certainly not so condensed a volume as this present one. It is not a dictionary of biblical theology, or of apologetics, or of fundamental theology; but we take into consideration the difficulties that non-Catholic Christians feel with regard to Catholic dogma. We have tried to accomplish our task, thus circumscribed, so far as a concise edition will permit. It is these considerations of space which forced us to dispense with bibliographies, to curtail articles on the history of dogma, to distinguish between fundamental articles of some length and brief notices, to provide such sparse references to Scripture and the latest edition of Denzinger, and so on. We are keenly aware of the sacrifices which our strict confinement within this scope has required, and fair criticism of the book must take this into account. As each of the two authors has contributed about half the text, it seemed unnecessary to specify the precise authorship of each section. Some new explanations are by Kuno Füssell.

For the new edition we have revised all the articles, and rewritten many of them substantially or entirely. We have included a number of new articles and removed those which now seem inappropriate. Where necessary, we have included references to Vatican II.

Theology in the last quarter of this century has had to answer more attentively to criticism than when the first edition of this book was conceived. We have tried to confront several new aspects of theology, but without seeming to claim that Christianity knows the answer to everything.

Karl Rahner
Herbert Vorgrimler

Publishers' Preface

We can only repeat what the late Cornelius Ernst, OP, wrote when prefacing the first English edition: 'This edition pretends to be no more and no less than a translation of the original. The special disadvantages of such a policy for a dictionary are obvious. Even where a firm theological terminology exists in English, the meanings of correlative English and German terms often only overlap and rarely coincide. Articles will therefore sometimes carry unfamiliar titles and provide instances of faintly unfamiliar usage. Again, articles which one would expect to find in an English dictionary of theology are notable by their absence; there is for instance no article on Anglicanism, though it is fascinating to speculate on the kind of article Fr Rahner might have written under this head: few topics, it might seem, would be more resistant to the *Begriff*. Or perhaps the more specifically philosophical articles might have been rewritten with an Anglo-Saxon audience in mind. In fact the field of possible adaptation is enormous; but one overriding consideration finally excluded all such tentative policies of adaptation: the unity of inspiration which makes this dictionary unique of its kind had as far as possible to be preserved (I may say that Fr Rahner himself would not have been in favour of any considerable adaptation).' We acknowledge our debt to Father Ernst's edition. The new material and references of the tenth German edition have been included.

The Publishers

Abbreviations

CIC	*Codex Iuris Canonici*
D	Denzinger, *Enchiridion Symbolorum,* edited by Adolf Schönmetzer, Freiburg i. Br., 32nd ed., 1963.
Gr.	Greek
Heb.	Hebrew
Lat.	Latin
NT	New Testament
OT	Old Testament
Vat. II	Vatican II

An asterisk (*) preceding a word indicates a relevant article in the Dictionary under that (or a closely similiar) heading.

OLD TESTAMENT

Gen	Genesis	1 Chr	1 Chronicles
Exod	Exodus	2 Chr	2 Chronicles
Lev	Leviticus	Ezra	Ezra
Num	Numbers	Neh	Nehemia
Deut	Deuteronomy	Tob	Tobit
Jos	Joshua	Jud	Judith
Jg	Judges	Est	Esther
Ruth	Ruth	Job	Job
1 Sam	1 Samuel	Ps	Psalms (numbered as in
2 Sam	2 Samuel		the Hebrew Bible)
1 Kg	1 Kings	Prov	Proverbs
2 Kg	2 Kings	Eccles	Ecclesiastes
Song	Song of Solomon	Obad	Obadiah
Wis	Wisdom	Jon	Jonah
Ecclus	Ecclesiasticus	Mic	Micah

ABBREVIATIONS

Is	Isaiah	Nah	Nahum
Jer	Jeremiah	Hab	Habakkuk
Lam	Lamentations	Zech	Zechariah
Dan	Daniel	Mal	Malachi
Hos	Hosea	1 Macc	1 Maccabees
Joel	Joel	2 Macc	2 Maccabees
Amos	Amos		

NEW TESTAMENT

Mt	Matthew	1 Tim	1 Timothy
Mk	Mark	2 Tim	2 Timothy
Lk	Luke	Tit	Titus
Jn	John	Phm	Philemon
Acts	Acts of the Apostles	Heb	Hebrews
Rom	Romans	Jas	James
1 Cor	1 Corinthians	1 Pet	1 Peter
2 Cor	2 Corinthians	2 Pet	2 Peter
Gal	Galatians	1 Jn	1 John
Eph	Ephesians	2 Jn	2 John
Phil	Philippians	3 Jn	3 John
Col	Colossians	Jude	Jude
1 Thess	1 Thessalonians	Rev	Revelation
2 Thess	2 Thessalonians		

VATICAN II

Bish.	Decree on the Bishops' Pastoral Office in the Church *(Christus Dominus)*
Church	Dogmatic Constitution on the Church *(Lumen Gentium)*
Church/world CW	Pastoral Constitution on the Church in the Modern World *(Gaudium et spes)*
East. Church.	Decree on Eastern Catholic Churches *(Orientalium Ecclesiarum)*
Ecum.	Decree on Ecumenism *(Unitatis redintegratio)*
Educ.	Declaration on Christian Education *(Gravissimum educationis)*
Lay P.	Decree on the Apostolate of the Laity *(Apostolicam actuositatem)*

ABBREVIATIONS

Lit.	Constitution on the Sacred Liturgy *(Sacrosanctum concilium)*
Min. Pr.	Decree on the Ministry and Life of Priests *(Presbyterorum ordinis)*
Miss.	Decree on the Church's Missionary Activity *(Ad gentes divinitus; Ecclesiae sanctae)*
Non-C. rel.	Declaration on the Relationship of the Church to Non-Christian Religions *(Nostra aetate)*
Priests	Decree on Priestly Formation *(Optatam totius)*
Rel. Lib.	Declaration on Religious Liberty *(Dignitatis humanae)*
Rel. Life	Decree on the Appropriate Renewal of Religious Life *(Perfectae caritatis)*
Rev.	Dogmatic Constitution on Divine Revelation *(Dei Verbum)*
Soc. Comm.	Decree on the Instruments of Social Communication *(Inter mirifica)*

DICTIONARY
OF THEOLOGY

A

ABSOLUTE

That which exists in and of itself altogether exempt of any dependence. In general the absolute is conceived as existing of itself, as true of itself, and as good of itself, without dependence of any kind.

ABSOLUTIST CLAIM OF CHRISTIANITY. Christianity absolutizes neither the finite, the conditional, nor the relative in anything human—even in religion. But since in Jesus Christ God has absolutely accepted the finite and communicated himself to it in an absolute manner, Christianity lays claim to being unique among religions, their final fulfilment which in the course of history will in no way ever be superseded.—See also *Non-Christian Religions, Christianity.*

ABSOLUTION

See *Penance, Sacrament of.*

ACCIDENT

By the term "accident" Thomistic philosophy and theology (in the context of discussion of the connexion between essence and appearance) chiefly understand that which concurs with a substance and perfects it (entitative accident). In the real world one encounters only the whole which is composed of substance and accident. Though the substance is known through its accidents, the distinction which exists between the two is clear enough. Substance persists through change whereas the accidents inhering in any substance might well be present

1

or absent. Accident inheres in a substance but can have no independent existence; it has *being only analogically. Nine supreme genera of accidents are distinguished, the most important of which are quantity and quality (absolute accidents), action, affection, position in space and time (relative accidents). These concepts are adopted in the doctrine of the Eucharist: after the consecration only the accidents (*Species) of bread and wine remain, not their substance (*Transubstantiation).

ACT

THOMISTIC PHILOSOPHY. Act (perfection) and *potency (possibility) are the two basic modalities of being, because all being undergoes change, passing from one state to another. "Pure act" signifies *absolute, eternal, unlimited perfection, thus excluding all potency. *Actus purus* is the Thomistic "definition" of *God.

MORAL THEOLOGY distinguishes between the *actus hominis,* an act of man but not specifically human in character—such as instinctive reactions—and the *actus humanus,* specifically human in character, involving the exercise of judgment and free will. Every *actus humanus* is a moral act because it implies a more or less conscious attitude towards the norms of morality. Catholic moral theology finds this norm in reference to the natural or supernatural last end, and makes the subjective virtue or vice of a human act depend on its subjective (conscious) ordination, actual or virtual, to the last end. The Church teaches that sinners and unbelievers are also capable of morally good acts in the natural order, which through actual elevating *grace may become salutary acts—as probably happens in practice with all good acts. In view of the union of body and soul in *man, the traditional division of acts into *actus interni* (internal and spiritual) and *actus externi* (external and bodily) can be regarded only as a rough description for practical convenience. The *freedom of an act is limited by psychological or pathological factors such as age, habits, or neuroses, and by four direct restraints: violence, passion, fear, or ignorance. Whether a human act is objectively good or bad depends on its formal or moral object; that is, it depends on whether or not the object is rightly related to the last end of man. This moral object is composed of two elements: an intrinsic objective purpose which shapes the very structure of the act, and the circumstances, notably the subjective purpose or the motivation of the agent. It follows that in the concrete

2

there can be no such thing as a morally indifferent human act. At the same time it must be noted that a variety of *motives will influence a single act. An act becomes the "weightier" as those motives that prompt it to conform to its intrinsic purpose are consciously purified and reduced to the most perfect unity possible. In a Christian this is to act by *faith.—See also *Moral Theology, Ethics.*

RELIGIOUS ACT. God himself is not an object with which man has the option of establishing a relationship supplementary to his relationships with other objects, since man's very nature refers him to the *mystery of God (*Anthropology). The religious act is that by which man finds access to the *transcendence of his own nature. Such an act includes the following elements: (1) It exists *a priori,* that is, it cannot be avoided, because it is part of man's self-realization and can therefore only be accepted or suppressed. (2) It is integral and rational, that is, it signifies a greater self-possession and perfection for man and therefore also for his reason, arising out of the unique relationship between God and humanity. (3) It springs from the centre of the person (the *heart), where intellect and will are still one—thought and devotion, understanding and emotion, objectivity and reverence, judgment and persuasion. (4) It is personal, the acceptance of one's human condition and thus a response and surrender to *mystery (*Love). (5) It is also categorical, responding to God in every human dimension, even in those dimensions where human experience is most concrete and particularized; and thus (6) it is "incarnational", orientated, consciously or not, to the concrete shape of God in Jesus Christ as an earthly creature, the profoundest possible affirmation of the world. Consequently that love of God integral to the religious act is love of realities that are not God, and love of these is love of God. One Christian understanding of faith is also characterized by the historically covenantal (i.e., promissory) nature of the substance of faith (for that reason too the religious act is not extra-mundane) and is accordingly intersubjective in structure, so that the subject (a human being) of the specifically Christian religious act is a man or woman in his or her common humanity (i.e., also his or her public responsibility).

ADAM

In ancient eastern languages Adam means "man", "humanity", "from earth and to earth". The word can mean a "connective personality". The biblical *creation narrative, which uses mythical elements,

3

relates in its different levels: that the body of the first human being, a man, was taken from the earth, whence he is obviously a part of natural history; and that he received the "breath of life" directly from God; that a woman, Eve, man's equal, was ordered to him as he to her, that both are God's image, and that this couple was the beginning of mankind. Adam was placed in a *paradise to which he had no natural claim and which God did not owe him (*Original justice). As the first progenitor of all men he is also the ancestor of Jesus Christ (Lk 3:38), the second progenitor (second Adam), who surpasses him. Adam transmits earthly life to those who by his disobedience are sinners and the slaves of death (*Original sin), Jesus Christ imparts spiritual life to those whom by his obedience he has made just and partakers in his resurrection (1 Cor 15; Rom 5). In the second Adam the will of God is realized in a free spiritual partnership of men with the incarnate God.

ADOPTIANISM

Collectively designates all those opinions which chiefly out of concern for pure *monotheism regard *Jesus Christ as simply a human being, in a special manner possessed of the divine spirit and "adopted" by God as his Son. Its principal adherents were the judaizing Christians of the first century, Paul of Samosata in the third century, and Elipandus of Toledo and Felix of Urgel in the eighth century.—See also *Monarchianism*.

ADORATION

The NT commonly uses the expression "fall down (before someone)" in the sense of reverencing a great man; but in NT theology the term means the true worship of God—as the basic mode of the religious *act in general—and of the Lord Jesus, which according to the Apocalypse is rendered to the latter by all creation. God is no longer adored in one particular place alone, but according to John 4 in spirit and in truth; in the true house of God, according to St Paul and the Epistle to the Hebrews, that is to say in the community assembled as the body of Jesus Christ to celebrate the Lord's Supper. In order to preclude any possible misunderstanding, dogmatic theology emphasizes that adoration is due to God alone (D 601). Adoration uniquely realizes the aspect of worship in every relation with God, recognizing the infinite difference between God and every creature, his infinite sanctity and glory. This acknowledgment may be purely interior, or may be expressed and supported by religious ceremonies, and it may be further embodied in our practical conduct. The object of all adoration is the personality of God in its most concrete form, namely, in the humanity of Christ, his presence in the Eucharist. Saints, pictures, and objects can and may not be adored (*Veneration of saints, *Veneration of images, *Relics), but may be psychologically helpful towards real adoration.

AEON

In Plato's *Timaeus* (37d) αἰών has the meaning of "world", "age", "epoch", "long time", "timeless eternity". The term already had a personified meaning in the writings of Euripides and is to be found later in Syria and Egypt, then in Gnosticism. For the biblical notion of aeon as eternity see the article *Eternity.*

Scriptural terminology is based on the notion of aeon to be found in the *apocalyptic literature of later Judaism, where two aeons are mentioned, one superseding the other (this—that; transitory—everlasting; pain, affliction, corruption—grandeur, newness, justice, truth). The advent of the future aeon is associated with the Messiah and is located either on the new earth or in the heavenly world. In the latter case we often find that one aeon no longer annuls and transcends the other: though divergent in character they are contemporaneous (earthly and visible—heavenly and invisible). This doctrine of the two aeons does not figure in the kingdom proclaimed by Jesus (*Basileia), though its terminology appears in the synoptic Gospels: "this" aeon and "that" future aeon which is to come. St Paul often deliberately ignores the future aeon and speaks chiefly of "this" present, evil aeon complete with its own god (2 Cor 4:4), out of which the Christian has been rescued by the death of Jesus and to which he may never again conform (compare St John's analogous notion of "this" *world). In spite of St Paul's negative attitude, however, we must remember that unlike Judaism, he takes "this" world seriously, as a place of simultaneous decision and discrimination. According to Hebrews 6:5, Christians have already experienced the powers of the future aeon.

AETIOLOGY

In the broadest sense aetiology (Gr. $\alpha i \tau i \alpha$, cause) means advancing a reason or cause for some reality. In a narrower sense it means stating that a prior event is the reason for a condition we have experienced or for some other occurrence in the human sphere. This retrospect of a previous event may take the form of an imaginative picture that is simply intended to supply the consciousness with a graphic clarification of the present condition: mythological aetiology; or it may be the genuine deduction of an historical cause *from* the present condition, a deduction which is objectively possible and justified though it is perhaps expressed in picturesque form: historical aetiology. In this case the present is more clearly grasped by the clarification of its origin, the real cause and the present consequence are seen in a single perspective. In this sense the concept is applicable to scriptural statements about the primitive history of mankind (*Creation narrative).

AGAPE

See *Charity*.

AGNOSTICISM

A vulgar agnosticism (Gr. $\alpha\gamma\nu\omega\sigma\tau os$, unknown) denies the possibility of any certain knowledge beyond our ordinary, immediate experience or of any science which corresponds to this experience (*Knowledge of God).

A subtler agnosticism would have religion take refuge in a domain where it is *a priori* unassailable. On this view rational knowledge simply collapses when confronted by questions of ultimate significance, thus clearing the way for "faith" (*Modernism). Religious agnosticism contains some truth in that it realizes that God is only known as God when he is known and acknowledged as incomprehensible *mystery. Popular piety often reduces God to something with which the human mind can cope.

ALEXANDRIA, SCHOOL OF

From the end of the 2nd century there existed at Alexandria a catechetical school and several theological academies for the educated classes. Alexandrian theology, as it is called, is characterized by its profound sense of the mystery of the written and the Incarnate Word of God. This is to say that it particularly emphasizes the divinity of Jesus—whence, later on, the danger of *Monophysitism. Its exposition of Scripture, influenced as it was by Philo, is predominantly allegorical and typological (*Type). The most eminent doctors of the school are Clement of Alexandria and Origen.

ANABAPTISTS

See *Infant Baptism.*

ANACEPHALAEOSIS

Literally a summary of recapitulation (Gr. ἀνακεφαλαίωσις); its theological usage, relating to saving history, derives from Ephesians 1:10 and was employed notably by St Irenaeus. It denotes that the whole of creation is referred to the Incarnation of God in such a way that creation as such must be understood as a preparation for collaboration with God made Man. In the present economy, therefore, Jesus Christ is not only the goal of creation and the apogee of Adam's race, but having borne our sins and risen as the first-born from the dead, his radical acceptance of every phase of human history has redeemed and "re"-constituted that creation which up until his coming had been subjected to vanity.

ANALOGIA FIDEI

A theological concept occurring in Romans 12:6, which Karl Barth understands as an analogy of "similarity but greater dissimilarity" between "human decision in faith" and the "decision of God's grace". In the Catholic sense it means that every affirmation of revelation or faith must be understood in the light of the Church's *objective* faith as a whole. The *analogia fidei* also requires that it be quite clear that the terms used in any dogmatic formula bear a merely analogical meaning. This principle is recognized by the magisterium (D 3283, 3543–3547, 3887).—See also *Schools, Analogy, Mystery.*

ANALOGY, ANALOGIA ENTIS

The attempt to consider the connexion between finite and infinite, so that there can be no mention either of necessary relation (dialectics) nor of absence of relation (positivism). An analogical concept is one which, while preserving the unity of its connotation, undergoes an essential change of meaning when applied to different beings or realms of being. It is to be distinguished from both equivocation where a single word has two or more totally different senses, and univocation where the sense of a concept is always precisely the same and whose uses are differentiated only by characters, notes extrinsic to the concept. The analogical concept embraces the common and the proper, like and unlike, in a community which is logically indivisible. The analogy of being as such, the *analogia entis* (real analogy), and the analogy of the concept of being (logical analogy) are both founded on that community and diversity which is present in every existing thing precisely in its *being. If the univocal element in being is expressed, the logical consequence is an ultimate community of infinite and finite being, of human and divine knowledge. On the other hand if the equivocal element is expressed, being falls asunder into ultimate diversity and radical separation. In its present state the human mind can attain being itself only in individual things that are, but it does so in such a way—owing to its *transcendence—that its analogical understanding of being provides the permanent basis for all its (univocal) comprehension of individual objects.

Two kinds of analogy are distinguished. Where the analogous content of a concept is transferred from a primary analogate to a secondary, derivative analogate, we have the *analogy of attribution.* If the content—as well as the word and a relationship with the primary analogate—is intrinsically proper to the secondary analogate, we have an *intrinsic attribution.* There is, for instance, an analogy of intrinsic attribution between God and all finite being, because all that exists intrinsically possesses being and in its being depends on God. *Analogy of proportionality,* whether it be intrinsic or extrinsic, is found in the analogical similarity of the relationships which exist between each analogate and some specific attribute. An analogy of true proportionality obtains between God and all finite being because God bears a relationship to his own being which is similar to, yet essentially different from, the relationship of all else that exists to its respective being. To see analogy as the form of our thought and language about God and his relation to us and the world is not a logical trick by which human knowledge masters God; it is to paraphrase the basic datum of human knowledge: that it is always and from the first referred to absolute *mystery presented to our minds in a non-objective mode, though the mystery does not do away with the datum, nor the datum do away with the incomprehensibility of God. "For no similarity can be said to hold between Creator and creature which does not imply a greater dissimilarity between the two" (Fourth Lateran Council; D 806).

ANALYSIS FIDEI

That analysis of the act of faith which investigates why, as an assent of the intellect, it is immediately and ultimately based upon the authority of God revealing and not ultimately upon one or the other intellectual motives that are present (*Praeambula fidei). That is, it investigates how the believer can *directly* attain that same God revealing upon whose authority he bases his act of faith. The theologians reply as follows: (1) Suarez maintains that the authority of God revealing is itself an object of faith. However, this results in a vicious circle. (2) De Lugo sees the authority of God revealing as immediately recognizable of itself; it "speaks for itself" when the Church preaches in virtue of the grace of faith. But such an opinion would seem to attenuate the intellectual motive. (3) For Straub the authority of God revealing is affirmed in the act of faith as the ultimate motive, but not as a truly objective intellectual motive (which would need to be the case). (4) Billot concludes that neither the external intellectual motive nor the authority (simply recognized) of God revealing is affirmed in the act of faith, but only the revealed truth. But in fact the intellectual motive must at least be included in the affirmation.

Today theologians lay more stress on the personal nature of faith, the encounter with God in Christ and the resultant experience of his "authority", and the illuminating action of *grace in *faith, though this may not be accessible to consciousness.

ANAMNESIS

Anamnesis (Gr. ἀνάμνησις, "recalling to mind") is natural to man, reflecting as he does upon important historical events (by the nature of things, unique) that form the basis of his life. By thus reflecting he is able to realize those events for himself. The OT witnesses to the anamnesis of the Exodus as the decisive and still valid act by which God saved his people (*Pasch). The eucharistic anamnesis in the NT is of an analogous nature (*Eucharist). Both take the form of cult. Thus anamnesis may be theologically defined as the ceremonial re-presentation of a salutary event of the past, in order that the event may lay hold of the situation of the celebrant. Unlike many liturgical acts in other religions, Judaeo-Christian anamnesis presupposes that although the event has and retains its historical uniqueness, it is at the same time present, that is, remains in force as an accomplished fact. It also presupposes that man is able to actualize the effectual presence of this event in his own time in a manner superior to a mere subjective recollection. The event must have a specific texture: it must be accomplished in a personal act and anticipate its ceremonial representation in anamnesis; it must affect the celebrants and be of significance for salvation, or more specifically, it must commemorate in advance their future salvation. Anamnesis of this sort is exclusively a human possibility, because the fact that man is a being permanently established within the universe and the unity of history means that those deeds which he has accomplished in time retain their validity and remain likewise historically established.

The salutary event envisages all mankind; and consequently authority to re-enact it is primarily vested not in the individual but in the Church which represents humanity and was herself founded by that event. The theology of anamnesis arises in connexion with the humanity of Christ as instrumental cause of grace for man, the sacraments, and the Eucharist. The presence of the Lord's death must not be reduced to the merely moral and juridical presence of an event in the past; to do so would exclude the real anamnesis which Scripture declares to be necessary. See *Memory*.

ANATHEMA

See *Excommunication*.

ANGEL

Since the Middle Ages the term "angel" (Gr. ἄγγελος , messenger) has been used to designate superhuman created beings, "pure" spirits.

THE TEACHING OF SCRIPTURE. Scripture assumes familiarity with beings variously called "angels", that is to say, "messengers", "men",

"Yahweh's host", "heavenly host", according to their function, their appearance, or their relation to God. In the post-exilic period they are more precisely conceived as "sons of God", "gods", "princes", "powers", "spirits", which either have no body or only one that is apparent. They come as God's messengers to aid or punish, are assigned to the individual person or nation, and often have a name of their own (Michael, Gabriel, Raphael, Uriel).

NT statements about the angels reflect late Jewish views of these beings but on the whole are more sober. Jesus Christ standing at the right hand of God is exalted above all the angels; the Church proclaims God's plan of salvation even to the angels (Eph 3:10). Consequently they are seen in the service of Christ and his disciples (Mt 4:11; Acts 5:19f.); they act as messengers to men on behalf of God's salvific will and are to surround Jesus Christ at the Last Judgment.— See book of Revelation.

TRADITION. The Fathers defend the created nature of the angels against Greek and Jewish apocalyptic notions: they do not (as in various forms of *Gnosis) take part in the creation of the world (*Demiurge), but are nevertheless more powerful than men. The purely spiritual nature of the angels becomes a thesis of angelology (St Thomas Aquinas) only on the occasion of a definition of the Fourth Lateran Council which presupposes the existence of the angels. Finally, a recent declaration of the magisterium (*Humani generis;* D 3891) takes to task those who question the personal character of the angels or the essential difference between spirit and matter.

TEACHING OF SYSTEMATIC THEOLOGY. The theological doctrine of the angels must begin with the fact that the original source of doctrine about the angels is not the revelation of God himself, either in OT or NT; that in this revelation the angels are merely taken for granted and their existence experienced, as created, personal, structural principles within the harmony of the cosmic order. Nevertheless, references to the angels in revelation have the important function of purifying conceptions of the angels derived from elsewhere and of confirming what remains as human experience legitimately handed down by tradition. The mention of angels serves to shed light on more comprehensive truths of greater religious importance: God's dominion over all things, and the hazards of the human situation. Revelation is not interested in the details (the names, number, rank of the angels and so forth). Consequently a theological angelology is integrated into the one event on which everything in human existence depends, namely

God's entrance into creation in Jesus Christ. It prevents man from foreshortening the dimensions of his environment; he stands in the midst of a wider than human society of salvation and damnation. It is only from this point of view that the very first determination of the nature of the angels should be made: they are part of the world on the basis of their very being, they are naturally united with man in both actuality and history, and have *one* supernatural saving history with him which has its first exemplar and final goal in Jesus Christ. But since theological *anthropology and *Christology are essentially connected, angelology must be considered an intrinsic element of Christology. By nature the angels are the personal environment, the entourage of the uttered and exinanated Word of the Father, who is in a *single* Person the Word uttered and the Word heard. The difference between angels and men should be conceived as a "specific" modification of that ("generic") nature common to both angels and men, which itself attains its supreme, gracious fulfilment in the Word of God. It is from this point of view that we should understand the grace of the angels as the grace of Jesus Christ, Jesus Christ as the head of the angels, the original unity of the world and of saving history with angels and men in their *mutual* super-ordination and sub-ordination, and the change which the function of the angels undergoes in saving history. As aspects of *this* world *before* Jesus Christ, the angels had a greater function of mediation in regard to God than they have now.—See also *Devils, Principalities and Powers.*

ANGELOLOGY

That part of theology which deals with the *angels; more precisely, it is the doctrine of man's preter-human contemporaries and environment in saving history as an element of theological *anthropology. But its nature is partially determined by the essential connexion between theological anthropology and *Christology (compare the grace of the angels as the grace of Christ, Christ as head of the angels, the many and various functions which the angels have in saving history, and other themes which are closely similar).

ANIMA NATURALITER CHRISTIANA

An expression of Tertullian ("the soul is naturally Christian": *Apologeticum* 17:6) by which he means that the soul is endowed from the outset with the knowledge of God and that whatever God imparts in this manner can at most be obscured, but never entirely extinguished.—In a broader sense the expression may be used to signify: (1) that the capacity to know God and the natural law is part of human nature (such knowledge also being part of Christianity); (2) that it is part of human nature to be open to a possible verbal revelation in history (*Potentia obedientialis); (3) that human existence is always determined in part by the whole of human history (tradition) and, therefore, consciously or unconsciously, by Christianity; (4) that man lives always and everywhere under the universal *salvific will of God, is ordered to a supernatural end (*Existential, supernatural), and is capable of faith. Thus the historical, explicit message of Christianity never encounters a human being conceived of as a merely pre-Christian "nature", or as one shut in on itself by sin, or pursuing its course without an active relation to possible revelation (*Grace, *Nature).

ANIMISM.

See *Religion.*

ANOINTING OF THE SICK, "LAST" ANOINTING

That sacramental action of the Church in and for the sick which shows the Church victorious in eschatological hope over approaching death and its darkness. According to Vatican II, the sacramental action is better not called the "last" anointing, since it is not the sacrament only of those in the last extremity (Church, 11; Lit., 73). The Roman constitution of 1972 states that it is intended for those whose health is severely threatened, and for those in danger of dying.

THE SCRIPTURAL BASIS for this anointing is traditionally located in James 5:14ff. According to this text the leaders of the Christian community are to pray over the sick man, anointing him with oil—in accordance with the ancient association between anointing and the hope of healing and salvation—and invoking the name of the Lord. The effect of the anointing is the forgiveness of sins. The people are to confess their sins to one another and pray for one another so that they may be healed. The power to forgive sins, here enunciated and attached to an office, can only be bestowed by God, and so the whole

13

action has the essential characteristics of a *sacrament. If the Church is seen as the *primordial sacrament, whose basic and essential actualizations in view of the salvation of the human individual in his crucial situations, are necessarily *opus operatum, sacramental, then it is clear that Jesus Christ did institute this sacrament without our having to postulate any express words of his to that effect.

THE DOGMA was defined against the Reformers at the Council of *Trent (D 694–1647, 1716–1719): extreme unction is a true sacrament instituted by Jesus Christ, announced by St James. It should be received by those who are gravely ill and have or have had the use of reason; it may not be repeated during the same illness, unless death again becomes imminent. The minister is the priest, or several priests in the Eastern Church. The matter is olive oil consecrated by the bishop and the anointing of the senses, or of one in an emergency. In the Latin rite the form is the (essential) sacramental words.

THEOLOGY. Anointing of the sick is regarded as a sacrament for the dying in the strict sense only from the ninth century (the earliest tradition concerning the consecration of oil for the sick can be found in Hippolytus, A.D. 215), but theology has always regarded *sickness as the physical proof that we are forfeit to death. The first indispensable sacrament in this situation is the *Eucharist; but it is reasonable that part of what is bestowed in this sacrament should be set into still sharper relief by another sacrament—anointing of the sick, which communicates the more abundantly what it more clearly signifies. The Church also calls this anointing the completion of the sacrament of *penance (D 1694). We may conclude from both these facts that the effect of the anointing is to immerse the sickness of the recipient in the victory of Jesus Christ, who has overcome sickness and death, because these are the consequence and expression of sin. Thus if the sick man is well *disposed, his sickness has become a saving situation which, regardless how the sickness may end, will lead to salvation. Since the effect of this sacrament, as of every other, depends on the dispositions of the recipient, there is no need to labour the point that the sick man must be anointed in good time and that the priest must speak to him in a confident and encouraging fashion. Anointing of the sick, like every sacrament, also has an essentially ecclesial aspect. Both in the sick man himself, who by a postive act of faith allows himself to be anointed (young children do not receive this sacrament) as a member of the Church, and in the action of the Church herself confidently standing by him and declaring her solidarity with him as

14

his agony approaches, the Church realizes her being as she who lifts the lamp of faith as night falls in the world, and goes forth to meet the bridegroom.

ANOMOEANS

See *Arianism, Semi-Arianism.*

ANONYMOUS CHRISTIANITY

A brief phrase (which like all such phrases is open to misunderstanding) summarizing a fact which, especially since Vatican II, is now indisputable; namely that a person can deserve God's grace and thus find salvation even if he, inculpably, is not formally a member of the Church, is not baptized, indeed even considers himself to be an atheist. The theological question is *how* in such a person that faith which Vatican II declared to be necessary for salvation for all men can be said to exist in even a rudimentary way. Faced with this problem one can refer to the "ways which God alone knows" (Miss. 7), as the Council itself does, or one can try to show that every positive moral decision based on the dictates of conscience, because it is supported by *grace, already implies a belief in revelation, for this "edifying" grace already includes an ultimate *a priori* horizon of understanding (of unconditional hope of salvation in God himself), which can be seen as (transcendental) *revelation.

The doctrine of "anonymous Christianity" is of great pastoral significance. First, it is the source of hope for the success of all explicitly Christian proclamation because it presupposes that a person is already impelled by the same grace first proclaimed by Jesus Christ. Second, this doctrine calls on those who preach the *Gospel to make constant efforts to discover and appeal to those inner experiences undergone by the recipient of the Gospel message which are brought about by his "natural" inclination towards God, although this is always moved and affected by grace—a grace which is always offered to him—even before he hears the word of God.

The essential principles of this doctrine are also propounded by those (e.g., de Lubac, Hans Urs von Balthasar, and so on) who themselves object to the ways in which it is formulated.

15

ANTHROPOCENTRISM

May be described as that opinion and practical attitude which regards "man as the measure of all things" and accordingly denies God's love, turns man in upon himself, and imprisons him in a pretended autonomy. This includes all *atheism, all personal unbelief, every personal mortal sin, and every philosophy that does not make man receptive to that absolute *Mystery which is beyond human control. Yet there is a sense in which anthropocentrism means that the true theocentrism of man is, like any personal deed or attitude, necessarily the orientation of a personal subject. It is only by a return to oneself that an absolute departure from oneself becomes possible; the absolute dignity and propriety of a moral action derives from the dignity of the subject, who is grounded as such in God, by reason of his own personal transcendence. From this point of view, when both are rightly understood, anthropocentrism and theocentrism are not strict opposites at all. The Christocentrism of God is implied in the anthropocentric reduction of Christianity (Mt 25:31– 45).

ANTHROPOLOGY

The conscious effort of *man to achieve an understanding of himself by *a priori* and transcendental arguments, or by a divine revelation, or through *a posteriori* sciences (medicine, biology, psychology, sociology, and the like). A genuinely theological anthropology must appear *a posteriori* to the extent that it presupposes what has already been said about man in the historical message of the faith. At the same time this presupposition does not necessarily exclude the possibility that an interpretation of man, derived as a matter of historical fact from without, should be the final, basic, and conclusive interpretation. Man's very nature ineluctably refers him to historical fact, which he cannot rationalistically dismiss as "non-essential". In his every reflection he grasps himself (only) as involved in history, controlled by, and himself controlling, historical fact; in no science can he adequately reflect this concrete historicity, divesting himself of it as a being grasped and understood *a priori*—though an original self-possession is of his very essence (*Person, *Existential state). Hence the *a posteriori* anthropology of revelation need not confront man's comprehensive, *a priori* understanding of himself as an alien norm; and theology can legitimately proceed from the actual understanding of himself that man has derived from historical tradition and active faith.

16

ANTHROPOLOGY

Revelation in the OT and NT contains declarations of binding force about man which claim that they alone lead him to an experimental knowledge of his own real (concrete, historical) nature. Man is represented as a being without equal in his world, so truly personal as to be God's partner, for whom everything else by the will of the Creator —and therefore by its own *real* nature—is merely environment. His position as a free spirit having eternal personal significance and value for God; his capacity to become a partner with God in a genuine dialogue or "covenant-relationships" which leads to absolute intimacy "face to face" in light inaccessible, to "partaking in the divine nature" where we shall know even as we are known; his capacity to disclose his own existence as an expression of God himself (God-becoming-man)—these are the things which really make man a being who is not in the last analysis a part of a greater whole (world). Quite uniquely he himself is the whole—a subject, a person, an individual rather than a thing. From first to last the truly historical (that is, non-cyclical) history of the universe is an element in this history of God and man. The history of man is not an element in all-embracing cosmogony, rather the world is simply the necessary precondition of human history and finds in that history the ultimate reason for its existence; the end of the universe is determined by man's history in the eyes of God. Within this historical process the believing Christian knows that God has historically spoken to him despite his creatureliness and sinfulness. Indeed, precisely in them was spoken the absolute, free, gracious word by which God reveals himself in his own intimate life. On the one hand this affirmation is immediately comprehensible to the Christian as a summary of what he learns of himself by faith, and, on the other hand, it forms a suitable point of departure for theological anthropology.

It follows from this basic approach that creatureliness is the most comprehensive characteristic of man, but primarily and specifically creatureliness as personal subject (of which the createdness of mere things is only a diminished mode), that is, the infinite receptivity to God of him who is not God. This characteristic is at once positive and negative, and each aspect deepens in the same measure in the presence of the incomparable God. Although the fact of *Revelation can be known by natural reason (*Praeambula fidei), the person who really hears divine revelation is he who so accepts it in that absolute (loving) obedience of faith made possible by God's self-communication in grace, that the quality of the divine word as *self*-revelation is not lost, or so debilitated by the pre-conceptions of finite man that what he hears is a human word. Here we may discern the original difference

17

between nature and grace: *grace is a predisposition to the connatural acceptance of God's self-revelation in the word (believing and loving) and in the *beatific vision of God; *nature is the permanent constitution of man presupposed by this disposition. This nature is such that the sinner and unbeliever can close himself against the self-revelation of God pressing in upon him, and such that this self-revelation made to man subsequent to his personal creation can still emerge as the gratuitous miracle of personal love, to which man "of himself", that is to say of his nature, has no claim, although it can be promised him and he is essentially receptive to it (*Potentia obedientialis).

The *historicity of man, both as his fundamental attribute and as a theological principle, clearly emerges from the fact that the word of God is heard historically. It is amply confirmed by man's susceptibility to his environment, by his bodily and sexual nature, by the *unity of mankind, by man's inclination to society, by the character of his existence as a striving, and by the historical relativity and irretrievable unicity of his situation.

Theological anthropology must particularly attend to the relation between itself and *Christology. The Incarnation is not rightly apprehended if Christ's humanity is seen as the mere instrument— ultimately external, after all—through which an ever-invisible God makes himself known. It must be seen as precisely what God himself becomes when, whilst remaining God, he empties himself into the dimension of that which is other than himself, of the non-divine. Even though God could create the world without the Incarnation, it is not incompatible with this thesis to affirm that the possibility of creation is grounded in the more radical possibility of God's self-exinanition (because the possibilities contained in the simplicity of the divine essence are not simply diverse without subordination). But then man's primary definition is to be that possible Other which God becomes in self-exinanition, and the possible brother of Jesus. Thus Christology, whether regarded from the divine point of view or the human, appears as the most radical and perfect recapitulation of theological anthropology.

No unified theological anthropology exists at present. What divine revelation has to say of man is divided among the individual theological tractates, especially those assigned to *dogmatic theology, and the systematic basis of all anthropology still remains to be worked out.

ANTHROPOMORPHISM

From the Gr. $\overset{\text{᾿}}{\alpha}\nu\theta\rho\omega\pi os$, man, and $\mu o\rho\phi\acute{\eta}$, form; it denotes the use of human characteristics to describe the reality of God. It is often found in the OT, where human feelings, actions, and even limbs are attributed to God (regret, laughter, sorrow, anger; mouth, nose, feet, and so on). As it still occurs in the purified diction of the prophets, it is chiefly intended to convey the dynamism peculiar to God without obscuring the qualitative distance separating God from his creation. Nevertheless, anthropomorphic language raises difficult problems concerning God's relation to evil and the theology of our knowledge of God. Undoubtedly it is inadequate to apply human characteristics to God, implying as they do concrete representations. But because of the transcendence of the human mind in relation to God, every concept possesses a certain transparency towards the divinity (*Analogy) that makes a true knowledge of him possible—albeit analogical and in constant need of adjustment to God through new negations. In such knowledge man is aware of his anthropomorphisms and by that very fact surmounts them to "penetrate" the mystery of God. Any attempt to justify the use of anthropomorphisms on the basis of our necessary dependence upon sense perception should take into account God's own intervention in history. If we are to bear witness to this historical intervention we must necessarily make use of concepts derived from historical experience and it is precisely this latter kind of testimony that constitutes a more exalted justification for the use of anthropomorphisms.

ANTICHRIST

In Scripture and Tradition the "Man of sin" who pretends to be Christ and who, despite great successes, is overcome by him. This doctrine need not be thought mythological or explained as merely symbolizing the struggles of the Christian and the Church, since the history of salvation and damnation is made by personal agents capable of controlling history, and its warlike character is intensified as the end approaches. On the other hand, it is possible to understand the statements of Scripture as meaning that the Antichrist is the embodiment of all those historical forces hostile to God which are under the control of man. Unchristian polemicists and apologists identify specific individuals with the Antichrist.

19

ANTINOMIANISM

An attitude which denies the justice and validity of all *law. In particular it represents the assertion that once the Gospel was promulgated the moral law is not binding on Christians as such.

ANTINOMIAN CONTROVERSY refers to two conflicts within Lutheranism. In the first half of the sixteenth century J. Agricola defended the total worthlessness of the law against Melanchthon and Luther. Again in the latter half of the same century a group of Antinomianists (M. Neander and A. Poach) argued against the disciples of Melanchthon that the Christian as a believer is above the law, while as a sinner he is subject to it (*Formula concordiae,* 1580). For the theological problems and a critique of Antinomianism see also *Law.*

ANTIOCH, SCHOOL OF

The common feature of the theological trends which developed at Antioch was not so much doctrinal as methodological. It was characterized by a preoccupation with the literal—contrasted with the allegorical—sense of the critical text of Scripture and the perfect humanity of Christ. Subsequently the danger of *Nestorianism arose. Principal representatives of the school were: Malchion (third century), Lucian of Antioch (fourth century) with Arius and the Arian leaders, Diodore of Tarsus and his pupils, Theodore of Mopsuestia, and St John Chrysostom.

ANXIETY

See *Dread.*

APHTHARTODOCETISTS

A Monophysite sect founded in the first half of the sixth century by Julian of Halicarnassus. The name derives from the Greek ἄφθαρτος (imperishable), because they regarded Christ's body as impassible, immortal, and imperishable from the moment of his conception. For other teachings see also *Monophysitism.*

APOCALYPTIC LITERATURE

A comprehensive name for a literary genre found in later Judaism and also employed in Christian circles. Of the major non-biblical apocalypses dating from the period between 200 B.C. and about A.D. 800 seventeen are pre-Christian—though remodelled in a Christian sense —and eleven derive from the Christian milieu. To compensate for their lack of authority they are often ascribed to important personages of the OT and NT (Abraham, Baruch, Elijah, Enoch, Isaiah, Moses, the Apostles, and others). OT passages employing apocalyptic imagery are to be found in Ezekiel, Isaiah, Zachariah, Joel, and Daniel; in the NT similar imagery is found in the book of Revelation, the discourse on the Second Coming, Mark 13 and its Synoptic parallels, and 2 Thessalonians 2:1–12, and numerous other individual passages. The subject-matter of apocalyptic writing usually consists of visions of the future coupled with admonitions and often takes the form of instruction reserved only for disciples. Apocalyptic writing in Scripture, in contrast to that of later Judaism, is no longer marked by unseemly intrusion into divine mysteries and fantastic description—such as advance "coverage" of the future as such without existential relevance to one's own present. Similarly, in the NT pseudonymity is generally displaced by reference to the author's own prophetic *charism. The authenticity of the visions recounted in biblical apocalyptic writing must be judged in light of the inerrancy of Scripture by the theological principles governing *apparitions. Furthermore their whole content —especially predictions of the end of the world and the termination of history—is to be interpreted according to the theological hermeneutics of *eschatological statements. In modern theology apocalyptic is conceived as projects for change and drafts for the future expressed in the language of myth (see *Demythologization).*

APOCATASTASIS

The only scriptural reference to ἀποκατάστασις (restoration) is to be found in Acts 3:21, where it refers to the restoration of the blessings of paradise to be accomplished by the Messiah. In later Judaism (see Mk 9:12) the restoration is ascribed to Elijah; Jesus himself, in Mark 9:12, applies the restorative role to John the Baptist in the sense that he was preparing the people for the Messiah. In later theological diction the term comes to mean the restoration of all creation—including sinners, the damned, and the devils—to a state of

21

perfect bliss; it signifies in fact a universal reconciliation. It is perhaps defended by Origen, but certainly by St Gregory of Nazianzus, St Gregory of Nyssa, Didymus the Blind, Evagrius Ponticus, Diodore of Tarsus, Theodore of Mopsuestia, John Scotus Erigena, and individual theologians of medieval and modern times. The Church's magisterium has condemned the positive assertion of an *apocatastasis* as heretical (D 411, 801, 1002). This judgment must be taken as a positive reference to man's freedom and responsibility and to the inviolable unrestrictedness of his decisions in this world. On the negative side, the Church has determined that conversion after death is impossible. Divine revelation does not inform us in what manner God will realize that plan for human salvation which he has fixed from the beginning (*Salvific will), nor whether few or many are actually damned. The Christian invention behind *apocatastasis* is more appropriate to the theology of *hope.

APOCRYPHA

From the Gr. ἀπόκρυφος , hidden; books not used in the liturgy or in theology because of their fantastic tenor, unknown origin, and heretical authorship. Despite their Jewish or Christian origin, which is sometimes quite ancient, they have not been included in the canon of Scripture. In Catholic theology the term OT apocrypha is commonly used to refer to *apocalyptic literature of later Judaism. In Protestant theology the OT apocrypha are known as pseudepigrapha, and here they generally understand the so-called "deuterocanonical books" (*Canon). Catholic and Protestant theology concur on the NT apocrypha, namely the apocryphal gospels, acts of the Apostles, epistles, and apocalypses. They are very numerous, and important discoveries of them have been made in the twentieth century.

APOLLINARIANISM

The heresy of Apollinarius, Bishop of Laodicea about A.D. 360. He taught that the second Person of the Trinity, the Logos, took the place of the spiritual part of Jesus' soul, with the result that Christ's humanity was something incomplete. It was Apollinarius' personal wish to emphasize Christ's divinity. But since he regarded human flesh to be essentially corrupt, in Christ it had to be deprived of an active principle of its own and subjected to the essentially sinless will of the Logos. He affirmed but a single nature in Christ, formed of the divinity of the Logos and the human flesh.—See also *Monophysitism.*

APOLOGETICS

See *Fundamental Theology.*

APOSTLE

From the Greek ἀπόστολος , envoy; the name which the NT gives to the Twelve in particular but also applies to other missionaries and messengers of the Church. The latter meaning is probably the more ancient. The envoy was an established feature of later Judaism, in which it was axiomatic that "the envoy (delegate) is like the sender." In the older letters, Paul calls himself and his fellow workers "apostles" (1 Thess 2:7). The Apostles had the task commissioned by Jesus of preaching the *Gospel; a later criterion of the apostolate is testimony to the *Resurrection of Jesus. The service of proclamation is exercised in responsibility before God in the spirit of Jesus for human redemption (Rom 2:4, 11f.). Acts stress the sending of the Apostles by Jesus; they are only the Twelve and Paul. We are told in Matthew 10:5 (Lk 9:2) that Jesus sent forth the Twelve whom he had called (Mk 3:14 and parallel passages) and in Luke 6:13 that he named them Apostles. The number twelve signifies Jesus' claim upon the twelve tribes of Israel; it was to them that the Apostles were primarily sent with the authority to preach the kingdom (*Basileia). This function, which was limited in duration in Jesus' lifetime, became an office after the Resurrection, by the gift of the spirit (Mt 28:18 ff.), which was collegial in structure and whose head was Peter (cf. Mt 16:18f.). The unique functions of the Apostles as foundation of the Church and witnesses to Christ, especially as eye-witnesses of his Resurrection, remain permanently efficacious—whence the Church has a duty to preserve them. But the Apostles have no true successors in these functions. Consequently it is defined teaching that the Church has received the whole of *Revelation exclusively through the Apostles (D 1501); it is theologically certain that public revelation ceased with the death of the last Apostle (D 3421), so that a *development of dogma may certainly occur but nothing can be added to its content. With all due reverence to the unique origin of the apostolic office, Catholic theology (Vat. II: Church, 18ff.; Rev. 18f.) recognizes a legitimate development of that office with regard to those apostolic functions which are also necessary for the continuance of the Church. Development of the apostolic office in this specified sense also applies, therefore, to the ministerial service and duties of the *Pope and the college of *bishops, as the true successors to the Apostolic college in governing the Church, in maintaining the purity of revelation, and in explaining its sense according to that foundation already laid down in the New Testament (Acts 20:28; 1 Tim 4:14; 2 Tim 1:6).—See also *Apostolicity of the Church.*

APOSTOLICITY OF THE CHURCH

An essential characteristic and distinctive note of the Church. It means the essential identity of the Church throughout her development in space and time with the Church of the Apostles (D 468f., 732, 2886ff.; in the fourth century inserted in the Creed). The Church is apostolic because she was founded by Christ in and through the Apostles; because her doctrine and sacraments are essentially those of the Apostles; because Pope and bishops, being links in an unbroken chain reaching back to the Apostles, are in a true sense successors of the Apostles. There are also bishops outside the Catholic Church— notably in the Oriental Churches separated from Rome—who by reason of their valid episcopal consecration are materially, but not formally, true successors of the Apostles (*Apostolic succession). According to Protestant doctrine a church is apostolic if the word of God is preached in it in conformity with the teaching of the Apostles (Declaration of Barmen, 1934); but recently it has been appreciated that the legitimate preaching of apostolic doctrine and administration of the sacraments would have to be the function of a ministerial *office deriving from Christ.

APOSTOLIC SUCCESSION

The legitimation of office and authority by their valid derivation from the twelve *Apostles, whose office and authority derive from the aim of Jesus Christ and the Holy Spirit. Corresponding to the two powers of order and jurisdiction, the apostolic succession is one of sacramental consecration by validly consecrated *bishops who can thus trace their succession back to the Apostles, or one constituted by an office-bearer's full communion with and subordination to the society of

Christ's Church and thus to its supreme office-bearer the *Pope, the legitimate successor of the head of the apostolic college, through whom jurisdiction in the Church is received. The former apostolic succession is also called material, the latter formal. The principle of apostolic succession, as part of the Church and as a criterion of the true Church, cannot be abandoned; otherwise instead of being a tangible, historical reality the Church would be an abstract idea. Furthermore the continuity of an historical human society cannot be based on a book (Scripture alone) but requires a legitimate succession. In fact Scripture itself declares that the legitimacy of the gospel that is preached and demands the assent of our faith is necessarily known by the legitimacy of its preachers (see Mk 16:15; Mt 28:18–20; Lk 10:16). The universal episcopate with the Pope at its head is the successor to the apostolic college with Peter at its head, and it is in and as a member of this episcopal college that the individual bishop is a successor of the Apostles (See Vat. II; Church, 20, 22). The evangelical question of the meaning of such a "chain of succession" or traditional link has an important function for the Church because the question constantly reminds us that a mere succession in office is nothing without a succession of the whole Church in the faith of the first disciples and Apostles.

APPARITIONS (VISIONS)

In theological language the name given to those psychical experiences in which invisible and inaudible objects or persons become perceptible to the senses in a supernatural manner, although their being is inaccessible to normal human powers. Theology makes it quite clear that apparitions of a supernatural kind are possible. God remains the free, omnipotent master of the natural laws of his creation and thus can make himself and realities that are beyond the reach of our powers perceptible to the senses. Where a divine operation occurs and leads to an apparition, it is likely to be primarily a gracious influence upon the spiritual core of the person, which afterwards radiates upon the person's senses in a manner partly governed by the psychological character of the visionary and his environment. This "consequence" need not be considered the work of God in the same measure and manner as the primary divine influence. It is always important to remember the Catholic principle that where visions are alleged, supernatural influences are not to be presumed but must be proved—just as, analogously, the divine origin of any revelation must be proved.

Concerning the question as to whether a supernatural apparition has in fact occurred, theology legitimately appeals to a psychology which for its part must remain open to a "theology of existence in grace" (in the full sense, including the psychological sense, of this term).

APPROPRIATION

Attribution to a single divine Person of those characteristics or activities of God which are in fact not proper to an individual Person but rather common to the three Persons of the Trinity. Catholic theology preserves strict *monotheism, taking great p̶͟ ̶̶̶̶̶̶̶̶̶̶̶̶̶̶ ̶ example, in Scripture what is appropriation f̶ṟ̶ọ̶m̶ ̶w̶ḥ̶ạ̶ṭ̶ ̶ị̶ṣ̶ ̶ṇọ̶ṭ̶, and adheres to the defined teaching that the divine Persons are a single creative, operative principle as regards the world (D 800, 1330). For instance, it is appropriation to attribute omnipotence to the Father, wisdom or truth to the Son, charity and holiness to the Holy Ghost. But if appropriation is recognized as a mode of expression to be carefully taken into account in the doctrine of creation and redemption, it does not follow that one may simply transfer it to the doctrine of grace. The *indwelling of God in the justified—because it is *self-communication—is not merely attributed to the respective divine Persons by appropriation; rather *grace establishes a special relation between each divine Person and the justified man. Consequently it is not a case of appropriation when Scripture states that the Father in the Trinity is our father or that the Spirit dwells in our hearts in a special manner.

ARGUMENT OF CONVERGENCE

The proof of a proposition by showing that it is supported by several independent considerations. This argument begets either certainty or probability, according as the convergence of several indices can *only* be explained in logical terms on the assumption that the thesis put forward is correct, or is merely *best* explained on that assumption, though other possible explanations are not altogether excluded. Theoretical probability is equivalent to (indirect) practical certainty; one need only realize that in view of the modest degree of certainty that can reasonably be required in practical matters, one is absolutely bound to act on the basis of theoretical "probability" supported by the argument of convergence. Taking into account the concrete opportunities for knowledge which are open to the average person, with his very limited time, talents, and education the arguments used in apologetics and *fundamental theology become in effect arguments of convergence.

ARIANISM

After Arius, a priest of Alexandria from the School of *Antioch; a heresy propounded from about the year 315 concerned with the relation of Father and Son in the Trinity and with the Incarnation. In its solution to the problem of the Son it adopted a "dual Logos", of which its declarations on the Holy Ghost are mere consequences. It held that the *Logos is always with God, a characteristic of God, not eternal like the Father but, rather, that he received his being immediately from the Father, though not from the Father's substance, before the beginning of time. Accordingly, he is at once begotten and created; he is as it were God only by participation. The Logos is the mediating being between God and the world. As a trial he had to become radically human in such a way that the Logos substituted for the human soul in the man Jesus.—These doctrines were condemned in 325 by the First Council of Nicaea, but they found strong support in the Eusebianite party, which had close connections with the court at Constantinople (Bishop Eusebius of Nicomedia). On this account the champion of Nicaea, St Athanasius, was several times forced into exile. Arianism split into several schools of thought: the extreme party maintained that Christ was radically unlike ($\dot{\alpha}\nu\acute{o}\mu o\iota o$s) the Father, whence their name "Anomoeans"; the moderates or "Homoeans" insisted that he was similar ($\ddot{o}\mu o\iota o$s) to the Father; a conciliatory third party, given the name "Homoiousians" or "Semi-Arians", with their notion that the Son is "of like substance" ($\dot{o}\mu o\iota o\acute{v}\sigma\iota o$s) with the Father approached the central conception of Nicaea, where it was defined that the Son is consubstantial ($\dot{o}\mu oo\acute{v}\sigma\iota o$s) with the Father. Arianism was finally overcome theologically in 381 by the First Council of *Constantinople. It lasted among Germanic tribes until the seventh century.

ASCENSION

The event is reported in Acts 1:1–14 and there is a derivative account in Mark 16:19; many other texts in the NT refer to it as well. According to the NT, after his crucifixion, death, and resurrection, Jesus was taken up to God in a manner that "manifests" the abiding validity of his humanity. The accounts of the Ascension should be considered in connexion with those of his appearances subsequent to the *Resurrection before "preordained witnesses" (Acts 10:41). They tell us nothing of the day on which the Ascension itself occurred, but report the day on which the Ascension was made visible to the witnesses. For Jesus the Ascension means the consummation of his work begun on the cross and in his Resurrection; it is his triumphant exaltation, his disarming of the unruly powers, his making all things full in him their Head, and a new, radical relation of lordship over the world. For us the Ascension means a new presence of God in the Holy Ghost, who was given to the Church which the Ascension of Jesus has made his body. *Heaven was thrown open; absolutely speaking, it is salvation for mankind. Yet at the same time the Ascension reminds us that definitive salvation is yet to come and despite appearances to the contrary, must be hoped for in faith. Jesus has been withdrawn from our senses and the consummation of the world in *parousia, *Judgment, and the *resurrection of the flesh have only commenced in secret.

ASCETICAL THEOLOGY

The systematic consideration of the existential truths and problems of concrete Christian life with a view to their mastery by the individual Christian. It has hitherto often been misconceived as the doctrine of the pursuit of perfection. When correctly understood it is distinguished from both *mysticism and *moral theology. The term first occurs in 1655; the discipline has existed since the 17th century.

ASCETICISM

From the Gr. ἄσκησις , training, renunciation. In popular Stoicism the term denoted deliverance from all ties with the world in order to attain the free imperturbability of the wise man. The scriptural foundations of renunciation for God's sake belong in the OT to the sphere of ritual *purity; later on in Scripture and in later Judaism the desire to be free for God and the reward due to this as to any other good work are motives for asceticism. Christian asceticism must not be governed by conscious or unconscious contempt of the world, unfaithfulness to or flight from one's earthly duties. It cannot be denied, however, that in Christianity there is an asceticism which is but the masked resentment of an incompetent individual, who despises the world because he is too weak and too cowardly to grapple with it and master it in both its grandeur and gravity. The essence of specifically Christian asceticism is not primarily moral, consisting in a struggle against everything sinful, all the dangerous powers of nature, in training to achieve undisturbed harmony among the various human faculties—in short, it is not asceticism as a means to virtue or as anticonsumption, important and meaningful as such asceticism is. Nor is Christian asceticism ritual, in which man offers sacrifice to the deity because the profane or pleasurable absorption in the world is felt to be the antithesis of the sacred, while sacrifices great and small are believed to bring one nearer God. Neither is Christian asceticism ultimately mystical ascetism, a preparation of the subject (by dying to the world, to self and one's own will, and the like) for a mysterious experience of the divine. Rather, Christian asceticism must spring from the exclusively Christian interpretation of human life in its totality. Man must frankly and existentially accept that phenomenon which casts doubt on the self-contained intelligibility of human life as a whole within this world, namely, *death. Man practises asceticism in the true Christian sense when he positively confronts his mortal condition, personally affirming that he is forfeit to death (by consciously and explicitly dying together with *Jesus Christ, or by implicitly believing in him) and giving his affirmation existential reality by voluntarily anticipating this death which is suffered gradually all through life. It is Christian asceticism when a man verifies that his preparedness for death is existentially serious and inwardly genuine by freely laying hold upon something of the passion of death above and beyond that which destiny itself imposes on him. This is the systematic consequence of those statements of the NT concerning asceticism, according to which we must identify ourselves in mysterious and paradoxical fashion with the "it must be"—the following of Jesus Christ, the Passion, cross, and death—by personally willing and accepting it, even though our own efforts can never fully correspond to that "must" and its import. Neither can Christian asceticism ever be total, or constitute the only path to God (compare the reproach that Jesus was a glutton and winedrinker in Mt 11:18f.). Rather it must be a *vocation, like the vocation to particular forms of asceticism such as the religious life. Intensified exhortations to asceticism in St Paul and early Christianity are to be explained by the expectation of an imminent *parousia (*Imminence of the end).

ASEITY

A technical term meaning that God exists of himself *(a se)*, in himself, and through himself, grounded in no other, and that, accordingly, existence and essence are identical in him; he enjoys plenitude of Being. In their detailed explanation Thomists understand God's being as pure *act, pure Being as the basic reality prior to the duality of essence and existence; *ipsum esse* is indentical with *actus purus;* non-Thomists understand God's Being as essence which is simultaneously reality because of God's perfection; *essentia subsistens* is identical with *a se existens.*

ASSUMPTION OF THE BLESSED VIRGIN

The defined teaching that even now a perfect and glorified corporeality is part of the total fulfilment of *Mary since the close of her earthly life (D 3903f.). This teaching, which had clearly emerged by the seventh century, is based on fundamental passages in Scripture. Mary's physical motherhood, there attested, is after all no mere biological occurrence, but her supreme act of faith; with and through her the salvation which is Jesus' alone is given to the world. For this very reason the Church has always believed that she was redeemed in the most perfect and radical manner (*Immaculate conception). If she is believed to be the model of perfect redemption, it has further to be considered that Jesus' *resurrection cannot be an individual occurrence, since corporeality—being the external form produced in matter by the spirit to make it accessible to something else—necessarily implies physical association with another physical being (see Mt 27:52f.). It is also to be noted that this world has already achieved a new mode of existence (*Heaven) in Christ through its history, which is simultaneously a history of both the material and spiritual. Hence, the dogma of the Assumption means that our present postion vis-à-vis salvation is clarified; she, who by faith has received salvation in her body for herself and for us all, has received it *totally,* for it is the salvation of the *whole* human being. Consequently this dogma has important consequences in ecclesiology and eschatology. The Assumption does not necessarily imply the proposition that only Mary (in addition to Jesus) has "already" experienced this fulfilment, even though these are also special grounds for positing such a fulfilment in the case of Mary.

ATHEISM

ASSUMPTUS-HOMO THEOLOGY

A type of *Christology which (1) regards the Incarnation rather as the elevation *(assumptio)* of man than the abasement and self-emptying of God (A. G. Sertillanges, O. P., d. 1948); (2) holds that in the *hypostatic union not only a humanity but a psychologically autonomous human being, with his psychological ego, is united with the Logos (P. Galtier, S. J., d. 1961, and others); (3) calls the *assumptus homo,* the human being Jesus Christ, "someone" distinct from God's Son (D. de Basly, O F. M., d. 1937; L. Seiller, O. F. M.). This latter opinion was condemned by the magisterium in 1951 (D 3905).

ATHEISM

The denial of the existence of *God or of any, not merely rational, knowledge of him. When this *theoretical* atheism has no proselytizing aspirations its adherents may be tolerant, or even distressed; it is "militant" when it conceives itself as a doctrine to be propagated for the welfare of mankind and combats every religion as a destructive aberration. A conduct of life which is not influenced in any significant degree by one's (theoretical) recognition of God's existence, is known as practical atheism or indifferentism. Where atheism exists and where it does not exist will depend on the exact conception of God that one has in mind. The history of civilization shows that atheism as a philosophical system has always appeared at crucial moments of transition between successive spiritual, cultural, or social epochs, when a particular experience of human finiteness seemed to have become antiquated or to have been exploded with the result that recognition of radical finiteness itself was undermined, creating an impression that there was no room for a truly infinite and absolute reality distinct from man. Philosophical criticism of atheism must first make use of a transcendental method to demonstrate that metaphysical scepticism or positivistic empiricism cancels itself out both epistemologically and metaphysically and that consequently the possibility of metaphysics implicit in man's necessary knowledge is always affirmed. In this way God's being and attributes may be given explicitness by suitable arguments (*Proof of the existence of God) and the absolutely unique nature of this knowing as an analogical knowledge of the *mystery of God's incomprehensibility pointed out. Thereby both the possibility and the limitations of atheism are clarified. If atheism sees its own nature and grasps what is meant by God, it denies that the question of being in general and of the questioning individual as such can and should be posed. Such criticism must be supplemented by a sociological and cultural analysis of the milieu in which the phenomenon of mass atheism arises and by an explanation, in terms of depth-psychology, of the "psychic mechanism" that underlies doubt of the transcendent and "incapacity" with respect to it (atheism as "flight" from God). Philosophical criticism of atheism should always as well be a criticism of current forms of theism, both popular and philosophic, on the grounds that atheism's chief sustenance is misconception about God, from which theism suffers in its actual historical forms. Note must be taken that in the long run theoretical knowledge of God survives only if it finds higher expression in the affirmation of God by the whole person and that person's whole life.

It is a defined teaching that God can be known (*Knowledge of God); and persons professing atheism are excommunicated (D 3021, 3023ff.).

Scripture is concerned with combating idolatry, not atheism. In teaching that the whole reality of the world is created and enables natural reason to know God (Wis 13; Rom 1:20), Scripture already suggests the modern conception of the world as subject to investigation and control. The price of Scripture's dispelling the magic of the world by presenting it as a creation—necessary as this is for the true adoration incorporated in theism—is that it opens the door to the danger of modern atheism, tempting men to "explain" the world without God (see Acts 17:22f.; Eph 2:12; Rom 1:21f.). In view of the relative case with which God can be known (Wis 13:9) and the fact that "vain" atheism is "inexcusable" (Wisdom and Rom 1) Catholic theologians generally teach that over any considerable period under normal circumstances *negative* atheism, that is failure to form a judgment on the existence of God, must involve some fault. They recognize *positive* atheism, which denies either that God exists, or that he can be known, as a possible fact or fixed attitude, but term it culpable. This doctrine admits of many nuances however. Billot emphasizes the individual's social and cultural dependence on his environment, and accordingly holds that many "adults" are under-age where the existence of God is concerned. Blondel and de Lubac lay such stress on man's essential ordination to God that in fact they hold that there are no atheists, only people who *think* they do not believe in God. Theological reflections on atheism were seriously considered by the magesterium of Vatican II. In the Constitution on the Church (16), an "inculpable" atheism, which does not exclude the atheist from eternal divine salvation, is seen to be a real possibility. In Church/world, 19–21, it is stated that it is possible for atheism to reject only a God who in fact does not exist, that it often originates in an atrophy of genuine religious experience, that it is often sparked off by the *theodicy problem, also has social causes and is often a false interpretation of an essentially legitimate experience of freedom and autonomy on the part of modern man, or arises from his desire for active liberation from economic and social bonds or an absolutization of human values. It is stated that Christians also bear guilt for atheism as a critical reaction to inadequate forms of theism in theory and life. It is stressed that belief in God answers a question which man cannot obviate in the long run and in the decisive moments of his existence, and that active construction of the future in this world is not attenuated by Christian faith and eschatological hope. In connection with atheism, theology should observe that a nominal theism is possible, which either does not attain the true character of *transcendence genuinely and in personal freedom or else at heart atheistically denies it, even whilst objectively discoursing of God. There may well be an atheism which only *supposes* it is such, because though obediently accepting transcendence in implicit fashion it fails to make that transcendence sufficiently explicit; while, on the other hand, there may be a total atheism—one therefore necessarily culpable—which consciously and explicitly denies transcendence, closing the self against it out of fear or pride. Which of these possible forms of atheism occurs in a particular person or at a particular time ultimately remains the secret of God, the only judge. Christianity must show atheists through dialogue where in their lives they can find God, even if they do not call the ultimate whither and whence of their ethical freedom and love by the name "God," do not wish to "objectify" them, and often see institutionalized religion as opium or as a contradiction of this unutterable *mystery of their being. An *atheist ethics* is possible, in that there are values, and norms derived from them, distinct from God (the personal nature of man and all that is appropriate to it, such as society) that can be perceived and affirmed without explicit knowledge of God. But if these values and norms are to carry any absolute obligation it can only be on the basis of man's transcendence, even in morals, with relation to God—though affirmed only implicitly. Thus even an atheist ethics which is subjectively self-contained is just as impossible as atheism itself. Admittedly a person who thinks himself an atheist may in fact affirm God by his absolute deference to the demands of morality, provided of course that this deference be genuine and not the insufficient product of bourgeois respectability. A

33

person might actually realize this fact in the depths of his conscience, and yet falsely interpret his own actions in the conceptual system of his objective consciousness.

ATONEMENT

See *Redemption, Satisfaction.*

ATTRITIONISM

The doctrine that attrition (from the Lat. *attritio,* repentance) suffices for the valid reception of the sacrament of penance. The theory can only be understood historically: attrition was first advanced in the twelfth century as incomplete repentance resulting from insufficient effort towards the perfect repentance of contrition (*Contritionism), but nonetheless ordered to the latter. Later it was conceived as a separate type of repentance, serious and prompted by moral motives (for example, fear of divine justice) but not yet by charity, not yet rejecting sin as such. Luther violently attacked it as the "repentance of the gallows" (*Fear of God). Before the Council of Trent declared attrition to be a morally good preparation for the sacrament (D 1678), it was disputed whether sacramental *penance could change attrition into contrition. Subsequent to Trent, discussion was concerned with whether attrition sufficed as a proximate disposition to the sacrament of penance or whether an additional explicit act of charity—be it ever so faint—might be required.—See *Contrition.*

AUGUSTINIANISM

IN THEOLOGY. The term primarily refers to a doctrine on grace which rightly or wrongly appeals to the authority of St Augustine (A.D. 354 – 430). It maintains that man in his original paradisiacal state was able to will and do good unaided by an intrinsically efficacious grace; primal man was merely sustained by the general assistance of divine grace. This capacity was forfeited by his fall. Intrinsically efficacious grace, that is to say every grace, even the merely sufficient or imperfectly efficacious to which man is predestined apart from any merit of his own, overcomes *concupiscence as the consequence of original sin. Insofar as this Augustinianism denies the real possibility of a state

34

of pure *nature it is highly questionable theologically (D 2616, 3891). The chief exponents of Augustinianism (as opposed to Calvinism, *Baianism, and *Jansenism) are H. de Noris (1631–1704), F. Bellelli (1675–1742), and J. L. Berti (1696–1766).

IN PHILOSOPHY. Some principal theses: All human knowledge is derived from direct divine illumination; at the moment of creation certain *"seeds" *(rationes seminales)* capable of development were "implanted" in matter; there is more than one substantial form in man (pluralism): the will (love) enjoys a priority over the intellect. These views were borrowed in part from the Arabian philosophers Avicenna and Avicebron. Best known among its exponents are William of Auvergne (about 1180–1249), Alexander of Hales (about 1185–1245), St Bonaventure (about 1217–74), Peter John Olivi (about 1248 –98). Augustinianism reached its climax in the attack on St Thomas about 1270.

AUTHENTICITY OF SCRIPTURE

In *juridical* reference, that normative authority which Scripture enjoys in matters of faith, founded upon its inspired, infallible, and canonical character; in the full sense it is proper to the original manuscripts (none of which survive), but accurate copies and translations of the originals are also authentic when the Church as guardian of revelation declares that they may be used in matters of faith. In the context of *textual criticism* the authenticity of Scripture means that its various individual writings derive from the men who are seriously alleged to be their authors and that the text has been preserved in a substantially unaltered state. Authenticity of Scripture in this latter sense is established by the biblical sciences.

AUTHORITY

The palpable, demonstrable trustworthiness or legal claim of a person or thing (a book), capable of convincing another person of some truth or of the validity of a command and obliging him to accept it, even though that truth or valid character is not immediately evident. Any serious claim to persuade or commit another person presupposes that at least the intention exists to give him direct insight into something. True discernment presupposes the most thorough information, a grasp of complex associations, education, and so on. If participation and dialogue in this sense are denied by authority, authoritative behaviour becomes authoritarian domination (*Democratization, open decisions; cf. *Enlightenment). Authority in the Church is legitimate only if it serves the mission of Jesus. It cannot simply be identified with the authority of Jesus; nor by calling on Jesus' authority, can it avoid objective criticism that examines the appropriateness of ecclesiastical authority to an element essential to an attentive and believing Church. The acceptance of a command on authority is called *obedience; the similarly motivated acceptance of a truth is called *faith. Both are modes of *indirect* recognition as they are based on the authority of an intermediary.—See also: *Philosophy and Theology,* for the relation of philosophy, which as a system of direct evidence recognizes no authority, to theology.

B

BAIANISM

The doctrine of Baius (1513–89), a theologian of the Augustinian school, according to whom God was unable to withhold from man the gifts of *original justice. Original sin quite reverses this order: without grace, fallen man necessarily sins in all that he does, even in striving after virtue for its own sake. Consequently he enjoys freedom of choice only with respect to indifferent values; even involuntary *concupiscence is sinful. The penalty which the justified thus incur is forgiven them. Seventy-nine propositions excerpted from Baius' writings were condemned in 1567 (D 1901–1980) in order to end the violent controversy they had precipitated; however, there was no decision whether or not a number of them might be understood in an orthodox sense.

BANEZIANISM

A doctrine of *grace based on the teachings of St Thomas; it takes its name after D. Bañez, O.P. (1538–1604). In his view, and in that of nearly all theologians, before man makes a free choice *(in actu primo)* God bestows an actual *grace which enables him freely to perform a *salutary act. According to Bañez this actual grace is a sufficient grace *(gratia sufficiens),* and the salutary act is not actually performed until the person is granted an additional efficacious grace *(gratia efficax)* that is really different from the first. More specifically, God himself infallibly causes the human will to pass from a state of *potency to a particular free *act by a "physical premotion", which by its own inner nature produces a free choice. In a mysterious manner this does not prejudice human *freedom, for God gives both the act and the act's quality of freedom.—See also *Predetermination.*

BAPTISM

The first and fundamental *sacrament (D 150, 802, 1614ff. and *passim).* Consequently it must always be considered in closest connexion with the Catholic notion of the Church. Baptism is the purifying and sanctifying sacrament of rebirth (Jn 3:5; see also Ezek 36:25f.; D 223, 231, 247, 1314ff., 1730 and *passim)* in the Spirit and grace of Jesus Christ through a simultaneously juridical and sacral incorporation in the Church, where the salvific theandric life of Christ—the new yet most primordial beginning of mankind, fallen in Adam—has already established its indestructible sacramental and bodily presence in the world. This incorporation into the sacramental corporeality of salvation in the *body of Jesus Christ, which is his Church, (D 394, 1314f., 1513, 1671f., 1730, 3705)—animated and sanctified by his Spirit—is once and for all indelibly sealed (2 Cor 1:21f.; Eph 4:30) by the baptismal *character (D 781, 1314ff., 1609, 1767–1770), thus making a repetition of baptism impossible (D 10, 123, 183, 214, 810, 1609, 1624, 1626, 1671f., 1864f.). Understood in this manner, incorporation into the Church is the primary basic effect of baptism (D 632, 1050, 1314ff., 1621, 1627 and *passim;* CIC can. 87; see also *Membership of the Church).* At the same time, assuming the appropriate *disposition, it is likewise the means by which we attain the fullness of baptismal grace—the renewal of the "old man" in justification (Eph 4:22; Col 1:10 and *passim;* D 1671) by an interior divinization and conformation to the death and resurrection of Christ (Rom 6), by the strength of his Spirit present in and through the Church; the obliteration of all sins (D 150, 231, 239, 540f., 632, 793, 854, 903, 1314f., 1515f., 1671f.), and the remission of all the eternal and temporal *penalties due to sin (Eph 5:26; D 854, 1314ff., 1515f., 1542f., 1689ff.). Since only baptism bestows rebirth into the new life in Christ, this same life cannot in principle be had without baptism (Jn 3:5; Mk 16:16). But since baptism bestows it as the sacrament of initiation into Jesus' community (1 Cor 12:13) and thereby into the grace therein embodied in historic tangibility, its *necessity for salvation is closely bound up with that of the Church, so that there are various degrees of actual participation in its saving sacramentality (analogously to the case of membership of the Church) in what is called the baptism of blood and the *baptism of desire. The baptism of blood, accomplished through *martyrdom, justifies man because it is a real participation in the Church's function of witnessing to the presence of that salvation wrought by Jesus Christ's death. The *baptism of desire, the explicit or even implicit desire (*Votum) for the sacrament of baptism accompanied by perfect *contrition, also effects justification, because by this desire man freely affirms and accepts his human nature in faith and love insofar as it is objectively ordered to Jesus Christ himself through the mystery of the Incarnation and thus is already configured to Jesus Christ's sacred humanity in a quasi-sacramental fashion.

Against *Donatism and those who advocated the rebaptism of *heretics, the Church teaches that in principle everyone can validly administer sacramental baptism (D 110f, 123, 127f., 183, 211, 1314ff., 1348f.). Only certain Church officials can confer solemn baptism: a bishop, a priest, or a deacon. The baptismal rite has adopted the primitive religious symbol of ritual ablution (manifest, for example, in the baptism of John the Baptist, in the ablution of Jewish proselytes, in the gnostic mystery cults, in Mandaeism, and the like). However, the specific idea in Christian baptism, that of supernatural regeneration, cannot be derived from the pre-Christian baptism studied in comparative religion; but within the world of the Bible it is possible to regard Christian baptism as perfecting and superseding the baptism of John, which was intended to testify to faith in the coming Messiah (see Ezek 36:25). Valid Christian baptism is administered by pouring (or sprinkling, or immersion in) natural water, at the same time designating the act of baptism ("N., I baptize thee . . .") and invoking the Blessed Trinity ("in the name of the Father and of the Son and of the Holy Ghost") with the *intention of doing what the Church does when she baptizes. Any person who has not yet been baptized, including infants, can receive baptism. When the child of non-Catholic or apostate parents is to be baptized certain conditions must be fulfilled, for after all the child is to be baptized into the Church (*Infant baptism).

BAPTISM OF DESIRE

A theological concept arising out of the question whether a person can attain *salvation who is not outwardly and officially a full member of the Church as she fulfils herself in the sacraments, does not explicitly believe in *Jesus Christ, and has not received the sacrament of baptism. On the one hand the answer must be in the affirmative, for while God's *salvific will extends to all men, the Gospel has neither in the past nor in the present reached all men nor reached all in the appropriate manner. On the other hand, however, the answer must not be allowed to prejudice the Church's doctrine that *membership of the Church is *necessary for salvation (*Extra ecclesiam nulla salus). From the Middle Ages the Church has taught that the *votum sacramenti, the desire to receive the sacrament, may fulfil the requirement of baptism. It has similarly been taught that the votum ecclesiae or desire to belong to the true Church of Jesus Christ may satisfy the requirement of membership in the Church (D 741, 788, 1524, 1604, 1677f., 1932, 1971; CIC can 737, § 1). The Holy Office declared in 1949 (American Ecclesiastical Review, 127 (1952), pp. 312–14; D 3866 –3873) that where faith and charity are present this desire need not be explicit. Vatican II did not take up the doctrine of the votum or that of baptism of desire, but simply declared that whoever is inculpably unaware of Christ's Gospel and the Church, but honestly seeks God and obeys his or her conscience, can attain to eternal salvation (Church, 16). This doctrine does not compromise the Church's rôle in saving history, for the grace which God freely bestows outside the Church and the sacraments is always both the grace of Jesus Christ, the *primordial sacrament, given in him and for his sake, and the grace of the Church, because she is the sign of grace eschatologically victorious and present in the world. Baptism of desire may be said to exist in anyone who lives according to his *conscience, since such a person is accomplishing the will of God. As to how such a person can satisfy the necessity for faith and charity, see the article Jesus Christ.

In terms of saving history, baptism of desire is to be seen as that type of *beginning which impels a person towards its fulfilment in full membership of the Church and the reception of baptism; but in the manner of a genuine beginning it contains the whole (salvation) concealed within itself even when its full development is in fact frustrated. For the separate question of whether baptism of desire is possible for children who die unbaptized see the article Limbo.

BASILEIA

In the NT always the basileia (Gr. βασιλεία, kingdom, sovereignty, reign) of God or the basileia of heaven ("heaven" here being a circumlocution for God in later Judaism); it is the central concept in the scriptural message of salvation. Even the most ancient parts of the OT are acquainted with God's dominion over Israel, other peoples, and the rulers of the world; *Yahweh is the true King of Israel, which serves him by its worship and its fidelity to the covenant. Later Judaism witnesses the development of two particular conceptions of the *basileia:* (1) An eschatological reign of God, inaugurated only by the judgment of the nations and the end of the world in its present form, or already mysteriously present as the new *aeon. According to *apocalyptic literature the salvation this basileia brings will not be confined to Jews. (2) An earthly kingdom of God to be established on earth by the triumph of the *Messiah. The *basileia* of God is the substance of Christ's preaching; in him and his deeds (subjugating the devils) the *basileia* is at hand (Mk 1:15 and parallel passages, *passim)* and with it the *salvation of mankind. This is accorded to everyone, but above all to the disadvantaged and peripheral. Though the *basileia* is the quintessence of all human joys *(basileia* as a banquet, wedding-feast), in fact Jesus repudiates the earthly and national notion of the kingdom (Mt 8:11; 21:43). The promises of the *basileia* (already offered by the prophets as peace, justice, freedom, reconciliation) must be affirmed by those who follow Jesus. Its presence is that of the mustard seed, a seed that has been sown, a sprouting plant (parables of growth). On the other hand it is emphatically represented as a reality that will assume its full magnitude in the future (the mustard tree grown out of the seed, the harvest sprung from the sowing) for which the Christian must pray and for which the Church itself makes petition in the Our Father (Mt 6:10); we are explicitly told that we have yet to enter the *basileia,* or more precisely we have yet to inherit it, it is brought about or bestowed by God (Lk 12:32; 22:29). Only the Father knows (Mk 13:32 and parallel passages, *passim)* when it will come (*Day of the Lord, *Parousia) and who will be received into it. Thus the *basileia* cannot be identified with the *Church, however much the Church calls for its prerequisites, namely, penance (*Metanoia) and *faith, prepares the field for the *following of Christ as the condition for sharing in the *basileia,* exercises *power over those who hope for the *basileia,* since the keys of the *basileia* were promised to Peter (Mt 16:19), and celebrates the Eucharist as a mysterious anticipation of the banquet of the *basileia.* St Paul distinguishes between a *basileia* of Christ which is the Church (Col 1:13 and *passim)* and a *basileia* of God in the sense of Christ's preaching.—See also *Kingdom of God.*

BASLE

Eugenius IV inaugurated the Seventeenth Ecumenical Council on August 23, 1431 at Basle and transferred it to Ferrara (*Florence) on September 18, 1437; prior to the transference no important decrees had been formulated. The adherents of *conciliarism who remained at Basle declared it as dogma that a Council is superior to the Pope. They deposed Eugenius IV and elected the anti-pope Felix V. In 1448 Emperor Frederick III expelled them from the city.

BEATIFIC VISION

In Scripture the perfection of the personal creature as a whole; more precisely, it is that direct and, so far as the creature is capable of it, perfect contemplation of himself (1 Cor 13:12; 1 Jn 3:2), which God gratuitously imparts to the pure of heart as beneficiaries of his promise (Mt 5:8). By this, Scripture does not mean intellectual knowledge alone, but the experience of God's nearness and an absorption in his *glory which is grounded in our possession of the Spirit (*Pneuma) and our conformity with Christ. Theology declares that the vision of God is essential to the glory man has been promised, but in comparison with Scripture, theology often unduly stresses the intellectual aspect. It is the defined teaching of the Church that an intuitive vision of the divine essence independent of any created mediating *species* is granted the souls of those who have been perfected by death (and *purgatory), even "before" the resurrection of the body (D 1000f., 1304ff., 1314ff.). The Church has condemned (D 895) the opinions that every rational nature is in itself blessed and that the soul does not need the light of glory in order to be capable of the beatific vision. It is indirectly defined that God remains incomprehensible even in the beatific vision (D 3001). Traditionally it is possible to conceive a temporal difference between the realization of a person in the spiritual and personal dimension, and fulfilment in the physical dimension, but ultimately it is inconclusive. Since Scripture always intends the single complete fulfilment of a human being, the realization of human physicality should be included in the full notion of the beatific vision. If it be asked what the nature and prerequisites of the beatific vision are, the reply will depend on certain fundamental conceptions of the nature of knowledge in general. The primal notion of knowledge is not an "intentional" reaching-out of the subject to an object, not "objectivity" in the sense that the knower emerges from his very self in order to fasten upon something else, but primarily the presence of the entity to itself, its inner clarity to and for itself because its being is of a certain grade, namely, immaterial; its state of being reflected upon itself. In this sense the beatific vision must perfectly actualize man's being: the highest fulfilment of his nature is a transparency to the absolute God himself. Empirical knowledge of other things is based on an adequation of the subject's being to that of the object through the "species", is an entitative reality both of the knower and the known, whereby the knower and the known truly become "a single thing". Knower and known are not made one by knowledge, but the knower knows the object because the two are entitatively one. The ontological prerequisite for the beatific vision is a "relationship" between the creature and God which is above all categories and does not depend on an intrinsic though accidental modification of the creature by God's creative power (because nothing finite and created can mediate the direct vision of God). It involves a quasi-formal causality of God himself with respect to the created mind, with the result that in the beatific vision the reality of the mind as a knower is the being of God himself. This new "relationship" of God to the creature—which cannot be classified in the category of efficient causality, as a production of something external to the cause, but must rather be conceived as a formal causality, a taking up into the source—is a supernatural *mystery in the strict sense. It is only in the intuitive beatific vision that God's utter incomprehensibility is contemplated in itself with all its radicality; there is the vision of that very infinity which alone makes God God and thereby the object of true beatitude. We ought not to construe this formal divine causality acting upon the human mind too narrowly, as exclusively affecting the intellect; for according to Scripture it is man's *heart that sees God. That final grace which disposes the mind to receive the formal causality of God's being, theologians call the *lumen gloriae,* the light of glory: that created grace which is absolutely necessary for the beatific vision and the seed of which is already present in man by grace, and can grow because created grace is capable of growth.

BEATITUDE

The total ultimate perfection of the whole man who has been blessed by grace in the supernatural order: the *beatific vision, the *resurrection of the flesh, the definitive *basileia of God (*Heaven) in the perfected *communion of saints (*Eschatology).—The same thing is ultimately meant by the beatitudes contained in the *Sermon on the Mount, though the exact import of "blessedness" in this case, saving acceptance by God, is not yet clear.

BEAUTY

According to St Thomas beauty is the splendour of *form, an immediate and necessary, essential character of *being, the completion of all other essential characters. In practice it is inseparable from *contemplation, in which man rests in a consent and content exceeding his desire; it is also inseparable from *hope, since the beautiful—often, perhaps, unconsciously—is necessarily loved in its relation to the infinite, which is pervasively present in everything beautiful as both exemplary cause and promise. Every being is beautiful in a germinal sense; beauty and life grow in direct proportion to one another (in material things, as symmetry, balance, harmony, or as functionality; in organic beings, as vitality and rhythm); God therefore, the supreme being, is absolutely beautiful. If theologians today with few exceptions (Hans Urs von Balthasar) ignore beauty, in contrast with their own tradition from Plotinus through St Augustine, Pseudo-Dionysius, and St Bonaventure, it still has a certain place in the sacred play (ludus) of liturgy and in Church art. A theology of beauty would begin primarily with reflections on *bridal mysticism (see the Song of Solomon) and from thence proceed into ecclesiology. The *praeambula fidei could also draw attention to the beauty of *revelation as a whole. There can of course be no purely aesthetic Christian attitude to life (Kierkegaard), since pure beauty is to be found only in the *salvation to come; but for the believer beauty is at least the hidden essence of the world. What lies at the heart of the world is not the suffering servant of God, without form or beauty (Is 53:2), but rather the *doxa of God through the sufferings of his servant (see Mt 12:40).

BEGINNING

Not the first element in a series of comparable elements, but that initiation of a whole which alone makes the history of the whole possible; hence, the concept of a beginning transcends the notion of formal, external time. The beginning presents the whole with its nature and with the therein implicit concrete conditions for its realization. It is something apart from that which begins, for it ordains the boundaries of concrete created existence and is thus the irrevocable prerequisite of such existence experienced as fulfilment. It is a genuine beginning only when it is the beginning of a personal being, where what is inaugurated is a new whole and not merely a phase of another movement. The beginning remains open with respect to its end and only attains itself in its end. The growing presence of the end in man's progressive self-perfection is simultaneously the growing presence of the beginning. We must speak of a real beginning in the theological sense (creation or re-creation) wherever God acts immediately. A beginning, therefore, above all, implies createdness, for the existence of an intellectual person can only derive from an immediate divine act of creation (*Soul), and thus direct dependence on God necessarily involves the irrevocability of the beginning. Such a beginning, as it commences a process of becoming, is obscure and only reveals itself in the history of the individual existence. Since the beginning is the beginning of a definite individual, the potentialities implicit in it are the exclusive endowment of this particular individual and, therefore, constitute that inescapable responsibility which the individual must bear. Insofar as the beginning is genuinely potential and of itself enters into the dimension of time wherein the perfection gradually matures, and insofar as it exposes itself to God's incalculable disposition, the *end is certainly the preservation, perfection, and revelation of that beginning. But this perfection is not merely the process whereby the beginning gradually achieves self-identity; rather, the beginning lives on the movement towards perfection, the final completion of which is produced by God, who alone is simultaneously beginning and end.

BEING

That reality and concept which is the chief concern of metaphysics (see also *Ontology, Philosophy and Theology);* some understanding of it is important if we are to grasp what is meant by "God". We call "a being", or entity, any conceivable object of knowledge, anything that is not nothing. The concept of entity is reached by bringing all possible objects under the broadest possible heading by radically abstracting from every distinguishing characteristic; in turn this concept must be able to include the entirety of those elements from which we originally abstracted. To this extent "being" may be taken to mean that which makes "a being" of this something which is not nothing. But it would be superficial and wrong to regard "being" as nothing more than the ultimate abstraction drawn simply from our experience of particular things. Rather, the individual mind grasps an individual object in accordance with the antecedent laws of intellectual judgment in general. A concept emerges by way of the mind's (implicit) prior grasp of the fontal totality of possible reality. The individual object is encountered within a "horizon" which is non-objectively and implicitly involved whenever the mind grasps individual objects. This non-objective, non-thematic knowledge is a kind of properly metaphysical experience which the metaphysically blind always pass by unawares but which begins to become articulate in the phenomenon of infinite love, longing, dread, of the entirely open question as such. It is the *a priori* condition of all particular knowledge; without it we could neither compare things nor relate them nor form unqualified judgments. For to associate or to distinguish between two objects that are given empirically (the basic function of intellectual judgment) presupposes, but does not create, a common measure, even though one first becomes aware of the latter in the empirical material one is dealing with. The term of this *a priori* grasp (*Transcendence) which simultaneously distinguishes and unites individual objects, reaching out in knowledge and love to the fontal totality of possible knowledge and love, we call Being. Now this already postulates the incomprehensible and infinite, for if being were apprehended as finite of itself it would already be comprehended and so understood within a wider horizon which alone would really be the horizon of Being *simpliciter*. That which is called *actus purus,* absolute Being, *simpliciter,* absolute mystery, *God, is not the abstract notion of being which we build up from each particular, finite entity, but rather the fontal infinitude of Being *simpliciter,* to which as to incomprehensible *mystery the transcendence of man is ordered in every act of knowledge—though he does not conceive of it for itself—and which is the source not only of the knowledge but of the reality of every being.

BIBLICAL CRITICISM

This discipline examines the Bible by the method of historical criticism and with the aid of the secular sciences, especially history, archaeology, and philology. As textual criticism it notably contributes to the restoration of the original text; as literary criticism it is concerned to investigate the date of composition, authorship, literary character, and theological purpose of the individual books of the Bible (*Literary genres). Because biblical criticism first appeared in liberal and rationalistic forms (18th and 19th centuries) in which religio-historical and philosophical suasions were to the fore, the magisterium treated it with reserve and the theologians disapproved of it. But since Pius XII's encyclical on biblical studies (1943) the Church has encouraged a sound biblical criticism, which does not adopt an attitude of pseudo-scientific neutrality towards the theological datum of *Holy Scripture as a whole (D 3825ff., 3862ff., 3898). It was further encouraged by Vatican II (Rev. 12, 23).

BIBLICAL THEOLOGY

A relatively independent science of biblical theology is necessary in present-day Catholic theology, not only for the sake of an orderly classification of the sciences but also on the basis of the specific, unique position of *Holy Scripture itself. Certainly *dogmatic theology is concerned with certain propositions which demand the assent of faith although not simply and obviously identical with the statements of Scripture; it is after all regulated by the *magisterium. Furthermore, *Tradition is another one of its sources and norms and there is a real *development of dogma. But, nevertheless, Scripture is not simply one of two equally important sources of dogmatic truth. Biblical theology, in the strict sense of *theological* exegesis, not exegesis in terms of the development of religion, or in terms of mere historical philology, must of course, like all dogmatic theology, interpret Scripture in the Church according to the "proximate rule" of the faith as actually preached by the ecclesiastical magisterium which Christ has commissioned. But this very preaching of the faith here and now by the Church's magisterium necessarily has constant recourse to the concreteness of that permanent origin and beginning which God himself has guaranteed to be "pure" and which can be distinguished from its fulfilment in the Church's later teaching. This concreteness is to be found in Scripture and in Scripture alone, since the bare survival of tradition as an objective "block" apart from the magisterium's diacritical function, offers no guarantee that the tradition has not been tainted by purely human accretions. For in order to differentiate between divine and human tradition by a recourse to tradition itself is after all an act of the magisterium which has this recourse and thus already presupposes the difference between the material norm and that which the norm regulates. To this extent, despite the existence of a divine and apostolic tradition, Scripture remains not only an excellent but an incomparable source and norm for the Church's present teaching and thus also for dogmatic theology, which is regulated by that teaching and at the same time humbly helps to prepare it (see D 3281f.; Vat. II, Rev., 21, 24). Consequently, when dogmatic theology as a whole listens to God's written word in and with the authoritative Church, which itself is bound to listen attentively to Scripture, something totally unique occurs. Here and here alone, dogmatic theology is directed and does not direct, listens without really passing judgment as it does in its other functions ("historical" and "speculative"). Though it is a *beginning, the *pure* beginning of the *kerygma of the faith which is everpresent in Scripture always remains something greater and more comprehensive, a principle constantly giving rise to new development which it pervades and governs. Biblical theology consists in a return to this principle, not in the collection of proof-texts (*Scriptural proof). Biblical theology has a liberating effect as against a stultified dogmatic theology (e.g., neo-Scholasticism), but runs the risk of theological naivety if changes in the forms of experience between biblical and modern times are ignored.

BINDING AND LOOSING

This power signifies the authority that Christ conferred on Peter (Mt 16:19 and 18:18) and the "disciples" (Mt 18:1). The exact import of this binding and loosing cannot be gathered with certainty from the NT alone. In rabbinical terminology it means "to inflict *excommunication (from the synagogue)" on some one and then "to free from excommunication"; probably by derivation from this sense, it also means "to declare with authority", "to forbid" and "to allow". But the demonological expressions "deliver to Satan" and "deliver from Satan", widely current in the biblical milieu, represent an even older sense of binding and loosing that frequently occurs in both OT and NT (see Mk 7:35; Lk 13:12, 16; Acts 2:24; Jn 3:8; Rev 9:14f.; 20:1, 3, 7 and *passim)*. These three usages are not mutually exclusive, and taken together they show that binding and loosing is the power by which the Church survives in an *aeon ruled by devils; he who submits to Satan is simultaneously bound and excommunicated; he who by God's grace breaks with Satan can also be validly loosed before God in virtue of that power and is forgiven (*Penance). From the same power derives the Church's right to lay down what it is that binds or looses one, that is the right to forbid or permit.

BISHOP

A bishop (Gr. ἐπίσκοπος , overseer) is one who holds the *office willed and established by Jesus Christ in his Church by pneumatic endowment, who by virtue of a divine right and of his membership in the episcopal college—above all in virtue of his communion with the *Pope, with the episcopal see of Peter—rules a local church (his diocese) as a microcosm of the universal Church. The office and notion of a bishop as well as membership in a college of elders as the characteristic sign of such office seem to find their prototype in the Jewish milieu of NT times. This office of administration and government is already linked in the NT to the theological conception of the pastoral office (Acts 20:17–36): the office of a bishop is plainly to be seen, for example, in Phil 1:1; 1 Thess 5:12; 1 Tim 3:2ff.; Tit 1:5ff. The development of the office of a bishop from the pastoral supervision of several *episcopes* within a community to the "monarchial" episcopate occurred by and large in the first century. It is a defined teaching that the episcopate exists by divine right (D 1767ff., 1776, 3050ff., 3061, 3804). The Pope, therefore, cannot abolish the episcopate, his primacy of jurisdiction over the whole Church and each of her members, including the individual bishops, notwithstanding. Bishops must not be regarded as officials or representatives of the Pope. They feed their flocks not in the Pope's name, but in Christ's name and their own as his true ambassadors; consequently by divine institution they are the very successors of the Apostles. Their divine right and divine institution are evident from the fact that Christ willed his *Church and willed this specific *office in her, and that the universal episcopate is the college of the *Apostles perduring in history. The universal episcopate (whose head is the Pope, who is Pope precisely as its head) has rights and duties in the Church precisely as a college, rights and duties that are original, inalienable, and of divine right, such that the Pope does not have the same rights vis-à-vis the universal episcopate that he has vis-à-vis the individual bishop. The individual bishop is not the successor of an individual Apostle, but the individual bishop is in legitimate succession to an Apostle by belonging to the Church's universal episcopate, which for its part succeeds the apostolic college as a body. As in the apostolic college, so in the universal episcopate: the college as such is the entity willed and preordained by Christ, and is not composed of persons each invested in advance with his own individual authority who subsequently decide to unite. The primate is primate in this college, not vis-à-vis the college, as though he had later decided to associate a college with himself and to confer authority on it. The college is primary, the successor of the apostolic college, with its preordained head the Pope, and inconceivable without him; yet the Pope is and can be Pope only as a member of this college and as its head.

From this point of view the Catholic doctrine that a *council possesses supreme power in the Church (CIC, can. 228; Vat. II, Bish., 4) becomes intelligible and obvious. This implies no diminution of the papal primacy, since the episcopal college always has the Pope for its head and could not exist, in council or out of council, without him. Unless the Pope is acting as a private individual, his acts are in effect acts of the college. This clarifies the *infallibility of the Church's *magisterium and shows where infallibility resides: an infallible *definition of the magisterium pronounced by the Pope alone and one pronounced by the Pope together with a council are not distinguished as the acts of two different subjects; they are two different procedures of one and the same subject, distinguished only by the circumstances. In the first case the one moral subject is dispersed throughout the world, while in the second case it is gathered in one place, thus throwing into relief the collaboration of the members of the college with its head and their harmonious participation with him in the definition. The same is true of declarations by the "ordinary magisterium". We can now grasp the significance of the episcopal college: the Church is to be constituted not only by *many* members but also by members *qualitatively* different from each other. The pluralism that God wills to exist in the Church must also make itself felt and respected at the summit of the Church and at the same time find its fulfilment there. Now a bishop of the episcopal college can properly discharge his function for the universal Church only if he authoritatively represents a particular member (diocese) of the universal Church in which the difference from her other members which the Spirit wills can and does really exist. But insofar as he is an individual bishop he is allotted his clearly defined territory by the Pope, who confers pastoral authority on him and can intervene to restrict these rights in case of emergency. The bishop receives his power of orders, essentially the same as the Pope's, at his consecration (Vat. II, Church, 21, 26; Bish., 15); this gives him the full powers of the one *Order, in virtue of which he administers confirmation and ordains priests in his diocese. The consecration of churches and altars, the blessing of abbots and abbesses and of holy oils are also reserved to the bishop. In virtue of his pastoral authority he rules his diocese as chief shepherd (teaching of doctrine, charitable works, cure of souls and its supervision, legislative and judicial power, administration of temporalities, etc.).—See also the constitution *de Ecclesia* of Vatican II, ch. 3.

It is clear that these theological considerations do not exclude, but on ecclesiological grounds require, a sociological critique (lest the goal and nature of the *Church are traduced). The danger of an absolutist control and use of office (not obviated by such commitments as outlined in Bish., 11–17), the inadequacies of the appointment procedure (from "above" with overwhelming influence allowed to bureaucratic administrators), the disadvantages of a period of office practically unlimited in duration, the superfluity of suffragan bishops and so on, are far from insignificant.

BLESSEDNESS

See *Beatific Vision.*

BLESSING

Since all that is good in reality exists by God's creative word (*Creation, *Conservation), the Christian recognizes all good that happens to him as a "blessing" from the God of all blessing (Gen 1:22, 28). Prayers of the individual or the Church begging the favour of God, often in special liturgical form (*Sacramentals), are also called blessings. Such blessings are known both to the OT: blessings given by patriarchs, parents, and kings, and by priests during worship, and the NT: blessings given by Christ or an Apostle, and similar instances. Blessings may also be given when office is bestowed, or on behalf of those who are to use certain objects (*Consecration).

BLOOD

In the OT blood was considered to be the seat (symbol) of life (Gen 9:4f.) and therefore to belong to God. Already called a means of atonement in Leviticus 17:10 (*Sacrifice), blood acquires soteriological significance in the blood of Christ; Christ freely shed his blood for many to the remission of sins (Mt 26:28), thereby instituting God's New Covenant with a new, redeemed people, the Church. Thus the blood of Jesus is the source of the Church's life (Jn 19:34 –37), and she attests her institution in that blood by re-presenting Christ's blood-sacrifice—in the Last Supper and the sacrifice of the cross—in the sacrifice of the *Mass. The blood of Jesus represents his personal surrender of his life and does not indicate any magical power on the part of his blood. The reference in Romans (3:25) is an expression conditioned by contemporary usage though derived from the Old Testament and does not refer to an angry God demanding a bloody *Sacrifice.

BODY

Two conceptions of the body which figure in the intellectual history of the West still mould men's understanding of themselves, as expressed in their thought and behaviour, and sharply divide them. The Greek conception is a more (Plato) or less (Aristotle) extreme *dualism. In the one instance the body is the "prison" or "tomb" of the soul; mitigated dualism, on the other hand, would have man consist of "parts", such that he can only be said to "have" a body—the *soul is the substantial *form of the body (*Trichotomism).

The other basic conception, the biblical one, is already elaborated in the OT. Here there is no notion of the body but in its stead the terms "flesh" and "soul" as "breath of life" are used to designate the whole man in his original unity. Belief in the *resurrection of the flesh, which first emerges in later Judaism, represents an advance in thought about the body, but one that still springs from the soil of the OT. This biblical conception does not admit of a body external to the "I" which is possessed as a mere "instrument" (even when, prior to a real understanding of the resurrection of the flesh, the dead man is thought to live on as a shade in *Sheol): his body too is something which man "is". In the NT St Paul further develops the theology of the body. His conception is *soma* rather than *sarx. Soma* is the earthly as well as the heavenly body, the unity of the whole man, here on earth subject to concupiscence, sin, and death, but destined to be exalted and transformed by the *Pneuma; *sarx* alone can mean the morality of the body, it is the "locus" of human sin, the earthly-minded man.

It was the task of Christian philosophy and theology (not yet fully accomplished even today) to harmonize Platonic anthropology, in whose historical ambience the Church's first theology arose (*Neoplatonism), with that of the Bible. Steps in this direction were taken by the Church's declaration on the unity of the human being (D 902, see also *Creation of Man*) and the anthropology of St Thomas Aquinas, who tried to convey the Christian notion of the body in terms of the Aristotelian categories of *form and *matter: the body is the substantial "expression" of the soul in which the soul first achieves its concrete reality; the soul cannot fulfil itself without making use of matter; the greater its self-fulfilment, that is to say, the more man becomes *spirit, the more the soul (the man) becomes the body. This means that the body is the medium of all *communication and that conversely the soul fulfils itself in proportion as man lives with bodily men in a bodily world (*Sensibility).

The current theology of the body is in agreement with these principles. On the basis of biblical anthropology the "becoming-man" of the Logos is called "incarnation", "becoming-flesh" (Jn 1:14); Jesus Christ is one man, not split up into parts as *Arianism and *Apollinarianism would have him. He effects the redemption in his body, which is delivered up and whose blood is shed. We may gather, principally from the revealed truth that our body is conformed to his, that the assertion that *death is the "separation of body and soul" is at very least inadequate in terms of biblical theology and a deeper metaphysical notion of man, and requires careful interpretation. The fact that in accordance with her constitution as People of God the Church realizes herself essentially in the *sacraments and the announcement of the *basileia, shows that an essential feature of bodily life—communication by sensible signs—is also an integral element of human *salvation. We may gather from the biblical theology of sin, in particular from the words of Jesus himself, that the body is not the preferred site of sin, but rather that the sin of the whole individual—like everything that is alleged to be purely spiritual or purely interior—must necessarily come to light in the body. But the salvation Christ has wrought must also necessarily come to light in the body, though by no means as an accidental, external beatitude of the body finally added to a beatitude of the "soul" that has long been perfect without it. This is accomplished not only in the sense that bodily we are already "temples of the Holy Ghost" (1 Cor 6:19), but in the Resurrection-Body. There it will be seen that it was an error ill beseeming Christians to banish grace to the realm of the "soul alone", for in that Body, possessed by grace and become the expression of grace, is the one entire man and the whole of humanity, blessed bodily in the bodily presence of Christ.

BODY OF CHRIST

The entire tradition of ecclesiology from St Paul onwards (principal texts: 1 Cor 6:12–20; 10:14 –22; 12:4 –27; Rom 12:4 –8; Eph 2:11–18; 1:22f.; 4:4, 12, 15f.; 5:30; Col 1:18, 24; 2:19; 3:15) has called the Church a "body" (a metaphor which is not to be arbitrarily pressed), insofar as it possesses the historical tangibility and unity of a society (is "embodied"), displays in the manner of an organism a plurality of "members" within this unity who have various specific functions (*Pope, *Bishop, Holy *Orders, *Layman), some institutional and some charismatic, belongs to Christ, who is its Lord ("head", see Eph 5:23, D 870ff.), and is so preserved by the Spirit of Christ in the grace of God's truth and love (D 600f., 380ff.) which has been vouchsafed to it with eschatological conclusiveness and animated by that Spirit with organic life that she remains till the end of time the historical, efficacious presence of Christ (his "primordial sacrament") in human history (Vat. II: Church, 7f.). If this body is one and composed of many members, it is only so on the basis of two concrete presuppositions: (1) that the human race, according to that one salvific will of God which destines all in Jesus Christ for the same supernatural end, namely, God's direct self-communication, and consecrates the one human race as the "People of God", is one in virtue of its nature, its history, and its goal; (2) that the Word of God through his Incarnation belongs to this one human race in his own "physical" bodiliness, and that the "People of God" is constituted a society through the Spirit. Accordingly, the celebration of the Eucharist—as the *anamnesis of the institution of the new covenant in the sacrifice of Christ's body and blood by the assembled community displayed in its hierarchical structure—most perfectly manifests the Church as the body of Christ.

BRETHREN OF JESUS

In various passages of the NT James, Joseph, Jude, and Simon are called brethren of Jesus (Mk 6:3 and parallel passages). The following facts militate against the supposition that we are here concerned with blood-brothers of Jesus (or step-brothers, as the Greek Orthodox still hold): (1) Jesus alone is called *the* son of Joseph and *the* son of Mary; (2) Luke 1:27 shows that the brethren of Jesus cannot have been older sons of Mary; (3) they cannot have been younger sons of Mary, otherwise her paschal pilgrimage to Jerusalem would have been impossible (Lk 2:41–52); (4) on the cross Jesus entrusted his mother to John (Jn 19:26f.); (5) it is established that in texts which were exposed to semitic influence the Greek word ἀδελφός (brother) was also used to designate more distant relatives.

BRIDAL MYSTICISM, BRIDAL SYMBOLISM

Bridal mysticism in the strict sense is inspired by supernatural *love, in which each human being understands that he is God's beloved and seeks through the concentration of all his vital powers to offer a loving response to that love of God, which he experiences "as a bride". The measure of more or less sublimated sexual and sensuous resonance in this response depends on the character, sex, and personal history of the mystic. Written records of such bridal mysticism often rely heavily on the bridal symbolism and theme of the Song of Solomon. The bridal symbolism of the OT is based on the idea of the unique and free *election of the people of the covenant by their God. Jesus' own preaching leaves the rôle of the bride in abeyance for the time being; but in apostolic times the Church was increasingly understood as the bride whom Christ woos and eventually leads to his home (see Eph 5:22–32). The final union with the Bridegroom is seen in the image of the wedding.

BUILDING, EDIFICATION

In the Church's usage this notion derives ultimately from that salvific action of God in the OT which with reference to the "house of Israel" is called "building", by contrast with "tearing down", "destroying". The concept is elaborated, with regard to the new situation in saving history, in the synoptic and Johannine tradition of Jesus. A comparison of the statement about the rebuilding of the temple (Mt 26:60f.), which was ascribed to Jesus, with Mt 16:18 reveals the specifically NT affirmation that by Christ's action the building of his new People (*Church) will be definitive and permanent in history, and at the same time will make entry into the eschatological *basileia possible. This conception, now Christological, becomes an ecclesiological one in St Paul; the individual Christian community is indeed built (edified) by God's collaborators (with authority), but also by every individual member (1 Thess 5:11), by *charity, bearing with one's neighbour's weaknesses, by *gnosis, and prohecy (1 Cor 8:1, 13:1ff.).

C

CANONIZATION

See *Veneration of Saints.*

CANON LAW

The Greek κάνων, derived from the Semitic, means "reed", "measure". Canon Law is the name of the law in force in the *Church, which governs its activity as a society. It is called divine law insofar as it derives from divine revelation or forms part of the *natural moral law. For a closer understanding of divine law it should be borne in mind that *revelation is not necessarily a passive phenomenon, but that in certain circumstances it can represent an active choice on the part of the recipient from among a number of given possibilities. With reference to the revelation of divine law in the Church, this means that on a crucial issue closely connected with its self-fulfilment the Church reaches a decision *appropriate to its nature.* Seen in these terms as an appropriate, divine law can be "posited" at least still in the apostolic period up to the complete constitution of the Church. Purely ecclesiastical law is composed of legislation by the Church, which of course often contains elements of divine law, and consuetudinary law. The *Codex Iuris Canonici* (CIC) is the principal source of canon law in the Latin Church. It came into force in 1918, but since then it has been found to require revision in many respects and is now being revised. Divine law in the Church is not fossilized; rather, knowledge of it and its application to concrete circumstances is governed by principles similar to those that govern the *development of dogma. Purely ecclesiastical law is of course most susceptible to change and adaptation to different times. The criteria governing changes in canon law do not derive solely from contemporary considerations appropriate to the nature of the Church. Rather, they are based on critical hermeneutical interpretation of the original context of canon law (e.g., with reference to marital law and administrative law). Where the norms of canon law provide the essential framework of the Church's life, they have the same salvific significance as the Church herself (the different conception Protestants and Orthodox have of the nature of the Church accounts for their different view of canon law), but the binding force of these norms is not always easy to demonstrate in a particular case. The Church is very considerate where a number of purely ecclesiastical laws are concerned (the Church grants dispensations; *epikeia* [i.e., later interpretation of the lawgiver's intention] ranks as a virtue, and it is a generally admitted principle that purely ecclesiastical laws do not bind in case of serious hardship).

The study of canon law is one of the oldest theological disciplines, being based on collections of conciliar canons as early as the 5th century. Gratian made an important collection of decrees about 1142.

CANON OF SCRIPTURE

A technical term in theology designating the collection of *inspired books that composes Holy Scripture and forms the rule of faith.

POSITIVE DATA. The collection was formed in successive stages. The *Law (Tora, Pentateuch) was the rule of faith for Israel by the time Ezra was preaching (probably 398 B.C.); the prophetical books attained this status in the 2nd century B.C. The present canon of the OT, including "other writings" which were already much esteemed in the NT, was certainly in existence about A.D. 100 when a Jewish synod was held at Jabneh (Jamnia); but certain books (Tobit, Judith, 1 and 2 Maccabees, Wisdom, Ecclesiasticus, Baruch, and the Greek portion of Esther and Daniel) cannot be proved to have formed part of the Jewish canon in the strict sense, though there is no doubt that they were highly regarded. Since the time of Sixtus of Siena (d. 1569) they have been infelicitously called "deutero-canonical books". Just as a quotation from a book establishes its authenticity by purely historical means, so the beginnings of the NT canon are proved by quotations in the early Fathers and ecclesiastical writers during the first half of the 2nd century. The first orthodox list of the books of the NT is the fragment known as the "Muratorian Canon" (of Italian origin, second half of the 2nd century), which, however, omits five epistles of the present canon. The canonicity of certain books of the NT was only established after a long hesitation; in the West it was not established until about 380–390, while in the East, where there was still question concerning the status of the book of Revelation, it was not established until the end of the 7th century. St Athanasius gives the first complete NT canon in A.D. 367. As in the OT, so also in the NT, books which were highly regarded but whose canonicity was in dispute were known as "deutero-canonical": Hebrews, James, 2 Peter, 2 John, 3 John, Jude, and Revelation. Doubts cast by the Reformers and some Catholics, like Erasmus, not only on the canonicity but also on the authenticity of a number of books in the Bible first made it necessary for the Church to pronounce a dogmatic definition of the canon. This was done in 1546 at the Council of Trent, which required equal reverence for all forty-five books of the OT and all twenty-seven books of the NT on the grounds that God is their author (D 1501ff.; see also D 3029). Vatican II qualifies this with the statement that the Gospels enjoy precedence over all other biblical writings, including those of the NT (Rev., 18).

THEOLOGY. The divine authorship of *Holy Scripture through *inspiration is, like all God's saving deeds known to us by divine revelation, authentically proclaimed and interpreted by the Church's magisterium. That the books of the Bible are inspired and therefore canonical we know directly from the teaching of the Church, which cites divine revelation as the original source of this knowledge. The Church has always claimed the right to determine the canon in this way, whether by declaring books canonical or by relegating them to the *apocrypha. The distinction between proto- (indisputably) canonical and deutero-canonical writings is primarily a matter of the Church's certainty of their inspiration and has no bearing on dogmatic definitions fixing the scope of the canon. The same applies to the question of the canonicity of some shorter individual passages within the traditional biblical text. The problem of the canon from the point of view of dogmatic theology and the history of dogma is how precisely we are to understand the revelation of the fact of inspiration and canonicity and the Church's knowledge of this (apostolic) revelation, in such a way that our account of this twofold process may be seen to be historically probable and, in particular, consistent with the slow and halting formation of the canon. For on the one hand revelation must be closed with the first generation ("with the death of the last apostle"), so that the Church can indeed reach a clearer understanding of revelation but cannot receive a new revelation. On the other hand, in many matters touching the scope of the canon, the Church has long wavered before taking a final decision, a fact which could hardly be explained apart from new revelation, if the original revelation on this point, given in apostolic times (for there must have been one), had been conveyed by an apostle in explicit declarations about each of the books at issue. The problem is thus whether one can conceive of an original revelation imparted in apostolic times, yet so implicit that its explicit formulation requires time and even falters (*Development of dogma). If we begin by supposing that it is of the essence of Holy Scripture to be willed by God as an essential element of the *primitive Church which is normative for all time, and thus belongs as norm for the future to the God-wrought constitution of this Church, so that the fact of its inspiration is contained *within* the revelation of this wider truth of a normative primitive Church, then we have the explicit datum from which the Church can gradually learn the extent of the canon of Scripture without new revelation. For those of the writings of the period which she recognizes by gradual reflection to be pure objectifications of the primitive Church (and that Church's OT past) are thereby also recognized as constitutive elements of the primitive Church and hence inspired and canonical—which is not to say that the Church's recognition *constitutes* the inspired and normative character of the writings.

CARDINAL VIRTUES

Those *virtues which are the chief foundation (Lat. *cardo,* hinge) of man's moral life. Since the time of St Ambrose the name has been given to the four moral virtues (as distinct from the theological virtues): *prudence, *justice, *fortitude, and *temperance.

CARDIOGNOSIS

Literally, knowledge of the heart (Gr. καρδιογνῶσις); a special gift making it possible to know the moral and religious condition which a man has attained by his own free choice (and therefore also his relationship with God). According to Catholic theology such knowledge cannot be acquired; by reason of its very nature it belongs exclusively to God, as Scripture testifies, and is a *charism granted to individuals, which, in particular cases, is hardly distinguishable from parapsychological phenomena.

CARTHAGE

The sixteenth Synod of Carthage, A.D. 418, formerly confused with the council of Milev, A.D. 416, formulated nine canons against *Pelagianism (D 221–230). Their doctrinal content was sanctioned by Pope Zosimus, but it is now disputed whether his approbation was a *definition. The matter is of interest at the present time in the context of the controversy concerning *limbo.

CATECHISM

From the Gr. $\kappa\alpha\tau\eta\chi\tilde{\eta}\sigma\iota s$, oral instruction; at present, the manual of elementary Christian instruction. A catechism is an important document of the ordinary magisterium if, and insofar as, a bishop approves it as an outline of the faith. Yet a truth is not necessarily a dogma or even a Catholic truth simply because of its inclusion in the catechism, for a catechism is not designed to present truths of this order exclusively, rather, it usually contains an undifferentiated mixture of *dogmas, *Catholic truths, truths that are theologically certain, and other material, all as seen by men rooted in their own times.

CATHOLIC ACTION

See *Layman.*

CATHOLICITY

An essential characteristic and one of the four marks of the one true Church of Christ. In virtue of God's universal *salvific will, humanity's radical redemption in Jesus Christ, and the operation of the Holy Spirit, the *Church, unlimited by space or time, necessarily stands open to all men, who in turn have an objective obligation to belong to her. On the basis of this truth the Church must affirm in every age that pluralism which by God's will is intrinsic to history in all the manifold spheres of private and public life. Her preaching and modes of life can never be confined to any one culture or race to the exclusion of all others. Catholicity further indicates that the Church is in possession of the fullness of God's *revelation in Christ. This catholicity or universality begins to take shape in those writings of the OT and later

Judaism which expressly affirm God's will to save all peoples; and it is finally established with St Paul's vocation to be the Apostle of the gentiles (see especially Eph 2:11–3:11). The catholicity of the Church is professed in the creeds (DS 2; end of 2nd century). In the patristic age (the Church is first called "catholic" by St Ignatius of Antioch [*ad Smyrnaeos,* 8, 2]) as today, catholicity especially signifies an interior, qualitative characteristic of the Church, whereas at the apogee of apologetics it rather meant the external, actual universality of the Church.

CATHOLIC TRUTHS

Veritates catholicae or *doctrina catholica:* in the strict theological sense all those truths which the Church teaches authentically but not infallibly—wherein they differ from *dogmas and *dogmatic facts. Many theological conclusions and much of the teaching of papal *encyclicals can be included in this category. The Church requires our internal assent to these truths, but not the absolutely irrevocable assent of faith. A person may withhold this assent, which is posited on the basis of the *Church's authority, if in view of certain considerations which supersede the state of the question as it has hitherto been expounded, he becomes convinced that an opinion proposed authentically but not infallibly by the Church no longer does the matter justice.

CAUSALITY

A favourite theme in Greek philosophy arising out of the question what "moves", that is to say changes, an object. Out of what was there before (*Matter) something new comes into being through the infusion of a new intrinsic *form. Thus matter and form are regarded as intrinsic causes (*Principle) (material and formal cause). Since there is always some *purpose motivating the execution of some change, this efficient element and its accompanying finality are considered its extrinsic causes (instrumental and final cause). This classical quartet of causes is supplemented by the extrinsic form of the prototype or ideal on which an existent is modelled (exemplary cause). In scholastic philosophy, where the problem of causality was more carefully scrutinized, we find a "principle of causality": Every finite entity, since it is not absolute *being, is *contingent, that is, not absolutely

CELIBACY

necessary; but if it actually exists it must have been produced by an efficient cause. The principle of contradiction provides this principle with its philosophical support. A contingent being is not of its own nature ordered to existence; since its own nature is not the source of its being, it may or may not exist. Granted its actual existence, however, it must have been brought into existence by something other than itself, for otherwise it would simultaneously enjoy an ordination to existence (since it does exist) and non-existence (since it supposedly has no cause), and this would be a contradiction. Of course this is relevant to theology only if the activity of the human mind presupposes a grasp of what being is; if being itself were not always the goal and foundation of thought, if thought did not affirm being and occur within the horizon of being, then the application of the principle of causality to the relationship between God and the world would not lead to a correct notion of God.—See also *Proofs of the Existence of God.*

CELIBACY

See *Virginity.*

CENSURES

See *Notes, Theological.*

CERTAINTY

That confidence in and freedom from misgivings about his knowledge which a subject considers to be justified. Its subdivisions are: (1) certainty prompted by immediate evidence, when an object directly shows itself or a fact is immediately obvious; (2) compelling certainty, when all *doubt and all justified hesitation is immediately excluded; (3) strict but free certainty, the true moral certainty, when the subject sees that he is morally justified in dismissing a doubt which he can still entertain psychologically, and proceeds to act.

CERTAINTY OF SALVATION

A concept of Protestant theology which signifies a belief in justification so firm that this belief is inconsistent with any doubt of a man's ultimate salvation. Such a certainty of salvation—which Catholic theology describes as *absolute*—was repudiated by the Council of Trent (D 1533f., 1540f., 1563ff.), because whereas the Christian is absolutely forbidden to doubt what God has done in Jesus Christ or to doubt his universal *salvific will, this does not exclude all possible doubt of one's own eternal salvation. In this matter the recourse of the Christian is to entertain that "firm hope" which is a *practical* certainty of salvation and at the same time to commit one's eternal destiny to the sovereign discretion of the gracious God. The problem of the certainty of salvation is part of the wider problem of the relation between *faith and *works (*Hope, *Synergism, *Predestination). Thus Catholic doctrine not only does justice to the practical certainty of salvation plainly expressed in St Paul but also to the other texts of Scripture which bid us work out our salvation "with fear and trembling" (Phil 2:12; 1 Cor 10:12; Heb 12:29).

CHALCEDON

A city in Asia Minor where the Fourth Ecumenical Council assembled between October 8th and November 1st, A.D. 451, during the pontificate of Pope Leo I. At the council the following christological dogma was formulated: *Jesus Christ, God's *Logos made Man, is a single *Person in two *natures, which exist in this one Person without confusion, without change, without division, and without separation (D 301ff.). The dogma was defined against *Nestorianism, which alleged that there are two persons in Christ (see *Ephesus), and against the strictly *Monophysite doctrine of Eutyches (that the two natures in Christ coalesce in one). St Leo, whose legates presided over the council, confirmed its decrees with the exception of canon 28, which, to the detriment of Antioch and Alexandria, accorded Constantinople the first rank after Rome.

CHARACTER, SACRAMENTAL CHARACTER

Character (Gr. χαρακτήρ, distinctive mark) signifies the "spiritual and indelible mark" that is impressed on the individual Christian by

63

*baptism, *confirmation, and holy *order (the permanent validity of these sacraments, independent of the subjective dispositions of the individual). For the defined teaching of the Church, see D 1609. The scriptural foundation for the doctrine of sacramental character is the "seal" (*Sphragis) of God with which the elect are marked (Rev 7:2–8). It was first developed by St Augustine on the basis of the recognized fact that none of these sacraments could be repeated. The indelibility of the sacramental character places it beyond the sphere of human decision and the individual's personal history of salvation, referring each interior, invisible, salvific appeal that God graciously makes to the individual person, to the historical and public sphere of the Church and her worship instead (Vat. II: Church, 11). Since it actualizes the permanent vocation of the person who is baptized, confirmed or ordained, therefore, the Church's worship is the visible representation of God's permanent, unrepentant will to love and of its acceptance by the Church as a whole (*Sacrament). The sacramental character is distinct from *grace itself, but refers the Christian to his duty to possess grace and also offers him grace.

CHARISM

From the Gr. $\chi \acute{\alpha} \rho \iota \sigma \mu \alpha$, gratuitous gift; in the NT it has the meaning of unmerited salvation in general. In the plural in the NT and in modern theological usage it refers to those operations of the Spirit of God upon the individual believer which can never be wrung from God by man, nor foreseen by the official organs of the Church, nor effected by the sacraments, and yet are always and everywhere to be expected, because like office and the sacraments they belong to the nature of the Church. By contrast with the *virtues, the purpose of the charism is to make the Church visible and credible as the "holy People of God", and thus it completes ecclesiastical *office in its proper rôle. The forms taken by charismata (in apostolic times it was wisdom, knowledge, miracles, the discerning of spirits, gifts of government, and the gift of tongues that predominated; see especially 1 Cor 12–14) cannot be foreseen, precisely because they belong by their very nature to the saving history of the Church; and therefore they must be constantly rediscovered and accepted (D 3807f.). The novelty of their form, the movement for evangelical poverty in the Middle Ages for instance, cannot be held to show that they are unecclesial and do not come from the Holy Spirit, but must rather be recognized as a new impulse of God's Spirit (to be examined with care, of course) who wishes in this way to confront the Church with her ever novel present and engage her with it more thoroughly, in a more highly differentiated way.

CHARITY

In the NT charity (Gr. ἀγάπη) is usually the term for love in general, primarily the love of God for men, but also the love of men for one another and for God. It is a fundamentally distinctive mode of love, since it is realized by the Spirit of God; for God's part it is realized in working out the plan of salvation, in his will to create that which is other than himself, to become that other, and to communicate himself to it; man for his part realizes charity in his response, which itself is a gift of the Spirit of God, establishing him in communion with God and with his fellows (Rom 5:5; Jn 4:16; 1 Cor 13:8–13).

CHRISTIANITY

Both in its hidden nature, as an object of faith (*grace), and in its visible appearance (Incarnation, *Church) Christianity is that relationship between man and God that God himself has established in *Jesus Christ by his free, gracious, historical disposition and by his verbal revelation. Thus Christianity is rooted in the being and work of Christ the Mediator. Insofar as Christianity is based on the concrete Person of Christ, embraces the whole man in his entire reality and world, and is a partnership with the infinite, incomprehensible God, it is not possible to give any exhaustive, abstract definition of its nature. The question "What is Christianity?" can legitimately be asked from two different standpoints: (I) from without, that is to say, by the person who is not yet a believer; his question is answered by what fundamental theology has to say of Christianity in its relation to other religions; (II) from within, when Christianity seeks its own genuine understanding of itself, which can be discovered only by itself; this question is answered by Christianity's dogmatic affirmations about itself.

I. CHRISTIANITY COMPARED WITH OTHER RELIGIONS

(1) CHRISTIANITY IS A RELIGION FOR THE WHOLE WORLD AND FOR ALL MEN. It regards absolutely every human being as the recipient of its message, gifts, and promises. It considers itself to be, not one

particular manifestation of generic religion among others, but the only relationship between man and God, because God himself has established it as the only one. In fact Christianity has never been confined within a single civilization. In the course of history, while always remaining itself, it has truly become a world religion, universal in time and space.

(2) CHRISTIANITY IS A RELIGION OF CIVILIZATION. While tracing its presuppositions and preparatory history (even and precisely as God-woven *saving history) back to the beginnings of mankind (*Primitive revelation, *Grace of Christ, *Covenant with Abraham, *Old Testament), Christianity by its very nature presupposes a certain degree of human culture, inasmuch as it treats the whole gamut of human capabilities as material for embodying religion.

(3) CHRISTIANITY IS AN HISTORICALLY REVEALED RELIGION. Though Christianity makes affirmations of permanent validity about the nature of God, the world, and man, which in themselves and in principle are accessible from any point in history, yet it conceives itself to be essentially an historical, revealed religion. That is to say, the reality which Christianity represents and the truth it proclaims are *in* the world because at one quite particular point in time and space (one that history and geography can ascertain) the work and gospel of the living God, who is distinct from the world, freely and graciously occurred (in the *prophets and in *Jesus Christ); are therefore *in* the world because *revelation (by God, not by the world) came to pass. The Person of Jesus, in whom God's revelation has taken place definitively in historical time, is the irreducible, original datum of Christianity, incapable of explanation in syncretistic terms.

(4) CHRISTIANITY IS A DOGMATIC RELIGION. Though the reality which the Church presents and announces is God's deed done to man, which passes all understanding because it is the *self-communication of God to man-who-is-not-God, yet this communication of God by God himself is conveyed in human terms (which have a long history behind them). Despite the analogical nature and the imperfection of human ideas, therefore, this verbal communication is truth absolute and unalterable, and (as can be empirically demonstrated) is transmitted, unaltered, by Scripture and Tradition notwithstanding the progressive development of new formulae for its expression (*Development of dogma).

(5) CHRISTIANITY IS AN ESCHATOLOGICAL RELIGION. That is, it takes its own historicity and that of man in radical earnest and yet understands itself to be absolute. This means: (a) It is the final, definitive religion for this age of the world and can never be superseded. Despite its own historical origin it is not a phase of religious history, to be succeeded perhaps by some other religion, for in principle there is room within it for all genuine religious productivity and for all the work of grace that the one God may do even outside Christianity, and as the religion of God's absolute *self-communication in Incarnation and *grace it really yields only to the *beatific vision. (b) Christianity regards itself as provisional and conditioned insofar as it is itself "on pilgrimage" towards that end (to which its own dynamism refers it) in which God's glory is to be made manifest and time and the scene and history of Christianity's activity will cease. (c) As an eschatological element "in the flesh of this world", Christianity opposes all attempts at absolutism on the part of any power in the world by making the world, history, and civilization relative to the salvific will and absolute salvific sovereignty of God. Yet precisely this limitation preserves the world, history, and the rest in their validity (and autonomy), since Christianity, representing God's eternal salvific will *in* the world and *in* time, hopes and longs for the final, gracious accomplishment of this will. Thus Christianity regards itself precisely *as* an eschatological religion and not as an administrator and ruler of earthly things.

(6) CHRISTIANITY IS AN INTEGRAL RELIGION. Christianity, as the work of the Creator of all earthly realities, addresses the individual and society in the same manner and in mutual dependence. Because Christianity is the salvation of the individual before God in grace and personal decision, it can never be a mere cultural institution set up by society. But when God addresses all he does so historically tangible in his incarnate Son, and therefore by the will of Jesus its founder, Christianity in its fullness exists only in the one visible *Church* with its social constitution, articulated according to offices and duties, which in unbroken historical continuity (*Ministries, recognition of, *Apostolic succession) propagates God's saving activity in the sacraments and God's truth in her teaching everywhere and in every age and represents the complete historical tangibility of God's saving deed in Christ.

II. CHRISTIANITY'S DOGMATIC AFFIRMATIONS ABOUT ITSELF
  (1) In Christianity the infinite, personal and holy God acts upon

man and with man. The world and man, freely created out of nothing, he clearly sets apart from himself, yet in such a way (dependence) that in all things they are continuously referred to the infinite *mystery that is God. For this reason the creature cannot determine his concrete relationship with God by himself alone but must remain open to God's disposal.

(2) By his free grace this God has admitted the world he freely created, and especially the intellectual creature, to participation in his divine life, so that God is not only the efficient cause by which creatures come into being, but (in free grace) he who communicates himself in his own being. Thus he has disclosed his own glory and his intimate life as the goal gratuitously set for the intellectual creature and in so doing he has at once superseded all human self-development in this world and opened it to its infinite fulfilment. The structure of this, God's super-natural self-communication, is the interior reality of God himself: the unoriginate Communicator of himself (Father), the uttered "Word", ever possessing the fullness of the Source (Son), and the loving Affirmation of union between outgoing Source and declarative Issue as these have permanently arrived in the divine plenitude at the goal of their egress (Holy Ghost), form the real tri-personality of the one God in himself (*Trinity).

(3) The history of the acceptance or rejection by human freedom of God's self-communication is enacted in every human life that reaches self-fulfilment in spiritual freedom and is possible at any given time in virtue of the historical situation in which the person concerned finds himself at that time. Where this history of grace becomes a conscious datum, acquires social tangibility, authenticated expression, and is embodied in institutional forms, *saving history in the stricter sense is enacted (*Covenant with the people of Israel, *Old Testament, *Kingdom of God, *Basileia).

(4) The assumption by the second divine Person of the one God, of a human reality (*Nature) as his own in *Jesus Christ is the supreme and qualitatively unique realization of God's self-communication to the world and his will to save all men. In this sense Jesus is the mediator of salvation between God and creatures; and from the beginning the creation and history of the world are ordered to him, the "Head". When the believer acknowledges Jesus as the Man whose being is God's own existence in our midst, and in whose life, destiny, death, and resurrection God himself has shared our existence, he (the believer) knows himself to have been revealed, and finally confirmed, in his own reality (as the partner whom God has graciously chosen; *Redemption, *Resurrection).

(5) God's saving deed, perduring in history, reveals to Christianity a deeper knowledge of what man is: the recipient of God's free self-communication in grace, who through his own *sin is positively unworthy of this gift and therefore of himself would be lost (*Death, *Original sin), but who relies wholly upon the forgiveness of sins that is proffered in Christ.

(6) Christianity regards man as a *spirit (always embodied) of absolute value, endowed during the one earthly life that is his with the real capacity to make a final decision in spiritual knowledge and free choice, for or against God and thus for his own salvation or eternal damnation. The meaning of life that has been fixed by God's work of creation and salvation is at the same time the standard of human behaviour: in *faith, *hope, *charity (towards God and our neighbour), and gratitude (*Eucharist, *Church).—See also *Judaism and Christianity, Paganism, Non-Christian Religions, Anonymous Christianity.*

CHRIST-MYSTICISM

This is chiefly based on St Paul's conception, "in Christ". It is inspired by the experience of the gracious gift, already radically accepted, of the union of one's own person with Jesus Christ. Though this personal union occupies the foreground of mystical experience and dominates the terminology of Christ-mysticism, the latter does not overlook the fact that each individual is incorporated in the "Body of Christ" and thus remains permanently ordered to the community of those who live in Christ (St Igantius of Loyola: the mysticism of serving Christ visible in the Church).

CHRISTOCENTRISM

A Christian theology is christocentric insofar as it rightly shows Christ's position in the history of creation and salvation to be central, that is, conditioning and ordering everything else. Insofar as the will of God which sustains all creation—transcending the permanent distinction between *nature and grace and, within the order of grace, between the grace of *original justice and redemptive grace—may be conceived to depend in actual fact, though freely, on the original will of God to express himself, in his Logos, in terms of the non-divine and to communicate himself to this latter, it can be said that *everything,* even nature and natural human history, has been created in order to *Jesus Christ the God-Man and subsists in him. Though there is no unanimity among Catholic theologians on this point, it can then be said: (1) The natural world was created as at once the condition and the recipient of God's *self-communication in the Incarnation of the Logos. (2) Even the grace of original justice was already the grace of Jesus Christ. (3) Sin, as opposition to God in *Christ,* is permitted by God because in Jesus Christ it is comprehended within God's unconditional will to this self-communication, which by the very fact becomes a redemptive self-communication. (4) The grace which justifies and divinizes us, as in fact it is granted to us, is essentially so much the grace of the Incarnate and the Crucified that grace and Incarnation are two inseparable elements of the one *mystery of God's self-communication to his creature.

CHRISTOLOGY

That part of theology which deals with *Jesus Christ, and in a strict sense with his Person, whilst the theology of his redemptive work comes under the heading of *soteriology. It must above all remain closely connected with *Trinitarian theology, thus making it clear that the economic is the immanent Trinity and vice versa; though the Incarnation must be recognized as absolutely voluntary, still it is essential to see *after* revelation and on the basis of revelation, that it is precisely in the Son that God assumes a reality which is other than his own and makes it the manifestation of his own truly self-declaratory presence. This is to say that the true Christian interpretation of the world and of history is to be sought in this nexus between the theology of the Trinity and Christology (*Christocentrism). The affirmations of Christology itself since the Council of *Chalcedon have been based on a very few conceptions: those of the two *natures in Jesus Christ, of one *hypostasis, and of the assumption of human nature by the Person of the divine *Logos (*Hypostatic union; *Homoousios). But this does not necessarily mean that Christology is concluded for the rest of time. Its openness to understanding follows from that tension which exists by the nature of the case between a Christology "from above" and a Christology "from below". It would be the business of a Christology "from above" to show the possibility and significance of God himself becoming that which is other than himself, (based not only on an adequate theology of the Trinity as shown above, but also on a theological *anthropology) which is indicated in the biblical terms "Son" and "Word". Christology "from below" would have to present the real history of Jesus (with the help of *exegesis), the concrete figure of Jesus, the *mysteries of the life of Jesus as fundamental theology, not confused with dogmatic theology and yet inseparably united with it. Further, it would have to demonstrate satisfactorily that *this Jesus* is the absolutely real presence of God in the world, that the work he has done as Man is really the *redemption of the world (see also *Knowledge of Jesus, Death*). Both would then make it clear that the very Incarnation of the divine Logos is God's supreme, historical, irrevocable self-communication to the world and that Christology and soteriology at least must be regarded and treated as an internal unity. These sections of dogmatic theology must be immediately followed by a dogmatic *ecclesiology which will give expression to the permanence of Jesus Christ in history, community, and grace, to his redemption in the world and the acceptance of that redemption.

CHURCH

From the Gr. κυριακή, "belonging to the Lord", supplementing the Greek ἐκκλησία, the holy people, especially its assembly for worship. Church, therefore, means the Lord's holy congregation.

IN SCRIPTURE. The starting-point of the foundation of the Church is to be found in the preaching of *Jesus Christ to his people Israel, whom he wished to call into God's *basileia*. This nation was the people of God, whose solemn assembly was called *qahal* in Hebrew, ἐκκλησία in Greek. The call first went forth to Israel within the *covenant, the *Old Testament; Jesus chose twelve *Apostles so as to lay claim to his whole people, to all twelve tribes. To convey this call Jesus uses the idioms of the Jewish world of his time. He becomes an itinerant religious teacher, training a body of disciples, and thus already constituting a Church, though this community differs from similar groups, notably in welcoming sinners and the abandoned (Mk 6:34; Mt 10:6). After the rejection of Jesus' call by large sections of Israel he does not preach a purely spiritual Church, the "holy remnant" of a special messianic community, but rather initiates his disciples more deeply into the mystery of his mission and death; he reckons with an interval between his death and the open manifestation of the *basileia* (see Mk 2:19f.; 13:9f.; especially the mandate to repeat the commemorative meal: 1 Cor 11:24; Lk 22:16, 19f., 30a; see also

22:31f.). Jesus himself did not further institutionalize this approach. But the NT writers relied on him in their understanding of the Church in which they were already living, cf. the words instituting the Church in Mt 16: 18f: On the foundation of Peter (which must therefore last as long as the building does) Jesus will build "his Church", which is not yet the *basileia* and yet is dependent on the *basileia,* for its keys are given to Peter (*Keys, power of).

This Church will exist in this age, for the gates of hell will assault though cannot overwhelm her. This is so because the death of Jesus, the *Ebed Yahweh,* "for many" (Mk 14:24), has established the New *Covenant and the Church in it as the means of salvation for all who are to inherit the *basileia.* This Church is to be governed by an apostolic hierarchy (Lk 22:31f.; Mt 18:18; *Binding and loosing); its fuller development and interior inspiration will be the work of the *Holy Ghost, the *Paraclete whom Jesus has promised. The relationship with the Spirit of God, imparted eschatologically and irrevocably, is an important link between Jesus and the early Church. (See *Primitive Church.)* In this spirit the Church maintains her claim to Israel (Acts 2:36; 3:17–26) and opens her doors to the gentiles (Acts 15:14). St Paul's theology of the Church regards the union of Jews and gentiles in the Church as the mystery of Jesus Christ *simpliciter* (Eph 3:4ff.). If by "church" St Paul often refers to the local Christian community, nevertheless, the Church in his thought is ultimately a theological entity, not an organization. Through all the difficulties of his mission to the gentiles he clings to the original community at Jerusalem and by "Church" he really means the universal Church, realized and represented, of course, in the little local communities.

THEOLOGY

(1) THE FUNDAMENTAL NATURE OF THE CHURCH is best sought in the nature of *revelation; it is the community, lawfully constituted as a society, in which by *faith the eschatological fullness of revelation in Christ remains present for the world as reality and truth. Therefore, the Church can only exist in the definitive phase of revelation, God's victorious self-communication in his efficacious divine Word, through which, as human word, he addresses himself definitively to the world as mercy and grace: the word, then, that goes forth to create a *community* of believers, that makes the promise of grace explicit and conscious in its confession of faith, and that is preserved inviolate and authentically expounded in it by its appointed leaders (magisterium).

CHURCH

The Church is the abiding presence of God's definitive (and therefore fully articulate) Word to the world, in the world and for the world. Since this Word in the final analysis is Jesus Christ, he founded the Church through his very reality (D 1330, 3050 –3075, 3537–3542 and *passim;* Vat. II: Miss., 5: the Church formed after Jesus' resurrection).

(2) THE ESSENTIAL LAW OF THE CHURCH. In accordance with its nature as the abiding presence of the theandric word of God, heard, proclaimed, and efficacious in the world, the Church is a kind of "sacramental" union of sign and signified, neither identified with nor yet separable from each other (Vat. II: Church, 1, 9, 48; Church/world, 42 and *passim;* *Primordial sacrament); it is an external society, a "visible" Church with a constitution (*Pope, *Bishop) derived —at least in certain respects—from Jesus Christ (D 3050ff.), a tangible community of worship and profession. But all this is precisely the sign of God's efficacious utterance of himself to the world: the infallible doctrine of the Church (*Infallibility) is the sign of his truth; the efficacious word of the *sacraments, of his grace; the gracious union of believers and their service to the world, of his love. This grace, of which the visible Church (in its being and activity) is the efficacious sign, itself belongs to the Church.

(3) THE HISTORICAL CHARACTER OF THE CHURCH is rooted in this twofold mode of existence. The Church is present, yet it can only be understood in terms of eschatology (of the consummation that has already begun in Jesus Christ): "The pilgrim Church, in its sacraments and institutions, which belong to this present age, carries the mark of this world which will pass, and she herself takes her place among the creatures which groan and travail yet and await the revelation of the sons of God" (Vat. II: Church, 48); it is the pilgrim people of God (1 Pet 2:10; Heb 3:7– 4:11) until Christ comes again. This historicity of the Church is not in contradiction with its binding character in particular concrete manifestations, in which alone (and not in any spiritualized "ideal" Church) the Church can be found at any given moment. The Church is history, yet ever preserved anew from ever impending ruin by the Holy Ghost (see D 302, 2288; *saving history), who constantly discloses completed *revelation anew in the course of history. The Church's interior dynamism not only impels it by faith and grace to represent this inner reality tangibly and sacramentally, but this "visible" sacramentality carries it back to faith and grace, and these two movements together impel it towards the final consummation. Thus the Church lives in three realms at

once: in the inwardness of faith and grace, in the visibility of representational office and sacramental action, and in a growing participation (realized here and now in committed love) in the future aeon where sign and signified are no longer distinguished.

(4) THE NECESSITY OF THE CHURCH FOR HUMAN SALVATION is to be understood in the context of this "sacramental" character: (D 1351, 2865ff. and *passim)* as Christ, faith, and baptism are respectively necessary (*Baptism of desire, *Membership of the Church, *Necessity for salvation). Just as theologians have long recognized that faith *(fides implicita)* and baptism *(votum baptismi)* may be explicit in various degrees, so the process of formation of the Church goes through various stages (Vat. II: Church, 13–16; Ecum., 4) but in such a way that all are genuine participations in the final sacramental and ecclesial stage because of their ordination to the latter. This is only possible because the reality of the Church (like that of Jesus Christ and the sacraments), though visible, is not confined to a single phenomenal embodiment. It is an expressive reality, bodily and spiritual at once; and as such it can more easily remain strictly identical throughout various levels of embodiment. Thus the dictum of St Cyprian, *Extra Ecclesiam nulla salus,* can be meaningfully reconciled with God's universal and salvific will, without denying either the real possibility of salvation for all (therefore even of those externally outside the Church) or the obligation of belonging to the Church. This latter is not fully safeguarded if one talks of "extraordinary" and "invisible" means of salvation and of people belonging to the "soul" of the Church. The Church's structure according to Catholic doctrine does not admit of any such dichotomy (D 911, 2885f.), but it does (because this structure is sacramental) admit of degrees, provided each degree objectively participates in the whole reality that unfolds itself in them, and provided man's obligation to accept the whole reality of the Church remains intact.

(5) NOTES OF THE CHURCH. Today the characteristic features which distinguish the true Church of Christ are usually reckoned to be four in number (D 2886ff.): (a) The Catholic Church claims for itself alone the mandate to realize the one Church which is also visibly one (*Unity of the Church: Vat.II, Church, 8). (b) The Catholic Church sees itself as holy (*Holiness of the Church: Vat. II, Church, 8ff., 39, 41, 48). (c) The Church of Christ must be catholic in principle, that is, it must be a global Church (*Catholicity of the Church: Vat. II, Church, 8, 13, 23; Ecum., 4). (d) It must be based on the Apostles

and follow them; it must be apostolic (*Apostolicity of the Church: Vat. II: Church, 8; Ecum., 17).

(6) For the CONSTITUTION OF THE CHURCH AS AN EXTERNAL SOCIETY see the following articles *Apostle, Pope, Bishop, Office, Laity, Magisterium, Pastoral Office of the Church, Order, Ministries, recognition of, Apostolic Succession.*

(7) IMAGES OF THE CHURCH. In accordance with Holy Scripture and the Fathers, the Church expresses her nature in analogies and images, whose reference to the Church and exact meaning can of course only be gathered from the whole of revelation. (a) The readiest comparison derives from the sociological sphere itself: the Church is the people of God (1 Pet 2:10 and *passim*). From this point of view the vocation to salvation becomes a principle which draws men together. Modern individualism takes unkindly to the idea that man's relationship with God is bound up with a common external activity (or a common suffering). Yet this theme runs through the whole of saving history (*Principle of solidarity). God's grace has always been linked with a human group, beginning from the summing up of our humanity in Adam our common father (*Monogenism), the patriarchs Noah, Abraham, and Moses, down to the New *Covenant, in which "those near and those afar off" (Eph 2:17) have come together in the blood of Christ in the peace of the "New Israel" (see Mt 21:43 and *passim*). There is no escaping this connection without losing the way to that very transcendence for whose sake, and against illegitimate claims upon it, one is tempted and perhaps bound to protest that here the human element has been over-emphasized. (b) The term *Kingdom of God is on the same plane (for its correct use see *Basileia).* It presents the Church as the historical sphere in which God's will is publicly carried out and shows the Church to be the preliminary phase of that definitive order of creation where "God is all in all" in the true *basileia*. (c) Following St Paul (1 Cor 6:15ff.; Eph 1:22f.; Col 1:24) and in harmony with tradition (St Clement of Rome, Origen, St Augustine, Boniface VIII) the Church calls itself the "Mystical Body of Jesus Christ". The doctrine of the mystical body is important to our new sense of the Church today, because it links the Church more intimately with Jesus Christ and provides a solid foundation for the solidarity of its members with one another. As to the former point it can be said that the Church is an expression of the reality of Jesus Christ himself (1 Cor 12:13); it is the specific manner in which, since his glorification, Jesus Christ lives on through the

sending of the Holy Ghost (see 1 Cor 10:3f.; Eph 2:15, 17f.) among the men whom he drew to himself by his death to be his "body", his "fullness" (Eph 4:12f.). They become conformed to him and "one in Jesus Christ" together (Gal 3:28). If this form of continued existence is called mystical, this is not to diminish its reality in any way but simply to differentiate it from other ways of being a body (for example the unity of biological substances). The Church is thus a living unity that transcends mere institutions; Jesus Christ is not only the origin but the ground and principle of its life present within it. The bond uniting all believers with one another (*Communion of saints) which is symbolized by the image of the mystical body and manifested by partaking of the one Bread (1 Cor 10:17, 21) is the basis of that sense of ontic solidarity among its members "in Christ" (Rom 12:5) and provides the motive for the demands for action in the liturgical, ascetical, pastoral, ecumenical, and social fields. (d) Since the Church of the New Testament succeeds to the heritage of the Old Testament, it naturally takes over not only the general idea of the People of God but also the metaphorical language of *bridal mysticism in the prophetic books; God unites himself with redeemed mankind with the tenderness and constancy of a lover. It is only at first glance that this image seems to fall short of that of the mystical body, for this love is precisely one which makes the two partners "one flesh" (Gen 2:24) and this body is precisely one which preserves the personal identity of the members. The two images are combined in the New Testament (Eph 5:23–32; Rev 21:9f.); and, supplementing one another, keep reverence and intimacy in equilibrium. (d) The mingling in Scripture of mechanical and organic imagery serves the same dialectical purpose. On the one hand the Church is compared to a building, in which many stones compose a house (1 Tim 3:15; Heb 3:6; 1 Pet 4:17) or a temple (Eph 2:21f.), so as finally to reach the perfection of the city of God (Gal 4:25f.). On the other hand it grows from within like a grain of mustard seed, a vineyard, a tree (Mt 13:31f.; Jn 15:1–8) towards the fullness of life in paradise. But a city and a garden are not antitheses; rather they indicate that the metaphors seek to raise the mysterious being of the Church above the concepts both of aggregation and of the animate. Ultimately, however, the total reality of the Church, wrought by the Holy Ghost, escapes any given category of earthly existence, whether imaginative or conceptual. The principle which makes the Church possible at all is "from above", and it does not become accessible to human thought by our pretending otherwise.

(8) LOCAL CHURCH AND CHURCH. Vatican II saw the local

Church as primarily the Church presided over by a bishop (diocese). Theologically, the local Church may be understood thus: The one Church of Jesus Christ is available and present in each local parish (Vat. II: Church, 26) which is constituted by the proclamation of the Gospel of Jesus Christ, the Eucharist and the practice of love. This (in certain circumstances very small) local community is a particular manifestation of the new people of God in the Holy Spirit. It makes Jesus Christ present to believers and unbelievers in sign and spirit. The whole Church is constructed from many such (perhaps widely scattered) basic communities of faith (local cells).

(9) CHURCH AND STATE. On the grounds of its nature the Church claims a thorough-going independence of the State (it is not bound to any political, economic or social system, or to any specific culture, Vat. II: Church/world, 42, 58, 76), but it fully recognizes the autonomy of the State and civil society as independent of the Church ("perfect society"; *Pluralism) (D 683ff., 943, 2895, 2919f., 3168f., 3171, 3685). Although it claims to be the sign and defence of the transcendence of the human person (Vat. II: Church/world, 76) and preaches norms of the *natural moral law which are objectively valid even for public life and the behaviour of governments, and, by declaring that offences against these norms violate the conscience of the nations, binds the conscience of its members, yet this does not make the Church a superstate; for it acknowledges the basic laws of toleration and freedom from compulsion in regard to faith for the State, particularly the State which permits ideological variety, and does not claim to be able to issue detailed instructions as to what political or social measures should be undertaken in any particular historical situation. The Church which, according to Vatican II, has no mission in the political, economic or social spheres (Church/world, 42), is nevertheless duty-bound to contribute actively to the more human shaping of the human family (40). Members of the Church have justifiable differences of opinion (43, 75) regarding the precise political option to that end, though of course that does not mean that they are free to stand on the side of sole proprietors, oppressors and exploiters (63–72). The tasks of the Church in state and society arise from its existence *for* others, even *for* unbelievers, and therefore must be *against* injustice, but do not include the defence of its own privileges, not even its "legitimately won rights" (76).

(10) THE CHURCH AND CHRISTIANS TODAY. The attitude of the mature Christian towards the Church today will be guided on the one

hand by the realization that complete individualism in religion is impossible. God wills the salvation of all, and this salvation, being that of the whole man, is realized and embodied in every human dimension: there is no such thing as a separate, "specifically" religious dimension (such as inwardness, the heart, the feminine world, worship, or the like). Consequently, the social dimension in which God's salvation is made actively present also belongs to the Church. The Christian, of peace, reconciliation, and unity, knows no separatist individualism where religion is concerned, however much, as *homo religiosus,* he may remain the *individuum ineffabile.* On the other hand, for all his unqualified loyalty to the Church as the permanent sphere of his religious life, and obedience to its doctrinal and pastoral authority, the Christian knows that the Church is a pilgrim, painfully seeking its way through time in its historicity, and he patiently bears with it in critical loyalty as he is borne up by it. And he sees the Church as the sign of salvation that God has raised up in history, salvation for the whole world, not excepting those who do not yet tangibly belong to it. This basic and wholly concrete affirmation of the Church does not exclude the individual or a group anticipating (in charism and commitment) the Church's intention, and only identifying in part with a local Church in which that intention is inadequately realized.

CHURCH AUTHORITY

The sum of the powers with which the Church is endowed for the fulfilment of its mission. Theologians and canon law divide these into the power of order and the power of jurisdiction, although we must not fail to observe that the two are closely related to each other. The power of order is conferred on a particular person by the sacrament of holy *orders, in its various degrees, through the rite of the *laying on of hands. The power of jurisdiction belongs to holders of office in the Church and can therefore be passed on by delegation. It need not be delegated in full measure and may be withdrawn from the holder (from the *Pope, who holds the primacy of jurisdiction, only by his abdication, or by his ceasing to be Pope because of public heresy or error). It is possible to conceive of the power of order being conferred on occasion, as at priestly ordination, in its fullness, yet so that its exercise is precluded or restricted. This is the simplest explanation of the fact that in an emergency a simple priest can administer confirmation (indeed in the Middle Ages was able in a few cases legitimately to ordain priests) and yet cannot validly absolve a penitent without "jurisdiction" for hearing confessions. In the latter case the restriction of both powers is obvious. Vatican II applies the schema of three offices (sanctification, teaching and leadership) which are all imparted through ordination, and tries to express the unity of *all* powers of office in the Church, and the sacramental ground and pneumatic character of all authority (legal as well) (Church, 21,n. 2; Bish., 2).

CHURCH HISTORY

That discipline which scientifically investigates and sets forth the history of the *Church's original life and thought as an entity in theological and saving history. Only if it is thus understood, if its subject-matter, the history of the Church, is treated in the light of divine revelation itself and the Church's understanding of herself in the past is disclosed, can Church history be a theological science, different from the Christian portion of general comparative religion— even though this portion were written by a Catholic. It should not be studied in such a way that the Christian doctrine and conviction of the divine institution of the Church serves only to exclude certain hypotheses from a purely empirical investigation of the religious history of Christianity. *A posteriori* research can assist the task of the Church's self-criticism by examining the errors of the Church in theory and practice and reconstructing what the Church has suppressed.

CIRCUMCISION

In the OT it primarily meant removing the foreskin of the male sex-organ. It is found as an *initiation rite among many ancient peoples. In Israel it was a sign of the covenant, indicating that the male Israelite belonged to the people of the covenant and was entitled to take part in its worship. Thus circumcision was a pledge of the Jew's salvation, but compare the spiritual interpretation of the prophets in Jeremiah 4:4 and Ezekiel 44:7.

Catholic theology regards Jewish circumcision under the old dispensation as a *sacrament effecting justification through the faith of the people of the covenant (D 1602, 1614). The NT expressly records the circumcision of Jesus and John the Baptist. The Jewish Christians of the primitive Church in Jerusalem took it for granted that circumcision was necessary for all believers, but it proved a serious difficulty for Gentile converts, who were finally exempted from any obligation to undergo the rite (Acts 15:6 –31). Credit for this is due to St Paul, who recognised only the circumcision of the heart (Rom 2:25–29) and *baptism as the "circumcision of Christ" (Col 2:11f.; see Phil 3:3), thus dismissing the old circumcision as unavailing (Gal 5:6).—For the wider context in saving history see also *Old Testament.*

CIRCUMINCESSION

See *Perichoresis.*

CLERGY

That group of persons in the Church who share (Gr. κλῆρος , lot, share) ecclesiastical *office and *power to an extent which the Church itself must determine in detail. Regarding office and ordination in the Church, see *Order, Priesthood.* In the Latin Church the diaconate (after an antecedent vocation and acceptance by the Church) aggregates one to the clergy. The clergy are not the whole Church; as is clear from their very name they have no precedence over the laity, but a greater responsibility. Their function within the Church is essentially one of service, and is exercised, according to the share each cleric has in *Church authority, in the government of the Church (not of the world). In addition, clerics of the Latin Church have a function of service and witness in and for the world through their permanent obligation to celibacy and canonical obedience.

COLLEGIALITY

The classical theological issue of the relationship between *Pope and Council or, more precisely, between the Pope as the chief pastor of the Church and all the bishops as the collegial bearers of this same highest authority becomes less problematical if the principle of collegiality is used as the basis of explanation. (It may be compared to the problem of avoiding two adequate and distinct subjects of total and highest authority in the Church). Accordingly, the episcopate as a whole, together with and under the Pope as its head, bears the highest power in the Church. This single bearer can exercise its power either in a specific collegial act or in an act carried out by the Pope, for he always acts as head of the college of bishops, even without their specific legal authorization. Any papal act is therefore always an act of the college of which he is the chief, and a constitutive member. Hence there is only one instance of supreme power (the college of bishops united under the Pope as its head), but there are two ways in which this highest authority may be exercised. This explanation in no way reduces the importance of the papal primacy. The Pope was entrusted with his particular rôle not by all the other bishops but by Jesus Christ, but insofar as the Pope would be the visible head of the entire episcopacy and of the Church in all his prerogatives and actions. Christ's intention in constituting the Church was directed towards an episcopate which by its collegiate nature has the same power as the Pope, although it can exercise this authority only with and under the Pope. This interpretation is both consistent and in keeping with the teaching of the Church. See also *Bishop, Church authority*.

COMMANDMENTS OF GOD

In the OT the name for those decrees which the God of the Covenant announced to the people of the Covenant (*Decalogue). The later elaboration of these until they became many individual *laws—liturgical, cultic and the like—Jesus calls "the tradition of the ancients" (Mt 15:3ff.), but he does not confirm them as commandments of God. Insofar as they were summed up even in the OT in the great commandment to love God and our neighbour as its concrete expression, they are included in that fundamental divine law which God himself has promulgated for man in Jesus Christ. But Jesus Christ does this, not by appealing to tradition, but in a way that is explicitly novel, by appealing to his mission (*Sermon on the mount). Thus very early in the primitive Church the commandments of God become "commandments of the Lord", even the "law of Christ" (Gal 6:2). The evident will of God that "his" commandments shall be interpreted by Christ himself and transformed into the law of Christ may therefore not be overlooked, especially when (as frequently happens in church pronouncements) it is affirmed or assumed that an adequate knowledge of God's commandments can be gained from man's experience of his own nature or by reflection on natural law alone (*Natural moral law).

81

COMMANDMENTS OF THE CHURCH

In the stricter, catechetical sense, those "five commandments" formulated in 1555 which bind all baptized persons from their seventh year onwards provided they have the use of reason: (1) To sanctify Sundays and Holy Days; (2) To hear Mass on Sunday and Holy Days; (3) To abstain and fast on certain days; (4) To confess one's sins, if they be mortal, at least once a year; (5) To receive Communion during the Easter period. In a wider sense the commandments of the Church are those ordinances of the Church which follow from its theological and social constitution and are so designed as to protect them: the form of marriage, the upbringing and education of children, and so forth. The commandments of the Church are historically necessary because without concrete "minimum requirements" the spontaneous, charismatic development of the Church in a widely diffused, pluralistic society—such as the Church has become—is not to be looked for, indeed is ultimately impossible. Because of this very historical and social structure of the Church its commandments are also the outflow of the Church's actual understanding of itself as constantly actualizing itself here and now; they also share, therefore, in the legitimate modification of this actual understanding which the Church has of itself insofar as the change affects the ever historical actualization of the Church but not its abiding theological nature. Hence in recent years the commandments on fasting, censorship, non-cremation, etc. have been changed or cancelled. The Church lawgiver cannot "be" the will of God, and cannot as God's representative demand by direct moral suasion obedience to laws which are only "of the Church" unless they are an essential concomitant of the Church as conceived by Christians.

COMMEMORATION

See *Anamnesis.*

COMMUNICATION

Designates that active exchange, based on personal ability to hear and free openness, that creates a community between the transmitter and the recipient (hearer) which is best called communion. In its very highest form, namely, *self-communication, the source of the communication itself is given to the recipient. Communication is natural to *man, who cannot be merely individual substance or immanent subject; rather, his very "being" is always to be with others, thus communicating by language, gestures, signs, and the like. In the personal encounter ("I and Thou") (which is not necessarily restricted to two, but can also include groups, classes and so on), the I which is addressed by the Thou is constituted in the complete sense of the word, since the freedom and uniqueness of the *person is only released by adopting an attitude towards this address. Man's natural bent for communication always implies the capacity to be addressed by the absolute, universal Thou and to be called to ultimate, cosmic community. According to revelation, man is enabled to receive connaturally this address of God which is God's self-communication and so to be a permanent partner of the Absolute. But this latter reveals itself in the form of the incarnate brother, so that communication with God in Christ is true mutual exinanition and radical surrender of self, culminating in the communication of *heaven (*Beatific vision). "Spiritual communion" is a special form of communication. It is longing, in faith and love, for the actualization and growth of one's abiding union with Jesus Christ in his *Pneuma, without sacramentally eating the Eucharistic bread—but with an explicit or implicit desire for it. The Church teaches that this "spiritual communion" is a real personal communication with Jesus Christ, for it effects the sacramental grace of the Eucharist in non-sacramental fashion (D 881).

COMMUNICATIO IDIOMATUM

Literally, from the Latin, communication of properties. It primarily means that because of the *hypostatic union the properties of both natures can and must be predicated of the one Person Jesus Christ. True communication of properties in the logical sense occurs when Christ is deisgnated by a name that directly identifies his Person as the bearer of one of the two natures and the properties of the other nature are predicated of this subject; for example, "The Word of God was crucified". Scripture and the Church have employed this communication of properties from the first. The Scholastics lay down six rules for its use: (1) Concrete divine and human attributes of Christ are interchangeable ("God is man"). (2) Abstract attributes of God and man are not interchangeable and abstract attributes cannot be predicated of those which are concrete; it is false to say, "Christ's humanity is the Word made flesh". (3) A proposition which denies

Christ an attribute that is his in virtue of either of his natures is false; thus it is false to say, "The Logos did not die". (4) Expressions designating the "becoming" of hypostatic union cannot be predicated of the man Jesus. It is false to say, "man became God". (5) Derivatives or compounds of "God" or "man" must be treated with caution; Nestorius erroneously says, "Christ is a God-bearing man". (6) Expressions used by heretics should only be used with circumspection; for example, the Arian proposition "Christ is a creature", which is susceptible of a correct interpretation. These rules for the communication of properties are, as it were, the translation into logical terms of the reality of the *hypostatic union.

COMMUNION OF SAINTS

An article of faith which has been explicit in the Apostles' Creed since the 5th century. It is based on the NT concept of κοινωνία (community), which connotes fellowship in the faith at the celebration of the Eucharist of each member with all and all with Christ. The sense which should be chiefly borne in mind today is this: the "saints" are primarily the members of God's people, who are one in the Holy Ghost, in the grace of justification, in love, and in the sacraments, and accordingly they intercede for one another in prayer and deed. Hence the communion of saints also signifies union with the dead who have gone before us and with the angels (*Purgatory, *Indulgence, *Veneration of saints).

COMMUNITY

In general, the union of a number of personal beings who are joined in society by certain relationships, personal *communication, juridical bonds, proximity in time and space, or transcendental relations. From a philosophical point of view community is natural to man, who can only arrive at his unique self by experiencing existence shared with other bodily, spiritual persons. Since fulfilment of the "I" can only occur through and in community, self-discovery and union with community grow in the same, not inverse, proportion. The various kinds of community within the world and their elements are based on the various dimensions of human existence: *marriage, family, friendship, nation. Theology explains and interprets man's nature as a social being in more detail; man is always the partner whom God himself has chosen, in such a way that he must realize his personal uniqueness *in* the community of all men and *in its service*. Thus God's self-communication to all men in Christ has not created a series of private saving histories for atomized individuals, but the *one* history of the *one* human race. Yet this history keeps each individual in view for his own sake; but he finds his way to himself—to himself as the person God has in view—only by finding that saving community which God himself has set up and personally realizing his membership of it (*Church), and by practising solidarity with those whom God loves (the poor and disadvantaged). Theological thought on community consists to date of attempts to view the question of society theologically, and to study the relationship between individual and collective identity.

COMPULSION

A situation interior or exterior to man which makes it impossible for him to reach a given free decision or to give that decision physical effect. Such compulsion (even interior) does exist: man in his finite, creaturely freedom is not always capable of everything. When there is compulsion, responsibility, merit, and sin are alike impossible (D 1950f., 2003; these references contain the official teaching of the Church). But this fact must not be so magnified that we embrace *determinism and deny *freedom of choice altogether. Since compulsion is not necessarily pathological, it is not possible for man in a certain concrete case to determine precisely with certainty where internal compulsion ceases and where freedom begins. In a concrete case a man may falsely imagine that he is free, or may conceal his real freedom behind the pretext of compulsion.—See also *Certainty of Salvation*.

CONCILIARISM

A theory emanating in a variety of forms from canonists of the 12th and 13th centuries, according to which an ecumenical council was held to be superior to the Pope. Whereas the earlier forms of conciliarism, which envisaged a council rather as a representation of the whole Church than as an assembly of autonomous bishops, arose principally for theological reasons (decisions in questions of faith, combating schism and anti-popes, and other reforms in the Church; most prominent exponent: Marsilius of Padua, d. about 1343), its later forms attempted to enhance the position of individual bishops or their Churches, and were often supported by particular nations and their rulers (Gallicanism) for political reasons. Conciliarism was solemnly condemned by the Church at Vatican Council I (*Pope). It overlooks the fact that a council always reflects the abiding structure of the Church. Now, the apostolic (episcopal) college only exists with and under its head (Peter–Pope) and forms the governing body of the Church together with him, not parallel to him or in opposition to him.

CONCILIARITY

See *Bishop, Council, Pope.*

CONCUPISCENCE

A desire which directs human freedom towards a partial *good antecedently to any decision taken by that freedom and not altogether subject to such decision. According to Scripture it is principally in concupiscence that sin manifests itself in saving history since *Adam; yet concupiscence is not identical with sin (Rom 7:8; D 1515f.), so that it survives even in the justified (Rom 13, 14, and *passim)* and that in all its dimensions. Thus it must not be thought to reside in the *body alone, which is not synonymous with the biblical "flesh" (*Sarx). The Church teaches that concupiscence is something natural (D 1979f.); but as compared with the life that God originally bestowed on man, it is also, especially as we experience it, a lack of that power of decision that God originally bestowed. To this extent, then, concupiscence is a result of *original sin and an inducement to personal sin (see *Temptation),* but as the latter it can be overcome by the grace of God (D 1512, 1515f., 1521, 1536 –39, 1568). Modern theology has abandoned an interpretation of concupiscence deriving from St Augustine which materially identifies it with the guilt of original sin, and also the opinion of most post-Tridentine theologians that concupiscence is merely a penalty for original sin in a juridical sense, being in itself purely "natural", that is, to be taken for granted, even considering man in the concrete. It regards concupiscence as a natural instinct of man, not in itself vicious, but contradicting the supernatural *existential so long as it has not become subject to the moral decision of the individual; as a real manifestation, therefore, of guilt, which in the

86

justified leads to active acceptance of *death (*Asceticism) and thus to the conquest of concupiscence. This concupiscence also has an "outward aspect" in regard to social rather than merely individual states. In a world profoundly affected by concupiscence, freedom (justice) will always be experienced also as something still outstanding, which is prevented by unnecessary social structures and has to be opposed.

CONFESSION

The declaration of personal decisions and circumstances within the confines of a community. Thus in Scripture we find the confession of Yahweh's saving deeds of power, confessions of guilt and gratitude, and above all confessions of praise (liturgical homologies and doxologies). Confession is revived in the NT by Jesus' demand that men confess him in faith (Mt 10:32f.), and St Paul calls it a necessary testimony of faith (Rom 10:9f.). Public confession in both its aspects —the praise of God's mighty deeds in Jesus Christ on behalf of man who confesses his guilt—has always figured in Christianity, necessarily arising from man's psychosomatic unity and his essential ordination to society, and as constituting the Church (*Creed).

CONFESSION

See *Penance, Sacrament of.*

CONFIRMATION

One of the seven *sacraments of the New Covenant (D 1259, 1317ff., 1628, and *passim),* which is to be regarded as completing *baptism (D 1311) and, like baptism itself and priestly ordination, impresses an indelible *character (D 1313, 1609, 1767, 1864). Confirmation must be understood in the context of the scriptural theology of the *laying on of hands and of the *Holy Spirit. He is bestowed on the baptized person, in what Scripture calls an "anointing" or a "sealing", as a special gift, which is different from the grace of conversion and baptism (see Acts 8:12–17; 19:1–7) and permits him to share in the permanent prophetic and charismatic gift which the Church received at Pentecost. For insofar as the grace of Jesus Christ is the grace of the Incarnation and not simply the grace of dying together with Jesus Christ, which in baptism rescues the individual from the law of death and sin, this grace of confirmation must make the acceptance of the world, for the latter's transfiguration, visible *in* the world (*World, responsibility for). Therefore the grace of confirmation, rightly understood, is God's grace for the Church for carrying out the mission to the world and for announcing the world's transforming fulfilment. What functions this grace allots the individual as his first and particular duty God will determine by the vocation he gives and by his distribution of the *charismata of the Spirit, which are nothing else than preferred styles of expression of one and the same Spirit whom all receive in confirmation.

In the Latin Church the Spirit is mediated by a rite which includes (1) the *laying on of hands, already in use in the apostolic Church; (2) anointing with chrism (prepared of olive oil mixed with balsam), a later feature, dating from about the 3rd century; and (3) the words. The ordinary minister of confirmation (the minister of first choice, Vat. II, Church, 26) is the bishop; in exceptional cases (as is the rule in the Eastern Churches) a priest. The beginning of adolescence is to be considered a suitable age for confirmation (school-leaving, consecration of Christian maturity), although any baptized person can be validly confirmed whatever his age. Liturgical interests would like to restore the ancient process or Christian initiation: baptism, confirmation, Eucharist.

CONFIRMATION IN GRACE

A technical term in the scholastic theology of grace. It means that a person has received the special gift, unmerited and impossible to merit, not only of actual sinlessness but also of impeccability, either as an intrinsic incapacity of the will (which is still free) with respect to sin (as St Thomas and St Bonaventure teach) or as a prevention of sin by God's external disposition though the power to sin remains (thus Suarez). These theologians hold that the Blessed Virgin, St Joseph, St John the Baptist, and the Apostles, among others, were confirmed in grace on account of their rôle in God's plan for salvation.

CONFLICT

The term often used in a modified sense to describe a combative confrontation. As a sociological term it also embraces any kind of dispute, regardless of its intensity or mode of development (conflict theory, theoretical conflicts, conflicts regarding standards, rôles, wages and race between generations, and armed conflict). The various manifestations and world-wide appearance of conflicts leads to the conclusion that they are containable if inevitable basic social phenomena. Hence, whatever form a conflict may take, certain basic questions may be posed: Under what conditions do conflicts arise? To what extent can they be analysed? How can they be contained or resolved? The decisive factor for a theological approach to conflict is that the doctrine of *original sin and concupiscence provides a rational explanation for the inevitability of conflicts. Furthermore, the doctrine of *salvation and atonement as well as the commandment to love one's neighbour offer models for restraining and overcoming conflicts, without in any way requiring that we should disregard the productive function of social conflicts in the continuing development of social formations, as often happens in the Church.

CONSCIENCE

That element in man's experience of freedom which makes him aware of his responsibility. The biblical term for conscience is the *heart, in which God's will is written (Rom 2:15); which can be a heart of stone (Ezek 11:19) or a divided heart (Jas 1:8), which must be circumcised, in which the light of divine truth shines (2 Cor 4:6). He who acts out of inner conviction, that is to say in obedient acceptance of the reality which is prior to freedom and which is implicitly posited anew even by the denial of freedom, has a pure heart and will see God (Mt 5:8, see Mt 12:34f.). Conscience in the sense of "self-consciousness passing moral judgment" figured in Greek popular philosophy in the first century B.C. (*Syneidesis) and found its way into the apostolic writings of the NT. St Paul in particular developed it as a Christian concept (Rom 2:14f. and *passim*) approaching the notion of the "heart": "All that is not done from conviction is sin" (Rom 14:23). That is, the responsibility of the *person entails the establishment of inner conviction, which therefore must relate to everything that "person" connotes (responsibility to God the sovereign mystery, to the ego itself [and its intrinsic truth—its reality], to each *community to which this person belongs, to his world). But this means that conscience can be formed, or rather that one's reflection on the reality that has been given from the first can be given depth and precision,

89

and must affirm that the pre-conditions of the free act (the objective norms which are made known *a posteriori*—historically and collectively; *natural moral law) are to be willed, in other words, are imperatives. It also means, however, that these objective norms can be presented to man only by the judgment of his own conscience, so that this judgment of conscience absolutely binds man in all his decisions. Hence freedom of conscience can be understood in several different senses: (1) as the freedom of the will to recognize or to ignore the demands of conscience; (2) as freedom to obey conscience alone, independent of any external influence, even of the highest authorities if these do not address themselves to conscience itself (these two kinds of freedom constitute an obligation inseparable from what it is to be a person); (3) as freedom of conscience in society, the natural right to live according to one's own conscience (*Tolerance; *Religious freedom*). What has been said does not settle the question whether in fact the conscience adequately recognizes truth itself when passing its concrete judgment or not. In the latter case we speak, somewhat unsatisfactorily, of an erroneous conscience. The Church teaches that in the concrete situation of humanity since Adam an undistorted and sufficiently developed knowledge of man's natural being, as the norm of his (natural) moral behaviour, is attainable only with the help of explicit divine revelation. Thus, having to make decisions in his concrete situation and yet knowing that his decisions may be wrong, man finds himself referred to the grace of God, which liberates his freedom.

CONSECRATION

The action by which a thing is set apart from profane use, or a person is appointed to a special liturgical service of God. In Catholic Christianity the consecration of an object is nothing else than a prayer of petition for the user of the object and does not give the thing itself any magical powers. Consecration of a person (apart from the consecration of abbots, virgins, and such persons) is his "ordination" (Holy *orders) to clerical office (*Priesthood, *Bishop, *Deacon).

CONSENT

Consent (Lat. *consensus,* agreement) has several meanings in theology: (1) *In *marriage:* The free, unconstrained resolution of man and wife by which they enter into a community of life and love intended to last until death. (2) *"Consent of the Fathers"*: Agreement among the *Fathers of the Church on a matter of faith as *such*. In principle it is also to be presumed if agreement is proved to exist among all the Fathers who explicitly taught a doctrine *as* revealed and were not contradicted. The binding force of the consent of the Fathers was acknowledged in practice by the first *council, and formally by the Council of Trent (D 1507). (3) *Consent of theologians:* The agreement of *theologians who have distinguished themselves by their orthodoxy and the importance of their theological work insofar as the teaching of the Church's magisterium is recognizably reflected in that work (D 2879, 3881f.). (4) *Universal consent:* When all the faithful express their general agreement on a matter of faith of morals, they cannot err (Vat. II, Church, 11).

CONSERVATION OF THE WORLD

The concept of *creation as the free "causation" of the world by God's unique act, without reference to anything anterior, but wholly containing both the "what" and the "how" of this act (in contrast to creaturely causation, which affects something already extant, resting on it and entering into it), connotes so radical a dependence of the creature on the Creator that in this "creation" both the *beginning and the permanence of "createdness" are settled once for all. Thus the conservation of the world is simply another aspect of the causation of the world. Like the act of creation it can only be understood as a permanent, positive production of the world by God, not as an indirect preservation of the world by guarding it against the forces of dissolution. Though not expressly defined as a dogma, the conservation of the world is an integral part of that conception of the world which the Church teaches everywhere through her ordinary magisterium (see Rev 17:28). It follows from the necessity of conservation that God can preserve the world in Christ and for Christ's sake in spite of its sinfulness, and that thus by God's saving disposition this world itself remains open for its own "renewal" under God's eschatological sovereignty.

CONSOLATION, COMFORT, ENCOURAGEMENT

The religious experience (still in the *hope of a future consummation) that our life, though it seems hopelessly ruined, is sustained by the supreme, incomprehensible love of God in Christ. This experience comes only to one who entrusts himself to God in faith without reserve, without asking any "pre-payment" to reassure him (2 Cor 1:7–11), who steadfastly accepts the sorrows of life (Mt 5:4), obediently hears the word of God in Scripture (Rom 15:4), regards consolation as an aid to the salvation of others (2 Cor 1:3–7), and is prepared to communicate this divine consolation to others (Acts 15:31f.; 16:40; 1 Thess 2:11f.; 4:18).

CONSTANCE

The Sixteenth Ecumenical Council, which sat from November 5, 1414 to April 22, 1418 at Constance, was chiefly concerned to end the Great Schism (abdication of Gregory XII, deposition of the antipopes John XXIII and Benedict XIII, election of Martin V). It is theologically important because it condemned the errors of John Wycliffe (D 1151–1195) and John Huss (D 1201–1230; see also D 1247–1279) and defined that the whole Christ with his body and blood is present under each eucharistic *species, under the species of bread as well as that of wine (D 1198f.). The interpretation of the Council's teaching (fourth and fifth sessions before the election of Martin V) is still controverted, in Catholic theology as well.

CONSTANTINOPLE

The "New Rome", capital of the Byzantine Empire, now Istanbul. Four ecumenical councils were held at Constantinople: (1) The Second Ecumenical Council, convoked in the pontificate of St Damasus from May to July, 381, condemned all the heresies that denied the divinity of the Holy Ghost (*Macedonianism) and issued the Creed still recited in the Roman and Byzantine celebration of the Eucharist (D 150). (2) The Fifth Ecumenical Council, assembled from May 5 to June 2, 553, in the pontificate of Vigilius, renewed the condemnation of *Nestorianism (D 421–438) and repudiated *Origenism (D 403–411). (3) The Sixth Ecumenical Council, also called the Trullan, took place under Popes Agatho and Leo II from November 7, 680 to September 16, 681. It condemned *Monothelitism (D 548, 553–559) and Pope Honorius I, because he had declared—not defined—that the Monothelite controversy was a mere dispute about words. (4) The Eighth Ecumenical Council, from October 5, 869 to February 28, 870, in the pontificates of Nicholas I and Hadrian II, condemned the Patriarch of Constantinople, Photius, for his schism (see D 650 – 664) and is no longer recognized as ecumenical by the separated Eastern Churches.

CONSUBSTANTIATION

The theological notion, rejected by the Catholic Church, that in the *Eucharist the body and blood of Christ indeed become present but coexist with the *substance of bread and wine, so that the empirical forms of bread and wine—which certainly remain after the consecration—are still bread and wine in an absolute sense, not merely their *species. The Catholic doctrine of *transubstantiation was elaborated because of certain confused notions of consubstantiation current in patristic and medieval times. Luther revived consubstantiation and this view is widespread in modern Lutheranism. It was repudiated by the Council of Trent (D 1652).

CONTEMPLATION

The tranquil abiding in the presence of God. Christian *mysticism differentiates between acquired contemplation, achieved by psychological effort, and infused contemplation, in which God gratuitously makes himself known to the individual. This latter is true contemplation, directly engaging man in the *transcendence that is natural to him but elevated by grace—without a controlled operation of his mental faculties determined and effected by an object. Since this deprives man of certain peripheral natural operations, such as discursive rational knowledge, contemplation first manifests itself as "aridity", a "dark night" in which man is purified of his preoccupation with external things.

CONTINGENCY

In philosophy, the fortuitous character, that is to say, the non-necessity, of an existing being, for essence and existence are distinct and not necessarily united. This contingency is perceived when through our experience of freedom and change we grasp the transcendental necessity of recognizing certain judgments ("I did this") as purely declaratory. Now when existence is not part of the very nature of a thing, so that its mere being there before us is enigmatic, that thing refers us to some outside principle which must explain why essence and existence are in fact united here (since every mere matter of fact is rooted in something necessary, though the two are not identical; as every declaratory judgment implies, and yet is not, an apodictic one), thus plainly revealing itself to be produced and sustained by the absolute *being of God, incapable of existing without him, or of being affirmed unless he be (implicitly) affirmed. At the same time this relationship, by the nature of contingency and our experience of it, can only be conceived as one freely established by God. Thus contingency is the (somewhat weaker) philosophical counterpart of the theological notion of createdness, since this latter more explicitly grasps the free production of the contingent and knows that the "first" creative efficient cause is identical with the living God whom man encounters in saving history.

CONTRITION

In theological language the conversion (Mt 3:2; 4:17; *Metanoia) of a sinner to God in faith, hope, and love in response (under the impulse of grace) to God's merciful willingness to forgive him in Jesus Christ. Thus there is no question of the sinner redeeming himself. But he has personal dealings with God who gives man both divine grace and his free, responsible answer to grace. God's love overcomes man's guilt by bringing man to love him freely in return. Contrition may have two phases. We speak of "imperfect contrition" (attritio; *Attritionism) when a consideration of God's justice, which demands the rejection of the sinner, moves him to turn from sin (in thought and deed) as offensive to God's goodness and holy will (D 1677f., 1705). When contrition attains its full stature, as it must, and becomes real love of God for his own sake, either through the sacrament of *penance or outside it (though with an explicit or implicit desire for the sacrament, D 1677f.), so that this love (D 1677f.) turns a man away from sin, we speak of "perfect contrition" (*Contritionism). Whenever and however some person rejects sin as an offence against God it is easy for him to love God; for man's own nature compels him to give his heart either to God or to some creature he has deified. What matters in practice, therefore, is that the disillusioned sinner shall be freed, by the light of the grace he has besought from God, from the tyranny of a good that is only finite and particular but without which life seemed unbearable and for the sake of which he has even prepared to defy God's will. The rejection by someone of what he freely did in the past that is involved in contrition is aimed at the moral worthlessness of this past deed and at the attitude of which the deed was the concrete expression. This rejection does not mean sentimental regret or an attempt to flee from or suppress the past. Rather, it is the right way for a man to come to terms with his own past and to accept responsibility for it. This rejection does not involve any fictional play-acting or make-believe; it does not contest the undeniable fact that even this evil deed that was done in the past had as its purpose something "good" and that often it has resulted in much good (with regard to human maturity, and so on). From the psychological point of view this means that repentance often gives rise to a problem that seems almost insoluble, when what has to be rejected is some occurrence that because of its good consequences the person concerned is hardly able to unthink. Here the better way of repentance will be an unconditional turning to God and to the forgiveness he offers in love, instead of becoming bogged down in analysing the past.

CONTRITIONISM

This term may refer to one of three theories. (1) The view of early scholastic theology that all efficacious and true repentance (then called *contritio)* must necessarily be justifying *love; that the sinner who approaches the *sacrament of penance with *contritio* is already justified, the absolution effecting only remission of temporal penalties due to sin and reconciliation with the Church. Thirteenth century scholasticism transformed this theory into something of an *attritionism: sincere *attritio* does not justify of itself, it can only become perfect *contritio* by virtue of absolution in the sacrament of penance. The early scholastic view that absolution did not obliterate sin but merely showed the forgiveness already granted, as Luther also held, was thus rejected (also by the Council of Trent: D 1677f.). (2) A theory advanced in Baianism, Jansenism, and the like that the *motive for all genuine repentance must be perfect love of God (already condemned at Trent). (3) A still later view, that in the sacrament of penance all repentance springing from *fear of God must necessarily include an incipient, feeble love of God, but not a love of desire, even though this alone does not justify without the sacrament. A controversy ensued between Contritionists and Attritionists, the latter maintaining that the love of desire in *attritio* sufficed for reception of the sacrament;

Alexander VII in 1667 forbade either side to pronounce theological censures on the other (D 2070).—See also *Fear of God*.

CONTROVERSIAL THEOLOGY

The methodical reflection of theologians on the doctrines of non-Catholic Christian communions. It has existed in this form only since the Reformation, though there were beginnings as early as the *patristic age. Its subsidiary disciplines are the comparative study of the different communions and church history, which together seek to give as accurate a picture as possible of the rise, development, and nature of the separated communions. Three methods of controversial theology have emerged, not always clearly distinguishable from one another: the polemic method, characterized by an aggressive attitude that seeks to expose an opponent's weaknesses; the irenic, which consciously abandons animosity and deliberately seeks to understand the separated brethren (here there is a danger of relativistic irenism: D 3879f.); and *symbolics, where the attempt of understanding and comparison, in view of uniting the parties concerned, is confined to their dogmatic formulations, the confessional documents or "symbols". We may call "ecumenism" that type of controversial theology which deliberately tries to work for church unity, stressing existing unity in essential matters of faith, presenting the non-dogmatic tradition of each "church" as its special character which ought to be preserved and positively seeking to incorporate this in the future union (*Ecumenical movement).

CONVENIENCE, ARGUMENT OF

A method of studying a theological truth, used by theologians in both medieval and modern times, which demonstrates that it is "fitting" (in terms of other revealed truths, the divine attributes, and so forth), without claiming to prove the necessity of this truth. Where such a truth is already established, the argument of convenience simply investigates more thoroughly the nature of this truth, of its connection with other truths, and thus is indispensable to theology. The argument of convenience as such cannot prove a truth which is not already established. But it must be observed that arguments that are objectively conclusive, producing at least moral certainty, may strike other people as mere arguments of convenience. This fact must be borne in mind if one is to judge the *history of dogma correctly.

CONVERSION

The biblical *metanoia;* primarily any sort of religious or moral transformation, especially the radical venture of entrusting oneself to God and his gracious guidance by a radical and fundamental religious *act. It is always a matter of religious *experience and of the subjective certainty bound up with this latter, though the personal question whether God has effected a particular conversion by an intervention that can be direclty ascertained must often be left in abeyance. Conversion of this kind can and must often occur where faith has already been received and within the Church.

Conversion is also taken to mean the adoption of a different Christian belief. Finally, it can mean entering a religious community (from change in one's manner of life). "Lay brothers" today correspond to the old institution of the *conversi.*

CONVERSION, THEORY OF

(1) A theoretical explanation of the sacrificial character of the Mass: if *sacrifice in general consists in changing the offering into a superior form (not destroying it), whereby it is made over to God, then the sacrifice of the *Mass formally consists in *transubstantiation as such, whereby the earthly offering is changed into the body and blood of Christ and is thus made over to God. (2) A theoretical explanation of *transubstantiation itself: the body of Christ becomes present solely through the changing or conversion of the bread.

COREDEMPTRIX

A term in Catholic theology (*Mariology) whose possible meaning has not yet been precisely determined. It seeks to express *Mary's rôle—unique in personal and saving history and ever valid and efficacious—in the historical beginning of redemption and its fulfilment by the Redeemer Jesus Christ and in the communion of saints (D 3274, 3370).

COSMOS

See *World*.

COUNCIL

GENERAL NOTION. Councils (synods) are meetings, chiefly (though, theologically, not perforce only) of bishops, which deliberate upon Church affairs, make decisions, and lay down regulations. At particular, formerly also national, councils each bishop represents his local church. A council at which the Church as a whole is represented in accordance with prevailing canon law (one which the Pope convokes, presides over, and ultimately confirms) is called an ecumenical council.

THEOLOGICAL PROBLEMS. In Catholic doctrine the bishops, deliberating and reaching decisions under the leadership of the Pope and together with him in an ecumenical council, possess supreme authority in the Church (CIC can. 228) and are infallible in matters of faith when the council pronounces a solemn *definition (Vat. II: Church, 25). But the same is also true when together they exercise and exhibit the ordinary *magisterium. In both cases they exhibit collegially their rôle as successors of the apostolic college. Though the ordinary magisterium and the collegiality of the bishops exist and are visible apart from a council, an ecumenical council makes it possible to display the unity of the Church more clearly and at the same time to bring into clearer view the multiplicity of the bishops and their local churches. A special problem in theology and the history of dogma arises from the fact that some of the 21 councils now recognized as ecumenical were formerly not considered so, and that on the other hand certain councils are recognized as authoritative in matters of dogma which so far have not been considered ecumenical. Furthermore, earlier councils do not fulfil all the requirements cited above, not having been called or confirmed by the Pope. As to these problems, it should be said that a council represents the Church's understanding of herself at a particular time, an understanding which can develop and change in accordance with the *development of dogma and canon law. Now what binds the councils of the Church today is not that earlier conception of herself which it may be possible to ascertain by historical methods, but only her present developed conception. If the Church finds her later conception of the faith in an earlier council which, for example, was only called by the emperor or even was a mere local synod, there is no reason why she should not declare such a council ecumenical, that is equivalent to an ecumenical council in the present sense, and accept its authority even for our time. Of course if an ancient council certainly represented the whole Church in a manner consistent with the state of ecclesiastical law at that time and there is no doubt that it proclaimed a doctrine with the intention of unconditionally binding the whole Church, then it has been infallible from the first. Often, however, only the sources (conciliar acts), the general aims of the council, and the mentality of the relevant period can show whether an earlier council actually meant to pronounce infallible judgment. Thus, for instance, exegesis of a scriptural text by a council is only binding if the council expressly intended to pronounce on the interpretation.—The 21 ecumenical councils up to the present are: *Nicaea (2), *Constantinople (4), *Ephesus, *Chalcedon, the *Lateran (5), *Lyons (2), *Vienne, *Constance, *Basle-Ferrara-*Florence, *Trent, *Vatican (2).

COVENANT

A term in biblical theology; in the OT it means Israel's unique relationship with Yahweh as his chosen people, a relationship based on that gracious choice by which God undertakes to be the people's partner, yet in such a way that he remains the Lord of the covenant and that neither party thereto can renounce it. In the aetiology of OT saving history this covenant is described as a consequence of individual alliances before Moses' time: with Noah, Genesis 9:8–17 (already an "eternal covenant"); with Abraham, Genesis 15:9–12, 17f. (*circumcision as the sign of the covenant is associated with Abraham's covenant: Gen 17). The covenant is entered into with all Israel on Sinai (the real Old Covenant with the *Law and above all the *Decalogue; Ex 20; 34); then with David, 2 Samuel 7 (the messianic covenant, since David is promised a descendant who will be God's Son and will ensure the continuance of David's house forever); other accounts where the entrance into covenants are described are to be thought of either as renewing the covenant or as exhorting to fidelity. The Sinaitic covenant is of central·importance (on the pattern of ancient eastern contracts of sovereignty and vassallage): The love given to Israel binds it to obedient loyalty: i.e., to remain commonly loyal to Yahweh in fidelity and friendship. For the theology of the covenant see also *Old Testament*. The translation of "covenant" as "testament" (last will and testament) does not quite convey the theological essence of the covenant, which is partnership; it indicates, rather, God's sovereign mastery and derives from the Greek translation of the OT. In the NT too, God's salvific activity in the OT is called the "covenant". When the covenants of the OT were entered into, the blood of animals was usually shed in sacrifice, and the NT too knows of a blood in which a covenant (Mk 14:24), a "new covenant" (Lk 22:20; 1 Cor 11:25) is instituted, namely, the Blood of Jesus. Henceforth it is clear that official, public *saving history comprises two successive covenants (Gal 4:24; 2 Cor 3:6 –18). An authentic theology of the New Covenant, in which the partners are God and redeemed mankind, is developed in Hebrews (7–10), which fully acknowledges the dignity of the Old Covenant (*New Testament).

CREATION

In every affirmation it makes, the human mind affirms, at least implicitly, absolute being as the real ground of the metaphysical principles of being and knowledge that are assumed without qualification when any statement is made, and further affirms absolute being as *mystery and—in the eminent sense—as personal being (*Person). This nameless being we call God. This absolute, incomprehensible reality, which ontologically is always the silent horizon of all intellectual encounter with being, is thus always implicitly conjointly affirmed in every affirmation as infinitely different from the knowing subject that is man, and from the particular finite beings that are known. Accordingly, man can only ascertain the relation between knower and known— finite being and absolute infinity—in two respects: firstly, God, being absolute and infinite, must be utterly distinct from finite being (D 3001), otherwise he would be an object of comprehension instead of the *principle and ground of comprehension that always "lies beyond" it; this he is and always remains, even when metaphysical reflection names and "objectifies" him. Consequently he cannot "need" finite being (called the *world; see D 3002). Otherwise he would not be radically different from the world but would be part of a greater whole, the world being something of God himself, as it were God's body, the mode of his manifestation, the means by which he is himself (*Pantheism, *Emanation). And secondly, the world must radically depend on God (see D 800, 3021, 3025), without God depending on it as the master depends on the servant; no part of its being can be independent of him, any more than the variety and oneness of earthly things can be perceived apart from the "prior reach", the *transcendence of the mind to God. It is defined Catholic teaching that God must freely establish this dependent being (D 3025), for being finite and transient it cannot be absolutely necessary; it could only be absolutely necessary if God necessarily willed the world, and in this case the world would be necessary to God, he would be dependent on it. This radical dependence must be permanent (see D 790, 3003), that is to say must characterize more than a "beginning", because finite being now and always refers us to its absolute source. This peculiar relation between God and the world (which cannot really be subsumed under a general [univocal] concept of *causality) is known to dogmatic theology as the "createdness" of the world, its permanent rootedness in the free enactment of the personal God, whereby the world, totally and at all times, remains dependent on him (*Conservation of the world, Divine *concourse). This creative enactment, therefore, does not imply any "material" already in existence. It is defined teaching that God creates out of "nothing" (D 3025) and is therefore not a mere *demiurge; what God makes, exists. It is no mere appearance behind which God is concealed, but real being different from God, so that genuine reality and radical dependence grow in the same, not in inverse, proportion. Faith affirms this creation out of our prayerful experience of our own autonomous, responsible being and the complete surrender of that being to the unmasterable mastery of utter mystery; and it sees the creatureliness thus experienced as the fundamental structure of all finite being with which man has dealings. At the same time this Christian doctrine of creatureliness "demythologizes" the preterhuman world: that world is not God, it is not really "numinous", and therefore is rightly looked on as "material" for the creative powers of man, who encounters in it, as such, dull finitude and in himself (and the world so far as he knows and controls it) the limitless spiritual openness—which nevertheless is fulfilled, and in this sense is finite—of his own genuine creatureliness, and so finds God. Through this utter dependence, finite being at every level "reveals" (*Revelation) something of the nature of God, because an *analogy between Creator and creature must and does exist to the *glory of God.—See also *Creation of Man, Beginning, Evolution, Principle of Economy.*

CREATION, DOCTRINE OF

The theological doctrine of the creaturelines of man, which is based on *creation. It treats not only in general of the createdness of all that is not God (Gen 1:1; D 800, 3002) but especially of that creatureliness which is proper to man and thus becomes the fundamental structure of man's relationship with God: *humility, *adoration, trust in him who sustains the life we can no longer control, readiness to believe, hiddenness in God, docility to God (*Potentia obedientialis), the inner dialectic of the attitude which accepts both utter dependence on God and real, responsible autonomy and independence in dialogue with God. The doctrine of creation does not merely state what human *nature is, but in elaborating the notion of the creaturely, embraces every sphere of human life—and therefore also man's supernatural elevation by grace. The doctrine of creation is closely connected with theological *anthropology since creatureliness is only fully realized in man.

CREATIONISM

By contrast with *generationism (*Traducianism) creationism is the Catholic doctrine that God creates every individual soul out of nothing (*Creation), uniting it with the cells of the parents, which have fused in generation to form a single human being (D 1440f., 2015, 2017, 3896). The soul does not exist before its substantial union with the body (D 403, 456, against *Preexistentianism and the theory of the transmigration of souls). The majority of Catholic theologians agree that the soul is infused at the moment when the cells of the parents are united (not at birth: D 2131; and not upon the first intellectual act: D 3220). Creationism does not deny that the parents are in a true and proper sense the cause of the new human being but it also affirms that the production of what is truly new in a spiritual, free person transcends the created cause through which God works, though in such a way that the dynamism of God's absolute being remains "in" this cause so that in spite of the act of creation the new person originates through a genuinely natural event, regardless of the moral character of the parents' act of generation. The unification of the actual reproduction of the body and of the soul of a human being by his or her parents with the creation of the soul by God as taught by the Church is made more accessible by the notion of self-transcendence (*Creation of man).

CREATION NARRATIVE

The two creation narratives (Gen 1:1–2:4a; 2:4b–25), the one (from the priestly writings and much more recent) more concerned with the world, the other (from the Yahwist tradition and older) with man, set forth in dramatic and picturesque fashion our primordial metaphysical and religious experience: the creatureliness of the world and man, their origin in a spiritual, wise, free God who wills his creature's good, (optimistically) rejecting any absolute dualism, emphasizing the fact that the division of the human race into two sexes, the equal dignity of both—however widely the two natures may differ—, their union in *marriage, all are part of the original order of creation, which always remains the exemplar of man's historical development, both individual and social. Because all reality is God's creation, because man is one being composed of a spiritual *soul and a *body (see D 800, 3002) and as such—as a spiritual person the elements of whose nature interact—cannot be accounted for "from below", man must be created by God, body and soul (*Monogenism, *Creation of man). This does not mean that the origin of man had no prehistory in the world, under the creative governance of God which sustains all earthly being and enables that being at every level to rise above itself as it could never do by its own powers. On the contrary. Man's prehistory in the world is the general history of the evolution of material things and biological life. The creation narratives do not "report" the *way* in which creation happened at the beginning but state the *fact* of creation, which the human authors—working under the guidance of divine illumination with the aid of existing popular theological reflection and therefore using the imagery familiar to the latter (D 3862ff., 3898)—deduce from their own intellectual, social, and religious situation. Thus we may enunciate the principle that whatever can be learnt of the beginning in and through this situation (which also includes religious experience of grace, of men's universal entanglement in sin, and so forth) is part of the context of the creation narratives, so that its truth is guaranteed by the inspiration of Scripture. Everything else is the mode of expression, designed to convey in bold outline, in figurative, childlike terms the createdness of the world and man's relationship with God.

CREATION OF MAN

DECLARATIONS OF THE MAGISTERIUM. (1) Man is one in his substantial nature in such a way that this unity has an ontological priority over a genuine, real, irreducible plurality in his natural life; he is one in his origin, existence, and last end (D 502, 900ff., 1440f., 2828, 3221f., 3224). This means that to make any affirmation about man under some partial aspect is to make it about man as a whole. (2) Yet there is a real plurality of realities in man which cannot be derived from each other. What we call the rational soul in man is not a mere modification of what we describe as his materiality and corporeity (D 1440f., 3022, 3220f., 3896) and conversely. (3) Man possesses a proper, specifying, constituent principle of his whole nature, a spiritual, simple, substantial *soul, which without prejudice to the unity of the one human being is essentially distinct from *matter. It can only come into being, therefore, through that act which—because it does not fashion things by simply making new combinations of what is already extant and given—is called *creation, and thus presupposes that absolutely independent power we call God. But because it originates a *single* being, at once spiritual and material, precisely this creative impulsion of God expresses itself in this its effect as a self-transcendence of material being. In other words: where something essentially new appears, such as mankind, the notion applicable is one of a "creative intervention" on the past of God (in contradistinction to the permanent origination of the matter of the world altogether by God). But this "creative intervention" is not to be conceived as a supplementary intervention from without which adds something new to a wholly passive given, but may be seen—because it directly intends something essentially new—as the manifestation of the self-transcendence of the advent within this world, of that which is new; including even the "spiritual" human soul. The meaning of "spiritual" is an *a priori* datum of human knowledge from which only metaphysics can work out what "material" really means. (4) Insofar as man in his ontological plurality is a bodily material being he has a causal connexion with the material universe. Not only is this not denied by the teaching of the faith, it is positively taught (D 800, 3002). As to the nature of this connexion the Church declares that, saving the rights of the magisterium even in these matters and provided the direct creation of the soul by God is upheld, it is permissible to suppose that there is a real, ontological connexion between the animal kingdom and the human body (D 3862ff., 3896, 3898). If the magisterium denies that the truth of the theory of evolution is absolutely certain and has been strictly demonstrated, it is not the Church's intention thereby to prevent the natural scientist from affirming that *evolution, within the sphere of his investigations, is pragmatically certain. For since the magisterium can condemn a scientific theory only if it directly or indirectly contradicts a revealed doctrine, its basic competence expires where it does not argue on this ground.

BIBLICAL STATEMENTS. See the following articles: *Creation Narrative, Adam, Eve*. For further related questions see: *Paradise, Monogenism, States of Man, Creationism*.

THEOLOGY. If the Church's magisterium today does not object to a moderate evolutionism, it does not follow that the theological problem has now been solved. The specific humanity of the human body, for example, has been too little investigated for us to be able to jump to such a conclusion. Precisely because of the substantial unity of man, the theology of the *body has to be considered in connexion with the *resurrection of the flesh and the theology of *death, which show that Catholic theology cannot hand over the body to natural science so as to save the soul, at least, for theology. It could be asked more clearly what the theological significance is for the fate of man and his religious vocation and destiny, if man—in a history which, being genuine history, may not lie *entirely* behind him—has risen above his animal element, which nevertheless is still present in him as a precondition which the spirit ultimately gives itself, as a possibility, as a promise of the embodied spirit; and perhaps is still in the state of hominization, or has even suffered a kind of regression through the fault of man, according to the testimony of revelation. The animal element, we may say, ought to have existed from the very beginning of history thoroughly informed by the personal and integrated in the spiritual personality; thus man begins as more of an "animal" than he ought to have done, and indeed the humanization of his material sphere will only be completed by the eschatological transfiguration of the body. A further task for the theology of the creation of man will be to work out a positive theological interpretation of the enormous length of human history before the historical age of official *Revelation and Jesus Christ, that is, before *saving history becomes distinguishable from profane history. It is necessary to reflect, for example, to what proportions the whole of saving history from Abraham to Moses and from Moses to Jesus Christ contracts, if we admit that it was preceded by more than a million years of human history in which we can allege no data of saving history, since we must conceive *protology as historical *aetiology; that is, we have a theological knowledge of the beginning of the world and man which is of a different nature from the knowledge of the tradition of the experience

105

of human history, from historical memory. In the perspective of a history of this enormous length the Incarnation of God in Jesus Christ appears as the end of a development of incalculable length, as a new beginning, or as the end *simpliciter,* or better, presumably, as both in one.

CREATURE

Everything that exists through *creation, that is to say everything whose explanation lies beyond itself, all that is finite, in jeopardy, open to God and at his disposal (*Potentia obedientialis), such that creatures are enabled to rise above themselves by grace-given acceptance of the divine self-communication (*Nature and grace).

CREED, CONFESSION OF FAITH

In theological usage this term does not primarily mean the act of confessing the faith but a series of propositions in which the magisterium and Tradition have sought to provide a more or less complete formulation of the content of faith. This is also called a profession of faith or *symbolum.* Even in the NT we find units of tradition, of either one, two, or three members, which probably derive from the very first baptismal liturgy, in which a confession of faith was required. While the one-member formulae confess the Lord Jesus (*Kyrios) the three-membered ones, following the pattern of Matthew 28:19, are trinitarian. It is established that the prototype of what is called the Apostles' Creed existed in the 2nd century: it professed belief in the triune God, Holy Church, and the forgiveness of sins. A more developed form was used in the 4th century as the Roman baptismal creed; the present form was used liturgically in southwestern France in the 6th century and in the 9th century was officially adopted at Rome for baptism (D 1–30, 36). Similarly in the East, during the christological and trinitarian controversies, the creed of the city of Nicaea was adopted by the first Council of *Nicaea (D 125f.). From the 6th century the Creed of Nicaea-Constantinople, that of the first Council of *Constantinople (D 150), was widely adopted as a baptismal confession of faith and in 1014 became the Creed of the Roman Mass. Later creeds were explicitly formulated in order to combat heresies. Confessions of faith in the present theological sense contain the principal *dogmas; whether their texts are binding depends on whether they are generally accepted by the Church, or have been formulated or sanctioned by a council or by the Pope *(ex cathedra,* invoking his *infallibility).

CROSS

The means (or type) of execution most commonly used in Roman antiquity for common criminals guilty of serious offences (the gallows of that time). Since Jesus Christ redeemed the human race by his *death on the cross this latter also stands for putting on the death of Jesus in faith, which has its sacramental foundation in *baptism (Rom 6:3), is given effect by the *following of Christ crucified during one's life, and is consummated at one's own death by dying together with Christ (Rom 6:8). The theology of the cross is the persistent character- istic of Lutheran theology which looks for God only in the crucified Christ. From the Catholic viewpoint too, the Christian can fulfil his existence only within the context of Jesus' cross. Similarly, theology must assign its positive statements through Jesus' death to the always greater, unfathomable *mystery of God.—The cross must not be employed to enervate or diminish an active interpretation of following Jesus by committed action on behalf of the suffering and the op- pressed.

CULT

The service expressly offered to God through sacred signs and inward dispositions of *adoration, praise, thanksgiving, and *petition (for forgiveness, salvation, and earthly well-being), which acknowledges God's supreme power. While the peripheral forms may vary both in the Old Testament and in the Church, cult is essentially an *anamne- sis* in its basic and permanent forms (*Passover, *Eucharist, *Prayer, *Sacrifice). Cult in the strict sense is due to God alone and always includes adoration. In the interest of clarity of thought it is preferable to call the Catholic cultus of the saints the *veneration of saints, its ultimate goal, like that of cult in the strict sense, being the *glory of God.—See also *God, Worship of.*

CULTURE

This term designates the shaping of man himself and of his world through the exercise of his own mind and freedom. Man can never exist without culture, for he necessarily exists as an embodied being (objectifying himself in his bodiliness and its surroundings) and as a personal being who has freely fulfilled himself; therefore, culture is his fundamental task (Gen 1:28), in accomplishing which he also realizes his relationship with God. Consequently, Christian life can never be hostile to culture or seek to be simply acultural. What is really "natural" to man is his genuine culture—corresponding to his essential being and that of the world, ever open to the mystery and the purposes of God. But this culture, remaining creaturely as it does, is thereby determined by all man's existential categories: finitude, jeopardy, sinfulness, ambiguity, openness to the incalculable, need of redemption, state of redemption. It is not the *kingdom of God, not grace itself (being activity from below), but the objectivating material medium in which (explicitly or implicitly) man accomplishes the act of faith of accepting God's gracious self-communication from above. *Religion, insofar as it is the work of man, is also part of his culture, which conditions and differentiates it; insofar as it is the work of God for man, it essentially surpasses all human cultural achievements. According to Vatican II the Church is not bound to adhere to any one form of human culture (Church/world, 42); it recognizes the pluralism of new, contemporary forms of culture (CW, 53f.) and deems it appropriate to enter into communion with different forms of culture (CW, 58). The Church makes a decisive plea for the rightful freedom of development and the autonomy of culture (CW, 59) as well as for the realization of the right of *all* mankind to human and civil culture (CW, 60). Christians are expected to get to know the ways of thinking and feeling expressed in contemporary culture and to ensure that their practice of religion and their moral behaviour keep abreast with their education and knowledge (CW, 62). Vatican II thereby provided the impetus for Catholics to participate in a critical, yet committed, way in any truly human secular culture, and to renounce any negative or contentious attitude towards culture.

D

DAY OF THE LORD

The name for the end of the temporal history of the world and mankind, in that this universal consummation will show that the cause, the measure, and the goal of profane and saving history was God's self-communication to the world, which reached its climax and irrevocable finality in the Incarnation of the Logos and his work. Thus, when the universal consummation is reached, the position of the incarnate Logos in profane and saving history will be manifested, he will have "come again" as pardon unveiled (*Parousia) and the *Judgment of the world. For this reason the public triumph of the kingship of God (OT) and Christ (NT), which terminates history, is called in Scripture the day of Yahweh, the day of the Lord, the day of the Son of Man, Christ's day, "that" day, the last day, or the Day simply (Amos 5:18–20; Is 2:2; 13:6ff.; 1 Cor 1:8; 5:5; Lk 17:24; Phil 1:6; Jn 6:39f., and par.).

DEACON

From the Greek διάκονος, servant; the holder of an ecclesiastical *office which is already clearly discernible in the Apostolic Church; it is directly coordinated with the episcopate (Phil 1:1; 1 Tim 3:8ff.) and its duties include alms-giving and administrative functions. If the seven men of Acts 6:1ff. were deacons and thus leaders of the Hellenistic community, then the deacons also had a duty to teach and govern.

In the primitive and ancient Church the duties which were attributed to the ministerial office of the deacon included: reading the Gospel and serving at the celebration of the Eucharist; distributing Communion, especially to those absent from church; supervising the Church's distribution of alms and administering her temporal goods, and also preaching. In the early Middle Ages (at the latest) the independent office of deacon disappeared and the diaconate became a mere stepping-stone to the priesthood.

In accordance with the common and certain doctrine, the diaconate is a sacramental order, at least insofar as Christ willed it when he established a hierarchical authority in the Church in which the deacon participates by imposition of the bishop's hands (*Laying on of hands) (D 1776, 3860). Here it must be observed that the concrete measure of participation in the Church's apostolic office may be variously determined at various times, provided that the intention to confer a permanent participation remains. Vatican II reintroduced the permanent diaconate into the Latin Church (Church, 29; cf, also Miss., 17) largely because of the lack of priests. The deacon's office in proclaiming the faith, in the liturgy and in serving his fellow Christians differs according to the particular pastoral outlook. However, the tasks undertaken (with fringe groups, in parish work and so on) demand both professional and religious training followed by continuous in-service training (regardless of whether the permanent diaconate is to be exercised full-time, part-time or on an honorary basis).

DEATH

Death is an event involving the whole man. But man is a unity of *nature and *person, that is, a being who exists antecedent to his free personal decision, who is subject to certain laws and a certain development, and on the other hand freely disposes of himself, is ultimately what he intends in his freedom to be. Thus death is at once a natural and a personal event. Since biology does not "really" know why all multicellular life, and especially man, dies, the only reason advanced to explain the indisputable universality of death is that advanced by faith—the moral catastrophe of mankind (Rom 5). And this theological basis itself provides the certainty that in all time to come the necessity of dying will continue to govern our lives, that we shall never be able to abolish death.

THE NATURE OF DEATH. (1) Christian tradition gives us a preliminary description of death in the maxim that death is "the separation of body and soul". That is to say that the spiritual principle of life in man, his "soul", assumes a different relation to what we are accustomed to call the *"body", but it says little more. Consequently, the

110

aforesaid maxim fails to satisfy the metaphysical and theological requirements for a definition of the nature of death. For it has nothing to say of death insofar as it is something that happens to man as a whole being and as a spiritual person: the conclusive finality of his free personal growth, which finality without doubt not only comes about "at" or "after" death but is an intrinsic factor of death itself. While plants and animals "perish", only man really "dies". The description of death which we have mentioned is unsatisfactory for the further reason that the concept of "separation" remains obscure and susceptible of very different senses. For if the soul is united with the body, then it obviously stands in relation to that totality of which the body is part, that totality which is the unity of the material world. This material unity of the world is neither a mere abstraction, the sum of particular things, nor yet the mere extrinsic unity formed by the effects particular things have on each other. Since the soul's substantial union with the body as its substantial form also relates it to this radical unity of the world, the separation of body and soul in death cannot simply abolish this relation to the world, leaving the soul acosmic, altogether otherworldly (as many are pleased to think in Neoplatonist fashion). Quite on the contrary, the fact that the soul ceases to maintain the body's separate identity vis-à-vis the world only serves to open the soul the more widely to the whole world, to intensify its pancosmic relation. In death the soul acquires a closer intimacy, a more interior relationship with that elusive but very real ground of the world's unity, in which all things in the world are in communion even before they begin to influence one another, and this is possible precisely because the soul no longer clings to the shape of its individual body. This view is also implicit in the scholastic doctrine that the substantial act of the soul is not really distinct from it, that is, could only cease if the soul too were to cease, were not immortal as philosophy shows and Catholic dogma authoritatively teaches it is. Here we must reflect that in principle the spiritual soul has opened itself to the world through its bodiliness even before death, that it is never a closed, windowless monad but is always in communion with the whole world. This pancosmic relationship means that the soul, by giving up its limited bodily shape in death and opening itself to the All, becomes a contributory cause of the whole world, even of the world as the basis of the personal life of other psychosomatic beings. This fact is indicated by many para-psychological phenomena, the Catholic doctrine of *purgatory (see especially *Intermediate State)*, the intercession of saints, etc. Purgatory, for example, would mean that by giving up its bodily shape the soul, with its free moral self-determination, experiences its harmony or discord with the objective moral structure of the world more keenly and on the other hand shares in making it what it is. (2) Another essential feature of death is the following: death is neither the end of man's existence nor a mere transition from one form of existence to another that essentially resembles it (that is in its temporality and incompletion), but the beginning of *eternity—if and insofar as one can speak of a beginning in connexion with eternity. The whole of created being, the world, gradually grows towards its definitive state in and through the incarnate spiritual persons whose "body", in a sense, is the world, and through their death, true though it be that this perfection which matures from within (like that of the human individual) is at the same time, in an obscure dialectical unity, a discontinuance from within and an end made from without through the external intervention of God by his advent in *Judgment on a day that no man knows. Death, then, befalls the human person, is something before which he stands exposed, which he must passively and helplessly undergo; but it is also his personal self-achievement, his "own death", an act of the man proceeding from within—that is to say, of course, death itself, not just the adoption of an attitude towards it. Thus death is both things: the end of man as a spiritual person is an active consummation from within, a bringing of himself to completion, a growth that preserves the issue of his life; it is total entry into possession of himself, the state of having "produced" himself, the fullness of the being he has become by all his free acts. And human death, the end of biological life, is at the same time necessarily a disruption from without that affects the whole man, a destruction, so that one's "own death", personally effected from within, is at the same time the event which reduces man to utter impotence, action and passion in one. And given the substantial unity of man it is not possible to assign one of these aspects to the body and the other to the soul, which would mean the dissolution of the true nature of human death. (3) This duality makes death essentially obscure: it is never possible for man to state with existential certainty whether the fullness of life that is achieved in death is the inanity and nothingness of man which was formerly veiled, or whether the emptiness that is seen in death is only the external seeming of a real plenitude, the liberation of the person's pure being. Because of this obscurity, death can be the penalty and expression of sin, but also the climax of sin, mortal sin in the truest sense.

THE DEATH OF CHRIST. Since Jesus Christ became a man of the fallen race of Adam, assuming our sinful flesh (Rom 8:3), he entered

112

into human life, which reaches its completion only by passing through a death that is equivocal and obscure. Thus he took death upon himself, which in the concrete order expresses and manifests the creation which fell in angels and men. He did not only make some kind of satisfaction for sin—what he did and suffered was death, the manifestation and expression of sin in the world. He did this in absolute freedom, as an act and manifestation of the divine grace which is his by natural right, which divinizes the life of his humanity because he is a divine Person. But this made death something quite different from what it would be in a man who did not possess the life of grace and complete freedom from the weakness of concupiscence, as of right. The very obscurity of Christ's death expresses and embodies his loving obedience, the free dedication of his whole, created being to God. Without ceasing to be dark and obscure, death which was a manifestation of sin becomes the manifestation of the obliteration of sin by Christ's obedience to the Father's will. Through Christ's death the spiritual being which was his from the beginning, and which he gave active expression to in the life that was completed by his death, became open to the whole world, has been inserted into the totality of the world and has become a permanent, ontological modification of the world in its root and ground. (In the perspective of this essential characteristic of human death as realized in Christ compare the biblical affirmation of Jesus' *descent into hell). But this has made the world as a whole and as the scene of human activity a different place from what it would be had Jesus not died. The significance of Jesus' death for salvation does not depend on the validity and on the possibility of realizing such not simply indispensable concepts as sin, sacrifice, satisfaction, and so on. In the history of mankind the fate of one has significance for the other. If (a) God wants there to be and lets come into being a man who in his reality is God's final and irrevocable word of promise to mankind, if (b) this promise of God must also be accepted at least in this man and an acceptance can only take place through the life-history of this man which reaches its final validity in death and only in death, and if (c) this man's answer of acceptance appears historically as accepted by God for his part and as having attained to God (which we call Jesus' *resurrection), then it can and should be said that this eschatological word of promise on the part of God that arises from *God's* free initiative is genuinely accomplished and made historically present for us in the life of Jesus, which comes to its conclusion in his freely accepted death. Hence this death first reaches its consummation in the resurrection and becomes historically tangible for us inasmuch as it is concluded in free obedience and surrenders life to God without anything held back. Jesus' life and death, taken together, are the essential "cause" of our salvation, because in them what is signified (God's will of universal salvation) provides the sign (Jesus' death together with his resurrection) and through it (and not without it) effects itself.

DYING. Our whole life is intrinsically affected by the knowledge, implicit though this usually remains, that we must inevitably die (though we know not when or how). Death is always "present" in human life through this knowledge, which alone brings home to us the necessity of action, the fleeting nature of life's opportunities, and the irrevocability of our decisions. Just as defaulting (*Sin) in face of the absolute demand of conscience is the crudest, so death is the most patent expression of human finitude (*Person). But the very fact that we explicitly and consciously anticipate death, in our natural dread of it, shows that life itself points infinitely beyond death. For in the dread of death, death appears (as it does not when death is merely feared) not only as a (perhaps painful) particular event at the "end" of life, but rather as an event which will free man from his servitude to all particular being and bring him into the presence of truth: the fundamental option of a man that governs his whole life becomes definitive (Jn 9:4; Lk 16:26; 2 Cor 5:10; D 839, 854–859, 923f., 1000f., 1304f.) in a way which he hopes will also mean his fulfilment, but he is never sure whether this will be so. Because man's purposive will, maturing from within, that his life shall be complete and definitive is constantly frustrated by the distractions of bodily existence and thus deprived of its integrating power, unable to complete his personal life with the certitude and mastery of a work of art, human life in the presence of death remains imperspicuous, in jeopardy from without, and reaches in death the height of contradiction; supreme will and utter impotence, fate self-made and merely undergone, plenitude and emptiness. Death, this obscure and paradoxical situation, is the consequence of *original sin, which affects all men and in them becomes the intrinsic expression of the Fall of man in *Adam from the *immortality that was his by grace (see Rom 5:11; D 222, 372, 1521) (human life on earth unfolding into transfigured communion with God). According as a man either attempts to understand and master by his own powers this (life-long) death which flows from original sin and lies beyond his control, or holds himself in faith at the free disposal of the incomprehensible God, the death of a human being will either be the personal repetition and confirmation of the first man's sinful emancipation from God and thus the acme of sin, the definitive

114

mortal sin, or else it will be the repetition and personal appropriation of the obedient death of Jesus (Phil 2:8) (by which he imparted his divine life to the world itself), the acme of his human salutary activity, because his lifelong configuration with Christ's death through the sacramental life of faith (*Baptism, the *Eucharist, *Asceticism) now finds its personal completion in a blessed "dying in the Lord" (Rev 14:13), in which the experience of the *end becomes the dawn of fulfilment. (Vat. II: CW, 18).

DECALOGUE

From the Greek δεκάλογος, ten commandments; the classic term for prohibitions that were laid apodictically with absolute binding force upon the people of the Old Covenant. They were embodied in ten principles (Ex 20:2–17; Deut 5:6 –21) and were intended to govern their social and moral life together and guarantee the survival of this people as a monotheistic cultic confederation based on the *Covenant, in the midst of the polytheistic world which surrounded them. The social and historical relativity of the decalogue does not admit of the fundamental attitudes (*Charity, gratitude) proclaimed and required in the NT being simply transferred into the decalogue. In the NT the decalogue is radically integrated into and subordinated to the commandment of love and henceforth binds only insofar as it remains the *natural moral law and concretion of NT ethics.

DEFINITION

In general the clear-cut, brief, complete, notional determination of the facts of a case or the meaning of a word. *Dogmatic definition:* that solemn dogmatic judgment (plainly recognizable as such by its form) of the *Pope (definition *ex cathedra)* or of an ecumenical *council whereby a proposition is definitively taught as true and binding on the universal Church, and is therefore to be believed with divine and Catholic (or ecclesiastical) faith, because this truth is revealed by God (or is so closely connected with a revealed truth that to deny the one is to deny the other).—See also *Infallibility, Dogma, Magisterium.*

DEISM

A view of *God which acknowledges his personal existence and accepts the world and the laws of nature as his creation (even in the fourteenth century: God as the clockmaker of the world clock), but denies any further assistance or intervention of God in his creation (especially any supernatural *revelation). Since the end of the 16th century this deism has appeared in a great variety of forms in connexion with the construction of a philosophical natural *religion. The undisputed spokesman of deism was Voltaire. Deism justifiably but too easily rejected a "God-of-the-gaps". Deism was condemned by the First Vatican Council (D 3000 –3020, 3027, 3031–3034) because of the explicit or implicit deist opinion that God necessarily created the world, and the denial of God's *freedom which this entails (whereby all deism involves itself in contradictions), and because of deism's denial of the *supernatural and of *revelation.

DEMIURGE

Plato first introduced the demiurge into philosophy as the architect of the world; in Gnosticism it is conceived as a being intermediate between God and the world, which forms the world out of pre-existing matter. Against this conception the Fathers of the Church defend the identity of the one true God with the Creator and architect of the one, good, visible world.

DEMOCRATIZATION

Critical public opinion; the principle behind the fundamental, universal socio-political demand for the abolition of something grounded in the long-outdated separation of state and society: that is, the reduction of democracy to the level of a formal principle of organization within the state. Democratization accordingly seeks to establish democracy as a basic political reality embracing all relevant social elements (economy, education, churches; each of course being treated in accordance with its own particular characteristics). In practical terms this includes any organized activity performed by various groups or classes with the intention of bringing about effective change in the structure of power, the forms of knowledge, modes of behaviour and standards, thereby increasing their own self-determination and sense

116

of responsibility. The fundamental mobilization of the grass roots of society this involves is chiefly intended to achieve a more effective control over economic and technocratic *power, while at the same time creating greater freedom for social creativity in the different spheres of life. Participation in the form of responsible sharing among those concerned with the use of their means of production can only be successful if it is also accompanied by a general willingness to learn and a readiness to assume responsibility on the part of the members of the social base. Hence the declared aim of democratization is the creation of a society of free, equal human beings. As a rule, therefore, the democratization of social infrastructures helps to improve the quality of life for everyone in society. The understanding of freedom in the NT is very close to the concept of the *Church as a mutually responsible community of brothers and sisters freely gathered together to live and act in accordance with democratic principles. In spite of the differences existing between State and Church, this shows that the Church as a social structure is based on the principle of openness and a considerable degree of democratization. Democracy in the Church should not only involve the comprehensive and active participation of all the faithful in the Church's decision-making; it should also aim to strengthen the principle of *collegiality and concept of the *people of God as well as the introduction of learning processes oriented to reform, and of self-critical discrimination.

DEMONSTRATIVE THEOLOGY

That style of systematic theology which seeks to clarify our understanding of revealed truth and our faith at any given time by deducing conclusions according to the rules of logic from a major and minor premise. Both premises may be revealed truths, or the major premise may be revealed and the minor a truth of reason. Probably a conclusion can only be accepted with divine *faith (Theological *notes) if the minor premise as well is at least implicitly revealed (*Dogma). When the minor premise is only a truth of reason the conclusion will probably be at most an object of ecclesiastical faith. This procedure is legitimate and genuinely theological provided that one does not pretend to achieve ultimate conceptual clarity about the basic revealed propositions, thus rendering the *mystery transparent, and provided that the goal in view is an improved understanding of the faith by way of a clearer idea of the inner unity of revelation.—See also *Development of Dogma*.

DEMYTHOLOGIZATION

The name (neither quite correct in fact nor authentic) given to the task, first explicitly set by the Protestant theologian R. Bultmann (b. 1884), of interpreting the NT in existential terms, that is, of laying bare its *kerygma in such a way that it shall immediately strike home to the man of today and make him see that he is confronted by an "existential" decision. According to Bultmann, what obscures the NT kerygma and must therefore be interpreted or eliminated so that this task may be accomplished, is briefly as follows: Even those portions of the Gospel of Jesus which biblical criticism has found to be Jesus' own historical words are mythological, that is, they use *myth as a mode of expression (for example, *Basileia, *Son of Man). All the later parts of the NT make even greater use of myth: thus the preaching of the disciples about Jesus which arose shortly after the latter's death (for instance, the myth of the resurrection). The still later Hellenistic stratum applies additional myths to Jesus (the myth of a redeemer, borrowed from Gnosis). Briefly, the conditions for and principles of the existential interpretation of the NT message, which lies buried under mythology, are these: Absolutely every statement must be interpreted existentially, for no statement concerns me at all unless it is understood in actual decision. I am not interested in learning objective facts which are merely "there" (like objects in nature). In the NT it is precisely what would summon me to decision that is obscured by being objectified in myth. Myth creates further difficulties for "modern" man: the closed natural world which is investigated by the natural sciences cannot stand open to the irruption of transcendence as is represented by myth (for instance in the accounts of *miracles). Consequently, the NT kerygma can on no account be the proclamation of objective truths and mysteries which are universally valid and salutary (this would be pure mythology). Rather the message of the NT which concerns me is that Jesus wishes to summon me to decision between God and this transitory world; for this summons it is "the last hour", the decisive "now". Just as Jesus died on the cross and never was the beneficiary of miracles, or worked any himself, but rather believed God by obediently accepting his destiny, so that in his death God's judgment was pronounced on this world of fallen men, so too faith, decision against this world and against sin is demanded of me, without my having any proof of the truth of the word of God that speaks to me.—According to Bultmann the NT itself undertakes this existential interpretation, though in general terms and obscurely, because it presents myths which contra-

118

dict one another, thereby showing that the objectivizing conceptions are not really asserted, especially in John and Paul with their demythologizing of eschatology (the end of the world is not a later event but an ever present event, i.e. existing in decision against this world). Scholarly criticism of Bultmann has convincingly demonstrated that the NT kerygma is not merely a summons to decision, but the communication of an objective event, the event of Christ, which including the *resurrection can be proved with sufficient historical certainty. As to philosophy, Bultmann's notion of *transcendence has been proved to be truncated and to rest on insufficient analysis precisely of *man's essentially transcendental constitution. This also shows that to reduce the kerygma to a distorted conception of existence, as demythologization proposes to do, must lead to a groundlessly paradoxical faith at variance with the nature of man, not least of the man of today. But this does not dispose of Bultmann's legitimate concern. It cannot be denied that OT and NT reflect the mythical cosmology of the age in which they came into being. This cosmology is not guaranteed by revelation, rather it has always been the permanent duty of theology (which would not indeed otherwise exist at all) to enquire what the traditional doctrines "really" mean and what they do not mean. Theology has always distinguished between the content of a doctrine and the terms in which it is couched, and therefore theology has always been demythologization in the true sense. On the other hand this must be said: if the transcendent, the transcendent God, is confined within a single human dimension, as Bultmann confines him within the single dimension of the existential, then in fact the transcendent is mythologized, not demythologized. On this matter see the principles formulated in the articles *Myth* and *World.* "This" world and its history may not be disposed of by a disjunction so radically unbalanced as Bultmann's extreme dualism, for God has truly entered into this reality and has permanently accepted it. However there still remains the task for theology, rightly pointed out by Bultmann and never wholly mastered, of endeavouring to present God's saving deed in *Jesus Christ in such a way that the hearer of the word is "existentially" moved, summoned to repentant decision and to faith.

DEPOSIT OF FAITH

This term signifies the "stock" or "treasure" of faith entrusted to the *Church, which she must faithfully preserve and infallibly expound (*Holy Scripture, *Tradition, *Faith; D 3020; Vat II: Rev., 10). By the nature of Christ's saving message and saving deed the deposit of faith cannot be thought of as a neatly tied up parcel of propositions, but as the sum of the blessings, in word and gift, which are entrusted to the Church, to be realized in ways that are ever new, so as to make her deposit of faith comprehensible, credible, and fruitful in the ever new historical situations on earth which she must face as her present. This realization is a matter which concerns all the members of the Church (*Hearing Church) and takes place through doctrine, *worship, and life.

DESCENT INTO HELL

At least ten texts of the NT as well as the form of the Apostles' Creed which has been current since A.D. 370 declare that Jesus was in the realm of the dead as a dead man. (For the defined teaching of the Church, see D 801, 852.) Individual texts add that there he announced or represented the victory of the *basileia (to the powers or to the dead). The underworld in question is not *hell but the *sheol of later Judaism, as is clear from tradition. If we carefully distinguish between the mode of expression and what is actually affirmed we shall conclude that the descent into hell is Jesus' dying, insofar as he obediently accepts and realizes *death which reduces man to impotence, and "in death" is exposed to (voluntary) total helplessness—wholly at God's disposal; but by this means his redemptive obedience wins him power over the universe and history, because his relationship with the whole of creation does not cease in *death but rather becomes manifest as existing "at the heart of the world" (Mt 12:40). The descent into hell is not a new act of redemption in addition to his death. By dying Jesus entered the company of those who had died before him and in the true sense shared with them what he had achieved—a lasting appeal for necessary human solidarity with the forgotten dead. It is pointless to enquire exactly when the descent into hell occurred and how long it lasted; because it can only be regarded as that moment, borne away by onrushing time, when he was dead.

DESCENT OF MAN

Scripture always sees man as a single being, composed of soul and body, who in his very bodily nature is God's intellectual and moral associate. Man originates as this unique reality through a special

120

divine initiative which directly intends to produce man and which effects the image and likeness of God, which did not exist until then. Consequently, according to the doctrine of the Church, man, being a personal spirit (*Soul, *Person), cannot be the product of infrahuman reality by the operation of that reality's own natural laws. (For the defined teaching of the Church, see D 3022.) The biblical account of the *creation of man, however, is not concerned to describe his origin in concrete detail but simply to express the fact in popular and picturesque language. Hence the magisterium does not condemn the scientific thesis that there is an historical connexion between man and the animal kingdom, but allows this question to be freely discussed (D 3896). For further discussion see *Creation of Man, Monogenism.*

DESPAIR

In theology despair is the sin of freely abandoning *hope, which relies on God's faithfulness, help, and mercy in all our jeopardy and distress, without or within, and thus clings to the realizable meaning of existence, which is salvation. Passive experience of one's jeopardy and impotence is not, as such, despair in the theological sense. Despair only enters when man, in ultimate (unadmitted) hubris, will not confess that God is greater than his own strength, which he experiences as impotence, and identifies what is possible for himself with what is possible through himself.

DESTRUCTION, THEORY OF

Those interpretations of the *Mass which see the essence of the *sacrifice in a destructive change in the offering, which withdraws it from human use, surrendering up the offering, as symbolizing man, to God. The most important of these theories sees the essence of Mass in the "mystical slaying", the sacramental separation of Christ's Body and Blood at the double Consecration (offering of Christ under the figure of his death).

DEVELOPMENT

See *Evolution, Stages of Life.*

DEVELOPMENT OF DOGMA

It is the task of the doctrine of the development of dogma to explain the undoubted fact that the Church defines propositions as divinely revealed which either (1) existed before but were not always expressly taught *as* divinely revealed, or (2) state the substance of the affirmations of previous tradition in quite a different terminology, one which is only in the process of developing, whereby the Church more explicitly protects that sense of the revealed truth which has always been known, against heretical misinterpretations, or (3) for which even tradition does not at once and directly furnish explicit propositions that are obviously equivalent to the definition and that can be proved to date back to the Apostles.

The problem raised by the development of dogma is the task of demonstrating both the inherent possibility of the later, "developed" exposition of the faith being identical with the apostolic exposition which was made in Christ, and also that actual identity in each instance. The difficulty here is that according to Catholic doctrine the *Revelation with which the Church has been entrusted (and which requires of the individual the assent of faith) was concluded with the death of the last Apostle (see D 1501, 3421), so that the Church can only continue to bear witness to what she heard from Christ in the apostolic generation and recognized then as belonging to her deposit of faith. True though it be that the Church's magisterium and its authority can now guarantee the individual believer that an objective connexion exists between "old" and "new" propositions, still they cannot constitute this connexion, much less form a substitute for it.

It follows from the terms of the problem, as we have posed it, that recognition of the connexion between "old" and "new" propositions must be rationally justifiable, if the "new" proposition is not to be a new revelation. And in fact the development of dogma has a rational aspect: it has never proceeded without the labour of theologians. Thus the development of dogma confronts theology with the question *to what extent* a truth that is later defined (or to be defined) is implicit in the whole deposit of faith as hitherto known. In what ways (in terms of formal logic) can a truth be implicit in the Gospel, in view of its structure (which after all is "logical" too)? Theology has as yet reached no unanimous solution to this problem, which does not directly bear upon the actual development of dogma, based as this is on the assistance of the Holy Ghost.

122

DEVIL

According to Christian theology the devil is not just a mythological personification of evil in the world but an existent being. On the other hand the devil must not be seen as God's independent and equal antagonist. He is an absolutely finite creature whose evil nature remains circumscribed by God's power, freedom and goodness. Teaching on the devil, as on *devils or demons, occurs in general in Scripture as a natural presupposition and as part of human experience: this natural understanding is corrected by the revelation of the victory of God's grace in Jesus Christ and the liberation of men which this has effected, and which needs to be continued, from all principalities and powers. If it is clear that the doctrine of the devil came into revelation from outside on the basis of widespread natural experiences, it is easily understandable that the concept of the devil brought with it many historical elements from outside Christianity. Reduced to its Christian content, the doctrine says that the lack of and need for salvation that *redemption both presupposes and overcomes is marked by freedom on the part of creatures, a freedom that precedes the individual human history of freedom. This finite super-individual freedom has been ruptured (the word 'devil' comes from the Greek *diabolos,* he who sets at variance, the opponent or enemy) and through this ruptured unity constitutes human history. For the Church's teaching on the devil see *devils, demons.*

DEVILS, DEMONS

In the Greek poets the δαίμων was often a benevolent tutelary divinity, the interior voice of man. The peoples of every age have been familiar with devils of different kinds, of varying status and power. The term devil is generally used in the stricter sense of "malignant spirits". The OT assumes the existence of these without attaching special importance to them. In later Judaism devils are depicted concretely: as a hierarchy led by the Devil, Satan and so forth; their destructive work; the origin of the devils in a fall of the angels. These characteristic features are carried over into the NT but entirely recast in terms of saving history: the devils form a kingdom (Mk 3:22–26) opposed to the *basileia and manifested in *possession. See also *Principalities and Powers.* A definition of the Fourth Lateran Council categorically declares that *evil has not existed from the beginning but that everything evil has temporal limits and arises from the free choice

123

of creatures (D 800). In this connexion it is stated that God created Satan and the other devils good by nature but that they became evil of their own accord. Thus this definition presupposes the existence of devils, which is not however expressly taught. A declaration (1975) of the Congregation for the Faith describes the existence of the devil and of devils as a *dogmatic fact but not, therefore, as dogma. These meagre data do not permit us to conceive of Satan (as popular piety often does) as an equal opponent of God, or to depict the character and doings of the devils. In view of the seriousness of saving history it would be untheological levity to look on Satan and his devils as a sort of "hobgoblins knocking about the world"; rather it may be assumed that they are the powers *of* the world (not independent of mankind) insofar as *this* *world is a denial of God and a temptation to man. This view preserves the personal nature of the devils, which is laid down by Scripture and the magisterium (D 3891), since every essential disorder in the world is personally realized; it also preserves their plurality, which is to be visualized in the context of the world's qualitative and regional plurality. It also means that the devils as elements of *this* world culpably close themselves to God, a fact to which the passing away of the fashion of this world aetiologically refers. Since Jesus Christ overcame *sin their power is only an arrogant sham, however real the power of wars, tyrants, and so forth is within the world; they are stripped of real power (Lk 10:18; Mt 12:28).

DIALECTICAL THEOLOGY

A fundamental change in Protestant theology after 1918 which largely displaced the *liberal theology dominant during the 19th century. Insofar as it can be briefly summarized (it never regarded itself as a system) dialectical theology proceeds on the assumption that crisis is man's fundamental condition. In this crisis man makes various attempts to find security, of which the worst and most perverse is religion, as a human defence and self-assertion against God. In the death and resurrection of Jesus man is negated by God; God and man, time and eternity are separated by a "barrier of death". But precisely in the death and resurrection of Jesus God's new world touches the old world "as a tangent touches a circle", neither empirically nor historically, nor yet in faith, which from man's side is only an emptiness. The centre of the new life, God's Incarnation, is neither utterable nor visible; its affirmation is clarified only by negation: "the new man that I am is not what I am". This form of dialectical theology, developed early in his career by Karl Barth (and based on Kierkegaard and Dostoievsky) was given more precision by E. Brunner, R. Bultmann, and F. Gogarten, so that the dialectical character of theology should be based not on the negation of man by revelation but (following M. Heidegger and M. Buber, among others) on the dialogic constitution of human existence. Since 1933 the views of these men can no longer be called dialectical theology.—For the Catholic attitude see *Mystery, Analogy.*

DIALOGUE

Any dialogue which is not a dispute or an explicitly one-sided attempt at conversion presupposes that *both* sides have the desire to learn something from the other. A Christian and a Catholic may set himself or herself the same aim when entering into dialogue with atheists and others of differing persuasions (as repeatedly recommended by Vatican II: Church/world, 21, 40, 43, 92; Rel. Lib., 3; Miss., 16, 41 etc.). Learning from others not only means that dialogue will provide better information about the attitudes, doctrine, and practice of the partner in dialogue, thereby leading to a more humane society; this mutual giving and taking is also based on the fact that the partner in dialogue often has ideas and experiences to contribute to a more humane *world-view or to an individual's struggle to come to terms with the world (meditation, etc.), which the Christian does not see so clearly or immediately and which, if they are really humane, he or she has to trace back theologically to the *grace of God. Given the mutual limitations of *theory and practice a dialogue can also be meaningful even when at the outset it aims 'only' to achieve standard practice, and when unification in matters concerning truth in the theoretical sense is not yet possible. Even a Catholic does not simply possess truth; he or she must continually learn anew the truth revealed to him or her by participating in the historical process of dialogue which aims to establish the truth. The concrete needs of the world and fundamental human values demand that dialogue between Christians and non-Christians should proceed towards co-operation (Vat. II: Church/world, 21, 90; Miss., 11, 41 etc.).

DICHOTOMISM

From Greek and Latin: the doctrine of duality; a view of human

125

nature according to which man is composed of two "parts" (part being understood as an entity, not a principle of being), body and soul (Descartes). This primitive conception attributes all consciousness to the soul alone and everything physical to the body alone, often in the context of a qualified *dualism. Neither biblical nor thomistic *anthropology can be called dichotomism, since each of these, though with unequal clarity, emphasizes the substantial unity of the whole *man.—See also *Body, Soul*.

DISCIPLINE OF THE SECRET

In the presence of the unbaptized it was customary in the ancient Church (as first indicated in the *Didache)* either to avoid all mention of baptism, the Eucharist, indeed any of the content of faith, the place of worship, etc., or else to speak of these things only in symbols. The practice reached its height in the fourth and fifth centuries. The discipline of the secret is of fundamental importance for us today. This will be clear if we consider that there are certain things which should only be shown to another subject to the continuous control and absolute discretion of the person disclosing them, and also provided that the former personally participates in the event he is witnessing, so that it is not exposed to the naked curiosity of a mere spectator (metaphysical modesty).

DISPOSITION

In general: the state (or attitude) in a thing or person which is a necessary precondition for the emergence of a particular characteristic of that person or thing.

In theology: that which places man in immediate readiness to perform a particular act or receive an influence, removing the attitude inconsistent with the influence desired and producing a positive capacity for that influence. Man is never capable of a disposition, or positive orientation, to justifying grace which would create any right to this grace or would arise without this grace producing the disposition for itself. Even where *metanoia, repentance, is required of the adult human being before his justification, this repentance itself is a gracious anticipatory effect of God's wooing, already at work within that person (see Mt 3:2 with Jn 6:44) (*Original sin, *Grace, *Sin, *Nature). Nevertheless that realization of the human person which is "right in itself" can be regarded as a "negative" disposition, in accordance with the axiom: *Facienti quod in se est, Deus non denegat gratiam.* (God does not refuse grace to him who [not: because he] does what he can); because on the one hand we must maintain the possibility of naturally good works and on the other hand God's universal salvific will is a gracious fact. More precisely, this negative disposition consists in the fact that no new hindrance *(obex)* is placed in the way of God's saving work. A positive disposition, initiated and sustained by grace itself, is necessary for adults, especially for reception of the *sacraments (D 1554, 1557, 1606).—See also *Intention.*

DISTINCTION

The plurality of the world is part of the primordial data of human experience, that is, the conviction, based on experience of ourselves as free and responsible "subjects", that this "plurality" is not simply the variegated appearance of something which is "one and the same in itself". When two things are different from each other, independently of any operation of the intellect, we speak of a real distinction. Otherwise, the distinction is "notional". But there are very different kinds of real distinction: the distinction between two things each of which can exist though the other does not; the distinction of the *accident from the *substance in which it inheres and without which (naturally speaking) it cannot exist; the distinction between principles of being which together compose a thing that is substantially one (*Form, *Matter), and the like. A real distinction does not rule out connexions of another sort (for example, causality, creation) which can and often must exist between two things that are really distinct. Even in the supreme unity of God (*Trinity) a real distinction is still a positive characteristic. Similarly, it is frequently the task of theology, in ways which are appropriate to the specific case, to insist on a connexion in distinction, the one intensifying rather than reducing the other: *nature and grace, the doctrine of the two natures in the *hypostatic union, sacramental sign and sacramental grace in the *sacraments, *Church and *State, since it is equally wrong and equally tempting for finite theological thought either to atomize reality or reduce it to a monolithic unity.

127

DITHEISM

This is the doctrine that there are two Gods with two different divine natures. It is encountered in *Manichaeism, which believes in two independent first principles, and in strict *Subordinationism.

DIVINE CONCOURSE

This term (Lat. *concursus divinus)* refers to the fact that God has created a world that can develop itself and yet while doing so remains at every moment, in its *actus secundi,* created and sustained by God in his *eternity. We must not imagine that God works on the world and with his creatures as one specifiable cause among others; he rather acts as transcendental cause sustaining the "secondary causes". Apart from the *conservation of the world and its causal activity, therefore, God's concourse is the divine dynamism that is necessary to the activity of creatures when it produces something really new, whereby God gives creatures the power of creative self-transcendence; so that where the leap is really taken to something qualitatively new, the history of the world is not broken off because something new appears, nor does the operation of God become superfluous because the old history continues. The direct physical concourse of God with his creatures (Acts 17:25, 28) is the common teaching of theologians against every form of *Deism. For the sake of theological clarity it is better not to describe God's supernatural elevation of the human act, by which it becomes a *salutary act, as "concourse", because this elevation as such is the establishment in man of a capacity for salutary activity; it is not the concourse with this latter.—In connexion with this problem see *Grace, Synergism.*

DIVINE SONSHIP

This concept, like that of the *image of God, is known only from revelation. It designates the relationship between God and man. In the OT Israel as a whole is the son of God; later, devout individuals are so called, and finally it is indicated that all men are the children of God (Is 43:6; see also Mt 8:11f.) and that this sonship is a gift of the eschatological age of salvation (Mal 3:1; Mt 5:9). St Paul develops its theology. He teaches that all men are children of God in principle (Gal 3:26ff.). Only Jesus Christ, indeed, is the Son of God by nature

(Rom 8:29), but in him (our brother, Heb 2:11f.) we are all delivered from the bondage of the law and adopted as sons (Gal 4:5); we are so conformed to Christ by the *Pneuma that in him we may call God "Father" (Gal 4:6). St John above all speaks of this sonship by grace. It is bestowed by rebirth out of water and the Spirit (Jn 3:5) and is based on a new generation (1 Jn 2:29 and *passim)* and in John, as in Paul, it is manifested by love for one's brethren (1 Jn 4:7 and *passim)*. Dogmatic theology uses the term divine adoptive sonship to describe the formal effects of *sanctifying grace; but the trust and tenderness that are essential to the NT conception need to be brought out with more freshness and clarity: with the astonishing courage that only God himself can give, we call absolute mystery—the abyss, the devouring judgment—"Father", and we are right.

DOCETISM

The name of a Christological opinion which maintained that *Jesus Christ had only an apparent body or a celestial (ethereal) body and only appeared to suffer and die (from the Gr. δοκεῖν, to seem). The cross was only to deceive unbelievers. This and similar views were attempts to solve the theological problem of how God's immortal, impassible Logos could at the same time be man and suffer. Docetism was not a sect, but appeared in numerous forms from the apostolic age onward (see John and Colossians). It was theologically defeated at *Chalcedon.

DOCTOR OF THE CHURCH

In the Catholic Church and in Catholic theology, a theologian who bears witness to ancient *tradition and who must be distinguished in four respects: for orthodoxy, personal sanctity, learning, and explicit commendation by the Church. The authority of Doctors of the Church is not the same as that of the *Fathers—for they have not necessarily lived in the patristic age, a number of them belonging to medieval or modern times—but is that of *theologians. From the 8th century the Latin Church recognized four Doctors: St Ambrose, St Jerome, St Augustine, and St Gregory the Great. Their number later increased to 30 (among whom were the first women thus acknowledged by Pope Paul VI: Teresa of Avila and Catherine of Siena). Since the 9th century the Eastern Churches have venerated only three, called the "three hierarchs and ecumenical Doctors", St Basil, St Gregory of Nazianzus, and St John Chrysostom.

DOCTRINAL FREEDOM

The nature of this freedom depends on the truth of the doctrine at issue and the criterion of that truth. The scope of the Catholic theologian's doctrinal freedom is both disclosed and fixed by the faith of the Church, since Catholic theology of its very nature bases its investigations squarely on that faith as proclaimed in the accredited *kerygma of God's revelation in Christ by the Church's magisterium. Catholic theology is "tied", and thus freed from its own arbitrary subjectivity, by the binding doctrine of the Church's *magisterium (D 3883). The freedom of the *schools of Catholic theology obtains within these limits, which faith recognizes as absolute and therefore not as restrictive but liberating. Since Catholic doctrine itself maintains, against *Traditionalism, that there are important sources of religious knowledge outside historical revelation (see D 3015, Vat. II: Church/world, 59) theology necessarily finds itself engaged in open and genuine dialogue with man's natural understanding of himself and the world, in which each partner assists the other (D 3019, Vat II: Church/ world, 62). Even though the believer knows that this dialogue can never lead to an absolute and final contradiction (for the defined teaching of the Church, see D 3042) or an essential change in our understanding of the faith hitherto (also defined teaching, see D 3043), since the supreme source of all reality and all knowledge is unique, yet this dialogue of mutual enquiry, and the task and the tension which result from it, is never finally terminated, but remains a constituent element of the abiding historicity of our understanding of *revelation. Hence it follows from the very nature of theology itself, that theology and secular science should allow each other freedom to pursue their investigations in accordance with their proper methods; thus while faith continues to be the supreme norm of all knowledge, this norm itself guarantees secular disciplines their own freedom. According to the declaration of intention made by the Second Vatican Council regarding the promotion of freedom in research and teaching, both in theology and in profane studies (see Church/world, 62), what are required are legal forms (these are also theologically quite possible) which would prevent church leaders from terminating (or hoping to terminate) any conflict which does not seriously endanger the

Church's faith by withdrawing a teacher's rght to teach, depriving him of his office, and so on.

DOGMA

From the Greek δόγμα ("what seems right").

NATURE OF DOGMA. In the present usage of the Church and of theology, clearly and generally taken in this sense only since the 18th century, a dogma is a proposition to be believed with divine and Catholic *faith, that is, a proposition which the Church expressly teaches in her ordinary *magisterium, or by a papal or conciliar *definition, as divinely revealed; the denial of which is, therefore, *heresy (D 3011; CIC can, 1323, 1325 § 2). Thus there are two decisive elements in the formal concept of dogma: the Church must expressly and definitively propose a doctrine as a revealed truth, and the doctrine must *be* part of divine, official, Christian *Revelation, in contrast to *private revelation, and thus be contained in the word of God. This may be the case even if the dogma is contained in another (dogmatic) truth; for the Church teaches a good deal today as dogma which (while contained in Revelation) was not always expressly taught or thought of as dogma. It is controverted whether a dogma must be formally implicit in another revealed truth in order to be derived from this latter, or whether it can also be logically deduced from a revealed truth with the aid of premises that are not revealed. In any case, we must be clear that the concrete fulfilment of the Christian faith can never be confined to formal dogmas, but must be related to other knowledge, views, and attitudes if it would be truly personal and Catholic.

The Church insists that a dogma may not be revised if this would imply that the Church's perception of the word of God (even in an individual dogma) had been mistaken. For the Church believes (and teaches) the knowledge imparted by God *as such* and assumes that there could be no viable grounds for believing in any knowledge imparted by God if there were a possibility that God himself could mislead those receiving this knowledge. The Church avoids such errors in receiving and articulating the word of God for the very reason that through this process of perceiving, formulating and testifying she preserves its identity. This process obviously rests on a number of specific conditions: in a dogma the word of God is combined with concrete models to facilitate understanding, perspectives, current attitudes, etc. Dogmatic pronouncements concerning God can only be formulated in analogous terms; dogmas are determined by social, psychological and other factors. The changing thought-structures of a given epoch can mean that a dogma no longer seems relevant or easily graspable so that in certain circumstances it is not even re-interpreted in a new, fresh way appropriate to the given historical situation. On the contrary, it is forgotten, even though it has to be retained in the historical "memory" of the Church in the hope that it might some day become relevant again. It cannot be discarded because the history of dogma does not necessarily have to proceed in any given direction. However, these components of the historical reality of a dogma do not signify any error on the part of the Church as an institution which perceives, formulates and believes in the word of God. See *Infallibility.*

DIVISION OF DOGMA. Although in principle all dogmas have the same formal importance, it is legitimate to distinguish between fundamental articles—general, fundamental truths of Christianity—and special dogmas, that is, the rest of the articles of faith. The most accurate criterion of this distinction is the question: Which dogmas must necessarily and explicitly be believed as such, always and everywhere, by everyone who would attain *salvation; or which dogmas is it sufficient, in certain circumstances, to believe implicitly?—See *Necessity for Salvation.* Vatican II specifically stated "that in Catholic doctrine there exists an order or 'hierarchy' of truths, since they vary in their relation to the foundation of the Christian faith" (Ecum., 11).

THE PLACE OF DOGMA IN CHRISTIAN EXISTENCE AND SELF-CON-SCIOUSNESS. Dogma claims to impose an absolute obligation on man, who is essentially free; it is therefore a truth that can be rightly heard and understood only in the free resolution of faith. Yet this free man always has a "dogmatic" existence, because as a spirit he cannot deny certain truths (even of the historical order) without destroying himself, though he may possess these only in prescientific, even subconscious form. Thus divine revelation and its acceptance do not violate human nature. The nature of dogma cannot be deduced from the abstract concept of a possible divine revelation alone, but must be deduced from what in fact God in Jesus Christ has said to man and what he has decided to do with man: (1) *Revelation is not bare speech, it is the actual occurrence of salvation, in that God "communicates" himself and this communication creates for itself a subject that obediently receives and explicitly "hears" it, namely, the Church.

In this sense dogma is not a mere proposition "about" something, rather as something received in grace (God's self-communication) it is essentially the very event, fulfilling itself in conceptual terms, that is communicated in the proposition. (2) This self-communication of God has reached its definitive, eschatological phase; revelation is "closed". (3) The character of dogma is essentially social and ecclesial, because the revelation underlying it was itself made to the Church; on the other hand, dogma makes the unity of the Church tangible (is a confirmation of general usage) and thus is the shape of the abiding validity of the word of God which was announced to the Church and is preserved by her (*Tradition). (4) Dogma itself is life insofar as the very self-communication of God takes place in it, since it can only be grasped in the reality of the very thing believed, that is to say, grace.

DOGMATIC FACTS

These are facts which cannot indeed be deduced from the revealed word of God but which the Church must nevertheless recognize and formulate as such with certainty, because they are necessary for the preservation of the *deposit of faith in all its purity (e.g., the legitimacy of a Pope, the ecumenical character of a council, the heretical character of a doctrine). Their theological locus is not so much dogma in the strict sense as the theology of the Church's normal self-fulfilment in practice (*Pastoral theology).

DOGMATIC THEOLOGY

The theological science of *dogma; its object therefore is the whole of Christian *Revelation and thus those dogmas, too, which concern the Christian fulfilment of the human person, that is to say, have "moral" significance (*Grace, *Anthropology). As part of Catholic theology it is a science of faith, a reflexive, methodical, systematic grasp, by the believer in the light of faith, of the salvific self-disclosure of the Triune God in Christ and the Church as his Body.

DISTINCTION FROM OTHER THEOLOGICAL DISCIPLINES. (1) From *moral theology: Insofar as God's self-communication is the concern of dogmatic theology precisely because it is the principle of man's supernatural conduct and moral theology, rightly understood, must concern itself with this very behaviour of man, moral theology, in respect of its subject-matter, necessarily remains part of dogmatic theology. (2) From *biblical theology: See that article in this book. (3) From *fundamental theology: This is a pre-condition of dogmatic theology, and at the same time dogmatic theology prefaces fundamental theology to itself as a "natural" element in the reflection of the whole man, in the light of faith, on God's word to him. (4) All other theological sciences may be considered together in their relationship to dogmatic theology, in that though *theological* sciences they are all concerned with the history and activity of the Church: see *Church history, including liturgical history, legal history, history of ecclesiastical literature (*patrology and history of theological literature); practical theology, including canon law, pastoral theology, catechetics, homiletics; liturgiology, including Church music. These disciplines concern themselves with the Church insofar as she represents the God-wrought response of man to God's word in the human contingencies of history, in autonomous action and the rules governing it.

METHOD. Insofar as dogmatic theology is a systematic, "positive" (historical) hearkening to God's word spoken by the Church, in an effort to understand this word, it is also "speculative" at the same time, because for the mind to welcome and assimilitate something is a positive activity which brings into play all the subjective factors in the hearer's nature. A truly inward appropriation of historically acquired truth demands confrontation of revealed truth as heard with the hearer's entire specific (transcendentally and historically conditioned) understanding of self and of the world. Thus philosophy and the *history of dogma are also essential elements of dogmatic theology itself.

INTERIOR ARTICULATION OF DOGMATIC THEOLOGY. The basic difficulty about ordering dogmatic theology in accordance with its nature is that its subject-matter is at once both "essential" and "existential": God's revelation, which forms the theme of dogmatic theology, affirms the *essential* relationship binding man and his world to God, and at the same time God's saving deed done to man in salvific *history*. This dualism forces dogmatic theology, in its necessary systematization, to present God's saving revelation in its (salvific-) historical structure; only thus can dogmatic theology bring out the fact that in the eschatological era in which the Church (as distinguished from the OT) practises theology, the contingent and the essential have found their ultimate and indissoluble intimacy with one another in their mutual relationship, itself historically various because the reality of this temporal world has once and for all been assumed by the ultimacy of God. This once-for-all nature of reality continues and is perceived appropriately in *anamnesis and "prognostication" (hopeful prediction of the future as completion of experience).—For the divisions of dogmatic theology see *Angelology, Anthropology, Christology, Ecclesiology, Eschatology, Formal and Fundamental Theology, Fundamental Theology, Grace, theology of, God, doctrine of, Mariology, Moral Theology, Sacramental Theology, Creation, doctrine of, Soteriology, Trinitarian Theology.*

DONATISM

A North African movement of the 4th century which arose from the political and social tensions and conflict between the surviving martyrs and those who had lapsed under persecution. It took its name from Donatus, the schismatic bishop of Carthage, and its adherents took the theological view that the sacraments of baptism and order could be forfeited. Whence, they also taught re-baptism. Furthermore, they repudiated the Church's peace with the State, considered the African Church to be the true one, and courted martyrdom even to the point of suicide. This enthusiastic movement, in part based on *Novatianism, broke up into numerous factions, was suppressed by the State, combatted by St Augustine, and condemned by the Synod of the Lateran (A.D. 313) and the Synod of Arles (A.D. 314), and ended with the Vandal conquest of Africa in 430. Theological reflection on the *Church and on the sacramental *character fructified through the disorders of Donatism.

DOUBT

Doubt must not be confused with questioning, which seeks better and fuller knowledge, so as to integrate into it the knowledge already found and retained. Nor is doubt involved even when adherence to some insight encounters objective or subjective (but not compelling) difficulties and therefore requires effort and resolution. Doubt is the deliberate suspension of personal assent to knowledge of which the import and (at least to some extent) the basis were and are known to the doubter. In the theological sense, doubt is the free and morally culpable suspension of assent to the truths of *faith. Doubt of this sort is possible because, however objective and well-founded a truth may be, knowledge of it in the sphere of personal life (and therefore even of *revelation) presupposes a certain moral disposition in the hearer: candour, reverence, modesty, docility, a proper appreciation of the light which a difficult truth sheds on human existence, and such similar dispositions. When and insofar as man perceives that God has truly spoken, he cannot in practice doubt what he has thus heard, but he can freely and culpably adopt, or resume, an interior attitude that prevents him recognizing part or all of revelation as the word of God, or suspends the judgment he has already formed that it is such, thus permitting him to doubt the fact. This is not to say that doubting the authenticity of concrete divine revelation is in every case morally culpable. In practice it is often all but impossible to tell the difference between doubt and critical questioning.

DOXA

From the Gr. δόξα, glory; a term for the manner in which God's celestial majesty is outwardly manifested, for instance (already in the OT) in the form of "fire", a "cloud", an "apparition". During the time of his abasement Christ is the "brightness of God's *doxa*" (Heb 1:3); the *doxa* of God is incarnationally present in him; since his *resurrection he is the "Lord of *doxa*" (1 Cor 2:8). *Doxa* is also, in "transitive" terminology, the immanent "honour" which Father and Son show one another within the Trinity. In principle, man has already acquired a share in God's eschatological *doxa* through the self-communication of God to man which has occured in Christ (the bestowal of the Spirit, *Grace); but, under this soteriological aspect, that *doxa* is still essentially a hidden thing, to be revealed only when the sufferings of this age are over (Rom 8:18).—See also *Glory of God*.

DREAD

Theologically, a fundamental condition of man in the personal history of his salvation. It figures in the OT as terror of Yahweh, his appearances, and his day—heightened by the still indeterminate issue of God's dialogue with his people in saving history—and as the sinner's dread of God's inescapable and always unattainable demands. The NT declares that Christ's redemptive dread (Lk 22:44f.) was an endurance of the sinner's culpable alienation from God, and thereby heralds a blessed Christian fear (2 Cor 6:4) which is a share in the suffering of Christ (Rom 8:17). Theological reflection discovers the root of dread in *original sin, that is, in the fact that it should not exist for man, and also shows that in Christ it can be transmuted into a saving event, so that we can now see as a task an element of dread antecedent to morality and common to all men: man (composed of a soul and a passible body) has been launched into the world, into time and death, and thereby exposed to a divine claim ever more demanding. We may either seek safety in independence, which does not allay dread but only makes it a sign of flight from God; at least this is true of fear in humanity as a whole, though such flight in the case of an individual whose anxiety is neurotic may not be blameworthy. Or we may accept fear in *hope, which is to share in Jesus' saving dread.— See also *Certainty of Salvation, Fear of God.* These remarks on the theological character of dread do not mean that it should simply be accepted. Dread as a sociopathological phenomenon arises from the experience of the contradiction between actually possible and socially barred freedom, and is to be combatted in the struggle for *emancipation.

DREAMS

In Christian tradition dreams have two aspects which must both be borne in mind if we would evaluate them correctly. Dreams occur during sleep when consciousness yields to the depths of human nature that exist antecedent to rational planning and decision and now emerge in those deceitful dreams against which Scripture warns us (Job 20:8; Ps 73:20; Is 29:7f.; Ecclus 34:1–7). But for the same reason dreams may reveal depths in us which our waking consciousness wrongly ignored and through which God may communicate his instructions to us in a dream; thus dreams may also be a form of divine revelation (Num 12:6; Gen 20:3ff.; 28:12–15; 37:5–10; Mt 1:20; 2:13 etc.).

DUALISM

In the strict sense, the doctrine that from the very beginning reality consists of two absolutely antagonistic realms of being. In religious history it is chiefly important in *Manichaeism, which splits the world into two absolute principles, one good and one evil, which restrain each other and are mutually hostile. Dualism in this extreme form is

137

nowhere to be found in Scripture, though the NT exhibits the unmistakable influence of the world-view of later Judaism (demonology; the kingdom of Satan opposed to the *basileia* of God, whose own supremacy is never in doubt; doctrine of the *aeons). But the NT's faith in Christ explodes every dualistic system (originating in the contradictions experienced in existence), however diluted and relatively reasonable, by its teaching of God's Incarnation, in which the "heavenly world" definitively and redemptively assumes the "earthly".

DULIA

See *Veneration of Saints.*

DUTY

As the basic experience that through our transcendence to God we are free for the good, duty is the unlimited claim the (ultimately personal) good lays upon another person in his freedom as such (obligation). It is ultimately a modality of the relationship of *person to person and therefore in the deepest sense is proper to love. But on the other hand it affects the relation of all the values which belong in the concrete to the nature and perfection of a person, so that even material things can impose an obligation. In other words, moral values—those values, that is, which constitute the personal domain, and insofar as they do so—are of themselves imperative, and as such willed by God (*Natural moral law) since they can be conceived only within the transcendental ascent to God's absolute being and therefore willed by God. Duty loses its heteronomous character when it is thought of as a "duty" of love and this love is experienced as the gift of grace, in the widest sense.

E

EASTER

See *Pasch, Resurrection of Christ.*

EASTERN ORTHODOX CHURCHES

This article is not concerned with the historical origin of the Eastern
Churches separated from Rome since the schism of the ninth and
eleventh century, nor with the repeated attempts at reunion, especially at the Second Council of *Lyons and the Council of *Florence,
nor with the history of the Eastern Churches in communion with
Rome, who keep their own liturgy and are comparatively autonomous
(cf. Vat II: East. Church.) Rather this is a brief summary of those
points in which the theology of the Eastern Churches separated from
Rome differs from Roman Catholic theology. Even so we can only
deal with the larger of those Churches (Greek and Slavonic). These
Eastern Churches did not participate in that development of Western
theology whose beginnings in a juridical ecclesiology and theory of
redemption can be traced back to Tertullian and St Cyprian in the
third century, which then took shape in St Augustine, especially in his
theology of the Trinity, and was consolidated by the Scholastics. This
theological difference, so often overlooked, meant that the East
thought in terms of a dynamic saving history and an ascending order
of things, beginning with the economy of the Trinity and closely
bound up with soteriology. Even where the *cross was thoroughly
understood, redemption was regarded in the East as a real ontological
process that begins with the Incarnation, discloses the immanent
economy of the Trinity, ends with the divinization of the world (in
which Christian practice has no part), and first proves its triumph in

Jesus Christ's resurrection, leading, according to some important early theologians, to an *apocatastasis*. In contrast, Western theology regards the Incarnation of the Logos almost exclusively as the means of constituting a fit agent capable of making satisfaction for sin. Though aware of the divinization of the world, it lays much more stress on Christ's atonement for sin on the cross and on forgiveness. This fundamental difference of approach, which might have led to a fruitful synthesis had there ever been a true meeting of minds between the two sides, was the obvious reason why the Eastern Churches were always able to cite the *Filioque* as the cause of their separation—a very minor point in itself, historically and theologically speaking, but one symptomatic of a deep-seated divergence in intellectual and spiritual outlook. The theology of the Eastern Churches, absorbed in meditation on the truths that were vindicated during the great Trinitarian and Christological controversies of the first five centuries, refused (despite the history of those very controversies) to entertain any idea of a legitimate *development of dogma and to this day receives only the first seven ecumenical *councils. The Eastern Orthodox reject the Catholic doctrine of *purgatory and the dogmas of the *Immaculate Conception and the *Assumption, though they believe in both these truths and practice a greater veneration of the Blessed Virgin than does the Roman Church. They hold that the sources of the faith are Scripture and Tradition, the latter embodied in the Creed of Nicaea- *Constantinople; but in fact the eucharistic liturgy is also considered a rule of faith in that the Eastern Churches have always made their relations with Protestantism depend on the latter's view of the Eucharist. The Orthodox consider external Church unity helpful, for instance, in the form of the World Council of Churches (where they figure as witnesses to the truth, not seekers after it), but not necessary, provided the Churches preserve internal unity by recognizing Christ as their invisible Head and administering the seven sacraments. Otherwise, each nation is left to determine the details of the constitution of its own Church. While all Orthodox patriarchs and bishops are in the *apostolic succession, Church government is frequently vested in a lay synod. Accordingly, the Orthodox recognize the Pope of Rome only as Patriarch of the West. Some would accord him a primacy of honour, but on no account primacy of jurisdiction over the whole Church and an infallible magisterium. A theological union with the Eastern Churches requires that they concern themselves, in a fraternal spirit, with theological developments in the West for the past eleven centuries or more; of primary importance in this connexion are the findings of a sound biblical theology (concerning

ECCLESIOLOGY

the Petrine office and biblical ecclesiology in general) and a fuller appreciation of *theology itself, together with a re-evaluation of Christian practice in active, concrete love and so on. On the other hand Catholic theologians must expect to be asked by the Orthodox whether they have as yet given due weight in the Church to the *patristic age and to the episcopal office (*Bishop), and whether they have offered sufficiently open resistance to a bureaucratic centralization in the Church which has no theological justification. Vatican II made advances in this direction (Ecum., 14–18; East. Church., 24–29 and *passim*).

EBED YAHWEH

From the Hebrew, meaning "servant of Yahweh", an OT term for all pious Israelites, but especially for a mysterious figure in Isaiah 42; 49; 50, 52–53, who is to appear prophetically and suffer an atoning death "for many". The term is sometimes understood collectively (of all Israel or of the righteous remnant of the people), sometimes mythologically (alleged Babylonian influence); there is also discussion as to whether the Ebed Yahweh is an ideal, or a man belonging to the past or the future. The NT adopts the term and applies it to the devout in Israel, including Jesus. But the life and death of Jesus especially are interpreted according to the texts of Isaiah (see Lk 22:37 with Is 53:12 and *passim*). Thus the NT revelation of Jesus allows the Ebed Yahweh texts in Isaiah to be read as messianic prophecy, presenting in moving language a picture of the Messiah which was certainly alien to the Judaism of the time: a Messiah unknown and afflicted, dumb, without beauty or comeliness, despised, struck by God, who bears our iniquities and is buried with the ungodly and thereby gains the many for his own.

ECCLESIOLOGY

The theological doctrine of the *Church. The place of ecclesiology in theology as a whole is still shrouded in such obscurity that we can hardly speak of a real tractate devoted to it. Ecclesiology is usually presented in apologetics (*Fundamental theology) in a twofold way; once in historical, pre-theological form for the historical proof of the Church's institution by Jesus Christ and the nature of her teaching authority (including the notes of the Church, the hierarchy, the magisterium, the pope and infallibility); and then in dogmatic form, since all the important affirmations which theology makes about *Holy Scripture (*Inspiration, etc.) and its relation to *Tradition—beyond their historical reliability—presuppose the dogmatic doctrine concerning the Church. It should be observed that the notes of the Church (oneness and uniqueness, holiness, catholicity, and apostolicity), whereby the true Church of Christ can be recognized, have been included in the Creed and thus must be believed. The affirmations about the real nature of the Church can only be understood in the light of the *Christology of the Word made flesh, which must therefore precede ecclesiology; the doctrine of the *Eucharist as the central mystery of the Church is an essential part of ecclesiology, and so is the doctrine of the *sacraments in general, which must present the sacraments as fundamental realizations of the Church.

ECONOMY, PRINCIPLE OF METAPHYSICAL

A concept ancillary to theology which is of great importance in our metaphysical and theological knowledge of God (*God, doctrine of). It means that God's transcendent causality intervenes in the world sparingly and with the utmost discretion. God, the transcendent and abiding causality, endows creatures with their own activity, which he himself sustains (*Creation, *Conservation, *Concourse, divine), then fortifies this created dynamism with his own power so that the creature outdoes himself and produces an effect, in and with this divine power, of which he would never have been capable alone. Thus God remains the transcendent cause of the natural occurrence and his activity does not make him a link in the chain of secondary causes. Where God's activity manifests itself *within* the succession of events we have saving history, culminating in the Incarnation. The world must do what it can in the noblest possible way. God himself develops to his own glory the potentialities he has given to creatures, and claims their realization as his own work; he need not create what can come about by *evolution.

ECUMENICAL MOVEMENT

(Sometimes known by the less appropriate, abstract term "ecumenism".) A collective name for all attempts to reunite Christians of different confessions, in the first place by taking temporary steps involving organizations (for example, by membership of the World Council of Churches, which does not see itself in any sense as a "super-Church"), and finally by achieving the one Church of all those who believe in Jesus Christ which accords with the will of Christ. This is not the place to discuss the history of the ecumenical movement, which only really began in the twentieth century. All that can be done here is to point to a few aspects of the movement in the light of Catholic theology. The Catholic Church knows now, as it knew in the past, that it is the *Church in which the one Church of Christ "subsists", as the Second Vatican Council expressed it (Constitution on the Church, 8), but it no longer regards the other churches and church communities as confessions which ought not to be in existence, which should become absorbed into the Catholic Church as quickly as possible through individual conversions and which have to be anathematized as "heresies" or as "schismatic". On the contrary, it sees the other churches now above all as partners in dialogue and co-operation, with more in common than what separates them and a shared task with regard to the *world. What all the churches have in common is, for example, a common faith in God and Jesus Christ as the only Lord and redeemer, a mutual concession to each others' good faith, in accordance with human and Christian duty, an unconditional and mutual respect for religious freedom and a mutual recognition of each others' baptism as valid and of its effective incorporation into Jesus Christ. The Catholic Church also has the duty to contribute certain aspects of faith to the ecumenical movement and it is, moreover, also theologically possible for it to do this. These elements include, for instance, an appreciation of the existence of other sacraments in the non-Catholic churches, a conviction that grace and justification are also present in non-Catholic Christians, a recognition that the non-Catholic churches as such have a positive function with regard to salvation for non-Catholic Christians and that they also have a positive and living Christian heritage that is not necessarily present in every respect and with equal clarity in the visible form of the Catholic Church—a conviction, in other words, that the churches are not separated from each other in every respect and that their members are not simply "separated brethren"—a knowledge that all Christians share in the guilt of the division in Christianity and that non-Catholic Christians cannot be regarded as "formal heretics", an open admission that the Catholic Church is always in need of repentance and reform and finally an acknowledgment that members of the other churches also live Christian lives (even to the point of becoming martyrs), and that this also contributes to the extension of the Catholic Church.

The ecumenical movement has the character of authentic *dialogue, which is fundamentally a conversation orientated towards an open future. It is not a question of approaching other church communities as such, nor is it simply a "return" on the part of the non-Catholic churches to the Catholic Church. This is because the Church of the future towards which Christians are working, even if it is seen as Roman Catholic, must contain the positively Christian treasures of the past from the other churches and must therefore in a sense be a different Church from the present Catholic Church in its present, historically conditioned form. The theme of ecumenical dialogue is everything that can be of service to the unity of Christians in faith, Church, Christian life and responsible action with regard to the world. It is therefore concerned with the exchange of information about Christian life and doctrine, a better understanding of each church's theology, an attempt to translate the theology of each church into the the theological language of other churches, an effort to overcome real doctrinal differences and arrangements for shared activities. There are several obstacles to the effectiveness of the ecumenical movement. The first of these is the inertia of those who do not suffer from the separation of the churches and the second is the immobility of the institutions (on all sides!). All the church institutions must inevitably change considerably in the course of the ecumenical movement, if a really serious attempt is made to reach the final aim of the one Church of all Christians. Many existing possibilities are as yet unexploited. There is still, for example, mutual intolerance and un-Christian competition, both of which could be to a very great extent removed from society. There is also the question of mixed marriages. It ought to be possible for theologians of the various churches involved to work together in a concrete, organized way to solve some of the problems raised by such marriages. Increasing use could also be made of the liturgy, church music and religious practices that the churches have in common. New obstacles to unity in teaching and practice could be avoided in advance by mutual consultation. Everything that is theologically possible in the matter of full shared worship should not simply be tolerated—it should rather be tactfully promoted. The problem of the mutual recognition of offices (*office) should be tackled more energetically.

Another area in which members of all the churches could work together is to be found in the task of all Christians to give the secular world a more human and therefore also a more Christian form. In

EMANATION

many ways, the churches ought to be able to commit themselves together (boldly going counter to any resistance in their own ranks) to peace, the abolition of discrimination and prejudices, social justice and the cause of the poor and the oppressed. Institutional presuppositions and structures could be created to deal with all these questions.

ELECTION

The dominant theme of the history of God's people as recorded in the OT. The object of this election is the people of Israel, considered as a collectivity descended from Abraham. Free and inscrutable choice of God's love though this election was, it is afterwards looked on as God's fidelity to his promises. This election is radically confirmed by Jesus' "mission" to the whole people of Israel. A limitation of this mission to a remnant ("little flock") is accepted for a time only after by contemporary Israel. The final formation of God's new congregation (Mt 16:18), however, is conceived not as a sect but on a worldwide scale: it opens salvation to all men. Insofar as men sanctified in Jesus have accepted their election as the gift of God's grace, they are called God's elect in the strict sense (Rom 8:33; Col 3:12; 1 Pet 1:1f. and *passim).* Beyond this biblical interpretation of election, election in the theological sense is to be understood as that sovereign, positive, salvific activity of God which flows from a loving resolution of his purpose and precedes the *individual* too, without abolishing his personal decision and tried fidelity but rather creating these (*Predestination, *Reprobation).

EMANATION

From the Latin *emanare,* to flow forth; in philosophy and theology Emanationism means the efflux of all things from the divine substance and, by derivation, that which has flowed forth. The emanation is held to be necessary; and the emanations progressively lose their perfection (like rays of light) as they proceed farther from the divine source. Emanationism as a form of *pantheism was condemned by the first Vatican Council (D 3024), since it contradicts the absolute simplicity and immutability of God and the doctrine of *creation taught by that Council.

EMANCIPATION (LIBERATION)

The concept is derived originally from jurisprudence. It refers on the one hand to the freeing of a slave, and on the other to a child's release from parental tutelage, and thus to his or her coming of age. Stemming from this emancipation generally, it signifies the liberation of individuals, groups, classes, and peoples (women, workers, Jews, Blacks) from various different states of dependence (legal and political, economic, educational, natural) which prevent them from realizing their full potential as human beings. The concept can thus signify socio-political liberation from systems based on domination and exploitation, the liberation of thought from external control, censorship and taboos, liberation from need, war and existential fears. Although emancipation is of fundamental significance as the central aim of the *Enlightenment it must be distinguished from the latter on account of its links to a specific period in history. Emancipation was conceived by the Enlightenment as implying a new quality, the liberation of the self through critical understanding. The revolutionary perception of freedom conceived by Marxism in conjunction with economic analyses and the class struggle caused emancipation to assume a far more progressive form than in the Enlightenment. With Marx, emancipation became a critical challenge even to bourgeois-liberal values and to the suppression of religion as the "opium of the people", and grew to symbolize the complete attribution of all situations to man's nature as a social being. In the present day emancipation has become the ideal according to which society and education should be structured. Through it we shall be able to overcome not only the most extreme instances of dependence and inhuman inequality; it will also effectively prevent the emergence of any new forms of social privilege and discrimination by the *democratization of all aspects of life.

EMOTION

An especially strong, spontaneous movement of the feelings tending to issue in impulsive or rash action and to inhibit the reaction of the intellect and the will; its physical function is to protect or intensify life. Responsibility for impulsive action is diminished to the degree in which freedom of choice and the use of reason are impaired.

146

ENCYCLICAL

Literally, a circular letter; this name, applied to circular letters of the Popes since the 7th century, has been a technical term since the 18th century. An encyclical is cited by the words with which it opens (for example *Quadragesimo anno*). The theological problem raised by encyclicals is the question of their authority. An encyclical as such is a pronouncement of the ordinary magisterium, but not in itself a new dogmatic definition by the extraordinary or the ordinary magisterium. Its teaching requires an assent that is positive and internal, but not absolutely final. Therefore reservations or a later withdrawal of that assent are not ruled out. By its nature, of course, an encyclical will reflect more of the language, the emphasis, and other features of its time than a final definition. The Pope can indeed make use of an encyclical to pronounce final judgment on matters still controverted, but in that case his intention to do so must be clearly indicated (D 3884f.).

END

The completed existence of that which in virtue of its very *beginning must mature in order to exist; or the limit which contains the whole of existence.

The end of the material world. It can be left an open question whether the material world has an end (in the sense specified above) which can be known by means of the material world and beyond which absolutely no further phase of the "world" can be conceived, because a purely material world as such does not exist; it exists necessarily (in the theological sense), by God's disposition, as the condition and the scene of the spiritual history of creatures and transcends its (hypothetical) "material end", if only by reason of what is taken up into the perfection of the created spirit and is there preserved.

That end of biological beings which as such is a renewal of the beginning (generation), suffices to show that the end is not the cessation of something which existed hitherto and now simply does not exist any longer, but a taking possession of the potentialities inherent in the cause of the beginning (the cause transcending the beginning itself).

The end of spiritual and personal being is a free acceptance of its true beginning and thus corresponds to the nature of spiritual and

147

personal being, which knows itself and takes free possession of itself. Insofar as this end is enacted before God in a history of freedom, it signifies the real theological conception of the end (*Death). This end is neither a negation of existence nor an arbitrary caesura in indefinitely continuing *time, but the fulfilment of time, because here time has been taken up into the absolute validity of a freedom which has realized itself temporally. Man's end is at once ever present now and yet to come, because he always takes up an attitude with regard to it (so that his present is either a hopeful or a fearful anticipation of the future). This open futurity discloses a responsibility, a challenge, and an obligation. Since man is essentially the being who exists historically, and since retrospection into the real past and foresight into the future are part of his actuality (and existence), this reference cannot be excised from his "sheer actualization" without "mythologizing" man. For this reason the *now of the individual man remains ordered to the end precisely in being referred to a supernatural goal (*Grace, *Beatific vision, *Saving history, *Death) and precisely as (eschatological) actuality.

ENLIGHTENMENT

The Enlightenment is crucially linked to fundamental Christian values. First, in terms of its origins in the eighteenth century in the work of Diderot, Voltaire, Wieland, Lessing, Shaftesbury and Hume; second, with regard to the problems it poses (*theodicy, the rational reconstruction of the historical process, criticism of tradition and sovereign authority in both state and Church, the natural law, reason and revelation); and third, in its aims (transition from the natural state to the political and legal state, encyclopaedic and moral education and the progress of society towards greater freedom, tolerance and maturity). Even Kant's subsequent definition of the Enlightenment as man's emergence from his self-imposed tutelage and the resulting demand to use his reason directly can only be interpreted as a criticism of Christianity if the latter is held to be among the powers which promoted and exploited this ignorance and antagonism to criticism. The debasement of the Enlightenment during the early Romantic period and the political restoration of the nineteenth century finds a theological echo in the fact that it is simply identified with a rationalism hostile to faith, or is considered to be an atheistic element and thus by extension the modern crisis of Christianity.

Given its original intentions, we cannot see the present as an extension of the Enlightenment nor conceive the latter as the outdated illusion of an earlier phase of bourgeois history. Instead, following Kant, Hegel and Marx, the Enlightenment should be interpreted as the incomplete task of pursuing the as yet uncompleted history of freedom. Critical theology is then faced with the necessity of coming to terms with the question of its own practical contribution to the fulfilment of legal and political freedom in history. This seems all the more promising in that, despite the criticism levelled at Christianity by the Enlightenment, even the enlightened Kantian intellect could not eliminate the discrepancy between man's destiny to struggle towards freedom throughout history and the concept of human endeavour being brought to final perfection by the intercession of a merciful and just God. The differing historical consciousness this implies not only makes the actual progress of history the decisive criterion of any contemporary contribution to the realization of freedom, but allows a distinction to be made between a free society and the eschatological kingdom of God.—See *Political theology.

ENTITY

See *Being, Soul.*

EPHESUS

A city of Asia Minor in which the third Ecumenical Council was held from June 22nd to July 17th, A.D. 431, during the pontificate of Pope Celestine I. It condemned *Nestorianism, laid down fundamental principles of *Christology, and in consequence expressly accorded *Mary the title of "Mother of God" (Gr. θεότοκοs) (D 250 –264).

EPIPHANY

From the Greek ἐπιφάνεια, apparition. In comparative religion epiphany means the sudden, fleeting appearance of deity. The scriptural conception of epiphany, in marked contrast to this, means the historically tangible invasion of the world by the personal God. Theology differentiates between theophanies, Christophanies (baptism of Christ, his Transfiguration, his walking on the sea), pneumatophanies, and angelophanies (*Angels). *Apparitions in the sense of purely *private revelations are completely unknown to Holy Scripture; all epiphanies contain some message intended for the entire community.

EPISTEMOLOGY, THEOLOGICAL

The doctrine of the formal principles and rules which are to be observed in the understanding of faith and the systematic reflection on it which is *theology. Thus it deals with man's permanent dependence on and orientation to divine revelation (*Mystery); with the nature of such understanding as *faith, the science of faith, and genuinely human (both rational and historical) knowledge of truth and the sources of this knowledge: *Holy Scripture (*Inspiration) and *Tradition (and their interrelationship); with the proper and original knower of this knowledge, who is not the individual but the hierarchically structured *Church; with the relation of the individual believer and the individual theologian and his knowledge to the Church's doctrine and dogmatic definitions (*Magisterium, *Infallibility, *Dogma, *Theological notes); and with particular theological methods, namely historical, speculative, and kerygmatic theology.

ESCHATOLOGY

The theological doctrine of the *last things (Gr. ἔσχατα). It is not an anticipatory reporting of events that are to happen "later" but the prospective view—necessary for man with his spiritual freedom of decision—from his present situation in saving history, governed by the event of Jesus Christ, to the final fulfilment of this his own existential situation, which is already eschatologically determined. The purpose of this prospective view is that man shall understand his present as his definitive *future hidden in the present and already offering him *salvation now if it is accepted as the deed of God the only ruler, the time and manner of which remain incalculable. This eschatological understanding of the present does not distort perception of the contradictions that still exist to the salvation already made available in Jesus Christ, and does not adversely affect the action of Christians too in the planning and construction of the (world's) future, without which God will not introduce the absolute, ultimate future (productive eschatology).

(1) A *hermeneutics of eschatological statements must establish

150

norms that preclude a false "apocalyptical" interpretation of eschatology (*Apocalyptic) as well as a "demythologizing", absolute existentialization of eschatology (*Demythologization). The latter forgets that man lives in genuine temporality ordered to a future which is really yet to come, and in a world which is not simply abstract existence but must rather attain salvation with all its dimensions (including the dimension of profane temporality). These norms make it clear *inter alia* that the discourses about *heaven and *hell are not on the same plane; that in the last analysis God's grace will certainly be victorious. This triumphant proposition about heaven becomes a proposition of the pilgrim when he accepts the proposition about hell as a genuine and open possibility of his individual damnation, and both are embraced in the individual act of hoping for salvation (*Hope). The propositions of eschatology must always be kept open as statements about *our* given possibilities now which we cannot bypass. They must be kept open against claims to esoteric knowledge of an alleged *apocatastasis and also against claims, anticipating God's hidden judgment, to certain knowledge of any case of actual concrete damnation. These norms help to distinguish between the content of the eschatological statements of Scripture and Tradition, and the manner of their expression.

(2) Eschatology affirms *inter alia:* the intrinsic finitude and historical nature of time, stretching as it does from a genuine *beginning to a genuine *end that is not to be superseded; the "once-for-all" character of every moment of *saving history; *death, and the God-wrought event of "transmutation" as the necessary mode of the genuine consummation of time; the fact that the end is already given in the Incarnation, death and *resurrection of Jesus; the fact that the "givenness" of this end is the established reality of the victorious mercy and the *self-communication of God; the special character of time "since" Christ; the permanent element of strife and contest in this time (*Antichrist), which is intensified as the end approaches; then the final abolition of the cosmic powers of law and death; the *Judgment as the consummation of the world; the abiding significance of Jesus' humanity for beatitude; the *beatific vision as vision of the abiding *mystery; the relation of the *heaven of the redeemed to the rejected world of the *devils; the metaphysical nature of glorified corporeality; the one *basileia* composed of angels and men.

A difficult theological problem in eschatology is the dialectic between individual eschatology (death, the particular judgment, the heaven or hell or purgatory of the individual) and general eschatology (the general Judgment, eternal heaven, eternal hell). The statements we have about these matters cannot, after all, be reconciled by assigning them to different realities to be treated of separately (beatitude of the "soul"—resurrection of the "body"), since man is one being, composed of body and soul, and all biblical statements about him invariably refer to the totality of his nature.

In present-day theology "eschatological" applies to the present insofar as the last days have begun in Christ ("God's eschatological action"); where it seems to refer to the future alone, it means the future as interpreting the present ("eschatological statements of Scripture").

ESSENCE

However much a being may change, however true it be that it must become what it is only "potentially", this growth proceeds from something fundamental in the being concerned which remains itself throughout the process of growth and is the *a priori* law of that growth (positively, determining what the being can and shall become: *goal; negatively, excluding from the outset what is beyond the powers of that growth). This permanent basic structure of a being is called its essence, or (as the principle of its operations) its *nature. Essence or nature are not abstractly detectable apart from being and its becoming. The more perfect an essence is, the greater are the (active and passive) potentialities for its growth, the more will the end-term be something inwardly determined by that which is actualizing its essence (*Freedom); hence essence is not unaffected by history. When the essence is that of a spiritual *transcendence (*Spirit, *Person, *Man) the potentialities for growth are unlimited. This essence is identical with the *potentia obedientialis, the power to receive God's absolute self-communication in *grace and the *beatific vision. Less than human beings are confined by their essence to a particular sphere of spatio-temporal reality. Herein lies the essential distinction between spirit and anything merely material.

ETERNITY

Eternity is predicated of God in Scripture as a characteristic of him who stands in radical contrast to man set and living in time and contingency (magisterium: D 75, 800, 3001); it is also attributed to all that belongs to God and to anything insofar as it depends upon his

152

absolute will: his Son, his dominion, his dwelling places, etc. God's eternity is essentially to be understood as continuance without any kind of succession, which not only has no beginning and no end but is a present that has always been in absolute possession of itself and for which, subsisting in itself, there is no such thing as "before" or "after". To this extent, therefore, eternity is simply the plentitude of being. *Time, on the other hand, is not a category of being itself but only the mode of being of the "temporal", of decaying created being, which realizes itself only in constant succession. Therefore no parallelization of time and eternity is possible. The world has a beginning, but not in a moment of eternity (which knows no moments); God was *never* without a world, since *before* time there was no temporality; the world is temporal, not God's relation to it—which is eternal. In the *creation God's eternity already shows itself not the pure negation of time but the master of time. It is most fully revealed by the fact that in the human nature of his Son God accepts the temporality of man, with its subjection to destiny and to change, and thereby raises it into his own eternal self-possession. From this point forward "time" becomes the dimension in which occurs the communication of God's eternity (that is of his plentitude of being) to temporal, mutable man, who through this very communication is graciously opened to the eternity of God, with the object of allowing man thus to possess eternity, so that he may be granted a share in the possession of God's plentitude of being.—See also *Immortality, Soul.*

ETHICS

Ethics as the fundamental part of practical *philosophy* is the science of morals; that is, it seeks to analyse and explore the moral facts from which the norms of human behaviour may be derived. To this extent it is to be sharply distinguished from theological ethics (*Moral theology), which must derive the norms of moral behaviour from the revealed word of God (attested in the Church) and his economy of salvation. So far as (philosophical) ethics concerns the moral aspect of man it subjects a fundamental aspect of man's self-understanding to scientific analysis: Man experiences himself, in his self-fulfilment, as a being who wills and who in actualizing his will "voluntarily" directs himself to *good or *evil. The free self-fulfilment of the person always includes a consciousness of this difference between good and evil. In freely fulfilling himself, the rational person experiences himself as the basic moral value. Ethics elaborates this "experience of basic value"; starting from it, the rational person can be shown to be one who at the same time morally fulfils his "nature" and his ordination to a last end. This person is absolutely willed as such, a fact from which we can and must deduce the absolute character of those moral values which serve the fulfilment of the rational person who is absolutely willed. Ethics now proceeds by subjecting each ontic relation of this person—his relation to himself, to other free persons (fellowmen), to human society, and finally to God—to thorough scientific analysis and sets up (ethical) norms for the fulfilment of these relations. This analysis leads to a subdivision of ethics, corresponding to the different spheres of life, into an individual ethics and a social ethics. The immediate subjective norm of each person's moral behaviour—the individual *conscience, whose decision ultimately determines the value or worthlessness of a concrete action—must be conformed to the resulting objective moral order, which takes into account the fact of the human person's ordination to certain environmental data and structures. Hence follow the ultimate principles for conscience (*Natural moral law), e. g.: objectively evil means are not justified by a subjectively good purpose; a moral value that is obligatory (because the rational person is absolutely willed) may not be sacrificed to a pre-moral partial value of human existence. Insofar as ethics reflects the free moral fulfilment of the human person in a pre-ordained order, it must remain open to anything that God may have decreed about the human person and his ordination to his end (*Moral theology).

EUCHARIST

From the Greek εὐχαριστεῖν, to give thanks (εὐ, good; χάρις, gift); literally and in the original sense, the thanks of one who has received "goodly gifts" and who, consequently, is "thankful". Eucharist also means gratitude, and prayer of thanksgiving. Later, eucharist acquired the further sense of Jesus' "Body", so far as the latter, under the species of bread and wine, is the point of departure and the centre of the Eucharistic action in the Church.

(1) The reality called the Eucharist is based on the Last Supper (especially Lk 22:19f. and 1 Cor 11:23ff.; see Mk 14:22ff.). There, according to his own words, Jesus gives his "Body" and "Blood" as food and drink to be eaten and drunk under the appearances of bread and wine. The meaning of this action emerges from the situation and the terms used. The thought of death is fundamental: Jesus conscious-

ly accepts his fate and brings it into line with the essential point of his preaching. Jesus also understands this meal eschatologically as the anticipation of the joy to be celebrated, ultimately. Finally, the concept of community is basic to this meal (Jesus' relationship with his friends and the foundation of the community of his friends). The terms used show the following: against its Semitic background "body" signifies the bodily tangibility of the person of Jesus; in the rider to the words about the bread Jesus is simply declared to be the *Ebed Yahweh (see Is 53:4 –12); but the *Blood is more precisely defined as the blood shed by Jesus in instituting the New *Covenant (see also Is 42:6; 49:8); thus Jesus is described as dying a bloody death. Jesus' gifts, therefore, are identical with Jesus himself the giver, God's suffering servant, who accepts a violent death in free obedience, thus establishing the New Covenant. The identity of the Church's eucharistic meal with the Body and Blood of Jesus is clearer in 1 Corinthians: it is the Body proffered by Jesus at the Last Supper; it is the crucified Body of Jesus, so that when it is eaten the death of Jesus is proclaimed as possessing saving efficacy and is made effectual; it is the flesh and blood of him who has been lifted up, by consuming which individuals are united in the community of the one pneumatic body of Jesus Christ (1 Cor 10:16f.). The permanence of this food in the Church and as the food of the Church follows from the command directly linked with the words of institution: "this do in commemoration (*Anamnesis) of me". The commission to do "this" henceforth ensures the constant efficacious presence of the whole reality of Christ wherever "this", namely, the Lord's Supper, is legitimately celebrated by the disciples of Jesus. In this re-enactment of the Last Supper, willed by Jesus himself, Christ's bloody sacrifice on the cross becomes present at the same time, because the Flesh and Blood of the *suffering* and *dying* servant of God become present, and only can become present by Jesus' own institution, as delivered and shed for "many" (that is, for countless multitudes), and because this presence of Christ's sacrifice is given to the Church in the form of a liturgical act of *sacrifice. Thus the Church's celebration of the Eucharist always remains both a true meal, since Christ's body and blood are really there as food, and at the same time a new sacrifice, since in it the *one* sacrifice of Jesus *in* history remains constantly efficacious and is constantly made effectual in the celebration of the Eucharist through the liturgical act of re-presentation performed by the essentially historical entity that is the Church. Consequently, theology cannot study these two realities, in the one eucharistic celebration, in total isolation from each other; reference to the sacrifice of the *Mass must therefore do duty for a

EUCHARIST

complete explanation of the Eucharist.—The Incarnation, resurrection, and ascension of the Lord are also made present (see Jn 6:57f.; Heb 10:5–10).

(2) In the fullest and most original sense, the Eucharist is a *sacrament (D 802, 1601, 1866 and *passim*) directly instituted by Christ (D 1320ff., 1601, 1636ff., 1866), in which the true Body and Blood of Jesus (and therefore the whole, saving, concrete reality of the Lord) are really present (D 700, 793f., 802, 860, 1320f., 1636f., 1651ff., 1658, 1866, 2535), under each of the "species" of bread and wine (D 1198ff., 1257, 1320ff., 1636f., 1729, 1733, 1866, 2535) and in every one of their parts (D 1320ff., 1639ff., 1653, 2535, 3231). The Body and Blood of Christ and his sacrificial death become present in the Church's sacrifice of the *Mass (D 793f., 802, 822, 834, 854ff., 1739ff.) through the consecration pronounced by the priest (D 793f., 802, 1072ff., 1320ff., 1771ff.). Jesus' own words of institution, spoken by the priest are the "form" (D 782, 793f., 834, 1320ff., 1352, 1639ff., 1739, 1752). More specifically, this consecration must be understood as a genuine change of one *substance (that of wheaten bread and grape wine as the "matter": D 1320ff.) into another (namely the Flesh and Blood of Jesus; D 700, 802, 860, 1018f., 1320ff., 1642, 1866, 2535, 3891 and *passim;* *Transubstantiation). True though it is that the consecration occurs in view of the consumption of this Body and Blood of Jesus by the faithful who receive them in *communion, and that it is through the consecration especially that the renewal of the sacrifice of the cross is effected (by the Church) at this concrete moment within history (D 1739ff.), yet its actual realization in event remains in a permanent form: so long as the appearances of the "meal" (meant to be eaten) are given, Christ too is present (and to be adored) (D 1639ff., 1654). This abiding real presence of Christ remains however necessarily referred to the effectuation of this presence in the Church's eucharistic rite and to its purpose—a reception ("eating") by the believer.

(3) In celebrating and receiving the Eucharist the Church, and the individual believer, really celebrates "eucharist", that is, thanksgiving, in its highest possible, specifically "ecclesial" form, which is the privilege of the Church of Jesus Christ alone and at the same time a fundamental law binding her: by really "possessing" Jesus Christ himself within her and really, though in the bold reality of faith, partaking of him as her food, she "declares" (realizes, performs) that grateful response to God's offer of grace (his self-communication) which is his supreme gift of himself because it is "formulated" by the life of Jesus, in flesh and blood, ever loved and absolutely accepted.

156

The "effect" of the Eucharist, therefore, must not be conceived to be purely personal, occurring in the individual, giving him a personal share in the life of Jesus Christ and the grace to realize this in a life that is "Christian" (in the strict sense: representing the life of Jesus Christ by charity, obedience and gratitude to the Father, forgiveness and patience), but above all ecclesiological (social): in the Eucharist God's gracious unrepentant salvific will for all men becomes present, tangible and visible in this world, because it turns the tangible, visible community of the faithful (the Church) into that sign which does not simply point to a grace and salvific will of God that may exist somewhere, but *is* the tangibility and permanence of this grace and of salvation. Thus the sacrament of the Eucharist and the sacramentality of the Church are intimately connected (*Church, *Primordial sacrament).

EUCHITES

See *Messalianism.*

EVANGELICAL COUNSELS

Jesus' teaching aimed to put an end to men thinking about God in terms of laws or obligations. Instead, he wished to confront each individual with the demands expected of him by God (*Sermon on the Mount) Jesus conceived this demand neither as an enforcible programme nor as the mere proclamation of an attitude of mind; rather, he gave it concrete form in various suggestions or "counsels" by means of which the commandment to love God and our fellow men and women is formulated and interpreted in response to various existential situations. These exhortations have not been uniformly adopted by ecclesiastical tradition. While some things which Jesus states quite clearly and unequivocally (e.g., the counsel to renounce force) are frequently overlooked by the Church, others concerned with the vocation of the individual have been established as three "classic" counsels. These three evangelical counsels (*Virginity, *Poverty, *Obedience) depend on scriptural evidence of unequal clarity as to the nature of Jesus' counsel. Jesus recognizes and recommends that celibacy which a man accepts as his personal vocation for the sake of the *basileia* (Mt 19:12). There is no question of a demand upon all; in this matter Paul has no command from the Lord (1 Cor 7:25), but for his part commends celibacy in view of the Christian eschatological situation (*Virginity). *Poverty and *obedience (which latter, however, in its scriptural sense, must be understood vis-à-vis the Word of God present in Jesus Christ and in relation to "service") may similarly be understood as special individual vocations from God, which as such are the gift of God and possible pointers to the saving kingdom of the last days. As a response of man, freely given under the impulse of grace, they can be regarded as a possible means to *perfection, provided that other means to the same end are also recognized in principle; insofar as the former vocation calls a concrete human existence in a particular situation (namely, that person's own) within the world, it cannot be *directly* compared with, or claim any superiority over, another vocation. As a direct manifestation of the eschatological Christian situation, the evangelical counsels in themselves, in renouncing earthly values, take precedence over the affirmation of earthly values as such (D 1810; see 3911f.).

EVE

From the Hebrew *hawwah,* derived by the Bible from the root *hayah,* to live; in the aetiological account found in the Bible, the "helper" the wife of *Adam. The parable of her production from Adam's rib declares that she is of the same nature as man, different in character but of equal value, a point which is elaborated by the very giving of her *name (Gen 2:23; *'ishshah,* the woman, displays the completeness of man, *'ish):* she stands on the same level of existence as the first man and is thus raised above all other forms of life. Together with the man she is the image of God in the world. Scripture regards the relationship between Adam and Eve as the archetype of *marriage according to the mind of God, the mutual intimacy of man and wife, the orientation of each to the other, parenthood.—See also *Protoevangelium.*

EVIL, WICKEDNESS

The real cause of evil is always the free choice of a created will, setting itself by this free choice in opposition to *good (God, purpose of existence, goal of life) (*Sin), so that evil is inconceivable without good. Evil is not only an absence of the good but an express and decisive renunciation of the good. In itself, therefore, it has no independent reality, it is not a primeval being opposed to God (Gnostic-

Manichaean *dualism), but the mysterious power God allows the free creature *(mysterium iniquitatis)* to disregard the beginning which has proceeded from God's goodness and the sense of creatureliness he has graciously imparted—to ignore the appeal, behind that personal freedom, of the God who has created for himself a free being to confront him, to deny him—and to persist in this incongruity, that is to say, in evil. According to Catholic doctrine such a rebellion (primeval rebellion) occurred among the first human beings (*original sin). The basic "entity" of evil already emerges in this first sin, rendering the creature (and all creation) autonomous vis-à-vis the Creator, diverting the course of the world from the creative and selfless love in which it began, to seek fulfilment in its own self. Hence the reality of evil in this world is to be seen not so much in disorder and disruption as in the organized attempt of the individual, of peoples, of the world as a whole, at self-sufficiency within this world. The end of the power of evil has been proclaimed and ushered in by the setting up of the *basileia* of God in this world which has occurred in Christ. By this means the original acceptance of man in Jesus Christ (*Christocentrism) as God's partner is itself shown to be a mighty encroachment upon sin, and thus not only to have made possible the return to God's dominion of each individual human being who by his own sin has ratified the evil intended in the first sin, and also by the power of grace to have effected that return at least for mankind as a whole, but also to have made God's loving control of his creation a palpable, historical power precisely where man's historical decision between good and evil occurs, that is, *in the midst* of the world.

Wickedness is the attitude of the human intellect and will which seeks evil not so much out of human frailty (uncertainty, blindness, lack of will-power) but rather for its own sake, deliberately, resolutely, treacherously, mercilessly, in contempt of God.

EVOLUTION

Connotes the alteration of something which at the same time perdures. It appears in human life in a great variety of forms (development of human thought, evolution of the world, of the environment, and similar cases) and is therefore an essential topic for theology. It is only in more recent times that theology has systematically treated of evolution and development, that is, since a somewhat parallel philosophical evolutionism (doctrine of development), found in Leibniz, Schelling, and Spencer—who regarded evolution as the principle of all reality and a revelation of the Absolute—and a biological evolutionism were first fused in Darwin's thesis of the origin of man. Faced with these doctrines of evolutionism, Catholic theology primarily emphasizes the difference between *creation and evolution. Creation connotes the pure beginning, the original institution of a being in its development. Evolution presupposes something already extant and denominates its temporal mode. Admittedly theological discussion of just how a thing can exist by creation and yet develop really only begins at this point. We should start from the principle that by producing the *creature God endows it with the power of self-fulfilment and the conditions necessary to that end, so that it is not to be assumed that God will himself produce what can be achieved by the immanent development of the creature. Once a theological *anthropology shows that *man is the goal of all creation, that creation has a real beginning (which is a theological concept, not a concept of natural science) and that every product of evolution remains in creaturely dependence on God (the measure of which dependence is of course the measure of the creature's independence), theology can be content to learn from natural science *what* can actually evolve within creation. As to the special problem which stirred up this discussion, see *Creation of Man, Descent of man*. Like the notion of the beginning, the genuine notion of the *end lies beyond the reach of natural science (*Basileia). To the extent that everything which has come to be in *historicity is taken up into eschatological fulfilment, there is a genuine development—even in respect of the ultimately and definitively valid—in which the personal spirit "becomes" itself while tending towards its goal. The best example of this type of development is the *Church.—See also *Development of Dogma*.

EXCOMMUNICATION

The custom already observed in the Old Testament of removing the serious offender from the sacred sphere of God's chosen people, and thus consigning him (even officially and tangibly) to the realm of uncleanness and vice which is exposed to the wrath of God. With the rise of the synagogue in Judaism, excommunication was developed into a formal disciplinary procedure, with a gradual and temporary separation as opposed to total exclusion (thus also in Qumran). This preliminary development only reaches fulfilment when adopted by the people of God which is the Church. Not only is St Paul familiar with excommunication, which he terms *anathema* (thing under a curse) and uses authoritatively in his communities (1 Cor 5:1–5; 1 Tim 1:18f.; Tit 3:9f. and *passim),* it also forms the substance of the power of *binding and loosing. Total exclusion from the Church of Christ is incurred only by wilful *heresy and wilful *schism, but excommunication exists (CIC c. 2257, § 1) as a corrective punishment whereby one who seriously offends against the ecclesiastical community (by a delict) can be excluded in three stages *(ipso facto,* after judicial sentence, and as a *vitandus)* from participating in the Church's self-realization (sacraments, liturgy, and the like). In former times political abuse often weighed upon ecclesiastical practice. The significance of excommunication in our present pluralistic society is small, but its permanent essence is authentically preserved in the sacrament of *penance. Since the Synod of Elvira about A.D. 300 councils have often attached the word anathema to heterodox propositions as a warning of excommunication and the judgment of God. Since the First Vatican Council it means that the proposition contradictory to the one condemned is a defined dogma.

EXEGESIS

From the Greek ἐξήγησις, interpretation; the name of that theological discipline which interprets *Holy Scripture by truly scientific methods—among them philology, *biblical criticism, and biblical history—but must not confine itself to applying these. As a Catholic science, exegesis must not merely accept the doctrine and direction of the Church's magisterium as a negative norm. It is among the tasks of Catholic exegesis to carry out the scholarly spadework which enables the Church's magisterium to offer a secure judgment on One meaning of a biblical text (Vat. II: Rev., 12), and to show the genuine compatibility of its findings with Catholic dogma and at least in principle with such teaching of the magisterium as is not defined (*Scriptural proof). Hence Catholic exegesis often becomes *biblical theology, which ideally is the same biblical theology presupposed by *dogmatic theology. Its principles are elaborated by *hermeneutics. Exegesis in the more restricted sense, as taught in theological institutes, gives a commentary on the individual books of Scripture, critically examines the text, considers the question of authorship and earlier sources, and draws upon historical, geographical, and archaeological data to elicit the *kerygma of the text. Where the scriptural text is to be translated into a modern language, all this preliminary work is indispensable.

EXEMPLAR CAUSALITY

See *Ideas, divine.*

EXISTENCE

In scholastic philosophy existence is real being as contrasted with merely notional being. It is in virtue of its existence that a thing can be encountered in the outside world; in virtue of its "being-such", or its *essence, it is some particular thing. Existence and essence are really distinguished in finite, contingent being, since not every conceivable essence is necessarily realized, but will be so if it also acquires existence.

In the philosophy of M. Heidegger, and similarly in the "philosophy of existence" in general, the concept of existence is confined to man, since man is that privileged entity which possesses the understanding of being, that is, understanding of itself, of its "there-ness" and of being in general. Hence human existence displays the real presence of *being; and therefore all philosophical enquiry into the nature of being must begin with the analysis of this existence (Theological *anthropology).

EXISTENTIAL ETHICS, PERSONAL ETHICS

Insofar as a man's moral behaviour is not merely an "instance" of a general, essential moral norm but the realization of himself in his unique individuality and this fact can and must be systematically investigated, an existential ethics can and must exist. The realization of a person falls within the scope of existential ethics insofar as it is possible to, and incumbent upon, him in a manner intimated to himself alone and is not adequately covered by general norms. To this extent existential ethics remains a necessary complement to "essential ethics", but not a substitute for it as *situation ethics maintains. The general moral norms worked out in the latter must be "applied" to each particular situation in which the agent finds himself; and by this situation we must understand that historical point of transition created by the unique personality of the individual, his personal relationships, his position in his own career and the kind of thought about general morals of which he is capable and from which his concrete moral action follows. In this "application" of the general moral norm to the individual's situation, the "thou" plays the part of generality in concrete form (community), for its part positively determining the situation of the agent, insofar as it is not only affected by the agent's activity but itself provokes and modifies this latter by concrete demands and restraints. Of course, this "thou" is not to be misconceived in an individualistic sense, but depends on larger social contexts. Within and behind the situation of the individual, even as determined by the demands of the "thou", a concrete call of God is legitimately presented to the individual concerned; and this call engages at once the agent in his moral behaviour, whose self-realization this call demands and bends in a particular direction, and the general moral law reflecting God's fundamental plan for man, society, and their environment, which is meant to be given effect through the activity of the individual and can only be given effect by that means.

EXISTENTIAL STATE

A technical term in M. Heidegger's philosophy which means the "self-confrontation" of the human existent, a "tempered" awakening to his condition, not reflection on his discovery of himself and, therefore, neither a feeling nor a mood but a basic disposition, characterized by "thrownness" and "being-in-the-world". This concept, akin to the scriptural notion of the *heart, is a suggestive one for Catholic theology since it recognizes and expresses the fact that once man begins to reflect on his own *historicity he awakens to himself as a *person, someone who has already achieved his *freedom by the very fact of achieving his subjectivity. Subsequent reflection (for instance on faith, conscience, the experience of grace), decisions and attitudes can neither adequately reflect this fundamental decision nor yet rescind it, still less adequately distinguish between the subject and his reflexive achievement of himself as a subject.

EXISTENTIAL, SUPERNATURAL

Underlying the concept of the supernatural existential is the following fact: antecedently to justification by *grace, received sacramentally or extra-sacramentally, man is already subject to the universal salvific will of God, he *is* already redeemed and absolutely obliged to tend to his supernatural end. This "situation" is not merely an external one; it is inclusively and inalienably precedent to man's free action, and determines that action; it does not exist only in God's thoughts and intentions, but is a real modification of man, added indeed to his nature by God's grace and therefore *supernatural, but in fact never lacking in the real order. It follows that even in the rejection of grace and in perdition a man can never be ontologically and subjectively unaffected by the inner figure of his supernatural destiny. Through his membership of the human race, a human being is however lastingly, inescapably and really conditioned by that human denial in regard to God which theological tradition calls *original sin. It is therefore permissible to call "original sin" an existential—but one which is of course encompassed and dominated by the more powerful supernatural existential of the *grace of God.

EXORCISM

See *Possession.*

EXPERIENCE

A form of *knowledge which arises from the direct reception of an impression from a reality (internal or external) which lies outside our free control. It is contrasted with that type, or aspect of knowledge in which man is an active agent, subjecting the object to his own viewpoints and methods and to critical investigation. An eminent degree of certainty ("evidence") attaches to experience since that which is experienced irresistibly attests its own presence. Religious experience in the strict sense, that which constitutes *faith, and inso-far as it does so, embraces at once the metaphysical, moral and existential experience of *being and *existence, and the experience of God's self-attestation in the occurrence of revelation, in which the fact of a divine self-attestation announces itself to the "conscience" (as the organ integrating all existentially meaningful knowledge, whether internal or external); as such, therefore, it includes the transcendental experience of man in which he has intuitively experienced himself, at least initially, that is, in his essential features (in a "first" experience), as one who is referred to things and the world, as the subject and ground of his thought and his acts. Religious experience as the inner self-attestation of supernatural reality (grace) is only possible to man, or to mankind, in the history of faith, in conjunction with objective, conceptual reflection of the mind upon itself. A clear-cut, adequate distinction between the creative working of God's grace and this its conceptual interpretation (on occasion incorrect) is not possible; no clear line can be drawn by reflective introspection between the natural transcendence of the mind towards God and the mind's participation by grace in the inner life of God (through Christ in the Holy Ghost), because God and his operations can never be grasped in isolation and clearly distinguished from the reflective activity of the created mind. The justified, in spite of the experience of grace, cannot be absolutely certain that they are in the state of grace (D 1533f., 1563f.; *Certainty of salvation). But since God's grace characteristically operates in the "theological virtues", which are supernaturally produced by God but precisely *as* virtues and as human acts, supernatural realities are revealed in these "responses" by the experience of peace, joy, confidence, consolation, light, and love.

EXTRA ECCLESIAM NULLA SALUS

Literally, from the Latin, "outside the Church there is no salvation". A principle formulated by Origen and St Cyprian and maintained by tradition, which does not signify that no grace is imparted "outside" the Church (D 2429), but that the grace which once for all has been offered to the individual for his justification through God's gift of himself in his incarnate Son and tangibly endures in history, remains historically present and tangible in the *Church; that where that grace is sought as *tangible* it is to be found only in the Church of Jesus Christ and her elements (Scripture, the sacraments, the example of a perfect Christian life); and that where it is given by God "outside" the Church that grace intrinsically still tends towards its historical embodiment in the Church. Since Vatican II takes into account the possibility of salvation for (guiltless) atheists and polytheists as something assured (Church/world, 22; Church, 16; Miss., 7), there is no cause for serious doubt that *all* human beings are *always* admitted to God's offer of his *grace which actually takes effect in them. The principle of "no salvation", etc., must therefore be interpreted in the light of this more inclusive teaching. See *Salvific will of God.*

EXTREME UNCTION

See *Anointing of the Sick.*

F

FAITH

In the widest sense faith means freely accepting what a person says because of one's confidence in that person. This is to say that faith always entails a relationship between *persons which stands or falls with the credibility of the person who is believed. In this way faith differs from knowledge which can be proved and from the arbitrary paradox of "blind faith". If this concept of faith is used in theology one must be quite clear from the first that it can only be applied to Christian faith analogically. For here it is God himself who is believed, God whom one believes and in whom one believes, provided of course that he makes himself known (*Revelation), and that for their part the witnesses chosen by God are credible—since the individual is not normally the direct recipient of revelation. Christian faith shares these formal characteristics with faith in general. But the fundamental difference between the two is that in Christian faith God's disclosure to the human person is not mere intellectual information, where God is merely an external motive of faith; rather the disclosure appeals to all the dimensions of man so as to order them all to God (*Self-Communication, *Grace) and its complete fulfilment is love. At the same time God the revealer communicates himself in such a way that this ordering of man to God lays claim to all man's subsequent life; discloses himself both as a lover and as man's surpassing (supernatural), final goal, containing in itself the perfect fulfilment of all hope.

FAITH IN SCRIPTURE. Faith is already presented as a personal relationship in the OT, above all as the relationship between God and the fathers of faith (Abraham, Gen 15:6; the Jews obediently leaving Egypt and traversing the Sea of Reeds, Ex 14:31; Isaiah trusting in the *hidden* God, Is 8:17); the word generally used for faith signifies "to be confident", "to hold fast". Faith, in the OT, also connotes the fidelity of the whole people and of the individual to the God of the Covenant in response to his fidelity (thus the Prophets in particular). Hence faith can take on the sense of *obedience, that is, to the will of Yahweh as revealed in the *Law, and of *confession, in face of Israel's later environment which had become too powerful to be defeated in war and had simply to be endured (*Monotheism). The basis of the Israelite's faith remains the mighty deeds that God has done for him, his people, or the fathers.

Passing over the use made of the word faith by Jesus himself and his precise purpose in working his indisputable *miracles in particular cases, we must say that Jesus demands faith when he requires recognition of the signs of the new and final dispensation which is inaugurated in him, signs which include all his activity (the preaching of the *basileia whose presence and power is proved by the casting out of *devils, the healing of the sick and the raising of the dead); and when he summons men to follow him (*Following of Christ): "Believe the Gospel" (Mk 1:15). This faith expresses itself in *metanoia, which means such a change of heart in man that he now hopes for things from God which before seemed impossible (Mk 9:32; 11:23f.). The faith of the later period which begins with the *primitive Church Jesus himself entrusted to witnesses, by gathering the disciples about him, clothing them with authority and founding the *Church (*Apostle, *Tradition). Accordingly, faith is not only confidence (Rom 4:24f.) and hope (Gal 5:5 and *passim*), but also believing the truth (Acts 6:7; Gal 5:7; Rom 1:5 and *passim*) and confessing it (Rom 10:9f.); faith may also mean the content of preaching (Gal 3:2, 5; Rom 12:6 and *passim*). St Paul and St John develop a very cogent and pregnant theology of faith. St Paul approaches the theology of faith in the light of the Jewish conception of the *Law as the means to salvation, showing instead, by the example of Abraham (Rom 4), that faith given in grace by God himself is the only way to the *justice which God demands. This faith, of which all men are capable (Gal 2:15ff.; Rom 3:21–31; 10:3–10 and *passim*), is regarded as one with *baptism and must preserve and manifest the new life given in baptism by active love (Rom 6; Gal 3:26f.; 5:6). St John constructs the theology of faith on the basis of the theology of the new life (Jn 3:16; 5:24; 6:29, 40, 47; 8:51; 11:25f.; 20:31 and *passim*), so that here too faith is a unique relationship both with God who begets us anew and with our brethren in the faith (Jn 13:34f.; 17:26; 1 Jn 3:23). As St Paul defends "his Gospel" by appealing to the tradition of the primitive

Church which he himself has received (1 Cor 11:23; 15:3 and *passim;* faith comes by hearing, Rom 10:17), so St John likewise stresses the fact that faith is based on the testimony of witnesses (Jn 5:31–47; 10:38 and *passim).*

SYSTEMATIC THEOLOGY OF FAITH. (1) Apart from formulating the content of faith in the *Creeds, the magisterium of the Church first concerned itself with faith in the decrees of the Second Council of *Orange, where it firmly maintained against *Semipelagianism (as Prosper of Aquitaine had done earlier in his *Indiculus*—the doctrine of which was afterwards adopted by the Church, D 236 –248, especially 244 –248—against *Pelagianism) that the first impetus to faith and the disposition to believe are gifts of God's *grace (D 373–378, especially 375). The Council of *Trent defined, against the Protestant conception of *fiducial faith, that faith is not mere confidence, but an act of assent to those things which God has revealed and promised (D 1526f., 1562); this faith is the gift of God's grace in us (D 1525, 1553), it is the beginning of human salvation, the foundation and root of all *justification (D 1532). Without works (that is to say hope and love) it is dead (D 1530f.). In the 19th century the magisterium defended the supernatural and gratuitous character of faith against *Rationalism (D 2738) and the reasonableness of faith against *Traditionalism (D 2751–2756, 2811–2816). The First *Vatican Council defined faith as follows: "Since man is wholly dependent on God, his Creator and Lord, and created reason is entirely subject to uncreated Truth, we are obliged to render God revealing the perfect obedience of our intellect and will in faith. This faith, which is 'the beginning of human salvation', the Catholic Church acknowledges to be a supernatural virtue whereby, impelled and sustained by grace, we believe those things to be true which God has revealed, not because we have perceived the intrinsic truth of these things by the light of our natural reason, but on the authority of God himself who reveals them, who can neither deceive nor be deceived. For 'faith', as the Apostle says, 'is the substance of things hoped for, the evidence of things that appear not (Heb 11:1)' " (D 3008). The Council then enlarges upon each of these qualities of faith (D 3009–3020). At Vatican II (Rev., 5) they are freed from a certain degree of intellectualistic restriction.

THE THEOLOGICAL PROBLEM. (1) *Faith as an act.* It is clear from contemporary discussion that since the Council of Trent the magisterium has increasingly drawn attention to faith as an act of the intellect. At the same time a *fundamental theology has been elaborated which concerns itself with the actual "preconditions of faith" (*Praeambula fidei), already worked out by St Albert the Great, St Thomas, and St. Bonaventure, and distinguishes the following elements in the preconditions for faith and the act of faith: the judgment of the intellect that the fact of revelation is credible, the judgment of the intellect that one has a duty to believe, that is an exercise of cognition as fulfilling the real *praeambula fidei;* then the free act of the will, which either commands the intellect to assent or does not (since the motive of faith is not so obvious as to compel assent); and finally, the intellectual assent as the real act of faith. This description of the act of faith raises two important theological questions. The first question is whether in practice, in concrete existence, knowledge of the *praeambula fidei* can be purely natural when the "beginning of faith" is a gift of God's interior grace: see *Praeambula fidei.* The second question is whether the act of faith is completely and adequately described as an act of the intellect, or whether this description merely throws into relief one essential aspect of the act of faith. With St Thomas we should regard the act of faith as primarily the ordination of the whole human person to God, since the act of faith totally concerns and engages the whole man; where we have such a radical and total fulfilment of man (which will of course pre-eminently affect the human mind: *spirit) it automatically becomes impossible adequately to distinguish between the individual elements of this act; but an analysis *a posteriori* depends on the ontology and psychology of the *one* human being.

The theology of the act of faith also investigates *what* is believed (material object) and the reason *why* it is believed (*Formal object, *Motive). Prior to any dispersion upon individual truths, the radical act of faith engages man in the self-communicating, incomprehensible *mystery of God, which reveals itself as the triune and incarnate God, who by his *grace establishes the believer in the *beatific vision of God, of which (according to St Thomas) faith is the beginning. Properly speaking the individual propositions which are believed are not the object of faith but the "means" of faith in which the whole is mediated under various aspects. Yet close examination of revelation (*Biblical criticism), and the selective denial of individual revealed truths on the part of heretics, show that it is necessary and wise to work out various propositions. Thus Catholic theology declares that it is possible and obligatory to believe only what is vouched for by the authority of God himself—what is formally (and virtually) revealed. A truth is formally revealed if it is directly contained as such in God's original revelation and does not require to be deduced with the help of other truths. It need not, indeed, be explicitly revealed; it may be found, in the course of human thought and experience, to be formally but implicitly revealed, so that the intrinsic elements of a truth already known stand out in a new light (*Development of dogma). That faith in a truth formally revealed, as revealed, Catholic theology calls divine faith; if in addition the truth is expressly proposed by the magisterium of the Church, then faith in it is called divine and Catholic faith (*Dogma). Those truths are virtually revealed which can only be deduced from revelation with the aid of other truths (*Demonstrative theology; *Dogmatic facts). Most theologians call faith in truths virtually revealed ecclesiastical faith, since it is directly based on the authority of the *Church. See also *Catholic Truths*.

As to the question *why* something is believed, we must distinguish between the motive of credibility (the reason for holding that the witness is sufficiently credible and that he in fact testifies to something) and the real motive of faith, that is, the sole authority of God, who is truth itself, incapable of deceiving anyone when he reveals himself (D 3008, 3537–3542): see *Analysis fidei*. Catholic theology holds that the act of faith is essentially supernatural, reasonable, and free. Faith is supernatural because it is only made possible by a supernatural interior *grace. This is known in Catholic tradition as the "light of faith", whereby we grasp what is materially revealed in terms of our conscious, though unthematic, dynamic supernatural ordination to the possession of God by direct vision (*Formal object, supernatural) and, spurning all weary scepticism, interpret the marks of credibility *as* marks of the supernatural credibility of God's revelation. Faith is reasonable, as *fundamental theology must show, because it engages man as an intellectual creature (*Spirit), demanding the total fulfilment of the human intellect, and because the *praeambula fidei* can be known with sufficient certainty; but not as if faith could comprehend absolute *mystery and subject it to rational analysis (D 3008f.). Faith is free because it is a personal act, and its *freedom is that freedom wherewith God in his grace has made us free so that we may believe. It also follows that faith is confident and certain (1 Jn 5:9; Rom 4:16–22). This does not mean that it is psychologically impossible to doubt or impugn it (see below). But the fact that God may reveal himself in an obscure manner, so that it is possible to doubt the revelation, does not mean that the believer's relationship with God is likewise contingent and open to doubt: this relationship means an unshakable decision for God, regardless of how clearly he is revealed, and for the truth of his testimony, a decision which acknowledges no other norm or judge. If one admits God is "given" only in an obscure manner, that faith in him does not always produce a positive solution of all the problems raised by existence and death in this world, if even after study and prayer one is tormented by anxiety that a proposition which the Church teaches as divinely revealed may after all not be revealed, all this does not amount to "doubting the faith". Doubts as sins against faith are usually complex acts which equally offend against the *Church, for instance presumptuously assuming that what the Church teaches is of "doubtful value". The First Vatican Council condemned that positive, not merely "methodical", scientific *doubt which G. Hermes had declared to be the necessary foundation of rational faith.

(2) *Faith as a virtue* (*Habitus). Insofar as faith, hope and love radically order the whole nature of that personal spirit which is man to the triune God of everlasting life in *sanctifying grace (as God's *self-communication), or as the "residue" of sanctifying grace, they are supernatural, "infused" *virtues which make acts elevated by grace possible and are the source of such acts (see D 1578, 3008).

(3) See also *Justification*. For the acceptance of the incarnate God by faith, see *Jesus Christ*.

(4) Since the grace which bestows faith enables man to accept the truth believed (the God believed) connaturally, the believer can achieve a grasp of the detailed content of faith which is based on a certain "instinctive" insight rather than on logical analysis; and this is equally true of the Church as a whole, in which the faith comes to be understood according to a kind of "collective sense" (J. A. Moehler)—there develops a sense or consciousness of the faith. Without doubt this sensibility of faith, already attested in Scripture, has played a considerable rôle in the *development of dogma, particularly in recent times; the magisterium indeed is its authentic interpreter, yet this magisterium itself rests upon the faith of the whole Church (cf. Vat II: Church, 12), which is alive and can mature and grow in knowledge. Insofar as the Church's sensibility of faith can be assessed "statistically" we speak of a *consensus (of the faithful).

FALL OF MAN

In Catholic theology it signifies chiefly the free decision of Adam to turn away from God (Rom 5; D 800), whereby he lost his holiness, justice, and exemption from death (*Original justice) (D 370f., 399f., 1511, 3514); thus the Fall is Adam's own personal *sin as distinguished from *original sin in his descendants, which can only be called "sin" in an analogical sense (D 780, 1006). The result of this free decision (the penalties of sin) does not mean that after the Fall Adam became a "pure nature", which after forfeiting its supernatural vocation to a share in the divine life could understand and round itself off merely in its own terms. Even after the Fall, man still has this supernatural *existential, this supernatural vocation remains incumbent on him as a real modification of his intrinsic being; it is finally fulfilled in the grace of the Second Adam (*Saving history). The scriptural account of the Fall (Gen 2f.) describes it as the transgression of a commandment of God, essentially disobedience and pride. We may assume that the rest of the description is simple popular imagery (D 3862f.); certainly it may not be taken to mean a primitive theft of fruit or illicit sexual intercourse (Gen 2:24). Similarly, whatever damage the first man suffered in body and soul (D 370f., 399f., 1511, 3514), the consequences of the Fall for himself, apart from the loss of *original justice, cannot be described as reduction to a lower morphological and cultural level, for Scripture says nothing of any such "miraculous punishment".

FATE

Fate exists for the Christian insofar as the free conscious activity of his life always takes shape against a prior and permanent exposure to the otherness of the world, to the incalculable and uncontrollable (since God himself remains essentially mysterious), so that the course of his life is governed less by his own plans than by what happens to him from without. Besides this, *death reduces man to impotence, and his greatest, most comprehensive, final act is to accept this utter impotence in the obedience of faith. But for the believer this fate is no impersonal force before which he can only hold his peace, or, if it be such a force, at least Christ has dethroned it (Rom 8:31–39). For the very Spirit of that God whom the Christian calls Father, has stripped the uncontrollable event, the inescapable burden, of their power. God is indeed mystery, yet he knows himself, he communicates himself and therefore also the meaning of all he "sends" to man; he is wise Love, who reverences his creature, and by the Incarnation has made fate his own destiny. Because it happens in grace and as *revelation, obedient acceptance of fate, which transfigures it, is already *faith and, where it reaches its perfection, *love; it is already anonymous Christianity, acceptance which is conquest, the redemption of fate.

FATHERHOOD OF GOD

In a wide sense God can be called the father of men because he is the wise, merciful, mighty, personal cause of the world and especially of men, by *creation, *conservation, and *providence, to whom men owe reverence (*Adoration) and whose laws they must obey. This analogous statement (*analogia lutis) affirms neither closeness to God in the form of crude trust or identification of God with a super-father-figure. But in the specifically Christian sense God (strictly: the first *Person in the *Trinity) is the Father of men because he makes them his own children (Divine *sonship, *Regeneration) by the self-com-munication of his own divine being (*Grace, *Justification, *Holy Spirit) in supernatural grace, so that they are conformed to the image of his Son and vivified by his *Pneuma (Rom 8), made partakers of the divine nature (2 Pet 1:4), born of God (Jn 1:12f.; 3:3–5; 1 Jn 3:1–9).

FATHERS OF THE CHURCH

According to the definition of Vincent of Lerins (mid-5th century), Fathers are those writers of Christian antiquity who each in his own time and locality were accredited doctors of the one faith in commu-nion with the Church. They are distinguished in the following ways: (1) orthodox doctrine, which, to be sure, does not imply infallibility and does not exclude actual errors in particular matters; (2) a holy life in the sense of Christian antiquity; (3) recognition by the Church, which need not be explicit but may be expressed by quotation from their writings; (4) they must have lived in patristic times, that is, before the death of Isidore of Seville in the West or St John Dama-scene in the East (about the middle of the 8th century). They are of special authority when they teach a doctrine by unanimous *consent, for then they can be unreservedly taken to be transmitting and bearing witness to the teaching of the Church. For their doctrine see *Patristics, Neo-Platonism*.

FEAR OF GOD

Holy "fear" of the absolute, incomprehensible, holy God is an element of the religious *act by which the human creature presents himself to God in *adoration, because here man recognizes that he is utterly

174

dependent and a sinner. It signifies no contradiction of confident love but rather an element of the latter (even in heaven: D 735) which characterizes it precisely as love of *God:* God is recognized and loved because the utter difference between God and oneself is recognized and loved. It would serve little purpose to explain this fear in terms of human fear or terror since it is a relationship *sui generis.* Fear for one's own salvation is not unworthy, though it may not be inspired by *love of God, since to accept one's own creatureliness is to recognize one's need of salvation. Indeed an unselfish, absolutely fearless unconcern about one's salvation would amount to presumption, an attempt to be like the God who is self-sufficient and never in jeopardy. Thus fear for one's own salvation (D 1533f., 1541, 1563; Mt 5:29; 10:28; Jn 5:14; Phil 2:12; Rom 11:20 and *passim),* considering God's unfathomable *justice, is another element in the complete concept of the fear of God, and accordingly plays its part in the process of justification (D 1526f., 1558), it may be the morally justifiable motive which (as servile fear, *timor simpliciter servilis)* brings one to the act of *repentance (D 1456, 1558, 1677f., 1705 and *passim;* *Attritionism). There is of course no moral act if God's punishment is simply feared as a physical evil, without any realization of the sinfulness of offending God, for then there is no interior aversion from sin as such *(timor serviliter servilis,* craven fear). Even that repentance which springs from fear and is morally justifiable as a preparation for justification only reaches its goal (justification) if it is transformed by a personal act and (or) a sacrament and integrated by the love of God in which God is loved for his own sake, so that the fear of God becomes a loving reverence *(timor filialis:* D 1677f.), so that one fears God out of love instead of loving him out of fear (St Francis de Sales).

FEELING, RELIGION OF

Feeling is a necessary element of piety insofar as feeling must be understood as an awakening to the objective world or (in relationships between persons) to the other person in his specific otherness, resulting in a subjective emotion. To exalt this element into an absolute, in the religion of feeling, is to ignore the fact that the true religion has been founded in the rationally intelligible word of the self-uttering God and that a correspondingly rational acknowledgment of this divine economy cannot be excluded from the nature of true religion.

FIDEISM

In particular a doctrine which emerged towards the end of the last century at Paris (in the faculty of Protestant theology), according to which the concepts and propositions of faith are only symbols of a faith which has been acquired antecedent to any conceptual formulation and independent of historical certainty and theological analysis. According to fideism, only the conviction and devotion of the heart avail to salvation, not the mind's certain knowledge in faith.—See also *Traditionalism* for a Catholic version of fideism which gives little weight to human reason and the conceptual presentation of faith.

FIDELITY OF GOD

See the following references: 1 Corinthians 1:9; 10:13; 1 Thessalonians 5:24. God is always faithful to his promises. His fidelity gives man, who can neither adequately plan his history nor gain a general view of it, the assurance that despite the apparently disconnected vicissitudes of his life it all has a single goal, a meaning, an inner coherence, though the ultimate significance of God's pledge may only appear in the course of the history of this salvation of mankind and the individual, though the redemption that engulfs human sin remains the sheer grace of God, for as such it cannot be reversed even by man (Rom 11:29; 2 Tim 2:13).

FIDUCIAL FAITH

A term in apologetics for the notion of faith put forward by the Reformers; according to them justifying *faith is identical with that "strong, firm confidence *(fiducia)* of the heart" in God's forgiveness in Christ despite the continuing sinfulness of man. They stress the passive character of fiducial faith (as against free assent), its reference to individual salvation as such (as against dogmatic faith in general revealed truths), its power to justify of itself. The difference between this doctrine and the Catholic doctrine of justification, rightly understood, is almost purely verbal, assuming that both sides can see today that grace and freedom are entities that grow in the same proportion, not in inverse proportion; that justifying faith is in fact the individual's firm hope of salvation; that faith which attains the complete fulfilment of its nature in total self-surrender to God is that charity which makes faith justifying faith.

FILIOQUE

From the Latin, literally "and from the Son"; an addition to the Creed of Nicaea-Constantinople first made by the Latin Church at the end of the 7th century. It means that the Holy Spirit proceeds from the Father "and the Son" as from a single principle (*Trinity). The addition was not adopted everywhere with the same readiness; not at Rome, apparently, until about A.D. 1000. It was opposed in particular by the Greek Church and has been the principal issue in that Church's dispute with the Latin Church since A.D. 867. To this day the Greeks consider it the original cause of the schism, though there was agreement between the two parties, both as to the expressed truth and as to the inclusion of the Filioque in the Creed, at the Council of *Florence (1439) which effected their reunion.

FINALITY

See *Goal, Purpose, Teleology.*

FLESH

See *Body, Sarx.*

FLIGHT FROM THE WORLD

Conscious and positive withdrawal from this world (with the intention of saving the world insofar as it is God's creature and the recipient of his salvation) is the duty of every Christian (a part of Christian life) insofar as the *world in the biblical sense means all those human beings who by sin have closed themselves to God and the divine *self-communication that is proferred in *grace, together with the relationships they have created, when these are a *temptation to further sinful rejection of God. In a stricter sense flight from the world is active renunciation of earthly values which in themselves are positive (*Evangelical counsels) in order to give practical expression to one's readiness in loving faith to accept the self-communication of God's love, even when the finitude of a world forfeit to death and the tragedies of life seem to belie this faith (when the "world" flees man) and when one must recognize and accept participation in Christ's death as such: this is flight from the world as practice for sharing the death which is the world's fate, and as a concrete expression of the God-given will to grace beyond all earthbound sense and meaning— all this in and for the Church. The "worldly" form of flight from the world also has something to teach Christians: since human *hope *also* requires critical distance in practice, flight from the world in a "secular" form often appears as refusal (protest against injustice, partial identification, etc).

FLORENCE

Pope Eugenius IV translated the 17th Ecumenical Council (*Basle) to Ferrara in 1437 and to Florence in 1439, where it brought about the (temporary) reunion of the Roman Catholics with the Greeks (July 16th, 1439), Armenians (November 22nd, 1439) and Copts (February 4th, 1442) and, after a further removal to Rome in 1443, union with the Syrians (September 30th, 1444), many Chaldaeans and Cypriot Maronites (August 7th, 1445). The definitions of the Council concern the *Filioque, the admission of the justified to the *beatific vision immediately after death, and the primacy of the *Pope (D 1300–1307). The decree for the Armenians sets forth in detail the doctrine of the seven sacraments (D 1310–1327), the decree for the Jacobites deals with the doctrine of the Trinity, Christology, the Old Law, infant baptism, the goodness of everything created, and membership of the Church (D 1330–1351).

FOLLOWING OF JESUS

This demand which Jesus makes of the believer (Mt 8:22; 9:9; 10:38; 16:24; 19:21; Mk 8:34; Lk 14:25–35) means neither merely following Jesus' example, as the paragon of obedience to a general law, nor "copying" Jesus' life, nor—according to all our NT texts—the actual, physical relationship of the disciple and assistant with Jesus the "Master" and teacher in the manner of the teacher–pupil relationship of that time, but the readiness in faith to yield full power over oneself to the kingdom of God (*Basileia) which is present in Jesus, definitively present in this way only in him, and which lays claim to every human being; denying oneself (*Self-denial) and accepting the cross of Christ.

FORCE

See *Violence.*

FORM

In general that ("shape", "structure") which imprints a particular way of being on a thing (material or otherwise). In Aristotelian-Thomistic metaphysics form means the intrinsic principle which determines the real character of any being and gives it being; to this extent form is a concept correlative to *matter and exists only in the determination and realization of matter. God—in whom there is no distinction between form and a matter which has to be shaped by form and is never quite exhausted by it—can be conceived as "pure" form. Hence *spirit, even a created spirit, is free, immaterial presence to itself and can, like God the pure spirit, be called *forma formarum,* because it embraces all being.

In sacramental theology the form is taken to mean the words that "shape" and give sense to a given "matter" (an action of the priest and the material things used in it; or, as in penance, the outwardly expressed receptivity to be displayed by the person receiving the sacrament), thus wholly "forming" it into the sacramental sign.

FORMAL AND FUNDAMENTAL THEOLOGY

This term might be used for that part of strictly systematic theology (*Dogmatic theology) which works out the "formal" and permanent basic structures of saving history (basic relationship of God and creature; general concept of personal revelation in word and deed; concept of redemptive revelation). It could be called "fundamental" (not to be confused with *fundamental theology) in that it presents these formal categories as means to the understanding of *saving history (to be described in the "special dogmatic theology" corresponding to "formal and fundamental theology"). It would be "fundamental" as confronting this general and formal pattern of revelation in Christianity with the formal structures of the life of the human mind in general, within which, after all, this history of revelation occurs, into which it is plunged, and out of which some way of access to this historical revelation must be shown. *Fundamental theology would still retain its own field: the rational justification of faith in the fact of Christian revelation; the fact and the "material", actual structure of revelation.

FORMAL OBJECT, SUPERNATURAL

Behind this term lies a problem of Catholic theology which has long been discussed but to which as yet no agreed solution has been found: Is the supernatural *salutary act of the person whom *grace has capacitated for such acts, salutary solely on the grounds of the ontic structure grace gives it, or is the person's consciousness (in the most comprehensive sense of this word) graciously elevated ("affected" by grace)? Is a man's knowing affected by grace or only his being?

Insofar as grace is in germ, that is, really and efficaciously, a participation in the life of God and the whole spiritual activity of man is thus already (here and now) directed towards the essentially supernatural *beatific vision (possession of God), we can speak of man's cognitive intentionality being elevated by grace ("illuminated", Scripture says) and directed to a supernatural formal object—the infinite reality of God himself; and this intentionality, so directed, forms the non-objective and non-specific "horizon", in a kind of fundamental existential situation, within which everything of moral and religious (that is, existential) significance is contained and ordered to its last end. There are no compelling grounds for maintaining the limited, merely ontic elevation of the human supernatural act, even though no clear distinction can be drawn by introspection between this intentionality and the transcendentality of the spirit.

FORTITUDE

In the Thomist doctrine of the virtues fortitude is the third *cardinal virtue, whereby man stands firm in *hope against the overwhelming pressures and tragedies of the world and against fear, especially the *dread of death; it is ordered to *prudence, since fortitude is not meant to be pointless daredevilry. Traditional doctrine often confuses fortitude with Stoic indifference ($\dot{\alpha}\pi\dot{\alpha}\theta\epsilon\iota\alpha$).

FREEDOM

Human freedom necessarily forms part of the object of *anthropo-logy, philosophical as well as theological. What sets man apart from everything else in his environment is the basic fact that he does not "exist" harnessed to a universal natural order which totally deter-mines the fulfilment of his nature, but rather is set in "openness". This means that by *work, etc., he must himself realize the various histori-cal possibilities of his self and through this effort discover the charac-ter of his nature (individually and as a member of the human race). To renounce this freedom would therefore be to renounce this con-stituent of human nature and so ultimately an abandonment of him-self. Man must accept his summons to personal freedom. The "positive" freedom (that is, the "freedom for"), based on this commis-sion, also entails a "negative freedom": man's free power to do this or that, to refrain from doing this or that. In realizing his personal freedom the individual human being meets with other free "independ-ences", which can either open or close themselves to his own pur-poses, and which can limit the scope of freedom and thus its objectivization, but not freedom itself. The "freedom of choice" in-volved in man's spiritual personality is also the condition, confirmed by revelation, for the existence of guilt (*Sin), and is also realized in the acceptance of justification in faith and love and in every salutary act. The existence of freedom and its realization in sin and *salutary act is defined as a truth of faith (D 330–339, 685, 1486, 1515, 1554ff., 1927f., 1965ff., 2002ff., 2409ff., 2621, 3010, 3875ff. and *passim*). Ini-tially, therefore, freedom is a transcendental peculiarity of all being, which is accorded to a creature in accordance with the level of being, and is known as freedom proper where spiritual persons are con-cerned. Created freedom is intended in the factual order to make possible the personal, free self-communication of God to a free part-ner in a reciprocally free dialogue. A conception of existential freedom of choice as an essential dignity of the *person—developed from the nature of the love of God and the partner necessary to it—provides the foundation for the doctrine of freedom of conscience rightly un-derstood, of the right to the scope necessary for the concrete realiza-tion of freedom as against all forcible abolition or undue restriction of this scope by the power of civil or ecclesiastical society (*Tolerance, *Emancipation). As a *theological concept* in the strict sense (within theological anthropology) the "freedom of the children of God" is the fundamental kerygma of Jesus Christ's gospel (Rom 8:15). This text deals with freedom as a fruit of *redemption in Jesus Christ and as

181

the unfolding of the Spirit he has given. This Christian freedom connotes liberation from the determining factor of sin, external legalism and *death and thus from slavery to worldly powers in general. Positively, it signifies the Spirit-given vitality of the heart, released from above, which springs from the revelation and communication of God's redemptive love in Jesus Christ and has its true basic form in love as the "great gift of grace". This means both candid, confident, cheerful freedom towards the Father and, in the spirit of God's redemptive love, loving intimacy with everything created, primarily with men and above all with "all that labour and are burdened". This liberated freedom has been proclaimed, and by God's gift in Jesus Christ established and begun as an "earnest" (Rom 8:23), yet it is still cloaked in and menaced by the conditions of existence in this world (D 330–339, 378, 383, 396, 633, 1521 and *passim)*. This means that is is often in danger of being used as a pretext for self-seeking and excess (Gal 5:13). By its nature Christian freedom has an eschatological structure: though it has truly begun, it must with all creation patiently await final, complete deliverance from bondage into the freedom of the glory of the children of God (Rom 8:21) in which the freedom wherewith Christ has made us free is to issue.

FREQUENT CONFESSION

Frequent confession of such circumstances and occurrences of everyday Christian life as do not oblige one to confess them as sins in the sacrament of *penance (venial sins) was unknown for centuries, but is recommended by the Church and prescribed for seminarists and religious by the CIC. Frequent confession is not a *necessary* means to obtaining forgiveness of venial sins and an increase of grace, because both are possible without the sacrament. Nor should one overlook the danger of excessive frequency arising from a misunderstanding of the rôle of the sacraments. But the practice is sound because the opening of conscience is valuable, together with personal direction in the objective context of the sacrament and under the seal of confession; because it repeatedly acknowledges that God's deed alone blots out our sins and that human contrition requires the divine response that has been historically established in the Church; and because it exercises fraternal charity.

FUNDAMENTAL ARTICLES

A term used in Protestant theology to designate those truths of faith which, by contrast with the non-fundamental articles, a person must believe in order to be saved (*Necessity for salvation). In the Catholic view, the duty of faith extends to everything revealed by God, though there is a "hierarchery" of truths of faith, in accordance with the different relation to the foundations of Christian belief (Vat. II, Ecum., II).

FUNDAMENTAL THEOLOGY

(1) Fundamental theology arose from the conflict of Christianity, from its earliest days, with its non-Christian "intellectual environment" and from the responsible thrust of Christian belief (1 Pet 3:15). Its earliest form, the "apology", directed against paganism (*Judaism, *Gnosis, *Manichaeism), developed into a more and more systematic apologetics (St Thomas Aquinas: *Summa contra Gentiles)* no longer, as such, necessarily directed against those who denied Christian Revelation, but designed to clarify "fundamental" problems so that Christian theology might better understand itself. Influenced by the subsequent need to defend the faith against Deism, Rationalism, Idealism, and Materialism, this "apologetics" enlarged on the following themes: questions of existential ontology as to the possibility of knowing revelation (motives of faith, disposition to faith, *praeambula fidei,* miracles, *prophecies); that is, the nature, possibility, and knowability of a possible *revelation; possible forms of such revelation; the fact of the Revelation that has occurred in Christ; its historical structure; its historical proofs. Another section of this apologetics develops the historical permanence of this Revelation through the establishment of the *Church; the Church's structure as an historical society (*Apostles, hierarchy, primacy, *magisterium, *Pope, *infallibility); her essential marks (unity, sanctity, catholicity, apostolicity).

(2) Fundamental theology today, above and beyond this form of apologetics and proof of the occurrence of Christian Revelation, seeks increasingly to take the place of that part of systematic theology (dogmatic theology) where it tries to take stock of itself in a "formal and fundamental" way. Fundamental theology would then approximate to "formal and fundamental theology" and thus explicitly become part of *dogmatic theology itself, so far as the latter, within its appropriate sphere, must as a science seek to explain and substanti-

ate itself; yet in method it remains separate, because the "material" enquiry of dogmatic theology into what is conceretely contained in Revelation can, and for didactic reasons should, be distinguished from the enquiry of formal and fundamental theology into the "formal modes" of Revelation. Fundamental theology enlarges the horizon of dogmatic theology to include general anthropology and comparative religion; and conversely brings the data of these sciences into the formal and fundamental investigations of this systematic theology. Thus man is shown to be a being capable of hearing (*Potentia obedientialis) a possible revelation from God; but also one, in his ever individual situation as one who hears, wishes to believe, doubts or in fact believes, who is a particular concretion of religiousness-possible-in-the-world and religiousness actually verified or else a concretion of possible and actual resistance to God's transcendent disposition. Nowadays fundamental theology has to reflect not only on internal problems for faith but on threats to it from the social world without. The relationship between theory and practice has to be considered when examining that between theology and philosophy. The factors affecting historical understanding, including the category of the future, and critical solidarity with the oppressed must enliven theology (*political theology). This integration of man's historical, social and religious disposition into the domain of theology through the scientific, methodical labour of fundamental theology, would complete theology itself as the genuine "dialogue" which God himself has begun by making his Word flesh (Incarnation) in the situation of this world, and which he absolutely wills to be continued.

FUTURE

Man's future in the theological sense is not only what has not yet happened, what in fact will one day happen, but that obligatory and accessible *goal which was already set man in the *beginning by his nature (*Essence) and his supernatural *existential, the goal towards which he can and must tend in order to win it both as his own achievement and as the gift of God's free grace. This true and final future, made possible by God's *salvific will, has "already begun" because the definitive future of the world has already started to exist in the *resurrection of Jesus, which in virtue of the principle of *solidarity is also the actual beginning (more than the mere promise) of our own future. By man's openness to it in faith, the future which seems not yet to exist, becomes the perspective in which the past is

184

interpreted and the present endured. Christianity sees itself as the expectation of a future which of itself draws close to and brings about the consummation of history so that no further greater future may be awaited behind or beyond the approach of this future that leads to consummation: this approaching future is therefore for Christianity an absolute future; i.e., "absolute future" is a hermeneutically suitable term for God. The future of the world considered in purely secular terms is, with the *world's increasingly secular nature, increasingly a matter of rational and deliberately planned construction by men and women. Christianity regards humanizing work towards this secular future, provided it is not subject to *ideology, as a genuinely religious task of bringing about openness in faith and hope for the absolute future in the progressive liberation of men and women.

G

GALLICANISM

See *Conciliarism*.

GENERATIONISM

The doctrine that parents produce the body *and* the soul of their offspring out of inanimate matter (thus theologians of Antiquity like Tertullian, and the adherents of *Traducianism). The magisterium has condemned the opinion that the human soul is generated by the parents alone (D 360f., 1007, 3220); the Catholic doctrine, instead, is *Creationism (D 3896). The problems posed by generationism remain unresolved: children are not generated out of inanimate matter but out of living substance. Natural science generally accepts ontogenesis (development of the organism out of a germ), but theology has not yet arrived at a very satisfying conception of the special creation of each soul and the union of the parents' activity with that of God. The notion of the self, transcendence of matter (of which it is incapable by its own unaided efforts) may offer some clarification of the problem.—See also *Creation of Man*.

GLORY OF GOD

Scripture regards the glory of God as man's recognition of God's *doxa*, as this appears in the various (self-) revelations of God. Such are the numerous doxologies (formulae of praise, most of which already had their place in the *liturgy of the primitive Church). Dogmatic theology, at the same time, sees the glory of God *(gloria)* as an

186

ontological perfection of God (*Holiness of God) which is known and acknowledged (honour in an analogous sense), but also as supreme recognition (praise, glorification) of this perfection itself. The internal glory of God is God's self-possession in knowledge and love (formal glory of God); the external (formal) glory of God is knowledge and recognition on the part of the creature. The internal (formal and material) glory of God is identical with God's communicable plenitude of being (communicated by creation and grace), which for its part is the "sense" of the divine act of creation; the external (formal and material) glory of God is thus that perfection of being to which creation, as a participation in God's plenitude of being, is itself ordered. Thus, by God's gracious *self-communication in Christ, the creature's spiritual recognition of God is based on that which God himself possesses as his own internal glory (*Doxa).

GLOSSOLALIA

See *Charism.*

GNOSIS

From the Greek γνῶσις, knowledge. (1) In a genuinely Christian sense gnosis means the charismatic knowledge comprised in ἀγάπη (*Charity), as an element of faith, not something surpassing faith, which St Paul attributes to the perfect "spiritual" man, who is in the πνεῦμα (*Pneuma); that knowledge in which, by faith, man ultimately "grasps" in ever increasing measure God's incomprehensible love revealed in the cross of Christ, and thus allows himself to be engulfed in ever increasing measure by this love as that which is wholly and ultimately real. This growth means a *unifying* understanding of the *whole* of revelation as such and of its ever more personal relevance to one's own existence. This theological knowledge is ordered of its own nature to *contemplation, should be shot through by the *wisdom of the *Holy Spirit, should become "charismatic", "prayerful theology", should spring from the realization in the liturgy of what is believed and occur in love in a personal "connaturality" with the mystery of faith (D 2324). All *theology needs such gnosis.

(2) Gnosis in a heterodox sense means at once a recurrent attack on Christianity (leading even to estrangement in heresy) and a fundamental attitude. The gnostic phenomena are usually referred to under

the collective name "Gnosticism", on the basis of particular views which are common to all gnosis. Among the most important of these are: a rejection of the concrete present; a "flight" into the sphere of the divine, reached by philosophical knowledge and by asceticism (and pictured in speculations about spirits and angels); *dualism, absolute or relative (limited by the end of the world); rejection of legal norms (*Antinomianism). Gnosis of this kind existed in the Jewish environment of the NT, for instance in the Qumran brotherhood; it was found in those circles which St Paul attacked in the Epistle to the Colossians (for diminishing the position of Christ) and in the Pastoral Epistles (myths, hostility to marriage) and against which the Apocalypse is directed. At the same time it must be recognized that the NT makes partial use of gnostic terminology precisely in order to reject this sort of gnosis out of hand (*Demythologization). Among the radically anti-gnostic features of the NT are the emphatic teaching that the perfecting of the world and of the individual are the business of God alone, who alone gives *salvation, the emphasis on the fleshly, bodily existence of God's Logos become true man and the scandal of the cross, the once-for-all and gratuitous nature of redemption. From the beginning of the 2nd century a gnosis of Eastern origin, incorporating fragments of Christianity in its system, was most dangerous because it was based on genuine religious experience and was a powerful opponent of the early Church. An early gnostic group, found at Antioch about A.D. 120 (teaching *Docetism and absolute sexual continence), the disciples of Basilides at Alexandria, A.D. 120–145 (noted for gnostic exegesis of the Gospels and composition of hymns), and the adherents of Valentinus at Rome (A.D. 145–160), who set up a dualistic myth of redemption, are of chief importance. Marcion, who was excommunicated at Rome in A.D. 144, rejected the "Jewish God" (the whole OT) root and branch and set up a canon, which he had purified of "Jewish elements", consisting of St Luke and ten epistles of St Paul, was not a real gnostic, but his followers were. The reaction against this gnosis was the Church's earliest *development of dogma, a splendid Catholic literature (St Justin Martyr, St Irenaeus, Tertullian, Hippolytus) and theological efforts to "baptize" the profounder and valid insights of the gnostics (*Alexandria, school of). The Catholic defence concentrates on a thoroughgoing affirmation of Christ's genuine humanity and therefore of the dignity of the flesh (*Resurrection of the flesh). Gnostic opinions have frequently been revived in medieval and modern times (Theosophy, Anthroposophy, Rosicrucianism, etc.). Above all theology must reject gnosis because of the following features which it exhibits; gnosis is knowledge derived from the discovery of human nature itself, not from a gratuitous, personal self-disclosure of God—ultimately, that is, it is "self-consciousness", not obediently hearing the word of God, not faith. The gnostic "redeemer" only helps man to penetrate to his own buried nature and is not a true man in concrete history, first creating the salvation that he bestows. Knowledge redeems as such and of itself alone; love and moral behaviour are at most a consequence of knowledge, so that objectively and subjectively gnosis is everything. Thus gnosis affirms that at the last man finds the absolute, all-embracing unity of all things in himself; it ignores the fact that man in his creaturely *pluralism is ordered to the unity of God which always transcends him, so that his existence will resist being reduced to mere knowledge. Knowledge, in gnosis, becomes a "closed" system reflecting a world which takes its course by necessity, logical or physical, and therefore excludes all real personal freedom and *historicity, all that is unique, leaving no room for the *mystery of the heart of being—that incomprehensibility of God which abides although it has "drawn close" to us—but treating it as though it had been unveiled and mastered.

GOAL

An ontological notion which has to be grasped by a transcendental act of the mind. A being in *time which owing to its temporality possesses the elements of its being "disjunctively" and yet experiences its time as a single complex, does not already possess its "end", its perfection, and herein its whole history in its *beginning (initial *essence); and yet this beginning is not indifferent to the end (the perfected essence), but is ordered to the end as determinate and already foreseen in the beginning: the end is "the goal" of the beginning. When man freely and deliberately sets himself particular goals we have a distinct kind of goal and teleology but not the real foundation of this notion, which is supra-anthropomorphic. The notion is important for an understanding of theological propositions concerning divine *providence, the creation of the world to the *glory of God, man's *supernatural destiny, the *natural moral law. A sound grasp of the concept of goal enables one to perceive that essential and teleological ethics are basically the same.

GOD

Latin, *Deus;* Greek, Θεός ; Hebrew, *El, Elohim, Yahweh.* God is the name for him who reveals himself in the OT as unbounded (Is 6; Kg 8:27), the incomparable (Ps 139:7–12 and *passim),* radically alive (Ps 90), the absolute master of being, future and trustworthy (Ex 3:13f.), whose omnipotence is not proved in the abstract but historically by the mighty deeds he has done for his people Israel before the gentiles, who shows himself beyond all doubt to be personal by his loving choice of the people of the *Covenant and of the individual. Jesus acknowledges this same God as his Father, who has graciously forgiven and accepted man in Jesus and in Jesus has granted him access to his *basileia.* Of his nature he is invisible (Rom 1:20; Jn 1:18; 6:46), known only to the Son (Jn 1:18 and *passim),* but he is recognized as love by his self-communication to the Son and through the Son to the brethren (Jn 4:16f.), and finally he has become visible in Jesus, his true image (2 Cor 4:4; Col 1:15). Christian philosophy and theology conceive God in terms of the analogy of being as absolutely holy, supreme, exalted above the world, personal, absolutely necessary, uncaused, existing of himself, and therefore the eternal and infinitely perfect being (D 3001), who has created everything else out of *nothing (*Creation; *Conservation of the world). Of course these reflections and analogous formulations *(*analogia entis)* cannot possibly include all possible experiences of the human history of faith and hope. The following considerations, which offer a theoretical summary of the "practical statement, God", are primarily of theological import:

(1) Since God exists absolutely of himself he cannot be called "being" in the same sense as created being. *Being can be attributed to him simpliciter and absolutely *(esse ipsum subsistens)* since he possesses the *principle of his existence in himself, that is in his own nature (*Aseity); whereas created being only possesses being as derived from God (*Contingence, *Causality) and therefore is only being by *analogy. Because God is absolute being in eternal self-possession he can neither be limited nor "added to"; no unrealized positive potentiality is to be found in him, he is pure *act. God's absolute spirituality is grounded in this absolute, original, unlimited self-possession. Though reason can know God through the world which resembles him, "concluding" from our multifarious experience of the abiding contingency of being and the very contingency of this experience itself to the principle (cause) of this contingent reality (*Knowledge of God, possibility of, *Proof of the existence of God),

190

yet God in his infinity, his absolute perfections and his absolute other-ness is incomprehensible for this same finite human thought because God's infinity cannot be grasped in itself or understood in the light of anything else, but being the principle of all understanding remains unfathomable, never entering the realm of human knowledge as an "object" (only after the manner of an object). Thus he remains the absolute, insoluble *mystery and must be thought of as such if God is to remain HE for us. As such, God is the principle and the goal of the transcendental movement of the finite human *spirit which is open to the infinite, and the affirmation of God is always (if un-thematically) included in the operations of that spirit (knowing and willing). Since God is given to man as this kind of mystery and nevertheless is considered to be accessible to natural human knowl-edge (D 3005, 3875ff.) that reason to which the dogmatic definition of the First Vatican Council refers must be understood to mean the capacity for openness to the mystery; but in that case all positive analogical statements about God the infinite mystery will only be understood aright if they are interpreted, in absolute union with their positive content, as referring us to the unutterable mystery and at the same time as protecting that mystery from violation.

(2) In actual human life this statement about God owes neither its content nor its incisive force solely to metaphysical knowledge of God derived from the world at large. For this very statement is in part an effect of medicinal *grace and an affirmation of faith, that is it derives from God's self-revelation in history (D 3005) and is realized as faith (D 800, 3001). Indeed the Church expressly emphasizes how vulnera-ble, how liable to distortion a purely "metaphysical" knowledge of God, unsupported by grace and revelation, is in this present world (*Polytheism). Our statement, then, should always be understood in the light of our experience of *Jesus Christ acting in saving history and grace, so that we shall always say that HE is God. Our ultimate and adequate affirmation of faith therefore will not be, "There is a God", but: "This being with whom we have to do in the history of Jesus Christ, who appears there, who reveals and communicates him-self as the *Trinity, is God, is the only God, the principle of total, multifarious, mutually conflicting reality, is utter Mystery." Conse-quently all the (above) abstract metaphysical statements about God in dogmatic theology do not refer to an abstract metaphysical subject but are always an acknowledgment that in our history we have con-crete dealings with him of whom we predicate these unutterable things, that we predicate them of him because in our history this is

what he shows himself to be like, he whom we are permitted to call THOU.

(3) The more particular purpose of this specifically dogmatic affirmation which faith makes about God is thus to declare him in his absolute uniqueness and hence to infer the absolute obligation of *faith in *this* God of the revelation that has occurred in Christ: God is the being who keeps himself absolutely and essentially distinct from the world (D 804ff., 957, 2842f., 3001, 3201f., 3875f. and *passim*), although he is the abiding, all-pervading principle and ground of the world, conserving all things in their own being (D 75, 800, 3001). He cannot therefore be conceived in pantheist fashion as a personification of the sum of all reality (D 3023f.; *Pantheism). There is only one such reality, not a quality of this world but existing absolutely in and of itself (*Monotheism); it is absolutely "simple" (D 800, 1880, 3001) precisely because of the infinite plenitude of its being, which shares no dimensions with any other entity and therefore is not referred to anything else (simplicity of God). This one and unique reality is described as the "totality of infinite perfection" (omnipotence, omniscience, etc., D 3001). Only the divine incomprehensibility can offer any theological elucidation of this infinitude of perfection. Since an entity can never outstrip its first cause but must rather be eminently contained in the latter, spirit, will, self-consciousness, life must reach their acme in that unique, absolute reality that is God. God therefore is *("intellectu et voluntate infinitus"*: D 3001) the absolutely free, living, personal God, who has imparted himself to man in saving history, through Christ, in this same plenitude and in impenitent love.—See also *God, doctrine of, Trinity, doctrine of, Theodicy.*

(4) See also *Fatherhood of God, Yahweh, Son of God, Jesus Christ, Logos, Holy Spirit, Pneuma, Mercy, divine, Justice, divine, Fidelity of God, Worship of God, Religion, Holiness of God.*

(5) The present day experience of God is characterized by the gradual abolition of notions that God is a specific reality in the world and that he is a partial cause in a state of perpetual mutual reciprocation with all other realities. The legitimate secularization of the world is seen increasingly (if slowly) as the transcending of world and finite objects which is necessary for a genuine experience of God. A "personal relationship" to God is at present characterized above all by an attitude of "silence", man's verbal communication with God being merely the prerequisite for this silence. This experience of God is linked to Jesus' own experience of God the experience of worshipping without comprehending. However, this sort of experience finds little support in the purely social tradition of Christianity (the Church).

GOD, DOCTRINE OF

It has always been agreed in Christian theology that if *dogmatic theology is to be systematic at all it must begin with the doctrine of *God, just as the *Creed does. Revelation and saving history (and therefore the formal nature of *theology) as God's self-disclosure and man's transcendental, literally "ec-centric" nature, which is radically summoned to the obedience of faith in this self-revealing God, is only at home when it finds God and would not find the true God if he were considered only in his being so far as it affects us, bid man speak first of God, not first of his own salvation. This does not mean that even this first tractate is allowed to forget that our real knowledge of God derives from Christ (*Christocentrism). Thus it is important not to expound the general doctrine of God *(de Deo uno)* as if no theology of the *Trinity existed. The God who is the lord of history and gives himself to the world in a progressive self-revelation *is* by that very fact the God who progressively reveals and communicates himself as One in three Persons. The "nature" of God is not really defined, in theology, until it is recognized as internally communicable and this communicability is understood as a consequence of the nature of the being with which we have to do in the doctrine of God. The possibility of knowing God is quite rightly discussed in the doctrine of God, for reflection on the character of man's transcendental and gracious ordination to God of its nature shows us who God really is. The doctrine of God in the strict sense raises the whole question of the relation between the natural order and the supernatural order of grace and the knowledge corresponding to each, between essential and existential knowledge and the kind of objectivity corresponding to each. It would be untheological to pretend that theology, as systematic reflection on the revealed word, can dispense with metaphysics (*Philosophy and theology, *theism). The theological doctrine of God, it is true, can only concern the statement of what has been experienced through God's historical witness to himself in his salvific activity and in his word, but in this very experience, and in the statement of it, man unavoidably exercises his metaphysical existence, and the clearer the thought he devotes to it—precisely so as to be quite open to God's self-attestation—the more accurately he can state that witness in his turn. This statement must not be confined to the necessary attributes of God's nature but must also embrace the basic structures of God's free attitude towards the world which characterize all saving history. As a rule these two things are not clearly enough distinguished. God's *fidelity, *mercy, *love, etc., which we experience in actual fact and explain in this tractate, are not merely the (theologically attested) necessary "attributes" of God's metaphysical nature but far more. For he could deny us *this* fidelity, love, etc., which in fact he shows us, without thereby ceasing to be faithful, loving, etc. in a metaphysical sense. Nor can these attributes be reduced to a synthetic unity of content. For example we must praise his *mercy more than we fear his *justice for it is his grace, not wrath, which he has allowed to overflow.

The doctrine of God represents the divine nature as absolute *being. But note that the infinite plenitude of being proper to "pure act", and its *aseity, can only be "understood" when it is adored as the sacred *mystery.

GOD, WORSHIP OF

The "embodied" (visible and audible) acknowledgment of God as God (*Adoration). The specific nature of this "embodiment" is implied by the fundamental constitution of man, who in the first place can only realize an "interior" attitude if he also "expresses" it and in the second place is summoned to such an external manifestation of his internal acknowledgment, because this acknowledgment must "occur" in a total ordination of the self (that is, of man's whole corporal-spiritual being) to that which is acknowledged (Religious *act). Further, the ultimate necessity of a social structure for the worship of God is obvious from the fact that man's whole being is summoned to the acknowledgment of God and that at the same time human nature destines him for society (*Cult, *Church). The acknowledgment of God expressed in divine worship is in its turn directed and specified by the knowledge of God that is available. Thus the object of Christian worship of God is not the metaphysical abstraction of absolute being as such but rather the God who is perceived in his self-revelation through Jesus Christ to be radically distinct from the world and yet to have disclosed himself to this world in absolute self-communication.

Specifically Christian worship, therefore, is the acceptance and recognition, made possible by God himself, of God's self-communication. This God-wrought acceptance has been made historical and permanent in the Church. Thus the attempt to specify Christian worship resolves itself into the attempt to specify the cult of the Church. Apart from her proper and public cult (services) the Church also recognizes a private cult (prayer, pilgrimages, devotions, etc.).

194

Cursing, blasphemy, sacrilege and idolatry are direct offences against the worship of God; *superstition also, insofar as it expresses a real recognition of a transcendent power hostile to God.—See *Religion.*

GOOD

Primarily a transcendental attribute of entities in general; it designates that which befits the entity in its final and perfect form (and is therefore sought after). The entity itself is pre-eminently "good": insofar as it posits itself by actually realizing its nature it is ontically "good" in regard to itself *(bonum sibi).* Whatever assists this realization of its nature is also good *(bonum alteri).* If an entity is aware of itself in view of free self-realization (*Freedom) under the horizon of absolute *being, then its ontic goodness is an ontological good, that is, an objectively moral good *(bonum honestum),* and being present under the horizon of absolute being it is also an absolute "value": because an entity (a good) has an absolute validity, a rightness, that does not abolish but presupposes freedom and is a summons to definite decision, insofar as it is harmoniously related to the goal set for human nature and insofar as man, in free and conscious self-possession, is "absolute" before God, that is, is no longer a means to an end. Therefore "objective moral value" connotes (1) a spiritual *person (God or man), and (2) everything else so far as it may help the primary objective moral value to affirm its self-awareness, its realization or recognition of itself. The free spiritual *act of recognition and realization which attains such objective moral good is a subjective moral good *(bonum morale).*

GOSPEL

The literal translation of εὐαγγέλιον, "good news", most clearly expresses Jesus' claim for his own message. This message is addressed to the poor man (Mt 11:5) who has so comprehended himself, his situation in the world and in relation to God, that of himself he would have to expect a sentence of rejection. The purport of this news is the fact that the gracious reign of God in Christ has now become present and liberatingly efficacious in this world which was thought to be already rejected (Mk 1:14f.).

In the later writings of the NT the concept of the Gospel is extended to the communication of the news of that which occurred in Jesus

Christ and was seen and heard by his disciples. So the content of the Gospel comes to include the existence, the words, the life of Jesus. The Gospel in this sense thus immediately becomes a "gospel", a joyful message from God to man. In keeping with the unique character of this intelligence, Scripture uses the term Gospel exclusively in the singular. Only later does the term (now used in the plural) signify the written formulation of the disciples' message, as contained in the four Gospels (the Gospels of Matthew, Mark, Luke, and John). The application of this name Gospel to these writings indicates their character as missionary writings or missionary preaching. As such this formulation is the *preaching of the Church about that word and event whereby she herself was established (*Holy Scripture).

GRACE

In theology God's personal condescension and absolutely gratuitous clemency to man; but grace (Gr. χάρις , Lat. *gratia)* also signifies the effect of this clemency, in which God communicates himself to man.
   (1) The Christian believer, in and despite his creatureliness, and although he recognizes that he is a sinner both of himself and by his origin (*Original sin), must understand that he is (the) one who has been historically summoned by God and the efficacious Word of God's free, absolute self-disclosure to enter God's own intimate life. The vital point here is that God does not simply grant man *some* kind of salutary love and intimacy, such as is necessarily implied in the abstract concept of a relationship between the Creator and his still innocent creature, but allows him to participate in the divine nature itself, to be joint heir with the Son, called to eternal life face to face with God in the intuitive *beatific vision of God, that is of God's own life (in *doxa).
   (2) This grace is in itself God's free gift to man, not only insofar as he is a sinner (that is, he who culpably shuts himself against this offer God makes of himself, against the divine will which seeks expression in *all* human reality), but *antecedent* to sin (*Original justice). The acceptance of grace needs to be sustained by God just as the gift of grace is, lest finite man (in accordance with the nature and measure of a finite creature) reduce the divine *self-communication to the level of an event which remains merely something which is of the finite order, thus eliminating God's *self*-communication as such. The self-communication as such effects its own acceptance, so that the actual and proximate ability to accept it is the sheerest grace.

196

(3) Because this free self-communication of God in *Jesus Christ and his Spirit must be accepted by the spiritual creature in a dialogical partnership that is equally free, it presupposes a permanent human constitution (freely determined by God)—(a) one prior to God's self-communication in such a way that man must receive this latter as an event that is free favour, unforeseeable in the light of man's constitution, that is to say not transcendentally implicit in human self-realization, though man is essentially open to this self-disclosure of God (*Potentia obedientialis, Supernatural *existential) and involves his whole being in calamity if he forgoes it; (b) one that persists (as something senseless) even if man closes himself to this self-disclosure of God. This "addressee", this precondition of God's self-communication, is known in Catholic thought as human *nature (*Nature and grace).

(4) In this sense the grace of God's self-communication is *supernatural, in other words man can have no claim to it—quite apart from his unworthiness as a sinner—nor can any creature: it is not entailed by man's inalienable being (his "nature"), so that in principle God could deny it to man though sin had never been committed.

(5) The declarations of the magisterium have chiefly stressed this supernatural character of grace (D 895, 1917 and passim, 2435, 2616, 3005, 3008, 3891)—the ground on which the Church early laid down that man has no sort of claim to grace and is wholly incapable of meriting grace by his own unaided powers, being unable of himself either to ask for grace or to prepare himself for it in any positive way (D 243f., 248, 273f., 1525, 1553 and passim).

(6) This does not mean that grace as forgiveness is relegated to the background (Rom 3:23f.). For the concrete human being always finds himself in a situation which has two inseparable aspects: he is both a creature and a sinner and in his concrete experience each aspect conditions and illuminates the other. The fallibility of the finite creature is indeed no sin, but it is pitilessly laid bare in sin; and his sinfulness forces on man the plain recognition that he is the absolutely finite creature, for whom God's divinizing favour is invariably grace. Hence it is small wonder that the whole Tridentine doctrine of justifying grace (*Trent, Council of) is not conceived as the "elevation" of a nature but as the pardoning of the ungodly (D 1513f., 1521–1534).

(7) Insofar as this grace is given to man in the state of original sin, elevating him by pardoning him, it is purely the grace of Jesus Christ (D 127, 1513, 1521f., 1551f. and passim; *Redemption, *Christocentrism). This origin in Christ gives grace, even divinizing grace, the character of an eminently historical dialogue, that is although it is

God's favour, *always* intended for all men everywhere and in every age (see D 340ff., 2305, 2406, 2464, 2618 and *passim),* yet it depends on the "event" of Jesus Christ, is therefore incarnational and sacramental in character (*Church as mystical *Body of Christ, *Sacrament) and incorporates pardoned man into the life and *death of Christ.

(8) In view of the foregoing (see 1, above) it will readily be seen that strictly supernatural grace, grace as such (the grace of *justification), is primarily God communicating himself in his own being; uncreated grace (see also *Appropriation, Indwelling, Pneuma, Sanctifying Grace, Justification).* Hence any objectivist conception which would hand over grace to man's autonomous control is categorically put out of court. The Tridentine doctrine of "inhering" grace (D 1530f., 1561) was not formulated either to deny this or simply with an eye to the problem of distinguishing created from uncreated grace (the latter is mentioned, D 1528f., 1677f.); its purpose is only to state the fact that justification is a true rebirth, that it produces a new creature, a temple truly inhabited by the Spirit of God himself, a man anointed and sealed by the Spirit and born of God; that this just man is not forensically "deemed" to be just, but actually *is* just (D 1528ff., 1561). The very term "uncreated" grace implies that *man himself, in himself,* is truly created by this divine self-communication, so that in this sense there is a "created" and "accidental" grace.

(9) Because of the struggle with *Pelagianism, in which grace was defined to be necessary for salutary acts, the Western theology of grace (St Augustine) regards grace primarily as assistance for an act—as "actual" grace in this sense (D 238, 249, 330 –339, 340ff., 1551ff.). But in the defined teaching of the Church the distinction between actual, supernatural, elevating grace and habitual grace appears only from the fact that the unjustified may perform salutary acts, with the absolutely indispensable help of prevenient grace (D 1525), which prepare them for justification. The only distinction here that is binding on faith is this: grace is "habitual" insofar as God's supernatural self-communication is permanently offered to man (after baptism) and insofar as it is freely accepted (by one who is of age); this very same grace is called "actual" insofar as it actually sustains the act whereby it is accepted—an act which is intrinsically graduated in existential depth and can be renewed indefinitely—and thus actualizes itself.

(10) It follows, from the fact of God's universal *salvific will on the one hand and human sinfulness on the other, that there is an assistance of grace which is offered but does not take effect, that is, is

merely "sufficient" *(gratia sufficiens;* D 1525, 1554, 2002, 2305f., 2621, 3010). Its character therefore cannot be sought in God's irresistible omnipotence (D 2409–2415). The difference between merely sufficient and efficacious actual grace, according to the (almost) common teaching (of Banezianism as well as of *Molinism), is grounded in God's election prior to man's acceptance or rejection of grace and despite man's freedom either to accept or reject it. Actual grace is an illumination and an inspiration (D 244f., 377, 1525, 2621, 3010). It is regarded not only as gratuitous (D 244f., 1525f., 1532, 2618) but as supernatural in the same sense as justifying grace (see D 3008ff.). Accordingly it does not consist merely in external circumstances which God's *providence has shaped so as to favour man's religious activity, but is an "interior" grace in the same sense as sanctifying grace.

(11) In spite of *original sin and *concupiscence man is *free* (D 1515f., 1526f., 1554f.,); thus he freely consents to prevenient grace or freely rejects it (D 243, 247, 330 –339, 393, 1521, 3875ff.). *To this extent* we must speak of a "collaboration" between God and man (D 379, 397, 1525, 1554). But this does not signify any kind of *"synergism", any apportionment of the work of salvation between them. For it is not only the ability to perform salutary acts (the infused *habitus or the prevenient sufficient grace) but the very free consent to grace which is the gift of God (D 373f., 379 and *passim).* Thus it is grace itself which frees our *freedom for salutary acts (giving us both the power and the deed), so that the situation whereby man is able to say Yes or No to God is not one of emancipation and autonomous choice (D 397, 626f., 633); but rather, where man says No it is his own doing, and where he freely says Yes he must thank God because that is *God's* gift. For the speculative attempts that have been made to understand how man's own salutary free decision can be the gift of God, see also *Grace, systems of.*

(12) The magisterium also distinguishes between elevating grace (which is necessary for *salutary acts) and "medicinal" grace, the divine assistance which is necessary for the observance of the *natural moral law (D 225, 241, 244, 383f., 387, 1541, 1572 and *passim).* However, this does not answer the question whether *in fact* there are moral acts without any positive relevance to salvation or, if they exist, whether an elevating grace makes them all salutary (G. Vasquez, J. M. Ripalda). External "medicinal" grace could be considered an element in a gracious event whose purpose, given the actual universal Christocentrism of human history, is the realization of man both as a human being and as a Christian.—See also *Faith.*

GRACE, SYSTEMS OF

(13) Grace may be experienced in the most diverse forms; it differs from person to person: unutterable joy, unconditional personal love, unconditional obedience, a feeling of loving unity with the "world", the uniqueness of one's own existence, and so on.

GRACE, SYSTEMS OF

The name for the speculative attempts to understand the working of the *grace of God while preserving human *freedom. (In every case these include the doctrine of *God, *sin, *original sin, the relations of *nature and grace, the character of the *supernatural, the *states of man, *predestination, *reprobation, etc.) The principle systems are *Augustinianism, *Banezianism, and *Molinism. The Church tolerates them all without preferring any particular one. None has satisfactorily solved the basic problem, chiefly because of the inadequate biblical theology of earlier times and because of the temptation to try to fathom the incomprehensible *mystery of God by a kind of syllogistic *gnosis. As a result the systems of grace now have little importance in modern theology. Utterances of God concerning himself and man (and likewise experiences) that seem to contradict each other are best left side by side as an expression of the plenitude of reality which man can never master; in our case we must realize that the incomprehensible coexistence of God's absolute sovereignty with man's genuine freedom is only the most extreme instance of the incomprehensible coexistence of God's absolute being with the genuine being of creatures: the incomprehensibility *must* be permanent if God is to be God. Such propositions as these are maintained in praise of God's sovereign saving grace, which frees us for true freedom.

GRACE, THEOLOGY OF

That division of the dogmatic *anthropology of redeemed and justified man which essentially and originally deals not with *grace in the abstract but with pardoned men. For where the being of man does not appear in its multiple dimensions, grace remains a formal concept, an abstract elevation of a nature or a moral assistance and falls short of the concrete grace of biblical theology. The doctrine of the supernatural *virtues is an essential component of this division of the anthropology of redeemed humanity (which should properly take its place in dogmatic theology after the doctrine of the *Trinity, the

200

doctrine of *creation, *Christology, *soteriology and *ecclesiology), which as a whole provides the dogmatic basis for a *moral theology that is dogmatic from the outset. The principal topics of the theology of grace are the following: (1) God's fundamental act of Trinitarian self-communication in Christ to man who is not God, the act therefore which distinguishes and embraces *nature and grace, the supralapsarian and infralapsarian dispensations (the order of things before the sin of Adam and after *original sin). (2) From this act the concept of the (uncreated and created) supernatural grace of *justification should be elaborated, with due attention to its christological, infralapsarian, individual and social, anthropological and cosmic character. (3) Then follows the doctrine of the actual (existential) realization of the supernatural grace with which man has been favoured. This includes: justified life in Christ (sovereignty of grace, grace hidden in the living of an upright life, consciousness of grace, freedom under grace and freedom's liberation by grace, law and grace, conscience and grace, corporeality of grace in the Church, knowledge and grace, the virtue of faith, action and grace, the virtues of hope and love and their embodiment in all the breadth of human life, in the so-called moral virtues), the process of justification, the growth of supernatural life and the threat to it of the Christian's residual sinfulness, the basic forms of spiritual life, the ecclesiological and active side of life in grace: *charism, *vocation, witness.

GUILT

In the theological sense guilt is another word for *sin, but especially connotes the profane aspects of the matter (the psychological experience of guilt, the problem of guilt in penal law, etc.). We speak of subjective guilt when the offence against the *law, understood as the expression of God's gracious holy will (*Commandments of God) is committed knowingly and freely (which knowledge and freedom need not, of course, take reflex form). We speak of (merely) objective guilt when there is an actual discrepancy between what a man does and what he should do but the discrepancy is not freely intended. Personal guilt must be carefully distinguished from what is called *original sin and therefore cannot give rise to the possibility of a collective guilt which is more than the sum of the guilt of individuals; but the guilt of original sin is analogous to collective liability. Guilt may also mean the deed (actual sin) and the permanent state to which it gives rise (habitual sin): a wrong frame of mind, consequences of the deed in the person concerned (loss of *grace, *concupiscence, perversions, the *penalties of sin), and God's right because of the offence to withhold the free grace of his personal self-communication, even if the person "of himself" would give up his wrong frame of mind; so that habitual sin in the last analysis can only be overcome by God.

H

HABITUS

The name given in Aristotelian-Thomistic philosophy to the determination of a *potency, which so shapes the latter that it perfectly and permanently corresponds to its own nature *(habitus perfectivus)*. If an operative potency is so shaped as regularly to produce acts of a particular quality the habitus is called operative. The natural foundation of a habitus is a *disposition; a habitus based on a disposition can be "acquired" by constant repetition *(habitus acquisitus)*. If the (acquired) habitus refers to an objective moral good the good habitus thus acquired is called a *virtue. The scholastic theology of the virtues, which speaks of "infused" virtues, describes *grace as an "infused" habitus inhering in the soul, making supernatural salutary acts possible, if not always easy and stable (then the concept is close to that of *existential). A habitus may also be an evil one, in which case it is generally called a "vice".

HEART

A basic concept of primitive anthropology ("primordial word") which designates that single centre of the personal spirit's self-control and psychosomatic autonomy which can only be reached asymptotically. It cannot, of course, be localized in the physical heart, but the latter is its primordial symbol. Strictly speaking, the heart is peculiar to man, being the primordial unity of man who is naturally and substantially composite (at once body and soul). The heart is also the dynamic principle which drives man to seek that ultimate and ultimately unattainable understanding of himself which can only be found in his own heart.

HEATHEN

See *Pagans.*

HEAVEN

Theology uses the term "heaven" in two senses that must be distinguished from each other.

(1) As a figure of speech in the OT and NT heaven means the upper region above the earth, in accordance with the cosmography of the ancient world with its various levels, the uppermost of which is quite figuratively conceived as God's dwelling-place. The OT itself "demythologizes" this idea when it says that heaven and earth cannot contain God (1 Kg 8:27; Jer 23:24). In later Judaism heaven is also pictured as the abode of those who are saved: *paradise was in heaven, the "heavenly Jerusalem" will be there. The NT likewise says metaphorically that Christians are to strive for the things that are "above" (Col 3:1); our true country is there (Phil 3:20; Heb 13:14). Heaven is also a circumlocution for the Name of God: the "*basileia* of heaven" therefore does not mean that the NT transfers God's eschatological kingdom to the next world, since that kingdom is characterized by a glorious transformation of all creation into a new heaven and a new earth.

(2) In theology heaven can be a metaphor for the fullness of salvation enjoyed by those who are finally saved in God. Whether this heaven can be called a "place" depends on the manner in which *matter is likewise finally saved in God; but apart from the fact (the resurrection of the flesh) nothing on the subject has been revealed. In no circumstances may this heaven be conceived as a place existing outside time "at" or "in" which one arrives. This follows from the essentially christological structure of heaven: heaven is based on Jesus Christ's conquest of death and on his exaltation (*Ascension), which are the preconditions for the ability of creatures to enter the life of God himself; this abiding of personal creatures in the presence of God essentially means the gathering of mankind into the definitive *Body of Jesus Christ, into the "whole Christ", to commune with God who is made (and remains) *man;* hence it is that we shall "see one another again", that the human relationships of this world continue in heaven. This union of man with God and with his fellows means no loss or absorption of individuality; rather the closer man approaches to God the more his individuality is liberated and fortified. This is clear from

the language of theology, which defines the essential nature of heaven and beatitude in God as the *beatific vision of God (thus the Thomists) or as utter personal *love between God and his creature (thus the Scotists). Taken together, these two views show how beatitude can be differently conceived without ceasing to be beatitude: the individual who is finally saved by God's grace alone (which is what theology means by saying that man must necessarily be transformed by the "light of glory" in order to be capable of heaven) remains conditioned by what he has done and what he has become in history, and it is in this historical measure and "mould" that God wholly fills and loves him. Although heaven is based on the entry of Jesus Christ into his glory, which is the abiding validity in God of his sacred humanity and the admission to this beatitude of those who have died after him, and at the same time inaugurates a new relation between the world and Jesus and those who dwell with him, yet it must be borne in mind that "heaven" is still growing, since salvation is only complete when everything is saved (the world, history and men), so that salvation is only consummated in the consummation of all things in the *parousia, the *Judgment and the *resurrection of the flesh.

HELL

The term derives from the North Germanic *hel,* "realm of the dead"; a popular expression for failure to reach the blessed society of God (*Heaven) and the positive punitive consequences of the state of final personal alienation from God and final personal antagonism to the divine order of creation. The magisterium declares that this hell exists (D 72, 76, 801, 858, 1351), that the punishment of hell begins immediately after death (without awaiting the Last Judgment) (D 1002) and that it lasts forever (D 411). Freely adopting the notions of later Judaism, the NT rather assumes than affirms the existence of a special place of punishment; what it says in this matter is to be interpreted according to the principles governing the interpretation of apocalyptic and eschatological texts of Scripture. That is, such statements are not "advance coverage", as though Scripture were reporting a future that had so to speak already arrived; rather their purpose is to shed light on the present existence of men before God. Thus the dogma of hell means that human life is threatened by the real possibility of eternal shipwreck, because man freely disposes of himself and can therefore freely refuse himself to God. Jesus directly states this possibility when he warns of the consequences of arbitrary and obstinate self-closure (lack of love, on which we shall be judged) in imagery which was current at that time. He proclaims the seriousness of one's present situation and the significance of human history, whose fruits are taken as man's own work, thus rejecting all trivializing (*Apocatastasis) and all superficial views of the relationship between man and God and as it were negatively stressing the utter love of God which nevertheless establishes us in individuality and freedom. Whether and how far man does in fact avail himself of his power to reject God (*Devils) revelation does not inform us, nor has the magisterium made any pronouncement on the question. Such information, indeed, would be inconsistent with the purpose of the doctrine of hell, which is not to provide abstract data or to satisfy our curiosity but to bring us to our senses and to conversion. Without seeing how they can be reconciled, we must confess the two doctrines: the omnipotence of God, who wills all men to be saved, and the possibility of eternal perdition, though we do not see both of them as equally powerful.

HENOTHEISM

See *Polytheism.*

HERESY

From the Greek αἵρεσις . The verb αἱρέομαι means to choose, to prefer. Heresy means primarily an error in matters of faith. The heretic takes a truth out of the organic whole which is the faith and, because he looks at it in isolation, misunderstands it; or else he denies a *dogma. Jesus himself predicted that this would happen in the Church (Mk 13:6; Mt 13:24–39 and *passim)* and the apostolic writings of the NT provide ample evidence that it did. The tendency of "false brethren" to separate from the Church and form a church of their own is already clear in the NT (Acts 20:30; Col 2:18 and *passim),* and thenceforward it is a hallmark of heresy. Present-day theology distinguishes between material heresy (adhering to what is objectively heresy without realizing that it is such) and formal heresy (obstinately adhering to an objective heresy out of malice). As long as the false belief or the denial of the dogma remains interior and is not expressed to anyone the heresy is called a sin rather than a delict. A person who has fallen into heresy in a way of which juridical cognizance can be taken is no longer a member of the Church in the full sense (D 1351, 3802 and *passim)*.

A theology of heresy must start from the fact that heresy can only occur in baptized persons who wish to remain Christians. It is also under obligation to interpret the doctrines of others in a benevolent sense and with "understanding". And finally it must note that the Christian truths that have been "retained" develop an objective and subjective dynamism which tends to eliminate the heretical doctrines or transform them into true ones. The first aspect which will strike someone who looks at heresy with really Christian eyes, therefore, is the virtual preservation of *total* Christianity in heresy and in the heretics' conception of Christianity as a whole. This could lead on to the notion of a purely "verbal" heresy which in fact is only a misguided objection to Catholic terminology and therefore rather *schism than heresy. It is quite conceivable that in the course of its history a real heresy might unconsciously work its way back to the position of a purely verbal heresy. Nor should we ever lose sight of the possibility that both in doctrine and practice realizations of the nature of Christianity *may* be found within the history of a heresy which potentially, indeed, have always existed in the Catholic (that is, true and universal) and historically legitimate form of Christianity (namely, in the Roman Catholic Church) but have not yet been actualized there to the same extent; may become the occasion of development in Catholic doctrine and practice and thus have a positive rôle to play *vis-à-vis* the Church in saving history. The marrow of the theology of heresy, then, is this: according to St Paul heresy is a "necessity" of saving history in which man's fault in truncating divine truth is comprehended within God's will for his revelation and its custodian the Church. This "containment" gives heresy a positive significance (not of itself, of course, and without legitimating the deeds of men): it is by heresy that the truth of God—insofar as it is the truth of man—is constantly humbled and in practice first grows in the human mind; heresy is the means which "must be" by which the Church is led into all truth. Consequently there is no question of the Church taking up a static position, when she is confronted by heresies, and simply persevering in the defence of truths which she has already adequately understood. Rather it is only by hearing contradiction and rejecting it as repugnant to her truth and her (still evolving) understanding of herself that the Church acquires a clearer grasp of her own truth. And yet the history of truth and its development (*Development of dogma) is a history of division, of the Church's ever more exhaustive and categorical repudiation of heresy, a history of the necessary "discrimination of spirits", the beginning of God's Judgment which parts human truth and falsehood as well, although this judgment of the Church judges the historical objectivizations of man's relationship with primoridal truth—which are never unequivocal evidence of man's interior belief —and not that relationship itself, not men.

HERETICS, BAPTISM OF

A major theological problem of the 3rd century was whether converts from a heretical sect should be baptized on their conversion if they had already been baptized by heretics, or whether it was sufficient to subject them to ecclesiastical penance (*Penance, sacrament of), as was done when re-admitting fallen-away Catholics to communion. The African Church (represented by such weighty theologians as Tertullian and St Cyprian) and many Eastern Churches advocated and practised re-baptism, whereas the Churches of Rome and Alexandria disapproved of it, so that a breach occurred between the two parties in A.D. 256 which was not officially healed but gradually faded away. Several synods dealt with the question and decided that those persons should be re-baptized who had not first been baptized with a form of words acknowledging the Blessed Trinity (D 123, 127f.). This has remained the attitude of the Catholic Church down to the present time (D 802, 1617). Thus we have a good example of how even in *heresy true faith in the triune God is possible and valid baptism is conferred if this faith is objectively confessed at its administration; we see too that the validity of baptism, as of all other sacraments, does not depend on the "holiness" of either the minister or the recipient (*Sacrament, *Opus operatum).

HERMENEUTICS

From the Greek ἑρμηνεύειν, to interpret; a body of principles which govern the interpretation of any statement. The establishment of such principles is necessary, if, in spite of its chronological distance from the present, changes in ways of thought, ideas and language, one wishes to understand the "real meaning" of a statement. As the "theory of understanding", hermeneutics attempts to reconcile the process of tradition with aspects of one's own experience; the universal medium in this procedure is language (*linguistics). *Tradition is the inclusive horizon of theological hermeneutics. Only biblical hermeneutics has become an autonomous science in Catholic theology; it establishes the criteria according to which the Catholic theologian must interpret the text of *Holy Scripture (cf Vat. II: Rev.): the dogmatic criterion—the character of Scripture as the word of God (*Inspiration)—and the various literary criteria for judging Scripture, like any other document written by a human author (language, original text, historical background, *literary genre). Reconciling the literary criteria with the dogmatic one presents serious problems and Catholic theology has not yet succeeded in giving each type the same thoroughgoing treatment. Interpretation itself is separately undertaken in the two disciplines of *dogmatic theology and *exegesis, between which there is often little or no contact. Nor can the difficulties (already perceived by the Fathers of the Church) be satisfactorily resolved by recourse to the different *Senses of Scripture they distinguished.—See also *Biblical Theology, Scriptural Proof.*

HEROIC VIRTUE

See *Holiness of Man.*

HISTORICITY

That fundamental attribute of man which sets him in *time and provides him with a world that he must accept in *freedom. That is to say that he must first overtake his own nature in the very course of transforming time and the world itself with which he is provided, turning physical time into "his" time, the mere "environment" into a real world, in the *now of his responsible decision; thereby coming to himself as one-who-exists. This task, which the very possession of his *spirit sets him, is one indeed which he never fully accomplishes; he is frustrated by finitude. Nonetheless the historical, though always unique, always "event", is at the same time always transcended in the free decision reaching out towards absolute validity. Consequently man's historicity stands in need of healing which is not to be looked for from the internal dynamism of history. So that it becomes clear that *revelation alone brings man's historicity to itself by showing the genuine *end of history to be the final consummation of history and the world in *salvation; that historicity is also a fundamental property of Christian existence: as a theological term man's historicity means that man remains open to God's disposal in such a way that he may expect the *salvation of himself, of his world and history from an historical and personal event. It also means that his remembrance of the saving event as something that has happened (*Anamnesis) can have the force of a commemorative *repetition (*Eucharist, *Tradition, *Development of dogma). Finally, in accordance with the communicative nature of the saving event (*Covenant, *Old Testament, *New Testament) the event and its remembrance are historically preserved (*Church).

HISTORY, THEOLOGY OF

The name for the *theological* understanding of history. Only for theological understanding do the *beginning and the *end of history have a certain concrete content, because they are revealed; both bear the character of an event. The course of history too, like its beginning and end, is subject to God's unfettered sway, which the theology of history shows, by theological analysis, to be a single, unchanging plan which progressively reveals itself in history. In accordance with this plan God enters into *historicity by a free, supernatural intervention; in *Jesus Christ and his *grace the world becomes the history of God himself; only from the point of view of *Christocentrism can the intrinsic differentiation of history into saving history and profane history be understood. In the light of these basic theological data the theology of history understands the forces of history within the world such as *sin, *death, *law, the *State, the *unity of mankind (*Monogenism), *angels and *devils. For the realization of this plan God calls upon man as his partner set in *freedom. (*Primitive revelation, *Revelation and the *Covenant are the principal factors here in the theology of history.) The history of man's No forms a subordinate theme of the theology of history: instructed by revelation, it regards this No to a certain extent as the frontier which has constantly to be overcome, as the "necessary" (Lk 24:26; 1 Cor 11:19 and *passim)* rejection of God's free gift of salvation. But within history ever new epochs of *saving history (*Original justice, *Paganism, *Old Testament, *New Testament, *Christianity, *Non-Christian religions, *Church) spring from God's action and man's response. The theology of history investigates these with the aid of genuine epistemological types: *aetiology (as reaching back to the remote past), kerygmatics (as evocation of the salvific present; *Kerygma), *anamnesis (as the mutual implication of past and future in saving history), and finally the *hermeneutics of eschatological statements (*Apocalyptic, *Eschatology). This theology of the phases of God's plan of salvation is the proper task for the systematic theology of history. The findings of the theology of history require to be developed at two essential theological points: as the foundation of a really theological *Church history and as data of a genuine *pastoral theology, which in view of the theology of history should include in its thought the attitudes of the Christian as the only human being whose historical existence (in *patience, *hope, etc.) is genuine and redeemed. Catholic theology, to be sure, has not yet addressed itself to this task. So far as it thinks in terms of the theology of history at all, it clings to those patterns which were worked out in the first four centuries (by St Irenaeus, Eusebius, and St Augustine), whereas Protestant theology has a whole series of important theologians of history which it can count to its credit (Karl Barth and Oscar Cullmann among others).

HISTORY OF DOGMA

This is the methodical and systematic presentation of the history of individual *dogmas, of the dogmatic formulation of individual truths of faith, and of the Christian understanding of the faith as a whole since the close of *Revelation itself. It is based on the essentially historical character of dogma as divine truth heard, believed and formulated by man in this world and as a living function of the Church, which must receive, explicitate and proclaim the truth that is given to her—guaranteed by God himself—according to the ever varying understanding (ability to hear) of the world about her, a process essentially historical and socially structured. The dogmatic decisions of the Church (*Dogma, *Dogmatic facts, *Magisterium) as they are formulated in the *creeds, and in definitions of councils and Popes, are the proper study of dogmatic history. Its method is the theologico-historical one: ascertaining the original formulation of belief, and the motives (*Heresy) and forces (personal or social) behind it, which played their part in the evolution of the dogma (*Development of dogma), and understanding the thrust of this development in the future. Thus dogmatic history helps to illuminate both the individual dogma and the whole dogmatic self-consciousness of the believing *Church (*Christianity II). It is not generally taught as a special subject in theological institutes, but merely treated of in dogmatic theology and in books (by Protestants since the Enlightenment, by Catholics since the 19th century). Because dogma does not appear solely in the explicit definitions of the extraordinary magisterium, the distinction between the history of dogma and the history of theology (which is possible in principle) is not always precisely possible in practice.

HOLINESS, HUMAN

In Catholic doctrine an effect of man's *justification by *sanctifying grace; essentially a participation in the *holiness of God, since it is a strictly supernatural *grace, that is a self-communication to man of God who is holy by nature. Whatever is said of "grace" necessarily applies to human holiness: it is supernatural, gratuitous, essentially personal and dialogic, both christological and eschatological, at once a gift and a task. Since this justification is inextricably bound up with the capacity given one by the supernatural *virtues of *faith, *hope, and *love (D 1530f. and *passim*), human holiness is an absolute surrender to the God of eternal life as he is in himself. If this surrender grows and bears fruit, by the grace of God, in a more or less total, existential appropriation of God's gracious offer, and in such a way as to become a distinct component of the *holiness of the Church, then this Christian holiness attains that maturity which is known in present ecclesiastical terminology as an heroic degree of the theological and cardinal virtues and becomes sanctity in the sense associated with beatification and canonization and the *veneration of the saints.

HOLINESS OF GOD

The name in Scripture for that characteristic of the divine essence—revealed by God and displayed in the history of revelation—whereby he is infinitely exalted in his sacred majesty, *doxa* and overwhelming vitality (*Life) above all that is not God, yet stoops in his merciful love to forgive man's sins and translate him into the *holy realm that is proper to God alone. The NT preserves both these aspects of the OT revelation of God by showing him to be the Father of Jesus and the Father of us all in Jesus and at the same time acknowledging him the Lord whose will is incomprehensible and terrible and who is enthroned in light inaccessible. In the doctrine of God theology specially emphasizes the lofty majesty of God's holiness (D 3001 and *passim*), his objective holiness, which absolutely demands *adoration of his creatures, and his subjective holiness, whereby God is the final and supreme norm of all morality, so that he necessarily has an infinite love for his own goodness.

HOLINESS OF THE CHURCH

One of the essential notes, according to Catholic theology, whereby she can be recognized as the Church willed by Jesus (D 3013f.). Recognition of the Church's holiness is older than the Creeds (D 1-2, 11, 41, 150 and *passim)* and determines the attitude of the Apostles towards sinners in the Christian communities (*Penance, sacrament of). Objectively, the holiness of the Church means that she is the means of salvation and grace in the world, herself a sign of God's eschatologically triumphant grace (Vat. II: Church, 1, 9, 48, 59; Church/world, 42, 45 and *passim)* (*Body of Christ, *Primordial sacrament, *Church, *Extra ecclesiam nulla salus). Subjectively it means that the Church will never lack her "cloud of witnesses" (Heb 12:1), subjective *holiness in her members (*Veneration of saints). This doctrine must be correlated with the doctrine (defined since *Constance) that sinners are members of the Church (as the Church has constantly maintained against *Montanism, *Novatianism, the Albigenses, Wycliffe, Hus and *Jansenism), so that the Church is a Church of sinners (Mt 13:47–50; 18:17 and *passim)*. This means not only that there are sinners *in* the Church but also that the Church herself is sinful, in that her own members—not excluding Church officials—are sinners and will continue to be sinners (so that the Church itself is in constant need of renewal and purification, Vat. II: Ecum., 4, 6 and *passim)*. In this sense then, the Church's holiness simply means that the Church, though stained by sin, can never, unlike all other historical organizations, including the "Church" of the OT, be so disfigured by sin that the Spirit animating the Church will depart from her or cease to be historically perceptible in her (Mt 16:18: the gates of hell shall not prevail against her). The sinfulness of the Church can never be regarded as a manifestation of the essential principle of her being. God has preserved the Church, in advance of the actual behaviour of her members, from falling fundamentally and essentially from divine favour and promise. The sins of the Church never disclose the essential nature of the Church.

HOLY, THE SACRED

A basic religious concept variously understood from time to time by the history and philosophy of religion and by biblical and dogmatic theology. In religious history anything men worship may be called holy but especially the powers that manifest themselves in any sphere of life (in hierophanies and cratophanies, etc.). Their differences are investigated by comparative religion, which is thus compelled to make use of the basic categories of the philosophy of religion (such as religious *experience). A searching analysis of religious experience by the philosophy of religion proves that the basic experience of the sacred, in this historical ("profane") world, takes the form of an experience of its absence, showing itself in its true nature at the summits of human life (such as love and death) but immediately withdrawing into obscurity and ambiguity. Thus the sacred is seen to be at once necessary (since it alone can make any sense of existence and the world: *Salvation) and free (since man can lay no claim at all to this salvation but only hope that *mystery, the sacred principle and ground of being, will give it him of *grace). In this way the philosophy of religion reveals the character of the sacred as an event (B. Welte). Biblical theology clearly shows the sacred to be event by demonstrating the *holiness of God as a power which shapes history by its healing interventions even in the revelation of the OT. Yahweh is the Holy One of Israel because his *election and his *covenant with his people make them a domain of his own embedded in history and "separated" (the Hebrew root of the word "holy") by both nationality and religion from the profane, the *world in the pejorative sense. Moral holiness is only required as a consequence of membership of a nation that is holy. The NT continues to use this language (Rom 1:7; 1 Cor 1:2; 1 Pet 1:15f., 2:9), with the fundamental difference, of course, that definitive and universal salvation is only given in Jesus, so that the holy or sacred is no longer that set apart from the world, in a special place. This religious experience and the data of revelation set theology the difficult task of preserving the distinction between God and creatures whilst attributing holiness to man as a real, intrinsic quality (D 1512 and *passim).—See also *Self-Communication of God: Sanctifying Grace*.

HOLY GHOST

See *Holy Spirit*.

HOLY SCRIPTURE

POINT OF DEPARTURE OF THE THEOLOGY OF SCRIPTURE. God's *revelation is: (a) historical, that is, it is a spatio-temporal event, and thus needs a *tradition that will continue to attest it; (b) verbal, namely, human concepts and therefore human words are a constituent element of it; (c) social, not addressed solely to man's interior privacy but to the "Church" as the equally original recipient of this message, to the Church which must bear permanent witness to this now definitive revelation; (d) eschatological, it will not be superseded in this world by any new revelation. If this divine revelation, with these four essential elements, penetrates a human civilization which is already literate and possesses written material, then God intends that this definitive verbal revelation, which requires a tradition, shall be recorded in writing. What we call Holy Scripture is this written objectivization of the original message of revelation (the apostolic *kerygma) in the Church of the *Old and *New Testament up to the moment when the original process of revelation ceased, composed under a special divine influence (*Inspiration) such that God is the author of this objectivization. It can and must be looked on as an objectivization of the kerygma—the original process and content of revelation—that is pure and undimmed, contains at least the substance of the kerygma and is differentiated from other non-normative objectivizations; and thus it becomes of itself the source and norm whereby witness continues to be given to this revelation.

POSITIVE DATA. Another name for Holy Scripture is the "Bible", from the Greek βιβλία, written pages, scroll. The Bible calls itself "the holy books", "the Scriptures", "Scripture". The OT is composed of the Law, the Prophets and the Writings (Jewish classification), or the historical, didactic and prophetical books (Catholic classification); the NT of the Gospels, Acts, Epistles and Apocalypse. The place and date of composition and the authorship of the individual books are investigated by the biblical sciences (*Exegesis). The OT (the original language of which was Hebrew, except for certain parts that were composed in Greek and Aramaic) is preserved in Hebrew manuscripts of the 9th, 10th and 11th centuries A.D.; there are also several fragments and individual sections from 3 B.C. to A.D. 68, including a complete manuscript of Isaiah of about 100 B.C. and fragments on the Nash papyrus (probably pre-Christian or 1st century A.D.), etc. The ancient Greek translation of the OT (Septuagint) exists in numerous manuscripts and in fragments dating from the 2nd century B.C. to the

4th century A.D. The original manuscripts of the NT are also lost. The original Greek text survives in fragments of the 2nd to the 7th century A.D. and in fifty complete manuscripts of the 4th to the 10th century. The numerous readings and textual variants are theologically unimportant. Among translations of the Bible into ancient and modern languages St Jerome's revision of the old Latin text (especially the NT) and new Latin translation (especially the OT) known as the Vulgate (= version in common use), which dates from the end of the 4th century, is of special importance in Catholic theology, since the Council of Trent declared it to be reliable and authoritative (*Authenticity) (D 1506). At the same time the Church has ever increasingly recommended the use of the original text as established by scientific methods (Vat. II: Rev., 22).

ORIGIN OF SCRIPTURE, see *Inspiration*.

DIFFERENTIATION OF SCRIPTURE from other written objectivizations in the early Church and the recognition of this differentiation, see *Canon*.

THE INERRANCY OF SCRIPTURE follows from its inspiration and its divine authorship (as regards scriptural doctrine concerning faith and morals properly speaking: D 1501, 1504, 3006, 3029, 3291, 3629), and its normative rôle for the Church as the pillar and ground of truth and for her infallible *magisterium. Vatican II makes a more precise distinction than scholasticism between God as the "originator" of Scripture and human beings as its "real authors". It avoids the concept of "inerrancy" and teaches instead that the books of the Bible "firmly, faithfully and without error, teach that truth which God, for the sake of our salvation, wished to see confined to the sacred Scriptures" (Rev., 11). Apparent "errors" in Scripture are to be examined as follows: (a) by investigating what the statement in question really means and says, and precisely how far the human author wishes the statement to go, with scrupulous regard to the relevant *literary genre (D 3373, 3862ff., 3898); (b) taking note of the lack of marginal sharpness that is unavoidable in every human statement, even one which is perfectly true, (and appears, for example, in the parallel accounts of Scripture); (c) noting the *Sitz-im-Leben* or sociological setting of the statement; (d) by accurately distinguishing between the form and the sense of the statement, between the human author's own assertion and mere reporting of current opinions or mere outward appearances (implicit quotations: D 3372, 3490f., 3654); (e) by realizing that if lack

216

of knowledge shows itself in a statement this is not a denial of the thing not known; that the fact that two statements do not tally on the plane of the human author's scheme of things does not mean that they are irreconcilable; (f) by realizing that a statement made in a false perspective is not necessarily false; (g) by plainly admitting that much is still obscure and may always remain so, so that there is no need for artificial and pettifogging solutions of such problems. The foregoing does not exclude the possibility of the exegete calling certain biblical passages incorrect if, taken alone, they do not refer to any salvific truth and they are judged in accordance with modern notions of truth.

INTERPRETATION OF SCRIPTURE, see *Exegesis, biblical, Hermeneutics, Biblical Theology, Biblical Criticism, Literary Genre, Senses of Scripture.*

SCRIPTURE AND THE MAGISTERIUM. (1) Since it took its origin as the objectivization of God's word in the word of the authoritative teacher and minister of revelation, since it is only in the living witness of the authoritative teaching *Church that this objectivization can invariably be recognized *as* such, and since there is a succession in the teaching authority, Scripture (together with tradition) is always essentially and from the start closely associated with the magisterium (Vat. II: Rev., 10). Scripture is never a rival authority which private persons could invoke against the Church: the Church's magisterium is the legitimate interpreter of Scripture, because Scripture by its very origin is an element of the primitive Church, whose nature and doctrine is a permanent norm for all time coming. Scripture being by God's will an essential element of this norm, the Church and the magisterium are not "above Scripture" but above private interpretations of Scripture. The relationship between the Church and Scripture can only be understood aright if we reflect that they spring from a common origin and are not rival authorities adequately distinct from each other: the Church always remains bound by her God-given origin, of which Scripture is an integral part; her abiding fidelity to this beginning is guaranteed by the Spirit and so, therefore, is her dutiful conformity to Scripture (D 1507f., 1863, 3007, 3284, 3402, 3404, 3826ff., 3886) (2) Since the magisterium can only teach and transmit what is taught in the revealed apostolic kerygma of the primitive Church (D 3011, 3020, 3056 and *passim)*—though historically explicitated by the *development of dogma. Furthermore, since Scripture is the pure, unadulterated objectivization of this kerygma, Scripture remains an obligatory source and norm for the magisterium (D 1501; *Inspiration). The Church's observance of this norm, it is true, is not subject to the cognizance of any judicial authority distinct from herself, but is guaranteed by the promised assistance of the Holy Spirit which she enjoys.

SCRIPTURE AND TRADITION. It is clear from the manner in which Scripture first took shape and from the nature of the Church, with her authoritative magisterium, that the oral apostolic kerygma accounts for the recognition of the formal authority of Scripture and not vice versa. *Tradition in the theological sense is the authoritative transmission of this kerygma by the actual preaching of a doctrine precisely *as* part of apostolic revelation. Tradition takes permanent precedence of Scripture, at least insofar as it is the carrier of knowledge of the nature (inspiration) and delimitation (canon) of Scripture. To this extent, at any rate, Scripture and oral Tradition are each a norm and source of the Church's teaching in the same manner (D 1501 and *passim;* Vat. II: Rev., 8–10; Church, 25). This is not to deny that the Church's oral Tradition must have recourse to Scripture as a source and norm, nor does it settle the question whether, since the formation of Scripture, Tradition transmits material which simply cannot be derived from Scripture, in addition to delimiting Scripture and witnessing to it as source and norm. This question is still controverted among theologians and was explicitly left open by Vatican II, according to which Scripture and Tradition are comprised in the "apostolic proclamation" which has been "expressed with especial clarity" in Scripture. Tradition is charged with the functions of definition of the full canon (Rev., 8) and assurance about revelation. In any case the magisterium of the Church has made no concrete declaration concerning any doctrines known by Tradition alone, and seeks to prove that there is an "ultimate foundation" in Scripture even for defined doctrines which appear to be far removed from it (see D 3900ff., 434, 1512, 1514, 1615, 1642, 1703, 1726f., 3053f.). Furthermore it is no easier in practice to trace a doctrine of faith which has only recently become explicit back to an explicit original apostolic kerygma with any historical probability than to prove according to the principle of the *development of dogma that such a doctrine is the explicitation of what Scripture teaches implicitly. Finally, in doubtful cases, it is only possible in practice to determine by Scripture what in the content of tradition (not clearly distinguished from Tradition itself) is merely human and what is divine apostolic Tradition.

SCRIPTURE AS THE SOURCE AND NORM OF CHRISTIAN LIFE. Even

the OT celebrates the importance for life of reading the Scriptures; Jesus recognizes this importance (Mt 22:29; Jn 5:39), as do the Apostles (Rom 15:4; 1 Tim 4:13; 2 Tim 3:16f.; Heb 4:12 and *passim*). The practice of the primitive Church, modelled on that of the synagogue (1 Thess 5:27; Col 4:16), and her liturgy show the same attitude. See Vat. II: Rev., 31–25.—See also *Word of God.*

HOLY SPIRIT

The "Spirit of God" (Heb. *ruach,* a feminine word; Gr. πνεῦμα) is an expression in the OT for God's efficacious power; the Holy Spirit is not yet clearly discernible as the "Person" of the blessed *Trinity. The NT is aware of "another advocate" (*Paraclete), who proceeds from the Father (Jn 14:16 –16:15; Mk 1:10f.; Mt 28:19). He and his operations are usually presented in symbols: the dove, symbolizing the creation of the new people of God (the dove is a favourite symbol of the holy people: see St Augustine; Mk 1:10f., and parallel texts); a gale, symbolizing strength (Acts 2); tongues of fire, symbolizing the ecstasy of the witnesses (Acts 2).—See also *Pneuma.*

In accordance with Scripture the "personality" of the Holy Spirit is confessed and defined in the Creeds and in all the Church's doctrinal judgments concerning the divine Trinity against *Modalism and *Macedonianism (D 112, 151f. and *passim*). He is the "Spirit of the Father and of the Son" (D 178), who proceeds from the Father and the Son (D 188, 527 and *passim;* *Filioque) as from a single principle and by a single "breathing" *(spiratio:* D 850, 1300ff., 1331). It is by him that Mary conceived (D 11, 30, 41), although he may not be called Jesus' "Father" (D 533); he is active in Jesus (D 178) and in the *Church (D 3807f.; *Magisterium); he is bestowed in a special manner in the sacraments of *Confirmation and Holy *Orders (D 1269, 1774). On the procession of the Holy Spirit in the triune God see *Trinity.* The "nature" of the Holy Spirit's "mission" in the world can be grasped without considerable difficulty (within the terms of the mystery). Divine revelation to the world is founded on two basic modalities: self-revelation as the truth which manifests itself in history and is freely offered to us by God's trust, and self-revelation as the love which in turn reveals man's transcendental being and makes him receptive to God's absolute future. Thus God imparts himself to man, the needful, finite and sinful being. To give of oneself without seeking to find or attain to oneself, indeed to "risk" oneself by being so generous as to freely "belittle" oneself in regard to another person is what is meant by *love. Because God creates as God, he creates as Spirit everything in the world that is constantly new and fresh, free and vital, unexpected and mighty, at once tender and strong. He is the Spirit of grace: God within us as our anointing and sealing, our earnest of heaven, our guest, comforter and advocate, the interior call, freedom and sonship, life and peace, holiness and unity, we call the Spirit. He who causes the "fruits to mature in us—*love, *joy, *peace, *patience, *chastity—is the Spirit, the stern adversary of the flesh, of sin, of legalism, the secret power of transformation within us that presses forward to the resurrection of the glorified body and the transfiguration of the world. He is the Spirit of the Church, the unity of the *body of Jesus Christ. Pentecost reveals that this Spirit is not only offered to man, but that man's acceptance of the Spirit is itself the Spirit's gift; that this communication of the Spirit is no longer a sporadic breathing, as it was for the prophets, but has happened definitively and irrevocably. The primordial sacrament of Christ's grace in the Spirit, who is not only promised but given, is the *Church. In her he lives, both in prudent laws and in awakenings to new life, in *office and *charism. He is the Spirit of the individual, who may possess him and be guided by him in a Christianity that is still name-less and does not understand the Church but that can be perceived wherever men refuse by the grace of God to conform to legalistic mediocrity.

HOMOEANS

See *Arianism, Semiarianism.*

HOMOOUSIOS

From the Greek ὁμοούσιος , "of the *same* nature" (it is not to be confused with ὁμοιούσιος , of a *similar* nature); a technical term in theology, already in use by the 3rd century, which signifies that the Father and the Logos in the divine *Trinity are of the same nature (better: of *one* nature) or "substance". The Trinitarian and Christo-logical controversies of the 3rd and 4th centuries established that Christ is of one nature ("con-substantial") with the Father (D 125f., 150, 301ff.) and of one substance with us (D 301ff.) by reason of the two *natures in him. The Greek theologians conceive the divine na-ture to be absolutely simple: it cannot be divided by generation but is communicated without division. The philosophical and theological problem that still remained after the First Council of *Nicaea was how to distinguish between "nature" (*Essence) (Gr. οὐσία) and *hypostasis.—See *Arianism.*

HOPE

In the NT sense, hope is ultimately constituted by the intersection, on the one hand, of that divine predestining plan for man whereby the love of God—which, being incarnate in Christ, has become human history—has efficaciously and permanently affected man, and on the other hand of the responsive attitude towards this plan shown by the person (or the *Church, in which the highly personal response of which each individual is capable is preserved and sustained) who confidently awaits the final consummation of the divine economy of salvation in the coming of Jesus Christ (Heb 6:18f.; Rom 8:24 and *passim),* in reliance on the saving plan which has already and irrevocably been intiated by God, as he knows with the certainty of faith. Thus hope is a God-wrought ("theologal") *virtue, closely bound up as such with *grace, but at the same time a genuinely human act (effected by God) and thus closely associated with personal *faith and *love, thereby forming a sort of intermediate stage in the historical development of *general* dogmatic faith into the absolute personal intimacy of love (1 Cor 13:13; see D 1530f., 1545ff.). Christian hope is ultimately not only a modality of faith and love for the time being, but also the continual banishment of things provisional on the way to the absolute and pure illimitability of God, the permanent destruction of appearance. The ground of hope is the universal *salvific will of God which is only concretely present and attained to (though not wholly comprehended) in hope. The following, according to theological tradition, form the material object of hope: the forgiveness of sins which is already known by faith, grace both as justification that can never be claimed or merited and as efficacious help to persevere in this state of grace, but above all the ultimate *beatific vision—all as gifts that God has "always intended for me". Christian hope finds its certainty in the person of Jesus Christ (see Col 1:27; 1 Tim 1:1), in whom God's gracious assumption of human destiny and of man himself has become history; that very assumption (transformation) of human history as a "must" that is part of God's own plan and issues in the definitive new creation, gives its "rightness". Hope keeps the memory of the as yet unfulfilled divine promises fresh—whose fulfilment man strives for by working to construct the future of this world. Hope is the category of a theology with practice as its goal (see *Political theology*).

HUMILITY

The disposition of the human being who, conscious of his radical distance from God, who is perfect Being, has gratefully and courageously taken to himself God's self-exinanition in his Son (Phil 2:2–8) and the transformation (elevation) therein revealed of the little and the weak of this world into the great of the kingdom of God (Mt 18:4 and parallel passages). This humble self-acceptance is expressed particularly in acceptance (forgiveness, endurance) of the weakness of one's fellow-man and in readiness to serve him and God.

HYLOMORPHISM

The doctrine of Aristotle, supplemented by the Scholastics, that every physical being is essentially constituted of *matter (Gr. ὕλη) and *form (Gr. μορφή), which combine to make a single entity. It is based on the notion that physical being has a substantial essence, constituted by a "prime matter" *(materia prima,* *potency, mutability) and a "form" (*act), a (variable) substantial principle of configuration which is produced by an external efficient cause (see especially *Causality),* is the basis of specific difference and makes matter what it was in potency to be. The structure of the resultant palpable "second matter" is thus always hylomorphic. Scholastic thought shifted the emphasis from cosmology to metaphysics. In this way, since the beginning of the 13th century, hylomorphism has also served to clarify theological matters. St Thomas and his followers (*Thomism) maintained that each being has only one substantial form, while the Franciscan school and Suarez accepted a plurality of forms (*Pluralism). An exception was admitted in the case of *transubstantiation, where it was held that matter does not continue in existence, both matter and form—the whole *substance—being changed. The relation between body and soul was also described in hylomorphic terms (see D 902), and hylomorphism figures in the scholastic doctrine of *sanctifying grace as the "formal cause" of justification (see D 904, 1528f.) and in the definition of the sacramental sign as the union of a ritual gesture (the *"matter") with a form of words (the *"form") (see D 1671ff., 1695, 1704 and *passim).*—A hylomorphic "metaphysical constitution" of things would not depend on the findings of natural science regarding the constitution of organic and inorganic bodies.

HYPERDULIA

From the Greek ὑπερδουλεία, best rendered, "greater veneration", or "especial veneration"; a term for the "greater" veneration of the Blessed Virgin *Mary because she is the *Mother of God and as such has a unique place in saving history. This veneration is "greater" as contrasted with that paid to the other saints (*Veneration of saints). Hyperdulia, which of course has nothing to do with *adoration, is accorded Mary by the Catholic Church and the separated Eastern Churches.

HYPOSTASIS

A philosophical expression for "concrete reality" (Gr. ὑπόστασις). This term originally had the same meaning as οὐσία (nature); so that the Latin *substantia* (*substance) was used to render both. But when theological reflection on the *Trinity began this usage proved unfortunate, given the relations that then obtained between Greek and Latin theologians. Origen described the three divine Persons as ὑποστάσεις united by an identical οὐσία; Tertullian spoke of three Persons in one substance. Nevertheless the First Council of *Nicaea still treated ὑπόστασις and οὐσία as synonyms (D 125f.). The classic theology of the Trinity was only formulated in the year 380: in the one divine *nature (essence) there are three ὑποστάσεις , that is, three *subsistences, or three *Persons (see D 421). A further confusion of language was met with in Christology. Ὑπόστασις was equated with φύσις (nature) (see *Monophysitism). The matter was not finally clarified until the Council of Chalcedon. Jesus Christ is one ὑπόστασις (one Person) in two natures (D 301ff.). In the 6th century Christ, the single ὑπόστασις , is called "one of the three divine "ὑποστάσεις " (D 401, 426). This concluded classic Christology as related to the theology of the Trinity. The problem raised by the undifferentiated use of the notion of ὑπόστασις (Person) in the theology of the Trinity (where the Person is constituted by *relation alone) and in Christology had not yet been perceived.

HYPOSTATIC UNION

A technical term in theology which means that in *Jesus Christ a human being became the created self-expression of the Word of God through the permanent union of a human nature with the divine Person (ὑπόστασις) of the Logos. (For the defined teaching of the Church, see D 252–263, 301ff., 426, 436f., 516). This formulation is the fruit of the great Christological controversies of the first four centuries. These arose out of intellectual speculations which unsuccessfully attempted to elucidate the fact, evident in Scripture, that Jesus Christ is true man and true God. The gravity of these Christological heresies was that they degraded the Incarnation itself, and therefore Christ's true humanity, into a mere disguise of the divinity (*Arianism, *Apollinarianism), for instance by denying that Jesus had a human soul and making the "soul" of the divine Logos the nexus between it and the flesh (which logically led to *Monophysitism, making redemption the work of God alone), or else by denying that the divine Logos is the subject of the human nature too (*Nestorianism: the sacred humanity would be left this side of an abyss yawning between God and creatures if Christ's truly human attributes could not in the strictest sense be predicated of God). The acknowledgment of the two *natures in Christ (at the Council of *Chalcedon) made it possible to fit the decisive, redemptive act of mediation firmly into the reality of this world—the humanity of Christ—so that the act of redemption is and remains an act of the Logos and yet a free human act. This doctrine implies that the human nature of the Logos possesses a central principle of genuinely spontaneous, free, spiritual activity, a human self-consciousness imbued with a sense of utter creatureliness, whose attitude towards God is the genuinely human one of adoration and obedience. For Jesus is not a God who deals with us in human form, but God who is at the same time true man, able in true human freedom to be our mediator with God. How this can be conceived is the problem in connexion with the hypostatic union that engrosses attention at the present day. The starting-point for its solution should be the fact that only a *divine* Person can possess a freedom really distinct from himself in such a way that freedom is his own, does not cease to be really free *vis-à-vis* the possessing divine Person, and yet is an attribute of this Person, who is its ontological subject. For we can conceive of no one but God personally constituting a being distinct from himself. The Person of the Logos is to be thought of as bearing a relation to his human nature in which independence *and* utter intimacy simultaneously reach a climax whose quality

224

is without parallel—the unique climax of relationship between Creator and creature. Accordingly Christ's human nature must of itself be conscious of this hypostatic union insofar as this union is a real and ontological specification of his human nature—indeed its supreme ontological specification—and this nature is itself "present to itself" (which follows from its spiritual character); the hypostatic union cannot be a mere datum of the objective knowledge the sacred humanity derives "from without", but Christ's human soul is "with" the Logos directly, both ontically and consciously (*Knowledge of Jesus). Hence it could be affirmed that Jesus is essentially "the man who lives unique, *absolute* self-abandonment to God", provided that an absolute self-abandonment to God implies an *absolute* *self-communication of God which turns what it causes—the God-enriched recipient of the divine self-communication which the latter creates— into the being of the cause itself, and provided that such a proposition in terms of lived experience is also a proposition about the very being of Jesus. See *Incarnation*.

I

ICONOCLASTIC CONTROVERSY

This controversy was provoked by an edict of the Byzantine Emperor Leo the Isaurian, A.D. 730, forbidding the *veneration of images. Under his successor Constantine V, a persecution of those who defended that practice broke out; it particularly affected the monks, against whose power the original edict was probably directed. The second Council of *Nicaea, A.D. 787, upheld the veneration of images, according them a relative worship (D 600ff.). When the controversy had flared up anew, the Empress Theodosia sanctioned the veneration of images by instituting the "Feast of Orthodoxy", A.D. 843.

IDEAS, DIVINE

An idea in general is an archetype, an illuminating image (contrasted with a "replica" and "concept"). In patristic *Neoplatonism the divine ideas are God's creative thoughts about creatable beings or the archetypes immanent in himself which are identical with his perfection and of which creatures are imitations. St Bonaventure and St Thomas elaborated this in their doctrine of God's exemplar causality. Bonaventure's view is christocentric: the Son of God is the image of the Father and imparts to creatures the *image of God.

IDEOLOGY

Every social reality requires for its formation, preservation and continued development a corresponding system of concepts, ideas and theories concerning social reality as a whole and its individual ele-

226

ments, processes and problematic areas. Nevertheless, ideologies are not merely reflections in human consciousness of prevailing material circumstances. They are also a concentrated expression of relevant class interests and hence form the basic rudiments of corresponding attitudes, values, decisions and conventions. An ideological system is thus composed of descriptive and explanatory statements and perceptions and of appeals, demands and values intended to shape motives and stimulate action. The history of human society contains many examples of ideologies which interpret social reality in a one-sided or false way yet continue to influence human actions and social structures. Conversely, every just value in a society does not necessarily have a corresponding effect on the actions of individuals or masses. The task of ideological criticism is thus to examine the connexion between the truth and the effectiveness of an ideological system, which are not automatically synonymous. Wherever *religion is seen as the expression of a false consciousness of the power structure in a society, and of class conflict, a critique of ideology assumes the specific form of criticism of religion. It is precisely this distinction between the truth and the effectiveness of an ideology which repeatedly proves the social location and interest of any pronouncements concerning social reality. An unbiased, impartial assessment of social relations is therefore not impossible. However, depending on the particular existential conditions and class affiliation, a social standpoint can amount to a decisive curtailment of understanding and source of error just as easily as it can lead to clear and exact understanding. A call for ideological freedom or for the abolition of ideologies may be interpreted as a veiled attempt to replace an existing ideology by a new one.

IDOLATRY

See *Polytheism, Veneration of Images.*

IMAGE, REFLECTION ON IMAGES

The image is the illustration or embodiment, proper to human thought, of reality as it affects man; and this reality for its part is conditioned by the "visual" (sensible) mode of human cognition (*Sensibility), whereby each "concept" is grasped only in relation to an imaginative representation. Such representation necessarily ceases where pure *spirit (*God) is concerned; thus the OT forbids making any likeness of God (Exod 20:4f.), chiefly for reasons which concern saving history (*Monotheism). But in Jesus Christ God has entered the world of human experience as "the image of the invisible" (Col 1:15; *Image of God). By using images as well as words for his *meditation, man can strive to "see" the truth behind its formulation. But what each individual "sees" is of course qualified and shaped both by his imaginative representation and by his power of vision (imagination) itself.

IMAGE AND LIKENESS OF GOD

A concept known from revelation, which describes the unique relationship between God and man. Man, that is, according to biblical anthropology, the *whole* man, composed of soul and body, as man and woman, is created in the image of God (Gen 1:26f.) as God's partner and ruler of the world. This at once differentiates him from all the rest of creation, especially living creatures, which are created each "after his *own* kind". Man still remains the image of God after original sin (Gen 9:6), because he can still be called and God still calls him. But *the* image of God *simpliciter* is *Jesus Christ (2 Cor 4:4ff.; Col 1:12–16; Heb 1:3) because as the *Son of God (*Logos) he portrays the Father and as the incarnate God he makes God visible; thus the splendour of the Father's glory lies upon him. By the divine *Pneuma he who believes in the Son also shares in his *doxa* and thus becomes the image of the transfigured Lord even in this world (2 Cor 3:18)— how much more so after the resurrection of the flesh (1 Cor 15:49; Rom 8:29). Dogmatic anthropology attempts to come to grips with this still figurative statement which maintains that the human being is the image of God, by defining him as open by *nature to God's *self-communication and this nature itself as a *potentia obedientialis* for the *hypostatic union and the *grace of Christ (given the *a priori* *Christocentrism of creation), and further defining supernatural grace as God's self-communication and as the power of *connaturally* accepting this divine self-disclosure within the word (faith-love) and the *beatific vision of God.

IMMACULATE CONCEPTION

This must not be confused with Jesus Christ's *virgin birth of *Mary, or be understood of Mary's own physical generation as such. The

228

dogma (D 2803f.) means that through the prevenient redemptive grace of Jesus Christ Mary was preserved from *original sin from the first moment of her existence and thus began her life possessed of the *grace of *justification (as the grace of Christ). If every human being is offered the grace of Jesus Christ, because of God's universal salvific will, and therefore has a supernatural *existential despite original sin, God considering him from the beginning a brother of Jesus and not only a son of Adam; if in addition, because of her indissoluble connexion with Jesus (who was to come into existence by the free consent of a mother's faith), she is redeemed in the most perfect manner possible (*Mariology); if she was predestined to salvation because of the union in her of office and person, then God's salvific will for her must have been given effect through grace from the first. The maternity which God predestined for her, which she was freely to accept, is for her from the beginning what *infant baptism is for others: the efficacious pledge of Jesus Christ's grace which excludes original sin and always precedes man's own free salutary acts.

IMMANENCE

Contrasted with *transcendence; it implies that something does not exceed a limit. Thus an epistemology may confine itself to subjective concerns, consciously abstracting from things "in themselves", or it may equate knowledge with sense-experience, declaring that whatever eludes the latter lies beyond the realm of all possible knowledge.—See *Spirit, Experience.* *Materialism, *Monism, and *Pantheism are philosophies of immanence, if and insofar as they confine being itself to the tangible or the finite. In this connexion Immanentism also means a philosophy which, while not denying God's own infinite being, holds that it is not substantially distinct from finite being, thus involving itself in contradictions. Immanence in a correct sense is an attribute of *life, since living does not connote an effect external to the agent but a self-realization *(actio immanens);* this is seen most clearly in the self-realization of a *spirit, but precisely this latter shows that immanence and transcendence need not be mutually exclusive.

IMMANENTIST APOLOGETICS

A collective name for various trends, especially in French theology during the late 19th and early 20th century, which sought to make the innate tendencies of man—as these are elevated by grace—and those data of revelation which as it were meet these tendencies halfway, the starting point for rational exposition of the *praeambula fidei, and accordingly undervalued the external motives of credibility (miracles and prophecies) which are highly valued by traditional apologetics (*Fundamental theology). The danger (not always avoided) is that immanentist apologetics may attach too much importance to emotion and the religious needs of human nature while belittling the intellect; insofar as it was identified with the false doctrines of *Modernism it was condemned by the magisterium (D 3878, 3882, 3894). The classic representative of immanentist apologetics, M. Blondel, has been expressly excepted from the condemnation. The encyclical *Humani Generis*, published in 1950, also shows that the sound and necessary efforts of immanentist apologetics are not condemned as such, since Pius XII (following St Thomas) points out that a truth may be known by "connaturality" with it. As to the proper approach for immanentist apologetics to adopt, see *Potentia Obedientialis, Supernatural Existential, Revelation.*

IMMINENCE OF THE END

The sound conviction of the primitive Church (one so basic to the Christian's understanding of his religion) was that with the death and resurrection of Jesus God has given himself absolutely and irrevocably to the world, so that it is no longer possible to look for a really new economy of salvation and that in this sense the end of the *aeons has already come. This conviction could not fail to create the impression that the total disclosure of this eschatological situation, Christ's *parousia, must follow within a space of time foreseeable and brief by earthly standards (see for example 1 Thess 4:17; Phil 4:5; Heb 10:37; Jas 5:8; 1 Pet 4:7; 1 Jn 2:18; Mk 9:1; Mt 10:23; Lk 9:27; also D 3433, 3628ff.), especially as the Christian necessarily hopes and prays for such an unveiling of the final order of salvation which is already established in substance and through his or her activity for the future of mankind assists its advent. In this perspective the length of earthly time intervening between that establishment and its full disclosure falls away. The NT often formulates its expectation in this perspective. Jesus himself, in statements about a temporal imminence, shows his conviction that God is acting *now*. In so doing, no more than the authors of the NT, he neither denies the intervening period nor provides any definite indication of its length, aware that this is the secret of God alone (Mk 13:32; Acts 1:7; 2 Pet 3:8–10; 1 Thess 5:1f.) which will only become known to mankind gradually. And if the extent of historical time remains obscure, the substance of Christian expectation of the end of the world loses none of its validity, indeed it becomes all the more important; the expanding world and its history (but also the scandalous aspects of the Church, increasingly institutionalized in consequence of the delay of the *Parousia) are embraced by the absolute imminence of God's self-communication, which has already occurred irrevocably and irresistibly in Jesus. So far as the individual is concerned the end is unavoidably imminent in his own *death.

IMMORTALITY

As referring to a characteristic of *life implying more than mere continued evidence, the term "immortality" signifies the exemption of this life from death, in that no finite temporality (such as that of merely biological life) can be discerned in its internal history which would make its existence apart from this temporal form meaningless, and neither is it "extinguished" from without. Absolute (metaphysically necessary) immortality is proper to God; being the fullness of life and absolute freedom from jeopardy, it is in fact a divine prerogative. Man is immortal, not as though his biological life had no finite temporal form ending in *death, but because within this very biological time man freely perfects himself as a spiritual person and for this reason gives up his spatio-temporal biological form (of his own accord, even though this task is accomplished against the resistance of biological life and by external causes). Thus he does not "continue to exist" "in time", but possessing his living completion, which can no longer be lost, he exists above time on a higher plane. Man has this immortality because his *soul is a substantial, "supra-material" principle which has a far more exalted function—as we realize by *transcendence even now—than that of merely shaping and informing temporal and material being. This conclusiveness, which man freely fashions for himself, may be either the perfection of supernatural good (*Salvation) or ultimate rejection of God turned in upon itself (*Hell). We speak of a conditional, bodily immortality of man in *paradise insofar as, but for sin (*Original sin, *Original justice), man could have attained his perfection not by actual death but by a transfiguration of bodily existence in space and time (which it is hardly possible to conceive of in more detail). The doctrine of the resurrection shows that even now,

231

since sin, God has promised to perfect the whole man in eternal salvation, and has already begun to do so in Christ.

IMPECCABILITY

As distinct from merely factual freedom from *sin consequent on free decision, the simple state of not having sinned, impeccability is the condition of a created will, brought about by internal (for example, the *beatific vision) or external causes (for instance, an efficacious *grace of God), whereby sin is excluded in advance of the creature's decision and without prejudice to his freedom, so that it is true to say that the creature "can" not sin although he is "free" to do so. The different systems of *grace variously explain how such "antecedent" impeccability is compatible with freedom. But it is the common teaching of all theological schools that a free impeccability of this kind is conceivable, and the concept is of importance in explaining the impeccability of Christ as man, that of Mary and the blessed, *confirmation in grace, and the preservation of the Church as a whole in truth and love (*Holiness of the Church).—See also *Sinlessness*.

IMPUTED JUSTICE

A name for the view of *justification held by many of the Reformers (Melanchthon), according to which God ceases to impute the sinner's sins to him because he imputes Christ's justice to him in justification. This forensic imputation is purely external, the sinner remains *simul iustus et peccator* and justice does not really become his own. As against this view the Council of Trent, following Holy Scripture, lays down that the sinner is also interiorly justified (Rom 8:1 and *passim;* D 1561). Nevertheless imputed justice can be understood in a perfectly Catholic sense, since Scripture obliges us to admit that it is only by the grace of Christ that our sins are not imputed (Rom 4; Gal 3:6; 2 Cor 5:19) and that nothing in the sinner can constitute any claim to justification. If this doctrine is considered in the light of the Catholic doctrine of the abiding sinfulness of the justified (D 225ff., 1533f., 1540, 1548ff., 1573 and *passim)* and the Protestant teaching now widespread that imputed justice stresses the gratuitous character of justification but does not deny that the sinner is made really and truly just, then it appears that imputed justice is no longer a real doctrinal issue between Catholic and non-Catholic Christians.

232

INCARNATION

(Lat. = becoming flesh). The central mystery of Christianity. The doctrine of incarnation states that Jesus Christ's human nature was assumed by the divine person of the Logos in a *hypostatic union as his alone for ever.

The *"human nature of Jesus Christ"*, the person of the Logos, must be understood to mean that Jesus Christ is really and truly a human being with everything this implies: a human consciousness which in worship is aware of its infinite distance from God; a spontaneous, human subjectivity and freedom with a history which, since it is God's own, possesses more rather than less independence, increasing rather than diminishing through the unity with God. Oneness with God and independence are essentially aspects which grow in equal measure rather than disproportionately. The divine act of union is itself the act of freeing created reality by making it actively independent in regard to God. This means that contemporary Christology (in proclamation and in theology) must so to speak retrace (and preach) the history of the "ascent Christology", which even within the NT rapidly changes from the experience of the historical Jesus and the descent-formulae found in Pauline and *Johannine Christology to a doctrine of the incarnation of God's pre-existent Son and Logos. The incarnation must be taught so that the experience of *Jesus* as an historically concrete person takes root more and more firmly, so that through it we are able to experience God's absolute and final closeness to the world and to our own existence, which can only be deduced and accepted without reservation if the classical formulae of Christology remain valid and comprehensible. In the *first* place Jesus can be seen and experienced impartially as the human "prophet" who in a creatively new way is affected by the mystery of God while at the same time naturally existing in the history of his own world, and who preaches the urgent proximity of the victorious kingdom of God emanating from God's mercy. Even within orthodox Christology we have the possibility and the right to discern Christ's genuine historical consciousness, because the ultimate, spiritual, eternally given transcendence of his being to the immediacy to God (in scholastic theology, the direct perception of God by the soul of Jesus) does not preclude, as the final horizon and justification of his human existence, the genuine historicity of his religious life with regard to God. But this "prophet" sees himself as more than just one of the many constantly recurring figures calling attention to man's genuinely radical religious relationship with God throughout history, with the future always unknown. Rather, he sees himself as the final, absolute Saviour, in whose life, death and resurrection the ultimate union between man and God is manifested, sealed, and made definitive through the experience of his resurrection. He does not see himself as the mere prophet of an as yet absolutely outstanding, purely futuristic "kingdom of God", nor of one (which *is* salvation) existing independently of his being, and of which he could only *speak*. Rather, he *is* this Kingdom, so that the salvation of every human being depends on his or her relationship to Jesus.

It is both possible and desirable in the present cultural and intellectual situation to translate ontic Christology (without eradicating it or refuting its continuing validity) into the form of a *transcendentally ontological Christology,* precisely in order to understand traditional Christology more efficiently. Put simply, this means that man from the foundation of his being *is* the absolutely unrestricted question about and quest for God, and does not merely pursue this question and quest as one of his many possible activities alongside others. This is evident in that transcendental relativity to God in a condition of knowledge and freedom (as a possibility permanently made available by God, not as a form of "autonomous" subjectivity) is the unreflexive and continuous condition of the possibility of all human knowing and free action whatsoever. This transcendence is realized in a spatio-temporal multiplicity of "accidental' human acts, which constitute human history, but this very multiplicity is borne by the fundamental act of *transcendence, which *is* the human essence. This fundamental act (insofar as it precedes the expression of human freedom) is at one and the same time that genuine origination from God and direction to him, that openness for God, which was permanently laid open by God in the act of creation in the form of a questioning of the freedom thus constituted to accept or reject that transcendence, and in the form of *potentia obedientialis* for the self-communication of God as the possible though free and radically highest answer of God to this question and quest which man *is* (see *Grace, Redemption).* If the question which man is and the acceptance of this questionability by God himself occur in *so* creative a manner that this question is posited *as* the condition of the possibility of the answer of the self-communication of God to mankind, and in such a way that *(a)* the will to this self-communication and to its acceptance from the human side as *absolute* will itself (not only as conditioned will) posits this *potentia obedientialis,* the everlasting question which man is, *because* the will to an answer on the part of God is absolute; and, (b) in such a way that this absolute acceptance (and therefore an acceptance which

234

implies its acceptance in formal predestination) of divine self-communication to the spiritual creature appears as something historically irreversible; then this unity of question and absolute answer constitutes (in an ontological proposition) what is called a hypostatic union (in an ontic proposition). For, on the foregoing presupposition, the "quest(ion)" which man is, is an inner aspect of the answer itself. If this answer is not something which emanates only from God as originator, but something which he strictly is himself, and if the question (as one accepted of itself in freedom, and of itself accepting the answer, as one which allows itself to be answered) is posited *as* an aspect or moment of the God who gives *himself* as the answer (as self-communication), then the positing of the "question" as an inner aspect or moment of the answer is a reality which is distinct from God and yet at the same time one which most rigorously belongs to God himself; one, then, which is proper to God himself. On this basis, it may then be shown (without further extension of the argument) how the "unmixed" difference between the divine and human in Jesus Christ arises *from* the unifying will of the *self*-communication of God; the creation of the human (as Augustine says) occurs through the "acceptance" itself, and the "covenant" (as Karl Barth in essence—and rightly—stressed) supports the creation. The foregoing can be properly understood and assessed only if it is understood in a rigorously ontological way: that is, the presupposition is made at the same time that spirit, self-consciousness, freedom and transcendence are not chance epiphenomena "in" some "given" which is ultimately conceived in a wholly materialistic manner, but constitute the very nature of being, which in the individual existent is only prevented from fulfilling itself by reason of the "non-being" of the *materia*. On the foregoing basis, it is also comprehensible that the self-pronouncement of God to the *world* (in divinizing grace) should occur and therefore be present irreversibly, victoriously and redemptively in history in the unique God-man.

An understanding of the incarnation (which of course does not eradicate the mystery) is attainable also from another viewpoint, and this necessarily has to be taken into account nowadays whenever it is appropriate to proclaim this mystery to the unbelieving "pagans" of the modern world. Contemporary man has an "evolving" understanding of the world. He sees himself as humanity implanted in the flux of history. For him the world has a "natural history"; it is not a statistical entity but a world in the process of becoming. Natural and world history form a single whole. This one history is experienced and seen as an history which is directed upwards, no matter how one might wish more exactly to describe the formal structure of this higher something at each stage, into which each single phase of this history moves in self-surpassing motion (for instance, increasing inwardness as self-givenness; growing extension from the whole of reality; increasing unity *and* complexity of the individual existent). If this history is to bring forth something which is really new (that is, higher, essentially more potent and not merely different), and to do so by its own means, then the transition from one form and phase of history to another can be characterized only as "self-transcendence". This self-transcendence towards something higher, although it is *ex supposito* the action of the historical existent itself, can occur only of the power of the absolute being of God himself who, without becoming an essential moment of the finite evolving being, in his creative reception and cooperation as future (at least asymptotically moving and therefore aiming from the basis of himself) effects this self-transcendence of the finite existent as the act of that being itself. It this notion of self-*transcendence* is conceived as divine movement and the divine act as the bestowal of *self*-transcendence, then the development of the materially spiritual world may be understood as an history, without that involving any denial of or oblivion to the *essential* distinctions within this one world and history. As we know from divine revelation, which reveals the ultimate existential experience of grace, the highest, absolute and ultimate self-transcendence of created being, which bears all precedent self-transcendences and gives them their ultimate meaning and their goal, is the self-transcendence of created spirit into the directness of the infinite mystery of the being of God himself. *This* self-transcendence requires the "cooperation" of God in an absolutely unique sense. Seen from the viewpoint of that transcendence, this cooperation is the gracious self-communication of God. The history of the world and of spirit occurring in stages of self-transcendence of created being is borne by the self-communication of God, a moment of which (which constitutes its presupposition) is the effective and original *creation of that which is distinct from God, while it is itself the prime cause and ultimate goal in the world of facts. The ultimate and highest self-transcendence of the finite, and the radical self-communication of God, are the two aspects of what happens in history. Here we must not overlook a dual process. On the one hand the goal of this ultimate self-transcendence is always the inconceivable mystery of God. All ways into the future are therefore co-determined by this uniqueness of the goal, and are ways into that openness which is as yet unknown to us. Hence all self-transcendence is hope and loving self-entrusting to that illimitable pure-and-simple which communi-

236

cates itself as the inconceivability of love. Furthermore, the history of
self-transcendence is the history of freedom, and therefore the history
of possible (and actually occurrent) guilt, and the rejection of this
thrust of history or of the false (that is, autonomous) interpretation
of this self-transcendence; the history of the possibilities of absolute
and ultimate deflection from the ultimate goal. Within this dual possibility of the history of freedom, abandonment, the "cross" and *death
have a necessary place.

This history of the self-communication of God and of the self-
transcendence of the creature, which is the history of the increasing
divinization of the world, does not occur only in the depths of the free
conscience, but—in the unity of the multidimensional human being
and of the thrust of grace towards the elucidation of *all* created
things—enjoys a specific historically categorical dimension. It appears
and produces its own accessibility in what we call *salvation history
in the specific and conventional sense; and this categorical, spatio-
temporal history is the history in which the self-communication of
God and the self-transcendence of the creature (therefore, of man)
occur. Where the self-communication of God and the self-transcendence of man categorically and historically reach their absolute and
irreversible apex—that is, where God is spatio-temporally, purely and
simply and irrevocably "there" and therefore the self-transcendence
of man attains to just such a full assignment to God—that has happened which in Christian terms is known as incarnation. Hence there
is a unified Christocentricity of the world which is cosmic and occurs
in the history of freedom.—But not as if the world reached its absolute
self-transcendence "only" in Jesus Christ. It reaches it as a whole,
insofar as all that is material transcends itself into that which is
spiritual and personal, and ultimately will exist only as an aspect of
the spiritual (in angels and in men) in fulfilment; and in the fulfilled
spiritual creation will have reached absolute proximity to God, to
absolute infinite being. To that extent, Jesus Christ is not really a
"higher stage" of the self-transcendence of spirit, or of the self-communication of God—such that one would have to ask why it is given
"only once", and is not attained to in all spiritual creatures in a
"panchristic" form. The incarnate Logos is the highest point and the
centre of the divinization of the world, insofar as it is necessarily given
as "unique", if the divinization of the world in grace and glory is to
reach its irreversible apex and victory, which occurs *historically*
within history itself. Because God bestows himself upon the world,
there is Jesus Christ; he is no merely possible mediator of salvation,

if he wishes to fulfil this communication, but is that communication itself, and that which is irrevocable and historically occurrent.

INDICULUS

See *Faith, Lex Orandi.*

INDIFFERENTISM

See *Atheism, Relativism.*

INDIVIDUALITY

In philosophy that determinateness of an entity which establishes it in its unicity and incommunicable oneness *vis-à-vis* the general (for example, genus). In the strictly qualitative (not merely numerical) sense it is an attribute of the *person only and the Fifth Lateran Council defined the individuality of each human soul (at least in the numerical sense) against Averroism and Neo-Aristotelianism (D 738).

INDULGENCE

Originally, the remission of public penance imposed by the Church for a certain period (whence its reckoning by years and days; *Penance, sacrament of). After centuries of abuse and misunderstanding, the practice of indulgences has now been largely abandoned. Theologically, a promise of the Church's special intercession with God for remission of the temporal punishment due to *sins the guilt of which has already been wiped out. The consequences of wrongdoing are not simply wiped out by the amendment of one's life. The Church, by her *prayer, can support the efforts of the individual to overcome them, and her prayer is certain to be heard because she is Holy Church and such prayer is always in accordance with the will of God. It will be effectual, of course, only where the individual is prepared for an ever deeper purification of his whole being—an indulgence is no substitute for penance. It is defined teaching that the Church has the power to grant indulgences; they are salutary and should be made use of (D

238

1835, 2537). Prerequisites: baptism, freedom from excommunication, performance of the good works enjoined, at least a general intention of gaining the indulgence. Scriptural term: do penance as a process of ending complete culpable alienation from God.—See also *Purgatory, Punishment of Sin.*

INDWELLING OF GOD

This is a general term for God's gracious *self-communication (*Grace) to the individual and so to the Church, insofar as what is given in this communication is God himself (or the individual divine Person). The testimony of Scripture brings out this fact by declaring that the *Holy Spirit is given, is poured out by the Father; that he abides and dwells in us, that God anoints and seals us with the Holy Spirit; that the Father and the Son come and make their abode with us (Jn 14:23); that the Son is in the sanctified and he in the Son (Jn 14:20). Accordingly the indwelling of God is based on the missions of the Holy Spirit and the (invisible) mission of the Son; the presence which is affirmed is based on the gracious benevolence of the abiding and indwelling Person; insofar as it is also bound up with that act of grace which creates supernatural *charity towards God in historical man ("created" grace), this divine indwelling also further signifies a mutual personal companionship of the utmost intimacy (see also D 1677f., 1913, 1915).

INFALLIBILITY

Infallibility means (1) that the *Church as a whole is protected by the power of God's grace (and not by the human strength of its members) from falling away from God's truth (and love); and (2) that by the power of God's grace the Church's teaching authority or *magisterium is protected from error in proclaiming absolutely binding dogmas. From the point of view of the history of dogma infallibility in the second sense developed—not uninfluenced by non-theological, political and ecclesiastical factors—out of infallibility in the first sense, which was always the conviction of the entire Church (cf. Church, 25). The Church's infallibility arises from the eschatological finality of salvation in Jesus Christ. Since God's act of salvation in Jesus Christ is both final and victorious and since truth, faith and the social organization of the Church belong to its inner constituents, an error would as a definitely intended interpretation of itself by this reality of salvation bring about its annihilation. The universal *consent *(Consensus universalis)* of the entire Church "in matters of faith and morals" is "infallible", i.e., cannot err in faith (Church, 12), but usually the Church's teaching authority acts as the mouthpiece for the *sensus fidelium* on the part of the whole people of God.

Infallibility is vested in all those who have supreme authority over the whole Church in accordance with its hierarchical constitution, that is (1) the universal episcopate, when under its head the *Pope it teaches with moral unanimity that God has revealed a certain doctrine to the Church (D 2879, 3011; Vat. II, Church, 25, see *Bishop);* (2) a general *council with the Pope (D 1478ff., 2923; Church, 25); (3) the Pope alone, when as supreme teacher of the Church *(ex cathedra,* that is to say, invoking the plenitude of his authority) he pronounces a doctrinal definition which is binding on the whole Church (Church, 25). This final decision by the pope is irreformable in itself and does not become so through the agreement of the Church. But this does not mean that it is not obliged to express the conviction in matters of faith of the entire Church. In reaching his decisions the pope, just like the bishops, is bound by Scripture, Tradition and the Church's previous decisions. The pope is never "infallible" in his personal conduct of personal views.

On the one hand, the inalienable possession of the reality of salvation as truth that is believed demands in the context of man's historical nature and his mode of knowledge an ever new appropriation in the form of a decision. On the other hand the doctrine of infallibility does not mean an absolute guarantee of the knowledge of any quite new reality and truth at all: its purpose is rather to guarantee that those who believe will remain in the old truths, and beyond this nothing. This expresses the correct content and the limits of this dogma. Applied to dogmatic definitions this means that theology has the task not merely of establishing who is proclaiming the doctrine and the contents it is intended to cover but also of illuminating its situation, and of establishing who it is addressed to, the (always limited) medium used for this doctrinal statement, the narrower historical context, the prevailing influences (never purely Christian), in brief, the historical factors conditioning this particular doctrinal statement.

Of future definitions it can be said that any genuinely new definition that does not simply repeat and re-present an old definition needs for its formulation one and the same theology (conceptual vocabulary, style of argumentation, etc.) which has to be the same as in the

Church as a whole. This single identity of theology, though in the past it used to exist despite all the theological *schools that flourished, no longer exists today and moreover cannot any longer adequately be restored (*pluralism). Alternatively, in any new definition the legitimate scope of interpretation would be so large as to preclude the possibility of any error. This final state reached by a teaching authority able to define genuinely new dogmas brings out sharply the historical limitations of the dogma of infallibility.

Nevertheless, the historical limitations attaching to a dogma do not mean that the Church's infallibility should be interpreted in such a manner as if God guaranteed merely an eschatological remaining in the truth on the part of the Church while dogmas proclaimed by the Church's teaching authority or statements in Scripture could always be wrong. Remaining in the truth is also realized in true propositions; the final fundamental decision by man that by the grace of God places him in the truth is always and inevitably expressed in true statements. The Church as a tangible entity would not remain in the truth if the objective expression of this remaining in the truth, and therefore its own statements of belief as the concrete form of this remaining in the truth, were wrong. Because of the unity and the still continuing history of human thought and awareness every human statement is of course exposed to misunderstanding, capable of interpretation, in need of development, and so on. But the truth of statements or propositions is not a purely supplementary delineation of the original truth and reality. Instead the realization of the truth of statements or propositions itself realizes that more basic and original truth which ultimately is God's revelation of himself in grace to man.

INFANT BAPTISM

The Church expressly teaches that *baptism incorporates a human being in the Church. This incorporation by baptism, according to the words of Scripture, presupposes confession of the Church's faith. Hence arises a problem which has aroused renewed discussion among Protestant theologians since the end of the war, owing to Karl Barth's decidedly negative attitude towards infant baptism, and which Catholic theologians have also taken up: can children be baptized who are not yet able to make a personal profession of the faith? The Church at the Council of Trent had already defined against the Anabaptists ("re-baptizers", falsely so called; from the year 1521 they rejected infant baptism and demanded adult baptism preceded by conversion) that baptized children are true believers and that no ratification of their baptism is required when they attain the use of reason in order for it to be valid (D 1625). This doctrine is based on church tradition and the practice, already attested in Scripture as apostolic, of baptizing a whole "house" (which in the language of the day included children) (1 Cor 1:16; Acts 16:15, 33). The theologians later taught, by analogy with *original sin, that just as this latter was contracted without personal fault, so the faith underlying infant baptism was the "alien" faith of parents, sponsors and the whole Church. This doctrine was further clarified by the realization that the capacity for faith (the infused virtue of faith) must in every case be a gift of God's grace. The whole matter is settled once we perceive that we are graciously enabled to perform free, salutary acts by God's pure gift, which in fact precedes all human activity, though not necessarily by a priority of time. This salvific will of God for each individual, which must first bestow life before life can develop and fulfil itself, is addressed to the child at his baptism, as a gift and an obligation, in terms that are historically and ecclesially tangible, because the reality of that gift and obligation does not derive from the assent of his faith. But there is no convincing theological necessity for infant baptism, and objections to it must be taken seriously. Talk of "proxies" is improper, since no one can substitute for another's faith. Except in danger of death, the Church does not allow a child to be baptized if there is no guarantee of his Christian upbringing.

INFRALAPSARIAN

See *States of Man.*

INITIATION

A technical term in the field of comparative religion meaning "introduction". It is applied to a great variety of rites whereby a member of a people, on reaching maturity, is received into the community or a "candidate" who is uninitiated is admitted into a religious association as a full member and initiate, often with rites that symbolize struggle, death and probation. Hence, if we use the term in a very general sense, *baptism and *confirmation can be regarded as rites of initiation into Christianity in view of their material resemblance, not indeed to the *mysteries of paganism, but to the customs of Christianity's Jewish environment. The term "sacrament" likewise derives from this source; *sacramentum* was the Latin word for initiation.

INITIUM FIDEI

See *Semi-Pelagianism.*

INSPIRATION

As distinguished from divine *revelation to and by a *prophet, inspiration is that charismatic divine influence upon the writers of the OT and NT whereby (without these writers ceasing to be the authors of their work) God becomes the author of these books in a speical sense and the books become the infallible word of God (2 Tim 3:16; for the defined teaching of the Church, see D 3006, 3029). This charismatic divine influence instigates and guides the composition of these books in all their aspects, internal and external, so that they contain what God himself wishes to say by their means—the genuine expression, free of all error, of the doctrine and being of the Church, which rests upon the apostolic preaching; so that these books are at once the word of the inspired human author and an embodiment of the faith of the primitive Church normative for all time coming, and in both respects are the *word of God. Vatican II repeated the teaching of the magisterium on inspiration but made a distinction between God as the "originator" and human beings as the "true authors" of Scripture, in which "the truth" is contained. The possibility is not excluded that biblical passages which are not connected with the "truth for the sake of our salvation" contain human errors.

INSTINCT

The attraction man feels towards a finite *good (real or apparent, and in relation to one of man's various dimensions), and the capacity to be so attracted, which precedes a person's free decision (acceptance or rejection) and is the necessary condition of such free decision (*Passion). Since this free decision is generally incapable of completely controlling these impulses and integrating them in the person's voluntary conduct, that is of ordering them wholly to the one good or evil thing the person chooses, the sum of these instincts is identical with *concupiscence, and is an expression of the fact that grace has not wholly enlisted the forces of *nature in the service of God's love—they can still at times impel to *sin.

INSTITUTION

Human actions and social interactions are not only determined by individual needs, inclinations and aims, but by mutual dependencies, reciprocal expectations concerning attitudes, judgments and norms. Institutions are mutually acknowledged, individually binding, permanently established patterns governing social interaction and communication and the opportunities for work and education. Institutions unite the general will of different groups in a common aim; they also presuppose the existence of an organizing force to implement and support their aims. There is however a danger that the social categorization of universal norms and principles might be given ontological precedence over the dignity and interests of the individual. Care should be taken to ensure that institutional organizations do not represent some abstract generalized interest contrary to the rights and expectations of the individual participants involved, thus leading to the denial both of the individual and of collective possibilities for development and self-determination. By relieving individuals of certain activities and by reducing the complexity of things, institutions should be able to make social relationships easier to grasp and increase the individual's chances of self-fulfilment. Hence one of the fundamental problems of all institutions is to strike a balance between the antitheses of order and freedom. In addition, as basic elements and structural guidelines of a society's renewal and compulsory self-criticism, institutions are bound to act as mediators between the individual's search for meaning and structure in his life and the overall meaning and purpose of society as a whole. Thus the essential function of institutions is to integrate the protection of the identity of the individual with the stability of the organized structure of society. Institutions can only guarantee the sense of order this implies if they can succeed in conveying the idea of their own legitimacy and by extension the principle of a general readiness to agree. When the legitimate function of a particular conception of the world ceases, the institutions representing it simultaneously lose their liability and organizing power. Conversely, institutions also encounter difficulties in their tasks of integration and orientation when they fail to keep pace with social change, thereby unjustifiably restricting the possible actions of their subjects. Such institutions must either make way for new ones or they must undergo some far-reaching changes. Bearing in mind its specific nature, the same applies to the Church as an institution.

INTEGRITY

In general integrity connotes completeness; in the theology of *original justice it means all those endowments to which man had no claim but which God freely bestowed on him in *paradise: supernatural *sanctifying grace, the preternatural gifts of freedom from (negative) *concupiscence, from *death and its preludes, sickness and suffering (the theological doctrine of which will be found in the relevant articles; Gen 2:25; 3:7; Rom 6:12ff.; 7:8f. and *passim.*—Gen 2:16f.; 3:3; Rom 5:12–21). All this was lost through *original sin. In the Christological sense, furthermore, integrity means that exemption from *concupiscence which characterized the divine Logos after his Incarnation in human nature (D 434) and which God by the grace of Christ also granted to *Mary (D 2803f.; *Immaculate Conception) and which finally will be an essential feature of the *resurrection of the flesh, which latter will be impassible (Rev 7:16f.; 1 Cor 15:42, 53; Rom 8:11). See theological discussion under *Suffering.*

In the sphere of morals integrity primarily means the physiological and psychological completeness of man, of which no "part" may become independent (as in the voluntary or morbid dominance of a particular impulse), or which may be interfered with only so far as the good of the organism may require (medical intervention); in moral theology integrity means the integration of a whole human being into a fundamental option that is morally good (*Love).

INTELLECT

Intellect and reason are hardly distinguished in Catholic parlance, where both terms signify man's spiritual faculty of cognition, which is characterized by *transcendence (*Spirit) and therefore (though this may take the form of a denial), an inevitable ordination to God. This one faculty necessarily discovers itself and its transcendence with reference to the world, sensible reality, "ideas"—images, the concreteness of human experience and knowledge as they exist in society, custom, and tradition. The intellect thinks conceptually, discursively, by drawing conclusions, and at the same time "intuitively", so far as it not only thinks in terms of sensible reality but by becoming aware of its own transcendence grasps ultimate and irreducible metaphysical principles. The basic actualization of the intellect is essentially related to the basic actualization of the *will; together they form the self-actualization of the *spirit (somewhat as there are two and only two "processions" in the Blessed *Trinity). Revelation invokes this faculty of cognition in all the breadth and variety of its being: in its transcendence, by *grace; in its orientation to the world, by the historic spatio-temporality of God's saving deeds and *miracles and the pregnant human words of the bearers of revelation; in its social articulation, by the ecclesial vehicle of revelation; in its historical development, by the history of the mind of the believing Church (History of *dogma); in its discursive rationality, by the scientific character of dogmatic *theology and by *fundamental theology.

INTENTION

In the original, philosophical sense it signifies purpose, direction; in present-day philosophy intentionality is primarily the transcendental reference of a *spirit or a *person. Moral theology defines intention as that property of the human *act which refers it to a goal (*Good, *Motive) and therefore fixes the measure of that act's morality. It is neither the external motive nor the general interior disposition but the concrete inner purpose, which, depending on the measure in which it is present, may be explicit or implicit and, according to how far it influences the agent's deed, is either actual (a motive expressly mustered and actually present in the deed), virtual (expressly mustered and still operative but not expressly present in a deed), or habitual (at one time expressly mustered but thereafter merely unrevoked). These distinctions also figure in sacramental theology, a minimum intention being required for the valid reception of a *sacrament. A positive will not to receive a sacrament always makes the latter invalid. The validity of matrimony, the sacraments of penance and anointing of the sick always requires a positive (if on occasion only habitual) intention; on the other hand the Church considers baptism, confirmation and holy orders pure gifts rather than self-realization, whence the doctrine that they can be received even before the age of reason (CIC, can. 968); once the age of reason is reached they can be validly received only with a sufficient intention. The minister of the sacraments, assuming that he can validly administer them at all, must at least have the intention of "doing what the Church does" (D 1611), that is he must intend the religious rite, willed and known as such, as it is celebrated in the Church.

INTERESTED MORALITY

Certain texts in the Gospels promise a "reward" for Christian conduct (though the reward does not follow in earthly form but is "great in heaven", Mt 5:12). Catholic morality was formerly reproached with affirming moral values for the sake of sub-moral values, because the Church invokes the motive of reward (and because of certain over-simplifications). This reproach is undeserved. As for the "reward in heaven", a Christian cannot do otherwise than act in view of it, because it consists precisely in his gracious, gratuitous, undeserved admission into the *basileia* and because *salvation is what every human being hopes and yearns for, so that God himself is what is envisaged and affirmed in it. (See the motivation in the *Sermon on the Mount.) The earthly reward is for the most part identical with the life-enhancing rightness inherent in morally good behaviour, and is therefore not a sub-moral value.

INTERMEDIATE STATE

Theological propositions which concern man when on the one hand his final destiny has been personally decided at his *death and on the other hand, because the world to which the dead man still belongs pursues its course, he has not been perfected in every respect, are said to deal with the "intermediate state". This imperspicuous situation is usually explained by saying that as to his "soul" the dead man is "already" enjoying the *beatific vision (*Heaven) or is already in *hell or *purgatory, and that he will undergo his *resurrection "in the *body" only "later". These statements are correct. But we must also bear in mind that given the substantial unity of man, which takes ontological precedence over the pluralism of his constituent principles, a statement about the "body" is also one about the "soul" and vice versa; that the dead man can neither be thought of as wholly departed nor yet as subject to space and time in the same way as those still living. Theological propositions about the intermediate state therefore themselves hover in an inescapable duality of affirmations about the one human being who can only be rightly described at any time as both a spiritual person and an earthly being. Consequently individual and cosmic *eschatology, the eschatology of the soul and that of the body, can neither be divorced nor one reduced to the other. The doctrine of the intermediate state is based on this fundamental anthropological situation.

INTUITION

From the Latin *intuitio,* insight; the direct evidence of a being for and in a given act of knowing. Thus it is to be distinguished from abstract discursive knowledge but in fact, given the reflexive character of the human *spirit (Transcendental *experience), there is never any dichotomy between them. A theory of religious knowledge which attempts to substitute intuition alone for rational, logical knowledge (an attempt foredoomed to failure) is called Intuitionism. Such Intuitionism is a feature of *Ontologism, the philosophy of value (M. Scheler), *Neo-platonism, theosophy, anthroposophy, and *Modernism. The latter sought to liberate theology from *dogma, as merely indirect knowledge, for direct religious experience.

IRRATIONALISM

A collective term for any interpretation of human consciousness which assumes the existence of cognitive powers separable from and (more or less) independent of the intellect, and adopts an attitude of hostility or reserve towards abstract reasoning. It is irrationalism, for example, to assume that feeling is a third basic spiritual faculty proper to man, like intellect and will (freedom, love), as in the view that knowledge of God is only accessible to a feeling for values, or to conceive the ultimate principle and ground of being as "something" irrational or obscure (such as a life-force). In the history of ideas it is sometimes a reaction to *Rationalism.

I-THOU RELATIONSHIP

See *Communication, Community, Self-Communication.*

J

JANSENISM

A tendency in doctrine and piety, named after C. Jansen, Bishop of Ypres (d. 1638), which affected large parts of France, Belgium, Holland, Italy, and Germany in the 17th and 18th centuries. Very briefly its basic features are: an aversion to philosophy; exclusive acceptance of Scripture, the Fathers, and a mysticism of the heart; moral austerity (bitter struggle against Laxism), and an emphasis on the rights of bishops in the sense of French Gallicanism. Condemned by the Church. In theology the Jansenist doctrine of grace was wholly erroneous: grace was due to Adam by right, the virtues of pagans are only vices, mankind is enslaved to sinful concupiscence and even the justified remain subject to it at least interiorly; sin is possible even without interior freedom of choice; Jesus died for the elect only and the mass of men are damned (*Predestination). This doctrine of grace, contained in five propositions taken from Jansenius' book *Augustinus,* was condemned in 1653 (D 2001–2005). The Jansenists agreed that these propositions were heretical but denied that they were to be found in *Augustinus.* Thereupon the Church laid it down in 1656 that the propositions were contained in that book (D 2012; see also 2020), and in 1715 the bull *Unigenitus* solemnly renewed the condemnation of Jansenism. The doctrine, however, lingered on till the beginning of the 19th century and survives even at present in the Jansenist church of Utrecht, which separated from Rome in 1723.

JESUS CHRIST

THE LIFE OF JESUS. The historical existence of Jesus, his life, death, and resurrection and his affirmations about himself are established with certainty by the four Gospels, the letters of the Apostles, non-Christian witnesses (Flavius Josephus, Tacitus, Suetonius, Pliny the Younger, the Talmud) and early Christianity.

Jesus (Yehoshua, Joshua, Josue ["Yahweh is salvation"]; for "Christ", see *Messiah)* was born a Jew before the year 4 B.C. at Bethlehem in Palestine. His mother was *Mary. Herod the Edomite ruled Palestine at that time under Roman suzerainty; the Jewish nation, divided as to religion, had lost its political independence; and the Graeco-Roman civilization of the Roman Empire had laid the foundations for the future historical unity of Europe (and hence of the world). After a youth spent in obscurity at Nazareth Jesus comes forward about the year 27 as an itinerant religious teacher in Palestine. He announces that in himself, the Son of the Father, the definitive reign of God (*Basileia) is victoriously and irreversibly at hand which redeems lost and sinful men if they uncompromisingly believe in him and are converted (*Metanoia). This is the central point of his message and mission, which initially is directed to all Israel as the chosen people of God. Within the framework of his summons to the radical conversion of *faith he demands a morality which must be the gift of God's grace, which while quite realistic about the concrete moral achievement human beings are capable of (as compared with unlimited truthfulness, purity, humility, self-denial and love of our neighbour) breaks through all ethical and religious formalism and establishes a personal relationship between a man and the living God (*Sermon on the mount). Jesus teaches that though God is infinitely exalted he can be loved; that morality is what it should be only when it rises above itself—when the human being who has received the message of God's love in faith loves God with his whole heart. Jesus makes this possible for man by making the kingdom of God a matter of concrete experience, taking up the cause of the "weak", anticipating the kingdom at table with the "unclean" and in healing the sick, and appearing with the disadvantaged and with sinners, so as to become a brother to man, like him in all but sin (Heb 2:17; 4:15). This message is addressed to each individual, because in each individual Jesus sees a person absolutely distinct and valid before God, freely deciding his eternal destiny in this one life that is his. Jesus confirms his doctrine by his own life. He accepts its narrowness and rigour without complaint. With a pure heart and as a matter of course he humbly loves every human being who encounters him. He remains inflexibly devoted to his task, unflinching in face of contradiction and threats, perfectly obedient to his Father's will which governs his life in every detail, in loving adoration of this Father whom he always has

250

before him, whether at solitary prayer, in daily life or in the abandonment of death. Jesus' life testifies more eloquently than any words to his joy in God, the merciful and loving Father.

His message and demands meet with growing resistance from his people in the person of their officials and religious leaders, who see in Jesus' independent attitude to the *Law an attack on God himself. Jesus avoids the summoning of a "holy remnant" of the good and those ready for conversion to form a messianic community apart. He makes his message universally applicable to the heathen and to all men and women, and consciously attends his violent *death under the Roman rulers, and he looks on it as the consequence of his mission. After fully two years' activity he dies on the 14th or 15th Nisan (about April 7th), probably in the year 30. Because of his claim to be *the* Son of God and the Saviour he is executed on a *cross at Jerusalem, having been betrayed by his friends and condemned by both religious and secular authority. On the third day his tomb, which has been sealed and guarded by his enemies, is empty. But he shows himself physically alive, though transfigured, to his disciples—on one occasion to more than five hundred of them at once (*Resurrection of Jesus, *Ascension). He leaves behind him a community he has founded, which believes in him as the Lord (*Kyrios) and Redeemer by the power of his Holy Spirit. This community, the Church, placed under the authoritative government of the Apostolic College with Peter at its head (*Church), is united by its confession of Jesus, its common faith in his truth preached by the Apostles in obedience to his command; by baptism, the sacrament of faith through which, confessing the Trinity, one enters his Church; by common celebration of the Last Supper, in which through *anamnesis* his death on the cross is made present and his Body and Blood are received; by expectation of his return (*Parousia), which will fully reveal God's dominion, already become an indestructible reality in the world through life and liberating work, death and resurrection.

JESUS' SELF-UNDERSTANDING AND THE NT CHRISTOLOGIES. The deepest meaning of this life of Jesus lies in what he himself is and what he progressively reveals about himself. He knows that he is truly a human being, a worshipper before God to whose incomprehensible will he submits himself, exposed to everything that is implied in human destiny. But he also knows and declares that he is the Son of the Father as no other human being is—in a sense quite peculiar to himself. He knows that all men's eternal destiny is decided by him because in the last analysis whatever men do they do for or against

251

him. He claims power to forgive sins, which God alone can do. He is therefore legitimately seen as Lord of the divine law, the Lord and Head of God's Church, the Judge of world history, the Lord of the angels, the only begotten Son who alone knows the Father and whose own nature is the secret of the Father alone. He knows that his place is at the right hand of the Father. Jesus' statements about himself in the Fourth Gospel are indeed—like St Paul's Christology—formulated differently, in more metaphysical terms (Christ's pre-existence before his earthly life, his union with the Father, his possession of the personal Spirit of God; the divine *doxa* and life "in itself" being proper to him as to the Father; Jesus himself simply called "God") than in the Synoptics (see also *Son of God, Kyrios);* but they do not materially add to what is said there about Jesus.

NT Christologies use numerous expressions of dignity primarily to designate Jesus' importance in the history of salvation, rather than his personal nature. The far-reaching conception of Jesus' pre-paschal self-understanding dates only from Easter. The resurrection should be seen in advance as the event through which God finally and victoriously reveals himself to the world. Through this event God's eschatological action is manifested to the world and for the first time it becomes fully apparent *who* Jesus himself was from the beginning.

If we today wish to gain a closer understanding of Jesus of Nazareth, we should reflect that any person who freely and unequivocally accepts his or her existence is in fact pursuing a kind of "questing" Christology. This may be represented as a three-fold call: for (1) absolute *love of one's neighbour, (2) readiness for *death and (3) hope for the *future. Where, except in Jesus, could these universally sought-after things be found?

DOGMATIC FORMULATION OF JESUS' SELF-REVELATION. In order to prevent this self-utterance of Jesus and the NT Christologies being distorted or truncated, especially in the sense of a mere unity of religious outlook between the man Jesus and God (thus *Nestorianism and, later, the liberal Protestant theologians), the Church (Councils of *Nicaea, *Ephesus and *Chalcedon) developed and, by recourse to problematical terms and formulae from abstract popular philosophy, formulated it (with reference to the Blessed *Trinity) as follows: the second Person of the Trinity, the Son of the Father, his divine Word (*Logos), possessed from all eternity of the one divine nature which the Father communicates (Creeds; D 301ff., 434, 595 and *passim),* has within time assumed a human nature from Mary as entirely proper to himself (Creeds; D 301ff., 424f., 502 and *passim).*

Thus Jesus Christ possesses a divine nature and a human nature, without confusion or separation, in the unity of the same divine *Person (*Hypostatic union), whereby he is truly God *and* man (D 301ff.), a mystery of faith in the strictest sense. His being, therefore, has nothing in common with the mythological idea of a god appearing on earth in human disguise (except, perhaps, that it fulfils the human longing for the nearness of God which keeps appearing in myth and which only an atheist can think suspect). On the one hand we have the historicity of Jesus and the incommutability of the one infinite God, whose Word, truly existing as God, took on a truly human reality without injury to it; and on the other a multitude of gods who are personifications of particular forces within the world, stand in opposition to each other and do not "appear" at any definite place. And because Jesus is not some being intermediate between God and man (a misinterpretation of the Gospel that was exploded long ago during the struggle against *Gnosis, *Docetism, *Monophysitism, and *Arianism), the doctrine of the Incarnation requires no *demythologization, so long as one believes that even today there exists the living God and true man, possessing an eternal significance, with something, nay everything to do with each other. The imagery of such expressions as can be misinterpreted in a mythological sense ("descent", "emptying", "sitting at the right hand of God", and the like) is readily understood by the educated Christian. Nor has belief in the Incarnation anything to do with ideas derived from oriental religions, for in all of these the "incarnation" is only a transient sign of the deity within the realm of that which has no real being, a sign which perishes, and therefore can always be repeated, whereas in the Word made flesh the created world, though always a creature, finds its definitive and permanent validity.

Thus the mystery of Jesus consists in the fact that he truly stands on both sides of the boundary separating God from creatures: he is the Son of God and the Son of Man. If human nature is conceived as an active transcendence towards the absolute being of God, a transcendence that is open and must be personally realized, then the Incarnation can be regarded as the (free, gratuitous, unique) supreme fulfilment of what is meant by "human being". Jesus Christ's "humanity" can be seen as that which results when God in his Word literally becomes other to himself in a creature. In this way Jesus Christ is the summit of creation, the Lord and Head of the human race because he is one of its members, the *Mediator between God and creatures. Because Jesus cannot be conceived as man without the world for his environment, God's gracious will for that whole world has become historically concrete, definitely real, in the world; God's decisive and final word, in his dialogue with the world that he has established in freedom, has already been uttered in his Word made flesh. The dignity of the divine Person invests Jesus' moral acts with infinite significance. His obedience, realized in complete surrender to the Father through his death, which he undergoes as head of the human race, is the *redemption of the world.

He who hears and believes the message of Jesus and has faith in him, comprehends the fact that God in his sovereign freedom has willed not merely to endow creatures with a genuine freedom *vis-à-vis* the Creator, but also to summon all creation, to a share in his very own life in glory by way of the historical life his own Word has lived in the world, in the totality of body and spirit, as the very being of the Word. The Christian believes that this event, on which the final and ultimate salvation of the world depends, has occurred precisely in Jesus of Nazareth, that consequently his doctrine and his spirit are absolute truth and life for men, his death their redemption; that the consummation of the world consists in the definitive revelation of this utter intimacy between God and his creature (*Christianity).

Many a man who rejects the formulae of theological *Christology because he understands them amiss, may yet existentially have a perfectly genuine Christian faith in the Incarnation of the Word of God. Anyone who contemplating Jesus, his cross and death, really believes that here the living God has spoken to him the final, decisive, irrevocable word that delivers him from all bondage to the existential categories of his imprisoned, sinful, death-doomed existence, believes in the reality of the Jesus of Christian faith, believes in the Incarnation of God's Word, whether or not he realizes the fact. To say this, of course, is not to deny the importance of these formulae, which are objectively correct and which provide the sociological basis for community of thought and belief in the Church.

Indeed, many a man has encountered Jesus Christ unawares, laid hold without knowing it on someone into whose life and death he plunged as into his blessed, redeeming destiny. The grace of God and the grace of Christ are everywhere as the secret essence of all that is open to choice, so that it is difficult to grasp at anything without having to do with God and Jesus Christ in one way or another. Any man, therefore, however far he may be from the explicit verbal formulae of any *revelation, who accepts his own existence—that is, his humanity—in mute patience (or rather in faith, hope and love, whatever he may call these) as the mystery that conceals within itself the mystery of eternal love and bears life in the bosom of death, says Yes to something which corresponds to his limitless surrender to it, because God in fact has filled it with the limitless, that is with his divine self, when the Word became flesh; though he may not know it, such a one says Yes to Jesus Christ. After all a man who lets go and jumps, falls into the abyss that is there, not only as far as he has plumbed it. To accept and assume one's human condition without reserve (and just who does so remains obscure) is to accept the Son of Man, because in him God has accepted and assumed man. If Scripture declares that he who loves his neighbour has fulfilled the law, this is the ultimate truth for the reason that God himself has become this neighbour, so that whenever we accept and love our neighbour we are at the same time accepting and loving that one Neighbour who is nearest of all to us and farthest of all from us.

JOHANNINE THEOLOGY

The revealed and inspired doctrine which is presented in the Gospel of St John and in the three epistles of St John (and to some extent in the book of Revelation). Being an essential constituent of the NT, it forms a permanent part of Christianity. Johannine theology is remarkable in the theology of the primitive Church for its breadth of vision (despite a relatively limited vocabulary) and its profound resolution of the kerygma to theo-logical statements. At the same time, as non-Catholic scholars increasingly concede, we must recognize that this theology is inseparable from the patently authentic *logia* of the Lord and that, whatever the differences in terminology, it is consistent in all its features with the affirmations of the Synoptics and with *Pauline theology. What perhaps chiefly characterizes Johannine theology is the fact that in it the primitive Church attains her most articulate and mature self-consciousness *vis-à-vis* the new and wider world into which she has emerged from Jerusalem. Thus this theology is of fundamental importance. It is tidings from God, who is Spirit, Light, and Love and has sent his beloved only Son into the flesh so that those who accept him in faith may be reborn, filled with light and grace even here and now, but destined one day for the most intimate communion with God in the glory that fell to the Son's lot on his return home. All narrowness and particularism is alien to this theology, which draws a luminous picture of a new world in the midst of the old world which is subject to darkness, a world whose newness expresses itself in love and joy; so too it is said of God that he seeks to draw all things to himself. In the deepest sense this is a theology of the Church, if office and reverence for office, the sacraments and commandments are as it were presupposed as general structures and accepted as the way, and yet our contemplative gaze is not directed to these things themselves but to the God who communicates himself in Jesus: to light in itself rather than to the radiance it emits and the shadows that resist it. Conscious as it is that the Judgment has already taken place, that the Life is already alive in those born anew, who form a community of brethren united in love, Johannine theology displays none of that aggressive and polemical attitude sometimes found in Pauline theology; looking with confident expectation to re-union with the Lord, it finds any rejection of him, any desire to linger in the flesh, almost imcomprehensible.

JUDAISM AND CHRISTIANITY

The Jews might be defined as that part of humanity which was con-stituted a people in the OT epoch of saving history by God's historical intervention, by the *election and the *Covenant, and has on the whole (despite all tendencies to secularization) remained a people through consciousness of its election, of its hope of salvation and of God's unequivocal promise. Particular treatment of the theology of this people will be found in the articles *Old Testament, Election, Covenant, Law.* This nation produced Jesus, himself a Jew, born of the Jewish Virgin Mary. He prayed in the temple of the Jewish people, he was circumcised according to their custom, he wished to fulfil their Law, their Holy Scripture was also his Holy Scripture. His disciples belonged to this people, the Twelve whom he called so as to manifest his claim to this people, the twelve tribes, as his own. It was this people he warned with loving solicitude and forgave as he hung dying on the cross, "for they know not what they do" (Lk 23:34). The primitive Church separated itself from this people, and was separated from it, because she confessed that Jesus is the Son of God (concern-ing this new theological situation, see *Church, New Testament);* this separation was a necessity of saving history, something that should not have happened yet "had" to happen, because it was the necessary means, in the history of this world, of forcing open the chosen people to all mankind. But this separation should never have become an occasion for Christians to fall upon the Jews and as Christians to do them indescribable wrong for the pseudo-theological reason that they were "deicides". An initial Catholic approach to coming to terms with this terrible injustice of the past was made in the "Declaration on the

Relation of the Church to Non-Christian Religions" *(Nostra aetate)* of Vatican II (4f.). We are still only on the threshold of a Christian and Catholic theology which meditation on saving history will have thoroughly purged of hostility towards the Jews. It must begin with the "great sadness", the "continual sorrow" of the "anti-Jewish" theologian St Paul who "wished himself to be an anathema from Christ for my brethren" the Jews, "to whom belongeth the adoption as of children and the glory and the testament and the giving of the law and the service of God and the promises" (Rom 9:2ff.); with the eschatological vision outlined in Romans 9–11, where St Paul sees as it were in retrospect how God included both Jews and gentiles in unbelief so that he might have mercy on all, bringing both through a wholesome mutual emulation into his *basileia* (see Mt 23:29). The rupture caused by the fact that Christians acknowledge Jesus of the Jewish nation as Lord, whereas the Jews think they cannot believe in him, is no "theoretical" and innocuous difference of opinion. But the Christian who believes that he is blessed in this life and hereafter because Jesus of Nazareth died for him, is as responsible for the death of Christ as any Jew and can only approach the people from whom Christ came as Christ himself approached them. And if he perceives that today the Jews are beginning to say of Christ, with diffident affection, "after all he was one of us", then the hope must grow within him that behind the people of Israel's denial of Jesus Christ a greater and more cogent affirmation may lie hidden, for many who knew not his name have already found him to their salvation.

JUDGMENT, LAST

The Judgment must be seen in the context of the consummation of the world and of history as a whole. It will then be clear that those NT texts which closely connect the Judgment with the *parousia* (Mt 25:31– 46; Mk 14:62) on the *Day of the Lord and with the *resurrection (Mt 10:15;11:21ff. with parallel texts) are part of our basic information about the Judgment. This consummation is called the Judgment of *God* because on the one hand the radical disclosure of the completion of all the history of the world that has been enacted in freedom is central to it, and on the other hand the consummation is not simply the result of a *development immanent in the world, but depends on the sovereign discretion of God (an *end that is fixed, not merely arrived at). This consummation is called the Judgment of *Christ* because its ultimate character is essentially determined by the nature and work of Jesus Christ—this on account of the *Christocentrism of all reality in all its dimensions. Because it comes upon all (in the framework of their interrelations, consummating both good and evil) it is called the *general* Judgment. Because it is the final consummation which terminates history it is called the Last Judgment.

(1) The magisterium of the Church bears witness to the general Judgment in the Creeds. ("He shall come to judge the living and the dead.") The particular judgment of the individual, which follows his death, is taught by the Council of *Florence (D 1304ff.); see the details in the article *Death*.

(2) The theological problem arises when we attempt to define the relationship between the general and particular Judgment. The nature of man calls for a dialectical unity of affirmations about the one man, whose elements are not completely interchangeable yet cannot be clearly assigned to one or other of the two "parts" of man (soul-body). Man is a terrestrial being ever unique, existing in matter yet at the same time a spiritual entity existing in itself, not reducible therefore to a mere element of the cosmos and its history, and caught up in the destiny of the one world. On principle the consummation of this one man can only be expressed in two indissociable dialectical affirmations, corresponding to the indissoluble dialectical unity of two groups of affirmations: in the propositions of an individual eschatology and in the propositions of a cosmic one. The modern attempt to arrive at a purely individualistic eschatology through *demythologization does not do human nature justice. But no more does the tendency, now coming to the fore in Protestant theology, for example, to pass over eschatology that is personally eschatological in favour of a cosmic eschatology, an event of which the individual is only an element. But neither is it legitimate to attempt to introduce a dichotomy among the material elements of the one consummation of man who is one, dividing them between two events which are separated by an intervening lapse of time and are quite unrelated to each other. For the consummation of man as a cosmic being (for instance, the *resurrection of the flesh") is also an element in the consummation of his uniqueness (so that even as a spirit he is only consummated in the full sense in that event), and the consummation of the individual human being as his unique self (for instance *beatific vision) is an element in cosmic world-history. This fundamental relation between what is different, yet not adequately divisible in our affirmations about general and individual eschatology also obtains between the general and particular Judgment. The pronouncements of NT and magesterium on the Judgment are not intended as instruments of ecclesiastical threat. As

against the image of a Judgment presided over by Jesus, there is reason to hope securely in the fulfilment of God's *justice through his mercy. Judgment is also mentioned in the Gospels. Statements about the Judgment and popular associations of "people getting their due" do not dispense Christians from doing all they can to make justice prevail here and now.

(3) The following additional information from the NT about the Judgment certainly amounts to more than detail illustrative of our considerations of theological principle above: It is impossible to forecast the Judgment (Mt 24:43–51; Lk 17:20f.). We shall be judged by our attitude towards *Jesus Christ and the *love we have actually shown during our life, especially to those with whom Jesus identified himself (Mt 25:31– 46; 18:23–35). The Christian can await the Judgment with confidence (1 Thess 5:3; Gal 5:5; Col 3:4; 1 Cor 6:1–5; Rom 8:1, 31–39; 1 Pet 1:8f.; Jn 5:24). Those who hold office in the Church must expect a rigorous Judgment (Jas 3:1).

JURISDICTION

See *Church Authority.*

JUSTICE

The "disposition in virtue of which a man has the firm and constant will to render everyone his due" (St Thomas Aquinas). In the classical doctrine of the *virtues justice is the second cardinal virtue, traditionally divided into three types according to the three aspects of life in society: (a) *commutative* justice in the relations of individuals with each other; (b) *distributive* justice in the relations of society (family, State, Church) with its individual members whereby they are given a share in the common good; (c) *legal* justice in the individual's relation to society, whereby for his part he subordinates himself to the common good. Though justice ranks as the highest moral virtue, in its Christian form it is inseparable from love, since more is required of the Christian than a non-partisan attitude which would allow everyone the same rights or respect for irreductible rights to things of an objective kind. A Christian cannot accept the contention that the economic sphere is ruled only by its own laws. (We always remain debtors where love is concerned: Rom 13:8.)

The biblical concept of justice is dominated by the *Law. Both OT and NT ingenuously assume without qualm that there are just men who obey the holy will of God by fearing God and loving their neighbour and are without anti-social guilt. In the OT the poor, the oppressed and the persecuted are the "just". Justice is promised for the kingdom of God. The NT of course conveys the news of that justice which makes man really pleasing to God, which God imparts to him of grace because of his faith: *justification.

JUSTICE OF GOD

In theology, that moral attribute of God's will which places it in the right relationship with creatures—a relationship, that is, corresponding to the nature of each term of the relationship. The sole norm of divine justice is God's own holy will, which is identical with the divine essence. By *creation and *grace God *makes* man the right object of his activity, at the same time preserving the *freedom of the creature, since God himself creates that freedom; and therefore God's will for the creature can be both justice and *mercy: his justice does not "force" him to any particular action, such as demanding complete *satisfaction. God in his freedom can either judge and requite as a real contradiction of his holy will the human guilt he has permitted, or as the "just judge" reward the *merit that he has bestowed by his grace. The fact that man cannot control the unity of God's mercy and justice shows the divinity of both these attributes. According to revelation we are made just (*Justification) and so participate in God's justice: thus God reveals how he is at once merciful and just, by transforming us into beings whom it is right for him to love both in principle and in actuality.

JUSTIFICATION

Catholic doctrine holds that justification is the event in which God, by a free act of love, brings man (not in a narrow, individualistic sense) into that relationship with him which a holy God demands of man and which the God of overflowing grace is prepared to give him. He does so by giving man a share in the divine nature (2 Pet 1:4). This happens when God causes the *Holy Spirit, his own Spirit, to dwell efficaciously in the depths of man's being as the spirit of the adoption of sons (Rom 8:15; Divine *sonship), of *freedom (2 Cor 3:17) and of holiness (Rom 1:4), divinizing him (*Grace, *Self-communication of God), and gives him proof of this new creation—which is believed in but cannot yet be reflexively ascertained—through the word of faith and the signs of the sacraments (*Baptism). This justice, which is not merely imputed in juridical fashion (D 1520, 1561, 3235) but makes a man truly just (Rom 1:17; 6:20; 8:10; 1 Cor 15:17ff.; Gal 5:5; Eph 4:24 and *passim;* D 1528f.), is at the same time the forgiveness of sins (*Original sin). Through the Incarnation of the Son of God (*Jesus Christ), his death and his resurrection, God's will to justify man is present in the world, eschatologically certain and irrevocable. That this salvific will of God is given to men in Christ is part of our *faith; that it has singled out each individual, though each can sinfully reject God's love (whether he admit the fact or not), we confidently *hope, but there can be no reflexive *certainty of salvation for any individual. God's justifying action does not trespass on man's free realization of himself as a person (D 1525, 1554f., 1559); rather it finds its reality through the very free acts of faith, hope, and love which accept this divine self-communication. Consequently this *justice, God-given and received, can also be lost if man rejects divine love by serious sin (D 1544, 1577). Because justification is an event which happens to man, the historical being, he genuinely and radically passes from the state of sin to that of justification (there is no dialectical co-existence of sin and justification), even though man remains exposed to the attacks of sin (*Concupiscence) (D1515f.), is not able to discover for certain what his condition is before God (D 1533f.), continues to sin (D 1573) and in this three-fold respect remains a man fleeing from his own perdition to the grace of God. Because salvation must be won historically, justification may be preceded by preparatory acts which the grace of God makes possible (faith, imperfect *contrition: D 1526f.) and man can both preserve and continually increase it (*Merit, Good *works: D 1574).

K

KAIROS

In Greek philosophy, the term for a period of crisis within a temporal experience at which the person concerned is summoned to historical decision. The *kairos* in Scripture is the time of salvation which God has chosen and decreed (Mk 1:15), the fullness of time (Gal 4:4), the final offer of God's grace in *Jesus Christ to Israel (Lk 19:44) and to all men (2 Cor 6:2), and therefore simultaneously a final warning, the beginning of the Judgment (1 Pet 4:17; Col 4:5). *Kairos,* like the biblical *now, expresses God's sovereign dominion even over *time.

KENOSIS

A term in biblical theology which seeks to express Christ's self-exinanition (Gr. κένωσις , emptying) in the Incarnation, in his positive obedience to the Father, in his conscious acceptance of death (Phil 2:6 –11). It signifies that in his earthly existence he chose not to manifest the *doxa* that is his own by nature (*Pre-existence of Christ), living the life of a slave for our sake (see 2 Cor 8:9). For a more analytical approach to the union of God and man, see *Incarnation.*

KERYGMA

A NT term which in modern use means the word that is preached (Gr. κήρυγμα, preaching) to the Christian community or individual ("unto destruction" or "unto edification") in the name of God, by lawful commission of God and the Church, as the very word of God

262

and Christ, and which efficaciously makes present its utterance in the situation of the hearer whom it summons. This word is something more than and distinct from either the propositions of Catholic *dogma, which merely "accord" with reality (whenever the Church does not preach the kerygma but discerns truth from error by her "extraordinary" *magisterium), or the principles deduced from these propositions by human thought (*Theology), because in this way the word, by being spoken and heard, becomes the historically tangible event of that utterance in the situation of the hearer: a word which brings with it what it signifies, the offer of the grace of faith. But the kerygma is the primary source and norm of dogma and theology and finds the most intense fulfilment of its own nature in the word of faith that is spoken to the individual in the *sacraments as the manifestation of God's salvation, giving itself by effecting its own manifestation (its "sign").

KERYGMATIC THEOLOGY

Kerygmatic or "preached" theology is in principle an acceptable term for any theology which is specially concerned (as all theology should be) to serve the Church's kerygma, the fruitful and efficacious preaching of God's saving message by the Church. Historically speaking, kerygmatic theology means the thesis, put forward in the 1930s, that besides scientific (scholastic) theology with its formal object (God, under the aspect of his divinity) there can and should be a second theology with its own formal object (Jesus Christ), which must not only definitely serve pastoral purposes but is essentially different from scientific theology. This view attracted little support, and rightly so: all theology must be saving theology; a purely theoretical, unengaged theology cannot and may not exist. Yet this theory voiced a deep concern that scientific theology does not clearly serve the purposes of a vital preaching that reaches the man of today in his religious distress —a portentous default which results from the present system of theological teaching at universities and seminaries, which, however, cannot withdraw from interdisciplinary dialogue and confict and the consequent requirement of responsible scholarship and science.

KEYS, POWER OF

According to Matthew 16:19 the "keys of the *basileia" are given to

Peter. It was the belief of Later Judaism that the keys (a metaphor connected with "entrance" into the *basileia)* are in the hands of God, who sometimes entrusts them to human delegates (see Lk 4:25; Rev 3:7 with Is 22:22; Lk 11:52; Mt 23:13; Rev 9:1; 20:1, 3); they signify the way of salvation but not salvation itself. If they are entrusted to Peter (the Rock), this means that he is appointed dispenser of the way of salvation which Jesus has opened, that is, he is the accredited High Steward of that means to salvation which is the Church. The power of the keys, it must be noted, is not to be confused with the power of *binding and loosing, being given exclusively to Peter. In modern terminology, the distinction means that the authority of supreme pastor in the Church belongs to Peter alone, whereas supreme pastoral authority also belongs to the Apostles.

KINGDOM OF GOD

This term means (a) the validity of God's holy, salvific will (as Creator, conserver, legislator, and bestower of supernatural grace) in all his creation but especially in men and angels, and (b) the actual execution of this will (*Basileia). Because history is still going on, God's will is still in process of being executed, and therefore the kingdom of God is still "coming" (Mt 6:10). When a creature freely carries out God's will his act is both his own and the act of divine grace; so that the kingdom of God is the pure gift of God, which he bestows and gives reality by his might and which must therefore be prayed for, and at the same time a human task given as an assurance of the promises of the kingdom of justice, love and peace (without any question of *synergism). Insofar as this triumphant grace has been vouchsafed to the world as a whole with eschatological irrevocability in Jesus Christ and his death and has become manifest in him, the kingdom of God has already come and the issue of world history, as the kingdom of God in which his dominion is the glorification, not the damnation of the creature, is no longer in doubt (1 Cor 10:11), though the fate of the individual is still uncertain and therefore his salvation is an object of *hope (*Certainty of salvation) and though it would be more scriptural to call this kingdom of God the "kingdom of Christ". This kingdom of God is not identifiable either with a State—which must always be provisional—or even with the Church of this age, which is the society of those who believe in the kingdom of God to be which will terminate the history of the world. The Church is the *primordial sacrament of this kingdom and, because

264

she is Holy Church, its secret beginning, precisely when she recognizes in her own weakness the manner in which God's redemptive might will come. Hence discourse on the kingdom of God has a critical function in Church and society (*Political theology).

KNOWLEDGE

See *Doubt, Experience, Gnosis, Intuition, Reason, Truth, Wisdom.*

KNOWLEDGE OF JESUS

The theological problem of Jesus' knowledge is not concerned with the infinite knowledge of the eternal *Logos in *Jesus Christ but with that of his human, finite *soul. We know from the nature of the creaturely soul that its knowledge is finite: its supreme act in the immediate *beatific vision is the blessed surrender of itself to the incomprehensible *mystery of God. Since the consciousness of a being, its "presence to itself", corresponds to the level on which it exists, the *hypostatic union means that from the beginning the human soul of Christ necessarily had presence to itself its immediate union with God's Logos and therefore had the immediate vision of God, though this was not necessarily beatific in every respect (*Beatific vision). But in view of the origin of this vision it will be understood that this non-conceptual basic existential state of Jesus, who gives himself completely to God and is completely ruled by him, does not necessarily mean that his knowledge takes, or can take at will, the form of particular pieces of knowledge. Despite (or rather within) this unique, basic existential state, therefore, Jesus was able to gain experience just as we do, to develop intellectually (Lk 2:52); it was possible for him not to know something in terms of objective concepts which would allow of explicit statement to himself or others (for example Mt 24:36), for the future to be veiled to him, even though his mission and all that he had to know to fulfil it were already present in and to him by anticipation in that basic existential state, at once entitative and cognitive, which formed the core of what he was and is.

KNOWLEDGE OF GOD, POSSIBILITY OF

In accordance with the testimony of Scripture (Wis 13:1–9; Rom

1:18–21) and Tradition the Church (notably in the First Vatican Council) declares against Fideism and *Traditionalism—which regarded all religious knowledge as given in purely historical verbal revelation alone, that is in faith as such—and against all *agnosticism in metaphysics, that the "natural light" of reason is able to know God with certainty from the created world (and hence, by developing this knowledge in a systematic way, to achieve demonstrative certainty). (For the defined teaching of the Church see D 3026; also 3004, 3878, 3890.) How this happens, in the concrete, is stated in the article *proofs of the existence of God. This doctrine that God can be known by natural reason does not assert that such knowledge is independent of the human outlook and attitude as a whole, nor does it necessarily apply to the *individual* concrete human being in his individual and social circumstances and difficulties, so far as concerns a knowledge actually attained and explicitly worked out. Nor does this doctrine deny that all knowledge of God that is in fact attained in the concrete order of sin and grace, especially when and so far as it has any relevance to salvation, is sustained by the grace of Jesus Christ. But it means that even when man closes himself to the obedience of faith he still has to reckon with God, that there is a basic possibility of religious agreement between believer and unbeliever (with reference to Scripture and the Church's magisterium) prior to agreement about the content of revelation, and that the distinction and unity between (spiritual) *nature and grace (and their theological principles) is relevant to this matter.

KOINONIA

See *Communion of Saints.*

KYRIOS

From the Greek κύριος, lord, ruler. It is primarily the term for *Yahweh (since it was forbidden to pronounce this name) in the Greek translation of the OT. In the NT it is the primitive Church's name of praise and adoration for *Jesus Christ (already found in Aramaic, 1 Cor 16:22). By calling Jesus κύριος, the Church ad-

KYRIOS

dressed him as God, a confession that is only possible "in the Holy Spirit" (1 Cor 12:3). This testimony to Jesus' divinity aroused the opposition which the Church had to endure from the synagogue as well as from the heathen emperors.

L

LAITY

See *Layman, Laywoman.*

LAPSE FROM THE FAITH

In theological language, the abandonment of supernatural *faith, either complete (apostasy) or partial, that is with respect to particular truths which form an integral part of revelation as a whole (*Heresy). On this subject the First Vatican Council, rejecting the positive *doubt demanded by Hermes, declared that a Catholic can never have a sound reason for changing his faith or calling it in question, once he has received the faith under the Church's magisterium (D 3013f.). This is of course to be understood of reasons which are objectively sound, for Hermes' theory denies the efficacy of grace, which bestows faith, and is injurious to the *Church as the visible community of believers which is in itself a motive of credibility (D 3013f.). But since the Church exists in the world as the means of grace and whilst preserving her essential subjective holiness may, by the fault of her official representatives or of her other members, happen to wrong an individual and thus as a sinful Church offend against her members (for the converse is not the only possibility), it may come about in a particular case (though not normally, as Hermes would have it) that a Catholic will without *subjective* fault renounce his faith, at least within his articulate consciousness. (There will, of course, be some *objective* fault.) It can hardly be denied that the image of the Church as she really should be and as Jesus would have her which such a person bears in his heart may imply the desire (*Votum) to belong to her and to share her faith.

LAST THINGS

Those realities which comprise or lie 'beyond' the boundary dividing time, history, freedom and their ultimacy from one another, and therefore the usual name for the various elements of the one total finality (either in the form of perfection or that of utter and eternal ruin) of the one human being, as a unique individual before God and as a member of mankind: that is *death, particular *judgment (*Purgatory), the *beatific vision (*Heaven), *hell (as aspects of the personal fate of the individual) (D 372, 1304ff., 1000f., 1820); and the *resurrection of the flesh, the general *judgment, the new heaven and the new earth (as aspects of the universal consummation of mankind as a whole) (D 76, 150, 540f., 801). If we really take into account the basic Christian view of the world with its genuine temporality (*Creation) and the nature of true freedom (as implying all eternity in one's personal choice), and if certain dimensions of human existence are not excluded *a priori* from the definitive salvation of the one human being (a spiritual person who is also a concrete body) as unsalutary or indifferent, then it becomes obvious that these last things are aspects of the one consummation. They must neither be conceived as the object of affirmations about the same indistinguishable thing, varied only by "mythologization" (for man is a *plural* being), nor yet as the object of affirmations about events which are adequately distinct (for man is a single being, above all when he is perfected, whose individual elements can only be adequately grasped by envisaging them all). The last things are not only outstanding events towards which man proceeds but are already actually anticipated in faith and hope. On the one hand, eschatological hope relativizes every concrete aspect of present reality in which Christians live; on the other hand, this hope which relativizes the present should also be made evident in social structures (Vat. II: Church, 35). The doctrine of the last things is called *eschatology; consequently it is a dogmatic *anthropology (which again only achieves full statement in Christology) applied to the manner in which its object, mankind and the world are perfected.

LATERAN COUNCILS

Of the councils held at the Lateran in Rome (First 1123; Second 1139; Third 1179; Fourth 1215; Fifth 1512–17) two are theologically important: the Fourth (the Twelfth Ecumenical Council, November 11th to 30th, 1215, under Innocent III) which defined the orthodox doctrine

LAW

of the *Trinity, *Jesus Christ and the sacraments of the Eucharist (*Transubstantiation), baptism and penance against the Albigenses, Abbot Joachim of Fiore and others (D 800 –808) and established the rule of the Church concerning confession and communion at Easter-time (D 812f.); and the Fifth (Eighteenth Ecumenical Council, 10th May 1512 until the 16th March 1517 under Julius II and Leo X), which defined the immortality and individuality of each *soul against Neo-Aristotelian views (D 1440f.). A number of local synods have been held at the Lateran, notably those of A.D. 313 (against *Dona-tism) and A.D. 649 (against *Monothelitism; D 501–522).

LAW

An ordinance for a society, promulgated by the authority in charge of that society. As a theological entity it has a rôle of special impor-tance in the saving history of Israel. The books of the OT (almost exclusively Genesis, Exodus, Leviticus, Numbers, Deuteronomy) contain an abundance of laws, developed out of the juridical thought of the ancient East, which in a few particular instances are clearly human dispositions but as a whole are regarded as revealing the will of the God of Israel, the God of the Covenant. Hence the five aforesaid books (Gr. πεντάτευχος) are already known collectively in the OT as "the book of the Law" (2 Kg 22:8, 11; 2 Chr 34:14; Neh 8:3) and later are simply called "the Law" (Heb. *Torah).* The heart of the Law is the relations that are to exist between Yahweh and Israel and between Israel and the individual (*Decalogue, *Commandments of God, *Covenant). Since the OT conceives these relations to be salvific, the Law which lays them down is also held to be a gracious gift of Yahweh and is extolled in hymns (Ps 119). It was considered illicit to add anything to the Law which had been faithfully preserved in exile or to omit anything from it, from at least the time when Cyrus (559–529 B.C.) allowed the Jews to return from the Babylonian cap-tivity. From what has been said it will be understandable that the Law (synonymous with "will of God") was esteemed above all the holy books of Israel, being preferred to the Prophets and the later "writ-ings"; it became the norm for what was to be received into the *canon of the OT. Late Judaism developed its own theology of the Torah. It is the very wisdom of God, immortal, the glory of Israel, that which sets her apart from the heathen. On the other hand he who knows not the Law is lost, not only he who disobeys it. There are parties who

270

will accept nothing which is not in the Torah (Sadducees, Samaritans).

The formal concept of the Law in the NT is taken over from the OT: the "Law" is all the ordinances of the Pentateuch (including the ritual ordinances), the Pentateuch itself, indeed the whole OT. This Law has been given by God himself. But it is authoritatively expounded by Jesus, who knows himself to be master of the Law: it is deepened and sharpened into the commandment to love God and neighbour (Mt 5:23– 48; 7:12; 22:34 – 40; Mk 10:5; 12:28–34; Lk 10:25–29); the prescriptions of the Law concerning ritual purity are abolished (Mk 7:1–23)—thus the Law is truly fulfilled (Mt 5:17). From the moment when the disciples began to preach the *Gospel of *Jesus Christ, conflict between the *primitive Church and Judaism was inevitable; it was sustained by St Paul. For him too the Law reveals God's will (Rom 2:27; 7). But the Law was given because of sin (Gal 3:19) and therefore was only our "pedagogue" until Christ should come (Gal 3); but looked on as a means to salvation it is a curse: *salvation is not to be gained by human efforts and the observance of the letter, but comes only from the *grace of God (Rom 3 and 4) which is given in Jesus Christ; in the cross of Christ and in baptism as a dying with Christ, we are delivered from the Law (Rom 8:1– 6; Gal 2:19). As other NT texts show, this theological refutation of the idea that the Law is a means to salvation must not be interpreted as a denial of the necessity for faith to be realized in every human dimension and therefore to express itself in obedience and love (*Works). But the Pauline theology of grace has by no means closed the discussion of law. This discussion was given its characteristic form by the theology of the Reformers (and the opposition of the Reformed Churches to any canon law; see also *Antinomianism, Natural Law)* and is still continued today when Catholic morality is reproached with being "legalistic ethics". The necessity for ecclesiastical laws and commandments, and the similar right of the State to make laws for the ordering of civil society, emerge from an analysis of fully achieved human *freedom whose inalienable free act implicitly affirms that the *a priori* preconditions of that freedom are to be willed and are therefore imperatives, but only recognizes these preconditions when they are made known *a posteriori* and thus, given the historicity of man, must in concrete behaviour be subject to an "external" norm, a norm which for its part must be historically "embodied" and made evident. This can only be called "Christian legalism" if the grace of Christ is regarded simply as a means to compliance with this norm or if affirmation of the norm is demanded for its own sake, regardless of the intrinsic justice of the

LAXISM

norm (*Nominalism)—dangers which find no kind of support in the pronouncements of the Church's magisterium but which are by no means always avoided in ordinary Catholic catechesis and preaching.

LAXISM

See *Moral Systems.*

LAYING ON OF HANDS

A cultic gesture of great antiquity. In the OT it particularly signifies delivering animals in sacrifice to Yahweh (Exodus and Leviticus), symbolically transferring the sins of the whole people to the scapegoat on the day of atonement (whereupon he was driven into the wilderness to perish like those sins); a blessing which people gave one another; and a rite of ordination or consecration (Num 27:21f.; Deut 34:9). In the NT the laying on of hands is encountered most frequently in connexion with the healing of the sick by Jesus, the disciples and St Paul, but also as a gesture of blessing (Mk 10:16 and 11). The NT accounts of the laying on of hands as a rite of ordination or consecration are suggestive; it is expressly stated that the rite was associated with prayer, and in one case with fasting. The laying on of hands confers the diaconate (Acts 6:1– 6); it officially assigns Paul and Barnabas to missionary work (Acts 13:3); and is again mentioned as conferring office in 1 Timothy 4:14 and 2 Timothy 1:6. The NT is familiar with the laying on of hands as a rite which is supplementary to baptism and bestows the Holy Spirit (*Confirmation: Acts 8:15–17; 19:5f.; Heb 6:2), and finally as a penitential rite (1 Tim 5:22). Thus there is good Scriptural foundation for the present practice of the laying on of hands in the sacraments of baptism, confirmation, order, anointing of the sick, and, in the rudimentary form of raising the hands, penance. It symbolizes the communication of the Spirit (even in reconciliation with the Church) and healing; it is the sacramental sign (*Matter) of *confirmation and *order (ordination of deacons and priests, consecration of bishops; D 3837–3861).

LAYMAN, LAYWOMAN

From the Greek λαικός, "belonging to the people". As a theological

272

LAYMAN, LAYWOMAN

term it means firstly, if only negatively, one who is not among those invested with jurisdiction of full sacramental powers in the Church, that is does not belong to the *clergy (even Vatican II defined the laity "negatively" as those believing Christians who are not consecrated or ordained: Church, 31). This distinction is found in the biblical terms "sheep" and "shepherd" (Acts 20:28, 31; 1 Pet 5:3), "garden" and "gardener" (1 Cor 3:5–9; see 2 Cor 3:4ff.), and in the early Church is plainly seen in Clement of Alexandria, Tertullian, Origen, and St Cyprian. But this is not to say that a "layman" or "laywoman" in the Church is a mere passive object of the Church and her power to teach, govern, and sanctify, or represents the profane milieu in which the clergy functions as the Church, as clericalists' views tend to imply even today. This is not so, if only for the reason that every member of the Church—and therefore every "cleric", including the Pope himself—always remains a recipient of the sacraments and a member of the obedient Church. Furthermore, Scripture declares that all brethren in Christ are called to the inheritance of sonship, all form God's holy house, his own holy people (1 Pet 2:5, 9f.; 1 Cor 3:16f.; Eph 2:19–22; Heb 10:21f. and *passim)*. The word layman therefore means positively that the baptized person (thus sancified in principle and favoured with the very life of God) who is a member not a mere object of the Church as an active function and responsibility, belongs to the holy *People of God (1 Pet 2:10), must bear witness by his life (and thus also by what he says) to God's grace in Christ as the triumphant redemption of the world and all men; he shares in the Church's task of taking up, elevating and fulfilling man's purely human vocation in all spheres of human life (culture and history) in the expectation and acceptance of the kingdom of God. It is his responsibility to join in the celebration of the sacrifice of the Church (*Eucharist) as a member of the whole celebrant body, to undertake the share that concrete circumstances indicate is his in the Church's total task and its external missionary endeavour. The layman or laywoman is also, by the *direct* mission of God, the potential vehicle of *charisms by which God blesses and guides his Church, however willingly the layman or laywoman, in readiness to serve, adapts his or her charism to the general life of the Church, submitting it to the "discerning of spirits" by the universal Church's higher and more comprehensive charism in both its hierarchical and free forms. In church practice the laity has not been sufficiently integrated into the essential structure and development of life in the Church, although the theological situation in fact demands it. The lay person's primary task is his or her worldly obligation within the scope of which he or she must give a practical demonstration of his or her faith and hope. In so doing he or she reveals the importance of a just, Christian approach to the history of the world and its structures (marriage, work, career) to the salvation of the world: for we see here the fusion of the individual and the cosmos which will ultimately lead to God (*basileia). Prior to distinguishing between clergy and laity Vatican II tried (in Church, 30 –38, etc.) to emphasize the unity between *all* members of the Church on the basis of their communal faith and their share in the threefold ministry of Christ. *All* Christians are called to participate in the Church's mission of salvation through baptism and confirmation (and not through hierarchical assignment). Which means that *all* the laity are dependent on one another. One of the distinguishing features of the laity, as Vatican II made clear, is its "worldly character"; just how this should in fact be realized it is left to the laity to resolve (ministers are not competent to advise on "worldly" obligations and activities and have no mission to do so: Church/world, 43). However, following Vatican II, the theological problem of the relationship between the *Church and the *world should not be settled by recourse to a kind of *dualism. That would result in the disintegration of the Church into spiritual pastors and worldly functionaries. Fundamental to the ecclesiology expounded by Vatican II is the assertion that the Church —as a whole—"is a sacrament, i.e., symbol and instrument intended to bring about the closest union with God and the unity of all mankind" (Church, 1).

LAY THEOLOGY

This term may be taken to mean theology itself as it has always (though in varying degrees) been studied in the Church by *laity and expounded for laity. The need for this theology is evident, not alone from the present acute shortage of priests, but from the fundamental yet inadequately realized equality of *all* Christians with respect to *theology, which should not simply be the concern of the privileged few in Christianity. The participation of the laity in theological considerations guarantees theological research a closer "link with the present day". For this reason Vatican II wished to see a considerable increase in the number of lay theologians studying theology as their main subject (Church/world, 62). The lay theologian does not function independently of the official *magisterium of the Church, even when working as a teacher of religion, a pastoral assistant, etc., rather than in the numerically limited academic sphere. Whenever he or she

274

participates officially in the mission of the Church he or she is subordinate both theologically and professionally to the official teaching ministry of the Church to which he or she owes his or her mission.

LEARNING CHURCH

In a strict theological sense this term does not so much indicate the fact that the *Church as a whole is a learner of God's revealed word, or designate that part of the Church which receives instruction from the *magisterium, by divine right exclusively vested in the Pope and the episcopate under him and by ecclesiastical right in those whom the Pope delegates to teach; rather it indicates the profound truth that the teaching and learning Church are united in learning, because the Holy Spirit is given to the Church as a whole, so that this whole Church has a "sense of the faith" (*Faith) and only one who believes, that is obeys and learns, can really be a teacher in the Church.

LEX ORANDI, LEX CREDENDI

The abbreviation of a statement in the *Indiculus de gratia Dei* (D 246), meaning literally, "the law of prayer is the law of belief". From this source there later derived the theological principle that the *liturgy is a norm of faith, a witness to the infallible belief of the (praying) Church. This proposition must be correctly interpreted: where the liturgy does not expressly affirm a credal statement or obviously presuppose it, no such statement may be drawn from it; nor does the liturgy propose matters to be believed that are not divinely revealed. For instance the fact that St Joachim has a feast on August 16th is not evidence that the father of Mary is this Joachim who appears in the *Apocrypha. It must be observed that the passage in the *Indiculus* has nothing to do with the theological axiom later drawn from it. The sense of the passage is that the necessity for asking God's help in prayer proves our duty to believe in the necessity of grace.

LIBERAL THEOLOGY

A trend in Protestant theology during the 19th and 20th centuries, which aims to show that Christianity is rational and expedient and

LIFE

reconcilable with the human desire for autonomy. Whereas its early exponents, like D. F. Strauss and F. C. Baur, still consider Christianity the highest form of all religion, liberal theology later becomes relativist under the influence of the school of comparative religion (E. Troeltsch). Another form of liberal theology, like Catholic *Modernism, regards dogma as mere objectification of subjective faith (influenced by F. Schleiermacher and A. Ritschl). The most far-reaching result of liberal theology has been a *biblical criticism that does violence to the scriptural data and is governed by arbitrary philosophical assumptions. Liberal theology as descended from Ritschl and currently influential sees divine love as realized *only* in love of one's neighbour and seeks the reality of the kingdom of God in a transformed society (ethical basis of dogmatic theology).

LIFE

In philosophy, an analogical mode of being which is progressively realized at each ascending stage of reality as a whole (in the perspective of the natural sciences, life is associated with protoplasm as the highest known form of organization of matter). On the basis of our experience of animate bodies life connotes the ordered unity of a multiple being which coheres and persists in space and time as a single thing *vis-à-vis* the environment despite the real plurality of the elements composing it; so that, containing within itself the principle of its movement and direction, it is not a mere dependent function of the environment, but the whole is always something more than the sum of its parts and their interaction. If the task of the living being, accordingly, is spontaneously to preserve and develop its spatio-temporal form, then (wherever it rightly understands itself and is rightly understood) it must by that very fact be more open than that which is dead (death is a *limit*) to the environment by "expectation"; by accepting and modulating impressions from without in its own characteristic way; by placing its self-fulfilment, only now become possible, at the service of others; by increasingly drawing the milieu into the field of its own being and extending its scope within the milieu. From the theological point of view this fragile "miracle" of life is evidently the gift of God because contingency and creatureliness are more keenly experienced in living being than in the inanimate world. Life is evidently verified on an essentially higher plane in the operations peculiar to the personal spirit: conscious free agency—as history, personal responsibility and ultimate self-realization, and as

276

transcendence towards God's absolute mystery, through which the environment becomes a world of personal communion (and can thus become the kingdom of God)—is life in an eminent degree. Henceforth, God is finally conceived analogously and metaphorically as the "living God": Life itself and the ever creative primordial source of all life. He is not unreal, like the dead, like the dead idols, he can act with absolute power in perfect freedom. His world is at once in his presence and in him, its Creator, in absolute otherness and absolute intimacy (Gen 2:7; Ps 36:10; Acts 17:24 –28). He perfectly abides with himself in exhaustive knowledge and love of his being, which is inexhaustible because it is infinite (*Trinity), which proceeds only from himself and therefore knows and loves all else in selfless communication. God's radical self-communication in Jesus Christ, therefore, is life in the supreme degree, which "now" indeed must still be lived by dying together with Christ (Rom 6:3f.; Gal 2:20; 2 Cor 6:9; Col 2:12), and so is "hid with Christ in God" (Col 3:3). But "I live, now not I, but Christ liveth in me" (Gal 2:20). The Christian shares the life of the Risen Lord in the *Pneuma (Rom 5- 6; 2 Cor 5: Jn 3:15f.; 5:24; 6:40, and *passim),* a life which continually grows and unfolds until it becomes manifest as the glory of eternal life (Rom 5:17; 6:5, 22; 2 Cor 2:16; Jn 14:2f.; 17:24, 26). Since 'eternal life' begins, is anticipated and may become open to experience in earthly life, from the theological point of view, *all* human beings also have a right to authenitic life.

LIMBO

From the Latin *limbus,* border; a technical term in theology for the place or state in which the dead are thought to be who have deserved neither beatitude nor damnation. The *limbus patrum,* where the just of the OT and pious heathen had to await the opening of *heaven by Jesus (see the following texts: Lk 16:22; 1 Pet 3:18ff.; *Descent into hell) was distinguished from the *limbus puerorum,* where those children are thought of as existing in a kind of natural blessedness who have died without baptism and therefore have not attained to the *beatific vision because they remained in *original sin. The doctrine of limbo, doubtless derived from the idea of *sheol* in Later Judaism, was especially widespread in the scholastic period. The existence of the *limbus puerorum* is questioned in modern theology, in view of the fact that there have been no declarations of the magisterium on the subject—those texts which touch on the subject having nothing directly to say about limbo. Scholarly investigation, which is still in progress, has established that there is no *consensus of theologians on this matter in early times. The underlying problem will have to be envisaged in the light of the universal *salvific will of God, the *baptism of desire, and an adequate theology of *death.

LINGUISTICS AND THEOLOGY

As the intellectual analysis and framework of talk about God, theology does not only have immediate reference to language as providing the objects of its study and the medium within which it develops but also has reference to linguistic theory, since as a scholarly discipline it must be concerned to provide a universally valid foundation for the meaning and truth of its statements through critical reflection on the structures, functions and conventions of rational discourse about God. Since theology is inextricably linked to religious experience and the interpretation of this experience through the medium of language, in the context of historical transformations and social patterns of life, and is also intent on arousing people to decisive action by bringing out the implications for the present, it can defend as legitimate a preference for those linguistic theories that place their chief emphasis not on *a priori* construction and deductive application (theory of formal languages) but on the reconstruction of actual linguistic usage and its system of rules and on the exposition of the secular transmission of meaning (theories of normal language). To the extent that beyond this the doctrine of *inspiration and *revelation presupposes that the conditions for God's revealed word to be comprehensible are *a priori* linked with langauge and can be immediately perceived, a further theological requirement of a linguistic theory is that the analysis of actual linguistic usage must be able to lay bare and make known the transcendental constitutional framework of language, its structures, rules and functions. Beyond a methodological symbiosis of theology and *hermeneutics as applied to the humanities, theology can enter into dialogue with a number of various theories from the tradition of analytical linguistic philosophy. Theology can be equipped in its linguistic argumentation with new models for providing discourse about God with a solid foundation by means of the theory of language games that arose in the context of Wittgenstein's later philosophy (recognition of the autonomy of a religious language game) as well as by means of the functional analysis of meaning further developed by Austin and Searle through consideration of the theory of action to become a theory of the acts of speech. There is too the move towards pragmatism introduced by Peirce and Morris by providing a semiotic foundation for a logic of research and of the truth of empirical statements: this brought out the significance of a universal community of communication as the framework within which the claim to truth of theoretical statements could be met. All this opens up new perspectives both in the way of providing a firm foundation for theology as a science with its own independent programme of research and in the way of clarifying the indispensable social aspect of theological reflection (the ecclesial character of theology) and the normative role of statements of faith with regard to the anticipation in practice that is to be offered in them of a fulfilled life.

LITERARY GENRES

A term in *exegesis and *hermeneutics for the literary forms or stylistic peculiarities of the books of Scripture; like all literature, these are roughly divided into prose and poetry. Study of the OT further distinguishes the principal genres of prose (including sermons, prayers and tales), proberbs and songs. In the NT literary genres are of special importance in the epistles (insofar as they incorporate hymns or sermons, for example. Form-criticism *(Formgeschichte)* examines the Gospels in detail in terms of traditional units, editorial history etc. The purpose of this scholarly analysis is to ascertain the concrete background (the so-called *Sitz im Leben* or sociological setting) against which the particular passage and the composite end product arose. This enables one to state with more precision than formerly whether the books of the Bible (and which of them) are intended to record history, in what sense we can speak of historical writing in the ancient East at various periods, what is literary trappings or early theological interpretation, and what is actual and literal historical statement. Since the pontificate of Pius XII Catholic biblical scholars have been encouraged to investigate these literary genres with great care (their existence being henceforth taken for granted by the magisterium); indeed it is even said to be possible that the biblical authors used these literary genres unconsciously (D 3829f., 3862ff.,). It is not in order to weaken the force of biblical statements that literary genres are studied, but to fix their meaning more accurately, because it is often impossible for us to grasp the sense of books that are products of cultures so ancient and mentalities so different from ours by merely reading them. Thus full account is taken of the genuine human authorship as well as of the divine *inspiration of *Holy Scripture.

LITURGY

From the Greek λειτουργία, "action of the people"; the term used in the Septuagint for OT *worship. Liturgy is the official service of God offered by the mystical body of Jesus Christ, Head and members (thus *Mediator Dei, Pius XII's encyclical on the liturgy, 1947; *Lex orandi, lex credendi). According to the Epistle to the Hebrews Jesus Christ as high priest is a λειτουργός, though not exactly in the liturgico-sacred sense. In the book of Revelation adoration is portrayed as offered to God and the Lamb with solemn ceremonies. The NT Epistles include hymns that may have been sung at services but no instructions for the latter. During the first few centuries religious services and the prayers used in them were certainly improvised according to the basic pattern of a meal commemorative of Christ's death, and a service of readings and prayers, with a sermon and a confession of faith; the earliest traditional formulae are only meant to be examples; such formulae were first made obligatory about A.D. 600 at Rome. Only with the progress of theological reflection did the official text harden into a fixed form, on order that none of its numerous elements should be forgotten: Jesus Christ's office as mediator, dramatic symbolism (either of Jesus' life or of the heavenly liturgy), anamnesis of the Lord's death linked with a commemoration of the Saints, etc. The final step in this process was the preservation of purely ecclesiastical languages (that is "dead" languages). In a fundamental document, the constitution on the liturgy of Vatican II, the Church laid down broad principles the application of which in pastoral practice must be one of the major tasks of our generation and the effects of which in the restoration of Catholic life are incalculable, in a recovery from within of the sense of the Church as a worshipping community.

LOCI THEOLOGICI

In Protestant theology, where the idea took shape in the 16th century, the term is used to mean the principal subdivisions of the faith; in Catholic theology, the sources of theological knowledge: the *magisterium of the Church, which preserves and expounds *revelation in *Holy Scripture and *Tradition, the *Fathers of the Church and the *theologians, the *liturgy and *canon law. For principles and method see the articles referred to and Dogmatic Theology, Theology, Epistemology.

280

LOGOS

From the Greek λογός , word; the title given in John 1:1–14 and 1 John 1:1 to the *Son of God, *Jesus Christ. According to these texts the Logos is *pre-existent; he is with God and is God; everything was created through him, he is the light and life of men, and he has become flesh. In the later sapiential literature of the OT, the (female) figure of Wisdom, as an emanation from God, is seen as his companion in creation and the providential ordering of history. The Jewish religious thinker Philo of Alexandria (d. about A.D. 50) made abundant use of logos-terminology in his speculations, in a similar but hardly personal sense. It is possible that St John found the properly Christian use of Logos in an early hymn to Christ; the emphasis on the Incarnation and the true divinity of the Logos suggest an anti-gnostic purpose, while what is actually affirmed is in harmony with the rest of NT Christology. An extensive theology of the Logos was developed by the Fathers of the first three centuries, which Platonist and Jewish tendencies, respectively, threatened to involve in *Subordinationism and *Modalism; but despite a confused terminology (*Hypostasis, *Person) the Fathers themselves always regarded the Logos as dwelling uncreated with the Father, over against creatures.—See also *Word of God.*

LOGOS-MYSTICISM

The mystical idea of the communion of the baptized with the *Logos, Jesus Christ, described in more detail as a mystical marriage of the individual soul with Jesus or the birth of Jesus in the soul (or *heart). It is described with beautiful clarity by Origen and, in dependence upon him, by the great Greek theologians. In the West it is found in Meister Eckhart.—See also *Christ-Mysticism.*

LOVE

In Christian usage, the free radical fulfilment of man's being which orientates the whole man—as God actually wills and summons him— to God, thus establishing him in God's grace (justification) and in salvation. This fulfilment takes place as an acceptance of God's free and absolute *self-communication and in virtue of that self-communication, and since it happens in relation to this self-giving God and is

LOVE

of a dialogical and responsive character God himself is conceived of
as love (1 Jn 4:8). The nature of man being (personal) self-transcendence towards what is higher (as a person), its fulfilment is the unselfish love of generosity *(amor benevolentiae,* as distinguished from
love of a good which serves as an element of or a means to [legitimate]
self-affirmation: the love of desire, *amor concupiscentiae).* Such love
is *grace, an "infused *virtue", inseparably bound up with *justification (D 1530f., 1561; Church/world, 38–52), insofar as this love
which surrenders itself wholly to God is freely created by God along
with man, is only enabled to penetrate God's closest intimacy (filial
love and the love of friendship, as contrasted with servile love for one's
master) by God's prevenient gift of himself to man and, in order to
correspond "connaturally" to this gift (to be "worthy"), needs to be
sustained by it, thus always implying a conquest by God of man's
sinful self-centredness. Love must also be understood as *charity or
agape because man's love for God depends on God's prodigal, condescending *agape* selflessly giving itself to his lowly creature (that is not
a love enkindled by the presentation of an "ideal": *eros)* and draws
the fellow-man God loves into participation in God's own love. Since
love is the total fundamental human act which integrates everything
else, it is on the one hand the sum of the salutary acts that are required
of man; but on the other hand love must declare itself in the multiplicity of those spiritual operations, distinct from each other and from
love (*Faith, *Hope, *Repentance, *Justice, etc.), which when "informed" by love can provide it with a concrete presence in the world,
a criterion of its genuineness and modes of growth without being
simply identical with it (D 1532, 1559, 1579, 2625) and thus without
conclusively showing forth its existence. In the development of man's
personal history such operations can precede love (as arising from
virtues not yet "informed" by it) and can prepare its fulfilment.

Love for our fellow-man, so far as it can and must be distinguished
from *love of neighbour, is the will directed to some person desired
as a *good (value) to be taken possession of and enjoyed. This love
is inseparable from the desire to perfect the beloved in his own being;
by attempting this the lover undertakes the endless task of self-development (*Spirit). In both these ways love shows itself to be the
means by which infinity shines through a finite form. This also means
that human love must come soberly to terms with the limitations of
the beloved, and while necessarily and unquenchably hoping for infinite fulfilment does not make the beloved suffer for its disillusionment.
It is also particularly important from the Christian point of view not

282

to overlook the public character of love and its power to change the world.

Christianity has never maintained that love is not expressed outside Christianity—for example in *atheism. Such an assumption would make it impossible to understand the true unity (this does not imply an identity) that exists between the love of God and the love of one's neighbour and to see love outside Christianity in the light of the knowledge that a really absolute love of one's neighbour includes a (non-thematic) theism and an implicit love for God. It is precisely for this reason that Christianity has tended to reduce the love of God as the concealed and at the same time supreme mystery of man's existence to a theme. The climax in the history of man's salvation and the ultimate guarantee of the unity existing between the love of God and the love of one's neighbour is reached in love for *Jesus Christ in his unity of God and man. He is also loved every time one man loves his fellow-man (see Mt 25:34 – 40), with the result that the fate of every man is decided in the unity of love for Christ and one's fellow-man, even if this unity is not consciously known (Mt 25:37ff.). This can be more easily understood if we bear in mind (a) that authentic love for a certain person opens that person to the love of all men and (b) that love in dialogue for a finite, unreliable and possibly even hostile person is also an act of acceptance of a man who is at the same time God as a presence or hoped for future and as ground and guarantee, if that love is to have the absolute quality by means of which it can fulfil itself through grace.

LUTHERANISM

See *Protestantism.*

LYONS

Of the two ecumenical councils held in this French city (namely, the Thirteenth Ecumenical Council from June 28th to July 17th, 1245, under Innocent IV, and the Fourteenth Ecumenical Council, under Gregory X, from May 7th until July 17th, 1274), the later is of theological importance because of the Catholic doctrine of the Blessed

*Trinity which it clarified and defined in the interests of reunion with the separated Greek Church, notably the procession of the Holy Spirit (*Filioque), and because it defined the existence of the seven *sacraments (D 850–861).

M

MACEDONIANISM

Wrongly attributed to Macedonius, bishop of Constantinople in the mid-fourth century, a theological doctrine which affirmed that the Holy Ghost—hitherto named together with the Father and the Son without special thought having been given to his nature—was probably a creature, or that at least his operations were never represented in Holy Scripture as those of a divine Person (hence the Greek πνευματομάχοι, "adversaries of the Spirit"). Others supposed he was a being intermediate between God and creatures. This trend, arising out of *Arianism, was condemned at the First Council of *Constantinople (where 36 bishops had supported it).

MAGIC

See *Mysticism, Religion.*

MAGISTERIUM

The Church's active competence, juridically embodied, to prolong by its witness God's self-communicative self-revelation in Christ, which necessarily inheres in the Church (as the eschatologically definitive community of believers in Christ, founded by him as an hierarchical society, empowered by a mission to bear testimony to Christ), and which demands obedience. The Church as a whole cannot fall from eschatological grace—hence from truth as grace either—because she is the concrete presence of the definitive self-revelation of God which has occurred in the God-Man. The Christ-event is its own testimony and requires the response of faith, and thereby also grounds the "authority" of the witnesses, but it is also testified to by the word of properly commissioned witnesses by virtue of the authority thereby granted (Lk 10:16; Mt 28:19f.), which is handed on from one witness to another in legal historical continuity (*tradition; *apostolic succession). The first and full bearer of this word of testimony, which makes the Christ-event historically present for all times, is the community of those who believe in Jesus Christ, the Church as such and as a whole. But this means that when the Church as a whole declares her faith, demanding unqualified assent, she cannot fail to proclaim the truth of Christ. Now the Church as a whole may in accordance with her constitution declare Christ's truth so as to demand assent in a twofold yet single manner: within the unity of her teaching witness, through the universal episcopate which as a body is the legitimate successor of the Apostolic College (*Bishop), and, accordingly, through the personal and competent head of this college, the bishop of Rome, the *Pope, as well. The essential feature of the teaching authority of the Pope and the bishops can only be understood in the light of the eschatological nature of the Church. The holders of this doctrinal ministry do not receive their authority from the members of the Church, but their authority and their "infallibility" can be conceived only within this eschatological community of faith and is an element in the realization of God's will in Jesus Christ by which the salvific truth of the Christ-event remains historically actual in the world. Seen in these terms, the magisterium is in no way a substitute for the sovereignty of the Spirit, but remains under its guidance. In the self-understanding of the Catholic Church, full power to teach belongs to the universal episcopate (D 3020, 3050ff., 3061; cf. 125f., 686, 1247–71, 1477–80, 1520, 3000, 3011; Vat. II: Church; Rev., 10) when united in itself and with the bishop of Rome at its head, and to the bishop of Rome (D 3073f.) as the authoritative head of this college, not a mere delegated representative or instrument of a college that would be complete without him. The governing authority representing the universal Church, the Pope and episcopate, may function as the "ordinary magisterium" (their doctrine binding in various degrees) in their day-to-day preaching of the *kerygma, by their government and their supervision over theology. When they teach this kerygma throughout the Church as divinely revealed, requiring of all the assent of faith, the kerygma is preserved from error by the Spirit of God. In this instance, therefore, the magisterium is infallible (D 2879, 3011; Church, 25). The same holds true when the Pope (for the defined teaching of the Church, see D 3073; Church, 25) or a general *council (D 1478f., 2923; Church, 25) issues a solemn *definition by an act of the extraordinary magisterium (or rather by an exceptional act of the one, normal—hence ordinary-magisterium), that is to say, invoking the plenitude of doctrinal authority and the assistance of the Holy Ghost which is vouchsafed the Church for the custody of the divine revelation of which she is the depositary, requiring the whole Church to give the absolute assent of faith to a certain proposition as divinely revealed (*Infallibility). The *definitive* decisions reached by the magisterium are on the one hand unalterable; on the other hand, they are subject to the historical nature of the human perception of truth, to concurrent misunderstandings, to linguistic change, etc. No *dogma can ever be "retrospectively" accused of error with regard to its ultimate meaning and content. "Prospectively", however, it is always open to reform, i.e., it can be stated afresh and better formulated. As far as the *non-defined,* yet authentic doctrines (i.e., those represented as obligatory) are concerned, the magisterium of the Church is open to error, and some errors have in fact occurred. Not infrequently the Church authorities have in fact acted inappropriately harshly and unjustly, i.e., immorally, in regard to the supposed preservation of the essential and ultimate substance of faith. Before issuing any doctrinal statements and directives all members of the magisterium are morally bound to gather as much information as possible. Since the magisterium should concern itself not merely with factual accuracy but also with the greatest possible efficacy of its decisions in the Church, it does not have the right *merely* to enforce its formal authority. The magisterium is duty-bound to see itself as an organ and function of the Church as a whole; it should make it clear to the faithful that it not only presents a true doctrine, but that it also wishes to bring mankind closer to the reality of salvation. Since the magisterium does not receive any new revealed truth when formulating its doctrines, it is bound to explain to the faithful *how* it has reached these decisions in relation to the totality of the unique divine revelation actively adhered to by the faithful. There can be no doubt that in the centuries since the Council of Trent the function of the teaching ministry has expanded considerably, insofar as the magisterium is no longer merely a guardian and arbitrator but also claims to teach and expound. In regard to the (*pluralism), pluralistic nature of theology this means that the magisterium selectively adopts a particular theology for its purposes. Here too the magisterium should be required to justify its reasons for a given choice.

MAN

Many sciences are concerned with man and are able to make statements about him which, while accurate as far as they go, are restricted in their scope. Faith and theology in effect have only one statement to make about man, a statement that is comprehensive, unrestricted, immeasurable, and hence states the mystery: that man is open and in need, a partner of God in absolute proximity to him, the incomprehensible mystery, so that the other sciences cannot conclusively grasp and express him. Thus theological *anthropology resolves all other anthropologies into theology (the doctrine of God) and Christology (the doctrine of the God-Man). Since man is utterly dependent on God, his source and maker, he is in every respect a creature, whatever earthly dependences and ties he may have besides (*Creation of man): these are all embraced and sustained by his creatureliness, in the form of a dependence on and an orientation to God that are abiding yet ever new (not to be thought of as having been brought about "once upon a time"). Man is a *spirit (*Soul) insofar as this creatureliness becomes conscious of itself in him; for it is only in and through a continual reaching out for the absolute Mystery that he encounters and experiences the things and persons of his environment—his experience of *contingency, *transcendence, *dread, the absolute character of the *good, *love, joy, etc. He experiences his *body as a permanent intrinsic expression of his concrete spiritual *person, since he is spirit only through receptive, reactive, historical experience of his environment and fellow-men, presented in the unresolvable given particularity of facts which thought can never quite absorb. Because he is capable of hearing a summons from God and answering it by entering upon a responsible dialogue, man experiences himself as a free, spiritual person, experiences this personality, since it remains his even in the act of repudiating God, as part of his *nature, and both, since they are clearly the condition of any partnership with God, as theological terms. Since man discovers by external experience (the historical and social experience of verbal revelation) and by the interior experience of grace (the former in dependence on the latter) that absolute mystery is near him in the free, gratuitous, forgiving, cherishing intimacy of God's total self-communication, he experiences himself as "supernaturally elevated" by the *grace that is constantly offered him. In other words, he recognizes his vocation to intimacy with God's condescending, gracious, self-disclosing depths (an intimacy which draws and constrains him) as the supernatural *existential of his human being.

MANICHAEISM

The religion founded in the mid-third century by a Babylonian named Manes. He believed that he was the last great prophet—in succession to Zarathustra, Buddha, and Christ, among others—and that his mission was to perfect their religions (incomplete, as he supposed, because the founders had not themselves committed them to writing). Manes was accused by the priests of the State religion (the Magi) and put to death for his faith (about A.D. 277). His religion, set forth in an enormous literature (it is lost, but fragments were discovered in the 19th and 20th centuries), is a form of *gnosis, based on a thoroughgoing *dualism, which is developed in terms of a "saving history" (primeval separation—mingling—the separation restored). During the middle period the Son of God, the *Urmensch* or primordial man, was defeated, his soul mingling with matter. God's envoys (Jesus among them) are repeatedly vanquished during a long process of redemption; they are not able to free the souls from their state of banishment in bodies, who can only return to the realm of light by accepting the gospel of Manes, the *Paraclete. Those who believe in him compose the Church of the mind. Salvation consists in entering into knowledge of ourself (this linked with strict ascetical discipline). The imperfect are subject to continual rebirth in the world of bodies. Manichaeism, which was also known in the West (St. Augustine professed it for nine years), expanded into Central and Eastern Asia, where it finally disappeared in the 14th century.

MARIOLOGY

Theological teaching about Mary. The NT and the Apostles' Creed show that we can and must make dogmatic affirmation about *Mary which are not mere historical notices necessarily but trivially involved in affirming truths of faith that have been realized in history. The references to Mary in Matthew, Luke, and especially John already display strong theological concerns (*virgin birth, infancy narratives, Son of David, a tone hostile to *Docetism, etc.). Consequently the Catholic Christian cannot regard our data about Mary as correct, indeed, but "of no concern to him"; they are part of his faith, though of course the question of how far they are or should be explicit— whether from the personal point of view or that of dogmatic history and religious pedagogy—is no more readily answered in this case than in the case of other revealed truths. The actual reason for a Mariology is that salvation, which must be accepted in the obedience of faith, is so identified with the incarnate Logos of God and the assumption of the creaturely into God that faith (Religious *act) necessarily has an "incarnational" structure, i.e., it believes not only in the saving God but also in the saved creature—man can and must accept by faith as such not only God but also himself. This invests Mariology with all the rights and tasks of a separate theological tractate, which must not merely proceed in genuine conformity with the principles of Catholic dogmatics but must recognize that it is part of a more important whole and lead men to that whole. Since Mary can only be seen in the light of Jesus Christ, Mariology must follow upon *Christology and *soteriology in the general scheme of dogmatic theology. But if one remembers that it is just as essential that a dogmatic *ecclesiology should follow immediately upon these two tractates, so as to deal with the historical, sociological and gracious permanence of Jesus Christ and his redemption in the world and its acceptance there, then Mariology can also be seen as an intrinsic element of a dogmatic ecclesiology and its first chapter. This view finds its justification in the well-founded parallelism drawn throughout Tradition between the Church and Mary, and is based on the fact that Mary belongs to the Church, as one of the redeemed, as a believer, and as a decisive actor in saving history, and represents the perfect and typical instance of those who compose the Church (see constitution *de Ecclesia* of Vatican II, ch. 8). If one also considers the fact that the NT portrays Mary as mother of the Lord, by the free obedience of faith as well as by generation, so that her motherhood must be envisaged in wholly personal terms and occupies an eschatologically crucial position in public, official saving history, then a fundamental principle of Mariology is shown to be scriptural—a principle from which, against the background of the whole economy of salvation, other dogmatic affirmations about Mary (*Immaculate Conception, perpetual virginity, sinlessness, and plenitude of grace, *Assumption into heaven) may be presented as dependent upon Scripture, though not given formal expression there. Ultimately of course the soundness of this development upon Scriptural bases in the universal Church's consciousness of the faith is guaranteed not by private exegesis and speculation but by the assistance of the Spirit promised to the apostolic magisterium.

MARRIAGE

Sociologically: a firm sexual union with changing structures: in the

290

MARRIAGE

Catholic understanding: The legitimate union of man and wife for permanent physical and spiritual companionship.

(1) *In the Old Testament* marriage is the only social institution expressly grounded in the creative will of God, a relationship of two sexually distinct, equally valuable and entitled people, a holy ordinance from the beginning (Gen 1:27f.); in the history of the Old Covenant—though not at the level of the creation narrative—it is wholly directed to the preservation and propagation of the husband's clan. Hence arranging marriage is the business of the heads of families and its purpose is the begetting of issue. The demands of "civil" law and morality are different for husband and wife; the husband who commits adultery can only violate another marriage, whereas the wife who does so can only violate her own. The unity of marriage is unknown to the OT; marriage there is essentially dissoluble. The single state of life is alien to the OT.

(2) *The specifically New Testament conception* regards marriage in the sense explained by Jesus, as the unity brought about by God, aiming at permanency, of a man and a woman, in which he restores to woman the equal status intended by the creation narrative (Mk 10:6–9; Mt 19:4ff.). Yet marriage as a state of life belonging to this age of the world can make man guilty before God if for its sake he turns a deaf ear to the permanent appeal that God has made in Christ (Lk 14:20; *Evangelical counsels). Both these themes are developed in the letters of the Apostles (see especially 1 Cor 7). In addition, the place of marriage in saving history is shown when it is compared to Jesus' marriage with the Church (*Bridal symbolism, *Church); because marriage is the image of Christ's gracious union with the Church (Eph 5:32), it is itself seen to be the efficacious presence, under a sign, of God's gracious will, that is, a sacrament. It is undeniable that both Christian attitudes to marriage were unequally transmitted by Paul and his later interpreters, so that theological tradition (under Augustine's influence) gave extensive consideration to the question of the justification of marriage.

(3) *The Church's teaching.* Every valid marriage between two baptized persons (even between two non-Catholic Christians, therefore; but not, on the other hand, between a baptized person who is a Catholic but does not observe the Catholic form of marriage, and a non-Catholic) is a *sacrament (D, 718, 761; for the defined teaching of the Church, see Church/world, 47–52). This is based on the fact that the loving common life of two persons implies a reference to God as ground and goal; that every fellowship of Christians in Christ includes an active presence of Jesus and therefore also of the Church

(Mt 18:20), so that this must be said in particular of marriage as the smallest, yet complete fellowship in Jesus Christ. The contracting parties themselves are the ministers of the sacrament when in a valid manner they express their willingness to marry. The priest (or deacon), whose presence is normally necessary for the validity of a marriage between Catholics, acts as an official witness. All baptized persons are capable of receiving this sacrament provided there are no impediments to marriage in the particular case (see below). "Natural" marriage, as opposed to sacramental marriage, is valid marriage between two unbaptized persons. The essential effect of contracting a valid marriage is the marriage bond, which by its nature is life-long and exclusive: a marriage between Christians which has been validly contracted, and consummated, can be dissolved only by death. (The Church undeniably has the duty to promote the lasting nature of marriage and the reciprocal duty of the parties in the spirit of Jesus. It also has the duty of concern in the spirit of Jesus, i.e., without contempt or discrimination, for the divorced and, under certain circumstances, the remarried. The Church has no possibility of issuing a judgment on the reasons for the break-up of a marriage or its state of disruption. By reason of the marriage bond each partner to the marriage has a duty to be faithful to the other, to share the other's life and to give him or her spiritual and material help. Vatican II tried to relinquish a legalistic and biological view of marriage in describing marriage as a union and sharing in the love of Jesus for the Church and elevating the love of the partners as a benefit of marriage in addition to procreation (Church/world, 47–51; Church, 11).

(4) *Catholic legislation on marriage* (CIC, can. 1012–1143). The Church claims the exclusive right to legislate for and to take cognizance of marriage, because the marriage contract among Christians is a sacrament, the contract and the sacrament being inseparable. In order to contract marriage in valid form a Catholic Christian must marry in the active presence of the parish priest of the place where the marriage is celebrated (or of his delegate) and of at least two witnesses. In danger of death (otherwise for the period of a month) a marriage contracted in the presence of two witnesses only is also valid if a priest authorized to marry the couple cannot be fetched without grave inconvenience (extraordinary form of marrying). The Catholic form for contracting marriage obliges all who have been baptized in the Catholic Church or have been reconciled to her, even though the person have fallen away from the Church after baptism, or reconciliation; even though the person baptized a Catholic, having secured the necessary dispensation, marries someone of another reli-

gion. The usual preparation for marriage consists of betrothal, instruction of the couple, and proclamation of banns, for which the bride's parish priest should generally be approached. Before the wedding is celebrated the local bishop must—so far as is at all possible—have dispensed the parties from any *impediments* to marriage *(impedientia:* simple vows, affinity, difference of religion; *dirimentia:* insufficient age, impotence, an existing marriage bond, infidelity, major orders, solemn vows of religion, consanguinity, infamy, adultery, etc.). From the earliest times the Church has given the nuptial blessing after the *consent of the bride and groom; if possible this should be done during the nuptial Mass.

(5) *Catholic married life.* In the Christian dispensation the personal love manifested in marriage is borne by God's grace which, by reason of that love, *always* sanctifies, elevates and brings it close to God. This does not only happen in an ecclesiastical, sacramental marriage. In the perspective of Eph 5 we can say that the unity which exists between Jesus Christ and the Church (mankind loved by God) is the source of unity between a man and a woman and pre-empts the question whether and to what extent the unity thus brought about has all the characteristics of an effective unity. An openly Christian marriage thus truly represents God's unifying love for mankind through Jesus Christ; it is a symbol of the Church in the world in the form of the smallest but genuine individual church. This symbolic function is due to the special grace endowed by the sacrament of marriage.

MARTYRDOM

*Death for the sake of Christian faith or Christian morals. As early as the second century one who accepted such a death was looked on and revered as a μάρτυς (witness). This term is scriptural in that Jesus Christ is the "faithful Witness" absolutely (Acts 1:5; 3:14), and the servant is not above his Master (*Persecution). According to universal Christian tradition, not all forms of persecution of the Church (making its position in society difficult) or sharp practice against individual Christians can be called martyrdom (see Vat. II: Church, 42). Martyrdom is part of the Church's nature since it manifests Christian death in its pure form as the death of unconstrained faith, which otherwise is hidden in the ambivalence of all human events. Through martyrdom the Church's *holiness, instead of remaining purely subjective, achieves by God's grace the visible expression it needs, which makes it in the fullest sense a motive of credibility.

Hence it is clear why from the earliest times theological tradition has ascribed to martyrdom the same power to justify as *baptism (martyrdom: "baptism of blood"). Martyrdom does not have this power simply because, like any act of loving faith, it jusitifies even before reception of the sacrament; the power of martyrdom to justify is in a sense sacramental, for it is the manifestation of a gracious reality, the tangible expression of God's gracious deed to man.

MARY

The virgin Mother of Jesus Christ. She conceived the Son of God by the free, God-given assent of her faith, and gave him in her womb that existence which enabled him to be a member of the one human race and thus its Redeemer (Mt 1:18–23; Lk 1:26 –38). Mary is "the Mother of the Lord" (Lk 1:43), the "Mother of God" (D 250ff.) by reason of the *hypostatic union of God's Son with the human nature he received from Mary. Thus Mary's deed is a central event of saving history.

(1) Mary, the human creature, does this deed, welcomes the approach of God's grace on man's behalf, in genuine partnership with God and in the name of the whole human race. Although modern theology styles Mary *Corredemtrix (see D 3370, note), it is evident at the same time that this office of hers, is qualitatively different from that of the theandric *Mediator and Redeemer. Since Scripture (Jn 19:25–27) points to Mary simply as the Woman (second Eve, mother of the redeemed) at the foot of the cross, the tree of redemption, she clearly exercised the function of conceiving salvation, which was proper to her as Jesus' mother, throughout her life, until the very "hour" of the redemption (Jn 2:4). Her rôle in saving history (divine motherhood) and her personal sanctity (blessed was she who believed) reflect and condition each other. Because of this central position in saving history (sanctifying herself by "conceiving" salvation for all), Mary is in the mind and faith of the Catholic Church the paragon of human redemption, the most perfectly redeemed (Vat. II: Church, 53), and therefore is the archetype of all the redeemed and of the Church itself (ibid., 53, 63, 65) part of God's will for the redemptive, victorious Incarnation of the divine Word (see Constitution de Ecclesia of Vatican II, ch. 8).

(2) Consequently, in spite of being a member of the guilty human race, Mary was preserved from *original sin (for the defined teaching of the Church, see D 2803f.), having been in possession of sanctifying

MARY

grace from the first moment of her existence through the "foreseen merits of Christ" (*Immaculate conception) because of her part in God's will for the Redemption (D 2015, 2017). For the same reason she is completely sinless (D 1573) and was never subject to *concupiscence (D 1515f.). Holy Scripture expressly declares that she conceived the Son of God without the intervention of a man (virginity *before* the birth; Mt 1:18ff.; Lk 1:34–35; D 533, 1880; *Virgin birth). The birth of her Son without a father, yet of a mother, emphasizes the fact that with Christ salvation begins absolutely anew: he does not prolong the guilt-entangled history of mankind but redeems it unto newness of life. Injury and pain, to the extent that these manifest the domination of sin (according to Gen 3:16), are absent from Mary's child-bearing (virginity *during* the birth: D 1880). The Catholic Church recognizes Mary as ever virgin *(after* the birth, D 1400, 1880; *Brethren of Jesus) because of the utter devotion of her whole being and life to the pure service of God and Christ (1 Cor 7:34) publicly manifested in saving history and in the Church which Mary represents (Vat. II, Church, 46, 63).

(3) The Catholic Church confesses that Mary, being perfectly redeemed, has already attained perfection of *body* and soul (*Assumption of Mary, D 3903f.), because saving history has already advanced into its final phase, the incipient transfiguration of the material world itself (by the *resurrection of Jesus; see also Mt 27:52f.). In view of her unique rôle in saving history Mary is revered as "*Mediatrix of all graces" (D 3274, 3370; cf. Vat. II, Church, 62)—not productive mediation, like Jesus Christ's, but a receptive one of merit and intercession and, as Vatican II said, wholly dependent on the mediation of Jesus Christ (Church, 60)—because those who have attained salvation through the final achievement of their perfected lives intercede with God for the company of the saints on earth. The Church has not as yet given any dogmatic decision on this matter.

(4) Little is known of Mary's life. Such accounts as we have, other than the sparse data provided in Scripture (see Lk 1–2; Mt 1–2; Jn 2:1–11; Mk 3:31–35; Jn 19:25–27; Acts 1:14), are legendary. Most of our information about her derives from Lk 1:26–38. Her descent from the house of David is established only if the words "espoused to a man named Joseph" (Lk 1:27) do not belong to the original sources (P. Gaechter). Mary's dignity remained hidden from her people, for her life, thanks to her legitimate marriage with Joseph, was led according to the laws and customs of the Jews. She shared the religious life of the pious among her nation (presentation and circumcision of children, pilgrimages to the temple). Her life was one of

labour, poverty, and willing acceptance of God's inscrutable decrees. During Jesus' public life she maintained, as he wished, an attitude which showed that what mattered was not mere physical motherhood but doing the will of God in faith (even as his mother). She then retires into the background, to come forward again at the Lord's decisive hour and stand at the foot of his cross. After Christ's departure she remains, praying, in the company of the disciples. No historical information is available as to the circumstances of her death. But (as against recent contentions of individual Catholic theologians) it cannot be doubted that she died in the true perfection of her earthly life, sharing the fate of all human beings and imitating the death of her Son, since she was meant to show forth not the glory of paradise but the perfect triumph of Christ's grace in the weakness of the flesh.

(5) Devotion to Mary. In view of the *veneration of saints which Christians may practise and Mary's unique position in saving history and the communion of saints, she is to be called "blessed" by all generations (Lk 1:48), because by praising what God has done for her in a special manner we praise what he has done for all mankind. A special religious veneration is due to Mary as Mother of God which is quite distinct from *adoration (*Hyperdulia).

MASS

The memorial in thanksgiving and celebration in Christ's Church, according to his commandment (Lk 22:19f.; 1 Cor 11:24f.), of his sacrifice of life and death as the foundation of the Church and the hidden advent, in forgiveness and *grace, of the *basileia. This celebration is *anamnesis; that is, it signifies that a genuine historical event which has happened once for all is truly made present. The ontological and logical questions raised by anamnesis need not be gone into here. Suffice it to say that this anamnesis is neither a mere "idealist" reminiscence on our own part, nor a successive repetition of Christ's death, nor a denial that this historical event really happened, and happened once only, in time, since (contrary to gnostic views) just this historical event bears our salvation. The anamnetic "celebration" takes place when the Church does in cultic gesture what Jesus himself did when celebrating the Last Supper: accepting in free obedience the real death whereby he offers himself to the Father, proclaiming the saving power of his sacrifice and its application to the disciples by delivering to them the symbols of his body and blood. Without being a *new* sacrifice, except in the ritual dimension, this anamnesis of Christ's death is a sacrifice (an offering to God of gifts in which a change is effected) in that it makes his historically unique offering to the Father present (in an unbloody manner: D 1793ff., 1743), and that through a rite which cultically speaking is itself a *sacrifice. In the Mass the Lord is truly and substantially present under the empirical appearances of bread and wine, because Jesus expressly declares that what he distributes to the Apostles under the appearances of bread and wine is his flesh and blood, that is, according to Semitic usage, himself in person in the concrete reality of his sacrificial existence (which through the permanent validity of his death has attained its definitive, "glorified" state) (Mt 26:26, 28; Mk 14:22, 24; Lk 22:19f.; 1 Cor 11:24f.); and because the reality of the total presence of his salvific deed implies the true presence of the person on whose substantial reality and eternity the continued presence of the historical deed is based. The Church knows from Jesus' own words that what it proffers, re-enacting his gestures at the Last Supper, is the body and blood of Christ (for the defined teaching of the Church, see D 1651), and therefore not bread and wine; so it is all the more ready to affirm that nothing has changed in the sphere of sensory human experience (the "appearances", that is to say the *"species"), including whatever is accessible to the natural sciences; it holds that the reality (called *"substance") underlying the appearances is no longer that of earthly nourishment but that of Jesus Christ himself. The process by which this is brought about can be called *transubstantiation, and can be regarded as the sacrificial action itself (D 1652): in virtue of Jesus Christ's commission a liturgical rite so transforms the intrinsic reality, the "substance", of a bit of mundane reality that the reality which displaces it (the body and blood of Jesus Christ under the appearances of bread and wine) is wholly dedicated to God and liturgically represents Jesus Christ's surrender of himself in sacrifice to God. But since this is the essence of cultic sacrifice in general, the Mass is rightly called a sacrifice in the sense just defined (D 802, 1739ff., 1751, 1866), Christ himself being both sacrificing priest (D 802, 1743, 3677, 3849ff.) and victim (D 802, 1739ff., 1743, 3677).—See also Destruction, Conversion, Oblation, theory of, Eucharist. For the teaching of Vatican II on the Mass, see Lit., 2, 7, 47; Church, 3, 10f., 28. The true presence of the efficaciousness of Jesus' life and death in the Mass affords an immanent critique of cultic worship; that is an end to mere liturgico-symbolical memories and an entry into Christian practice as anticipation of the *kingdom of God.

MATERIALISM

Materialism, as a theoretical and practical attempt to understand the world systematically, has always been characterized by a desire to explain the world that can be objectively experienced as a single, united whole on the basis of that world itself and therefore to accept it as an all-embracing reality, rather than by presenting a philosophical antithesis to idealism or a wilful negation of the Spirit as the essential characteristic of man. This is why materialism, including the so-called mechanistic form of materialism that prevailed in the seventeenth and eighteenth centuries (Lamettrie, Helvetius and Holbach) has always, as the middle-class philosophical and political movement of emancipation, had to combat the fundamental contradiction that *matter, which appears, not as a homogeneous substance (nature or matter), but in an infinite pluriformity of quantities, qualities and structural configurations, always has to be raised at least relatively to the level of natural knowledge in the status of a fundamental principle and therefore to the all-embracing foundation level of nature and society. This contradiction is reinforced by man's ambivalent experience of nature as chaos, or as his own terrifying limitation on the one hand and as creation to liberated on the other. Although it certainly contains many theoretical inconsistencies, this form of materialism indisputably has the effect of emancipating man and therefore has to be judged as an aspect of the history of human freedom in the modern era from a different point of view from that of the pure theory of knowledge. The historical and dialectical materialism of Karl Marx (it is not possible to discuss in detail here the differences between Marx's materialism and that of Engels or Lenin) is therefore a more advanced form, not only because the qualitative difference between conceptual thought and sensory preception is no longer suppressed, but also because man's whole objective activity and all his becoming, being and historical development are included in the Marxist concept of materiality. The concept of social *work and that of generic development mediate between nature and history and the individual and society, resulting in the disappearance of the rigid ontological contrast between being and consciousness, "by means of the naturalization of man and the humanization of nature" (as a dialectical change of matter between man and nature). By means of nature's entry into the historical context of human praxis, matter can be made visible as the real substratum of the acting subject and not simply as the arsenal of man's means and materials. There is no longer any question, in this form of materialism, of an optimistic trust in an

298

automatic advance in the development of nature and history. The most suitable form of materialist praxis consists of work and struggle. Any attempt to approach materialism and the mediation that it brings about of the reality of man and the cosmos from the theological point of view should be based, not on a speculative criticism established on ontological premises and the theory of knowledge, but rather on the connexion between this materialism and the history of human freedom on the one hand and a humble but serious consideration of man, developed in contrast to theories of idealism, as a frail, conditioned and therefore sensual but also suffering being. An open declaration of the presence of unhappiness and evil in the world might therefore be a first common step towards building up a mankind reconciled with nature and acting in solidarity.

MATTER

(1) In a technical philosophical sense, the sustaining ground of being, determinable by a *form (the determining reality of a "subject") but of itself undetermined and in need of determination: especially in Aristotelian *hylomorphism, pure "potency" (prime matter) as contrasted with form-giving "act" (form, entelechy, etc.). In a derivative sense we speak of the "matter" of a sacrament (water, bread, oil), the ritual gesture (anointing, etc.) whose meaning has to be more exactly determined by the sacramental words, the "form" of the sacrament.

(2) In ordinary parlance matter means concrete, physical, non-spiritual things, the object of everyday external experience, of physics, chemistry, biology and the anthropological sciences insofar as they are based on investigations of the human body. Christian faith declares that "matter" in this sense (and the determinable basis involved in it, that is matter in the sense of (1) above) is wholly created by God and subject to his shaping power: it does not face him as a co-eternal, equally temporally powerful independent principle. Consequently matter is good, is not the principle of evil, and in a true sense is immediately present to God. It is a permanent element of the world (the guarantee of this is the Incarnation of the Logos and the *resurrection of the "flesh"), even in the ultimate transfiguration of the world, although we have no positive conception of the state of matter in the consummation of the world, and only mean by this proposition that the reality of the pre-spiritual basis of finite spirit cannot simply be eliminated at the consummation. Hence finite spirit and matter (as something intrinsic to concrete spiritual being, their necessary envi-

ronment, the stuff of their own self-realization) form a unity that is permanent and good. There are various considerations in support of this view. Firstly, the angels themselves, if they are thought of as "pure spirits", may still be seen as essentially higher (personal) powers presiding over and controlling the material world, so that they do not breach the oneness of the world that is composed of spirit and matter, nor the essential ordination of these constituent elements to each other. Secondly, the (dialectical) openness to the spiritual world of material things in their *evolution in Nature, under the abiding creative impulse of that God who transcends the world yet remains immanent in it (and only thus), does not if rightly understood contradict the Christian doctrine of the essential distinction between spirit and matter and it is therefore permissible to conceive of a self-transcendence of matter in the direction of the Spirit. Thirdly, the doctrine that the divine Logos has become flesh means that the supreme spirituality still penetrates the lowest depth of being, has freely made this an eternal expression of the concrete reality of God himself and thus (the history of the actual world being always determined in advance by its real reference to Christ as its centre) has imbued the actual world, in its very materiality, with a real permanent dynamism tending towards this absolute life of the spirit. From the Christian point of view, therefore, the history of matter is seen to be essentially the pre-history of permanently corporeal *spirit.—See also *Creation of the World, Evolution.*

MEDIATOR

In general, he who in any way establishes or maintains between two others a relation which without the mediator neither would nor could exist. *Jesus Christ is the mediator (Lat. *mediator,* Gr. μεσίτης) between God and man in a unique and ultimate sense (1 Tim 2:5; D 1347, 1513; Church, 8, 14, 28, 49, 60, 62; Ecum., 20) because in him (that is in his personal being [*Hypostatic union] and his deeds [*Cross, *Redemption, *Resurrection]) God's absolute, final self-disclosure to mankind occurs definitively and triumphantly and in him (as Man, knowing grace, merit and the beatific vision) is accepted by man. Insofar as mankind as a whole was envisaged and created in and with Jesus Christ and despite its sinfulness is once for all affirmed, redeemed, and sanctified in and with him, he is the Mediator absolutely speaking, the only mediator. The condition of the possibility of Jesus Christ's mediation of salvation and its personal realization in faith is the intercommunication of all men in the ultimate depths of their existence, going as far as their salvation, and the existential "realization" and experience of this radical intercommunication. Insofar as every human being is of importance to every other *within* the unity of all the redeemed which Christ alone sustains (because each has the unique individuality and the place willed for him in this whole of being and action), it is possible to say with due caution and in a derivative sense that anyone living in the state of grace "co-operates" in working out the salvation of his fellows. Consequently the Church applied the term "mediation" (even "co-redemption") to *Mary in particular, in view of the unique position she holds in saving history as one redeemed (not by any means as the one and only Mediator who sustains the whole order of redemption).

MEDIATRIX

An expression coined by Catholic theologians in order to convey the idea that all graces are received through the Blessed Virgin *Mary because of her unique position in saving history. The magisterium of the Church has not made a dogmatically binding pronoucement on this doctrine yet Vatican II said that her "motherly task" and "salutary influence" rest wholly on the mediation of Jesus Christ (Church, 60): by her "maternal charity" and "manifold intercession" she continues to "bring us the gifts of eternal salvation" and therefore is invoked as Mediatrix, etc. (Church, 62). See *Mediator.*

MEDITATION

In the language of the Church, the consideration of the truths and imperatives of faith for a practical motive and in connexion with spontaneous *prayer. It is distinguished from *contemplation by the fact that it proceeds according to discursive reason and is governed by the will. Its method distinguishes it from mere rumination. This method in substance consists of a preliminary delimitation and subdivision of the subject matter for meditation, a preparatory prayer, an imaginative representation ("application of the senses") of the subject of meditation, an effort at quite personal participation, turning the whole man to God in unrestrained interior prayer. Really interior and personal prayer, at least during considerable periods of a person's religious development, is impossible without meditation, which is therefore prescribed in the CIC for clerics, religious and seminarists (CIC, can. 125 § 2; 595 §§ 1, 2; 1367 § 1), though as yet too little has been done to lift meditation out of a certain dry, rationalistic routine and adapt it to the several types of human psychology. The Christian should learn how to use modern psychotherapeutic methods and adapt them to his Christian purpose.

MELITIANS

Members of two quite different schismatic communities. The first followed a Bishop Melitius of Lycopolis in Egypt (d. about 325) in condemning those who lapsed under pressure of Diocletian's persecution; they seem to have professed no error apart from this rigorism. The second, named after Bishop Melitius of Antioch (d. 381), was not founded by him and its adherents were neither real schismatics nor real heretics but rather a party in the struggle against *Arianism. Melitius himself presided over the First Council of *Constantinople (in the course of which he died). The Melitian party was reconciled with the other Eastern Catholics at the beginning of the 5th century.

MEMBERSHIP OF THE CHURCH

The question of church membership is identical with that of the nature of the Church. The dialectical position of the ecclesiology of Vatican II, according to which on the one hand (a) everyone who is true to his or her conscience attains to salvation in Jesus Christ, whether he or she is Catholic or not, belongs to another Christian denomination, lives in another religion, or is a (guiltless) atheist, and on the other hand, however, (b) explains the Church of Jesus Christ, given in the Roman Catholic Church, in accordance with all tradition, as necessary for salvation in the case of all men and women (Church, 16, 14), is offered in its teaching on the Church as the fundamental sacrament of the salvation of the world (Church, 1, 9, 48 and *passim).* The grace of God offered through the Church can be accessible to people without the Church, but the Church is nevertheless the historically authentic manifestation of this grace of God and means of referral to it.

MAGISTERIUM. The members of the Church include sinners and those who are "foreknown" to be damned. (For the defined teaching

302

of the Church, see D 1201ff., 1205f., 1221, 1578, 2472–2478, 2615, 3803.) This dogma does not imply that the loss of justifying grace leaves the Church indifferent, the less so as the Church must never be regarded as a purely external religious organization and the Holy Ghost is among those things which constitute its very essence. Valid *baptism and nothing less constitutes one a "person" in the Church (CIC, can. 87; see D 1314f., 1620, 1627, 1671f., 3802). At least, therefore, it is *de fide* that baptism always creates a certain positive, indestructible relationship with the Church, a basic (pre-personal) ordination to it (D 1621, 1671f.). Only those are *full,* active members of the Church who are baptized, profess the faith, and are united with the Church and her leaders (D 718, 1351, 2803, 3802f.).

THEOLOGY. A sacrament may be invalid, merely valid, or fruitful: the chronological nexus between the possession of grace and the sacramental sign of grace may vary; and these differences may or may not be culpable. Similar differences exist in the relationship of a person with the Church, the primordial sacrament. Accordingly we have to say: (1) The Catholic who believes and obeys the Church and lives in the state of justifying grace is a *full* member of the Church (Vat. II: Church, 14). His membership really effects what it signifies. Here grace has achieved its maximum historical embodiment and membership of the Church is bound up with what it is meant to signify: with faith and grace. (2) Where an unbaptized person is justified by faith and love and his implicit *votum* of the Church (*Baptism of desire) he is not (yet) properly speaking a member of the Church, but in a condition which objectively and existentially tends to its social and historical fulfilment in Church membership: he is already "ordered" to the Church in such a way that for him too it is the means of salvation. Where baptism and faith are culpably lacking, this ordination remains intact as objective *redemption, supernatural *existential and obligation (Vat. II: Church, 13). (3) The various gradations of objective deficiency in man's relationship with the Church which are possible between these two extreme cases readily fall into place. They are possible because justification on the one hand and the visible social embodiment of salvation on the other are not synonymous, so that the two processes may sometimes be out of step with each other without ceasing to form a unity.

Together with Augustine, Vatican II (Church, 14) distinguishes between a membership of the Church "of the heart" and one "of the body". The Catholic Christian knows that he or she belongs to the Church of Jesus Christ "in the body". He or she does not know for

MEMORY

certain, and can and must only *hope,* that he or she also belongs to
it "of the heart", i.e., lives in it through faithful love. This form of
hope knows that a person can be a "Christian" (i.e., in this case an
individual who lives in the grace of God and his Christ, *Anonymous
Christianity), even if he or she does not know the name of Christ or
believes that he or she must reject it.

MEMORY

In the light of a *political theology (J.B. Metz), the concept of memory is seen as a fundamental concept both of critical theology and of
a practical philosophy of history. Memory represents the connecting
link between reason and history. Furthermore it incorporates the dual
effect of the Platonic doctrine of anamnesis based on the perception
of reason through *a priori* knowledge and the Judaeo-Christian approach whereby history and freedom are determined by eschatological recollection. The nature of Christianity as a community based on
the spoken word, recalling the historically unique event of the salvation irrevocably offered to man in Jesus Christ, using the forces of
history to open up the paths to the future, introduces the predomi-
nance of an abstract metaphysics of remembrance as the basic form
of valid general knowledge. As a result, it is possible to discern the
significance of history in shaping our perceptions, as well as to perceive the rôle played by the memory process in the practical application of reason. Thus the memory of Christ's passion and of the
sufferings of mankind as the basis for freedom-orientated action and
the history of liberation passed on by word of mouth becomes the
legitimate prerequisite for critically argumentative reason.—
*Anamnesis.

MERCY

Readiness to help those in need. The OT expresses God's mercy
chiefly by the verbs meaning to "be motherly" and to "bend down".
Throughout the OT, assurances of God's mercy, graciousness, and
fidelity to his covenant outbalance all references (frequently anthropomorphic) to the wrath of God; these qualities completely dominate the
NT conception of God. For Christian theology God's mercy is evident
from the fact that he is infinite in every perfection (D 3001), but he
who in fact has deserved judgment must not reckon up the terms of

304

MERIT

the divine mercy but only accept it gratefully as an experience in saving history. It does not abrogate God's *justice, because it makes even the sinner just before God, so that God simultaneously satisfies his mercy and his justice (*Justification).

Human mercy, according to Scripture, is not measured by any display of feeling but by concrete proofs. It is only mercy, according to the OT, that makes worship of God authentic and valuable; according to the NT, mercy is an essential part of the *love which Christ has revealed, made possible, and required (Mt 5:48: Lk 6:31): mercilessness is included in the catalogue of *vice. The Christian is the more obliged to show mercy in that he himself has been forgiven incalculably more (Mt 18:23–25). His duty in daily life is not limited to the corporal and spiritual works of mercy, which are only intended as examples, but extends to solidarity, to real *love and forgiveness.— See also *Neighbour, love of, Sermon on the Mount.*

MERIT

The NT itself expresses in legal terms the objective value which God's grace gives to the *works of the justified done in freedom and grace: the just God rewards these merits with eternal life, he who without respect of persons renders to every man—the good and the evil— according to his works (Rom 2:6; 1 Pet 1:17). This language rightly stresses the God-given moral dignity and value of these works: done in the Holy Ghost and his power, they are based on our "participation in the divine nature" (2 Pet 1:4), actualize this participation, and so are acts of eternal life—though still in the obscurity of faith and the indigence of our ordinary life on earth—intrinsically proportionate to eternal life itself in its glory. It is by these very acts that the life of grace connaturally grows into eternal life. Consequently we can put the matter in this way: through meritorious works there comes about a growth in grace (the ever more profound and existential appropriation of grace, which integrates the various spheres of human life ever more closely into itself) (D 1535, 1574, 1545ff., 1576); our merits "earn" an increase of grace. The word merit, however—the propriety of which is defined (D 1582)—must not be misunderstood:

(1) There is no question of offering God an achievement of our own, independent of him, which he himself needs and must reward. Both our capacity for supernatural and meritorious acts and those acts themselves are the gift of God (through an elevating and "efficacious" grace); just as we exist only through him, so we can act only through

305

MESSALIANISM

him, so that God the just judge "rewards" and "crowns" his own gift. The doctrine of merit, therefore, does not infringe on the freedom of God's decrees and of his grace. Man does not "co-operate with" God as if the two were independent agents, but God enables man to work freely and thus really "bring forth *fruit" (Mt 13:8).

(2) However true it be that the finite creature, who never partakes of the divine simplicity and therefore need not hesitate to entertain a legitimate plurality of motives, may hope and strive for eternal life as his beatitude and therefore seek growth in grace and hence merit, he ultimately gains this eternal life only if he loves God with the theological virtue of *love, for God's own sake and not simply as the cause of his own happiness; only if the desire for his own merit is superseded and transformed by love which desires God himself.

MESSALIANISM

The doctrine of a Christian sect which arose about A.D. 350 (also known as Euchites, Enthusiasts, etc.), that Christians should abstain from work and the sacraments as unprofitable for the desired experience of grace, and can attain to the *beatific vision even in this life through *ascetism. It was widespread in Asia Minor and was condemned by several synods and the Council of *Ephesus.

MESSIAH

From Heb. *mashiaḥ*, Gr. Χριστός , "the anointed one"; in the OT primarily a term for (anointed) kings, also used of the high priest and in one or two derivatives cases. Especially, in later Jewish exposition of OT "messianic" texts, the promised "king" (Gen 49:10; Num 24:17; 2 Sam 7; Ps 2, 72, 110) whose "messianic" kingdom was eagerly expected during the Roman occupation and was portrayed in a variety of forms, culminating in an independent kingdom of Israel which was to rule the whole world (see Lk 24:21; Acts 1:6). "Messiah", once the term had been theologically purified, was the primitive Church's favourite title for *Jesus Christ (Acts 2:33–36); in the light of which must be read the genealogies of Jesus (Mt 1:1; Lk 1:32, 69) and all the other texts where Jesus is called "Son of David". In addition the *Ebed Yahweh had probably been equated with the Messiah. Finally it must be noted that Jesus is called a "prophet" (Acts 3:22; 7:37; Jn 6:14; 7:40) since the prophetical office was attributed to the Messiah.

306

Because of worldly and political ideas of the Messiah prevalent at the time, Jesus is very reserved where the title is concerned, but he knows he is the absolute Saviour who is more than a prophet, who has the Spirit of God, who decides the eternal destiny of men, who is the eschatological Shepherd of Israel, he through whom God takes pity on sinners—in short, he is more than the Judaism of his day could imagine or hope for the Messiah to be. In Mark 14:60ff. Jesus unequivocally declares that he is the Messiah, because any other reply would have meant that he too was awaiting another and greater Saviour.

METANOIA

A religious term of OT origin, meaning conversion to God and already used in the OT of man in all his dimensions, that is *metanoia* (Gr. μετάνοια, change of mind) is not only based on a change of attitude (Jer 8:4ff.; 31:18f. and *passim;* Ezek 18) but must also be shown externally (confession of guilt, fasting, etc.). Similarly John the Baptist preached a *metanoia* which is above all the absolute demand, sanctioned by the threat of God's judgment, that all men without exception must comply with (Mt 3:7ff.; Lk 3:7f.). Instead of repeating traditional exhortations to *metanoia* he preaches and administers a "baptism of penance" (Mk 1:4f.). Jesus adopts this notion of *metanoia* (quite rarely), with less stress on the threat of judgment and more on the rôle of *faith in true *metanoia* (Mk 1:15). The idea of a repeated *metanoia,* already to be found in later Judaism, becomes a great problem in the later writings of the NT (Heb) in view of the slackening enthusiasm of the Christian communities; it is even said (Heb 6:6) that there can be no repetition of *metanoia* (psychologically, not theologically speaking) in the case of a Christian who falls away. The sense of *metanoia* is conveyed today by the genuinely theological notion of *faith and *contrition.

MINISTRIES, RECOGNITION OF

Once agreement is reached or close to being reached on the major, hitherto divisive theological issues (*justification, theology of the *sacrament based on the theology of the Word, etc.), the question of the mutual recognition of ministries between the various Churches is probably the last decisive problem facing the *ecumenical movement.

The discussion to date has been conducted largely on an historical level and cannot possibly lead to agreement. But before Catholic theologians (and the Church) call on God to intervene on behalf of unification they are duty-bound to seek a new level of argumentation (though obviously without denying their own principles). Any such consideration should bear in mind the following points:

1. A great deal (more than is generally supposed) concerning ministry in the Church (*office) is not based simply on the will of God and Jesus Christ, and *therefore* established and acknowledged by the Church as an element preceding its self-fulfilment. Many features of ministry exist *insofar as* and *because* they have been specifically designated by the Church, to some extent out of free impulsion, and partly as a consequence of her very nature. The Church as a whole is the ultimate and original bearer of all "authorities" or "powers" (*Authority of the Church) embodied in her various functionaries; in the full reality of her spirit and faith the Church is the sphere in which the commissioned powers of the office-bearers or ministers can in any way exist. Theology has the task of differentiating between the *substance* of an authoritative commissioner and the (individual or collective) *bearer* of this authority and of revealing open possibilities. Thus, for example, it is not definitely established and can certainly not be attributed to Jesus that the offices of the Pope and the bishops should always be exercised "monarchically" rather than collectively.

2. There is a fundamental law of the Church which is not identical with its constitutional law ("*ius divinum*", *Canon law). This fundamental law arises from the actual nature of the Church as the community of the faithful necessarily and definitively gathered together in the spirit of the crucified and risen Christ, testifying to God's eschatologically victorious communication of himself to the world which that community testifies to, and continues to keep historically alive. This fundamental law contains possibilities of creating legal norms, which are then established and put into practice. For example, the "validity" of the ordination of a priest or bishop is not ultimately guaranteed by the "normal rule", in the unbroken (yet historically frequently questionable) chain of valid ordinations. The ordination of a priest or bishop is only "valid" when he is recognized as such by the body of the Church.

3. The Catholic Church must distinguish between its relationship to other Churches (which from the Catholic point of view are heretical or schismatic) when they *first* came into being, and its relationship to them at a *later* date when these Churches no longer see themselves primarily in terms of their opposition to the Catholic Church. The

spirit of "good faith" *(bona fides)* by which the various Churches are now drawn together socio-collectively creates a kind of ecclesiological unity despite the known divisions. *This* unity cannot simply be equated with the established unity of all Christians in Christ and his grace, nor with those elements shared equally by all Christians, for instance Scripture, baptism, etc. The various Churches are able to acknowledge one another's publicly tangible *"bona fides"*, which implies a genuine salvific Christian faith. On this ecclesiological basis, the office of the Catholic Church can acknowledge acts established and practised by the separated Churches as valid and effective acts of a sacramental nature. With reference to ministry, it should be borne in mind that the normal rite of ordination is not necessarily the only legitimate one in extraordinary cases, and that it is possible that these ministerial powers are also present in the other Churches in a structure which is at least not categorically excluded by the nature of the Church.

Before such time as these sacramental acts are expressly acknowledged by the office of the Catholic Church, they may already be accepted by the—legitimate—body of the Church (if the latter recognized the validity of heretical baptism then it can also acknowledge the possibility of a valid celebration of the Eucharist). The existence of ministries and sacraments "outside" the Catholic Church does not mean that they constitute several churches. As historical and ecclesiastical manifestations of the Spirit they all point invariably to the one Church as the "full" embodiment of this Spirit.

MINISTRY

See *Office.*

MIRACLE

An event within the horizon of our human experience which defies explanation according to the intrinsic laws of this experienced world (regarded as accessible in principle) and therefore summons man in that depth of his being which at once communicates with his empirical world and transcends it in that special interior accessibility and universal openness of his intellectual nature which gives him a fundamental perceptivity for what lies beyond the world of his experience, a permanent proximity to God (*Spirit, *Transcendence). True, he must constantly renew this perceptivity, which worldly influences would dull or stifle, by simply opening himself up to the full extent of his innate scope through that ready faith, devotion to God and candid acceptance which make him conscious of an ultimate shifting uncertainty of his horizons. This preserves in him a humble sense of wonder, so that having conscientiously examined those events in the world of his experience that are inexplicable (not merely unexplained in fact) in natural terms, he concludes that these have been directly intended and caused by God and accepts their summons to an historical dialogue with God. Scripture itself recognizes that this disposition to believe is the necessary condition for a miracle (see Mk 5:34; Lk 18:42), which then leads to *faith (in the strict sense) in God's explicit message (see Jn 11:37ff. and *passim*). As to the fact that miracles can happen and can be recognized as such (a dogma defined by the First Vatican Council, D 3034, see D 3009), a fact frequently called in question by modern natural scientists and by theologians imbued with their outlook, we must observe that the sum of reality which is disclosed to man resembles a many-storeyed structure, no part of which exists solely for its own sake: all the parts are joined in a whole which transcends the natural powers of the parts. Infrahuman nature is intrinsically and theologically ordered to human nature, which in turn is susceptible of itself to the free historical activity of God. The historical intervention of God by a miracle, therefore, only brings into play a qualitatively new mode of the intrinsic function of material nature, which is to express the order of God's sovereign will: releasing nature, which is normally confined within the bounds of scientifically accessible natural law, into the higher realm of those laws which govern the divine economy of salvation, where God by his deeds in history summons man to share his own intimate life.

From the dogmatic point of view, then, a miracle is no lawless, arbitrary display of God's omnipotence. It is part of a universal context of saving history, part of the process of God's self-communication in free grace to man (*Revelation, *Praeambula fidei). It is the testimony which God gives within history to his salvific will and the deeds which flow from it in saving history, in the *prophets (since Moses) and above all in *Jesus Christ. Miracles primarily serve as external signs confirming that their work is approved by God, but also have an eschatological aspect which is clearest in the decisive miracle of Jesus Christ's *resurrection. The miracle of Jesus Christ's glorified, risen body visibly anticipates the final lot of man who is called to the companionship of God, so as to confirm the eschatological power of God the author of history (who has effected the resurrection) and at the same time bear testimony that the perfection God promises man is already secretly at work in our present stage of salvation.

MISSION

Because redemption in Christ is universal and because Christ intends his *Church for all men, she has the duty and right—the "mission"— to preach the gospel as intelligible truth and concrete love without hindrance among all peoples and in all historical situations in order to summon men to the free obedience of faith (Mt 28:19; Church, 16f.; 23ff.; 27; Miss., 6, 29, 35f.). This mission, being a public one, necessarily alters social relations but it has no aims which are directly social or political; it will always encounter the opposition of sinful man, will never be easily fulfilled. It is a positive blessing for the Church herself, affording her experience of the fullness of the world and men; by practising accommodation in her mission, as in duty bound, she more richly develops her own being, becomes what she is—the universal Church (*Catholicity). This accommodation is an expression of respect for the spiritual world of the hearer in the proclamation of the Christian message and therefore also in the doctrinal affirmation of the content of revelation and, what is more, in a valid and lasting way, not simply as a temporary concession to non-Christian cultures. In the past, the Church's mission was seen as necessary on the basis of the individual's salvation. Nowadays, however, we have a much greater knowledge of the extent of the non-Christian history of mankind and are better able to make a correct theological assessment of the power of the *salvific will of God and of *redemption, with the result that we can no longer assume that a great part of mankind will be lost to God. On the contrary, it is now possible to see far more clearly how, from the theological point of view, a man who has not been able to hear an explicit proclamation of the Gospel may be confronted, in a very unsystematic form, with an absolute moral obligation and still react positively to it, to his own salvation (Church, 16; Church/world, 22; Miss., 7). Despite this optimism regarding man's salvation, however, it is still possible for the Church's mission to have a positive meaning. God's grace, by which all men are really saved, has an incarnate character, so that it is present and effective in all aspects of man's existence, including his history and his life in society. Of its very nature, it is humanizing. It also brings about peace and creates the Church.

MISSION, TRINITARIAN

Regarded from the point of view of him who is sent: it is the scriptural name given (Jn 20:21; Gal 4:4 –6, etc.) to the operations of the second and third divine Persons of the *Trinity in creation and saving history, insofar as these divine operations (identical in their source with the Persons themselves) are regarded as based on the divine procession of the Logos from the Father and of the Spirit from the Father and (through) the Son. Thus the Father can "come" (Jn 14:23) but cannot be "sent" and the fact that the Son sends the Spirit (Jn 16:7) shows that he also proceeds from the Son (Jn 15:26; D 850, 1300ff., etc.).

MODALISM

From the Latin *modus*, manner. The term applied to any theory of the *Trinity which maintains that the one God becomes trinitarian only in respect of the mode of his operations *ad extra* (especially creation, Incarnation, sanctification). It is most pronounced in *Sabellianism (*Monarchianism).

MODERNISM

A collective term for certain false or distorted theological views which arose about the year 1900 out of the legitimate desire (indeed the abiding duty) to proclaim the Christian faith to the men of that time in an adequate manner. In this connexion the following errors came to light in France, England and Italy: that *theology is a matter of feeling; that *religion is a product of the subconscious; that neither of these must be constrained by reason, which has only a very minor rôle to play in religion; that *revelation is awareness of an interior religious need, the bearers of revelation being such merely because they best objectify this need; that these objectifications, when ossified, become *Tradition; that *dogma is only a symbolic expression of these objectifications, which like them must change with the progress of civilization; that there is a natural need to communicate one's own objectifications of religion to others, and that when this is done the *Church results. These views were coupled with *biblical criticism. They were condemned, together with other errors, by Pius X in the decree *Lamentabili* (D 3401–3466) and the encyclical *Pascendi* (D 3475–3498). It must be added that during the polemics against Mod-

312

ernism, which proposed wrong solutions to many problems it had grasped aright, numerous adherents of Modernism were embittered by clerical intrigues and driven out of communion with the Church. To this day "Modernism" unfortunately remains a term used for spiteful invective by arrogant people in the Church who have no idea how difficult faith is for men of our time.

MOLINISM

The theory of *grace propounded by L. de Molina, S.J. (1535–1600) as a counter to *Banezianism. Very briefly, Molinism affirms that original sin has not weakened *freedom in the sense of the power of decision. God's concourse with human acts does not involve a physical *predetermination, but simply means that God gives reality to the free human activity itself. To explain how this can be so without prejudice either to God's sovereign providence or human freedom, Molina has recourse to the notion of *scientia media. Because God knows, through this "middle knowledge", how a man would act in any concrete situation if God brought it about, he can bring about one of these situations (*Predestination), and therefore the free action as well, without prejudice to man's free choice. At the moment of the decision that God has foreseen, this freely given prevenient grace (the situation God has ordained) becomes a helping grace (adiuvans), the sufficient grace becomes an efficacious one, or not, always according to God's scientia media. The most serious objection raised against Molinism was that it seemed to take insufficient account of the data of revelation concerning *grace. During the controversy about grace which arose in 1588 Molina was further accused of advancing a doctrine that could not be reconciled with St. Augustine or the Tridentine decrees, and falling into *Semipelagianism. In 1607 Pope Paul V settled the controversy between the Dominicans and the Jesuits by forbidding either side to impugn the orthodoxy of the other (D 1997).

MOMENT

See Kairos, Now.

MONARCHIANISM

A theological movement which denied the *Trinity in God (thus certain Judaizing teachers at the end of the 1st century, Cerinthus, the Ebionites). Jesus, therefore, had to be declared a mere prophet whom God adopted as his Son (Adoptianist Monarchianism, represented by Theodore the Tanner [end of 2nd century], Paul of Samosata [3rd century]), or else recourse to *Modalism was necessary to explain Christ's divinity (*Sabellianism, *Patripassianism).

MONASTIC AND LAY CONFESSION

These are ancient, quite sound and legitimate means of mutual religious and moral assistance among Christians. One confesses one's sins to a fellow Christian though he be not a priest, so as to unburden one's conscience and receive advice and consolation from a more mature Christian (spiritual father) and to strengthen one's faith in God's forgiving grace. Such a confession was very common in Eastern monasticism but was rarely confused with sacramental confession. In the West, during the Middle Ages, non-sacramental lay confession was recommended and practised (sometimes even declared obligatory) in cases where sacramental confession to a priest was not possible.

MONISM

That type of *pantheism which in effect is equivalent to atheism, denying any distinction between God and the world, affirming that the world and the world-principle are identical. The world is the Absolute and adequately explains itself. Monism usually takes the form of *materialism and absolute evolutionism, since it regards *spirit, *matter, and *life as a single reality. Monism was also given organizational form in a body that has existed since the time of E. Haeckel.

MONOGENISM

Monogenism is the doctrine according to which the whole of living mankind (at least since the time of fall) is biologically descended from a single human couple. Monogenism is contrasted with polygenism,

314

according to which the evolution from the animal kingdom to man took place in the same species in a plurality of cases, and with poly-phylism, according to which mankind is descended from many differ-ent species of animal. Only one *Adam is mentioned in Scripture, but it is difficult to know what is a conceptual model in this scriptural Adam and what is really meant by it. In Gen. 2, Adam means simply "man" (including man in the representation of a "corporate person") or mankind in its unity. Like Scripture, the pronouncements made by the Church's magisterium before 1950 simply referred to the man, Adam and no explicit position was adopted with regard to the ques-tion of monogenism. Pius XII rejected polygenism in 1950, because it was not clear how it could be reconciled with the Church's dogma of original sin (D 3897). It is now possible to accept the view, however, that Catholic theology has developed so much further that it is possi-ble to reconcile the dogma of original sin and polygenism. Theolo-gians cannot, of course, base their arguments on natural science, but they can respond with five counter-arguments to a hypothesis of polygenism proposed by natural scientists. These are (a) Even if bio-logical polygenism is not assumed, mankind is still a unity. This is so because man has descended from the one God with his one plan for the history of the whole of mankind, because mankind has a common being, because all men and women are interdependent within a spatio-temporal history, because all men and women are really related to Jesus Christ and because all men and women share the same aim in the kingdom of God. (b) In and through this unity, the situation of every human's salvation is determined by the personal decisions of all men and women, which are not confined to the inner experience of each individual, but are based on the existential space occupied by mankind in its unity and on intercommunication between all men. (c) There must necessarily have been, in the history of this one "situa-tion", a transitional phase from an entirely innocent mankind to a mankind living in a situation determined by guilt. Since all men are in need of redemption, this transition must have taken place at the beginning of the history of mankind. (Although we may not know anything about the concrete circumstances, we can infer this original guilt from our situation in *aetiology.) (d) According to the doctrine of *original sin, God gives an individual man or woman sanctifying grace not because he or she belongs to this one mankind, but only because of his or her orientation towards Jesus Christ. Mankind ought to have had this grace from God's original will to create man and to have mediated it to the individual because that individual belonged to mankind. This belonging to mankind, which ought to mediate grace, lost its function when mankind came to exist (from the beginning) in a situation of freedom determined by guilt. (e) It does not affect the constitution of this situation of freedom that is determined by guilt (and has been so determined from the beginning) that it may have been caused by the will of one individual or by the sin of several individuals, especially as the actual sin committed at the beginning is not inherited by or imputed to descendents.

MONOPHYSITISM

In the strict sense, the doctrine given sharp formulation by Eutyches, the archimandrite of a monastery at Constantinople in the middle of the fifth century, who insisted so uncompromisingly on earlier acceptable formulae as to make them heretical. Thus the substantial union of the Logos with the human reality was held to give rise to a single *physis* (*Nature), in which the humanity was absorbed by the divinity, dissolved like a drop of honey in the sea. Eutyches therefore was not prepared to accept the terminological advance which took place between *Ephesus and *Chalcedon, in accordance with which *person (*hypostasis) and *"physis"* were no longer used to mean the same thing (thus departing from the terminology of Cyril of Alexandria: D 254, 429f., 505, 272f.). Further, for fear of *Nestorianism, he denied that the human reality in Christ continued to exist "without confusion" together with the divine nature in the one person of the Logos (condemnation of monophysitism at Chalcedon in 451: D 293, 301ff.). Later forms of monophysitism frequently represent a reactionary stubbornness with regard to the Church's official language rather than a real departure from the Church's dogma. Monophysitism persists as a pre-Chalcedonian, non-heretical doctrine (verbal monophysitism) in the so-called "monophysite" Eastern Churches (in Syria, Armenia and especially the Ethiopian Coptic Church). Whenever the human reality is devalued or suppressed in the relationship between God and man, it is possible to speak of monophysite tendencies.

MONOTHEISM

Philosophically speaking, the doctrine that there exists a single supreme, infinite, personal spirit distinct from the world, which spirit creates, sustains and pervades the whole empirical reality of the world. All statements, then, about the infinite personal God must be understood as analogical statements (*Analogy) about the infinite *mystery (*Pantheism, *Polytheism). From the theological point of view the monotheism of the OT and NT is the affirmation that the being and power which is experienced in operation "here and now" ("*our* God", the "God of our fathers") is not some numinous power ("a" God) but precisely that one, only, absolute God (God absolutely speaking, beside whom there are no other gods), the sole principle and the omnipotent Lord of all the world and all history. Thus monotheism is the acknowledgment of the possibility and reality of direct encounter between creatures and the person of God as he is in himself: the formal anticipation of the Christian doctrine of *grace, *revelation, and God's *self-communication. Thus monotheism is not only a philosophical truth but also the abiding foundation of the special character of Christianity (see D 1f., 11, 790, 3021; Mk 12:29; Jn 17:3: 1 Cor 8:5f.).

MONOTHELITISM

A doctrine advanced in the Byzantine Empire during the 7th century in an attempt to reconcile the adherents of *Monophysitism with those of the Council of *Chalcedon. To conciliate the former, the Monothelites attributed only one mode of operation (Gr. ἐνέργεια) to Christ, while accepting the two natures defined at Chalcedon. This doctrine, which arose in the entourage of Sergius I, Patriarch of Constantinople, was called Monenergism and to some extent facilitated the negotiations for reunion. In 633 it was agreed that mention of either one or two energies should be avoided; but Sergius asserted that to speak of two energies suggested that Christ had two contrary wills. Thus he implicitly affirmed a single will. This view became increasingly explicit at New Rome. In 649 at a synod in the Lateran Pope Martin I expressly enunciated the doctrine of two natural energies or wills in Christ, and finally the Sixth Ecumenical Council, *Constantinople III, defined the dogma that in Christ there are two natural operations (without division, without separation, without charge, without confusion), and two natural wills which do not conflict (since the human will is subordinate to the divine; D 553–559).—See also *Hypostatic Union.*

317

MONTANISM

A sect of enthusiasts in the 2nd century A.D., founded by a prophet, the Phrygian Montanus, and two prophetesses. He announced new prophecies of the Holy Ghost, of whom he claimed to be a sort of incarnation: the imminent end of the world, a more austere morality (for example, stricter fasting, forbidding re-marriage) as a preparation for this event, a severer penitential discipline, diminution of the rôle of the hierarchy in favour of charismatic prophecy. Its principal adherent in the West was the important African ecclesiastical writer Tertullian. The sect survived for many centuries in small groups.

MORAL STATISTICS

The description of the actual moral conduct of men (particular nations, groups, etc.) (especially with regard to certain types of behaviour: sexual morality, prostitution, suicide, etc.) with the assistance of demographic and statistical methods. Moral statistics can never ascertain whether moral offences are subjective sins as well, or merely objective (material) sins; they can neither justify nor invalidate moral standards, since the validity of the moral law in no way depends on the extent to which it is in fact observed. Moral statistics can indeed show that human behaviour flows in part from certain common motives and assumptions but cannot be used to deny man's fundamental freedom, for no one asserts that freedom is unlimited or that it implies unmotivated behaviour. Such misuse of moral statistics must be repudiated (Kinsey Reports): but they may help legislators to frame laws that will effectually educate the masses, may draw the attention of moral philosophers and theologians to problems they would otherwise have overlooked, warn them against formulating principles without sufficient nicety, may raise the question why there is a discrepancy between our standards and our actual conduct and suggest an answer, may (when we confront the fact that God seriously wills all men to be saved) deepen our realization that we can by no means assume every objective infringement of objective moral standards to be a subjective offence before God.

MORAL SYSTEMS

By this term Catholic theology means not the various philosophical

318

or theological systems of morality, law, etc., as a whole, but the various theories as to how one is morally bound to act where there is a serious doubt whether a law exists or whether it applies to the case in hand and this doubt cannot be directly resolved by closer study, etc. This question does not arise in a case where a specific end must be achieved without fail (for instance, for the validity of a sacrament: D 2101) and therefore the best means to that end must be used. In other cases the question is answered as follows: (1) absolute tutiorism: one must always decide in favour of the law, even when its existence is doubtful, so long as any doubt at all remains of one's freedom from the law; this is a rigoristic view which is impossible in practice, misunderstands the moral nature of freedom as such and is rejected by the Church (D 2303): (2) probabiliorism: a person may decide in favour of freedom only if the reasons against the existence of the law are substantially sounder and more probable. To this it can be objected that a law only binds if its existence is certain and that there is a *presumption in favour of freedom, a moral value willed by God. But the Church allows this opinion (D 2175ff.); (3) equiprobabilism: freedom may be chosen if the grounds for it are as good as those for believing that the law exists; (4) pure probabilism: the presumption is in favour of freedom if there are serious reasons in its favour and the claim of the law is not certain. Probabilism and equiprobabilism in practice usually lead to the same conclusion since it is no easy task to weigh the reasons pro and con and the matter is always left to some extent to one's prudent estimation. Together they represent the most common view and if they are presupposed, then room is left in these doubtful cases for other considerations (compensating for the danger of breaking a law by securing other values; considerations drawn from *existential ethics); (5) laxism: the merest trace of a right to freedom justifies one in deciding against the law. Since we are normally concerned with a certainty that is only moral—not physical or metaphysical—and therefore some semblance of an argument against the law can generally be found, laxism would undermine all obedience to law and general norms of conduct. It is condemned by the Church (D 2101–2165, especially 2103).

MORAL THEOLOGY

The doctrine, based on divine revelation, of how man should behave so as to be upright and pleasing to God. Moral theology is distinguished from a transcendental philosophical *ethics—whatever use it may make of the latter's ideas and insights—because its source and norm is the revelation of God in Christ, in whom man is seen as he should be and God reveals his own image to man, and because it brings man into line with his real goal, acceptance of God's absolute self-communication by a free grace that man by his own powers can neither wrest from God nor even conceive. Ethics sketches a formal structure of human nature as it exists and as it should be respected by man's conduct, but leaves open the question of God's sovereign dominion over this nature that is open to him, of man's alienation from or intimacy with God in his free self-communication. Thus philosophical ethics is to moral theology as the question (that must be put) is to the answer. Moral theology is part of Christian *dogmatic theology in content, sources, and method, and therefore has the same sources and norms (*Holy Scripture, *Tradition, *Magisterium of the Church). Moral theology presupposes and develops dogmatic *anthropology, systematically deriving from it the norms of man's conduct as a Christian (but with constant reference to this derivation as already given in Scripture and Tradition). Being based on the permanent concrete nature of man (in the concrete Christian economy of salvation) it is a science of essential norms; and since it takes account of the historical situation (never to be really superseded till the end of history, only more radically grasped) which has been brought about by the consummation of saving history in Christ and the Church and must (taking into account the experiential human sciences) constantly apply the norms of that situation as far as possible to the ever shifting present produced by constant (profane) historical change in every human dimension, it is also (without becoming mere *situation ethics) a science of existential norms, and clearly mirrors in its own history the continual transformation of man's secular and religious situations. Although moral theology must as far as possible work out concrete and mandatory solutions that are in accord not only with conscience but also with objective reality (because this reality itself is subject of the dominion of God and Jesus Christ) (*Casuistry), yet it must not suppose that it can simply relieve the individual of the task of finding out God's concrete will for him; analysis of the concrete situation can never be reflexively complete, because even within the scope of the general norms which offer a man several alternative courses legitimate in themselves, God may wish him to act in one particular way and may make this will known to him, and because man cannot escape having to entrust himself without reserve to God's mercy by satisfying his own mind that his conduct is in fact blameless. Moral theology therefore will give man obligatory rules of conduct and at the same

320

time train him in humility for his solitary responsibility to God alone. It would be appropriate for moral theology to comprise a first, formal part (corresponding to general anthropology about the nature of supernatural morality, about *law and *conscience) and then a second, material part, setting forth the individual dimensions as so many "spheres of duty" or rather realms of possible moral growth and perfection, both from the personal and the social point of view.

MOTHER OF GOD

The Blessed Virgin *Mary is the true mother of *Jesus Christ, who is the true *Son of God. Hence Mary's title "Mother of God" arose from the Trinitarian and Christological conflicts of the first three centuries (D 252, 301ff.). It must be observed that "motherhood" connotes more than biological conception and child-bearing; and if becoming a mother in the real sense is more than a merely physical occurence, how much truer is this of Mary's free, personal act of faith, which is inseparable from our saving history. Since we can say in all truth—in virtue of the *communication of idioms (not otherwise)— that the divine Logos was begotten in Mary, Mary is truly the Mother of God, and the title "Mother of Christ" (associated with *Nestorian-ism) was rejected because it involved the danger of diminishing Christ's divinity or the *hypostatic union.

MOTIVE

That value which induces but does not compel a free agent to perform an act. The motive may coincide with the formal object (the particular aspect under which an object is envisaged by an act) but need not do so, because the reason for doing a certain thing and the chosen aspect of the object may be different. Thus, for instance, attrition (*Fear of God, *Attritionism) rejects sin as violating God's rights over man (the formal object) from fear of punishment (the motive). Although motive and formal object may be of different value, therefore, it does not follow that the act must be morally wrong.

MOVER, FIRST MOVER

This term for *God in Aristotelian-thomistic metaphysics does not signify the cause of a physical motion but is based on the philosophical insight that things exist which change (being that is at rest becomes operative, a qualitative change), thus presupposing a cause distinct from themselves. Once it is established that everything in existence that passes from *potency to *act requires a cause, which for its part must be uncaused (*Causality), it can be readily seen that this supreme and all-embracing efficient cause must itself be pure *act, and that in such a manner that in it act and *being are identical. Hence the first cause is also a *spirit and personal (*Person).—See also *Proof of God's Existence.*

MYSTERIES OF THE LIFE OF JESUS

It is not the Incarnation, *Cross and *Resurrection alone that are of universal significance for the salvation of all in and despite their historical uniqueness and contingency, are therefore the subject-matter of dogma, creed, anamnesis, and praise, and in this sense are "mysteries". The same is true of all the events of Jesus' life. These events are not falsely sublimated or mythologized by being so regarded; we merely recognize that the one total life of Jesus with all it embraces (each detail in its own way and in its own place), deliberately directed to and unified in his death and resurrection, is the one event for the sake of which God is gracious to us. This means—so we must reflect when meditating on these mysteries—that we are redeemed precisely because the Word of the Father accepted our lowly, profane, death-doomed life, thereby making the humdrum character of our own life an event of the grace that is ultimately God himself. The individual events of Jesus' life are therefore always of the same character as his death and resurrection, which are most obviously mysteries: as the finite approaches its bitterest finitude the advent of transfiguring divinity takes place in it (not as what is released once the self has been stripped away). For this the whole life of Jesus (because of the resurrection) is the pattern and earnest.

MYSTERIES (PAGAN) AND CHRISTIANITY

The mysteries common in the milieu that witnessed the rise of Christianity were ritual celebrations (involving word and act, by initiation, a bath and a meal) of cults which were at least theoretically esoteric (the mysteries of Eleusis, Attis, and Cybele, of Dionysus, Isis, and

Mithras); the mythical fate of a god was represented and renewed through *anamnesis and the person thus initiated (Gr. μύστης) was believed to share personally in the salvation of this god (enlightenment, life, etc.). Christianity seems in many respects to resemble the heathen mysteries—which should really not be thought surprising since we are dealing with fully developed religions laying claim to every dimension of a single human nature; rites, initiation, anamnesis, a meal, hope of personal salvation. But baptism and the Eucharist have their roots in the OT and the Judaism of Jesus' day, which knew nothing of mysteries. The concept of the divinity in Christianity and its eschatological expectation remove it far from the mystery religions. Above all, the anamnesis practised in these religions only enacts the mythologically dramatized death and renewal of nature, so that they remain confined to the pre-personal dimension of the powers of nature. The salvation which Christianity celebrates in its worship is a sharply defined event that occurred once only in the history of mankind itself, an historical event that belongs both to us and to the one, absolute God.

MYSTERIES, THEOLOGY OF THE

A revival of early Christian theological thought begun by O. Casel (d. 1948) and I. Herwegen (d. 1946). It is chiefly concerned with the relation between general saving history and particular realizations of salvation, or rather with the real and efficacious presence of Jesus Christ's saving deed in the sacramental event. Starting from this point (the Mystery), the whole of theology is developed as a mystery theology (*Anamnesis, *Presence, *Repetition). Furthermore mystery in the NT and the Fathers primarily means God's dealings with historical human beings unto salvation or unto judgment, that is, God's eternal decree (primordial mystery), the work of creation, redemption (Christ-mystery in the strict sense), the Church, faith and the sacraments (cultic mystery), the actuality and consummation of salvation as contrasted with the "mystery of iniquity". Hence mystery theology is not only a new theology of the *Mass but also affects dogmatic, moral and pastoral theology. Though many of its features have been attacked and require further clarification, it has nevertheless been beneficial to the liturgical revival and Catholic piety (cf. Vat. II: Lit, 35, 102 and *passim)* as well as to theology. Since it sheds light on a number of controversial questions (for example, the nature of the sacraments, the sacrifice of the Mass, the doctrine of grace) it has an important contribution to make to ecumenical discussion.

MYSTERY

Since mystery cannot be understood as a defective form of natural human knowledge, but is rather a reality ordered to the *act of religion as such, we must call mystery that in reference to which man constantly rises above himself in the unity of his intellective and freely loving *transcendence. Thus mystery is a primordial aspect, essential and permanent, of total reality, in that reality as a whole (that is, as infinite) is present for the finite, created spirit in the latter's intrinsic openness to the infinite. *Spirit, as this openness to the infinite, is the capacity to accept the incomprehensible as such, i.e., as permanent mystery. The teaching of faith about the *beatific vision does not abolish the permanence of the incomprehensible. Indeed the vision of God will reveal his incomprehensible infinitude (D 800, 3001) as such and thus make it the object of the blessed spirit's real and eternal beatitude. There is only one fundamental mystery: that the inconceivability of God, in which he is God, is not merely given as the distance and horizon within which our existence proceeds, but that this same God, still inconceivable, gives himself to us directly, so that he becomes the innermost reality of our existence, and does so as himself. But at the present time (even in theology) mystery is often taken in a narrower sense to mean something which in the beatific vision will cease to be a mystery (D 2856f., 3016), because this sort of incomprehensibility is based only on the sensible and earthly character of our present knowledge. From this narrower sense of mystery follows the distinction between (a) natural mysteries, which concern truths about God whose existence and import we can know because of the analogical character of the terms employed, but which remain obscure; (b) truths whose existence God must reveal because they concern realities which spring from such a free (saving-historical) intervention of God that natural reason cannot gather them from the world of natural experience (for example, the Virgin Birth); and (c) truths whose possible and actual content can now be known only by divine revelation and otherwise are inaccessible to any created intellect. The existence of mysteries in this strict sense and the possibility of their revelation is a dogma of the Church (D 2732, 2841f., 2855f., 3015f., 3041, 3225, 3236f., 3422 and *passim*). It is certain that the divine *Trinity, the

*Incarnation, supernatural *grace and its culmination, the *beatific vision, are mysteries in the strict sense.

MYSTICISM

The term can refer to (a) an experience, the interior meeting and union of a man with the divine infinity that sustains him and all other being—in Christian mysticism, in Judaism and Islam, with the personal God—as well as (b) the attempt to give a systematic exposition of this experience, or reflection upon it (hence a scientific "discipline").

(1) Witnesses testify that mystical phenomena occur in all the higher religions. Mystical contemplation, submerging the soul in its source, is always the act of the individual, not of the community of worshippers: but the individual may have mystical experience during worship. Cases where the mystic is commissioned to proclaim a message to others are the exception. The mystic's declaration of his experience or his intellectual exposition always remain inadequate "stammering", for the supersensory mystical experience as such gives no warrant of the truth or adequacy of subsequent communication in ordinary human term. Whereas magic seeks to bring about the encounter with divine power through special means, mystical contemplation is always experienced as a gift. *Asceticism may (as non-Christian religions specially emphasize) help to prepare one for mystical union. Mystical theory is often in danger of explaining such experience in terms of *monism, *pantheism or "theopanism", for the mystic experiences the influence from the Absolute as that which is most inward in his own soul, while losing consciousness of time and external things; but mystical experience as such has nothing to do with these errors.

(2) Christians too may experience the divine infinity through *natural* mysticism; indeed it is already implicit in the experience of *transcendence, so that this experience may tempt one to reject out of hand any mediation of the incarnate Word of God as a means to divine union. Christian mysticism too is a mysticism of infinity, but is such because it elevates and liberates the experience of transcendence by *grace, (experienced as) God's *self-communication. But this means that mystical union, an imperfect foretaste of the blessed vision of God in eternity, is like this very vision, always transmitted through the historical fact of God's descent to men in his Son, who even in

eternal life remains the Incarnate, the Crucified, the Risen: *Christ-mysticism.

(3) Because Jesus Christ redeemed all creation in his love, along with mankind, genuinely Christian mysticism is neither a denial of the world nor a meeting with the infinite All, but a taking of the world with one to a loving encounter with the personal God. Of course, where the personal God is experienced in mysticism outside Christianity we must speak not of 'natural' but of supernatural mysticism, for here Jesus Christ is unwittingly experienced as the countenance of the Father. For every grace is given solely by the redemption Jesus Christ has wrought. Christian mysticism is *Trinitarian mysticism in that God's Trinitarian life is communicated by Jesus Christ in the Holy Ghost, and the graces of the Holy Ghost have an important rôle to play in it. They can explain the gradual nature of mystical progress. Asceticism is the preliminary step. But purification and renunciation do not destroy the personality, rather the finite soul is freed for the more distinct experience of grace. The soul is "passive", not "active", vis-à-vis the graces of the Holy Ghost as it makes its way upward towards illumination and union by stages which are variously described by mystical writers. But the gifts of counsel and fortitude may lead the mystic to engage in social activity or even to take action which will be historically decisive. Mystical experience may be accompanied by unusual phenomena (ecstasy, *stigmatization, levitation, etc.), but these are no essential part of true mysticism.

MYTH

This is one of the obscurest notions of comparative religion in its application to religious utterances and the interpretation of life. If we assume that every concept bearing upon a metaphysical or religious reality, remote from direct experience, must work with a sensible image (in an original synthesis, not one artificially worked out afterwards for didactic purposes) which is not the original phenomenal form of that reality but is arrived at from elsewhere; if we further assume that this image (without which every concept is empty, that is impossible; in thomistic language the "phantasm" to which all transcendental knowledge must have recourse) is not a static "picture" but a dramatic representation—an event—or can be developed into one, and that such a thing can then be called a mythical representation; then every metaphysical or religious utterance is a mythical one or can be interpreted in mythical terms. This would not be to deny the possibility of a knowledge of truth that is genuine and permanently valid. Rather, mythical utterance in this sense would always be essentially involved in this sort of knowledge, being simply another way of expressing the analogical character of such knowledge (*Analogy).

Supposing a critical consciousness of the variable but inescapable imaginative element in such utterances were lacking or even excluded, concept and image being absolutely identified, we would have myth in the proper and pejorative (formal) sense. Of course any such myth may again be true enough, or go astray by asserting plain falsehood or by taking a correct interpretation of part of human life to apply to the whole of it. Where the thing signified by the religious utterance turns the historical and phenomenal forms of human experience into its own reality and therefore its own phenomenal form through God's activity in saving history (especially in the Incarnation), the ultimate problem of myth is solved by the thing signified. God's own epiphany (2 Tim 1:10; Tit 3:5) is in the flesh, and therefore we may speak of God himself in very earthly terms.—See also *Demythologization.*

N

NAME

Man can only comprehend a thing, distinguish it from other things and fit it into the framework of his conscious life by giving it a name, or rather, quite apart from the phonetic features the word may exhibit, accepting a name suggested by the patent reality of the thing itself, at the same time subjecting the thing to his own law by giving it a name (see Gen 2:19f.). Small wonder that primitive man supposed he could gain power over a thing by discovering its correct name, was given to casting spells by magic words, and held solemn ceremonies for the conferring or changing of names. Similarly in the OT we find that names, by a curious duality, are both identified with and taken to represent the thing or person named. Hence the OT's reverence for the proper name of God (*Yahweh), which the *Decalogue (Ex 20:7) did not allow to be taken in vain or invoked in oaths (Deut 5:11; Lev 19:12; Ecclus 23:10f., etc.). The expression "in Jesus' name" may be taken to mean by the commission, authority and power Jesus confers on those who, openly invoking his name, testify that this name (his nature) is really "known" to them (Mt 7:22; 18:20; Acts 2:38; 4:30; Mk 9:37ff.; Jn 14:13f.; 16:2f.).

NATIONALISM

See *Religion, State.*

NATURAL DESIRE

Since St Thomas Aquinas this term means the tendency or directedness of the created spirit towards the *beatific vision of God. It is

328

based on the unlimited openness of the human *spirit, in itself, to the Infinite. This natural desire, in the "natural" structure with which human nature supplies it, is confronted by the offer of God's self-communication which God in fact has made in Christ, an offer which the natural desire was never able to call forth and which therefore human nature can in no sense claim as its due; yet the natural desire is the dynamic "opening" of man in which God's supernatural, gratuitous self-communication and the equally gratuitous Vision of himself as man's actual last end, could be and have been engrafted (*Potentia obedientialis, Supernatural *existential).

NATURALISM

A vague collective term for various attitudes and interpretations of life, whether practical or worked out in theoretical form, which identify the real with the "natural" (that is with immediate everyday experience), so that for this sort of *positivism there can be no serious question of a metaphysics, a revealed religion or an ethics which is anything more than banal worldly wisdom.

NATURAL MORAL LAW

The objective structures of human *nature which precede and make possible the *freedom of man, because they are implicitly affirmed by a transcendental necessity even in the act of their denial, whether in theory or in practice, are as many necessary objective norms of human conduct; because these structures objectify the will of God, their Creator, the law of obligation flowing from them is also called the natural moral law or (in quite a different sense from that which the term has in the natural sciences) the natural law. The sum of the rights and duties which of themselves follow directly from the nature of man, as a being endowed with reason and free will, is also called natural law in Catholic ethics; the mutability or immutability of this law and the possibility of knowing it are an important theme in Greek and Christian philosophy. Not everything that is in fact encountered in man ought for that reason to be there. Man's nature is such as to leave a certain sphere to the morally indifferent in him because that nature disposes him to activity whereby he changes himself. But those structures of his being which he implicitly reaffirms (by setting them in operation) even when he denies them—his true spirituality, his freedom, his orientation to the mystery which is God, his historicity, his masculinity or femininity, his social being, etc.—constitute his necessary nature, his dignity and his responsibilities under the natural moral law. Since this nature is open to God's absolute dominion (*Nature and grace, *Potentia obedientialis) those obligatory norms which flow from God's supernatural self-communication to man in the grace of Jesus Christ are of a still higher order and impose the same absolute obligations as the natural moral law. From the theological point of view, there is, in the concrete order determined by Jesus Christ, no "pure nature". A fundamental problem of natural law, then, is whether "nature" is a suitable key-concept for moral directives that are valid for all men. According to the official teaching of the Catholic Church, there are two orders of knowledge—that of faith and that of reason (see D 3015, 3019; Church/world, 59). If it were possible for man to know the norms of moral behaviour without depending on the explicit revelation of God's word and only by means of his reason (which, even in the case of non-Christians, is never "purely natural" reason), it might also be possible to achieve, on this basis, an effective ethical union between believers and non-believers. It would, however, have to be borne in mind that, in this process, there could be no unity with regard to what is "in accordance with nature", "contrary to nature", "valid beyond time" or "historically relative". The Church's magisterium has again and again claimed—most recently in its teaching about birth regulation—the right to make binding statements about data concerning the natural moral law. In these cases, the Church is making (in the form of interpretations of the commandment of love) authentic pronouncements which are promulgated by the *magisterium, which are not infallible (*infallibility) and are, for their arguments, dependent on justifications and proofs taken from the secular sciences and universal human reason.—See also *Moral Theology, Sermon on the Mount, Existential Ethics.*

NATURAL SACRAMENTS

Since St Augustine's time Catholic theologians, in view of God's universal salvific will, have assumed that in the pagan world there must have been certain acts of faith (of parents, etc.), expressed in a tangible cult, by which *original sin in children could be blotted out, analogously to *circumcision in the OT. Whatever is to be thought of this theologoumenon, it shows how convinced ancient and medieval theologians were of the universality of God's salvific will and raises the question whether the limbo of infants is a theologoumenon that does this conviction full justice. In the light of the idea of natural sacraments much in *non-Christian religions could be assessed more favourably.

NATURAL SCIENCE AND THEOLOGY

Christianity as such concerns itself with the absolute *mystery embracing all particular being which we call *God, and with his relationship to us as made known by *revelation. Natural science treats of individual things and the laws governing their interrelations, which it expresses as far as possible in mathematical formulae. Thus theology and natural science differ in their object, their method, and the source of their data. Christianity does make certain affirmations about the world, but only insofar as the world is God's creature and the recipient of his self-communication and further affirmations about empirical reality (both assumptions and consequences) follow from these facts (*Soul, *Immortality, *Creation of man, etc.). Moreover the empirical world is the object of theology because it is where *miracles occur and are known. But in neither of these cases do theology and natural science come into fundamental conflict or contend for ultimate competence since the orientation of the world to God and the body of knowledge derived from the abstract science of metaphysics and from theology transcend the experience available to purely natural science through direct observation of phenomena and the laws concerning their inter-relation; the existentially significant "sign" (miracle), unique in each case, defies investigation by the experimental methods of modern natural science. Conflict can be avoided altogether if each side will take care to pose questions accurately and confine itself to its own methods. So far as in particular cases theology and the natural sciences make affirmations about the same object—though under different aspects and using different methods—*apparent* conflict is always possible from time to time. These apparent conflicts can and must be resolved by mutual patience and self-criticism (cf. Vat. II: Church/world, 36). It is more difficult to bring about a meeting and synthesis between the theologian's and the natural scientist's "sense of things" (the sum of knowledge, with its emotional overtones, that each has at his finger-tips, feels is obvious, and underlies his whole position), the outlook that develops when a person is professionally concerned all his life with one of the two sciences (a thing hardly avoidable nowadays). The discrepancy, not a real or logical contradiciton, between these two attitudes, their mutual alienation, especially when the natural scientist has no "taste" or talent for religion and the theologian is still emotionally committed to the old cosmology, is in part a consequence of the pluralism which is unavoidable today, must simply be borne with patience, which of course gives the natural scientist no right to ignore religion, since he can never be the man he must be by simply being a scientist, and can be overcome, partly by fostering meetings between the men of each discipline, partly by enlarging upon those topics and problems in each discipline which point beyond it. In addition the theologian must still further refine his language in such a way that the natural scientist will perceive that by "God" is meant the impenetrable *mystery which embraces and sustains his world and his knowledge of it without either restricting or declaring that the investigable cannot or should not be explored.

NATURAL THEOLOGY

A term applied to metaphysical *ontology insofar as the general doctrine of being necessarily includes some statement about the absolute *being of God.—See also *God, doctrine of; Proof of the Existence of God; Theodicy; Fundamental Theology.*

NATURE

The name for the permanent structure of a being (not strictly as composite, but thought of as radically one) insofar as this is the principle and antecedent law of its activity (and therefore the presuppositon of human culture). To the Christian mind "nature" is in no way inconsistent with *creation but expresses the meaningful content and creaturely autonomy that God's creation establishes and sustains. Thus the naturalness of a thing increases in direct (not inverse) proportion to the "nearness" of God's creative causality. The nature of all beings below man is a closed one, they and their actions being referred to a particular and limited environment; it is either not self-conscious at all, unable to make itself the object of its own acts, or else able to know and seek only a limited number of objects connected with the creature's biological self-development. If the nature of a being is open, i.e., tends by the absolute *transcendence of its intellect and will beyond all individual objects to reality itself and thus to God, then that being can objectify itself, make its whole self the object of its acts, that is, it is "personal" and stands in a dialogical relationship with the absolute, mysterious ground of all reality, with God. This kind of creaturely openness implies the God-given capacity for a divine self-communication in free grace (*Nature and grace, *Potentia obedientialis). If a spiritual "open" nature, through God's action upon it, so transcends itself even in its ultimate substantial principle and enters into God that it belongs to God without reserve, both in its being and in its operations—that is its transcendence no longer remains to a certain extent imperfect, and imperfectible by its own human powers—then such a nature as such (precisely because of its complete self-fulfilment and independent reality) is no longer called a "person" by the Church, since a finite person, in her language, implies a negative limitation, a distance from God and confinement within oneself. This case has occurred only once in the human "nature" of Jesus of Nazareth, which belongs to the *Person of God's Logos through the *hypostatic union and thus is not a person in its own right.

NATURE AND GRACE

Because of its *transcendence (*Potentia obedientialis) the open nature of man is a possible recipient of God's own free self-communication in *grace and the *beatific vision. Since this transcendence of man, making him capable of objective knowledge and personal freedom, would be intelligible even if the offer of this divine self-communication had not occurred, it is not, even in the concrete human nature that exists, the inevitable consequence of God's act in creating the intelligible being "man", but a free grace, in no way "due" to man, even if we abstract from the sin whereby man made himself positively unworthy of this divine gift. Human nature is called "pure" or mere nature *(natura pura)* when conceived of in a hypothetical order of things where God's self-gift would not be the whole purpose of creation. This conception, it is true, includes the doctrine that grace is absolutely gratuitous even antecedent to sin but does not suggest that nature as such ever existed nor that what we know from our existential experience of ourselves can be identified with "pure nature". In concrete creation, rather, human nature is always summoned to grace and required to accept God's offer of himself, in which alone it finds its real goal, without which it is *ipso facto* in a state of wretchedness; indeed it is created only because God in his ecstatic *love (*Charity)

333

is thereby enabled to communicate himself absolutely to that which is not God. Where man culpably rejects God's offer he is not preserving his nature but corrupting it. It then remains not a pure nature but a potential recipient of God's forgiving grace and a nature that has offended against itself, because human nature is precisely man's unqualified, dialogical availability to God.

NECESSITY

Necessity of nature and existence is primarily a predicate proper to God alone in virtue of his *aseity, as distinguished from all else, the existence of which is characterized by *contingency. This does not mean that logical and real necessary connexions do not arise from the very nature of real beings, once these contingents do in fact exist.

NECESSITY FOR SALVATION

This concept of Catholic theology is founded on recognition of the sovereignty of God, understood in the sense that God can (positively) command man to do a particular thing in order to attain his salvation. When considering this notion—which has not always been proof against a certain "contractualization" and an impression of arbitrariness—it is important to remember that the necessary means to salvation must always be seen within the framework of God's universal *salvific will, which is manifested in a personal relationship between God and man. *Faith (D 375, 399f., 1532, 3008, 3012) and *membership of the Church (D 870ff., 1351, 2865, 3802), realized or actualized in *baptism (D 1314f., 1513f., 1524, 1618, 3442), and the reception of other sacraments (D 1604), are necessary for salvation according to Catholic doctrine. Theology distinguishes between absolute and hypothetical necessity for salvation: the latter means that where a person through no fault of his own fails to become fully aware of the necessity (as in the matter of belonging to the Church), his desire, even if it be not explicit, enables him by the grace of God to fulfil the requirement for salvation (Vat. II: Church, 16; Church/world, 22; Miss., 7: *Votum, *Baptism of desire). As to the absolute necessity of faith for salvation, it must be pointed out that every genuine moral decision which bows to the absolute claim of morality may, at least implicitly, entail a knowledge and recognition of the God who freely communicates himself in grace and reveals himself as such (*Revelation); so that an obedient readiness to believe, an attitude of faith, may exist where the actual revelation, the specific external, historical message of the Gospel, has not been perceived (see D 2291, 2063; Rom 2:12–16). Where the necessity for salvation is independent of men's knowledge and dispositions, good or bad, it is called a necessity of means *(necessitas medii):* where the necessity exists only because of a command (so that failure, without fault, to fulfil the condition is excused and does not jeopardize salvation) it is called a necessity of precept *(necessitas praecepti).*

NEIGHBOURLY LOVE

This is a sanctifying Christian love, brought into being and sustained by God's grace, a true personal generosity which seeks out the other for his own sake and not as a means of securing private advantage or pleasure, and thus affirms his unique individuality without subjecting him to one's own "ideal": a love which refers one to the other, not the other to oneself (but see *Love).* The "selflessness" of this love, which is the real and total achievement of the spiritual personality, does not imply coolness and distance; it means the bestowal of one's whole being, so far as this is possible and the other is capable of being the recipient of such a love. Love of one's neighbour "for God's sake" precisely does not mean making the neighbour into a mere external occasion for training oneself in the love of God; the expression indicates the context and the basis which make real neighbourly love possible, because in the supernatural order God himself is man's inmost mystery. Hence it is the common theological view that neighbourly love is an act of the *virtue of divine love, and thus an active participation in the inner life of the Trinity, brought about by the grace of the Holy Ghost, the *Pneuma which is God's personal Love. It should also be borne in mind that God is not an "object" alongside other objects for man's subjective intention. God is always given, in the original act that precedes a reflective thematicization, as the ground of experience that lies beyond this world and bears up the *act and its object both subjectively and objectively and as the origin and destiny of an act that aims objectively at the world. When God is considered and presented as a Christian theme and is himself proposed as the destiny of man's transcendentality, this takes place in the presence of a man or woman who is given in freedom to himself or herself through a loving entry into the environment and through personal encounter and communication with the other in experience

within this world. As a result of this, man's original and explicit
experience of God is always given in an experience within this world.
The act of neighbourly love is the only categorical and original act in
which man reaches the whole reality that is categorically present. It
is also the primary act in which man has experience of God. The
explicit love of God is also borne up by that trusting and loving
openness to the whole of reality that takes place in neighbourly love.
Openness on the part of the individual in neighbourly love which is
orientated towards the whole of reality cannot remain restricted to
only one other or to one's neighbour in the literal sense of the word.
Because of its orientation towards the whole of reality, Christian
neighbourly love always has a (more or less explicitly) social and
political dimension. (The Constitution on the Church in the Modern
World even referred in this context to a *caritas politica,* 75). This
political dimension also points to the fact that Christian love is not
expressed in sentimentality or artificial attempts to create harmony,
but, if necessary, in struggles for others and continuing inevitable
conflict.—On the unity of the love of God and love of neighbour, see
Mt 22:37ff.; Rom 13:9f.; 1 Jn; Mt 5:43ff.; 7:12: 10:40ff.; 25:40: the NT
Canticle, 1 Cor 13; neighbourly love as fullness of the Law, Rom
13:10; Mt 22:40.

NEOPLATONISM

The final period of ancient philosophy (predominantly but not exclusively Platonic in character), being the philosophical expression of the
spirit of the *patristic age, is of the utmost importance for understanding the first systematic elaboration, in philosophical terms, of Christianity's reflection on itself during that age. Origen and St Augustine
were Neoplatonists, each in his own way, which means that the whole
theology of the "Fathers" (various as it is) is Neoplatonist. And since
the historical process, even in metaphysics, does not mean that an able
mind vanishes without a trace to make room for another which is
quite foreign to it, but that the mind carries the intellectual past,
transformed, with it into the future; and since Christianity, being the
whole (Catholic), finds its own everywhere in history, Christianity
will always preserve the Neoplatonist inheritance—modified, of
course, and transposed into an entirely different frame of reference—
as a means to genuinely Christian understanding of itself: God the
absolute, transcendently permanent being, God the Logos; finite being
a "participation" in the divine being; the idea of an hierarchical order

of the universe; the movement of finite being back to its source; the spiritual soul ordered to God; ethics and mysticism as a "spiritualization", an ascent to God. But Neoplatonism was also a threat to Christianity that was only warded off with difficulty and an obstacle in the way of theological reflection on the properly Christian inheritance, and thus partially explains why this still remains an unfinished task, hindering the Church in her efforts to make contact with the world of the present. For creation; history unique and irreversible, with an evolution that God can accept as his own by becoming Man; the positive character of non-identity; the person; freedom; love that is more than the dynamism of the Logos; finite being which is good and has been accepted once for all; the perpetual validity of the individual person—all these authentically Christian themes are alien to Neoplatonism and therefore, though perhaps not as material objects, as fundamental structures (forms of thought) of the Christian view of life they have been relatively neglected by Catholic theologians as compared with those themes which Neoplatonism helped to elaborate.

NEO-SCHOLASTICISM

See *Theology.*

NESTORIANISM

The heresy of Nestorius, Patriarch of Constantinople (d. about 451). He belonged to the theological school of *Antioch and denied that the eternal Logos himself was the real and only personal subject of Christ's humanity (*Communicatio idiomatum). He asserted that "Christ" was the subject of whom both human and divine attributes could be predicated. Though Nestorius sought to preserve a close union between Christ's divinity and humanity and intended to be orthodox, on his premises he was only able to admit a "moral" union of the Logos with the humanity, not a real *hypostatic union. This is also shown by his "doctrine of probation": the man Jesus was able to sin and only entered into real possession of divine attributes as a reward for his having been "put to the proof". Nestorianism was condemned by the Third Ecumenical Council at *Ephesus (431) under the leadership of St Cyril of Alexandria (d. 444) (D 250f., 268). The opponents of Nestorius had made it difficult for him to perceive his error in that they themselves had no clear doctrine of the two unconfused *natures in Christ to offer such as St Leo and the Council of Chalcedon (451) propounded (D 293f., 301ff.), and Nestorius felt, not altogether rightly, that this justified his position.

NEW TESTAMENT

Here the term is considered as referring to a reality in the history of salvation. There is a permanent "fundamental law" inherent in all finite, created, personal beings: the power, dignity and duty of receiving God's gift of himself and sharing in the divine nature. But that permanent fundamental law, engraven in reality, nay identical with it, nevertheless has a history in and with this reality: (a) an objective history, because this divine self-communication to creatures must always occur in some particular situation (the constant renewal in man's spiritual history) in the personal history of the individual human being and as something he freely accepts, and in the Incarnation of God's Logos reaches a climax which turns this dialogical history of God's offer of himself, and man's acceptance of that offer, irreversibly (considering this history as a whole) into a history of the ultimate triumph of that self-communication; (b) a subjective history, because the knowledge of the history aforesaid, in the general, reflex, articulate community of human knowledge, has a history too. Therefore in *saving history there is only one absolute caesura: *Jesus Christ in his self-revelation as God's Word incarnate, in his *death and *resurrection (which three elements condition one another and form an indissoluble unity). In him the history of self-communication has irrevocably passed into that which basically was always operative and always intended: God has given himself to the world and the world (as a whole) has definitively accepted him in that which the grace of Christ has done for it, so that in the incarnate Word, in the self-abnegation of his obedience and in its total acceptance in the resurrection, both God and the world have said their last word. The expectation of the absolute future (bestowed as grace), as which God communicates himself to history as its entelechy and goal, does not destroy the significance and seriousness of secular history. This hope in the kingdom of God declares that history as a whole, and not only explicitly religious history, actually had to do with salvation *per se.* Every positively moral form of practice is a mediation of acceptance of the absolute future. Encompassed as it is by the course of the NT, *this* history as a whole is assured that it will not run into the emptiness of death. And the *Church, the community of the faithful, explicitly confesses, in the truth whose nature corresponds to this eschatological finality, what has thus happened and begun in Jesus Christ. This explains the Church's nature as the basic sacrament of this predefined salvation of the world, and the absolute character of NT faith—the new and eternal *Covenant which is never to be superseded in this world by a new dispensation—of which all other truth, including that of other religions, is only explicitation, incapable of superseding that faith or adding anything positive to it; it explains why the final application of salvation to the individual by the sacraments of the NT is *opus operatum*. The aeon of the NT will not be succeeded by another salvific aeon in this world because it is the proclamation of the ultimate, of the arrival of God himself; but its nature must still be revealed because only in the *beatific vision and the *resurrection of the flesh will it manifest itself of itself, no longer in terms of the preceding dispensation and the untransfigured world.

NICAEA

A city in Asia Minor where the First Ecumenical Council was held (325) in the pontificate of Sylvester I. This Council, summoned by the Emperor Constantine, was attended by about 300 bishops, nearly all Eastern, and chiefly concerned itself with *Arianism. It drew up the Nicene Creed, which solemnly declares that the Son is God, of one substance with the Father (*Homoousios; D 125f.).

The Second Council of Nicaea, September 24th to October 23rd, 787, under Pope Hadrian I (Seventh Ecumenical Council), vindicated the legitimacy of the veneration of *images during the *iconoclastic controversy in the Eastern Church (D 600 –609).

NOMINALISM

A school of thought, in epistemology, metaphysics and theology, in later Scholasticism towards the end of the Middle Ages (*Ockhamism), which held that universal concepts are empty of essential content, being mere words *(nomina)* applied to many things which in themselves are absolutely individual. This sceptical attitude to metaphysics entails a positivist theology solely concerned to establish the facts, a kind of *Traditionalism, a positivist morality with little regard for the *natural moral law, a type of thought that distorts the *principle of economy, in a sense hostile to metaphysics. On the other hand Nominalism marks a necessary crisis whereby Christian understanding of the world outgrew the Middle Ages: preoccupation with the historical particulars, with the thinking subject rather than with things, the inductive method of modern science, *existential ethics, all emerge for the first time in Nominalism and bring us out of the Middle Ages to a closer, more authentic understanding of Christian life.

NON-CHRISTIAN RELIGIONS

Since man is able to know God by the use of his reason and thanks to the universal *salvific will of God is always subject to the dynamism of supernatural *grace, so that he always stands within the history of *revelation (*Primitive revelation), *religion always exists among men and the elements aforesaid must necessarily express themselves in religious objectification of a social character, though they may not be readily distinguishable from one another. Vatican II explicitly acknowledges the possibility of authentic experience of God and of the existence of that which is "true" and "sacred" in the different religions (Non-C. rel., 2). Full moral and doctrinal purity must not be demanded of a religion outside and antecedent to Christianity before it be accorded a certain legitimacy as a way to salvation (even) positively willed by God's providence, because the Church's infallible *magisterium and *holiness only come into the picture with the eschatological situation created by the revelation which terminates in Christ, and even the Old Testament which God willed to be a realization of saving history (*Covenant) possessed no infallible institutional authority which could constantly and clearly distinguish for everyone between the divine and the human, between true religion, personal or organized, and its corruptions. Furthermore, if man, a bodily and social being, is to have a concrete religion, then this religion must be embodied in concrete, instutional form. So for all these reasons we cannot deny that non-Christian, institutional religions were in some sense a positive aid to salvation. Otherwise it would be impossible to assert that God seriously desires the salvation of all men who are not Christians. This is only to say that in fact these pre-Christian religions were a more or less inextricable amalgam of truths about God perceived by natural reason, of *revelation (through *grace and *primitive revelation), sound embodiments of religious knowledge and aspirations, and theoretical and practical misunderstanding, and corruption. The mixture of these elements varies, of course, from one religion to the other and has a history of its own. We should not be taken to mean by this argument that every pre-Christian religion was legitimate: whenever a form of religion that impressed the conscience of the men in a particular situation as being certainly "purer", that is, objectively more correct and more instinct with grace, confronted the established religion of these men in its concrete historical situation, either from without or by a movement of reform from within, then the earlier religion ceased to be legitimate for these men. In addition, the conscience of each person was always able to some extent to distinguish between the good and the evil in the religion in which he was involved as a member of society and thus could existentially exercise an openness to the fulfilment and supersession of the religion with which he happened to be in contact. All these religions have been completely superseded by Christianity (*New Testament), the tidings of the Incarnation of the Logos himself and of redemption, by the objectively adequate embodiment in Church and magisterium of the divine self-communication which God's grace reveals and offers to every human being. Christianity, because of its mission to all ages, peoples, and civilizations, by a slow historical process confronts the other religions and their adherents, even within their concrete historical situations, presents its concrete, existential claim, fulfils these other religions by uniting in its own substance everything assimilable in these civilizations and religions (the *"anonymous" Christianity present in them). In this sense Vatican II requires members of the Church to recognize, affirm and promote the spiritual and moral good and socio-cultural values of the non-Christian religions (Non-C. rel., 2). It is difficult to determine at what exact moment Christianity deprives a particular culture or religion of any legitimacy it may have had in isolation. In view of the sinfulness endemic in men (and the Church) it is only to be expected that the claim of Christianity should meet contradiction until the end of time, not only the stolid opposition of the other living religions, not only organized global atheism, but also the attempt of those religions to assimilate certain Christian truths and practices without finding their own truths in the Christian Church, just as Christianity itself can and will draw closer to the position of these religions by *accommodation and *mission in its concrete form. Though neither side contemplates union with the other, this rapprochement may have incalculable effects on the internal history of each.

NOTES OF THE CHURCH

See *Apostolicity of the Church, Catholicity of the Church, Holiness of the Church, Unity of the Church.*

NOTES, THEOLOGICAL

These are judgments by theologians, or occasionally by the magisterium of the Church, on (true or false) doctrinal propositions, stating with what degree of certainty the propositions can be seen to agree or conflict with revealed truth (called "censures" when negative). Such notes are expressed in concise formulae, which are not systematized in any authoritative way and are not always and everywhere understood in the same sense. Positive notes are attached to true propositions, negative notes (censures) to false ones. We can only mention the most important notes here. A proposition is "of divine faith" *(de fide divina)* if it is clearly and expressly contained in the sources of revelation, which demand unqualified assent (the contrary is error in divine faith). If this proposition is also taught as such by the Church's magisterium it is a truth "of divine and Catholic faith" *(de fide divina et catholica)* (the contrary is a formal heresy). If in addition this truth is defined by the extraordinary magisterium (Pope, council), it is "of defined faith" *(de fide definita)*. A proposition is "of ecclesiastical faith" *(de fide ecclesiastica)* if it is not held to be directly revealed by God but is guaranteed by the infallible magisterium (*Catholic truths) (the contrary is error in ecclesiastical faith). A doctrine which "borders on faith" *(fidei proximum)* is one which the common teaching considers to be revealed but which is not yet clearly and definitively taught as a truth of revelation by the Church (the contrary is "suspect of heresy"). A proposition is "theologically certain" *(theologice certum)* when the Church has not yet explicitly or definitely declared it to be true or necessarily connected with revelation but its denial, in the more or less unanimous opinion of theologians, would clearly involve the denial of a truth of faith or indirectly threaten it (theological conclusions of various kinds) (the contrary: false or temerarious, theological error). The other, lesser notes are self-explanatory: the common teaching of theologians, a probable opinion, a "pious" opinion, a tolerated opinion, a proposition offensive to pious ears, captious, scandalous. The ultimate purpose of theological notes is both to safeguard the faith and to prevent any confusion between real divine revelation and theological opinion.

342

NOTHINGNESS

The term is a way of objectifying "nothing", which is possible because man in his transcendence towards infinite *being conceives of finite objective being as finite, and in positively overshooting finite being grasps the idea of finitude. Now when he thinks of finitude as such, man thinks (in a kind of bipolar unity) of the pure but real potentiality of a real entity and, taking this entity over again as *finite,* thinks of its limitation as mere nothingness—nothingness which must neither be thought of as a "somewhat" nor yet as the object of an independent concept. Nothingness may not be introduced into God's absolute being even as potentiality and as it were a stimulus to negativity. It may be understood as the hall-mark of the creaturely, yet it is grounded in the positive character with which God endows creatures, since finite being does exist. If nothingness were seriously hypostatized it would be the perversion of spirit and love, for these only come to grips with "nothingness" insofar as they encounter the incomprehensible plenitude of God. (*mystery)—on creation of the world from nothing, see *Creation.*

NOTIONS

See *Properties, trinitarian.*

NOUVELLE THÉOLOGIE (NEW THEOLOGY)

For a brief period the collective name for very various efforts among French theologians, especially after the Second World War, to reconsider traditional theology in the light of biblical and patristic theology, modern philosophy, and comparative religion, so as to make the Church's doctrine more intelligible and more credible to the men of our time. Certain aberrations incidental to these necessary efforts fell under censure in Pius XII's encyclical *Humani Generis,* 1950 (D 3875–3899).

NOVATIANISM

A rigoristic heresy concerning penance, which arose in the mid-third century and had adherents as late as the sixth, so called after its

343

originator, the Roman presbyter Novatian. It taught that when apostates from the faith, or any who had lost their baptismal grace by grievous sin, repented and sought reconciliation with the Church they were never to be absolved of their sin and readmitted to communion but must be left to divine grace alone. St Cyprian and Rome opposed Novatianism, which was already considered a heresy at *Nicaea but was treated leniently (D 127).

NOW

In theology the term does not designate a particular instant in a continuous series of equivalent moments, as in the philosophy of *time (Plato, Aristotle), but rather a basic religious experience. The authentic present is realized as the "now" not by emerging into the world and time but by retiring into oneself, transcending space and time (St Augustine; similarly the "present moment" of Meister Eckhart and the "eternal moment" of Karl Jaspers). In Scripture "now" (Gr. νῦν) is essentially a dimension of saving history, of varying valency as the presence of Christ (the physical presence of Jesus as the beginning of the new *aeon; apostolic times; the presence of Christ in the *kerygma), which as a simultaneous whole presses restlessly on, from Now to Now, towards the *parousia. Corresponding to this Now, there is the Now which is the moment of absolute decision, the response that is always required of man Now (Rom 13:11; S. Kierkegaard). In the Christian stage of Kierkegaard's "stages" the moment is the Eternal, at once the decisive present and the future, what is past as repetition.—See also *Kyrios, Judgment.*

O

OBEDIENCE

Generally speaking, a recognition of legitimate *authority which must be expressed in one's opinion and behaviour. Three distinct types of obedience play a special part in theology and in Catholic life. (a) Romans 5:19 shows Adam's sin as the disobedience by which many were made sinners, and contrasts with it the obedience by the things which he suffered and became, to all that obey him, the cause of eternal salvation (Heb 5:8f.). Thus obedience in Scripture chiefly means submission to the "it must be" of saving history (Mt 16:21 and *passim),* of which by way of entry into the *basileia* the commandments of God and the Church are part. (b) Obedience is certainly the most difficult of the *evangelical counsels to establish; since these counsels are also part of the Church's witness to her own nature, there arises the difficult question of how we know that subjecting ourselves to a human authority is the most thoroughgoing obedience to God. The answer will appear if we reflect that here obedience is an essential part of permanent committment to a particular form of life in the Church. A formal obedience for obedience's sake is of no moral value; obedience does not give a superior a blank cheque, so that superior for his part can demand obedience from another human being, demanding it merely by virtue of a goal which is certainly intended by God. Rather it is the acceptance of a common religious life, under constitutions which the Church has approved as a true and possible expression of a life devoted to God, agreeable to the doctrine and example of Jesus Christ, as acceptance of an incalculable destiny. It is wise to obey even an absurd command—provided what is required is not immoral—only because commitment to the example of Jesus Christ can be lived in the Church. It is, of course, very difficult to distinguish a command which is objectively mistaken from one that is immoral.

345

In view of this difficulty it is downright un-Christian to fall back on the amoral maxim that "orders are orders" or on "blind obedience"; rather the subject has a duty openly to resist authority if it requires what is plainly absurd. The evangelical counsel of obedience is observed both in destroying secret or open egotism in surrender to that which is always greater than oneself and in courageous solicitude that the greater shall not remain a mere theory or ideal. (c) What we have said applies equally to the canonical obedience of a person appointed to ecclesiastical office.

OBLATION, THEORY OF

This theory holds that the true nature of the central act of the *Mass (*Transubstantiation) is not a symbolic immolation, a representation of Christ's death by the separation of the *species, but an offering of the gifts to God which transforms and elevates them, since the earthly gifts (bread and wine) are changed into the Body and Blood of Christ, which God has accepted once for all through his death and resurrection.

OCCAMISM

A "nominalistic" trend in scholastic philosophy and theology during the later Middle Ages, chiefly represented by the Franciscan William of Ockham (d. 1350). Its conception of God is voluntarist (*Scotism), so that the decrees of God's free will do not so much produce an objectively structured world that can be grasped by recourse to general notions and is grounded in the divine nature, as arbitrarily determining the nature of things. Occamism greatly influenced modern logic, the rise of modern science (Galileo), and Luther, an aspect of whose doctrine of justification is anticipated by Ockham: *justification without interior divinization seen as merely acceptance by God.

OCCASIONALISM

This philosophical view (represented by Geulinex [d. 1669] and Malebranche [d. 1715] denies the causal interaction of created things; these and their circumstances only provide the "occasion" for God, the sole cause, to produce the appropriate effects in other things (*Pre-established harmony), a theory which by distorting God's universal causality and his *divine concourse leads to the unreality of finite being.

OFFICE

In general it is the organ of a society whose functions consist of rights and duties and whose acts are objectively binding upon the society. Offices are necessary in the Church by her very nature, since she is an historical *society. Even in the Old Testament there are "ancients", "judges", "kings", and the *priesthood. The New Testament indicates a development from spontaneous structures to institutional ministries in the primitive Church, first discernible in the ministry of the twelve Apostles (D 700, 944, 1610, 1767–1770) (*Bishop, Deacon) whose nature and titles find analogies and parallels in her Jewish origins. A good many of these offices later lost their importance or disappeared. In Scripture office is generally called "ministry" or sometimes "power" in and for the community; the Spirit (or God or Christ) confers office by the Church's act of installation, which guarantees *apostolic succession by the *laying on of hands. God's will that the Church be a permanent institution, and the presence of the Spirit in her, imply the permanence of office in the Church, though the distinction between what is unique in the first institution of an office and what follows from it by legitimate development (the office remains but is differentiated as required) must be borne in mind. It is the defined teaching of the Church that Christians do not all have the same powers with respect to the word of God and the sacraments (D 700, 944, 1610, 1767–1770; Church, 10), but that there is a divinely instituted hierarchy, graded into bishops, priests, and inferior ministers.—See *Sacrament, Order, Pope, Charism, Ministries, recognition of.*

Since the end of the 18th century in particular, theologians have spoken of three *Offices of Christ* (as teacher or prophet, priest, and king or shepherd) and hence of three (thus Pius XII) or two Offices of the Church (the teaching and pastoral office as her power of jurisdiction, and the priestly office as her power of order), corresponding to the not altogether satisfactory duality of word and work.

OLD TESTAMENT, OLD COVENANT

In the context of the history of salvation, that phase of the narrower

history of *Revelation and human salvation which begins theologically with God's *Covenant with Abraham, on subsequent reflection,
especially by the prophets, finds its true centre in the exodus from
Egypt and the covenant of the chosen people of Israel, under Moses,
with God at Sinai, and is finally fulfilled by the death and *Resurrection of Jesus and the New and eternal Covenant of God with all
mankind thereby established. This epoch in the history of salvation
is circumscribed: temporally, by so-called "early" or "primordial"
history; spatially, by the fact that it concerned only the people of
Israel and so did not coincide with the history of salvation as such,
since *grace was also given outside the Old Testament. The special
history of salvation (*Saving history) in the OT consisted in God's
offering himself to be perceived through his historical activity and
bringing about the *monotheism of Israel by his intervention: Yahweh, the God of the Covenant, was ever more clearly recognized as
the only true and living God and worshipped as such. Thus the God
of the whole world entered into a special covenant with one small
people because this course of a particular alliance was the historical
means to a universal end, the union of God with all mankind in God
made Man. This phase of salvation, considered in itself, is not yet
concluded, still hovers between judgment and grace; the event has not
yet shown that the merciful word of God, not the negations of man,
has the last word in the dialogue between God and the world. Hence
the social tangibility of this non-eschatological saving history can still
be destroyed by the unbelief of the human partner (*law). Yet the Old
Testament is also the presence of that which is to come (Heb 10:1):
he who entrusts himself in obedient faith to God's inscrutable Providence enters into the hidden unity of the divine plan for salvation by
hoping for the future redemption God has promised and finds salvation through Christ even in the Old Testament. Jesus fulfils the Law
so that, according to St Paul, its further observance is a denial of
Christ and of the unique significance of his cross for salvation. But this
does not abolish the Old Testament as part of the real past: Abraham
is the father of all believers, the saints of the Old Testament are still
just men for us and witnesses to the faith, the books of the Old
Testament belong to our Bible: "salvation is of the Jews" (Jn 4:22).—
See also *Judaism, Christianity.*

ONTOLOGISM

The doctrine, condemned by the Church, that human knowledge is made possible only by way of a direct, though non-explicit, vision of the divine essence in itself. Thus Malebranche (d. 1715), Gioberti (d. 1852), Rosmini (d. 1855). (See D 895, 2841ff., 3201ff.)

ONTOLOGY

The philosophical inquiry into that understanding of *being and every entity which lies at the basis of any free and thoughtful concern with concrete things, interpreting them in the light of being as a whole and itself interpreted in its light. Ontology is at work in all *theology, to which it is an indispensable aid and also a threat. For if reflex philosophical exposition of this original understanding of being is imperfect, yet it is necessary to the understanding of any theological proposition, indeed is present in every theological proposition: it can explain as well as obscure. The rejection of an independent analytic ontology, particularly in its theological applications, would not make theology "purer" or "more independent" but simply expose it to an uncritical, merely implicit ontology. Theology is not at the mercy of ontology but can always deal critically with the form of ontology that men happen to have worked out; for theology is the self-discovery of man in the light of his experience of God's gracious, external revelation, and therefore provides a fuller experience of total reality than the purely transcendental reflection on which ontology is based. And since ontology for its part can grasp man as a "hearer of the word", as a being open to the sway of the absolute mystery to which his transcendence refers him, as a being who necessarily understands himself in his historicity and not merely in his abstract transcendence, ontology too is open to revelation and theology and, where it does not mistake its own true nature, makes no claim at all to be the sole and absolute explanation of human life.

OPTIMISM

When this term does not mean simply a morally indifferent though pleasant mood of confidence and cheerfulness, it can have two senses: (1) the persuasion that all evil in the world (pain, death, guilt) is only apparent and will eventually be eliminated by social and technological progress. This sort of optimism is utopian, craven, and un-Christian, the real "opium of the people", because it prevents them alleviating the evils of the present by forcing them to try to obliterate those evils at some time in the future, and because the fanatical violence which is used in the attempt to usher in Utopia and compel the people to be happy produces new and worse evils. Christianity does not predict what concrete social forms evil will take (for instance it may be that war in the old sense can indeed be abolished); but it is convinced that evil as the painful experience of interior and external finitude, as death and guilt, can never be altogether overcome in this historical world, although it remains the duty of the Christian to combat evil, one among the tasks for which he bears an eternal responsibility; it is convinced that perseverance in this *pessimism is not only part of human dignity but in fact is more conducive to progress in this world than utopian optimism about the future. Indeed the Christian may not make the unqualified prediction of an absolute, eschatological harmony the basis of the *hope he is bound to cherish for all men (*Apocatastasis, *Hell). (2) Optimism may mean that if his own voluntary fault does not deprive a person of that which perfects his life and gives it its whole meaning, the grace of God (*Salvific will of God) which elevates and resolves human history will not fail to bring that person's life to its happy consummation and suprahistorical finality. This beneficent optimism perfects man precisely by accepting and enduring, in faith and hope, the "pessimistic" (that is, unrepressed) experience of finitude and death; it belongs to the essence of Christianity and in effect abrogates both optimism and pessimism by making good and evil alike avail unto salvation.

OPUS OPERATUM

A *sacrament is called this (D 1608) because its validity and efficacy depend on God, not on the subjective disposition of man (even those produced by divine grace) as such *(opus operantis)*. This does not mean that the grace of the sacrament will in fact have its wholesome effect in the recipient if he frustrates it by unbelief or obstinacy in sin (D 781, 1451, 1606). But this subjective *disposition which is necessary to fruitful reception of the sacrament, the genuine readiness to accept God's forgiveness and sanctification, does not cause the efficacy of the sacrament, it is required as a condition before the grace of God proffered in the sacrament can become operative. The same is true of the attitude of the person administering the sacrament: be he saint or sinner, so long as he intends to administer the sacrament (D 1611) and uses the appropriate ceremonies, it signifies, even when administered by a sinner, the objectively valid pledge of God's grace, the historical tangibility of his salvific will in Jesus Christ for the life of the individual and of the Church (D 1612). Besides which, because of the eschatological conclusiveness of the *NT, its sacramental rites properly celebrated, unlike the rites of the OT or indeed of any other religion, can never fail to symbolize God's unconditional offer of salvation in Christ (*Heretical baptism; *Intention). So long as saving history lasts they remain the signs about which God is absolutely in earnest, and therefore they effect what they signify. The sacrament conceived thus is not an isolated, magically effective sign, but the actualization and self-realization of the Church as the fundamental sacrament (proclamation of the effective word and prayer entrusted to her) which is unfailingly promised a response. It is against this background that the "reviviscence of the sacraments" ought to be explained: sacraments that cannot be repeated (D 1609) and whose operation during the performance of the rite was in fact frustrated by the resistance of the recipient, take effect afterwards as soon as the recipient ceases his culpable resistance.

ORANGE

A town in southern France which gave its name to a provincial synod (Second Council of Orange) probably held in 528 at Valence. Certain decrees condemning *Semipelagianism, published in 529 as an appendix to the acts of the synod, were confirmed by Pope Boniface II in 531 (D 398ff.) and are of theological importance. These canons were unknown to theologians in the Middle Ages but since the 16th century it has been recognized that they express the Church's definitive doctrine of grace (D 366, 370–397; see 1510).

ORDER, HOLY ORDERS

The *ordo* was in Roman law a body governing class as against the people. Used for the *clergy since the second century; *ordinatio* being used for the sacrament of orders since the twelfth century. In the course of the differentiation of church ministries in the apostolic and post-apostolic Church, an institutionalized hierarchy came into being in which specific functions were concentrated. The following is an account of the basic features of the self-understanding of the Catholic hierarchy as the ordained body within the Church. Being an ordered society, the Church has an hierarchical constitution (D 1776; Vat. II:

Church, 28); it has a governing authority appropriate to its various functions (testimony to the truth, concrete application of the Gospel to life, adoration of God in sacrificial worship, imparting the efficacious word of grace to the individual at crucial moments in his life and that of the Church [*sacraments]), and therefore officials entrusted with these functions. The first repository of this authority, appointed by Jesus himself, was the Apostolic College with Peter at its head (Mt 10:1ff.; 16:16 –19; Lk 22:32; Jn 21:2, 15ff.; Power of the *keys), representing the whole college yet able to act on his own account. This authority had to be transmitted to others: Peter's successors, the Popes (D 3056ff.), and the successors of the Apostles, the episcopal college (Vat. II: Church, 21f.). But it is not necessary for the fullness of ecclesiastical authority (whether in its sacramental or its governmental aspect) to be transmitted in every case. As in any society, a particular person may receive only a limited share of authority, according to the circumstances and the need for its exercise. Since apostolic times ecclesiastical authority has been transmitted in three degrees throughout the Church (D 1776): that of *deacon, priest (*Priesthood), and *bishop (Vat. II: Church, 21f.). This gradation is most clearly seen in the different relationships to the Eucharistic celebration in each case (ministers, a principal celebrant, one entitled to transmit power to celebrate the Eucharist), where the degree most closely associated with the Church's central mystery normally possesses governing authority in the Church the content of this transmission is interpreted by Vatican II as gradational sharing in the mission and in the three offices of Jesus Christ. (*Bishop, *Pope). Since apostolic times the three degrees of this power have been transmitted by the *laying on of hands (1 Tim 4:14; 2 Tim 1:6) (as a gesture by which office is transmitted) with the appropriate form of words conferring the office (D 3857–3861). This act both confers office and pledges to the new office-bearer the divine grace necessary in order that he may exercise his office for the good of the Church and for his own salvation. Since this ritual transmission of office by its very nature is one of the Church's fundamental modes of self-realization, which could cease to be effectual only if the Church ceased to be what it essentially is, and since the Church in its being and activity is the permanent symbol of God's eschatologically triumphant grace pledged to the world without stint, this bestowal of office must be *opus operatum and a *sacrament: it confers power absolutely and irrevocably (D 1774), together with God's solemn pledge of grace for its exercise that can be frustrated only by culpable resistance to it on the part of the recipient. The sacrament of holy orders is conferred by the bishop, who possesses the fullness of sacramental authority in the Church (D 1777).

ORIGENISM

A tendency, rather than a doctrinal system, in Eastern (especially monastic) theology which exaggerated certain aspects of the doctrine of Origen (d. 254)—along with St Augustine, the greatest theologian of antiquity—in an heretical sense, thus causing a bitter conflict that lasted till the middle of the sixth century. The characteristic themes of Origenism were: the necessity and eternity of the world and of souls (*Pre-existentianism); the angelic nature assumed by the Logos; matter as a consequence of sin; *apocatastasis; perfection consisting in *gnosis (see D 403– 411, 433, 518f.).

ORIGINAL JUSTICE

This term in theology sums up the following truths of faith:
(1) The first man was created in *sanctifying grace, in that interior *supernatural endowment which makes man just before God and a sharer in the divine nature, and thus intrinsically orders him to the *beatific vision of God and the love that is appropriate to that beatitude (D 389, 1511–1514; see Rom 5; 1 Cor 15 and the scriptural concepts of "reconciliation", "redemption" and "regeneration"). The significance of this truth for us is that the whole history of mankind has had a single meaning and goal from the beginning. Man as man is created for eternal life in the immediate possession of God. In concrete fact a "state of pure nature" has never existed, and, therefore, the whole of human history from the first has been the history of the conflict between the acceptance and the rejection of this supernatural plan of God for man—so much so that this problem can never under any circumstances be evaded; God still demands of man what man lost in Adam. Any conception of man which would confine him within his mere humanity, any purely philosophical conception of man, sins against God's concrete, primordial creation of man. Man only rightly understands his nature when he perceives that it is open to a divine ordering which transcends it, and that in such a way that this ordering is not something adventitious, a mere "accidental" modification of a nature already constituted, but is the one thing necessary for man, the bedrock of his salvation. If, therefore, ordina-

tion to the immediate possession of God is part of man's original constitution and remains after Adam's fall, then God must have ordained it with a view to the God-Man—it must be the grace of *Jesus Christ. For otherwise he who is the mediator and source of our grace would only be the restorer, and so the servant, of an order that was conceived independently of him—he would give us his grace, not to set up his own order but to re-establish the more original and comprehensive order of Adam. The order of Adam must already have been the order of Christ, which the Crucified restored as his own; for God does not permit the human beginning of the divine-human order to fall away from his mercy though it was destroyed by human sin, but transmutes the original grace of the God-Man, which in man from the beginning ordered human history to the fullness of time, into the grace of the Redeemer who was delivered to a sinner's death on the cross. With St Paul we must say that God only permitted sin—the cause of the imperfection of our present state in comparison with Adam's beginning—so that the power and glory of divine grace might be the more abundantly manifested.

(2) The first man was free of "rebellious" *concupiscence, a freedom that was not due to him and was therefore a preternatural gift (D 1515f., 1926, 1955, 2616. See "sin" in St Paul, especially Rom 5–8).

(3) The first man, in virtue of a similar gift, was exempt from the necessity of *death (D 222, 370f., 1978, 2617, 3514; see Gen 2–3; Rom 5:12–21). As to (2) and (3), see what is said in the articles *Integrity, Concupiscence,* and *Death.*

This Catholic doctrine of original justice says nothing about the biological form of the first man, the cultural level of primitive humanity, nor the geological age in which Adam lived. Anything of the sort would lie outside the immediate content of the doctrine, which states that Adam was a *person. Furthermore, since the beginning of mankind is primordial history, it lies outside the scope of natural science; it has a certain historical transcendence and cannot be examined as if it were one element among others in our history. Of their very nature, the reality of primordial history and eschatology is farthest removed from our idea of them.

ORIGINAL SIN

The state in which all human beings are born, insofar as this (a) is caused by the *Fall of "Adam" (see *Monogenism);* (b) places every individual human being in a situation of inward alienation from God;

(c) yet must not be confused with a real, that is, personal, voluntary, sin. Original sin therefore refers to that negative quality of human existential experience which is derived from human sexual union as such, and which must always be seen in conjunction with that positive quality which is afforded out of God's *salvific will for all men, and is always available in advance by virtue of the powerful *grace of Jesus Christ.

TEACHING OF SCRIPTURE. Although tribulation, suffering, and death are accounted for by the sin of our first parents (*Fall of man) in the aetiological OT narrative of the loss of their intimate relations with God (Gen 2:8–3:24), the OT nevertheless knows nothing of original sin, in the strict sense, as a consequence of the Fall. Similarly the Gospels contain no more than allusions to the Fall; nowhere do they clearly teach that all men are in a state caused by the Fall of man. The decisive scriptural affirmation is found in St Paul, 1 Corinthians 15:21f. and especially Romans 5:12–21. In the latter passage Paul speaks of original sin (see the Tridentine definition, D 1510 –1516), in that he establishes a parallelism between Adam and Christ (and the effect of Adam's deèd and Christ's deed on all men) (v. 18), and derives from them respectively a situation of condemnation and a situation of salvation, which the individual man indeed ratifies by his own sin or faith, but which is antecedent to his attitude and which truly and internally characterizes him, either as a sinner, bereft of the Spirit because of Adam (v. 19), or as one sought by God's active salvific will because of Christ. Admittedly this account requires Catholic theology to see (more clearly than it usually does) "objective redemption", antecedent to faith and the sacraments, in Pauline terms as an *existential internally characterizing man.

THEOLOGICAL INTERPRETATION. The fundamental Christian belief about redemption and *grace is based on the assumption that this divine, forgiving mercy is granted to all people (a) by Jesus Christ alone, and not simply because they are human beings or members of humanity (seen as something apart from Jesus Christ), and (b) that it is intended for the forgiveness of sins. This is the case "for all" by virtue of Jesus' own interpretation of his life and death. Hence God's sanctifying *pneuma is not granted to people simply because they are human beings and members of mankind. We know from revelation that God was willing to give his grace (subordinately to and in dependence on Jesus Christ) to mankind in their totality as mankind and in their original "*covenant" with God, *inasmuch as* they were the successors of the first men to receive God's grace. Since God owes his grace to no one, he was able to make this a stipulation for any meaningful condition, including the test of the first human beings. If the initial condition is not fulfilled, men are not offered the divine pneuma as the "children of Adam", but solely on account of Jesus Christ in and for whom, as the Head of mankind, God's will persists, despite sin. People do not receive the divine pneuma because they have a direct historical link with the beginnings of mankind. They "inherit" original sin. This inappropriate absence of pneuma is specific to all people as a kind of negative *existential state. Insofar as pneuma intends the salvation of the *whole* man or woman, its absence implies the lack of that dynamic force which can overcome death (*death is the consequence and manifestation of original sin). According to Catholic doctrine, even in a state of original sin man remains what he is by "nature" (D 1955). Nevertheless, he can experience himself as "maimed", and "impotent" with regard to his natural abilities (D 1511) if he experiences and compares himself to "demands" proffered him, through grace and its (unreflexive) experience, by the supernatural existential of subordination to God's own life (*desire).

Thus it can be seen that the "condition of deficiency" which characterizes original sin (which can never exist in its own right) is not to be seen as a personal sin committed by each individual (D 456). Original sin is only *sin by analogy. Prior to man's decision (to believe and love *or* to accept personal guilt), his situation as regards salvation is dialectically determined. He has inherited original sin from Adam while at the same time finding redemption in Jesus Christ. Through his personal freedom to decide, this dialectical freedom can move one way or the other; either he freely affirms the state of original sin through his own personal sins *or* he ratifies his redemption through his *faith and *love. However, neither of these decisions simply removes the underlying existential state against which a decision has been made. In the same way that the sinner is always offered grace, original sin does not become an irrelevant issue of the past even for the baptized (*baptism, *justification). In his pursuit of justice and love, a Christian must bear concrete, historical witness to the power of grace to overcome death and suffering.

ORTHODOX CHURCH

See *Eastern Churches.*

OTHER WORLD

A term for God and his reality, his "world", and also for the life and state of man after death. This expression does not derive from the activity of thought itself (*Transcendence) but from spatial representations, especially that of an "above", and its imagery is mythical. (See the accounts of the "journey" of departed souls as it were over a "bridge" until they reach their destination in the "other world".) Consequently this term is ill-suited to convey Christian eschatological belief, since *heaven is neither the highest physical dimension nor (when complete) the beatitude of pure spirits but the new, perfected state of *this* world, in which the history of this world "finds its resolution".

P

PAGANS, HEATHEN

A concept of theology (not of comparative religion) which cannot be dispensed with out of deference to "non-Christians" so long as theology upholds the absolute claim of the Church, as an historical entity and as an institution, to the allegiance of all men since Christ. Terminology in this matter is neither uniform nor very precise. Were we simply to follow the analogy of the OT, we could call "heathen" all who do not belong to the historical ("visible") society of the people of God (Church), are not full members of the Church (*Church, membership of). But in fact only the unbaptized (*Baptism) are called heathen. And not even all of these, for the term is not applied to Jews or Moslems—not to Jews, because being monotheists and standing within official saving history (*Old Testament), though as a survival, they cannot be given the name which traditionally (in Scripture) meant non-Jews; not to Moslems because their religion arose during the Christian era, because they are strict monotheists and even worship the same God who is the God of Christian saving history (so that Moslems seem to be really the adherents of a Trinitarian heresy). We should also remember that the term heathen (in Scripture) primarily designates the religious and historical *group* (and the individual only as a member of the group) that does *not* belong to the People of the Covenant. To be theologically accurate we should have to say that the heathen are those historical peoples who as "nations" have not yet been informed of the claims of Christianity or who still reject it in the name of their own historical tradition. The individual who renounces paganism and embraces Christianity before his own nation and history become Christian could quite reasonably be called a "heathen Christian" even today. *Polytheism will at most be considered a crude but quite secondary feature which *de facto* characterizes paganism.

358

The notion of *neo-paganism—and attempts by modern unbelievers, who would pride themselves on being pagans, to invest paganism with a certain prestige—is theologically inept and must be repudiated, or used only with the utmost caution: post-Christian "neo-pagans", whether baptized or not, are at least people who reject the faith within an historical context that long ago became Christian and still is so, at any rate in the sense that the individual cannot possibly avoid an interlocutory relationship with the Christian gospel, has a relationship with Christianity, therefore, which from the theological point of view is altogether different from that of a person of whose tangible historical situation (culture, society, etc.) Christianity is as yet no part. Whether the dialogue aforesaid will always remain unavoidable is of course another question.—This theological conception of paganism must be purged of all depreciation of the cultural achievements of the people concerned and of all evaluations of religion derived from religious history: neither culturally nor religiously must pagans be regarded as "primitives".—For a theological appreciation of pagan religions see *Non-Christian Religions.*

If the essential element in the conception of paganism is not the *de facto* rejection of Christianity but the lack of an historical encounter (of sufficient force) with Christianity in the history of the people concerned, then paganism in this sense is ceasing to exist, or is slowly entering an entirely new theological phase, through the disruption of the West that is now ushering in a global history in which every nation and culture is becoming an intrinsic element of every other nation and culture: we have a single world history in which Christians and non-Christians (that is "old" and "new pagans" now living in the same situation) confront each other as interlocutors.

PANENTHEISM

This form of *pantheism does not simply identify the world with God in monistic fashion (God, the "All") but sees the "All" of the world "within" God as an interior modification and manifestation of God, although God is not absorbed into the world. This doctrine of the "immanence" of the world in God is false and heretical only if it denies *creation and the distinction of the world from God (and not only of God from the world) (D 3001); otherwise it is a demand that *ontology undertake thinking out much more profoundly and much more accurately the relation which exists between absolute and finite *being (that is, the reciprocal conditioning of unity and difference as they grow in the same proportion).

PANTHEISM

The doctrine, occurring in various forms, that God's absolute being is identical with the world; that the finite, changing reality (*Contingent being) which we experience did not originate through *creation by God's free omnipotence as something distinct from himself but is a development of his own being, his (ontic or logical) self-expression and manifestation. It alleges that "God" is a comprehensive term for the world, either because the world is called a divine *emanation, body, *development, appearance, or modalities of God or forms of his manifestation; or because God and the world are identified without qualification (*Monism). Real pantheism, not simply an imprecise description of the orientation of all finite being to God and God's immanence in all creation, is religiously impossible, because it would substitute for the adoration, prayer, acceptance of one's finitude, responsibility, acknowledgment of sin, etc., of real *religion, nothing more than a vague sense that one's life is "numinous"; or else it would make the individual's own finitude, which is meant to endure and enjoy beatitude, purely negative with respect to God. Pantheism is metaphysically false, because if God is grounded in finite being, instead of vice versa, then the radical difference between the finite object on the one hand and the incomprehensible source (horizon, mystery) to which the primordial, inabrogable experience of transcendence refers it on the other, disappears. Furthermore the change which finite being undergoes, and even evil itself, would be intrinsic elements of the divine nature, whereas God is perfect goodness because he possesses the whole plenitude of being. Pantheism is a doctrine which is entirely unknown to the OT and NT. The Church has explicitly and solemnly condemned it (D 201, 804ff., 3001, 3023f.).

PARACLETE

From the Greek παράκλητος , advocate, defender, helper, consoler; the name given in St John to the *Holy Spirit (once directly to Christ: 1 Jn 2:1), Jn 14:16, 26; 16:7, as taking Jesus' place ("another" Paraclete) among the Apostles (and derivatively in every Christian), as the Spirit of truth who "proceeds from the Father" (15:26) and is given by Jesus; who teaches, develops, bears witness to this guiding, saving truth of Christ—indeed is himself this truth—and enables the Apostles to bear witness to it. Since this Paraclete is to teach the Church "all things", she knows that he supports and guides her even today.—See also *Pneuma.*

PARADISE

In ancient Eastern languages, "garden". This term designates the interior and external conditions in which the first human beings (*Adam, *Eve, *Monogenism) lived before the Fall (*Original sin), as these are described in the popular imagery (D 3862ff., 3898) of Genesis 2 and 3. The pure, sinless *beginning of all human history, being authentic beginning, that is a true source of that which is to come, must contain that which is to come in its pure original character and fullness, and must also be the *mere* beginning of an historical development still to come: it must be germ and promise. If scriptural statements about paradise are to be understood, we must duly note this indispensable dialectic of a retrospective, aetiological statement (*Aetiology) about the beginning: the lofty conception of the first man's *original justice (*Integrity, *Immortality) is not incompatible with a beginning that was economically and "culturally" primitive, and this primitive state must not be thought a mere consequence of sin. There is no need to suppose that man's complete harmony with God through grace (in the form of self-mastery) lasted for a long period; if we envisage it as an "existential state at the core of man's being—which is perfectly conceivable even at a primitive cultural level—this complies with what Scripture and the Church (D 222, 1511, 3514) mean by the historical character of the narratives in Genesis.

PARENESIS

From the Greek παραίνεσις, exhortation; a term with biblical associations which draws attention to an essential element in Christian *preaching (in the broad sense): it does not merely instruct, but paves the way for and reveals the blessed reality that is preached, liberating, consoling, fortifying its hearers and enabling them to accept it: a law which gives them the power they need to fulfil it.

PAROUSIA

The Greek word for what we usually call in English Christ's Second Coming (See Mt 10:23; 16:27f.; 19:28 and *passim;* Acts 1:11; 2 Pet 1:16; Rev 1:4, 7). Its approximate meaning is "saving presence" of Jesus Christ, that is the manifest conclusiveness of the issue of saving history and the history of the world. The English word "second" is rather unfortunate, as it might be interpreted to mean that what happened once for all was going to re-occur. But the presence of the eternal Logos in the flesh, bound by the mortality of our historical existence, is not what the parousia will reveal: the consummation of history (Jesus Christ's and the world's) in God, who will be directly revealed in his glory (see Mt 24:36; 25:31ff.; 1 Thess 5:2; 2 Thess 2:2ff.; Rev 20:11ff.; 22:17, 20). And the experience of Jesus Christ's *resurrection was precisely the beginning (not the interruption) of that single process which began at that time, has become irreversible and now goes on in the saving history of individuals and nations (precisely through the individual's *Last Things)—drawing the world into God's transfiguring self-communication, the triumph of saving grace, or the final rejection of God's gift of himself whereby man pronounces his own judgment. The completion of this process—whose duration in earthly time none can know—is Christ's parousia, for the being of the Risen Lord (to "return" in that all will find their way to him) will then be revealed to all (all being definitively saved or damned) as the beginning of irreversibility, the source and support of this process, its central meaning and its climax.

This parousia of Christ for judgment is, however, a revelation of the love of God, since God judges the world by means of an act of love which will take all those who want to be taken into the hereafter, and which will give us the will to be taken in accordance with a disposition that is as yet unknown to us. During the period between Christ's first coming and the parousia (*imminence of the end), the Church anticipates the promises of the *kingdom of God in the Eucharist and the practice of Christian love, without forgetting that her sacraments and institutions will pass away with the parousia of Jesus Christ.

PARTHENOGENESIS

See *Virgin Birth.*

362

PARTICIPATION

A general term signifying the various ways in which the nature of one being may affect that of another. Every efficient cause which produces something different from itself inevitably gives the thing caused some likeness to itself, and thus a "participation" in itself. But in addition, the one may grant the other a participation in itself through self-communication, and this in turn may happen at the most various levels and in the most various ways. The soul gives the body a participation in its own life by actual ontic "information" (one of the kinds of "intrinsic" *causality). In mutual personal *communication two spiritual personal beings may each give the other a participation in itself (participation in the context of nature or in society is somewhat different). This kind of participation reaches its summit in God's communication of himself (*Self-communication of God). If everything has a single origin and thus participates in God, and if God's exinanition which is love, perfects itself in grace and glory as divine self-communication, it is clear that the concept of participation—very mysterious in itself (two beings remain two and yet are one by participation in each other)—must be of key importance in theology.

PASCH

From the Greek πάσχα, which in turn is derived from the Hebrew *pesach;* the annual repetition (*Anamnesis) of Israel's first Passover in Egypt, to commemorate the sparing of their firstborn and their exodus from Egypt. It was celebrated on the 14th of the first month (Nisan: March/April) by offering a lamb in sacrifice at the place of worship (later the Temple) and by a sacrificial meal in the household accompanied by certain rites (in readiness for a hasty departure, with unleavened bread, bitter herbs, a drink which is passed round four times, a reference to the exodus, and hymns of praise). The Pasch is the anamnesis of God's establishment of the people of the Covenant by freeing them from slavery in Egypt. The paschal lamb is a *type of Christ (1 Cor 5:7; see 1 Cor 5:6–8; Mk 8:15; Gal 5:9 for the typological meaning of the unleavened bread). Jesus celebrated the Last Supper, instituting the New Covenant in anticipation of his death, within the framework of the OT Pasch, acting as the father of the household when he distributed his offering of Bread and gave the chalice to those who were dining with him. The Christian celebration of the Pasch simultaneously commemorates the institution of the Old and the New Covenant (Easter Vigil). The 'paschal mystery' is a key term of Vatican II's notion of the liturgy. In OT and NT, the paschal celebration is also an expression of the expectation of a new exodus to final liberation.

PASSION

In scholastic philosophy and psychology, the faculty and act of sensitive appetition (*Sensibility), divided by St Thomas into appetition for pleasure and appetition for achievement. The former is actualized in successive stages: liking, desire, enjoyment (or in aversion from the unpleasant: dislike, flight, sorrow); similarly with the appetition for achievement: hope and courage (or depression, fear, anger). Catholic theology teaches that these passions, comparable with the "impulses" of present-day psychology, are good in themselves but when activated need to be controlled and guided by reason; they have a tendency to separate from the whole man in a morbid independence which would shatter the intrinsic *pluralism of human nature. In fallen man they may be the "site" at which the negative element of "concupiscence" makes its appearance; on the other hand they urge on man in the state of grace, by a(n also) salutary discontent because of an unrealized humanity. Therefore it is immoral, again according to St Thomas, to try to eradicate the passions, as Plato, Suarez, Kant and others advocated in various degrees and for various reasons.

PASTORAL OFFICE OF THE CHURCH

The pregnant metaphor of the shepherd and the flock is much used in the NT to describe God's personal relationship with his people as their provider and saviour. Christ is also the shepherd of his Church (1 Pet 5:4), but the metaphor (a just appreciation of which is difficult today since "flock", despite its original sense, is now too suggestive of stolid masses ruled from above) is also applied to those who hold office in the primitive Church and to their congregations (Jn 21:15ff.; 1 Pet 5:1ff.; Acts 20:28). Thus theology likewise describes authority to govern the Church in view of salvation as the pastoral office (cf. Vat. II: Church, 21, 22, 27, 28 and *passim:* on the pastoral office of the Pope, bishops and priests), for the exercise of which the power of jurisdiction is given (*Pope, *Bishop). This power and the power of order overlap; see *Powers of the Church.*

364

PASTORAL THEOLOGY

Preferably to be called "practical theology", that is theology of the Church's practice. In a comprehensive sense this term designates theological reflection on the self-realizing activity of the Church whereby God communicates salvation to the world, and the forms this activity takes and should take in view both of the unchanging nature of the Church and also of the situation in which the Church and the world find themselves at any time. Thus it concerns itself not merely with the pastoral work of the priest but also with all the Church's work for salvation, not as a mere "essential" (theoretical) science, which gives us timeless universal principles governing this work drawn from ecclesiology and moral theology, but as a practical (existential) science which seeks to ascertain what is to be done here and now and will only be recognized as obligatory if the present situation is subjected to theological analysis (which is also but not only a sociological analysis). The principles governing the priestly ministry in the narrower sense, both individual and collective, have of course their necessary place within this general context. A pastoral theology which would examine not only the "tactics" of the priestly ministry but also the "strategy" of the whole Church from the point of view of theology and theological sociology and establish critical norms for both, is still largely lacking.

PATRIARCHS

From the Greek πατριάρχης , forefather; the name given to the great figures of the OT saving history such as Abraham and Moses. Since the *Old Testament is the immediate prehistory of the Incarnation as interpreted by Scripture (a minute fragment of human history), since the grace of Jesus Christ already secretly controls this prehistory (because of God's universal *salvific will), Scripture interprets these patriarchs in the "Christian" sense as the fathers and exemplars of our faith (see Mt 17:3; Rom 4:1; 1 Cor 10:1–12; Heb 11, etc.), whose decisions during their saving history still form the groundwork of our own historical existence.

PATRIPASSIANISM

A Western name for those adherents of *Monarchianism who professed *Modalism: one who denies the real *Trinity of God in himself can only affirm—if he is not to deny the divinity of Jesus—that the only divine Person, the Father himself, suffered in Jesus (thus Noetus, Praxeas, and *Sabellianism in the second and third centuries).

PATRISTIC AGE

The term in Church history and the history of dogma and theology for the age of the *Fathers of the Church, that is the period with which *patrology is concerned. The theology and dogmatic development of this period are important from the point of view of systematic theology. So far as the history of dogma is concerned this is the period (above all in the East) when Trinitarian and Christological dogma is developed during the struggle with *Monarchianism, *Subordinationism, *Arianism, *Nestorianism, *Monophysitism (and *Monotheletism), and when St Augustine first elaborates the doctrine of grace against *Pelagianism. As to the history of theology, several schools of thought are encountered, especially the *Alexandrian and *Antiochene schools of theology. *Paganism has also to be combatted at the intellectual level, and the continual confrontation of minds in conflict increasingly tends to produce a philosophical and cultural synthesis between Christianity and the ancient world. Whereas the East, in the patristic age, thought above all in "cosmic" terms (saving history as a divinization of the world through the Incarnation of the Logos—the source of the world from the beginning—and his resurrection), the West thought in more "personalistic" terms (salvation as a dialogue between sinful man and God who enables man to love him). Everywhere the various trends in ancient *philosophy (especially *Neoplatonism) greatly influenced the form taken by Christianity's conception of itself. Without adulterating its original substance this philosophy provided the faith with considerable means for expressing itself. On the other hand there were latent dangers in it: too much dominance was given to the Platonic and gnostic monastic idea of salvation as an ascent, an overcoming of the world by a process of rising above it spiritually, at the expense of the permanent descent of the Logos which confirms the goodness of the world; failure to distinguish accurately between *nature and grace proved at once too heavy and too light a burden for the Church and the world (philosophy became theology and theology became too philosophical; the Church became a State Church and the State became an ecclesiastical State, etc.). Only Scholasticism at its apogee—the dawn of modern times—

PAULINE THEOLOGY

distinguished nature from grace more precisely, giving the world more freedom to attend to its own affairs and Christianity a deeper insight into its own nature.

PATROLOGY

The history of ancient Christian literature and the study of the life and teaching of the *Fathers of the Church and other ecclesiastical writers of antiquity. (Thorough analysis of their doctrine leads us into the history of *dogma). Owing to the importance of *Tradition, patrology is one of the most useful auxiliary sciences for historical and systematic theology. The period it covers is generally considered to have closed in the West with St Isidore (d. 636) and in the East with St John Damascene (d. 749).

PAULINE THEOLOGY

The revealed and inspired doctrine of St Paul's epistles, an essential and permanent part of the NT and therefore of Christianity. But however great its importance as a source and norm of faith, it remains the consistent development (conditioned by Paul's personality and circumstances) of what the historical Jesus said of himself and his work. For difficult or impossible though it may be to distinguish historically, in particular cases, between Jesus' original statements about himself and his mission and the (sound) theological interpretation which had already been given to this testimony in the primitive Church by the preaching of the Apostles and was therefore embodied in the Synoptics, fused with Jesus' own sayings, still it cannot be denied that Jesus knew he was more than a prohpet and religious reformer initiating only a phase of religious history that was open to the unforeseen: he knew that he brought absolute salvation, that his person and work are the salvation and redemption of all, that his resurrection proved he was the beginning of supreme salvation for the world. Pauline theology enlarges on this theme. St Paul is not the founder of Christianity; he is, and knows he is, only a theologian reflecting on a fact that has been handed down to him—Jesus, his cross, his resurrection. But for this very reason his theology is of fundamental importance. It is a theology of Jesus Christ's *pre-existence as the Son absolutely; of *Christocentrism that also embraces the cosmos; of the universal need of redemption; of the conquest of

367

PEACE

the enslaving powers of (mere) *law, of *sin, and of *death (and the angelic powers that lie behind it) by the *Pneuma* of Christ crucified and risen that alone can save men wholly unprepared for salvation; a theology of history, of the universal Church that is the *Body of Christ, of the sacraments of baptism and the Eucharist, and of the efficacious word of God, including his own apostolate.

PEACE

In Scripture peace is simply the gift of God himself to men; as such it was promised to the chosen people in the OT and brought to the world by Jesus Christ. For biblical theology peace has the more precise sense of that "well-being"—wholeness, health, safety—which Jesus' act of obedience, in "delivering" himself without reserve to God, has won, by totally defeating the power of evil and of the mere law, and of death, which held us in bondage, and graciously ending man's quarrel with and separation from God. Peace therefore is the peace which is Jesus Christ (Eph 2:14), the peace which Jesus Christ (as the revelation of God's unrepenting self-surrender) has made with man (Acts 10:36; Col 1:20); which he alone can bequeath (Jn 14:27); which remains in the world by the operation of the Spirit of Jesus Christ (Gal 5:22; Lk 2:14); which therefore, gift of God though it be, is the task of Jesus Christ's Church and must be preserved by her (Rom 12:18; Eph 4:3). Scholastic philosophy specially emphasizes this last aspect; in St Thomas peace is "the order of cummunity life based on justice". This order of things is not preordained, but has always to be brought about anew. The requisite assurance of peace is a task for all those forces which can make a contribution (Vat II: Church/world, 42, 78, 82 and *passim*). Those who claim to be Christians must hold in such deliberations to Jesus' requirements of non-violence, unconditional forgiveness and love of one's enemies.

PECCATUM PHILOSOPHICUM

The name given to a culpable offence against the *natural moral law said to involve no deliberate violation at all of God's legislative will, only a conscious sin against human nature. But where the moral unworthiness of an action in respect of the human person is really perceived (the only case in which there can be any question of *sin), God's being and will are at least implicitly apprehended, though not reflexively, so that in practice a *peccatum philosophicum* is impossible (D 2291).

PELAGIANISM

A heresy in the theology of grace, which was formulated and spread within the ancient Church by the monk Pelagius (early fifth century), his disciple Caelestius, and somewhat later by Julian of Eclanum (d. after 454), and combatted by St Augustine and his disciples (*Semi-Pelagianism). Pelagianism rejects the doctrine of *original sin, overlooks the pressure of *concupiscence and the nature of suffering and death as consequences of sin. It conceives of human freedom as (created but) complete autonomy which by itself can and must observe the law of God, thus denying the necessity of *grace for natural and salutary observance of the moral law. Pelagianism is a sort of Stoic version of *Pharisaism. It was condemned by the Church in the fifth century (D 222–231, 267, 238–249) and again at the Council of Trent (D 1510–1514, 1521, 1551ff.). St Augustine made it difficult for his opponents to grasp the Catholic doctrine insofar as he did not sufficiently stress the universality of God's *salvific will and the availability to all of sufficient grace.

PENALTIES OF SIN

Every *sin has its natural consequences. These may be internal or external, since they flow from the nature of the sin itself and affect to a greater or lesser extent the whole spiritual and physical being of the person concerned. Now this being which has set itself against the divine order by sin, necessarily exposes itself thereby to the reaction of the environment, in the complete sense of the word, which is what it should be and remains subject in its concrete form to God's sovereign control. Since the very structure of God's creation (man and the world) necessarily expresses and manifests God's will, never failing to uphold it even when it has been violated by sin, there is no need to imagine that God must suitably punish man's offences for punishment's sake, as if he were some lesser, earthly authority. The penalty of sin is the concrete being God has chosen to make: this itself (and the totality of being) is the undoing of the sinner when he offends against it. This is especially so when man has reached the end of his term in *death and by his own moral decision remains in undisguised,

PENANCE

eschatological contradiction with the total divine order which is now in force (*Hell). The objectifications of sin often continue in existence, within man and in the world about him, even when a person has redirected his fundamental option to God: the punishment due to sin is not always erased by contrition and the forgiveness of sin as such (D 1542f., 1580). Thus we must understand the purpose of *purgatory and *satisfaction.

PENANCE

Penance as a "virtue" signifies the proper moral and religious attitude of man towards *sin (his own and sin in general), granted him by the grace of Christ. Its most central act is *contrition (*Metanoia). Penance essentially involves: having the courage to fear God and face the truth about one's own existence, dispensing with all repressions (the upright acknowledgment of one's past); the grace-given disposition to let God's revealing word convince one by destroying the pharisaic self-righteousness of sin; the serious and active will to amend one's life, trusting in the grace of God which triumphs through human helplessness (attested by penitential works, biblically: vigils, fasting, and almsgiving); the will to the sacrament of the forgiveness of sin; willingness humbly to endure the consequences of sin that remain even after it has been forgiven (*Penalties of sin); actively helping to bear the burden of sin that assumes concrete existence in the general unhappiness and distress of the world. Precisely as a gift of God, penance is a human action and not simply a passive experience: man turns away from his past, which "pains" him (because he again accepts the unshakable validity of the divine order) and which he "abhors" (because he himself is freely renewing this order). Penance implies that what is believed and accepted in *hope is not our repentance but God's deed in us. It includes recognition of man's plurality, which in turn requires a plurality of acts (external and internal works of penance, faith and charity, satisfaction, stepping into the future with the "firm purpose").

PENANCE, SACRAMENT OF

That *sacrament of the Church in which the repentant sinner has the guilt of those sins he has committed after baptism blotted out by the

370

Church through the absolution which the priest pronounces by the authority of Christ.

DOCTRINE OF THE CHURCH. The sacrament of penance is one of the seven sacraments of the Church and is distinct from baptism (D 761, 793f., 1542f., 1601, 1668ff., 1701, 1703). Like baptism it is necessary for salvation by a *necessity of means (in case of emergency, therefore, can be supplied by the *votum) for all who have committed serious sin after baptism (D 1085, 1260, 1323, 1411, 1671f., 1679ff., 1683, 1706f.). It forgives sins in virtue of Christ's death (D 1668ff.) and by a judicial decision (D 1671, 1684, 1709) which efficaciously realizes God's forgiveness (D 1323, 1673, 1684f., 1709). It readmits one to the sacraments (D 129, 212, 308, 468), since the person in mortal sin is excluded from the Eucharist and thus in a certain sense estranged from the Church (D 1646, 1661; CIC can. 856). By this sacrament damnation is averted and deliverance to the power of the devil rescinded (D 1542f., 1580, 1668ff., 1715), but the *penalties of sin are not always entirely disposed of. The sacrament may be repeated (D 1542f., 1668ff.). The efficacious sacramental sign consists principally in the priest's absolution, to be given orally, which as a judicial pronouncement has an indicative sense (though not necessarily expressed in the indicative mood) and must be given in indicative form in the Latin Church, but the older deprecative form used in the Oriental Churches is certainly valid and licit. The acts of the penitent, *contrition confession, *satisfaction, are the quasi materia of the sacramental sign. Interior repentance springing from faith is a necessary condition for valid and efficacious reception of the sacrament (D 1323, 1461, 1542f., 1557, 1673ff., 1704); this disposition on the part of the penitent must in some way be apparent to the priest in the sacrament of penance (D 1464); imperfect contrition suffices (D 1677f.): *attritionism. By the nature of the sacrament, and therefore by divine ordinance, all serious sins must be confessed which have not yet been directly blotted out in the sacrament. Confession must include all grave sins of which the penitent, after a serious examination of conscience, knows himself to be even subjectively guilty; the penitent must tell their specific nature and the number of times each has been committed and also confess any serious sins forgotten in previous confession (D 1679ff., 1706ff., 2031). This confession is protected by the seal of confession, which also belongs to the nature of the sacrament (D 323, 814, 2195). If without fault some sin is not confessed, it is nevertheless forgiven by the sacrament (D 1682). Since the Fourth Lateran Council the Church's law has imposed a strict obligation to

371

make a valid confession once a year if one is consciously guilty of any serious sin (D 812f. and *passim*) (*Frequent confession). The severe crisis of the sacrament of penance at present has led to the introduction of (non-sacramental) penitential services, at which since 1972 a bishops' conference can allow—after a general confession of sins—the giving of a general sacramental absolution. Anyone guilty of a subjectively grave sin may receive the Eucharist after this general absolution, but must repeat the confession in private (unless that is morally impossible). The priest's authority gives him the right and duty prudently to require a satisfaction that will in some measure correspond to the seriousness of the sin and the spiritual capacity of the penitent (D 1692ff. and *passim*) and can also be performed *after* absolution (D 1415, 2316ff. and *passim*). The reason for thus imposing "a penance" is that the forgiveness of sins committed after baptism does not necessarily obliterate all the penal consequences of sin; that by patiently accepting these, unavoidable as they are, and by voluntarily doing penance, whether imposed in confession or not, man learns the reality of divine justice and the gravity of sin and shares more deeply in the suffering of Christ which overcomes sin (D 1689f., 1712ff. and *passim*). The minister of the sacrament is a priest who has the necessary faculties (jurisdiction *in foro interno*) for exercising his power of order in the sacrament of penance (D 308, 812f., 1684ff., 1710 and *passim*). For grave reasons the Church can grant this authorization subject to reservations (except in danger of death: D 1686ff.), that is she can reserve certain sins to the cognizance of a higher tribunal of penance or to those having a special faculty (D 1686ff., 1711 and *passim*).

SCRIPTURE. The self-realization of the *Church as the judging and forgiving presence of Christ in the *world of sin finds expression in the ministry of the word of reconciliation (2 Cor 5:18ff.) that convinces man of sin, in baptism and Eucharist, in confession of the Church's guilt (Mt 6:12), in works of *penance, in prayer for the individual sinner (1 Jn 5:16), in fraternal correction (Mt 18:15), in official censure (1 Tim 5:20), and finally in that mightiest of the Church's acts of judgment or, whenever possible, of grace—*binding and loosing (*Excommunication). Since the Church serves the presence in the world of Christ and his grace, she can only excommunicate in order to bless and save (1 Cor 5:5; 1 Tim 1:20); since she is Holy Church her reaction to sin in one of her members must be excommunication, for sin is incompatible with her nature. Since she is the efficacious presence in the world of grace triumphant, reconciliation with her is the tangible and efficacious actualization of reconcilation with God, and therefore a sacrament. It is to this end that Peter and the Apostles are given authority in the power of *binding and loosing. John 20:19–23 states the same thing in Johannine terms. This excommunication of the sinner does not mean that his *membership of the Church is simply terminated, but the very loss of grace entails a change in the Church's relationship with the sinner, a change that is proclaimed by excommunication in the form of exclusion from the Eucharist in every case of mortal sin. We find the Church of the Apostles, on Jesus' instructions, proceeding against the sinners in her midst. If admonitions prove fruitless and it is a case of such sins as "exclude one from the *basileia" then the sinners must be excluded from the common table and their company shunned. This proscriptive "binding" is solemnly pronounced in Christ's name by the congregation under the authoritative government of the Apostle (1 Cor 5:4f.). It extends into the dimension of damnation ("to deliver to Satan"). But if the sinner returns repentant, "charity", that is ecclesiastical fellowship, can be restored to him by an official decision and he may participate once more in the salvation which belongs to the Church of grace (2 Cor 2:5–11); so that the sinner is also "loosed in heaven" and his sins are "remitted". Nowhere in the Apostolic Church is the notion to be found that a truly repentant sinner cannot be received again into communion (though doubts are expressed whether sin will in fact be overcome by repentance: Heb 6; 10; 12). Thus the sacrament in the practice of the Apostolic Church is penance by excommunication, followed by a reconciliation with the Church (probably by *laying on of hands, see 1 Tim 5:10 ff.).

HISTORY OF THE SACRAMENT OF PENANCE. The essential problem here, and by the same token the essential difference between the practice of the ancient Church and present practice, is not the transition from "public" to "private" penance (auricular confession), as many still suppose quite unhistorically, but the fact that formerly in the Western Church the sacrament of penance was administered only *once*, whereas today it can and must be repeated. The most private confession still bears a public character even today, because the person in mortal sin is excluded from the Eucharist and after receiving the sacrament of penance is once more admitted to this sacred common table of the Church. In Christian antiquity, from the 2nd to the 6th century, the sacrament of penance could be received only once; in a number of churches there was much hesitation to believe that the interior dispositions of penance were really verified. Against the heresies of *Montanism and *Novatianism the ancient Church firmly maintained the principle that she is able to absolve *all* sinners. The rite of ecclesiastical penance is clearly discernible by the 3rd century: the repentant sinner confesses his sin before the bishop; if his repentance is genuine he is admitted to ecclesiastical penance, which involves wearing special clothes and sitting in a special seat reserved for penitents, and after a lengthy probation the bishop welcomes him back with prayer and *laying on of hands. It became more and more usual to seek reconciliation only on one's deathbed or at an advanced age, especially following the introduction of penances that continued indefinitely *after* one had been reconciled (such as forbidding the use of marriage for the rest of a person's life, etc.). In the 6th century Irish and Anglo-Saxon Catholicism broke with this rigorism (see also the introduction of *monastic confession): the simple priest can repeatedly absolve the same sinner. The frequency of confession (a term in use from the 8th century) and the variety of sins required some variation in the penances imposed and these were catalogued in the penitentiaries. The milder practice reached the Continent with the Celtic mission and prevailed everywhere there by the 8th century. Attempts to restore the severity of ancient practice were made down to the time of the Council of Trent but were unsuccessful. The Fourth Lateran Council declared the custom of going to confession at least once a year to be henceforth a commandment of the Church. For other problems in the history of penance, see also *Attritionism, Contritionism.*

THEOLOGY. Today the sacrament of penance is practically identified with confession, which has almost become a work of penance in itself: the humiliation of the avowal expiates the sin avowed. But it were well to recover our realization of its indissoluble connexion with the theology of the Church, to pay more heed to the damage that sin does to the Church and the community, to throw into relief the salutary effects of being restored to the peace of the Church (the notion is at least mentioned by Vatican II: Church, 11). There are particular deficiencies in the "penance" imposed, the *satisfaction. More than repentance and reconciliation with God is required before sin is wholly overcome: the *whole* reality of man which sin has injured must be integrated into a new and fundamental decision, in order for that charity to be won in which indeed *all* is forgiven. This charity is most available where it is most possible, in the compensation of injury. The unrelated, more or less mechanical and legalistic imposition of a few prayers, whether shorter or longer, hardly amounts to satisfaction in this sense. This is a very serious problem for our present-day understanding of the sacrament of penance for the additional reason that

374

often it is only by radically and systematically counteracting sin that one can win through to that repentance of which men of the present day are allegedly incapable, but which is nevertheless requisite for the effectual realization of the sacrament of penance and for the *salvation of the sinner, etc.

PENTATEUCH

See *Canon, Law.*

PENTECOST

See *Holy Spirit.*

PEOPLE OF GOD

(1) A biblical term recently restored to currency by Vatican II (Church, 4 –17, etc.), "people of God" is used to describe the relationship between God and a particular group of human beings (Israel, the Church, mankind). "People" is of course in its origins a secular reality and in the concept "people of God" is used in a metaphorical sense. (2) The people of *Yahweh (Jahwe) is what Israel calls itself in the Old Testament, because after its experience of the Exodus it had Yahweh and his historical deed to thank for its existence as a nation and as a religious community, and for that reason is his creation and his possession. The relationship thus expressed in the term "people of God" provides the foundation for the people's pledge of loyalty to this real and actual God of its history (*covenant) and for its hope in his promises. On the permanent foundation of Israel the believing community formed by faith in Jesus proclaims itself, as the people of the New Covenant, to be the genuine, true and ultimate people of God. But now this is no longer characterized by forming a nation but is intended to embrace all nations and peoples and is founded in the *Holy Spirit and in *faith. In a way analogous to Israel's sojourn in the desert, the Church appears as the people of God on its (temporary) pilgrimage (Heb 4:9; Church, 2, 21, 48, and elsewhere; Ecum, 2, 6, etc.). (3) The dogmatically certain content of the term "people of God" means that in his desire for human salvation God has called people not as isolated individuals but in the midst of their entangle-

ment in history and in society and of their relationships with each other, which latter also have a function in the mediation of salvation on account of the unity of *love of God and love of neighbour. In this historical and social unity these people have an inner unity through God's revelation of himself; this inner unity appeared in history and became eschatologically irrevocable in *Jesus Christ and his resurrection. Hence this unity too has itself a historical and social tangibility, even if as far as we are concerned this group of those who have been called and united in the spirit of God cannot clearly be marked off from other men and women. (4) The idea suggests itself, and is theologically possible, of understanding by the term "people of God" the sum total, united in the spirit, of all those who are justified. They include those who are not completely incorporated in the organized society of the hierarchical Church. To put it another way, belonging to the people of God, and doing so in different ways, are all those who in some (differentiated) way or another belong to the Church. The idea is also possible of calling mankind as such the people of God: by its origin and by its supernatural vocation mankind forms a single unity, to its one history Jesus Christ belongs, all men and women are embraced by God's desire for the universal salvation of mankind, all men and women are redeemed. Already in its one history there has already taken place in Jesus what formally determines *a priori* the blessed outcome of this history. Mankind as a unity and as a totality is therefore already an entity constituted through God's act of grace in Jesus Christ for the personal decision of the individual and for the formation of the Church—and therefore the "people of God".

PERFECTION

In accordance with Matthew 5:48, perfection is that moral and religious maturity of man, made possible and bestowed by God's grace, which man freely develops in accordance with the objective law of God and the ever various capacities of the individual: loving God and our neighbour with our whole heart and our whole strength (Mt 22:37; Rom 13:10). All other moral dispositions and achievements are only modalities of love or various means to the end which is love (*Evangelical counsels), for perfection is only the fullness of *love. Since this perfection consists in integrating one's whole life (in all its changing phases which one can never adequately plan) into love, while man remains a pilgrim in this world perfection is a goal he can only approach asymptotically. But since *grace can really grow (Mt

13:8; Jn 15:2; Eph 3:15–19) and it is man's duty to see that it does (Eph 4:15), it is perfectly legitimate for man to strive for perfection (*Asceticism, *Mysticism) in response to grace and the lessons of life. When the Church canonizes saints it also calls perfection "heroic" virtue.

PERICHORESIS

The Greek περιχώρησις is equivalent to the Latin *circumincessio;* both mean penetration. In *Trinitarian theology it is necessary being-in-one-another or circumincession (D 1331; Jn 10:38; 14:10f.; 17:21; 1 Cor 2:10f.) of the three divine Persons of the *Trinity because of the single divine essence, the eternal procession of the Son from the Father and of the Spirit from the Father and (through) the Son, and the fact that the three Persons are distinguished solely by the *relations of opposition between them. Somewhat similarly, the *hypostatic union of the divine and human natures in Christ is considered a sort of *perichoresis.* Care must of course be taken not to envisage *perichoresis* in spatial terms.

PERSECUTION

Christianity is aware that it cannot expect its career within history to be altogether peaceful and triumphant, free of contradiction and attack. Its ultimate victory will be brought about by God alone when he brings temporal history to an end. Continual persecution (whose concrete forms are various and unpredictable and may come from within the Church, from individual and social circumstances [the *world] or from external concentrations of political power [*Antichrist]) is the inevitable lot of the Christian and the Church in saving history ("necessary", Lk 24:26; Mt 5:10 –12, 44; 2 Tim 3:12; Rev). It is the situation of true *faith and *hope, in which the Christian himself, even while he prays, already embraces his enemies as friends to be, a situation which God ordains and in which he brings to bear the criticism he must always have of his Church (Lk 22:31; 1 Pet 4:17). The situation in regard to persecution has changed since the first Christian centuries: (a) the Church persecutes/ed those who think differently; (b) many persecutions are to be explained in terms of a past history in which the Church itself persecuted and suppressed; (c) Christian Churches have provided one another with martyrs.

These factors should prevent us from talking glibly of the *martyr-dom of others and too uncomprehendingly of the persecution of Christians.

PERSEVERANCE

The continuance of the justified in the grace of *justification, the virtue of the wayfarer which is authenticated by the acceptance of Death. It is the defined teaching of the Church that actual persever-ance to the end *(perseverantia finalis)* is impossible without a special grace (D 1562); it remains uncertain whether this latter will be grant-ed (D 1566) (*Certainty of salvation); it cannot be merited, but the Christian is to pray for it and cherish the firm *hope of it.

PERSON

The Latin word *persona,* as a translation of the Greek πρόσωπον, countenance, originally meant an actor's mask. The notion of the person (firstly in the modern sense) is of great importance in theology, because it draws attention to those human characteristics which are the necessary condition of his relationship to God and his salutary acts: his spirituality (as grounded in his *transcendence) and presence to himself, his permanent and inescapable orientation to *being as a whole and thus to God (the *a priori* condition of his ability to judge [objectify] and deal with particular being), his freedom of choice in relation to all that is recognized as finite, particular being, dealing with it in a certain critical detachment. To be a person, therefore, is to possess oneself as a subject on conscious, free relation to reality as a whole and its infinite ground and source, God. Man as such, of course, is a personal being who can only act in a concrete body, in history here and now, in dialogue with another Thou, constantly exposed with his fellows to painful experience of the world through his own deeds. We need not labour the point that this ontological constitution of man explains his eternal validity, his responsibility, his dialogical relationship with God, his vocation to a supernatural desti-ny (*Nature and grace, *Potentia obedientialis), his dignity and *im-mortality, the absolute character of moral values (*Natural moral law).

But besides and within this modern conception of the person, there

378

PERSON

is another conception, connected but not identical with the first, familiar to Christian theologians in *Christology and the theology of the *Trinity. (The word is not used in precisely the same sense in these two fields and the several schools of theological thought have their particular interpretations of the concept). Theologians single out one aspect of the subject (self-conscious and free) who is a concrete spiritual being (that is, person in the modern sense) and declare it to be the special, "formal" characteristic of the person (*Hypostasis): its "subsistence", that is that property in virtue of which a concrete spiritual being belongs to itself (insofar as it does) in utter immediacy; total and final self-incession; that which inalienably possesses this spiritual nature, or that which makes a being such a possessor. One reason why theologians make this distinction is that the one complete being of Jesus Christ contains everything that makes a man a man (all that we have included above in the modern "material" conception of the person), whereas all this in itself is absolutely creaturely, finite and created and so cannot be identified with God's divinity. Yet all this does belong to the Logos, is permanently and perfectly united with him who is the revelatory being and presence of God among us. Now that which enables the Logos to be truly man without prejudice to his divinity. is known in traditional Christian language (since about the time of *Chalcedon, see D 301ff.) as his human "nature" (a term not meant to materialize it, or to deny its transcendence and freedom and its creaturely, dialogical relationship with God). And in so far as just this reality belongs wholly to the Logos, this terminology has it that he, the Logos, is the "person" of this "nature", that is, the ultimate bearer, support, and possessor of it, and hence that Jesus Christ's human "nature" is not of itself "person" (in this scholastic sense). This is not to make the humanity of Jesus Christ less "personal" (in the modern sense). On the contrary: insofar as personality (in the present sense) means that achieved self-consciousness (or the ontological principle of that self-consciousness) of a being which necessarily (really and existentially) refers it to a Thou and to God, the "subsistence" of the humanity of Jesus in the Logos supremely exemplifies what is meant by personality. Personality in a mere creature, then, as something spiritual that is not wholly (really and consciously) surrendered to God, implies a certain negativity. So that the modern and the traditional concept of the person unite again: spiritual, conscious transcendence, which in its ek-stasy constantly falls back upon itself and becomes hypo-static in itself (that is, finite person in the modern sense, explicitly recognizing the finitude of personal being as such), becomes in Jesus Christ "anhypostatic" in itself (mere "nature" yet

379

just in this way perfected in what personality claims of it because by divine agency its ek-stasy has achieved itself absolutely) and enhypostatic in the Logos.

The second reason why scholastic theologians distinguish between the person and the spiritual nature of the individual is to be sought in the Christian doctrine of the Trinity. God's self-communication to man by Incarnation and grace is so radical, so absolutely gives God as he is in himself, that the threefold aspect of this self-communication (God's Trinity in the economy of salvation) must be proper to God in and for himself, must characterize his own interior life: the absolutely unoriginate Origin of plenitude of being and life, communicated yet undiminished; the self-objectified utterance of this plenitude of being; the effusion of this plenitude of being in an ecstasy of holy Love—are all proper to God in himself and may not be reduced, because of God's genuine and absolute unity, to a dull uncommunicated uniformity, a lifeless identity, which would make the economic Trinity—no longer the true God in himself—a finite, undivine realm intermediate between God and the beneficiary of his grace, destroying genuine *self*-communication. These three aspects of the divine plenitude of being and life which possess an ultimate inalienability through their relative opposition to each other and thus allow the one identical plenitude of life (as absolute being) to exist in three unique and mutually opposite ways, are now called *Persons* and distinguished from the one infinite plenitude of being, the divine "nature". Accordingly it is defined that in the one Jesus Christ, the incarnate Logos, there are one Person (the Word of the Father) and two natures (the divine and the human) (D 301ff., 801, 1339–1346); that in the one eternal God there are one nature (or essence) and three Persons (D 75, 150, 800, 1330). Here we must observe that the "triplicity" of Persons does not posit the *same* thing three times, but enumerates that which makes Father, Son and Spirit absolutely *different*, that is, relatively opposed to each other. Only in a very loose sense can we grasp through a single concept the grounds for the differences purely internal to the one God which in fact perfect his real unity, since those "Three" are only distinguished by what makes them "Persons" in our present sense, not equated. For "what they have in common" is the perfect identity of the "nature", whereby the characteristics we have noted of the "person" in the modern sense (presence to oneself as an interior illumination of one's being, freedom) cannot possibly exist more than once in the three divine "Persons".

All this is said only to make it quite clear that when theologians speak of "nature" and "person" we must not allow the long history of these concepts to make us forget the underlying reality which has led to the use of such halting analogies, lest we unwittingly read false meanings into our Christological and Trinitarian formulae. Thus Christ's human "nature" as such is not a static thing, nor does it lack anything that characterizes the human "person": presence to himself, freedom, a dialogical creaturely relationship with God through adoration and obedience that exercise his creaturely transcendence. And the three "Persons" in God are not three active "subjects", each with his own plenitude of knowledge, freedom, and life, in which case there would no longer be any mystery of the one divine nature.

PERSONALITY

In an ethical sense, personality may be said to be present when a human being's free decision really and unflinchingly accepts the fact that he is a *person: accepts the dialogical character of life ordered to mystery, accepts freedom, duty, responsibility, unrepressed sinfulness, his neighbour's, ineffable individuality, pain, and death. Complete personality is rooted in the genius of the heart, not of the intellect.

PESSIMISM

A basic mood with special physiological predispositions arising from a keen sense of the incompleteness of the world and life as we experience them, and a realization of the depth of our guilt. When this mood is not erected into an absolute, but surrenders itself in ultimate silent obedience to the greater mystery which, though not understood, alone "explains" everything, such pessimism is justifiable and is a means of approaching God. When pessimism declares the inmost being of existence and the world to be senseless, evil, absurd (a blind impulse, empty nothingness, unknown darkness, etc.), it itself becomes absurd, because it cannot explain how a search and a demand for meaning can arise from that which is wholly meaningless. In this case pessimism erroneously generalizes on the basis of a particular experience (for we also experience spirit and love as things intelligible of themselves which it is our joy to affirm); it ignores the becoming involved in our being, in which lies the hope that absolutely affirms a goal unattained but attainable; it regards finite being primarily as negative limitation, rather than openness to the infinite; and overlooks the fact that the very transcendence which makes pessimist criticism possible necessarily affirms the goodness of being. In the last analysis pessimism concerns not the intellect alone but freedom, which willingly accepts pain as the birth-pangs of love and is prepared to receive God's gift of forgiveness. But this is grace.

PHARISAISM

In the theological sphere Pharisaism does not mean hypocrisy or a double standard of morality, but refers primarily to a party of Jews at the time of Christ (Pharisee, from the Hebrew which means "the separated") who were patriotic, xenophobic, and morally austere, faithfully observed the Law and had a great reverence for post-biblical tradition (the opposing party was the *Sadducees). When the negative features of this party are systematized the result is Pharisaism in the proper sense, which Jesus combats and which occurs in every age as a corruption of all (rightly) institutional religion: a preoccupation with the externals of religion, zeal for the letter of the law with no understanding of its spirit, the dominance of casuistry in moral theology, above all a "righteousness of good works" by which man expects, of himself, to establish calculable good relations with God (in effect a "self-redemption"), to put God in his debt so that he will have to reward good deeds which are not themselves divine grace. This attitude may degenerate further into real arrogance and hypocrisy. Jesus completely rejects such Pharisaism. St Paul, once a Pharisee, shows in theological terms how absolutely incompatible a legalistic righteousness of works is with Christianity (Romans, Galatians). (See Mt 5:20; 6:1–6, 16; 12:1–14; 15:1–20; 23:13–36; Lk 18:9–14.)

PHILOSOPHY AND THEOLOGY

The fundamental problem of the relation between philosophy and theology is whether and how they can simultaneously be basic sciences (that is, shed light on being in general and existence in a reflexive, systematic way) in such a way that man need neither abandon, nor sacrifice the character of, either discipline, that is be faced with the choice of being either a philosopher or a theologian. In order to elucidate this problem we must first observe that Catholic theology draws an essential distinction between *nature and grace, and consequently between natural *knowledge of God and *revelation; so that by its very nature it does not simply tolerate philosophy but actually needs it. That is to say, Catholic theology does not raise the structure of revelation and faith upon the ruins of the human intellect, sinner though man be. This is further confirmed, in that this distinction is not a matter of isolation (in the sense of the positing of the existence of a mere nature); against the background of the relation of general and "official' salvific history, the history of philosophy clearly also belongs to the history of *revelation and is therefore a requisite partner in communication between Christianity and theology. Furthermore, history shows that *theology has always thought in philosophical terms, among others; and against *Modernism and all religion of *feeling Catholic theology holds tenaciously to the historical fact that from the outset revelation and grace address the whole man, not least his intellect—a pertinent fact when one is considering the nature of religion. The Christian believer as such lives in the conviction that intellect, nature, and history are the creation, revelation, and property of the God who is the one truth, the source of all being and truth, and has produced historical, verbal revelation to perfect and exalt his creation. The fact, then, that a thing lies "outside" a particular sphere of earthly reality (in this case outside historical revelation, the Church and theology) by no means removes it from God's domain so far as the Christian is concerned. So that it is neither necessary nor permissible for him to make a closed and final system of theology at the expense of philosophy. To do so would be to confuse theology with theology's God. The Christian above all knows that there is a *pluralism in the world which can be positively and adequately unified by no one (except God), not even by the Church and her theologians, though of course there is no question of a double truth. Conversely, if philosophy is to accomplish the intellectual mastery of human existence as it actually is in all its breadth and depth, even the philosopher with the most transcendental approach must take notice of the history of the mind, then it may not ignore the phenomenon of religion, because religion is part of the basic structures of human existence (even where *atheism is preached as the true interpretation of life, and therefore as a "religion"). A philosophy which was not also a "philosophy of religion" and a "natural theology", in whatever form, would be a bad philosophy, because it would fail to perceive its own object. (A contented atheism which behaves as though the question of religion did not exist either does not know what we mean by God or else is transparent escapism from God and a pose).

The following considerations are decisive:

383

(1) If philosophy wishes to be systematic, transcendental reflection (and to the extent that it does), of itself it does not wish to (and cannot) advance any claim to be the concrete, adequate, salvific interpretation of life and thus to substitute itself for concrete, historical religion (and therefore the theology of religion). Should philosophy attempt to be more than such transcendental reflection ("mediation"), in other words should it attempt to be the concrete maieutic to concrete existence, which always eludes reflex comprehension yet is inescapable and obligatory, and thus to mediate concrete religion, it would have united both theology and philosophy, reason and revelation, under the title of philosophy (or else it would be false, i.e., for the greater part secularized, theology). This would raise a problem of terminology, and analysis would show that this single global grasp of existence falls apart into the familiar elements of reason and revelation, theology and philosophy, which do not allow of being unified by reflection. But if philosophy, in accordance with its whole tradition, regards itself as transcendental reflection, then it must be said that such reflection can never wholly exhaust the concrete reality of existence, and not its unimportant remainder: historicity is less than real history, concrete love more (not less) than the formal analysis of subjectivity (the ability and the duty to love), the anguish that is experienced is more (not less) than the concept of this basic condition of human existence. But if this self-limitation of philosophy is one of its basic affirmations in that philosophy is a "first" (fundamental) science, acknowledging reality as greater than itself but no other science as the source of its principles, then philosophy—being the study of the transcendence of mind and spirit—points to God who is absolute mystery "in person", constitutes man the potential (it may be) "hearer of the word" of this living God (perhaps even under the influence of the supernatural *existential) through its *anthropology and philosophy of religion, and as *mere* reflexivity and incomplete mediation refers man, who mediates himself historically, to history itself as the locus of his self-achievement. Of itself, therefore, philosophy is not the fundamental science in the sense of claiming that it alone illuminates and masters concrete human existence. When philosophy rightly understands itself and its freedom (liberated by the secret grace of God) it is that first reflex illumination of existence which gives man the courage to take concrete reality and history seriously. But thereby philosophy opens the door to man's discovery in concrete history of the living God who has "mediated" himself to man through the Incarnation.

(2) It is true that in one sense concrete revelation and the Church

claim (necessarily, considering their nature) to represent the whole of reality (as its highest principle and its salvation). Hence the Christian, because he is already a believer and has already organized and unified his life in the light of faith, cannot hold that the Church and her doctrine are irrelevant to his philosophy and have not authority over him as a philosopher. Catholic doctrine, if not a material source of his philosophy, is at least a "negative norm". However—given the abiding diversity of philosophy and theology which theology itself demands—it does not follow by any means that a Catholic philosopher or theologian must always be able to perceive a positive synthesis between the two disciplines, that is one that is experienced by historical man. The ultimate unity of philosophy and theology may and must be left to the God of philosophy and theology, who is greater than either.

Theology (as distinct from revelation and proclamation) is a reflection about that revelation and the Church's proclamation. In this theological reflection, man (whose attitude is questioning and critical) is confronted in the whole of his understanding of his own existence (which is also, at least partly, subjected to philosophical reflection) by revelation, within the context of his own concrete situation. In this confrontation, he is able to make the content of revelation really his own, to interpret it, to purify it from misunderstandings and examine it critically. On the other hand, he is also able to question his own sphere of understanding with regard to revelation itself. This "philosophizing" in theology is necessary. His "philosophical" pre-understanding of himself (which may be either reflected or not reflected) is one of the forces that distinguish the theology of revelation as such and set theology in motion. It is possible for philosophy in this sense to set theology in motion because revelation, as a call to and a claim made on man's whole existence is always open to man's understanding of himself and because the process itself contains a self-understanding which is either philosophical, pre-philosophical or originally philosophical, but which is also present in the apparently obvious aspects of everyday life and "common sense". The theologian who believes that he does not need to "philosophize" either falls back unthinkingly on one of the existing, dominant philosophies of his time or else simply talks in an edifying way and consequently does not carry out the real task of theology. Philosophizing in theology does not imply that it is necessary to have a closed philosophical system as a prerequisite that has to be treated as valid, unchanging and irreplaceable. Philosophy should act eclectically in theology, reflecting the unsystematic pluriformity of human experience and spiritual history and at the same time being prepared to undergo change when it is used in theology.

Christian philosophy as such can only exist (if it can exist at all) if it remains, in principle and in its methods, simply philosophy and nothing else; otherwise it would cease to be philosophy as a fundamental science. Philosophy can only be the "hand-maid" of theology (in other words, a mere aspect of a higher total reality to which it is open) if it is itself free. Theologians must also take the risk of open dialogue that has not been subjected to *a priori* manipulation by man or the Church and consequently be prepared to say what they did not previously know that they were going to say. A philosopher can only be a "Christian" philosopher if he allows his Christian faith to act as a "negative" norm. It is not acting contrary to philosophy to do this. A philosophy can be called "Christian" if it has received historical initiatives from Christianity, changing it in such a way that it would not have been as it is without them. A philosophy, then, is "Christian" if the philosopher, who is himself a Christian, tries to find a convergence between his philosophy and his faith (and therefore also with his theology), without overlooking the essential difference and incommensurability that exists between the two disciplines or forgetting that the lines of philosophy and theology in this endeavour are asymptotic. The endeavour itself does not imply either a previously existing and unthreatened absence of tension between philosophy and theology or the possibility of flight into a "double" truth.

The relationship between philosophy and theology has changed in recent years. This change is not only due to the much greater number of philosophies today. It is also because philosophy is no longer the only or even the first way in which the "world" is mediated to theologians, who have to practise their theology in an encounter with that world. The more recently developed sciences (history, the natural sciences, sociology and so on) have been added to philosophy in the service of theology. These new sciences cannot, moreover, be treated merely as extensions of philosophy. Although their origin in philosophy is recognized by those who practise them, their methods, essential being and self-understanding have not been provided by philosophy. These methods and this self-understanding are, on the contrary, regarded as superfluous in the mediation of man's existence or even as a subsequent formalization of the methods used in many of the autonomous sciences. Theologians have therefore to bear in mind that the proponents of these new sciences are their partners in a dialogue with effects on both sides. The fundamental attitudes of these modern scientists in their approach to their work and the pluriformity of these

386

sciences (which cannot be adequately reduced to a synthesis) must therefore be taken as much into account by theologians as the individual methods and results of the sciences themselves. On the other hand, theologians have also to help these scientists to preserve the humanity of this situation (which is often in danger of verging on spiritual schizophrenia).

Despite the very great number of philosophies today—so great that it is no longer possible to survey them adequately—and the correspondingly great number of theologies, the following factors should be borne in mind. The one Church with the same confession of faith and the same single teaching office for all its members cannot do without a theology which is at least to some extent the same and which is required for the interpretation and preservation of that one confession of faith and in order to regulate the language used to express what is demanded by the matter itself. This scholastic theology, which is, in its terminology and other related aspects, to some degree unified and is used by the Church's teaching office (but is also always part of the stream of historical developments) also means that the Church must at the same time have its own scholastic philosophy, at least in its methods and its use of intelligible and currently presupposed concepts. It is, of course, questionable whether this "philosophy" is really a philosophy in the strict sense of the word or whether it is fundamentally only the language or sphere of understanding which are derived, it is true, from philosophy, but which form the universal consciousness of a given period of history in its existence as something that has not yet been subjected to reflection or systematized. There is a real need for an average scholastic philosophy of this kind in the theology that is required for the one confession of faith.

PHILOSOPHY OF SCIENCE

According to the view of classical philosophy science is fundamentally concerned with knowledge of immutable and eternal first principles and essential structures as well as with the propositions that can logically and with conceptual clarity be unequivocally deduced from them. This idea of science altered under the impact of the transition from the Middle Ages to modern times, a transition marked by the criticism offered by nominalism, intellectual curiosity, and a technological and scientific interest in mastering nature. Logical deduction from first principles retreated into the background in favour of experimental verification as the decisive criterion for safeguarding the validity of scientific statements. At the same time as this transformation was affecting the intellectual structure of science there arose the demand to provide an equally strong scientific foundation for scientific knowledge and for the norms that governed its procedure and contents. In this way the field of study of the philosophy of science was marked out as the consideration of the internal structure of scientific knowledge and the provision of an adequate intellectual foundation for it. Hence from the start the development of generally recognized criteria of scientific method has belonged to the primary tasks of the philosophy of science, and in this the differentiation of the different contexts of scientific knowledge—that which provides the intellectual foundation for a question, that in which the question arises, and that in which the question and its solution are applied—is to be regarded as a constitutive element, as is the distinction between formal and empirical sciences. The logic of science, the methodology of science and (in the strict sense) the philosophy of science can be seen as the basic disciplines of a general philosophy of science understood in the wider sense and operating at the metatheoretical level: in these a variety of procedures are used to test the extent to which scientific statements can be properly founded, are free from contradiction, and can be proved. Among the most frequent problems encountered in the contemporary philosophy of science three deserve mention. The first concerns the concept of experience and experiment and the intersubjective as assurance of scientific knowledge; the second concerns the relationship between theory and experiment and especially that between logic and observation; the third the dependence of science on history and language and the conventionality of knowledge. Beyond this the central factors of ideality, normativity and communicativity which are so important for the establishment of universally valid scientific criteria necessarily lead to further epistemological questions concerning, for example, the validity of logic, the intersubjective justification of analytical methods and the conditions for the possibility of rational reconstruction. The solution to the problem that is thereby posed of a philosophical explanation of a general and rational foundation of science is what all the major tendencies in the contemporary philosophy of science are concerned with: scientism (Carnap, Stegmüller), critical rationalism (Popper, Albert), constructivism (Lorenzen, Kambartel), and transcendental universal pragmatism (Apel, Habermas).

PIETISM

A movement within German Lutheranism (Spener, Francke, Bengel, Zinzendorf, the Moravian Brethren) during the seventeenth and eighteenth centuries, in reaction against dry academic theology and stereotyped institutional religion. It stresses a practical Christianity of active love, inwardness, the experience of subjective conversion and transforming grace, and a personal devotion to Jesus. The danger is that it tends to vitiate dogma and break up into sects. Though the movement came to an end with the Enlightenment and its theology, Pietism still considerably influences devout Protestants.

PIETY.

See *God, Worship of, Prayer, Act (Religious Act)*

PISTOIA

An episcopal city in Tuscany, where a small local synod was held (1786) under the Bishop of Pistoia, de' Ricci. The decrees of this synod, hostile to Scholasticism and the papacy, are marked by a Jansenistic and Gallican spirit. They advocate liturgical reform to be undertaken by local authority and attack devotion to the Sacred Heart, frequent confession, and the religious orders. Pius VI condemned these decrees in 1794 (D 2601–2700).

PLEROMA

A rare word of obscure meaning in the NT (Col 1:19; 2:9; Eph 1:23; Jn 1:16), probably borrowed, with reservations, from Gnosticism. St Paul seems to mean that Jesus Christ is not one of a number of spiritual powers in the world (as Gnosticism supposed in "polytheistic" fashion), but that in him the fullness (Gr. $\pi\lambda\dot\eta\rho\omega\mu\alpha$), the one absolute totality, of the divine salvific being is redemptively communicated to us with unequivocal reality ("bodily"), so that we have received from this "fullness" in such abundance as to be "the filled", simply speaking. Considered collectively as the Church we are fullness (received) itself, since in this way God is "all in all" (1 Cor 15:28).

PLURALISM

The inescapable fact of creaturely existence that man and his sphere of life (milieu), despite their oneness in God and their last end and despite the metaphysical structures they ultimately share, are composed of so many various elements that human experience itself springs from several original sources (whose interplay exhibits no immediate uniformity), and man is unable either in theory or in practice to reduce all this variety to a system, which alone would permit him to grasp its being and derivation and bring it under control. The transparent, concrete unity of all things exists for man as a metaphysical postulate and an eschatological hope but not as something available for his manipulation. This pluralism is the hallmark of man's creatureliness: only in God is there perfect unity; in the finite world the antagonisms within reality are invincible. Here we have the deepest roots of *tolerance rightly understood. This pluralism is found in every dimension of human existence, not least the social: it is neither possible nor desirable to set up a single concrete authority (only the uncontainable God is this) as sovereign judge of all social, even all human, conduct. Not even the Church regards herself as a single supreme authority, governing all human life as her proper domain. Since she teaches that both Church and State are sovereign powers (D 3168; Vat II: Church/world, 76), it is clear that neither is the earthly representative of God in his absolute, universal power. The foregoing does not imply a denial of the existence of a form of pluralism in the social and economic sphere that in no way serves to protect the person, but rather protects certain interest groups from changes that are in favour of universality. This kind of pluralism, which favours certain groups, was rejected by the Second Vatican Council, in its affirmation of legitimate socialization (see Church/world, 6, 25, 42, 75 etc.). Modern theology is characterized by the existence of a great pluralism of theologies, although this is not the same as a co-existence of many different *schools of theology. This new theological pluralism is characterized by the fact that the many theologies and their arguments, ways of reasoning and methods are found existing side by side in a very disparate and incommensurable way and often without the possibility of any shared horizon of understanding, within which (if it were at least tacitly recognized) a meaningful discussion could take place. In the present situation of pluralism, it is more difficult to express the legitimate and necessary postulate that there should be only one confession of faith because the Church's magisterium, which formulates that confession, is itself inevitably bound to use a certain theological language on the basis of a previous decision in favour of a partial theology. In this situation, the Church must, together with its teaching office, allow individual theologians to be much more responsible than they were in the past for conforming with the Church's confession of faith.

PNEUMA

From the Greek $\pi\nu\epsilon\hat{\upsilon}\mu\alpha$, breath, spirit. This term in OT and NT means the permanent interior principle of life in man, the gift of God and subject to his control. It gradually proves to be a very broad concept, comprehending many distinct but associated ideas—the vital principle in a living man as contrasted with a dead man; his spiritual nature, including his character (but with no suggestion of *Trichotomism); the "pneumatic" endowment he has received from God, which makes him just before God and godlike, bringing him really to life for the first time; God's own personal life of holy love (*Trinity) as the presence of the ascended Jesus Christ in the just; God's free gracious self-communication become the inmost principle of justified, sanctified man called to share in God's transfiguring glory; às the messianic, eschatologically victorious antithesis of mere flesh (*Sarx) and the *world; as the principle uniting and vivifying the Church, her sacramental life and her word. (See among many texts Lk 23:46; Acts 7:59—Lk 1:47; Jn 11:33; Gal 6:18—Rom 8:10, 13f.; 1 Thess 5:23—Rom 8:26; 1 Cor 2:10 –16; 3:16f.; 2 Cor 3:17—1 Cor 12:13.)—See also *Holy Spirit.*

PNEUMATOMACHOI

See *Macedonianism.*

POLARITY

The multifarious character of the being which God has created as one world necessarily means that the various and the contradictory are interrelated. Otherwise there would be uniformity or utter chaos and the world could not have one source and one goal. These relations which distinguish, unite, and sustain different beings (or different elements of the same being if there is a real, intrinsic *distinction among them) are chiefly, though not exclusively, to be envisaged as connecting two beings (even in the *Trinity there are two different "processions"), which suggests the image of a "polarity" (the two poles of electric current, etc.). A philosophy and theology of polarity can help avoid a monolithic or atomistic interpretation of reality and a false *dualism, since a polar relation simultaneously unites and distinguishes.—See also *Pluralism, Monism, Conflict.*

POLITICAL THEOLOGY

The critical factor in political theology (or at least in the political theology of J.B. Metz) is that it has two hermeneutical intentions. On the one hand, it attempts to correct a privatized and individualistic explanation of the Gospel and, on the other, it stresses the public and critical character and the eschatological aspect of the *kingdom of God, while at the same time taking account of practice as a means of changing society and regarding this as a criterion of the truth of faith. Political theology is therefore not in any sense a legitimation of political theory or practice, nor is it an application of theology to politics. On the one hand, it accepts the fundamental Christian axiom of the unity of the love of God and neighbourly love (1 Jn 4:20f.) in confrontation with the suppression of the potential power of this axiom to criticize society that is present in the forms of existential, ontological and personalistic theology that prevail today. On the other hand political theology also accepts the public political factor both as a framework within which biblical texts can be interpreted and as a means of discovering theological truth. At the same time, the attempt is also made in political theology to continue the process that began during the *Enlightenment of redefining the relationship between religion and society, eschatological faith and socio-political practice, by consciously investigating the theme that is included within this context of the mediation of *theory and practice. The situation of the subject struggling for political and social self-determination and the public use of his reason and not only having to justify his critical claim theoretically, but also having to follow this up in practice by the creation of appropriate social preconditions is also a paradigmatic point of departure in political theology for theological reflection and the Church's proclamation. Practical political reason and the criteria by which it makes decisions must therefore not only be a part of critical theological reflection, but also enable theologians to prevent religion from becoming absorbed into politics and therefore giving support to the political claim to total importance and to the absolute value of power, which would result in a loss of freedom. The practical political achievement of the unity of the love of God and neighbourly love is therefore the task both of the individual Christian and of the Church as an institution. The constitutive claim to public recognition of the New Testament message of the kingdom of God cannot be fulfilled, however, if Christians do not commit themselves in the political struggle to the cause of the underprivileged and the oppressed and form strategic alliances on their behalf. This does not necessarily mean that it is only on the basis of faith that a concrete political programme can be evolved or that there is a specific subject of the whole of history within the world. The socio-political function of the Gospel is, however, not exhausted either in pure motivation or in total legitimation. It is, on the contrary, a permanent source of critical innovation. The Christian expectation of the future and the Christian ethos of love both lead to the criticism of all structures that are hostile to man and the attitudes that support those structures. They also call to mind the need to revise and improve social institutions and the fact that these can be improved. By his or her dissatisfaction with what is instantly obtainable and his or her anticipation of the divine utopia of radical humanity, the Christian also exerts critical pressure on every worldly order. This pressure is able to go beyond positively hopeful promises, negative experiences of contrast and spontaneous protests to the point where it becomes a practice that can bring about change. Both protest and the concrete will to change society are nourished by confident hope in a better future. A new ethos of political action can, however, only grow from practice itself. Even the radical imperatives of the Sermon on the Mount can only appear clearly as unconditional in political conflict, since it is the aim of such conflict to allow change to begin on the basis of political action before it can be perceived as a possibility by everyone and to accept responsibility for the predictable consequences of that action. Political theology is therefore a practical form of hermeneutics of faith and an ethos of action aimed at change. As such, it cannot be confined to a single discipline, but, on the basis of its point of departure, it has to be allowed to have an effect both on all theological disciplines and on the institutional Church.

POLYGENISM

See *Monogenism.*

POLYTHEISM

The doctrine that there are many divine beings. All being has a "numinous" character and contains contradictory elements—especially those "powers" that dominate human existence—because it refers us to God, ultimately eludes human control and is irreducibly mysterious. When these powers are recognized as being of such a character and thus as "present" in human existence, we have a deeper and sounder approach to life than that of the primitive eudemonistic empiricism (*Positivism) which simply exploits physical things. This pluralistic, antithetical experience of "powers" is not polytheism (though it offers an occasion for such a degraded misinterpretation of genuine experience) where it seems possible to find God as God only by the mediation of these numinous powers because the unique, historical *revelation and self-communication of the one living God has never been known or has been withdrawn. But if God, the true source of all being and therefore of all "powers", God, exalted above the world, is identified with these powers (not out of sheer metaphysical stupidity but as a real religion, though a sinful one, inimical to God); if the genuine religious *act of absolute self-transcendence and adoration is (so far as at all possible) definitively diverted to these powers, then this is polytheism, whether the person or nation concerned tries to worship many such gods that would be God, or only one of them as "his own" (henotheism). Polytheism of this sort is not encountered in early religions. The polytheism found in the history of religions is an inextricable mixture of the attitudes analysed above. Consequently it is a constant threat to all religious life, even though it appears today in less explicit forms: a threat that ultimately can be overcome only where the concrete, historical God appears as the absolute, in the Incarnation of the Logos, not by the logical proof of metaphysical speculation which demands that there necessarily be a single supreme source of the world (see 1 Cor 8:4 –6).

POPE

The official title now given to the Bishop of Rome in his capacity as supreme head on earth of the universal Church. According to Catholic doctrine, Jesus Christ himself founded the inner circle of disciples as a college of *Apostles, one of whom he singled out: Simon, to whom he gave the name Cephas (Gr. $\pi\epsilon\tau\rho\sigma s$, $\pi\epsilon\tau\rho\alpha$, rock; Mt 16:18; see also 10:2). Jesus himself declared that Peter was to be the rock foundation of his Church; the steward or "vizier" in this Church, who holds the *keys, that is full power of *binding and loosing, whose decisions are valid before God; the shepherd of Christ's whole flock, whose duty it is to strengthen his brethren in the faith (Mt 16:16ff.; Jn 21:15f.; Lk 22:32). Since the Church is to last until the end of time, and Peter's death was foreseen (Jn 21:18f.), and since the idea of succession, even in the religious sphere, was then commonplace, it is not odd to suppose that Jesus willed the permanent government of the college of the Apostles and their successors to have a permanent personal head (see D 3056ff.). Since Peter was Bishop of Rome when he died and since in fact no one else in the Church has ever laid claim to Peter's permanent authority, the Catholic Church believes that the Bishop of Rome succeeds Peter in those functions and powers which were his as first head of the bearers of office in the Church (though not in the basic position Peter held—with the other Apostles—as a member of the first and founding generation in the Church). It will be obvious to anyone who has a really historical approach to the question (i.e., who recognizes differences as well as continuity) that the concrete implementation of the Roman Bishop's claim, as well as the reflex understanding and formulation of these papal powers, has undergone development (and fluctuations as well) in the course of time. The First Vatican Council, 1870, set forth the Catholic dogma of the papacy in the most precise and comprehensive terms, teaching that the Pope's supreme authority over the Church consists of a primacy of jurisdiction (D 3053–3058) and a supreme magisterium (D 3065). By divine institution this primacy of jurisdiction is a genuine, immediate episcopal authority over the whole Church, including the other bishops (for the defined teaching of the Church: D 3060, 3064), and therefore comprehends supreme legislative power, supreme right of supervision, and supreme judicial power in the Church. As supreme teacher of the Church the Pope possesses that *infallibility with which Christ endowed his Church (the defined teaching is to be found in D 3073f.), that is to say, the preservation by a special grace from error in matters of faith. This doctrine of the First Vatican Council, which requires the assent of faith, does not mean either that all theoretical problems concerning the Pope's relationship with the universal Church, especially with the episcopate as a whole, found a solution there (*Bishop, *Council), nor yet that the present concrete historical form of the papal primacy may not undergo further historical development. For example, the Pope's rôle as Patriarch of the Latin, specifically "Western", Church might once again be more clearly distinguished from his rôle as Primate of the whole Church (see the Decree on Eastern

Catholic Churches of Vatican II); the independent significance of the episcopate, which is of divine right (see D 3061) and cannot be abolished by the Pope, has since been more practically impressed on the consciousness of the Church (Vat. II: Church, 18–27); the fact that the Pope always acts *as* head of the *Church,* even when personally exercising his primatial power and infallible teaching authority, is likely to be more practically taken into account, as can be seen from the proceedings of Vatican II. Vatican II made an approach to a practical elucidation of the relation of the Pope to the episcopate with the thesis of the *collegiality of the bishops (Church, 22); subsequently this collegiality was expressed in various forms of committee, especially in the permanent synod of bishops. This did not alter the legal status of the Pope. On the other hand it is becoming increasingly clear that a religion which comes from God and must therefore be authoritative, a religion which is eschatological and therefore always obligatory, a religion that is catholic and must therefore be professed by a universal Church, a religion that is meant to be personal despite and even in its social structure, and in which God effects his salvation by preserving man from his own defectibility and not simply by a book or some other "objective" means—that such a religion must have a place in its constitution for the office which we call the papacy. Faith, confidence and patience—the gifts of divine grace—bear the burden involved in the human exercise of this office, until we reach God's *basileia.*

POSITIVE THEOLOGY

Theology is so called insofar as it attempts by historical methods to collect the data of revelation from its positive sources—Scripture, Tradition, declarations of the magisterium in former times—to interpret it as accurately and present it as methodically as possible. In contrast, speculative or systematic theology seeks to analyse this "material" as systematically as possible (that is, as an intelligible whole, setting the particular data in right relation to each other and to man's whole mental and spiritual world), to unify, to understand and to absorb it. The two tasks can only be accomplished by mutual cooperation, because all theology, being the theology of revelation, is historical and empirical, and any understanding of what is thus perceived (and therefore as such is always grasped to some extent) rests on the one ground of the mind and tends of itself to become one.

POSITIVISM

The sceptical confinement of certain and "scientific" human knowledge to the realm of direct experience and its classifications, which latter are justified only by their applicability (predictability) to immediate (sense) experience. The positivist attitude is very widespread in our day. It is nourished by the impression that the various religions, metaphysical, and ethical systems can never be reconciled and that the "exact" sciences can give us "certainty" when they confine themselves to what can be experimentally verified. But positivism overlooks the fact that it sets itself up as a theory and a system (as does all scepticism); that it is an impractical guide for concrete human life because it cannot provide any real basis for moral obligation; that a person of penetration will discover behind all the variety of opinions and terminology, in their changing historical garb, a broad unity of basic human convictions which are thoroughly metaphysical and religious; that a transcendental type of experience exists which natural science in fact presupposes (though unawares) and which logic, ontology and ethics elaborate in such a way as to engender certainty of a different kind from that of natural science but no less fundamental (*Transcendence). Obviously positivism as a system of philosophy (as distinct from the methods of experimental science as such) is incompatible with Christianity.

POSSESSION

It is a truth of faith that preter-human, evil *principalities and powers (*Devils) exist and are operative in the world (D 800, 1668, 1694, 1696). Scripture itself teaches (for instance Lk 13:16; 1 Thess 2:18; Heb 2:14) that we should not take the influence of these powers to be at work only where reason establishes by empirical methods that "extraordinary" phenomena are present in addition to, and as distinct from, normal (tangible and controllable) phenomena. Rather there underlies the "normal" chain of events in nature and history, quite explicable in "natural" terms, a supernatural dynamism of diabolic powers bent on evil. Hence *sickness, *death, and everything in human life that tends to self-destruction, invariably can and must be regarded as an expression of the influence of diabolic powers, even though the proximate causes of these things are natural and can and should be combatted by natural means. Hence, from the religious point of view, it is neither possible nor particularly desirable to draw

397

POSSESSION

a *sharp* distinction between possession and natural sickness, especially as the latter may be a symptom as well as an occasion of possession. Therefore there is no radical dilemma between combatting the phenomenon by exorcism (a solemn prayer to God in the name and by the commission of Christ and the Church for his protection against malign powers) and doing so by medicine, especially as every Christian should *pray* for health even in the most "natural" sickness. Even where a phenomenon is to be deemed possession in the stricter sense, it will be the manifestation of that fundamental diabolical dominion that becomes tangible for us only through the circumstances "permitted" precisely in this case; but which also merely reveals what is always present in the world and therefore does not eliminate natural causes but uses them for its own purposes. To distinguish adequately between diabolical influence on the one hand and the intellectual and imaginative world of a person or a period, dispositions, possible illnesses, even parapsychological faculties on the other, is not possible.

POSSIBLES

A being is possible primarily in that it does exist but is not eternal and necessary (*Contingency). Thus it is recognized as something that can exist, is possible, whose existence is intrinsically thinkable (its characteristics are compatible) and has an external cause (ultimately God). By experiencing our own freedom to choose among several alternatives and by having knowledge of God's, we perceive that there must be possible things that have not been realized, though we are often unable to say whether something intrinsically thinkable could find an actual place in the whole of reality (which our vision cannot embrace) without dissolving "this" world. The doctrine of possibles is theologically important as the background to the freedom of God and creatures, to the prayer of petition and to active human responsibility. Reality is set in the wider framework of the possible, which both limits it and frees it for greater things.

POSTULATES, THEOLOGICAL

This name can be given to a method of theological investigation whereby a truth that is not evident of itself or revealed can be inferred with more or less certainty from the fact that another known truth (for example, the wisdom or justice of God, the coherence of being,

398

the dignity of a person, etc.) seems to require its existence. This method must be used with great reserve in view of God's freedom, but should not be rejected out of hand (*Analogia fidei), because the plural world of the one God is genuinely and recognizably connected and because this method is often the only concrete manner in which a truth we already possess legitimately reveals the components already grasped globally.

POTENCY

From the Latin *potentia,* possibility, capacity. It is the antonym of *act. The reality which this term designates is originally encountered in the exercise of human freedom and in the experience of alteration in some part of the human environment: the thing ("subject") remains itself, yet becomes something it was not before. This capacity to remain the same or become other through the possession of an adventitious reality (determination, act), constitutes the (active or passive) potentiality of a subject. Thus potency denotes not an abstract possibility (a mere *ens rationis)* but the disposition of a real entity to be further determined and perfected by an accession of being that is distinct from it and yet possessed as its own, so that the two (the subject as potency—the determination as act) are really one (the determined subject as actuated potency) without being absolutely identical. A grasp of this metaphysical, dialectical structure of finite being is essential if one is to understand what is involved in creatureliness and finitude, the possibility (basic to our relationship with God) of a thing truly becoming something else which it was not before and need not be *(*potentia obedientialis)*—that is to say that God can endow man with his grace in such a way that it can really be predicated of man and yet remain a gift, so that man praises the giver and remains dependent upon him.

POTENTIA OBEDIENTIALIS

The intrinsic being of man is called an "obediential potency" for super-natural grace, insofar as, in virtue of his spiritual *transcendence to all being, man is open to God's self-communication, which can only be imparted to a creature whose nature does not confine it to a particular sphere of existence. This *potency (receptivity) is called "obediential" because what it really is would still be meaningful if God did not communicate himself; so that this communication remains free notwithstanding the potency—that is, remains grace. The potency has no claims to advance before God but remains obedient to his good pleasure. Human nature is an obediential potency for the radical self-expression of God, which is actualized in Jesus Christ.

POVERTY

In the OT synonymous with misery, exploitation, outlawry, an evil coming not from God but from the rich and powerful, partly a punishment for sin. After the final suppression of Israel "poor" becomes a religious term meaning "humble", "pious". In later Judaism the poor are the true Israel. Jesus, poor himself, denounces his woes upon the rich and satisfied (Lk 6:24) and declares the poor in spirit blessed (Mt 5:3). Present exegesis takes this to mean the really poor and afflicted, not the submissive, the beggars before God, the spiritless, the self-sacrificing. Jesus requires his own to renounce property (Mt 8:20), not for an ethical motive but for the sake of the freedom to follow him that is thus to be won (and insofar as it is), and on account of the equality of Christians and the unity necessary in his community (see the hostility towards the rich in the NT, for example in St James, community of goods in the primitive Church).

It remains the Christian's moral duty to combat involuntary poverty whilst at the same time using all means to overcome pauperism in society, though Jesus has warned him that it will never be possible to abolish poverty altogether (Mt 26:11), which however can never be interpreted as a requirement that impoverishment and social inequality are to be borne in resignation. Voluntary poverty is intended to be a form of Christian *asceticism and, like all obedience to the *evangelical counsels, a sign of the Church's belief that the last days have begun, and to point to the ground of Christian hope. Its actual practice becomes very difficult in the pluralistic world of today. Nevertheless, the Church follows Christ in the task of being, not a rich Church for the poor, but a poor Church together with the poor.—As a religious concept, poverty also remains significant in the sense of avoidance of self-justification, acceptance of divine *grace with empty hands, and generous bestowal of love.

POWER

The desire to enforce one's own will, to further one's own interests, to impose one's own convictions and to extend the scope of one's own freedom (*violence), often in opposition to (legitimate) counter-attempts on the part of others, is both a fundamental anthropological attribute of man (Hobbes and Nietzsche) and one of the distinctive characteristics of the structure of the State. In both cases, if power is to be properly defined, it is important to complete the psychological and social factors involved by adding the material and ideal potentials of power. These include natural resources, capital, industrial and military capacity, political and moral influence, information, bureaucracy, propaganda (recruitment) and authority. If the opportunities to make the will to power effective are regulated and institutionalized by means of a system of power-structures, either on the basis of delegation and recognition or on that of voluntary or enforced obedience or manipulation or open oppression, then a situation of rule is created. In all the social systems that have ever existed in history, the rulers have always been privileged if they have used the available potential of power to maintain the existing structures of mastery and control and have been able to prevent a new distribution of power. The power structures themselves to a very great extent define the possible ways in which power can be exercised (for example, by a hierarchical concentration of power, a democratic distribution of power or joint decision making on the part of all concerned). Attempts have been made since the beginning of the modern era to evolve, in a political theory based on the interests of those who are ruled, suggestions for the control, limitation and even abolition of power and to make this theory a reality in a practice that will change society and political structures (such as the division of powers, respect for human rights, parliamentary government and *democratization).

Moving beyond these recognized political motives, it is also quite legitimate to criticize from the theological point of view any attempt to give substance to power, rule, domination or any excessive concentration of power at all by making use of the liberating message and practice of Jesus Christ. The power and rule (or "kingdom") of God proclaimed in Jesus' message is revealed by his redeeming words and actions giving new life, through the fullness of divine power, to those who are abandoned and oppressed. The power of God is therefore irreconcilably opposed to any form of divisive self-assertion or quest for power on the part of any individual or group and any religious or

POWERS

metaphysical overemphasis or repression of political powers, power-structures or ideologies.

The final consequence of Jesus' message of the reconciliatory rule or kingdom of God was his acceptance of death on the cross. His suffering was an admonitory and liberating sign of God's solidarity with the impotence and powerlessness of the crucified and abandoned just man. It therefore became the historical foundation of the gospel with its power to create salvation. Whenever the Church shares in the power of the state, it is always in danger of being unfaithful to the original intention.

POWERS

The physical and juridical capacity, permanent or temporary, to act in such a way that others must accept one's acts as imposing a moral obligation on them. Such powers may derive from objective relationships (natural law) (that is, the right of parents to bring up their children), or from the free act of a third party who is entitled to confer them (as when judicial authority is conferred). In accordance with the will of Jesus and the Spirit of God, powers in the Church are partly sacramental (*Sacrament) and partly "dominative" (power to teach and govern). Accordingly they are transmitted either by ordination (Holy *orders) or by a non-sacramental juridical act of the ecclesiastical superior. These two powers are ordered to each other but not identical and so need not always be united in the same person (*Church authority).—See also *Apostolic Succession, Power of the Keys, Binding and Loosing, Office, Recognition of Ministries.*

PRAEAMBULA FIDEI

A Latin phrase meaning "the preliminaries or presuppositions of faith". God's verbal revelation in history, occurring as it does at a particular place and time (*Prophets, *Jesus Christ), is made to a spiritual person with particular experiences and opinions and a particular mentality, addressing his responsibility and free judgment. It must therefore be of such a nature as to win a hearing of such a person and to prove itself God's word to him. Any word spoken by one person to another that conveys a truth of any weight possesses a certain power to make itself understood and accepted; and this is especially true of the *word of God, which effects its own acceptance by the manner of its utterance, its content, and above all by the interior grace which always and necessarily accompanies it and which is part of *revelation as such. For the self-communication that God first willed establishes in the "natural" creation and government of the world its own precondition. Now if the grace in and through which the word is revealed itself always produces the subject who is "connaturally" to hear, understand and accept the word (so that God causes himself to be heard in *his* word as such which transcends every dimension of nature), then this word must affect every (spiritual) human dimension, must remain a word of judgment even where it is rejected, must claim man's whole spiritual responsibility, must not be left outside the sphere of concrete, earthly human experience (for in that case it could all too easily and justifiably be surmised that the word is only an illusory ideology). God's word must also situate man in the dimension of his metaphysical and historical experience, where he is by nature and from which there is no escape for him. Knowledge of the *praeambula fidei*—that knowledge which (logically, if not temporally) "precedes" the assent of faith (D 2755, 2813, 3009, 3013f., 3537–3542)—is provided by our reflex knowledge ("natural" in the sense that it does not presuppose belief in the existence of a particular divine revelation) of the experiences (of both kinds) which make the fact of Christian revelation logically and morally credible (in fact "certain") for free, responsible, spiritual man, without forcing or attempting to force his assent. These include (concretely for Christians who face the direct challenge of Christ's Gospel in their concrete lives): the natural knowledge, derived from the created world (including the world of personal spirits), of God as the personal mystery to whose unfettered sway man (as a metaphysical and historical being) must be open; rational, historical knowledge of the existence of Christ and of the essential content of his Gospel and personal testimony; the knowledge that the Kingdom of God is attainable by anticipatory fulfilment of his promises; the historically credible witness to the *resurrection of Jesus as the demonstration of the entry of Jesus into his definitive authenticity. All this can be demonstrated with the same rational, historical (analytical) certainty which can and must suffice every human being for a thousand important decisions affecting his life, especially when it is clear that a contrary decision would have no better logical and moral justification either as to its content (of gloomy scepticism) or its "basis" (which ultimately reduces itself to the fact that the first decision cannot be extorted). A further element of the *praeambula fidei* is the fact that the person concerned is inwardly attuned to the message he hears (*Potentia obedientialis, *Revelation): he knows that his life has a "meaning" (though only spiritual valour may be able to defend it against a weary scepticism), his existence opens upon a horizon of meaning (though the meaning seems to be infinite *mystery, the mystery of utterly intimate *love). This interior experience, which integrates the discrete plurality of the individual external elements (somewhat as in infinitesimal calculus), can then no longer be clearly distinguished from the interior light of the grace of faith, which as such indeed cannot be objectified in reflection but exists, integrates and sustains existential decision and the courage to take it, against the dissolvent forces of rationalistic scepticism, and imparts an inner connaturality with the object of faith.

PRAYER

The express and positive realization of human involvement with the personal saving God. It fulfils the very essence of the religious *act: man's self-entrustment to the transcendence of his own nature, and humble, receptive, respectful and responsive acceptance of the total condition produced by the relevance to and effect upon human existence of the mystery of God as a person. Prayer is a basic function of the Church, who is the successor of the OT man of prayer (she prays his psalms, without confusing the historical and redemptive situations underlying them with her own) and at the same time accepts her specifically NT position with regard to salvation. The Church always distinguishes this prayer of hers from the unique prayer of Jesus (so far as this was the expression and outflow of his unique self-consciousness), although she received the basic form and theme of her prayer from the lips of Jesus himself: the *Our Father* (*Fatherhood of God). From the earliest times the Church has prayed both to the Father and to the Mediator of salvation, Jesus Christ himself. The fundamental theme or mood of prayer, which follows from its theological nature and for which the Church very early showed a preference, is thanksgiving; it comes to the fore in the eucharistic prayers (*Eucharist) and ultimately underlies the doxologies (prayer of praise) as well. But her prayer of petition is always characterized by her prior acceptance of God's definitive assurance about the end (consummation) of the world and the final answer to all human prayer that occurs in it (Mt 7:7–11 and parallel passages; Jn 16:23f.; 15:7, 16). The Church's developed doctrine recognizes two types of prayer, one liturgical and public and one "private"; both are declared to be necessary (*Meditation). Insofar as prayer is the individual's acceptance of God's will to love and save him it is also an act of grace; but to this extent it is always "in Christ and the Church" (Eph 3:21) and always bears an ecclesial character. Though this character may not be adverted to as such it is nevertheless efficacious precisely when one prays for the forgiveness of sins, for the dead, for personal salvation, and to the saints (*Communion of saints). Despite the fact that one can and must pray for oneself and one's own salvation with a concern that God wills and that acknowledges one's own creaturely indigence, prayer as exercise of the theological virtues has an intentionality which issues in God-in-himself and for his own sake. Similarly prayer is characterized by *anthropocentrism rightly understood (because of its self-forgetfulness, which in the last analysis does not seek to draw attention to itself); but this means that it is objectively meritorious, as a "good work" (*Works), as a salutary act and as growth in grace, though this merit cannot be the primary and comprehensive motive for prayer. Prayer also has the effect of *satisfaction. Being a request of man for God, inspired by God's own loving will and loving act, prayer is absolutely certain to be heard, because whatever it seeks apart from God it wants only if this is consistent—by the disposition of God which has been unconditionally accepted—with the fundamental desire for God. Thus genuine prayer leaves the manner in which it is to be answered to God's discretion. All prayer is made "in Jesus Christ's name" so long as it is, consciously or not, prayer in the grace of Jesus Christ for the salvation that has become manifest and permanent in Jesus Christ.

PRAYER OF PETITION

This, with prayer of praise and prayer of thanksgiving, is one of the three principal types of *prayer. In prayer man lays bare to God his (or the Church its) own need of salvation and assistance, acknowledging that the exigencies of concrete earthly existence are in God's hands, and representing them to God without allowing human petition to lead to mere passivity. This affirmation expresses the partnership that God himself has established with man by *grace and always appeals to the *mercy of God, who has provided for us before we ask him (Mt 6:25–33). Trust in God's unremitting care for us closely links prayer of petition with the prayer of thanksgiving, as happened very early with the introduction into the *Eucharist (prayer of thanksgiving) of the primal prayer of petition, "Lord, have mercy on us". Prayer of petition raises the theological question whether and how

God can be "moved" from without. Closer analysis shows this question to be wrongly put, as it confuses God's *eternity, in which all man's activity and thought, and therefore also his prayer, is absolutely present, with man's temporality.

PREACHING

In the broad sense, preaching is the proclamation of God's word (see *Kerygma)* by those whom the Church has commissioned in Christ's name. It is not mere instruction about facts which in principle can be learnt without its help, nor is it simply instruction in moral theory, but the proclamation of God's eternal plan for human salvation (*Gospel)—hidden in itself—carried into effect when God attaches an efficacious (eschatologically victorious) grace to the word that is preached, and this grace, as the divine self-communication, secures its own acceptance by human freedom. Even when what is preached is human vanity (in the scriptural sense), God in the *Church still offers men both the proclamation of the truth and the gift of hearing it in grace. To this extent preaching is intrinsically connected with the *word of God (with which it must not be simply equated) which the Church addresses to the individual, in his particular religious situation, through the *sacraments, and with the proclamation of God's consummate saving act (of Christ's cross) which is efficaciously made present in the Eucharist. Thus the service of God's word and the celebration of the Eucharist are very closely linked, and preaching (explicitly or implicity, as a remote or a proximate preparation) demonstrates the way to the intelligent acceptance, in faith, of the efficacious word in Mass and sacraments—"mystagogical" preaching, in which of course doctrine has a vitally important rôle to play. These aims of preaching are not attained when it is dominated by a monological structure of communication. The remembrance of God's word and the process of learning are essentially *common* actions of *all* participants.

PRE-ADAMITES

See *Monogenism.*

PREDEFINITION

*Predestination in relation to the individual free act of a creature. God can and must will the positive, good, free acts of a creature and whatever there is of being and goodness in evil acts if they are to exist, because he is the necessary source of all reality, and this will is their cause, not their consequence. To this extent such acts are predestined or predefined (as free, of course). This predefinition is brought about by efficacious graces. The various *systems of grace variously explain how these graces cause the freedom of the salutary acts they make possible instead of destroying it. Predefinition has a part to play in other domains of theology, where the efficacious execution of God's plan must co-exist with the freedom of his creatures: in the case of *providence, *inspiration, the preservation of the Church and her *magisterium from error, the eschatologically indestructible *holiness of the Church, those acts of individual human beings which are important in saving history (Mary, etc.).

PREDESTINATION

The eternal decree of God's will touching the supernatural final goal of spiritual creatures, interpreted to mean either that *reprobation is a kind of predestination along with predestination to glory, or that predestination to glory is the antithesis of reprobation. God, the absolute cause who gives everything its reality by his own free act, does not merely observe the course the world takes but must will it if it is to be, and nothing determines this will of his but his own wise, benignant freedom (which is necessarily inappellable and incomprehensible). Consequently there is a predestination to glory for those human beings who attain blessedness (D 1540, 1565, 1567; Rom 8:29f.). The sole cause of predestination so far as it concerns the totality of human salvation (resulting from morally good decision which God makes possible by his efficacious grace, and the glory ensuing) is God's free love. But God's love as such desires the glory of man by way of his moral decision. So far as it concerns him as an individual, predestination is unknown to man in his pilgrim state in this world (*Certainty of salvation) but is the object of his firm hope and prayer. Because God wills both the free act and its freedom, this predestination does not destroy the freedom of God's creature, his responsibility and his dialogic partnership with God, but causes it. When predestination is conceived as destroying man's freedom to work out his salvation, we have heretical Predestinationism (D 596, 621ff., 625, 1556, 1567). There is no positive, active predestination to sin—a thing that would be repugnant to God's sanctity and his universal *salvific will, and unnecessary since the sinfulness of the sinful act is a privation of being and therefore requires no divine causality. God does not will sin even though he foresees it, permits it, and positively wills its punishment as a consequence of the sin, not as the cause of his decision to permit the sin (D 596, 621, 628f.). The mystery of the relation between God's omnipotence (which implies predestination) and the freedom of man is only the continuation (on the plane of conduct) of the mystery of the co-existence of God's infinite being with finite being, which truly exists, that is, is different from God, and for this very reason is constantly sustained in being by God.

PREDETERMINATION

Physical predetermination (in the Thomist *system of grace, in *Banezianism) is God's free decision to grant the *divine concourse that is necessary to every human act, a "physical premotion" of such a character that it infallibly determines the quality of the human act before the act is done or foreseen by the agent, so that God by decreeing this premotion knows by the latter's intrinsic nature what man will freely do (for the contrary position, see *Scientia media*). Thomists hold that the predetermination of the human act does not destroy its freedom but gives the act its freedom together with the rest of its being. In their view "physical premotion" to a supernatural salutary act constitutes efficacious grace as contrasted with grace that is merely sufficient. A predetermination which destroyed the freedom of either the salutary or the sinful act would be heretical (D 1525, 1554ff., 2002, 3010).

PRE-EXISTENCE OF CHRIST

Because the eternal divine Logos, begotten by the Father from all eternity, has become Man, the *Person* (traditionally conceived thus) who becomes man as Jesus Christ did not originate with the temporal beginning of Christ's human nature (body and soul), but was always in existence beforehand. Though NT Christology normally begins with the experience of the concrete Man Jesus, it is fully aware of the pre-existence of Christ (Phil 2:6; Jn 1:1–18; 17:5, etc.). If Jesus Christ is God's absolute eschatological revelation and promise of himself, and in keeping with these their freely-assumed expression in the form of a creature, something brought about by the promise of formal *predefinition, and only in this way can be the absolute achievement of salvation, then the one making the promise and revealing himself, in other words God, is "pre-existent" and radically different from what is the case if God exists before some other (ephemeral) creature who is not his revelation of himself. As far as exegesis is concerned it is possible (in defence against the obvious suspicion of mythology) to investigate without bias whether what Jesus himself means by Son of the Father is simply identical with the God revealing himself in time and thus also revealing himself as pre-existent, or whether it also includes a creaturely aspect that is not identical with this God and thus is not yet "pre-existent". Even this second possibility does not exclude the pre-existence of this self-revealing divine subject who in the classical terminology is called (besides the Logos) the "Son".—See also *Hypostatic union, Jesus Christ, Pre-existentianism.*

PRE-EXISTENTIANISM

The doctrine that human souls exist before their bodily existence, either having been created simultaneously at the beginning with a view to the latter or having attained the liberated existence of pure spirits, so that bodily life is a consequence of sin in one's pre-corporeal life, the body being a manifestation of sin that coarsens the spirit (*Origenism, *Priscillianism). This doctrine, which denies the unity of man, the goodness of the material world God has created, and the decisive importance of the one life man has, which must be definitively brought to achievement by the exercise of freedom, the Church has always condemned as heretical (D 403, 456, 1440f.). In effect this also condemns the Hindu, Orphic and Theosophical "transmigration of souls", the doctrine that the same spiritual subject lives many bodily lives. For the Church's positive teaching, see *Creationism.*

PRESCRIPTION, ARGUMENT BY

Proof from "immemorial practice". A theological procedure based on a principle of law, already used by Tertullian (early third century). We might express it as follows: If the Church as a whole (with moral unanimity) at any point in time knows that she is in peaceful possession of a proposition (a belief) as a truth of faith divinely revealed, this belief cannot be false—because the *Church is preserved by the Holy Ghost from abandoning genuine revelation—but must date back to Apostolic tradition and therefore to the revelation of Christ, even if the precise manner of its historical transmission or its derivation from other truths is obscure to the theologians (*Development of dogma). The real problem here is to see how this procedure, which is formally sound, can explain the transition from a truth which was not clearly held to be revealed to a truth which is recognized with certainty as revealed and definable.

PRESENCE

The phenomenon of presence primarily occurs in our original, ultimately irreducible, sensible experience of spatio-temporally separate realities, which while remaining plural are experienced under a certain aspect as a unity. The various possibilities of such unity in their turn form the basis of the various types of presence worked out in theology: (1) The presence, through a transcendental unity, of the principle in that of which it is the principle, as illustrated by the mutual presence of the divine Persons within the absolute God (*Perichoresis); God's presence in the created, contingent world as its efficient cause (God's omnipresence); and the presence of the absolute *principle (God) in man by self-communication (*Grace, *Indwelling of God). (2) Presence based on a unity conceivable in categorical terms, as found between persons united by knowledge and love (*Communication, *Representation, etc.). (3) The presence, based on the unity of space, of entities which are "in space". (4) The sacramental presence, for example, of the Body of Christ in the *Eucharist, where the real presence of Christ's pneumatic corporality, displayed by the eucharistic elements, must nevertheless not be identified with the localized presence of natural bodies in space.

PRESUMPTION

In a sense like that it has in law, presumption has a certain significance for theology because it is indispensable as a kind of inductive proof for human knowledge in general. Many rules could be laid down to govern theological presumption: the correctness of a doctrinal decision by the magisterium which is not a definition must be presumed until the contrary be proved (D 2879f., 3045, 3884f.); it cannot be presumed, but must be proved, that a doctrine is defined (CIC, can. 1323 § 3); where a law is not certain, the presumption is in favour of freedom (*Moral systems); the presumption favours sense over nonsense, etc.

PRIESTHOOD

Every person who is justified and sanctified by God's grace is a priest (D 3849ff.; Constitution *de Ecclesia* of Vatican II, ch. 2), shares in the royal priesthood of all believers in Jesus Christ (1 Pet 2:9), outside whom there is no priesthood and in whom every man is a priest, insofar as the priest (Gr. $\pi\rho\epsilon\sigma\beta\upsilon\tau\epsilon\rho os$, "elder", an ancient term for a sacral office) is one who may enter the presence of God; speak directly to him; offering himself and his existence in sacrifice to God's incomprehensible dominion; invoke Jesus' unique sacrifice in his life and on the cross as his own. But by the will of God (because of the historicity of the *Incarnation, cross and *resurrection of Christ as the source of this priestly grace) the community of the faithful, invested with this universal priesthood of all (Vat. II; Lit., 14, 48; Church, 9f., 26, 34; Priests, 2), are historically and socially tangible in the preaching of the *word and the *sacraments, and therefore by the will of Jesus their founder form a society with a juridical structure, so that visible unity and order may also be preserved, in truth and worship, love and action, in this holy congregation. We speak of a priestly office and call its authority the "power of order" (as contrasted with the "power of jurisdiction" by which the Church is externally governed). When it came to defining the nature of the ministerial priesthood, which is distinct from the universal priesthood of all the faithful in essence and not just in degree (Church, 10), the Second Vatican Council did indeed try to avoid starting from the power of orders and the full authority over the sacraments. It tried to make its starting-point the ministry of the *word (Min. Pr., 4 and elsewhere; cf. also Church, 25 on bishops) so as to be able to say: the priest is the person who, in relation to a community, proclaims the word of God on behalf of the Church as a whole and thus officially, in such a way that what sacramentally is the highest degree of intensity of this word is entrusted to him. Beyond this the Council tried to deepen the theological foundations of the ministerial priesthood through the idea of special participation in Jesus Christ's triple ministry of prophet, priest and king (Church, 28; Min. Pr., 1 and elsewhere). But since all members

411

of the Church of Jesus share this participation and are at least in principle competent to undertake the ministry of the word and to lead a local community, the authority imparted by ordination *(potestas ordinis)* emerges as what is specific to the ministerial priesthood. There are three principal degrees of participation in this power of the priestly office (for the defined teaching of the Church, see D 1776; *Order). Vatican II modified the tendency to think hierarchically in terms of rank by stressing the unity of the presbyterium composed of bishop and priests (Church, 28). Though the relation between them varies, the power of order and that of jurisdiction form one entity—a commission to serve the Church and the royal priesthood of all Christians. The authority inherent in this commission, especially as relating to Mass, confession and the other sacraments, is conferred through ordination or consecration (as sacramental apostolic *succession) by Jesus Christ, not by the faithful as such (D 1773); but Jesus Christ confers it because he wills the *Church* (that is, the interior holiness and external social unity of all the justified) to exist, and therefore it is to be used "unto edification" (1 Cor 14:3), in the service of the whole Church. The position of Church officials (if we may be pardoned the comparison) is like that of officials in a club of professional chess-players: their functions cannot be discharged by individual players. But their functions have only one ultimate purpose—that excellent chess shall be played. This purpose accounts for the activities of the club and gives them meaning. Similarly it is the function of the priestly office to serve the universal priesthood of those who believe and love, are marked by God's Spirit and redeemed, who unconditionally in a unity of love of God and neighbour surrender themselves to God in Jesus Christ—which in the last analysis is the higher good. But even in its possessor, official priesthood refers back to faith, grace and love. For if it is to be rightly used it requires the Spirit who is poured forth upon all members of the Church. Since the official priest must not only confess Christ in the "place" assigned to him by his natural life (his birth, family, country, time, profession or trade), as the *layman does in the normal way, but shares in the Church's official, specifically missionary duty (Mt 28:19f.) to master the new existential situations in which Christianity is not present, he needs his own specific spirit of responsibility, courage, disinterested service and self-sacrifice for others, and an imaginative sympathy for the circumstances and mentality of others.

PRIMACY

See *Pope, Bishop.*

PRIMITIVE CHURCH

The expressions "Apostolic Church", "primitive Christianity", not merely refer to the first period, in a temporal sense, of the history of the Church and Christianity—that is, the period from Pentecost to approximately the end of the first Christian century—but characterize this era theologically as unique and normative for the Church and her teaching in all succeeding times (*Development of dogma). This *Church of the beginning is an eye-witness of Christ's *resurrection, the eschatologically decisive religious event; those who bear her authority, the *Apostles, are the recipients of the definitive Christian *revelation, they do not merely transmit it; during this time *Holy Scripture takes shape as the permanent norm of the magisterium. And therefore this Church is the permanent *beginning, in the context of which occurs all the subsequent history of the Church and the faith— genuine history, not mere reiteration of the beginning. Even though the soundness of the Church's further development is ultimately guaranteed by the assistance of the Spirit, this does not dispense the Church from constantly having to establish her identity, through continuity of development in doctrine, law and liturgy, by recourse to the primitive Church and with all respectful acknowledgment of the rule of the Spirit.—See also *Canon.*

PRIMITIVE REVELATION

At least that minimum of divine *revelation which is involved in offering men elevating and illuminating supernatural grace must be presumed to have existed "from the beginning" since God's universal *salvific will calls all men to the supernatural goal which consists in the possession of God through his gracious self-communication. This does not necessarily mean, of course, that this revealed, supernatural horizon of man's moral and spiritual life and activity must always have been perceived in reflex and thematic fashion. Christian tradition assumes that the first human beings were acquainted with a fairly clear and reflex divine revelation of the sort that is found in official and public *saving history. Since we are dealing here with enormous

413

lengths of time and the most difficult and primitive of human relations, it is impossible to tell whether or to what extent the content of such a revelation was handed down to the first men. In any case it is certainly possible that such knowledge as can always be gathered anew—in however simple a form—from human experience and ontological reflection in the light of grace (man's orientation to the mystery of God, his creatureliness, the fact that God wills mankind to be male and female, guilt as a general *existential of all men from the beginning, the unity of mankind through its common origin and common goal, hope of a redemption), has always existed in some form or other (are primitive revelation in this sense), and constantly reappears, under the impulsion of grace, in the general history of revelation and salvation, so that here too what is ever new is also ever ancient.

PRIMORDIAL SACRAMENT

The distinctive character of the Christian *sacraments (unlike the rites of pre-Christian times that promised salvation) is dependent upon the *hypostatic union of the *Logos with a human *nature and (derivatively) upon the nature of the *Church. In Jesus Christ and the Church God has definitively and victoriously pledged himself to the world to be its salvation (not its Judge). The Church's historical tangibility, which is different from eschatologically triumphant saving grace yet inseparable from it, bears the same relation to this grace (as the grace of the world as a whole) as does the sacramental sign to the sacramental grace that is given to the individual and is based on the former. Hence Jesus Christ and, by derivation from him, the Church are rightly known as the primordial sacrament (*Opus operatum). Vatican II adopted this theological teaching in so far as it called the Church the visible sacrament of salvific unity (of all humanity, from God and mankind: Church, 9 and *passim.*

PRINCIPALITIES AND POWERS

In the NT, especially in St Paul, principalities and powers are dominant forces of evil (*Devils) insofar as they still try to exercise power in the present *aeon. Since the NT freely accepts the experiences of mankind and transmits them in purified form, we may take it that these principalities and powers are personal evil in the world as this is manifested, in the various spheres and dimensions of human life, in self-will which leads to *sin and *death (see especially Ephesians and Colossians; Rom 8:38; 1 Cor 15:23–26). These principalities and powers have been vanquished in the cross and resurrection of Jesus Christ, but their impotence has not yet been laid bare; they still saturate the atmosphere of "this world", so that it exposes Christians to *temptation and leads to their *persecution. From the dogmatic point of view, these effects are "permitted" by divine providence.

PRINCIPLE

According to St Thomas "everything from which anything proceeds in any manner" is a principle (Lat. *principium*). Aristotelian-Thomistic philosophy distinguishes between principles of knowledge and principles of being. Logical judgments are based on first (or ultimate) principles which need not be proved because they are immediately evident (for example the principle of contradiction). Where these evident principles are concerned the distinction between logic and *ontology disappears: they are already principles of being. Scholastic philosophy identifies them with causes: the first (ultimate) principles of being *(principium quo)* constitute an entity; they are the four causes: (1) *form *(causa formalis)* and (2) *matter *(causa materialis),* which are related to each other as *act (reality) and *potency (possibility), *essence and *existence, (3) *causality *(causa efficiens)* and (4) finality *(causa finalis, * purpose).* But the first principles can be reduced to one principle corresponding to the axiom of sufficient reason, that whatever exists must have a cause for being and not not-being (Nicholas of Cusa). This first principle is the *being to which man's *transcendence refers him in all his cognition as to incomprehensible *mystery, and which at the same time is also the principle of the reality of every entity, called in theology *ipsum esse subsistens,* "pure act", *God, in whose perspective alone *man can be understood.

PRISCILLIANISM

A Spanish sect (named after Priscillian, executed A.D. 385). A version of Gnosticism, it mingled *dualism, *modalism, and fatalism (see D 188–208, 451– 464). It died out towards the end of the sixth century.

PRIVATE REVELATION

Genuine (verbal) *revelation made to an individual which does not directly require the assent of faith from all and is not committed to the Church by God to be preserved and expounded. Mystical revelations of this kind for the guidance and salvation of the individual are perfectly possible (*Existential ethics); the individual may even have a duty to give them the assent of faith. In order to be considered genuine they must be consistent with ecclesial revelation (general revelation in Jesus Christ). Even a genuine revelation, occurring in the depths of the soul, may be distorted or misinterpreted by its recipient; religious enthusiasts and sectaries often falsely represent subjective fantasies or sudden manifestations of the subconscious as private revelations. Genuine private revelations may also give an individual a "prophetic" mission to the Church, though this must not imply any right to improve or even to complete Jesus Christ's definitive revelation; such revelations only provide the impetus for the action which the Church should take according to changing circumstances, and always in fidelity to the one unchanging Gospel.

PROBABILISM

See *Moral Systems.*

PROCESSIONS IN GOD

See *Trinity.*

PROOF OF THE EXISTENCE OF GOD

This term means systematic thought devoted to that affirmation of what we call "God" which is necessarily involved in every spiritual human act (of judgment or free decision). Its final purpose is not to convey knowledge by presenting man from without with an object previously quite unknown and therefore of no interest to him, but rather to convey the reflex consciousness that always and everywhere in his spiritual existence man has dealings with God—whether he call him "God" or something else, whether he reflects on the fact or not, whether he is willing to admit and freely affirm the fact or not. Hence

416

the peculiar nature, the obviousness and the difficulty of the proof of the existence of God: it is aimed at the whole man, at both his judgment and his freedom, although the only aspect of man that can be systematized is the realm of his abstract, general ideas; it deals with what everyone has really always known and for that very reason is extremely difficult to express in objective terms, because any such objectivization is bound to fall short of one's unthematic knowledge (as the average man knows better than he can explain to himself or others what logic, time, love, freedom, and responsibility are). The proofs of God's existence (the proof can be variously formulated so as to express this or that aspect of the matter) all come down to showing that all knowledge (even doubt, enquiry, or deliberate refusal to meddle with "metaphysics"), whatever it may concern, so long as this knowledge posits something real—at least its own act—occurs against the background of an affirmation of *being in general or of being as the horizon, the asymptotic destination and sustaining *principle of act and object; whereupon the secondary question arises what we are to call this anonymous, elusive presence (Being *simpliciter,* mystery, or—stressing the aspect of freedom in this *transcendence— absolute good, the personal absolute Thou, the principle of all responsibility, etc.). In grasping the objective reality of his everyday life, both physically and intellectually in a comprehensive concept, man has necessarily fulfilled the condition of such comprehension by unthematically, unobjectively reaching out to the one, incomprehensible plenitude of reality, which in its unity is the condition both of knowledge and of the (individual) thing known and as such is always (unthematically) affirmed, even in the act of its thematic denial. The human individual experiences this inescapable structure of his spiritual existence in the ever personal basic *existential state of his life: as the incomprehensibly luminous transparency of his spirit; as the power to consider absolutely everything, which man exercises even with respect to himself, thereby rising above himself; in the anxiety which creates a void (something different from fear of an object); in unspeakable joy; in moral obligation which really takes a person out of himself; in the experience of death, in which one knows one's absolute impotence—in these and many other modes of basic, transcendental experience of existence, that which is everything (and chiefly for this reason is personal) becomes intelligibly present without being objectively "seen"—that which man experiences as the principle and ground of his spiritual existence, though he, being finite, may not identify himself with this ground.

This basic constitution of man and its import become thematic in the explicit proofs of God's existence. The experience that every judgment one forms is reached because one is sustained and moved by Being *simpliciter,* which is not in being and at work in virtue of one's thought but itself sustains that thought, is given thematic form in the metaphysical principle of causality (not to be confused with the functional law of causality in natural science, according to which every phenomenon is co-ordinated as an "effect" with another phenomenon, "quantitatively" equal to it, as its "cause"): contingent, finite being, which is affirmed in fact but not necessarily, since it does not contain within itself a sufficient reason for its being, exists as an "effect" (like its very affirmation) of absolute Being, its cause (*Causality). The primordial causality of Being, as intelligible presence and universal support of the mind's functioning, with respect to every entity which becomes a thematic object of consciousness, can only be expressed in terms of the various formal aspects of an entity: An entity considered simply as contingent indicates that its cause is absolute being—the cosmological proof, the proof from contingency. (Here again individual elements can be distinguished: for example the inherent finality of the entity, which gives us the teleological proof; the essential dependence of every act on an antecedent act, from which we conclude the existence of a pure act free of all potency—the kinesiological proof [first *Mover]; the necessary first beginning of the world—the entropic proof; the fact that all finite beings only participate in the perfections of pure being—St Thomas's proof by the degrees of perfection). The absolute obligation incumbent on personal beings points to the existence of absolute value—deontological, axiological, moral proof; the absolute character of truth (when it is really admitted) points to the absolute character in reality of necessary being—noetic proof; the common belief of all peoples in the existence of God, which must be based on a real God—the historical or ethnological proof. These elaborations of natural theology, which Western philosophy has attempted since the times of Anaxagoras and Plato, have been rather inappropriately classified since the 18th century as metaphysical, physical and moral proofs of the existence of God, in disregard of the fact that the purpose of them all (which can never be to compel people to recognize God) is only achieved to the extent to which each of them reflects a particular aspect of the basic transcendental experience of existence.

418

PROPERTIES, TRINITARIAN

Those characteristics which distinguish the three divine *Persons in the *Trinity from one another and as distinguishing marks of our knowledge of them, also called "notions". These properties are not only the three opposed *relations which constitute the Persons in God (fatherhood, sonship, passive spiration) but also the "unoriginate-ness" of the Father and to some extent the active spiration insofar as it distinguishes Father and Son jointly from the Holy Ghost (See D 800).

PROPHET

In fundamental theology a man can be called a prophet (Gr. προφήτης, religious herald) in a general sense if he is the accredited witness of God's *revelation in such a way that he not only experiences God's gracious self-communication to man but declares it correctly, that is without error (though imperfectly), with divine guidance and attestation (*Miracle), expounds it in a manner appropriate to the concrete situation facing himself and his environment, and in obedience to a divine impulse proclaims it to this environment. The prophet has a unique experience of vocation—He is God's messenger. Insofar as an estimation of one's religious situation necessarily involves looking into the future, though not an advance report on it, the prophet has the ability (more or less explicitly) to interpret the present in the light of its dynamism for the future—"prophecy" in the usual modern sense. Genuine prophecy may be inextricably involved in error, contradiction, and the corruption of the particular religious situation. It may be met with in this form outside the Old and New Testaments. The NT enables us to recognize the authenticity and holiness of the prophets of the OT and their writings. Since God's self-communication to the world bears most eloquent testimony to itself in the hypostatic union, its eschatological climax, Jesus Christ is *the* Prophet, the divine self-communication and its expression in person. His prophetic destiny, death, answered by God with resurrection, shows clearly who and what he is. Though in him divine revelation has come to a close, prophets still have their para-institutional place in the Church, because ever and again there are people in the Church divinely sent to it to bear a personal testimony to the reality of God and Christ in the might of his Spirit (*Charism). Prophecy in the Church must be contained in the "order" of the Church (often

419

with considerable conflict), but this "order" itself is participation in the absolute prophetic office.

PROTESTANTISM

The term (derived from the so-called "Protestation" of the Lutherans at the Second Imperial Diet of Speyer in 1529) for all the religious bodies which sprang from the Reformation of the sixteenth century and for their theological doctrines. What chiefly unites them is that they all protest against the Catholic Church. Early Protestantism, following Luther's witness for the gospel of free grace in *Jesus Christ against its alleged "materialization" and legalistic perversion by the hierarchical system of the Catholic Church, clung in the main to the *dogmas of Christian antiquity. Liberal Neo-Protestantism, however, became a protest against dogma, against established Churches, and indeed against the Church as an institution at all. The principal theological doctrines of Protestantism may be set out as follows. *Faith, which alone justifies (*Sola fide), is a personal encounter with the historical Christ in the living "word of God", which saves by the very fact of being preached. Because the total sinfulness of man before God prevents him from co-operating in any way in his own salvation, this faith is bestowed by grace alone (*Sola gratia) and is a venture in Christian life according to the Gospel, undertaken despite the sinfulness of man that remains after baptism (Luther: *simul iustus et peccator, "at once justified and a sinner").Faith is based solely on Holy Scripture (*Sola Scriptura) and the only two *sacraments instituted by Christ, *baptism and the Lord's Supper (*Eucharist), not on the authority of the Church and her *Tradition. The Bible, at least according to Luther, is not to be interpreted like a legal code (biblicism) but as a message of grace: the principle sola Scriptura only applies "so far as it serves Christ". But Christ is Lord and Redeemer. He is not a legislator, that is the founder of a Church which is a perfect society with legislative authority, especially as represented by the papal primacy. Christ is present only through the Holy Ghost in word and sacrament (principally the word): the sermon is the central feature of worship. This presence of Christ in his Church is not a token of glory to come hereafter yet already dawning, but of suffering and the cross, of sin (theologia crucis), which is also seen as the cause of Christian disunity. Grace is God's graciousness to us in Christ. Grace does make man a new creature, does bear fruit in good works, but is never so given to man that he ceased to be a sinner. There is no infallible magisterium; Holy Scripture declares itself. As to ecclesiastical law very various opinions are held. Though *office is generally regarded as deriving from Christ, not as a mere commission from the community, the sphere of merely human law in the Church is thought to be much wider than in the Catholic Church. Protestant bishops exist in some areas but a sacramentally ordained *priesthood and the *Mass are categorically rejected; so that the Church is built up from the community on the basis of the universal priesthood of believers. The Catholic Church is reproached with teaching a *double standard of morality, favouring the evangelical counsels and the religious orders at the expense of a strict Christian vocation to serve God in our neighbour. The "freedom of a Christian man", which is usually taken to sum up Protestantism, did not originally mean freedom of conscience *vis-à-vis* dogma and confessions of faith, especially the divinity of Christ, as people assume today. Negatively, it meant freedom from ecclesiastical law and positively, constant loving readiness—the gift of the Holy Ghost—to do the will of God.

(1) The Catholic will reply to this: (a) From a Christian point of view mere rejection of unity with the Catholic Church obviously cannot create a *Christian* Church or any sort of unity. The same is true of baptism pure and simple, for since it is given the most various and contradictory interpretations, it alone cannot form a Church. (b) The Catholic recognizes that his own post-Reformation Church must at least be presumed to be the true Church of Jesus Christ (until the contrary is proved), because its historical continuity with the Church of the past is without doubt more substantial than that of the Protestant churches, since it preserves the unity of the episcopate and communion with the Roman See (which characterized the pre-Reformation Church), and since Protestant Christians themselves can only be a legitimate Church to the extent that the old Church is also their Church. Accordingly, a Catholic could only concede an objective right to secede from the traditional Church if the points of difference between Catholics and Protestants were all entirely irrelevant to salvation before God, and we were divided on no matter about which we ought to agree (which no Christian can seriously maintain, for otherwise intercommunion would be the universal practice), or if it were certain that a Protestant Christian found the Catholic Church patently denying a truth which his Christian conscience would have obliged him to continue to profess at the time of the rupture.

(2) But a Catholic Christian cannot agree that this second supposition is verified, for: (a) The doctrine of all-sufficiency of Scripture *(sola Scriptura)* can certainly not be allowed to mean that the living preach-

ing of the word of God did not precede the written word of God in the Church, demanding the assent of faith and efficaciously at work before Scripture existed; Scripture objectifies this spoken word and therefore is permanently sustained by the authority Christ bestowed to proclaim the word of God with binding force. Otherwise the fact that the Church fixed the limits of the canon of Scripture is really unintelligible. This it not to deny that the later Church—whose doctrine can contain nothing but the apostolic preaching and can be judged by no other standard—finds in Scripture the normative source of the faith and the permanent criterion of the (necessary) development of her doctrine and the fresh actualizations which it must constantly be given. But by the nature of Scripture this criterion is to be used by the Church as a whole, not a decisive critical weapon with which the individual can attack the Church's interpretation of Scripture.

(b) The Catholic Church too accepts the doctrine of *sola gratia* if it be rightly understood. For from first to last every salutary act of man without exception is the fruit of gratuitous grace; whether it be the capacity for such acts or the free act itself or the liberation of freedom for divine faith, hope and love, all comes from that grace which indeed is meant for all but which none can claim of right. Now this grace really happens, so that God by a true interior transformation makes man, who otherwise would be Godless, his own dear child—man is no more what he once was (or otherwise would be). Yet man cannot boast of this grace as his possession. For he hopes in faith that he possesses it, but can never be certain that he does. Daily tempted and sinning, he daily flees anew from himself to God's mercy, because he never knows for certain whether his temptations and the sins he hopes are venial may not forebode or conceal a real rejection of God. Thus the Catholic Christian also admits he is a sinner while clinging to God's grace as grace that alone can save him. But because grace truly transforms the justified, whatever he does in the Spirit of God deserves the reward of eternal life—gains that *merit of which Scripture is eloquent. This doctrine is a statement of fact in praise of divine grace, not a statement of Christian motivation, for in order to find God one must love him for his own sake and not simply be preoccupied with one's own blessedness.

(c) If, as most Protestants acknowledge, there are sacraments in the Church, that is words which when spoken by the Church in a sacred rite issue into act in the individual's concrete religious situation and what is proclaimed becomes in him by God's act (baptism, Lord's Supper); if on the other hand, as Catholic doctrine affirms, the sacraments vary in rank and dignity and are not all equally necessary and, needless to say, do not effect in adult man what they validly pledge unless they are received by (or produce) a repentant believer; if, finally, as Protestants believe, God's word spoken by the Church is not a mere abstract statement but the actual happening of what it announces, then it is difficult to see why Protestants should not agree with the Catholic Church that all those words in which the Church engages her whole being—as the sign of the fulfilled promise of grace —and pledges God's grace to the individual at decisive moments in his life, should be called sacraments. Especially since the words of forgiveness addressed to the sinner (*Penance, sacrament of) (Mt 16; 18; Jn 20), the bestowal of the Spirit by *confirmation (Acts 8), the anointing of the sick (Jas 5), the transmission of office by the *laying on of hands (Acts 6), are well attested in Scripture and St Paul considers *marriage to be the token of Christ's redemptive love for his Church (Eph 5).

(d) If Protestant theology does not wish to transform the Church which is a tangible reality in the world, confessing Christ her Lord before the world, into a purely invisible community of grace (which is not generally the case today at least); if *this* Church, despite all weaknesses and betrayals, has received the promise that the might of grace will always defend her against all the powers of death; if this Church, in order to be such, must exhibit a certain order and organization, that is, office invested with Christ's authority (however that office and authority may be interpreted in detail): then this Protestant theology must acknowledge that when it repudiates with all its strength unbelief or false belief which would dissolve its very being, founded as it is on personal faith in the apostolic kerygma of Christ, it must be able to pronounce a No that is absolutely final and permanently binding, though it must always fall short of the fullness of lived witness to Christ (not only must be able to but in fact intends to do so and does it—and this anathema and *damnamus* was uttered by the fathers of the Reformation and during the struggle against National Socialism); and that this No, if it is not to dissolve the Church as true witness to Christ, must be kept from going astray by the power of the Spirit, that is to say, it must be "infallible" (which does not mean "plenary"). Protestant theology must also recognize that this magistral No must be pronounced by appointed office in the Church if it is really to speak in Christ's name and by his commission. If this office of the Church is permanently organized in a college which succeeds by right to the apostolic college, under a personal head who perpetuates the office of Peter in the apostolic college, then this supreme authority (the universal episcopate in the Church and her personal head) must be invested with this power to pronounce "infallible" judgment in matters of faith when it acts on behalf of the Church as a whole in the authority of Christ. In other words, if the Church, whose faith is always threatened, is also constantly protected by grace, must constantly announce new historical articulations of the faith, and if its authority is vested in certain persons, then there must be a supreme teacher in the Church whom the divine mercy preserves from error when he engages his full authority as supreme teacher of the Church. Here reference should be made to what was said above under (1)(b), and we ought to add that the Church, which must at least be presumed to originate in Christ, has definitively made its own this conception of the permanent Petrine office, which at any rate is no more unscriptural than the doctrine of the infallibility of Scripture.

(3)(a) Though a Catholic feels he is in the comfortable position of being able to presume that Christ founded his Church, and, as a believer who has experienced the faith of his Church "from within", to perceive that nothing un-Christian can be found in his Church's idea of itself which would compel him to abandon the presumption, nevertheless it is his duty, and the Church's duty too, continually to rethink and pray over its interpretation of the faith and to elaborate it, asking himself what it is about Catholicism which makes it difficult or impossible for other Christians of good will to recognize it as the pure, complete development of that Christian faith which they too profess and practise.

(b) On the other hand it is obviously the duty of non-Catholic Christians not to attempt to justify the old separation by constantly devising new and more complicated theological formulae, but to consider how their own convictions can be expressed so that the old Church—which after all is their mother Church—may recognize these as deeper insights into her own faith.

(c) But the Catholic Church must fully realize that unity of faith and unity of the Church in and under the primacy of Peter does not mean uniformity in discipline and theology for the churches so united.
—See also *Schools, theological; Ecumenical movement.*

PROTO-EVANGELIUM

The "First Gospel"; the name given to Genesis 3:15, because according to the interpretation traditional in the Church it foretells (in its plenary sense; *Senses of Scripture) at the beginning of the history of mankind after the Fall, the continual struggle between the human race and the powers of sin, and promises the triumphant outcome of the struggle in terms of human salvation, including in its promise the Redeemer and his Mother (see D 3514, 3900ff.).

PROTOLOGY

A term formed on the basis of an analogy with *eschatology; the revealed doctrine of the beginnings of the world and mankind. See the articles *Creation, States of Man, Paradise, Monogenism, Original Justice, Integrity, Adam, Eve, Creation of Man, Original Sin.* Protology (Gen 1–3) need not be pictured as a first-hand account of those who took part in the "beginning" (God, Adam), handed down by tradition for the many thousands of years of human history before Genesis was written. Rather, it is the retrospective reflection of the author of Genesis, in the light of revelation and contemporary experience of saving history and damnation (Historical *aetiology), on what must have happened at the beginning if the present is to be made intelligible against the background of its past. The significance of protology for an understanding of human and Christian existence (*Creation narratives) lies in this mutual illumination of origins remote yet still in being (*Beginning, *Anamnesis) and the derivative present.

PROVIDENCE, DIVINE

The plan which God's knowledge—knowing all things, even the free acts of creatures—and will—holy and loving, mightily sustaining and controlling all things—have for the created world (D 3003). This plan even embraces human *freedom (without destroying it), and by it God in his *eternity guides the course of the world and its history, and, within the latter, human saving history, to the goal (*Eschatology) he has foreseen and forewilled in his *predestination, through the forces immanent in the world that he has created and by his dispensations in saving history (*Grace, *Miracles). A misconceived *theism depreciates human activity supported by God in his providence and sees providence only as the direct "rule of the world" by God. It is only at the consummation that the creature really discovers this plan for the perfection of the world (which is yet to be), which alone makes ultimate sense of the whole world and of everything in it. Only by faith in the adorable, wise, holy, loving God and by unconditional surrender to his mysterious providence does man overcome that proud though anxious need of reassurance in which otherwise he feels himself to be only the victim of conflicting earthly forces which can be reduced to no real unity.

PRUDENCE

According to scholastic theology that *virtue which gives one a knowledge of his moral duty and of the concrete means to its accomplishment. For this reason it is the first of the *cardinal virtues. According to Scripture, the prudent man is one who can interpret his own concrete situation and discern spirits, who keeps watch and is ever mindful of his own death and the coming of the Lord (Ps 90:12; Mt 25:1–13; 1 Jn 4:1ff.).

PSEUDEPIGRAPHA

See *Apocrypha.*

PURGATORY

A term that has come into use since the Middle Ages for that purifying growth of perfection ("after" death) in all the dimensions of man which according to the Church's teaching exists (for the defined teaching of the Church, see D 838, 856ff., 1304ff., 1580, 1820, 1867), to which a person who dies in justifying grace is subject insofar as the debt of "punishment" he has incurred has not necessarily been cancelled when his sins were forgiven in justification, and this debt can be paid by "expiatory suffering". As to the detailed structure of this process, especially its connexion with any place, we have no information either from Scripture (which tells us that it is holy and wholesome to pray for the dead, 2 Macc 12:42– 45; *Sheol, *Intermediate State) or from a detailed definition of the magisterium; so that the word purgatory ought not to stand in the way of a better and more accurate term for that process, especially as it causes concern from the point of view of the teaching of religion.

The following consideration may help towards an understanding of the matter: Only one who is truly perfected can be capable of the beatific vision; but such a one will be so, even as an individual, before the general consummation (perfection) of the world (D 1000f.). But the interior perfecting of man, who matures in genuinely creaturely time, is a temporal process and on account of the many levels of the structure of human nature cannot be thought to happen by some *fiat* which would accomplish everything at once. Only by phases does man become, through all the levels of his nature, the "one" he already "is"—by central, fundamental, personal decision (faith, contrition, love)—and by *death permanently and irrevocably remains. But the execution of this fundamental decision encounters a pre-personal resistance, at the many levels of man's being, that has been built up by earlier faults and wrong decisions. The "experience" of this resistance is "suffering" and as such is a consequence of human sin. On the other hand, since it is distinct from the fulfilment of freedom and the self-experience of the core of the human person, it is "external" punishment. Thus that process of integration whereby after death the totality of the human person is enlisted against the resistance arising from and built up by his own sin, is real penal suffering, but suffering radically supported by the grace accepted in the basic decision, and thus issues necessarily and without fail in the perfection of man, that is, the ultimate vision of God.

PURITY, RITUAL

Cleanness and uncleanness, in the ritual sense, signify a difference in things, food and actions of the most various kinds, which are all regarded as morally indifferent in themselves but (either permanently or for a certain period) as compatible or incompatible with worship or the worshipper, whether because the "unclean" thing is held to be specially holy (that is, reserved for God) or in some way inappropriate to worship. Such taboos (very variously interpreted) have existed in most religions, even in the OT: certain sexual events and actions, touching a corpse or a leper, made one unclean for a time; many animals and types of meat were not to be eaten, etc. (for examples, see Lev 11–17). Their explanation is not easy, especially since ancient customs which were taken for granted and whose meaning had often been forgotten, were incorporated in the laws of the OT. No doubt considerations of hygiene entered in. Thus everyday life was penetrated with a consciousness of religion and the Hebrews were set apart from the manner of life and the religion of other peoples (*Circumcision). These tokens raised men's minds to a higher being (Heb 9:13; 10:22 etc.; *Sacrament). Christ abolished the prescriptions touching

427

ritual purity (Mt 15:1-20; Mk 7:1-23) in favour of purity of heart. Giving effect to this emancipation led to difficulties in the first Christian community (Acts 10:15 etc.).

PURPOSE

That towards which the structure of a being or of an action tends (objective purpose). It is a primitive datum of our experience of a growing and directed being, which seeks of itself, in and despite a variety of conditions, to reach a certain objective (finality). Where the purpose lies within the being itself, that is, where the being seeks its own perfection, which it regards as good and which is not a mere means employed by someone else to some other end, we are given a genuine insight into the meaningful order of things, in which all beings are associated in a real unity and mutually illuminate one another. Through knowledge and love the spiritual person enters into himself, rests in his sense of meaningful order, and just so by his free and perfected transcendence in grace and glory dwells wholly with God, the primordial, antecedent unity of all the purposes of all beings, and thus gives *glory to God.

Q

QUIETISM

A heterodox, or at least an undesirable, trend in mystical theology in the Romance countries during the seventeenth century (principal representatives M. de Molinos, Madame de Guyon, Fénelon; opposed by Bossuet; there were similar tendencies in the Eastern Church in twelfth-century Hesychasm, and in the West the Béguines of the thirteenth century: D 891ff.). Quietism holds that perfection is selfless love of God in the sense of purely passive inwardness and resignation, from which all activity and all concern for one's own salvation has been eliminated (*Love). Hence active *asceticism, vocal *prayer, prayer of *petition, and non-mystical *meditation are more or less rejected. *Pietism is an analogous movement in Protestantism. Both Pietism and Quietism are reactions against dry academic theology and a voluntaristic asceticism on the Stoic model which stultifies man's deeper powers instead of freeing and orientating them to God. Quietism was condemned by Innocent XI in 1687 and Innocent XII in 1699 (D 2201–2268, 2351–2373).

QUMRAN

An archaeological site by the Dead Sea, in eleven caves in the neighbourhood of which over six hundred manuscripts and fragments have been found since 1947. They include the oldest known manuscripts of the Old Testament, dating from the third century B.C. to the first century A.D. With the exception of Esther, all the books of the Hebrew canon are represented. Qumran included the "monastery" and cemetery of the Essenes (a name meaning "the pious"), an ascetic Jewish community of priests and lay people who saw themselves as the holy remnant of Israel with their own rules and calendar (which are extant). When the community was destroyed by the Romans in A.D. 68, its library survived in the caves. Qumran is very important for the reconstruction of the oldest form of the text of the Bible and for providing numerous points of reference (but no more than that) for our understanding of the New Testament.

R

RATIONALISM

A theologian would be introducing rationalism into theology if he did not remain fully conscious that the terms he uses are analogical, that the Christian religion is ultimately adoration and praise, that doctrinal statements direct the mind away from themselves to a real Person (to God and his government of the world), that the search to comprehend the incomprehensible mystery arises from comprehension by it. Theology must be clear and precise: it cannot be the *kerygma that directly praises God and convinces man. But it is the science of faith, and therefore when it neglects to refer itself back to personal faith—the abandonment of self to the free disposal of absolute mystery—it becomes clever chatter, rationalistic subtlety that can beget nothing but unbelief. The many forms of philosophical rationalism (*Enlightenment) force theology to make intellectually respectable statements and to engage in dialogue with the world in the form of the modern theory of science.

REAL PRESENCE

See *Eucharist, Transubstantiation.*

RECAPITULATION

See *Anacephalaeosis.*

RECONCILIATION

See *Redemption.*

REDEMPTION

In the widest sense signifies that that condition of man in which, individually and collectively, he inevitably finds himself and which he experiences as miserable and not terminable by himself, is definitively overcome. *Christianity recognizes man as capable of redemption (in the last analysis because even his freedom is finite and remains encompassed by God's creative love) and as needing redemption, on account of his guilt. This guilt (the guilt established by original sin, and the act of individual freedom) cannot be removed by man. It is not only a repudiation of factual terrestrial norms, in such a way that man himself could overcome the consequences of his repudiation and thus remove the guilt. Guilt is the freely-chosen rejection (and, as freedom, one intended to be definitive) of God's intimate love directly offered to us through uncreated divine *grace, and thus an absolutely dialogical act (*sin). Only when this love freely asserts itself as something permanent against this rejection and by its divine nature overcomes that guilt is forgiveness possible (i.e., the reciprocal love inspired in man by God). Final redemption as personal ultimacy and the conquest of the human condition in its subjection to suffering is inconceivable without this forgiveness of guilt, because on the one hand suffering and death are manifestations of the guilt rooted in existence, and on the other hand total "bliss" in all respects can be granted only as an eschatological gift of God himself, and not an aim to which man can aspire on his own.

Redemption in the Christian sense is seen as something "objective"; i.e., as an event and its consequence (objective redemption) which in fact precede human *justification and sanctification (subjective redemption). Finite human freedom also presupposes as a condition of redemption a "situation" which is not synonymous with man's necessary nature and freedom. Objective redemption therefore signifies the divinely conceived constitution of that historically real situation of freedom in which God's forgiving desire for redemption freely offered to mankind is now rendered eschatologically irrevocable in the historical reality of Jesus Christ, in which and from which alone man can freely accept the forgiveness offered to him.

This redemptive event (referred to in Christianity as "the cross of

Jesus") is not the primal cause of redemption in any way that prevents it from also being the cause of the redemption of mankind before Christ. Because God's self-communication (oriented to Jesus Christ) has always been effective in the world, it is not a valid question to ask what has "improved" since Jesus Christ. The overall history of mankind remains always and everywhere open to God's forgiving love in Jesus Christ.

The idea of self-redemption fails to do justice to the true nature and absolute depth of our need of redemption (efforts towards *emancipation and the realization of justice are necessary manifestations of redemption, but are not its essence); on the other hand redemption by God is not a redemption by a "stranger", because God is no "stranger" but the self-subsistent ground of that which is most proper to us (and because in Jesus Christ "man" shares in the work of his own salvation: 1 Tim 2:5; D 261, 636, 641f., 801, 1739ff., 1743, 2015, 3677; *Mediator), and because precisely by his redemptive grace he grants us *freedom to accept his own forgiving and redeeming self-communication. Both the content (divine life given with the remission of sin) and the manner of appropriating redemption are the free gift of God; thus God does not owe man redemption. Proceeding from the Father by an absolute initiative (Eph 1:3–23), it is wholly bound up with the historical Person and work of *Jesus (Heb 10:5–9; Phil 2:5–11); it is not by simply setting aside sin and the provisional character of the whole man in need of redemption that God's mercy takes effect, but by giving his redemptive grace in Jesus historical tangibility, presence and power in a world that is to be preserved. Jesus' being (as the union of God's life and human existence) and activity (as the acceptance, in loving obedience, of human existence characterized by sin: Rom 5:12–21; see also 1 Cor 15:45ff.) taken together *are* the historically real, eschatologically victorious bestowal on the world of God's self-communication despite, and in, the world's sinfulness. Thus the presence of God's redemptive forgiveness, efficacious throughout history, has found its all-sustaining sense and centre, its definitive culmination, in Jesus Christ; and it remains inabrogably such because in Jesus God has definitively accepted the one world and humanity, as a whole, in spite of sin and precisely in their culpable destiny (Heb 2:11; Rom 8:29). This is shown by Jesus' *resurrection and the mission of the *Holy Spirit. This reconciliation with man, initiated and granted by God, applies to all men (2 Cor 5:18f.; see also Col 1:21f.; Jn 3:16) and is antecedent to the always personal acceptance of this atonement or redemption in *faith against all predestinationism (see 1 Tim 2:4ff.; D 391, 723, 1011, 1513, 1523, 1530f. and *passim).* It also bears the character of divine justice (already in St Paul though in a not unobjectionable presentation) in that God willed the human life of his Son to be a total surrender of loving obedience in the deprivation of *death (Jn 10:17f.; Mk 10:45; Heb) and thereby granted the one humanity in its solidarity a propitiatory sacrifice (sacrifice of atonement) (Phil 2:5–11). To this extent it can and must be said that by redemption God forgives the world's sin because Jesus Christ has made satisfaction in our stead and for us by his death on the cross (D 1513, 1522f., 1528f., 1545, esp. 3891) and has atoned to God, especially since even the free acceptance of this atonement by the individual human being is again God's doing: *justification.

The essential problem of the doctrine of redemption (*soteriology) lies in the question why God's original desire for forgiveness does not simply "work downwards", causing this same forgiveness to take effect immediately, always and everywhere, rather than reaching mankind from a specific historical event which is *the* "cause" of forgiveness. Here we must remark that God's "transcendental" desire for salvation becomes reality and affects mankind *because* it assumes a concrete historical form. In this sense we may say that its historical manifestation constitutes both its cause and its effect. God's "transcendental" will for salvation is accomplished in a *single* *history of salvation. This strives towards a culmination which renders the direction taken by this history (towards the victory of the will to redemption) historically irreversible, in short takes it towards "eschatological" fulfilment. The point of culmination is available when God himself makes this history his own (although it is also a history of sin and its historical manifestations), and God's acceptance of the sinful world is also echoed by the predestined acceptance on the part of the world set in that acceptance. This point of culmination thus contains objectively and (in exemplary fashion) subjectively their reversible redemptive acceptance as the unity of God and the world throughout history. But man's radical acceptance of God's self-revelation is achieved through death, because death (as an act) is the ultimate assumption of individual freedom, in which guilt is accepted and expiated through suffering (the Passion). Thus salvation is made comprehensible through Christ's death, without involving the model of atonement and reparation contained in the *theory of satisfaction.

REFORMED CHURCHES

See *Protestantism*.

RELATION

REGENERATION

The scriptural name (Jn 1:13; 3:5ff.; Tit 3:5 etc.) for the *justification (*Baptism) of the sinner, in that habitual (*sanctifying) grace gives him an abiding interior life, to enable him as a child of God to perform acts that conform to God's holy will and are positively ordered to eternal life (and so to be "alive" in the highest sense); and because the sinner who is deprived of *original justice through *original sin, or of justification through personal sin, is given this gift of divine life by God gratuitously as something *new* (hence "from above", Jn 3:7).

RELATION

A mode of being which need not be merely notional but may belong to a thing in itself (real relation): the being-for-something *(ad aliud,* the term) of the subject of the relation in virtue of some particular characteristic of the thing (the basis of the relation). Relations are of many kinds (relations of similarity, of origin, etc.) and may be necessary (transcendental, because they are necessarily given with a certain absolute being as such and are adequately identical with it), or accidental (categorical). There may be a reciprocal relation between two things, depending on the same basis, so that each is subject and term of the relation. The doctrine of relations is of importance for dogma since the Church teaches that the mode of being of the three divine Persons in the *Trinity is relational, as distinguished from the one divine essence, which as such is absolute, not relative being (D 528, 530f., 1330). The four divine relations (paternity, filiation, active spiration, passive spiration) being opposed, distinguish the three Persons and make it intelligible, at least negatively (non-contradiction), and so far as is possible when one is dealing with absolute *mystery, how God can be threefold in his (relative) Persons yet one in the unity of his one (absolute) essence, and shed light on the notion of *perichoresis. The axiom that two things equal to a third (in this case the Persons and the divine essence) are equal to each other, can be confined to absolute being and denied where relative being is concerned. This does not positively resolve the chief difficulty about the Trinity (which no one could expect) but at least shows that it is not a compelling argument.

435

RELATIVISM

The opinion that the truths man knows are valid only in the context of a particular finite system, that is the world of the individual's own sensibility, whereas there are other systems, equally sound, outside it. This relativism (as the assertion of its own universal validity) is nonsense for the simple reason that such an assertion contradicts itself: relativism in the context of any particular system can be rejected as false by that system. Relativism has an attractive plausibility for the theologian because it succeeds so easily (too easily to be true) in "reconciling" contradictory religious and theological systems: they are all right, and none wholly right. But theological relativism founders because doctrine relates to objective reality, and faith is convinced that objective reality and our relation to it—not theories—decide whether we are saved. The proposition that Jesus Christ is truly risen from the dead, for example, cannot be reconciled by relativism with the proposition that he is not risen from the dead. It must either be true or false. The truth which relativism seeks to express in such unfortunate terms is the analogical character (*Analogy) of our religious knowledge; its necessary reference to *mystery; the danger of *rationalism in theology; the possibility that the same thing may be expressed, from different points of view that are objectively tenable, in formulae that seem to be contradictory—may even be better and more fully expressed in this way; the danger of clinging fixedly to a form of words as if it were the thing itself.

RELICS

Mortal remains of saints which are reverently preserved by the Church and accorded a certain veneration (really directed to the saint: CIC, can. 1255 § 2) (*Saints, veneration of). This veneration is not to be rejected in principle (D 1822, 1867). Nevertheless its concrete forms largely depend on the tastes of the age and do not all appeal to everyone. Ultimately this veneration does not depend on the question whether or not such relics will be incorporated in the resurrected human body.

RELIGION

The root meaning of the word is uncertain: it may be derived from the Latin *relegere* (to go over again), *religari* (to bind oneself), or *re-eligere* (to choose again). In terms of usage religion is usually defined as "having dealings or relations with the *sacred", and this in the broadest possible sense so as to include speculative, aesthetic and ethical religious *acts. According to Thomas Aquinas it is the task of religion to sustain man's orientation towards God; the label "religious" applies to everyone concerned about the ground and purpose of the world that we call God. Religion in the stricter sense means the *worship of God that arises out of this concern and reflection (*proof of the existence of God) and that also takes on a social dimension. This general definition of religion takes no account of whether God's relationship to mankind is one of *self-revelation, whether he himself creates the condition of man being able to hearken to his word and whether he has made his self-revelation historically and irreversibly manifest in Jesus. These basic assertions of Christian belief doubtless include aspects which distinguish Christianity fundamentally from other religions and thus raise the question of the extent to which it is even legitimate to understand and classify Christianity as a religion (cf. Karl Barth's view of Christianity as a judgment on all religions as the creations of man wishing to justify and assert himself over against God). More recent positive valuations of religion see it as the concrete expression of man's infinite transcendence, as the expression of the absolute worth of his hopes, his genuine needs and his limitless desires.

The modern critique of religion by outsiders has arisen in connexion with its relationship to the *world. Religion is in general accused of hostility towards science (natural *science and theology), acting as an obstacle in the way of *emancipation and the growth of democracy (see *Democratization)*, false consciousness (see *Ideology)* and subjectivism. In all religious societies, including the Church, the critique of religion by insiders (something that has existed in the Judaeo-Christian tradition ever since the *prophets) has above all appeared in the form of conflict between the ministerial and charismatic elements. In Protestant Christianity there is a tendency, originating with Dietrich Bonhoeffer, to reject *theism as laying claim on God as an explanation of the world, as an assertion of God's active governance of the world in providence and as an ideological support for the *status quo* and thereby as the intellectual embodiment of religion, and instead to demand a "pure" faith, often without formal liturgy and prayer, and in particular the secular ministry of a "religionless Christianity" in solidarity with all those who suffer and are oppressed. This view cannot be accused of returning to the verification of faith by works, but it needs to be made clear to those who hold it that it is something that owes its existence to the tradition of an institutional religion and that it remains subject to an inherent compulsion to take on concrete social expression and thus tends unavoidably to become once again a religious society.—On the theological problem of which religion is true and legitimate see *Non-Christian religions.*

FREEDOM OF RELIGION. The freedom of a human being to follow his own conscience in acknowledging any *religion or none, and to give public expression to this acknowledgment to the extent that no harm is done to others thereby. The human right of religious freedom extends not only to individuals but to religious societies. The right of religious freedom derives from the right to freedom in general (*tolerance); it has no connexion with the "truth" or "falsity" of any particular religion; all it is concerned about is the relationship in matters of religion between individuals and groups on the one hand and on the other society as a whole, particularly the public authorities. Up till Pius XII the Catholic Church was wedded to the view that the question of religious freedom was necessarily linked with the question of truth and that truth took precedence over freedom. Only with John XXIII (*Pacem in terris,* 1963) and Vatican II did the Catholic Church officially accept religious freedom. In its declaration the Council defined religious freedom as freedom from any kind of coercion in matters of belief (Rel. Lib., 2; the limits of religious freedom are set by the demands of public order, *ibid.,* 7); according to Vatican II all religious societies have equal rights and no religious society may indulge in unfair methods of proselytism (*ibid.,* 4). The Council finds the theological basis for religious freedom in the appeal Jesus and his disciples made to man's freedom (*ibid.,* 9, 11).

REPENTANCE

See *Contrition, Metanoia, Penance.*

REPETITION

If we give the matter careful thought we shall see that in the specifically human dimension this word means more than doing the same thing over and over again, each act independent of the other. It means the induction of a unique event as such anew into a different place and

438

time in human history (*Anamnesis). Such a procedure, which may take very different forms and may achieve its purpose in very different degrees, is possible because the act of a personal spirit (especially where it is the permanent actualization of a person who has been perfected by death) does not simply perish with the physical and biological event whereby it occurred, but persists as part of the conclusiveness of free acts; because man must always enact his present out of his surviving past; and because not only his own earlier deeds belong to this past, but also to the history of other men, though in very varying ways and degrees, thanks to man's dialogical existence and the principle of *solidarity in virtue of which man lives in a history common to all men. Real repetition is recourse to the surviving past as the basis of our present freedom, a recourse whereby (especially in commemoration, celebration, meditation, etc.) the abiding power of history is freely accepted and actualized. This concept finds, or could find, many applications in theology: in the theology of *worship, the liturgical year, the *Mass, the celebration of personal anniversaries, *contemplation, the *mysteries of the life of Jesus, etc.

REPRESENTATION

The objective unity of the world, which one God has created for one purpose and destiny and which reveals itself in the comprehensive unity of man's intellectual horizon, must also obtain in the personal sphere, though in a special manner. Hence there can be no absolute individualism where supernatural salvation is concerned, though this salvation is the fruit of a free decision which is unique and which one must take for oneself. Even here we are in part sustained by the decisions of others and their consequences, and in a positive sense what we do affects others. Now when such a decision by an individual has special significance for the salvation of others (or everyone), because of the nature of the agent or of his decision, one can speak of representation in the theological sense: then this one man really stands for all, "represents" them, without, of course, depriving them of their own free decision, for they must at least decide whether they will accept for themselves the meaning and effect of the other man's representative decision. Thus Jesus Christ, the *Mediator, is the supreme representative of mankind in his vicarious redemption.—For another theological sense of the term representation, see *Mass*.

REPROBATION

When God foresees that his creature will freely and finally reject him (and only in this case: D 623f., 1567, 2005) he wills and brings about the damnation of that person (see Mt 25:41; Rom 9:15ff.) (positive, unconditional but "consequent" reprobation [following on the person's rejection of God]). To assert a positive unconditional reprobation antecedent to human guilt and thus its cause, would be heretical predestinationism (*Predestination, *Salvific will of God).

RESURRECTION OF JESUS

(1) The Easter message of the NT is not primarily concerned to offer apologetical proof of the historical fact that *Jesus Christ, after his genuine and actual death, deposition from the cross and normal burial, rose again in his total and therefore in his physical reality to glorified perfection and immortality (see 2). But in view of the difficulties for faith that are possible today it is important first of all to indicate the solid historicity of the fact. It is based on two experiences which fortify and illuminate one another and which even when subjected to critical exegesis and purely historical investigation defy serious contestation. The first experience is the discovery of the empty tomb (earliest evidence Mk 16:1–8), which critical exegesis proves *not* to have been used as an apologetical argument. (On the one hand the discovery was made by women, who in Jewish law were incapable of being witnesses—"idle tales", Lk 24:11; the account ends on the note of fear, Mk 16:8; but on the other hand the report could be checked in Jerusalem; and the anti-Christian controversialists there never contested the fact of the empty tomb.) The other experience is that of Jesus' repeated appearances (earliest evidence 1 Cor 15:3b –5, a traditional passage deriving from the first years of the primitive Church and originally composed in Aramaic, which according to Jewish anthropology can only refer to a bodily resurrection, and in any case cannot be an authentic "legitimating formula") to selected witnesses. It is not primarily on the grounds of the empty tomb that these proclaim their faith, but on the grounds of a personal conviction derived from personal observation and later, in the Gospels, made credible for others also by the report of the discovery of the empty tomb, which was not and could not be disputed in Jerusalem.

(2) Like 1 Cor 15:3–5, the sermons of St Peter (Acts 2:22–40; 3:12–16; 5:29–32; 10:34–43 and *passim*—evidence, incidentally, of the

controversy between Christians and Jews over the Resurrection), the value of which has been rediscovered by critical exegesis, reveal the primitive community's paschal belief in the mighty deed of God that restored Jesus to life and made him manifest, whereby the apparitions of the risen Lord are attested as *objective* events. (Original outline of the paschal preaching: resurrection; scriptural proof; testimony of the disciples. Later outline: empty tomb; Christophany; ascension.) Another essential element in the attestation of these appearances is the demonstration that he who rose from the dead is identical with the Crucified (for example Lk 24; Jn 20); that a function of unique dignity, foreseen by the Lord, vests in the *Apostles and above all in Peter when they bear their witness, a function purposely fortified by the accounts of what the risen Christ said. In the NT, the resurrection of Jesus is always supported by the presumption (inseparable from the testimony) of an objective event, which is inadequately (even if not unjustly) represented as "resurrection into the awareness of the faithful". In view of the novelty of the resurrected body, it is understandable that some should assert that the *resurrection of the flesh expected in Judaism served as an interpretament for the disciples' Easter experience; but this experience consists not merely of an inward process of reflection demanding interpretation, but is clearly grounded in objective events.

(3) In addition, the apostolic faith in the resurrection of Jesus and its preaching in catechesis and liturgy (especially at *baptism) may be summed up as follows: Jesus' resurrection is the Father's supreme act of power—the decisive testimony of himself given by the Son; the inauguration of the last days and their salvation—the experience of salvation in the present; the full recognition of Jesus as the *Messiah, the *Ebed Yahweh, the *Son of man, the second *Adam, and "inaugurator of life", the founder and model of the new creation, the cosmic (Eph, Col) last Man (1 Cor 15:45), the Lord (*Kyrios), present to his Church in his glorified state; hence the admonition to walk in newness of *life, to put on the new man, which to be sure can only be done by the grace of the risen Lord since it is ultimately his "Spirit" (see Rom 7:6; 8:9; 14:17 and *passim)* that renews the believer in the image of the second and heavenly Adam (1 Cor 15:47f.), indeed empowers him to have the risen Christ formed in him (cf. Rom 8:10; Eph 3:17; Gal 2:19).

(4) The resurrection of Jesus is acknowledged by all the creeds from the beginning. It must also form a central theme of theology today, being the consummation of God's saving activity for the world and mankind, in which he irrevocably communicates himself to the world

in the Son whom the Resurrection has definitively identified, and thus with eschatological conclusiveness accepts the world to its own salvation, so that all that remains is to disclose and give effect to what has already happened in the Resurrection. The Resurrection is properly a mystery of faith because, being the consummation of Christ, it can be adequately understood only in reference to the absolute mystery of the Incarnation. Theologically, therefore, the resurrection of Christ is not one instance of resurrection in general, as though the latter were a thing already intelligible to us of itself; rather it is the unique event flowing from Christ's nature and death that first provides the foundation for the resurrection of those whom he has redeemed.

(5) From the Christological point of view the Resurrection means that Jesus in his whole reality, and therefore also in his body, has risen to the glorified perfection and immortality (by contrast with raising a dead man to life) that is due to him by virtue of his passion and death, since these bring forth this concrete consummation by an intrinsic necessity of their nature. The death and resurrection of Jesus are a single process, whose phases are intrinsically and indissolubly connected (see Lk 24:26, 46; Rom 4:25; 6:4f.): the definitive being of every human being is something he dies into from within, so that this conclusiveness is the ripened fruit of an existence lived freely in time, and not a merely temporally succeeding period which may be marked by something totally heterogeneous from what has gone before. At the same time, however, this completion is the gift of God, for to die is to place oneself in every respect at the disposition of the divine disposer. Jesus' resurrection must therefore be the perfected and perfecting end of his own personal and particular death and each element of the one process must condition and interpret the other. When Scripture and Tradition therefore regard the Resurrection as the Father's real acceptance of the sacrifice of Jesus' death and part of the nature of that sacrifice, this is not mythology but a statement of fact.

(6) Because Jesus' bodily humanity is a permanent part of one world which has one dynamism the resurrection of Christ is soteriologically and objectively the commencement of the ontologically coherent event which is the glorification of the world; in this commencement the final consummation of the world has been decided in principle and has already begun. The resurrection of Christ is also more than his private destiny because it creates *Heaven and is not (together with the *Ascension, which basically is an element of the Resurrection) simply an entrance into a pre-existent heaven; because here too history and saving history underlie natural history and do not simply run their course within the framework of a fixed natural order

442

that remains unaffected by them. On the other hand these considerations must also show that because the risen Christ has been released from individuating corporeality, it is of a mere earthly kind precisely as the risen one—by his "going", then—that he has truly become he who is close to the world, and, therefore, his return is only the disclosure of this intimate and unlimited relationship of Christ with the world which the Resurrection has established.

(7) The experience of someone "from the other world", who has to "show" himself, who no longer belongs to human spatio-temporality, is not an event "comprehensible" in terms of human experience. Without the experience of the spirit: i.e., in this case without the faithfully accepted experience of the meaningfulness of existence, trustful surrender to the Easter experience of the disciples would be impossible. Only he who hopes can see the fulfilment of hope, and once that fulfilment is seen hope reaches the peaceful terms of its own existence. A "fleshly" resurrection is inconceivable because it is not the reproduction of an earlier state, but signifies that radical metamorphosis which free earthly human existence must experience as a whole if man is to attain his fulfilment in the conquest of time and the detemporalization of eternity.

RESURRECTION OF THE FLESH

Man is the creature that awaits the future, which is fulfilment. Since he experiences himself as an entity, he cannot conceive this completion simply as fulfilment of the *soul, even though he cannot imagine what true fulfilment would be "like".

(1) The OT Scriptures and Later Judaism bear witness to a gradual emergence of belief in the resurrection of the flesh. The first certain evidence of it in the OT is Dan 12:1bf. (Further evidence in 2 Macc 7; in the OT apocrypha it figures especially as a privilege of the just, but is later extended to all, both good and bad.) In Jesus' time the resurrection of the flesh was denied in particular by the Sadducees because it is not found in the Pentateuch, and Jesus refuted them on scriptural grounds (Mk 12:18–27). The resurrection of the flesh is clearly taught in the preaching of Jesus, in Acts 24:15, in St John's Gospel and in the Apocalypse, and St Paul develops its theology while definitely rejecting the Hellenistic notion of the body (as the grave or prison of the soul). No trace is found in the NT of a beatitude with the Lord apart from the *body. According to St Paul the Christian's risen body is "spiritual" (as the whole resurrection is governed by the

443

Spirit; *Pneuma), conformed to Christ's glorious body (Phil 3:21; 1 Cor 15:35f.; *Glory), but, analogous to the Jesus' glorified body, preserving continuity with the earthly body, though changed (1 Cor 15:36f., 51). St Paul does not mention the resurrection of non-Christians and the unjust but presupposes it in his theology of *Judgment.

(2) Christian belief in the resurrection of the flesh was obscured for centuries by Greek depreciation of the *body and individualistic concern for the salvation of the soul, and also by the cosmological theory of the ancients that represented *heaven as a place prior and external to saving history which one could reach by emigrating upwards. Against his predecessor John XXII, Benedict XII defined the dogma that the human animating principle may attain the *beatific vision even before its fulfilment in glorified corporeality and need not await the resurrection of the flesh (presumed to occur "later", and *therefore* left undefined) (D 1000f.).

(3) In order to form an adequate conception of the resurrection of the flesh it is necessary to observe that flesh in Scripture means the whole man in his bodily reality (for a differential use of the term, see *Sarx*). But this whole man in his unity is yet something plural, a being existing in various dimensions (matter—spirit, nature—person, action —passion, etc.) whose perfection need not necessarily be achieved in every dimension at once. Thus it is also conceivable that the permanent reality of the personal spirit will attain immediate union with God in *death and the dead man yet remain bound up with the world's reality, its destiny, and therefore its time, the more so because the personal spirit must be seen as the sense of all terrestrial reality, and the end of the world—which is the end of its history but not of its existence—as a sharing in the completion of that spirit (*Intermediate state). This completion is only perfect when it embraces that dimension which inseparably belongs to the concreteness of the spirit as its matter, and which once perfect must no longer be conceived as occupying a place in our physical spatiality. That does not mean that the resurrection of the flesh cannot be seen as a process beginning with death. For the resurrection of the flesh as the epiphany of a person's whole history, see *Judgment;* for the perfecting of human communion in the resurrection of the flesh, see *Heaven.* Speculation about the risen body is limited by the special character of biblical *eschatology.

REVELATION

The question of the meaning of revelation is the question of the supreme and most radical case of insight into how, on the one hand, a real development of what is higher, coming about from "below" and from what is lower, yet able to transcend itself, and, on the other hand, a lasting creation from "above" can be no more than two equally true aspects of the one miracle of development and history. There are two positions that are opposed to this view. The first is the immanentism of *Modernism. For those who support this view, revelation is no more than the development that necessarily takes place, and is immanent in human history, of man's religious need. In that development, this need is made objective in the most widely differing forms in the history of different religions and has gradually, throughout this history, assumed more pure and objective forms in Judaism and Christianity. The second of these contrasting positions is that of extrinsicism. According to this view, revelation is the event of a divine intervention that comes purely from outside, addresses men, communicates truths to them through prophets in statements that would otherwise not be accessible to them, and gives them moral and other directives which they have to follow. When God creates other being and this being, as finite, refers the *spirit—which by its transcendence recognizes finite being *as* finite—to its principle and sharply differentiates that principle as being qualitatively different from the finite, this is equivalent to a certain disclosure of God as infinite mystery, which is often called "natural revelation". But this revelation still leaves God unknown to the extent that (a) it makes him known only by *analogy as *mystery, by denying him the attributes of finite being, by mediate inference, not directly laying hold on God in himself, and that (b) his ultimate, unequivocal relationship with spiritual creatures cannot be known by this means, which does not tell us whether God wills (or is able) to be for us the absolute intimacy of radical self-communication, or silent, self-contained infinity keeping us at a distance, imprisoned in our finitude, whether his response to our sinful rejection of him is to be judgment or forgiveness. Beyond this "natural" revelation, which presents the fact of God as a question, not an answer, there is a true revelation of God. It is not simply implicit in the spiritual nature of man but exhibits the character of an event; it is dialogic. In it God speaks to man (Heb 1:1–2), makes known to him not merely what can be deduced at all times and in all places from the necessary reference of all earthly things to God, that is the search for God and the challenge which this mystery presents to man, but rather all that remains unknown in and for the world even when the world is presupposed: the intimate being of God and his free, personal relationship with his spiritual creatures. We need not discuss whether it is possible by our unaided human powers to know that God is able to express himself in such a way. The argument may be that by entering the finite reality of human knowledge this revelation becomes finite, thus destroying itself as such. God in fact has so revealed himself (D 3004) and from this fact, at least, we may conclude that such revelation is possible. This revelation obviously possesses two different aspects, both of them necessary, which must not be divorced and whose mutual relations are subject to some variation.

(1) This revelation (called historical, personal, verbal revelation) primarily addresses itself to man's unique, interior, spiritual being, that is to say as part of the whole process of revelation, not as a phase anterior in time or an isolated event, enabling man to hear and embrace this personal self-disclosure of God as God in such a way that it is not brought down to the level of finite creatures as such—in which case it could no longer "get through" as God's self-revelation. For God, divinizing man through Himself, becomes co-author of the act of "hearing" (faith), that is, the act which accepts God's self-disclosure and self-communication. This revelation is God's personal gift of himself to man in absolute, forgiving intimacy, so that God is neither absolute, chilling distance nor the Judgment—though he could be both—but gives himself to man to experience in this forgiving intimacy. The duality we have just described is what Christians call sanctifying and justifying *grace, firstly a divinizing elevation of man ("created" grace) whereby God gives not only something different from himself but his own self ("uncreated" grace)—habitual grace—and secondly empowers man to accept it—actual grace. The event of God's free, gracious self-revelation is always in being because this grace from God is offered to all men in all ages for Christ's sake and is efficacious by the very fact of being offered, and, we may hope, though it is impossible to know for certain, at least the majority of men accept it even when they are unable to reflect on this event happening in the inmost core of their spiritual person; because this grace alters man's consciousness, gives him, in scholastic terminology, a new, higher, gracious, but non-reflexive "formal object" (transcendence to God's absolute being as beatitude); because at least the horizon of man's spiritual being, that infinite question, is filled through this ineffable divine self-communication with the confident faith that God answers the infinite question with the infinite answer that is himself. Thus, always and everywhere, history is the history of salvation and of revelation. But this interior gracious self-revelation of God at the core of the spiritual person is meant, after all, for man

in all his dimensions, because all are destined for salvation. And this brings us to the other aspect of revelation.

(2) God's self-revelation in the depths of the spiritual person is a certain "state of mind" (in the spiritual, not the emotional sense) produced by grace, inarticulate, taken for granted, not an objective proposition—not knowlege but a consciousness. But this gracious, unobjective, nonreflexive self-revelation of God must be translated into objective propositions if it is to become the principle of man's concrete behaviour in his objective reflex consciousness. Now this "translation" has a history of its own which God governs and which is therefore another divine revelation, and this history of reflection forms an intrinsic part of the historical process of God's self-disclosure in grace, because this self-disclosure possesses an inherent dynamism that urges it to objectify itself. In principle the attempt is made in every religion (at least on man's part) to reflect on original, nonreflexive, unobjectified revelation and to declare it in the form of propositions, and in every religion we find isolated instances of such successful reflection, made possible by the divine grace whereby God gives man, even in the dimension of his objectivity, in his concrete historicity, an opportunity to be saved. But as God permits human sin in general and this obscures and corrupts every dimension of human life, individual and social, the history of man's attempts to objectify revelation is not excepted: the attempt is only partially successful, and revelation is mingled with error and culpable ignorance. But if God guides this objectification of revelation for the sake of the human community and not merely the individual's personal life; if the "translation", in men whom we call religious *prophets, bearers of revelation to others in the full sense, is so guided by God as to remain pure (though it may only convey certain aspects of interior revelation and only declare them pragmatically in terms of certain historical situations), if the purity of this revelation as objectified by the prophets and its claims upon us are established by what we call a *miracle (D 3009), then we have what is known as public, official revelation, embodied in Covenant and Church, and its history—revelation *simpliciter*. This type of revelation is an historical occurrence, not only in that (once creation is assumed) it is God's free decision and requires the free (historical) response of (every) man, but also in that it does not occur everywhere in this official, reflexively guaranteed form but has a special history within universal history and the general history of religions. Insofar as this revelation has a separate history—through the historical phases of reflection on God's gracious gift of himself to man (which reflection, being guided by God, is itself an element of revela-

447

tion)—within universal history, the history of revelation comes to its absolute climax when the divine self-communication, through the *hypostatic union in God's Incarnation (the substantiality of which intrinsically includes God's personal and spiritual communication as a union with a created spirit), culminates in the created spiritual being of Jesus; for here he who is expressed (God), the mode of expression (Christ's human nature in its being, life and conclusiveness) and the recipient (Jesus as he who is blessed and sees God) have become absolutely one personally (not a neuter identity). In Jesus, both God's gracious communication to men and its self-declaration in the tangible, bodily, social dimension have reached their climax, have become Revelation.

Such revelation (reflex, propositional, public, and official) as existed before is only properly appreciated if seen as the most immediate preparation (in the temporal sense) for Christ, since we know of a revelation displaying all these characteristics only in God's covenant with Israel from the time of Moses—that is for a period, and in an area, comprising perhaps one per cent of human history. The crucial nature of this revelation for us does not follow from the concrete content of this OT history—which is either accessible to human powers as such (*Monotheism, *Natural moral law) or concerns the political life of the chosen people and the historical conditions of their concrete social and religious relationships (which reveal God's will even in what seems to be the "natural" course of history). But it remains permanently valid for us in two respects: because this history and no other is the immediate, concrete prehistory of the Incarnation as the history of revelation, and because the basic outline of NT revelation is already to be discerned in it—God speaks and acts in person, he draws near to man, history is experienced as the history of God's personal acts, which show him to be free, holy, and forgiving. This history of grace and this divinely guided self-reflection before Christ and his resurrection indicated the possibility that revelation might be declared to such an extent as to constitute an absolute self-communication of the glory of God's own intimate love, this—not the terrible divine Judgment—becoming God's last victorious word in history; but this interpretation of revelation was not yet the public, official one, its soundness confirmed by miracles. The history of God's self-communication was always going on, of course (because of Jesus Christ and with him as its goal), but before Jesus Christ objective knowledge of it was no essential part of this history itself (*Old Testament, *New Testament, *Holy Scripture).

When the eschatological, reflex realization of God's self-communication revealed through Jesus Christ (the final climax of this communication) is explicitly embodied in an eschatologically definitive society, the result is what we call the *Church. She both receives and announces this absolute revelation. Because this truth of God's absolute self-disclosure is definitive, not only victorious in ideological terms but really and permanently extant in Jesus Christ, the Church infallibly confesses the truth; that is, her confession, in which the real, objective truth of God's self-gift in Jesus Christ exists, cannot perish, cannot err when engaging the whole Church without qualification, for otherwise the very truth of Jesus Christ would no longer exist (*Infallibility). Since this victorious truth of Jesus Christ in the Church constitutes a Church which is organized hierarchically, "infallibility" must attach to the acts of the Church's hierarchical government, her magisterium (Pope and bishops), which must be able to preserve, actualize and develop the abiding presence of Christ's truth in any historical situation.

REVIVISCENCE

See *Opus Operatum.*

REVOLUTION, THEOLOGY OF REVOLUTION

Society is involved in the denial of its own essential nature and conflict is perpetually latent in it to the extent that the division of labour leads not just to a freely-agreed, indispensable division of functions but to the unilateral domination of one class over another resulting from the division of society into groups that have directly at their disposal the means of production, social institutions and the means of communication, and into groups that do not have at their disposal these basic means of realizing their potential both individually and socially. The explosive potential of this contradiction leads to a crisis in the structure of society to the extent that the oppressed become aware of this conflict and that the social system is no longer able to provide any real fulfilment of the oppressed class's now explicit demand for more freedom and for the opportunity of social development and is thus only able to try to appease this demand by means of an ideology of reconciliation. Revolution in the strict sense is when this conflict comes to a head in the thorough and violent overthrow of the prevailing social system within a limited period of time. Revolution as the radical reorganization of a society and its system of production is thus distinguished from reforms conducted within the system by the fact that it involves a head-on attack on the principles of the social system itself and by-passes the opportunities that system provides for adjusting difficulties and solving problems. As far as constitutional law is concerned a revolution must therefore always be illegal from the point of view of the prevailing system of government, since it specifically does not avail itself of the opportunities provided by this system. A successful revolution on the other hand establishes a new legal framework. The goal of every revolution is the good in the form of freedom —freedom from want, exploitation, injustice and oppression. The means a revolution is forced to use are violent confrontation, without which it is not possible to eliminate the existing regime with the force and the structural power it has at its disposal. Usually a revolution is accomplished by a revolutionary group or party trying to seize political power in the State in the name of the people. This gives rise to the fundamental question of which comes first: is a revolutionary change in people's awareness needed first of all before there can be any question of overthrowing the existing social system, or is it the political revolution that creates a new awareness? Considered in the abstract, this question cannot be answered in the sense of one development preceding the other in time. Rather, against the background of a redefinition of the relationship between theory and practice, the first question to be put concerns whether a revolutionary situation exists in practice and who is to conduct the revolution. Only when both conditions are fulfilled can revolutionary awareness and revolutionary practice come into being as factors affecting each other and take effect. The oppressed class goes into the question of social relationships thoroughly to the extent that it is involved in the overthrow in practice of the prevailing contradictions in society. For their administration institutions that have been transformed in keeping with the revolution need people similarly transformed. If either occurs on its own without the other, then what results is usually either chaos and anarchy or the restoration of the previous regime. From the point of view of the understanding of history, the question remains open whether liberty and equality can simultaneously be established definitely or at all on the basis of social surplus. The contemporary theology of revolution (for the most part of Protestant origin, but encouraged by the social encyclicals of Popes John XXIII and Paul VI; cf. also D 3775–76) sees itself not so much as a satisfactory answer to these problems and to their implications for our understanding of history but rather as an attempt, taking into consideration the eschatological character of the Christian message of salvation, to react to actual social crises (particularly in the third world) by contributing towards the elimination of unjust oppression and towards making possible a social system in keeping with human dignity. In this sense the theology of revolution is seen not only as a technique of interpreting belief in the light of the critique of society but also as an actual political option which as such demands a strategic alliance with the political organizations of the exploited and oppressed classes.

RIGHTEOUSNESS

See *Justice.*

RIGORISM

See *Moral Systems.*

RULE OF FAITH

Either, in a very general sense, what is presented to the individual Christian as a rule or norm of faith (God's revelation as the word of *Holy Scripture and *Tradition, authentically interpreted by the *magisterium of the *Church), or, in a narrower sense, certain brief summaries of Christian faith, already current in the Church in the apostolic age, which were gradually expanded and fixed in the form of the *Creeds still used today, especially as designed to guard against heretical notions.

S

SABELLIANISM

A heresy of the third and fourth centuries which denied the *Trinity, named after Sabellius (excommunicated at Rome about 220), a type of *Monarchianism (*Modalism). It alleged that God is three only in relation to the world, as three manifestations to the world of God who is simply identical in himself, with the effect that God ceases to be the Father with the Incarnation, and ceases to be the Son with the ascension (D 112–115).

SACRAMENT

The fundamental essence of the sacrament is to be found in the words used: the "matter" basically has only a secondary function of helping to make clear what the words signify. Words pronounced in the Church in the name and with the mandate of God and Jesus Christ have in principle an "exhibitive" character, that is they bring about what they are pointing to, in other words God's grace. In the strictest and proper sense the *word of God can only exist as the effect of his *grace. The word of the Gospel is always sustained by a grace that is in fact effective because it derives from God and not simply from the good will of man. This word of salvation, in the mouth of the *Church making its proclamation in faith, is ultimately as the eschatologically victorious word directed towards the world: the Church is the bearer of that word of God's promise of himself to the world that creates the salvation that is eschatologically victorious. Hence the Church is the primal or fundamental sacrament (cf. Church, 1, 9, 48, 59; Church/world, 42, 45; Miss., 1, 5, and elsewhere). Through its belief in God's grace that is eschatologically

452

victorious in Jesus Christ, a belief that it hears and proclaims in faith, the Church is the sacrament of the world's salvation, since it proclaims and makes present as eschatologically victorious in the world that grace that will never again disappear from this world and that invincibly is moving this world towards the fulfilment of the *kingdom of God. This sacramental sign of grace is an effective sign, not because it is trying to summon up God's gracious will which does not exist without it, but because through it this very gracious will of God comes to manifest itself in history and thus makes itself historically irrevocable: the sacrament is effective as *opus operatum. The true nature of a sacrament will only be intelligible if the *opus operatum is seen in the light of the eschatological situation of salvation in Christ. Since this dispensation is final, definitive, and victorious, the pledge of salvation it contains is absolute and is not, in its God-willed solemn validity, made dependent on the moral state of the human minister of the pledge (for the defined teaching of the Church, see D 1612), nor is it efficacious in virtue of the *disposition or *intention of its recipient. These subjective dispositions are indeed the condition (sometimes produced by the pledge itself) of the "advent" of grace for the individual as such (D 1606); here again the victorious fulfilment of the pledge is brought about by grace itself and its concrete enactment proclaimed in its eschatological uniqueness. When the Church, engaging its whole being, makes absolute in God's name and Christ's this pledge of grace for the individual at the decisive moments of his personal saving history, this opus operatum exists in the form of the individual sacraments. Given the social nature of the Church and the incarnational structure of grace and salvation, this pledge must be enacted "ceremonially" (see D 1613), like every solemn, official act of a society, if the Church—the eschatologically victorious representation and presence of God's grace in Christ—is to be totally engaged. This ceremonial may consist of mere words (the *form: absolution, consent in marriage); or the words, which are always necessary, may be associated with a liturgical gesture (*matter: for example, laying on of hands); or it may consist of a liturgical action (baptism, confirmation, Eucharist, anointing of the sick) which explains words and gestures still more clearly by the use of some material thing (ablutions with water, anointing with oil or chrism, serving food). The sacraments are of divine institution if only because Jesus Christ has intended the Church, through his life's work of forming a community round himself, by his *cross and *resurrection, to be the representative presence of his eschatologically victorious salvation, and because the sacraments are absolute acts of this victorious presence of grace for the individual in his decisive situations. In addition, though this need not be thought necessary for every sacrament, we know from historical tradition the words by which Christ gave the commission to impart *baptism (Mt 28:19), the *Eucharist (Mt 26:26–28; Mk 14:22–24; Lk 22:19–20; 1 Cor 11:24f.), the sacrament of *penance (Mt 16:18f.; Jn 20:22f.) (as to *office itself, power of the *keys, *binding and loosing). By the nature of such social events, it is for the Church to fix the concrete details of valid rite or the several degrees of participation in a sacramental action. It is only since the eleventh century that the Church has given these manifold, intrinsically different performances the common name of sacrament (a permanent sign of grace, established by Jesus Christ, and efficacious *ex opere operato).* Since then, in agreement with the Eastern Churches, it has recognized seven sacraments (for the defined teaching of the Church, see D 1601): man's initiation into the Church (baptism); the express mission to the world (deriving from baptism and its extrapolation) from the Holy Spirit (confirmation); the reconciliation of the baptized and repentant sinner (by the restoration of his baptismal grace) with the Church and God by the words of absolution (penance); the central solemnity of Jesus's Supper and the anamnetic presence of his redemptive sacrifice in the liturgical sacrifice, the celebration of the Church's unity in love in anticipation of the kingdom of God (in the Eucharist); the prayers and unction with which the Church comes to man's aid when his mortality presses upon him in serious illness (anointing of the sick); the transmission of office and the charism of office (in holy *orders); and the sanctification of wedded love by drawing it into the mystery of Jesus Christ's forgiving love that unites the Church to him (matrimony). The sevenfold nature of such radical, express demonstrations of *grace in the Church is not merely confirmed as given by the Church, but implies an historical decision by the Church itself, in which the Church acknowledges with these words alone that radical commitment on the part of the Church which, by the very nature of the matter, is necessary for so radically expressive an idea of grace. The sacraments contain and communicate (as instrumental causes) the grace which they signify. The authorized minister varies according to the sacrament (in matrimony the minister is the layman, as may also happen in the case of baptism). On the necessity of the sacraments for salvation, see D 1604 and *Necessity for Salvation.*

SACRAMENTALS

SACRAMENTAL THEOLOGY

This deals with the general nature and special characteristics of the seven sacraments. It seeks first to establish what all have in common (origin in Jesus, structure of the sacramental sign, *opus operatum,* distinction between valid and fruitful reception of the sacraments, the sacramental *character imprinted by three of them, etc), and then examines the individual sacraments one after the other. There is a danger here of looking on the sacraments as homogeneous "instances" of the genus sacrament (D 1603). The individual sacraments are rather to be considered specifically different realizations of Christian life in the recipient, and of the Church's nature. They should therefore be presented in connexion with the existential attitude to each one which grace creates in the Christian (dying to the world; mission to the world in the Spirit; *metanoia* constantly renewed, constant readiness to appropriate the cross of Jesus, the Church, newness of life; priestly life; married life; acceptance of human weakness as the strength of Christ).

SACRAMENTALS

As defined by the Code of Canon Law, can. 1144, sacramentals are things or actions which the Church is accustomed to use, on the model of the sacraments, to obtain certain effects (chiefly of a spiritual nature) by her prayers. Among the sacramentals are liturgical prayers and rites ("ceremonies" in a restricted sense) used in administering the sacraments, exorcisms, blessings (of persons), consecrations and blessings of objects (chalices, rosaries, etc.), and the subsequent use of these objects. All sacramentals are intercessory prayers of the Church (or else are based on and related to such prayers); they may be offered for the person on whom she is conferring office (for instance, the blessing of an abbot), for the person who is to use an object in worship which has been consecrated or blessed (that is, officially set aside for exclusively liturgical use), for one who is to use some profane object in reliance on the Church's intercessory prayer (blessing of houses, cars), and for people in special circumstances (churching of women, exorcism, etc.). This "intercession" is not confined to the prayer which the priest says (perhaps hastily and thoughtlessly) when the sacramental is being performed—his is merely an expression of the true prayer, explicit or implicit, constantly offered for one another by the justified members of the one body of Christ. The sacramentals are meaningful and in themselves beneficial religious acts of bodily man in the tangible society of the Church (in a manner analogous to the sacraments). They may not be condemned (D 1255, 1613, 1746, 1775). The individual Christian is free to choose what private use he will make of them. The danger of their superstitious or magical use should be perceived and avoided.

SACRED AND PROFANE

Sacred means that which belongs to the realm of the holy: *worship, persons and things marked out by *consecration, etc. Profane—that which lies *pro* (before) *fanum* (the temple, sanctuary, or sacred enclosure)—refers to the secular nature of the *world in which it lays claim to autonomy *vis-à-vis* religion and the churches. Underlying this dichotomy is the idea that part of the world can be reserved expressly for what is holy, that people and things can be segregated in this sphere and be primarily concerned with worship (conceived overwhelmingly as looking back to the past: *anamnesis, and that only in this sphere is a direct relationship with God possible. Christianity sees the world as profane, i.e., established by God in a process of increasing autonomy (and at the same time of increasing closeness to God in the process of God's *revelation of himself which has taken its definitive and final form in Jesus). But Christianity does not see itself as sacred, since as a whole it is not separated from or out of the world but instead is established in the world to come to fulfilment there. The distance that Christianity needs to maintain between itself and the world with its desires, and the critique it needs to bring to bear on it, are not to be established by the creation of a special sphere of the sacred. Even the Eucharist, in which Christianity finds its most fundamental expression and in which Jesus' "profane" life and death are made present and strength is gained for the realization of the promise of the kingdom of God in the world, is not a sacred activity in which something or someone is trying to become detached from the world. Even less to be regarded as sacred are the Church's personnel and institutions, which in any case are always also marked by the spirit of the world. The dichotomy is thus not suited to express the way Christianity sees the world and itself.

456

SACRIFICE

Being one of the most ancient and widespread of religious rites, sacrifice is found in a great variety of form and significance over the enormous range (in time and space) of man's religious practices. The conception of sacrifice which directly concerns Christian soteriology and sacramental theology, and bearing OT practice in mind (though it does not apply to every sacrifice), is roughly the following: Sacrifice is the act whereby an authorized person, representing a group of worshippers, changes a material offering in such a way as to withdraw it from profane use, place it within the "sacred" sphere and thus dedicate it to God as an expression of adoring self-surrender in the holy God; to make it, when accepted and sanctified by God, the sign in the community's sacrifical meal of God's gracious will to enter into communion with man. For the NT in particular the whole procedure of worship, wherever it may occur, can only be the *symbol of man's adoring self-surrender and God's gracious acceptance of it (see already 1 Sam 15:22; Ps 40:7; 51:18f.; Is 1:11; Jer 7:22; Os 6:66; then Mt 9:13; 23:19; Rom 12:1; Heb 10).

Sacrifice, as expressing the religious *act *par excellence,* is conceivable and legitimate only in relation to God. It is disputed among Catholic theologians whether changing the offering and dedicating it to God necessarily amounts to a "destruction", an "immolation" expressing the fact that as a sinner man is deserving of death, or whether this is only a secondary aspect of some sacrifices. The *adoration of God which is expressed in sacrifice may take on the colour of sheer praise, of thanksgiving, of petition or of propitiation, which will then be reflected in the sacrifice as well. On the use of this concept in dogmatic theology, see *Redemption, Cross, Theories of Satisfaction, Mass.*

SADDUCEES

Perhaps named after the high priest Zadok, see Ezekiel 40:46 etc.; a religious and political party of liberal and sceptical views in the Judaism of Jesus' time (opponents of the Pharisees), represented by the ruling classes (priests and aristocrats); they received only such theology as derived from the older writings of the OT, denied the resurrection of the flesh (Mt 22:23) and the existence of angels (Acts 23:8), and exaggerated human freedom and self-reliance.

SALUTARY ACT

A human act that is positively ordered to *justification (*actus mere salutaris*) or, when a person is already justified, makes some positive contribution to the attainment of the *beatific vision (*actus salutaris et meritorius, *merit). The Church has defined the doctrine that the gratuitous *grace of God is absolutely necessary for each salutary act (D 375, 377, 1551ff.; see what is said of the beginning of *faith in that article). For a discussion of the theological problems connected with salutary acts, see *Grace, Synergism*.

SALVATION

A basic concept of religion and theology but not really a technical term of theology. It does not primarily signify an "objective" achievement (as, e.g., in movements and utopias immanent to the world), but rather a "subjective", existential healing and fulfilment of life. Even the *aetiology of the OT, but above all the existential experience of *contingency, of the continual hazards of existence, especially in the experience of sin and death, and the teaching of Jesus show that salvation cannot be won by human efforts. The primary purpose of the scriptural message of salvation is to expose the common ruin in which the one human race is involved by man's own doing (*Original sin) and then to show that salvation bears the same dialectical relation to the human race and to each individual: salvation at once constitutes all mankind as God's *basileia and grants the individual God's *self-communication in Jesus Christ. If this opens the way of salvation to humanity and the individual in Jesus Christ (and in the chief instrument of divine grace and mercy, the new People of God, the Church) and reveals history as *saving history, still the presence of salvation is not equivalent to the subjective appropriation of salvation; for apart from Christ's own appropriation of salvation, which we only know of through witnesses, to experience grace is not the same thing as to be certain of salvation (*Salvation, certainty of) and so does not give the certainty of permanent healing and consolation that salvation connotes. Accordingly, the concept of salvation should not simply be identified with grace but (again, in contrast to secular utopias) should retain that note of conclusiveness which characterizes the complementary theological concepts of the *beatific vision and the *resurrection of the flesh. These could well be comprehended in the term "salvation"—salvation which applies to the whole man in the totality

458

of his being and is not yet given in this transient world by any objective redemption, any grace of any Church, as constant human experience proves. Thus salvation remains the essential object of *hope even in the Christian dispensation.

SALVIFIC WILL OF GOD

According to the testimony of Scripture this will is not a necessary attribute of God but a free, personal "attitude" which was first definitively and irrevocably revealed in Jesus Christ, to whom its history (*Saving history) is ordered and in whom it has been fulfilled. *All* have one Redeemer (1 Tim 4:10), *all* are enlightened (Jn 1:29; 3:16f.; 4:13; 8:12; 1 Jn 2:2; clearest of all is the classic text 1 Tim 2:1–6; see also Mt 26:28 with parallel texts; Mk 10:45; Rom 11:31; Mt 23:27; Lk 19:41). If Scripture thus praises the might of God's merciful will, which embraces *all* and conquers sin (Rom 5:17f.; 11:32), it does not conclude from this to an *apocatastasis*. The salvific will of God is the basis of *hope *per se*, which is actually manifest only in the act of hope itself. Accordingly the Church can firmly maintain that Christ died for all men (Creed); that God gives all who are justified sufficient *grace to avoid or counter by *penance all formal (subjectively) serious sin and thus to be saved (D 1536ff., 1568 and *passim*). It would be heretical to suppose that Christ died only for the predestined (D 2005 and *passim*) or only for believers (*Atheism), or that pagans, heretics and others outside the Church do not receive sufficient grace to be saved (*Extra Ecclesiam nulla salus; D 2304, 2425, 2428, 2865f.; Vat. II: Church, 16). The Church has made no pronouncement on the question whether infants who die unbaptized (*Limbo) are included in God's universal salvific will. The universality and sovereign freedom of God's salvific will show us, as nothing else does, *who* the God of love is (*Reprobation, *Predestination). In so far as hope is supported by the eschatological salvific event of Jesus Christ, salvation is not *one* of two possibilities, with damnation as another of equal status, and between which human freedom can make an autonomous choice. By means of his own sovereign effective grace, God has already determined the entire history of freedom (which comprises the area within which an individual makes his or her free choice) in favour of the world's redemption in Jesus Christ.

459

SANCTIFYING GRACE

In the NT God's gracious act for man is a *justification which is not merely an eschatological promise or an external imputation but a present, abiding, interior, salvific possession bestowed in the event (of itself historically particular) of *metanoia, becoming a believer and being baptized (*Baptism). According to Scripture this is a new creation, a passage from death to life, a rebirth from above and above all the communication of the divine *Pneuma (*Holy Spirit, *Indwelling), which is the true, regenerative being of God himself (2 Pet 1:4). This abiding, interior, efficacious communication of the divine Spirit, with its effects, is known in Catholic theology as sanctifying grace.

The Catholic doctrine of sanctifying grace is contained in the declaration of the Council of Trent. Here it is stated, against the Reformers' conception of justification, that justification truly blots out a man's sins, so that he ceases to be a sinner and becomes just, and that solely by God's deed in the grace of Christ which can never be exacted and never merited (D 1524, 1528f.). This forgiveness effects an interior transformation and sanctification of a man; grace and the gifts really become his own (which does not mean that he can do what he will with them), so that this grace is called "infused", "inherent", and this *justice of God is the only formal cause of justification (D 1560). The theological *virtues are either identical with sanctifying grace or indissolubly connected with it. Being truly "infused" into man and gratuitously produced by God's "efficient causality" it is considered to be a "created" quality and is thus contrasted with uncreated grace. But we are also said to be anointed and sealed with the Holy Ghost himself (D 1528f., 1677f., 1689ff.: *Indwelling of God, *Self-communication of God, *Grace). In accordance with the doctrine of God's freedom with respect to grace, of the necessity of the correct *disposition and of the growth of grace, sanctifying grace exists in varying measure in various justified individuals (D 1528f., 1535, 1574, 1582). *Justification, that is the forgiveness of sins and interior righteousness, divine sonship and friendship with God (D 1528f., 1535), the indwelling of God, "qualification" for beatitude (D 1314ff., 1528f.), incorporation in Christ (and the Church: D 394, 1314ff., 1671ff., 1730, 3705), and participation in the divine nature (D 1921, 1942) are described as formal effects of sanctifying grace. It is possible to lose this grace by grave personal sin. This loss of grace by one's personal fault must not be confused with the lack of sanctifying grace which is due to *original sin, although the "state of sin" resulting from each is in vital respects the same: In the present economy of salvation, where sanctifying grace—which, being the self-communication of the essentially holy God, sanctifies a man antecedent to his own personal attitude (as can be seen very clearly in *infant baptism)—is lacking in a man, this very lack is of itself a condition of alienation from God that is counter to his will, and is therefore sinful. If the lack is the result of one's own free, personal fault, the condition is one of personal habitual guilt. If the lack is caused by the personal fault of another (that is, *Adam) and is displeasing to God as contravening the divine will and the divine order that was established at creation itself, we have the habitual guilt of *original sin (which is sin only by analogy).—As to the growth of sanctifying grace, see *Merit.*

SARX

From the Greek σάρξ, flesh. This term in Scripture does not mean what we now call the *body, but the whole man as a bodily being, with the weakness, corruptibility, necessary subjection to law, and mortality that form part of his spiritual personality (like "flesh and blood": Mt 16:17) (Mt 19:5; 24:22; Rom 1:3 etc.). God sent his Son in this *sarx* to save mankind (Rom. 8:3). Man in the *sarx,* as "natural", is distinguished from "spirit" (*Pneuma), the sanctifying and vivifying power of God that alone can save and transfigure the "flesh" (Mt 26:41; Jn 6:63; Rom 7:5f.; 8:3–14; Gal 3:3 etc.; see also *trichotomism). This flesh, thus distinguished from God's *Pneuma* (and the pneumatic permeation of man by the divine Spirit), finally becomes earth-bound human nature, ever begetting sin and death anew because it closes itself against this gift of the Holy Spirit (1 Cor 5:5; Gal 5:16ff.; 6:8 etc.). This existential *dualism in historical man who is compelled to take free decisions, must of course not be distorted into an essential dualism—human nature must not be thought evil in itself. Collectively, *sarx* can be used to mean the community (Gen 2:23), mankind (Gen 6:12), or all corporeal beings (Gen 6:17).

SATISFACTION

In Catholic theology, the grace-given moral effort, in faith in Jesus Christ and his grace, to make reparation to the goodness and sanctity of God—offended by sin—by actions that acknowledge and proclaim the sanctity of God. For treatments extending beyond this perspective, see *Death; Satisfaction, theories of.* The fact that satisfaction is strictly defined as bestowed by grace means that the initiative comes from God who inspires the desire for and implementation of satisfaction. According to Catholic doctrine satisfaction can be made for oneself or vicariously (by intercession) for others; it may be condign or adequate *(satisfactio condigna)*, or only congruous or inadequate *(congrua)*. Western theology holds that Jesus Christ has made superabundant satisfaction for all sinners by dying for all (D 1528f., 3891; *Redemption; *Satisfaction, theories of). It is at best for venial sins that someone in the grace of Christ can make condign satisfaction for the guilt of actual sin (D 1689ff.); but by voluntarily doing *penance or performing satisfaction imposed by the Church he can pay the debt of temporal punishment due to *sin (treasury of the Church) (D 1693, 1713). The satisfaction sacramentally imposed in the confessional is part of the sacrament; for its salient features, see *Penance, Sacrament of, Penance*. It is important that this sacramental satisfaction should also be consciously performed as satisfaction to man, who has been injured by sin, for example as reparation for injured love, for damage to reputation or property, etc. If the sacramental satisfaction is neglected after a person has seriously resolved to perform it, the sacrament of penance still remains valid but the person will still have to make satisfaction by suffering the painful consequences of sin: *purgatory.

SATISFACTION, THEORIES OF

The theology of *redemption must be as multi-dimensional as this supreme act of the God-Man necessarily is. Consequently it must (looking at *soteriology "physically") see the Incarnation itself as God's supreme, historical, irrevocable self-communication to the world, which already involves the realization of God's universal *salvific will for the world, *Christocentrism, and the supernatural destiny of all creation. Then this theology can regard Christ's act (living, and dying on the cross, in a personal history that is absolutely one)— which from the beginning was willed, accepted, effected by the Logos as his own history, the consummation of the human nature he has assumed—as "obedience" in the scriptural sense (Phil 2:6–11 etc.) unto exinanition (*Kenosis), and as "sacrifice" (1 Cor 5:7; Eph 5:2; Heb *passim;* D 261, 539), which of their nature make Jesus the exalted Lord. His very being (in risen glory) signifies the irresistible beginning of the redemption of the world, for as the being of the Son (and brother) of man (Rom 8:29) it is and remains part of God's one world and therefore cannot leave the rest of that world to a quite separate fate. Jesus Christ's act can be regarded as endurance of the tyranny of the forces of this world that enslave us (sin, law, death, time etc.), which are overcome because it is the Son who experiences them (Gal 4:3–7; Rom 6:6ff.; 8:19–23, 38f. etc.). But Christ's deed can also be analysed in more detail from a formal point of view: it is the free moral act (of obedience and love) which possesses "infinite" moral value because the moral value of an act before God derives not only from the content of the act but also from the dignity of the agent; so that in this case, the agent being the God-Man, the Person of the eternal Logos, the dignity of the act is infinite and divine. If we then regard this act as reparation for the *glory of which sin in the world deprives God, and assume that this "infinite" value of Christ's deed is freely accepted by God as *satisfaction for the offence of sin (which seems sufficiently clear from the fact of redemption attested in Scripture), it becomes possible to state that Christ redeems us by offering infinite satisfaction for the sins of the world as the representative of humanity. Such is the substance of the "theory of satisfaction" generally accepted by Catholic theologians since the time of St Anselm (d. 1109), which the magisterium of the Church has adopted but not actually defined (D 1025, 1027, 1528f., 3891; the Church's pronouncements usually state the revealed truth of our redemption without giving any further explanation). This theory of satisfaction (like the theory of *sacrifice) again has various nuances in scholastic theology, according as particular stress is laid on the idea of vicarious representation (identification of Christ with sinful humanity), sin as a personal insult to God (D 3891), the significance for the act of the dignity of the agent; and especially according to whether the idea of a "punishment of Jesus Christ" in place of sinners is introduced or (rightly) rejected, the suffering actually involved in Jesus Christ's satisfaction is considered essential to it or incidental, and the cross therefore regarded as an expression of God's holiness and justice or only of his merciful love—which again leads on to a profounder theology of *death in general. We should not forget that notions of satisfaction, sacrificial victim, etc., are time-conditioned and are really helpful only under certain spiritual and historical conditions and cultural circumstances, and can also give rise to serious misunderstandings (e.g., of a God who has still to be conciliated and is not the origin of his own reconciliation).

SAVING HISTORY

Firstly, a general term signifying the fact that God, on account of his universal *salvific will, has graciously embraced the whole of human history and in it has offered all men his *salvation and that his grace and justification have been concretely and historically realized in humanity. Saving history also means the history of these experiences and embodiments of salvation throughout the human race. And finally, saving history means that pre-Christian and extra-Christian experiences of salvation are dynamically ordered to the *kairos and the age of salvation *simpliciter* in Jesus Christ (as so many different epochs which the theology of *history seeks to ascertain). Thus this concept is based on the theological presupposition not only that man has to hope for and accept grace within history but that grace itself is historical and that history itself, with all it involves—for instance, the *unity of mankind—is grace.—See discussion of pre-Christian and extra-Christian saving history in articles *Revelation, Heathen, Non-Christian Religions.*

In the stricter sense saving history is the history of those experiences and embodiments of salvation which emerge in ever sharper relief from general saving history to culminate in the absolute event of salvation. (This can also be called official or special saving history.) The *covenant of Yahweh with Moses is traditionally regarded as the beginning of special saving history (and thus marks the historical derivation of special saving history from general saving history, since the OT traces the early history of the Mosaic covenant back to the beginning). General saving history "comes to an end" in the sense that where man encounters the saving event tendered in such a way that he can take up an attitude towards it and closes himself to it, he is shutting himself off from salvation itself. This process is reflected in the increasing hostility of the world. Within special saving history one can distinguish between collective and individual saving history. They have in common a characteristic tangible structure (*Covenant, *Church, *Old Testament, *New Testament), *Christocentrism and an eschatological orientation. Individual saving history is specifically dialogical: God's summons addresses the *freedom of the individual and is freely accepted by *faith if that freedom has been liberated by God's grace.

The Catholic theology of saving history is only just beginning to develop; the biblical theology of saving history has advanced farthest (in the discussion of *demythologization it was able to show that

464

saving history is not a metahistorical experience of faith but a genuine history coextensive with profane history).

SAVIOUR

From the late Latin *salvator,* redeemer, a translation of the Hebrew *jehoshua* (Joshua, Jesus: "Yahweh is salvation") and the Greek σωτήρ, deliverer. The Hebrew word emphasizes God's mercy, the Greek his sovereignty (*Kyrios). The full original sense of the word is unfortunately still overlaid by the sentimental idea we have of Jesus Christ owing to the doctrine of Pietism and the Pre-Raphaelite school of art.

SCANDAL

From the Greek σκάνδαλον, snare; in the NT primarily the scandal Jesus Christ gave (Jesus Christ as a "sign of contradiction": Lk 2:34; see Mt 11:6; 1 Cor 1:18–2:16), that is, to expectations of an earthly Messiah and to self-righteousness by his behaviour and doctrine. Scandal is wrapped in the incomprehensibility (paradox) of God's Incarnation (thus St John in particular), which radically transcends all earthly imagination and understanding (Jn 1:5–10), above all in the cross of Christ (thus St Paul in particular).

Scandal given by Christians, according to Scripture, is primarily a necessary expression of the evil *aeon (Lk 17:1) and draws upon itself the special condemnation of Jesus. According to moral theology scandal may lie in the person taking offence, that is if a certain action is good in itself but becomes an occasion of sin (scandal) to someone either lacking in judgment and humility (pharisaic scandal) or spiritually immature and of weak character (scandal of the weak). There is no reason to avoid pharisaic scandal, but scandal of the weak should be avoided as far as practicable. Where scandal is given out of malice (to induce another to sin) or by acquiescence (if another's sin is foreseen and one does not prevent it though able to do so) sins against charity and the relevant virtue occur, entailing a duty to make good the harm done. In our pluralistic modern world and civilization people should be encouraged to give positive witness (even if their environment is scandalized, in the biblical sense), instead of being exclusively warned against giving scandal.

SCHISM

A Greek term which means the breach of ecclesiastical unity. Schism occurs, according to the Code of Canon Law (can. 1325 § 2), when a baptized person refuses to be subject to the Pope or to live in communion with the members of the Church, who are subject to the Pope. The NT does not distinguish schism from *heresy. The theological problem is how, since the definition of the *Pope's primacy of jurisdiction, there can be a schism which is not also a heresy.

SCHOLASTICISM

See *Theology.*

SCHOOLS OF THEOLOGY

In this article we shall not name or describe the various schools of theology that have arisen in the course of history (in the patristic period, for example, the *Alexandrian and *Antiochene schools; later, *Augustinianism, *Thomism, *Scotism, etc.), but we shall consider the significance and limits of the formation of schools of theology. First of all we must point out that though the Church recommends the doctrine, for instance of St Thomas (D 3665f., 3894), it never identifies itself with any particular theological school. In his knowledge of truth, as in other respects, man is an historical being: he remains ordered to all reality that is accessible in itself to human knowledge, against a background, finite, historically conditioned, antecedent to himself, of notions, ways of approaching problems, of assumptions and doubts, personal and social experience (D 3893). Even if intellectually man rejects his point of departure, this still remains the fixed law governing his change of mind. (This, of course, must not be confused with theological *relativism.) It is in the context of a knowledge thus historically conditioned that man now hears God's revelation. Thus he hears and interprets it in a particular historical form, especially since *revelation itself is historical and has been proclaimed in a form that is historically qualified and conditioned. In order to be heard intelligently, indeed as "objectively" as possible, any message must engage the whole "subjectivity" of the hearer and then alter it. The schools of theology must be seen in this perspective: they express the variety of ways, legitimate and historically conditioned, in which finite men in the Church can make revelation their own. Just as there is a *development of dogma, so there are schools of theology. The former shows that revelation is genuinely historical and has been appropriated by the Church itself; the latter that even within the one Church there are various historically, sociologically and personally conditioned ways of hearing revelation. Vatican II explicitly recognized the legitimacy of this fact (Church, 23; Ecum., 14, 16 and *passim*). Because there is one divine truth, one Church and one public confession of the faith of the one Church, it is for the magisterium of the Church to distinguish between legitimate interpretations of revelation—that is, theological schools—and those which stray from the one truth of God or fail to preserve the profession of the one faith of the one Church as it is universally understood (*Heresy). It follows that a school of theology only remains Catholic if it always remains open to what is always the more comprehensive interpretation of the Church of all ages and all schools (without seeking, through a complete "system", to be what only the Church as a whole in all ages can be), always rethinking the bases of its system in a spirit of self-criticism, judging them by the standard of the fullness of revealed truth. These basic considerations also apply to a theological *pluralism that breaks out of the framework of the old image of theological schools. To wish to belong to no school would be the part of a proud and stupid man who imagines that here and now he can possess eternal truth outside historical time. To cling to a system as if it fully expressed the faith of the Church would be to deny the historicity of truth. Within time one communes with God's truth only through humble obedience (which can be reduced to no system) to the faith tangibly embodied in the universal Church (for only so can it be an objective entity for his own subjectivity), and by a humble courage about one's "own" truth.

SCIENTIA MEDIA

Latin, literally "middle knowledge". The system of grace represented by *Molinism gives this name to the knowledge which the omniscient God must have of conditionally future free acts of creatures (what X. would or will freely do if he were or is placed [ultimately by God] in such a situation), logically antecedent to God's decision to realize that situation. Molinism assumes that God knows this conditionally future act in himself, not in his own decision to bring it about (*Predetermination), and that this is the only way God can know it without

467

destroying human freedom. This particular knowledge has been given the name "middle" because the conditionally future act lies midway between the merely possible free act and that which will in fact exist at some future date.

SCOTISM

A school of Catholic theology, named after the Scottish Franciscan John Duns Scotus (c. 1265–1308, buried in Cologne), which still exists today and forms a certain antithesis to *Thomism within Catholic theology. Besides its metaphysical differences from Thomism, the characteristic tenets of Scotism are that the divine essence is best envisaged as *love, the consequent primacy of the will, of freedom and the individual, *Christocentrism, the identification of justifying grace with love, and the more "existentialist" and critical view of the function of theology itself.

SCRIPTURAL PROOF

Since *Holy Scripture remains the inexhaustible source of all Christianity, without which theology would become sterile (D 3886), *biblical theology must furnish "scriptural proofs" both as an independent science and as an essential part of *dogmatic theology. This means two things. (1) It is necessary to show that the teaching of the ordinary and extraordinary magisterium is explicitly or implicitly contained in Scripture (D 3886) or at least finds it "ultimate foundation" there (D 3900ff.) and how it does so, for the magisterium is subject to Scripture (cf. Vat. II: Rev., 10). All the rules and resources of biblical *hermeneutics must be applied in order to ascertain the true *sense of Scripture and the biblical text must neither be stretched, nor must its full import be truncated in positivist fashion. (2) But we must also constantly review our efforts to explore the inexhaustible riches of Scripture where these have not been sufficiently actualized in the current preaching of the faith, so that Scripture is not simply used to provide retrospective justification of this preaching but remains its living source.—Holy Scripture, "so to speak the soul of all theology" (Vat. II: Train./priests, 16), is the most direct and ultimate source of Christian revelation, and therefore the direct concern of theologians *of all* theological disciplines.

SECT

The name applied to religious groups of the most varied historical origin, aims, structure, organization and activity. From the point of view of the sociology of religion the sect can be regarded as a suitable social structure for cognitive minorities (Peter Berger), since these are forced to define themselves over against the surrounding world as small closed groups in order to stabilize their divergent definition of reality. The small number of members that distinguishes a sect from the major churches is therefore a social and psychological consequence of its divergence from the doctrinal mainstream. From the theological point of view, the particular characteristics of sects are their biblical fundamentalism and a rigorous ethical system, their spontaneous nature and a strong awareness of forming the elect, their anti-institutional tendencies and a strong emphasis on the lay element.

SECULARIZATION

As a theological concept, to be firmly distinguished from the historical and legal phenomenon of secularization in which the State takes over Church property. Secularization therefore does not mean the appropriation by the secular authorities of religious funds or the banishment of religious communities from public life but rather the recognition that springs from faith of the independence and comprehensibility of a secular world (J.B. Metz). With a proper theological foundation, secularization thus opposes any religious takeover of secular history just as much as it reckons among a Christian's most basic duties the service he or she can bring to society and the contribution he or she can make towards building a more human *world. A Christian's ministry in the social and political world does not therefore alienate him or her from his or her basic purpose but rather through giving it historical expression helps it to find its manifestation in reality.

SELF-COMMUNICATION OF GOD

The very essence of *grace, *justification and the supernatural order can be defined by the fact that here God does not reveal himself, working salvation and beatitude, by communicating to man (or to *angels), through creation out of nothing, the gift of a being different from himself, whose analogical similarity to God would reveal and as

469

it were represent him: rather he gives himself, giver and gift are one, the creature is healed, justified, made eternally blessed by God's own very being. Since this *self*-communication is an absolutely free act, which God owes to no finite being, even a sinless one, it shows what is meant when we say that God is love (1 Jn 4:8): he is the being who can bestow himself as gift in his absolute intimacy and infinite glory to the finite. The experience of the infinite gift remains creaturely, because the recipient of the gift is a finite creature. But the insoluble mystery of the relationship between God and man consists precisely in the fact that man must acknowledge that he is finite and at the same time that he is blessed with the infinite self-communication of God himself. Since divine self-communication to the creature, as a dynamic principle, is the specific ground of hope, the realization of God's love for the world, and the principle of the world's love for God, it is the origin of the world, the supportive ground of its history and the goal of this history as well as the substance of its ultimacy.

SELF-DENIAL

A biblical concept (Mt 16:24ff.; see Tit 2:12) which expresses a requirement for the *following of Christ: man may, indeed inevitably does, find himself in a situation where he must choose between something which he would consider best for himself, but for God's call in Jesus Christ (to faith, God's commandments, the cross of Jesus, etc.), and even given this call is still tempted to consider so, and obedience to the call. If he obeys God he experiences a kind of abandonment and death of himself, denial and negation of himself, the mortifying and vivifying conflict of the *Pneuma* against his sinful or purely earthly notion of himself, against the "flesh" in the biblical sense (*Sarx). By the *asceticism of the *evangelical counsels man seeks actively to accept this situation, so that he may not fall short of it by treating it as something provided by God unasked.

SELF-RIGHTEOUSNESS

Ultimately this does not mean a vain estimation of oneself, false by any standards, even earthly ones, but that attitude in a man which leads him to attempt to establish his moral worth before God by fulfilling the law by his own powers (see Phil 3:9), instead of receiving true *justice before God as a gift from God (*Grace) to which he has no claim. The abandonment of this self-righteousness is not to be looked for in a mystical *Quietism—precisely because the good decisions of our own freedom, and our own acts, must be recognized as graces of God (Phil 2:13)—but ecstatic selfless love of God that man experiences as the pure gift of God's love so that he no longer seeks, Pharisee-like, to secure himself with regard to God by his independent achievements.

SEMI-ARIANISM

A theory of the mid-fourth century, whose adherents, "Homoeans" and "Homoiousians", sought to bring about a vague compromise between real *Arianism (of the "Anomoeans") and Catholic faith in the consubstantiality (*Homoousios) of the Logos with the Father. They did not deny the genuine consubstantiality of the Son with the Father, at least explicitly, but admitted that he was similar to the Father (ὁμοῖος), even of like substance in all things (ὁμοιούσιος). Thus, for example, the Homoean Acacius of Caesarea, the Homoiousian Basil of Ancyra, and many local synods of this century, which had so stormy a dogmatic history.

SEMI-PELAGIANISM

The name of a crude and heretical attempt (from the end of the fifth century) by certain Gallic theologians (Vincent of Lerins, Faustus of Riez, etc.) to reconcile the orthodox (Augustinian) doctrine of grace with *Pelagianism. It was condemned by the decrees of *Orange (Caesarius of Arles) in 529 (D 352, 370–397). Semi-pelagianism divides salvation between God and man in a primitive *synergism: man begins his salvation by his own unaided powers; then God responds to this independent "good will" by granting the grace to complete the work of salvation. Its adherents rightly emphasize against St Augustine the real universality of God's *salvific will.

SENSES, SENSIBILITY

See *Sensuality*.

SENSES OF SCRIPTURE

The sense of the words of *Holy Scripture that is intended by God, guaranteed by *inspiration, and is therefore true, is the sense intended by the human author as conveyed by his words. To ascertain this sense (with the degree of certitude intended by the author), all the rules for the interpretation of the spoken and written word must be observed (the meaning of a word at the particular time, in a particular context), and above all the literary genre of the text in question must be precisely determined, so as to enable one to distinguish with sufficient accuracy between the context (sense) of a statement and its form. In this connexion, of course, we must note that complete reflexive clarity on the precise boundary-line between these two is not possible with any human statement and therefore cannot be demanded of the human author of Scripture. It is possible to speak of the "plenary" sense of a text, contained in the latter though unarticulated, insofar as the human author need not apprehend the total implication of what he is really saying, though it can be considered part of God's word (at least so far as it can be gathered from Scripture as a whole). If a truth that is enunciated is a *type of another truth and this fact is substantiated by divine revelation, the typological sense (as part of the plenary sense) can be accounted part of the literal sense. Pious applications of scriptural texts which bear no relation to the meaning intended by the author, may not be advanced as senses of Scripture and are best avoided. In view of the difficulty in ascertaining the exact sense of a scriptural text (as in any human discussion of matters that are more than commonplace) it is necessary to consider the *analogia fidei, the interpretation of *Tradition (D 1507f., 3007, 3281f.) and the teaching of the Church's magisterium (D 3886f. etc.) (Biblical *hermeneutics).

SENSUALITY

In an objective and morally indifferent sense (now rare in English), sensuality is that aspect of human consciousness which is bound up with the body, is directly open to determination from without, is presupposed by the transcendence and freedom of the personal spirit, and presents "material" things to the mind in concrete acts of "knowledge" and "will". As "instinctive basis" too, sensuality is necessary and good (*Concupiscence), it is not to be extinguished (in Stoic or Manichaean fashion) but more and more integrated (*Integrity) into

472

the whole person and its good decision and ordered to God. The fact that this task is never completed during our earthly life is part of the Christian situation, of the struggle in which faith involves us (D 1515f.). No doubt sensuality in the concrete in sinful man, is always effected by the *world and its sinful history, provides an entry for the evil "principalities and powers" in the world, is shaped, too, by the wrong decisions made in the previous history of our freedom. Thus our own sensuality not only faces us with a task (that of a growing integration), but is also the "objectification" of sin (*Original and personal sin) and therefore an occasion of sin which must be overcome by the grace of God. The derogatory sense of sensuality which is now its usual one has its justification, but it is worth trying to revive the first and more original sense of the word.

SERMON

See *Preaching*.

SERMON ON THE MOUNT

The most extensive collection of Jesus' sayings (Mt 5–7; see Lk 6:20–49), given the literary form of a single discourse by St Matthew and designed for the catechesis of Jewish Christians; it comprehends vital points of his teaching (especially in moral matters) and shows the new Moses proclaiming the perfect law of the new dispensation, in which God's Kingdom (*Basileia) and the conditions required for entry into it directly and imperiously confront man, "abrogating" the Old *Law. The problem is how to interpret this morality of the Kingdom with its radical demands: in other words, is it intended to set before all Christians an obligatory and attainable ideal? The answer is affirmative if what we envisage is not an attainment that can be objectively measured or a plan for society to be imposed on others as by law, with the effect of delivering man from God's unbearable demand for his very self, nor a mere inward sense of value that would dispense one from any tangible acts which could be specified by objective norms, but rather a demand for the deed of the *heart*. Borne up by the grace of God in which it believes, the heart, by a process never complete and thus never concretely calculable, seeks to surrender itself ever more completely to God by love *through* the concrete activity of life, which however is never quite identical with that of the heart and therefore, according to the particular situation, may either uphold the order of creation immanent in the world or reach out by renunciation and the cross towards God's redemption and his Kingdom which transcend the world. The Sermon on the Mount must be understood as a concrete formulation of the love of the *whole* heart which is possible to man in God's Spirit when he begins to long for that love and in its beginning seeks not the measurements of love but God, not enjoyment of his own sense of value but the service of others, whilst realizing that his variable achievement may never be completely identified with love ever the same yet ever increasing.

SHEOL

The Hades of the OT, especially in Later Judaism, the "abode" of the dead, where they led a gloomy, shadowy existence far from God and true life. Only afterwards was this place divided into a better one for the good and a place of punishment for the wicked (Lk 16:22–24). The idea of *sheol* is the objectification of (a) belief in the continued existence of the dead; (b) *death and the experience of it (not so much of an existence actually coming after death, so that the OT cannot be said to affirm anything false about life "after death"): the OT theology of *sheol* (especially in the Psalms) can and must be regarded as a theology, from the purely human point of view, of the human experience of death as the absolute limit with which man cannot come to terms just by saying that death is "the end of everything"; (c) the unredeemed character of this mortal condition, whose Christian redemption (Phil 1:20 –26; Rom 8:38f.; 1 Cor 15; Lk 23:42f., 46; 1 Thess 4:13–18) is anticipated by the very fact that the enigma of death, which *sheol* represents, is humbly and obediently left in God's hands.

SICKNESS

Dogma does not define sickness, but referring to our experience of it interprets sickness in theological terms, that is, relates it to God and human salvation. Thus sickness is one of the processes that deprive man of control over himself: a concrete but equivocal manifestation of his creatureliness (the jeopardy of his existence and his dependence on *God), of his sinfulness (like *concupiscence: original sin), of the approach of *death (as *suffering and as an act), of the inabrogable and ever mysterious declaration of man's position as both agent and patient. A sick person is faced in his jeopardy with the question whether in self-surrender to the fertile earth he takes himself for a mere element in an innocent rhythm of nature which kills so as to produce more life (which he is not and cannot be), whether he will unbelievingly protest against his existence as senseless, or accept it in faith and hope as the riddle (explicit or implicit) which he has not to answer independently but which God has already answered in the death of Christ. A Christian who learns of the sickness of others and who follows Jesus' example will never see sickness as punishment for sin and do anything other than help the sick person (not just with pious uplift) in his or her need and isolation, remembering that Jesus identified with the sick (Mt 25:36, 43).

SIGN

An entity which refers to another and thereby advertises it. This reference may derive from the nature of the sign itself or be purely conventional; it may be instituted by that to which it refers or by something else: *Symbol, *Sacrament. According to the nature and closeness of its referential connexion, the sign may indicate something that is absent, or actually make something present (*Presence), may conceal or reveal. For the biblical concept of sign, see *Miracle.*

SIMUL IUSTUS ET PECCATOR

Literally "at once just and a sinner", a Latin expression Protestant theologians are fond of using to convey the "paradox" of human life: man knows by faith that he is justified by God's grace, and yet experiences himself as a sinner. This expression has a good Catholic sense which well describes man's existential situation if it excludes any absolute *certainty of salvation (apart from firm *hope that relies on God alone), if it means that man must pray daily for the forgiveness of his sins (D 229f.) because he is really a sinner (D 228) and constantly sins (D 1573), or if it means that considering the sins one actually commits the fact that grievous sins which destroy justification *can* be avoided (D 1572) is no guarantee that the individual in fact avoids them. It becomes heretical (D 1528ff., 1560, 1562) if it means that man is always and in the same sense both just and a sinner, that *justification does not make a sinner who was not just into a just man, which he was not, and who now is no longer the sinner he was, that the justified man is not, by the communication of the Holy Ghost, in an objective state (ultimately to be judged only by God) which makes him inwardly just. If Catholics, then, protest against this formula it is because they reject the idea that God-given justice, when and where it is given, is only a forensic "as if ", a mere "imputation" (*Imputed justice), a fiction which leaves man a sinner as before, incapable of good and salutary deeds.

SIMULTANEITY

In itself a property of *eternity, predicable of *historicity only insofar as the latter is as it were the *potentia obedientialis for eternity. From the theological point of view this potency is not only realized in the genuine *end of history but also in the supreme moment of Christ's "hour" (Jn 2:4 and passim) and his alone, in which he alone is able to unite *beginning and end in a pure free act. Somewhat similarly one can speak of a simultaneity of the Christian with Christ (Kierkegaard), when the fulfilment of saving history makes the individual present to Christ and Christ to him (which does not of course imply any surmounting of historical difference): the relativization of the purely historical which is necessary for the performance of a genuinely religious act.

SIN

In the full sense ("grave sin") sin as an act is the free decision of the whole personality against the will of God as manifested in the orders of nature and grace and in verbal revelation (see D 1544, 1577f.; it presupposes clear knowledge, free consent and grave matter; see Act). By mortal sin a creature rejects the Creator's will for the basic structures of his creation and his *covenant (as in the OT conception of sin) and God's will to communicate himself to his creature in *grace, and thus contradicts his own nature and the purpose of his freedom, which is to love the highest value of all, the personal God. Sin is a perversion of nature, but we know it is possible, both from experience of our own freedom and from the testimony of *revelation (in the OT, rebellion against the Lord, Num 15:30 etc.). As the mystery of iniquity (*Evil) it is part of the mystery of how creaturely freedom not only comes from God but can be used against God in his presence despite (yet because of) his creative omnipotence and universal dominion.

476

SIN

The sinner keeps his sin in darkness to hide it from himself (repression). Though mortal sin presupposes knowledge and freedom and is committed in concrete "material" terms, yet the consciously sinful will may operate very unthematically as a general attitude and basic *existential condition in the depths of the person, and as one cannot adequately reflect on such things, the person cannot form any certain and reflex judgment about himself (D 1533f.; *Certainty of salvation). The admission of sin is in itself a first effect of the redemptive revelation and grace of God. As a condition resulting from one's acts (habitual sin; in St Paul we find for this the Greek ἁμαρτία; see Rom 5ff.), sin in the real order (of nature and grace) is the culpable lack of the sanctifying grace God wills us to possess, whether through *original sin or sins we have personally committed. Sin can be committed only when men are free and insofar as they are free. *Concupiscence (Gen 6:5; 8:21; Deut 10:16; Jer 17:9 and *passim)* is a consequence of original sin and an incitement to personal sin but is not itself sin (D 1515). Where an offence against God's will is committed which is not wholly voluntary (because of imperfect knowledge or restricted freedom) or does not violate an essential part of the hierarchy of values sanctioned by God's will, the sin is "venial" and does not destroy our ordination to God by grace (D 1679ff.). Though the fundamental nature of (mortal) sin—the radical rejection of God's will—is always the same, still there are various kinds of sin (*Vice and *Fontes moralitatis) specified by the matter, in our world of plural values, in which that rejection occurs. If a man's sin were to become definitive in death by the wholly voluntary decision of his temporal life, it would damn him (*Hell). Although sin arises from the use of freedom against God's will, the finite creature does not escape the divine will by sin, for in sin God can reveal his holy *justice and the abyss of his mercy. The Protestant conception of sin is the antithesis of the Catholic: it stresses the essentially sinful nature of man that lies at the root of every sinful act; this basic sinfulness is not primarily envisaged as moral failure through the violation of God's commandments but as personal unbelief arising from essential, that is, hereditary selfishness and egotism; man is a sinner, he cannot spontaneously love God and his neighbour unless the Holy Ghost converts him to *faith by grace alone; but this *justification does not abolish our sinfulness while we are on earth (*Simul iustus et peccator).—On conversion from sin, see *Metanoia, Contrition, Baptism, Sacrament of Penance.*

SIN, MYSTIQUE OF

The idea, widespread in modern literature and in our present general attitude towards life, that sin and evil are a necessary stage in the development of a genuine and mature human life and that by such sin man gives God the opportunity to be merciful and thus to realize his own nature; so that when all is said and done man may make arrangements for sin as a positive part of his life. However true it be that sin which has been committed in the uncompleted course of history is engulfed in God's greater mercy (Rom 11:32), we may not will sin in order to call forth grace (Rom 6:1f.). It would be vulgar arrogance and crass stupidity in a finite creature to adopt a viewpoint which befits God alone and reckon in advance with sin as part of his plan for good. There is no good end which can be achieved as such only by means of evil.

SINLESSNESS

Freedom from *sin in a free spiritual being. It may be a necessity of nature (as in God), or the result of the free act of one who (for whatever reason: grace, etc.) has not in fact sinned. It may be the consequence of an *impeccability that is bestowed by grace. It may be found in a man who has sinned but whose sins have been blotted out by God's redeeming grace (*Justification). Against every form of *mystique of sin we must emphasize that in the concrete order every kind of sinlessness in mere man is as much the effect and manifestation of God's redemptive grace in Jesus Christ (even, and indeed especially, in Mary) as is the forgiveness of sins that have been committed. The saint is more in debt to God than anyone else.

SITUATION ETHICS

The doctrine of an exaggerated existentialism, that the moral duty of the individual in any given case is to be gathered from his concrete situation, and that what he has to do "here and now" is in no way governed by the general, essential norms of the *natural moral law (derived from the recognizable, permanent, metaphysical nature of man which remains the same through all historical change and which is presupposed in Scripture). Situation ethics is based on the denial of any metaphysics of essence and so would make it impossible for the

478

Church to preach any Christian ethics containing specific obligations. It is extreme individualism, a short-circuit chosen by a mind that wishes to spare itself the trouble of patient reflection such as is necessary to clarify a complicated situation. Protestant criticism of *law and its function for the sinner who has been justified by grace is often stirred by a similar ethical ideal. Situation ethics is also often a reaction to the fact that universal norms are *also* elements of dominant images of the world and are always subject to ideological misuse. Situation ethics is then an attempt to break out of this actual situation. The nucleus of truth in situation ethics is *existential ethics.

SOCINIANISM

A form of *Unitarianism, founded by Fausto Sozzini (1539–1604) and especially widespread in Poland. On rationalistic grounds it denied the Trinity, the divinity of Christ, and the redemption (D 1880).

SOLA FIDE

Latin, literally "by faith alone". It primarily means the view of Protestant theology that man can find salvation only by accepting it as *sola gratia,* not as the result of his actions independent of God's grace, not as the result of *works given to God without first being received from him, but simply of faith. Now if "faith" is simply a general term for man's free acceptance of grace by the gift of that very grace (as is often the case in St Paul), then sola fide is a Catholic principle. The only question is how this process of the acceptance of *justification, which grace effects, should accurately be described. The Catholic doctrine of justification is capable of describing it more subtly and more scripturally than is suggested by the over-simplified theologoumenon equating sola fide with fides fiducialis (*Fiducial faith), sheer, absolutely certain confidence in the purely forensic and external imputation of Christ's justice. The Council of Trent teaches that this acceptance of justifying grace by historical man in time may consist of a series of different acts (*faith as assent to God's truth, *hope, *contrition [*Attritionism], etc.) and only attains its full stature in *love which, growing out of (dogmatic) faith as its foundation and root, alone is the fullness of this process of justification.

SOLA GRATIA

Latin, literally "by grace alone". As the material principle of Protestant theology it primarily means that salvation is wholly God's gift and that the sinner is wholly incapable of any *salutary act. Thus stated, this principle is a Catholic one, for the Council of Trent teaches man's utter incapacity for salvation without grace (D 1551ff.) and the Catholic doctrine of grace may not be interpreted in terms of *synergism. Consequently serious doctrinal differences connected with this principle can only arise (a) if it is understood as denying freedom of choice in salutary acts instead of recognizing the salutary *freedom of both capacity and act as the gift of grace; or (b) if the manner of the salutary acts man performs of and under grace is inadequately explained (*Sola fide); or (c) if in the interests of a purely forensic attribution of Christ's justice, which leaves man inwardly still a sinner, one denies that *justification actually transforms man in all truth and really turns a sinner into a just man (despite all the concupiscence [D 1515f.], liability to sin, sinfulness [D 1573] and obscurity that remains [*Certainty of salvation]).

SOLA SCRIPTURA

Latin, literally "by Scripture alone". As the formal principle of Protestantism it is the doctrine of the complete sufficiency of *Holy Scripture, which clearly interprets itself (under the Spirit of God) and therefore renders superfluous the Church's authoritative *magisterium and *Tradition as real norms of Christian belief. In the last analysis this doctrine cannot justify the *canon of Scripture, which is not to be found in Scripture itself; nor is it compatible with the origins of Scripture, which was formed as a deposit of the authoritative kerygma which, before Scripture existed, demanded the assent of faith with the formal authority which Christ himself gave the preacher (Mt 28:18–20; Mk 16:15ff.; Lk 10:16 etc.); and finally this doctrine cancels itself out by giving one the formal right and the material opportunity to draw the contrary principle from Scripture itself. On the other hand it is still an open question for Catholic theologians whether, without prejudice to a formal authority of Tradition in the correct interpretation of Scripture (D 1501), a material sufficiency of Scripture as containing the whole of revelation (apart from the matter of the canon, from which one cannot readily generalize) cannot be admitted.

In our day the doctrine of *sola Scriptura* should no longer be invoked as a reason for division among Christians.

SOLIDARITY, PRINCIPLE OF

In theology this principle indicates that unity in variety of spiritual creatures (above all among men) whereby they not only affect one another in the physical and material domain—antecedent to the free consent of those thus influenced—but the decision of each individual affects the specifically human domain as well, becoming a contributory factor in the situation of each one even as regards his salvation (though of course no man's free decision can be displaced or replaced by another's). The reasons for this unity are complex (the unity of the physical domain, biological linkage: *Monogenism; the necessary *communication of spiritual creatures, union in the gracious self-communication of the one living God, the one source of all being, etc.). The principle of solidarity finds its chief expression in the doctrine of our universal hereditary guilt in the first man (Rom 5:12; D 372, 1512; *Original sin) and the redemption of all by the one God-Man (D 391, 1524, 1530f.). The principle is also the foundation of many other Christian truths implying a sort of "communism of salvation" (*Church, solidarity of believers with the poor and oppressed with whom Jesus identified, petition for others, *Indulgence, the role of *Mary in saving history).—See also *Unity of Mankind.*

SOMA

See *Body*.

SON OF GOD

This term in Scripture refers to: (1) the second divine Person in the Trinity, constituted as the Father's *Logos by the natural communication of the divine essence ("generation") within God and of one substance with the Father, so that this eternal divine Person becomes man by the *hypostatic union (*Jesus Christ) but not thereby the Son of God (the Father) for the first time (*Adoptianism); this title of Jesus has a specific rich history in the NT which shows that Jesus knew himself to be in a unique filial relationship with God, but did not describe himself as "Son of God"; (2) the justified man, because by *grace he is "made partaker of the divine nature" in a way analogous to the generation within God and thus becomes God's "child", his "son". On the one hand this sonship is called "adoption" in Scripture (Rom 8:15; Gal 4:5 etc.) (thus distinguishing it from the trinitarian Sonship); and on the other hand, because of God's real *self-communication to man, Scripture plainly calls it being begotten by God, being born of God, *regeneration (Jn 1:13; Tit 3:5; 1 Jn 2:29 etc.; Divine *sonship). Because our relationship in grace with the divine Persons does not merely rest on *appropriations but corresponds to what is distinctive about each of the three divine Persons, our Father to whom we pray (Mt 6:9) is the Father of the eternal Son (Jn 20:17), not "God" in general.

SON OF MAN

The title designates a mysterious heavenly figure which appears for the first time in Daniel 7:13, and is given a more developed role in some later Jewish *apocalyptic literature. The origin and exact significance of this figure are still not satisfactorily explained. Biblical exegesis is uncertain whether Jesus described himself as Son of Man, though it is certain that he referred to himself as Son of Man before his judges (Mk 14:60ff.), and that by speaking of the "coming" of this Son of Man he was giving a warning testimony to his own power, which he could not deny in such a situation without weakening his utterly decisive significance for salvation and leaving the way open for expectations of another redeemer. The title played no further part in the Christ-theology of the early Church.

SOTERIOLOGY

The theology of *redemption, the salvation (Gr. $\sigma\omega\tau\eta\rho\iota\alpha$) of man. Soteriology is not (objectively) a special field in dogmatic theology. In the concrete economy of salvation, God himself in his literal *self-communication is the salvation of man, with the result that all reality with which *revelation and *dogmatic theology are concerned can be considered from a soteriological point of view. But it is customary for soteriology to confine itself to examining Jesus Christ's redemptive death on the cross as the continuation of *Christology: the death of the God-Man, suffered in loving obedience, in view of which God loves mankind as a whole and in which (because it is his own) he has accepted and assumed the world (*Satisfaction, theory of). It is not soteriology but the doctrine of *grace which deals with the subjective application of this "objective" redemption by the free acceptance of Jesus Christ's grace as God's self-communication ("subjective redemption"). But we must not forget that "objective" redemption has made the religious situation of every individual, prior to any consent of his, something quite different from what it would be without Jesus Christ and his cross, so that the soteriology of "objective" redemption is nearly the most important part of the soteriology of "subjective" redemption (Supernatural *existential).

SOUL

Anglo-Saxon *sawol,* akin to Gothic *saiwala,* "coming from the eternal sea(?)": Gr. ψυχή, Lat. *anima.* If we are to have an accurate understanding of the Christian (not the Platonic) doctrine of the soul, we must from the first observe the distinction between a being and a real principle of being. A being is a real and complete thing with one nature and one existence, even though it has several characteristics, parts, dimensions, etc. A principle of being is an intrinsic source of a being, because of which—without prejudice to its unity—that being exhibits a plurality of characteristics none of which can be sufficiently explained by any other, though each one, being part of the whole, is codetermined by the whole. The soul, in Christian teaching, is a principle of being, not an entity which exists for its own sake and has entered into an adventitious union with matter. For the soul, together with the other principle of the one human being, his physical spatio-temporality, constitutes a substantial unity, man, so that every empirical characteristic we find in man is an attribute of the whole man (each in its own way, of course): the *body is a specifically human body, the expression of man's spiritual personality; the spiritual part of man acts in space and in historical time (imagination, image, word, gesture, society) and seeks the perfection of the whole man (*Resurrection). Only the whole man, who is one, can be encountered and experienced. Of course an accurate and comprehensive knowledge of him is only possible if we see him as a spiritual *person, of genuine, incommunicable individuality, who is more than an instance of a general law; with an intellect that can perceive more than what is biologically useful, is capable of attaining absolute truth through its *transcendence to being as such and therefore to the *mystery of *God; with freedom and responsibility which make him more than a part of biological, technological society. The principle of humanity in this sense, which brings material, spatio-temporal being to its own perfection, allows it to determine itself and thus to rise above the mere determinateness proper to material being, is called the soul. It is contrasted with the intrinsic principle of transitory spatio-temporal, biological, social being which is called *matter (not to be confused with the "body", that which is constituted in its proper species by soul and matter). Since this personal spirituality cannot be derived from matter, this principle of being called the "soul" is substantial (D 567) (that is, does not exist as a mere mode of being of some other thing), independent, simple (that is, is not quantitative, since it stands over against quantitative being, knowing and embracing it (D 900ff., 1440f., 2828). It can never be identified with a particular manifestation of material being, ceasing to exist when the latter does, because it is a genuine reality which never simply disappears but at most manifests itself and operates in new ways, because it stands over against and independent of mere material being, because it has a significance and value of its own. Hence reason and Christian faith tell us that the soul does not cease to exist at *death, together with man's physical and biological consciousness. The soul is immortal (D 1440f.), though this *immortality is not to be considered mere continuance as before but a supratemporal fulfilment of the spiritual person who has finished the period when he was free to act in time, and though revelation testifies that ultimately this fulfilment will be manifest as the completion of the whole man.—As to the origin of the individual soul, see *Creationism;* further problems are considered under *Trichotomism* and especially *Body; Beatific Vision.*

SPECIES

This term may mean: (1) the species as distinct from the individual and the genus, especially in the biological sense; that is, that relatively concrete character common to many individuals (especially where they are descended from each other); (2) the empirical, "accidental" reality of a being, which is directly accessible to sensory experience, as distinct from the substance in which this manifest variety is rooted. In this sense the term is used to explain *transubstantiation in the *Mass, where the reality that is attained by sense experience, the "appearances" (which alone interest the positivist physicist and alone can be examined by his methods of observation) of bread and wine remain and become an "advertisement" (species in both cases) of the Body and Blood of Christ which lie beneath the appearances. How far species in this sense is to be identified with *accident in the strictly ontological sense depends on what is concretely meant by the *substance of the bread (and wine) which the Church teaches us (D 1642, 1652) ceases to exist at the consecration. Since this can hardly be determined either from the nature of bread as such or by the methods of modern physics, many questions remain open. But in the end it is sufficient for the believer to perceive that Jesus Christ truly gives us his Body under the appearances of bread, so that what he gives is his Body and, in this dimension, nothing else. This does justice to our sensory experience and to faith. How the two facts co-exist can quite well be left a mystery.

SPHRAGIS

From the Greek σφραγίς, seal; the term in patristic language, which was steeped in Scripture, first for "sealing" by the Holy Ghost in *justification, and then also in *baptism or *confirmation (as an act of God appropriating and saving men and making his covenant with them). Later it was applied to the sacramental *character.

SPIRIT

That entity which is characterized by an openness towards *being and at the same time by an awareness of what itself is and is not. The two fundamental aspects of spirit correspond to these two opennesses, to universal being and to itself: *transcendence and *reflexivity (self-possession in self-consciousness and *freedom). By rising to universal being the individual experiences what he is himself as "something alive", as "subject"; and the individual "other thing" which he encounters within the horizon of his comprehension of being and which is not himself, as something that encounters him, that is as "object". The distance between the individual entity and that which is objectively alien to it, and the ability to conceive and recognize the whole of being, gives spirit the power of voluntarily adopting an attitude towards a particular object freely chosen and therefore power to control its own nature. The finiteness of the human spirit is primarily shown by the fact that it is capable of only partial and incalculable encounter with the "other" and the "alien" which happens to cross its path, and therefore cannot dispense with a *body of its own to form a bridge between subject and object. Thus the human spirit is not "pure spirit" but essentially a "spiritual soul", whose ties with the body—and thereby with space and time—make it the specifically "human spirit". In its thinking, knowing and willing this human spirit is referred to the *sensuality of the whole man, composed of spirit and body, and therefore is dependent on experience, which however is the experience of the human spirit itself. Such experience must always fall short of that reaching out of the spirit in which it is permanently and necessarily engaged by reason of its infinite *transcendence as the very condition of its experience. Even in its summing up, the ever finite thought of the human mind leaves intact that vastness to which spirit is open, and can never adequately correspond to the spirit's absolute and infinite expectancy. The objective consciousness of the human spirit, which always falls short of the range of this spirit, knows (if only vaguely, or even by wishing this not to be the case) that it is itself made possible by that which is the goal of its endless movement, which sustains its transcendence (*Mystery, *God, *Proof of God's existence) and which as such is the ground of the finite human spirit. The knowledge and freedom of the human spirit is encompassed and sustained by this infinite Incomprehensible, which the finite spirit experiences as that by which and for which it has been entrusted to itself and its freedom, and to which the finite spirit is open in its intrinsic being (*Existential, supernatural; *Grace; *Self-communication of God).

STATE

So long as civil society uses its laws and power, at least on the whole, to provide a life for its members that is worthy of human beings, it embodies that State which is necessary for men by the natural law deriving from human nature, it conforms in that degree to God's will, and is protected by the divine command to obey legitimate authority. Thus the laws of the State may bind in conscience of themselves (if they substantially serve the common good) or indirectly (if refusal to obey them would destroy civil order). They need not be obeyed if they call on one to do the common good considerable harm; and if they require anything immoral, then to obey (saying that "orders are orders") is unlawful and a sin before God. The "subject" may not dispense himself from examining the laws and commands of the State so far as he is able in the light of the Christian moral law and his own conscience; this would be immoral. Normally one has a duty to take part as far as possible in public life, provided such participation clearly serves some real purpose. The concrete form of government in a State (constitution) is not, of course, of direct divine institution but is subject to historical change. There may be a moral obligation to alter it: an emergency or the need for self-defence may even justify revolutionary action outside the law (*Revolution; Vat. II: Church/world, 74). The State is the servant of the common good, not its master, and is not the only means to its achievement. The Christian and the Church can and should be critical of the State, and that not only when it threatens harm to specifically ecclesiastical interests (*Political theology). Church and State may neither ignore nor injure each other, but a clear distinction between the two powers can only redound to the benefit of both (*Tolerance). Vatican II declared for a "separation" of Church and State inasmuch as it describes each as independent and autonomous in its own field (Church/world, 76). By sharply distinguishing the State from the Church Christianity preserves man from regarding the State, or one's country or nation, as something sacred and "numinous". Just as it has done with nature, Christianity in the course of many centuries has "demythologized" the State. Christians must do their utmost to see that the deification of the State which now threatens us anew shall not take root throughout the world.

STATES OF MAN

The usual term for the various real or conceivable religious states which are the precondition of the individual's power and duty to perform free salutary acts. Apart from a purely notional state of "pure" *nature, which has never existed, three such essential phases of saving history are distinguished: (1) Man's condition in *paradise before original sin, the "supralapsarian" state of *original justice, when man was endowed with supernatural grace by God's self-communication, was free from concupiscence (*Integrity) and immune from death. (2) The condition of man under *original sin and before Jesus Christ or before his justification (through faith, love and baptism), the "infralapsarian" state of "fallen nature". (3) The condition of the just man who has been sanctified by the grace of Jesus Christ, but was formerly a sinner through original sin and personal sin, the state of "nature fallen and restored".

These three successive phases of saving history, which are in part mere aspects of one religious situation (in that original sin must always be thought of as simply co-existing with God's will to be reconciled with man for Jesus Christ's sake: *Existential) are all embraced from the outset by God's sanctifying and merciful will to communicate himself in Jesus Christ (*Christocentrism) and unfold this one ultimate and essential structure of salvation in history: the grace of paradise is already the grace of Jesus Christ; God only permits sin because it cannot nullify the religious situation of Jesus Christ's more abundant grace but can only exhaust itself in the infinite vastness and conclusiveness of this situation; and this basic and all-embracing religious situation, which is always Jesus Christ, merely becomes explicitly present, in the Christian era and in the salutary acts of the individual, in explicit faith and the eschatological tangibility of the sacraments on the one hand, and in its subjective acceptance (again by its own doing) through faith and the sacraments on the other.

STIGMATIZATION

From the Greek, στίγμα, mark, brand; an incidental phenomenon of mystical experience which has occurred fairly frequently from the time of St Francis of Assisi to the present day. Wounds appear in the body of the mystic which correspond with his or her idea of Christ's wounds and have not been made intentionally or in order to deceive. The stigmata in themselves need not be properly miraculous since similar phenomena of a parapsychological nature are observed outside genuine *mysticism. But where they are the expression and physical result of mystical love of Christ and his cross—and are not exploited in the interests of sensationalism—they may be accorded a religious respect.

SUBORDINATIONISM

An opinion, among others in the second and third centuries when the doctrine of the *Trinity had not been completely formulated, which held that the *Logos and the Holy Ghost not only proceed from the Father and receive their being from the unoriginate Father through the self-communication of his divine essence, but are in some way "subordinate" to him, do not fully possess the one divine essence (*Homoousios), are not really *God* but mere divine "powers" through whom God (the Father) "economically" orders the world and saving history. Subordinationism is a vagueness in the ancient theology of the *Trinity which was clarified during the struggle with *modalism and *Sabellianism and disappeared after *Nicaea.

SUBSISTENCE

The real, fundamental unity of the one *Person of Jesus Christ and the unconfused distinction between the divine and the human *natures in him force us to distinguish even in a concrete individual *substance between its substantiality and its subsistence (though originally the two words were synonymous). A real individual substance (at least in the case of the human nature of the divine Logos) may belong to a real unity of a higher order without becoming an accident or an intrinsic modification of another nature (the divine nature as such), and in this sense not "subsist" in its own right, not be a distinct *hypostasis. Subsistence, then, is the absolute uncommunicatedness and immediacy of a thing whereby it exists in its being in and for itself—that which makes a substantial being a *hypostasis and, if it is a spiritual being, a *person.

SUBSTANCE

A basic concept that can only be described indirectly; opposed to *accident. By "substance" is meant a being which (negatively) is neither a determination inhering in another nor a metaphysical component of something else, but (positively) possesses as its own the reality it connotes, "stands on its own" and therefore may (but need not necessarily) have accidents inhering in it. The concept of substance is analogically realized (in decreasing measure as one descends) at every level of being, so that it is difficult when we are dealing with purely physical things to state clearly when and how a "particle" is detached from the "field" of matter as a whole in such a way as to verify the concept of substance. God, who absolutely subsists in himself, is substance in the most eminent degree (D 1782). The individual, free, spiritual person is also invariably a substance (though only by *analogy with God's substantiality, since the person depends on God: *Pantheism). For the difference between substance and subsistence, which is basic to Christology, see *Subsistence*.

SUFFERING

In a first sense suffering means the way in which the world informs the human mind and spirit (*passio* in St Thomas) which always spontaneously exposes itself to the world and cannot do otherwise, and the experience of this exposure of the human mind to the world causes man to experience a debilitating contradiction, both within and without; this is the case when this relation has been antecedently turned against God and salvation (*Original sin). It is then man's duty to accept the anguishing situation as well as possible, to integrate and transform it into a positive element of his own self-fulfilment (by acting while he suffers and suffering while he acts—the antithesis of passive acquiescence), so that he takes a personal decision for God in his ruinous situation and that situation gives his decision a depth it would otherwise lack. In this sense suffering is "willed by God". This was uniquely and incomparably the case with Jesus Christ, who positively accepted his sufferings and made them an expression of man's total dedication to God. We cannot emulate this deed of Jesus to the extent that our power to endure suffering and personally transform it is never quite equal to the concrete situation (*Concupiscence). Since the transformation of suffering is an active process, it means that a Christian not only has to come to terms with (others' and his or her own) suffering, but combats it in solidarity with the suffering. When suffering is experienced as meaningless (the inherent experience of absurdity is often proof against Christian talk of salvation) in accordance with scriptural example the Christian has the right of complaint to God. In a Christian perspective, the human history of suffering is part of future freedom.

SUPERNATURAL

The supernatural (or preferably "supernature", since it is not an entity) in the strictest sense is whatever, being a participation in the meaning and life of God (see 2 Pet 1:4), absolutely exceeds the powers and claims of any created spiritual nature (so far as these are a necessary part of such a *nature) (D 1923): *Grace and the *Beatific vision. It is the free gift of God in Jesus Christ quite apart from the necessity to have our sins forgiven. In a broader sense other gifts of God to which we have no claim are also called supernatural, such as *revelation, the gifts bestowed in *original justice, *miracles, etc., since all these things are only preconditions, concomitant phenomena

490

or effects of the properly supernatural: God's *self-communication. This communication is not owed to any creature (D 1921, 3891), because in itself it is not a finite being created by God's efficient causality, but flows from his formal causality—is God himself in his personal intimacy.

SUPRALAPSARIAN

See *States of Man.*

SYMBOL

In the genuine and original sense a symbol is not a sign man has arbitrarily chosen and applied from without to a particular thing so as to give the latter historical expression in space and time, but (in very varying degrees, of course) the "phenomenon", other yet connected, in which a thing affirms itself and in which, therefore, it also "utters" itself. In the *Trinity the Father is himself when he utters himself in the Son who is distinct from him. The *soul exists, that is to say, fulfils its own being, when it embodies and expresses itself in the body which it "informs" and which is different from it. A person succeeds in adopting a certain attitude when he expresses it in a gesture: by "expressing" itself the attitude comes into being, or acquires existential depth. The fact that the symbol originates in what is symbolized does not prevent the latter being subject to certain external norms if it is to find genuine expression in the symbol (for example, the particular ecclesiastical "form" of marriage is prerequisite if the union is to be absolutely binding). This should clear the way to an understanding of the *sacraments (as historical symbols of God's dealings with men in space and time) and their causality *(*Opus operatum),* of the liturgy, etc.

SYMBOLICS

Either the theory of the *symbol and the meaning of individual symbols, or the theological doctrine of the development and meaning of the individual "symbols" or *creeds that have in one way or another been sanctioned by the Church in the course of time, and therefore particularly of the written confessions of faith that have arisen since the sixteenth century in the various Christian bodies to express their differences in faith and doctrine.—See also *Controversial Theology.*

SYNEIDESIS

From the Greek συνείδησις , consciousness, due to a scribal error, often called *synderesis* by the scholastics. The term signifies the basic and indestructible moral and religious *existential state at the core of the human being, that ultimate self-presence of the inabrogable structure of human nature which—though perhaps unthematically—orders man to God (*Transcendence, existential) and through which he grasps the basic principles of moral responsibility (*Natural moral law). These form the basis of his *conscience (*Spirit) and even in rejecting and protesting against them man unavoidably reaffirms them.

SYNERGISM

The idea that the God of grace and free man collaborate in the process of salvation in the manner of partial causes, almost as if each did half the work. Though the magisterium of the Church freely speaks of man's "co-operation" with grace, synergism is something quite different, for Catholic doctrine is always clear that both man's power to work at his salvation and the exercise of that power (by efficacious *grace) are the gift of God's grace, so that the dialogical partnership between God and man only brings out the force of one aspect of their relationship.

SYNOD

See *Council.*

T

TELEOLOGY

A thing which has its own constituent essence (*Nature) and yet is temporal and historical (*Beginning), that is to say, must become itself, is thereby directed to a *goal (Gr. τέλος): the attainment of its own perfection which was already outlined in its initial essence. In the case of a being which is endowed with spiritual *transcendence and freedom and thus is historical in the real sense, this achievement in the concrete must not, of course, be regarded as mechanically or biologically determined, but as the unfathomable mystery of divine and human creativity which only discloses itself in the *end and cannot be "foretold". Consequently it is impossible to dispense with understanding a being in the light of its perfection, with teleology, unless we are to have recourse to a blind positivism and dispense with all knowledge of essences. *Eschatology is the dogmatic teleology of the whole of God's creation and of every individual person. The question of whether and in what sense the methods of natural science can discover a teleology in infrahuman reality (biological and material) belongs to the domain of philosophy. At all events *life cannot be intelligibly described in biology without recourse to the categories of teleology (*Purpose, etc.).

TEMPERANCE

That *virtue which enables man to control his *passions and *emotions by reason and keep them in the "mean". In the Thomistic doctrine of the virtues temperance is the last of the four *cardinal virtues and is expressed in a series of subordinate virtues, for example in actual temperance (to do with food and drink); chastity, and modesty.

TEMPTATION

That which incites us to *sin. In order to become active, creaturely freedom needs a receptive, passive experience of (real or apparent) values. So far as this necessary incitement to activity in human life, as a result of the loss of the *integrity man enjoyed in *original justice, takes the form of *concupiscence, which pursues its particular good regardless of man's universal moral goal and can never be wholly integrated into a man's fundamental option for the good, incitement to moral evil becomes the characteristic form of temptation which we encounter in the infralapsarian order of things: temptation which persists in man despite his rejection of it in obedience to God, which co-exists with this rejection and thus makes man's situation obscure to him (D 1533f.; *Certainty of salvation). But we must be clear that even persistent temptation does not destroy man's *freedom and responsibility (1 Cor 10:13; D 1536–1539, 1568), that it can be overcome, in God's grace, if we watch and pray (Mt 26:41), by faith, hope (Eph 6:16), and active *asceticism, unless it become *compulsion, in which case of course subjective mortal sin is impossible. Scripture and Tradition describe as causes of temptation all the elements of the human situation that are antecedent to our free decision: cosmic *principalities and powers, the *world, and man's own inner dispositions (*Sarx).

THEISM

(From the Greek word for God, *theos*). That view of God which sees God as a sovereign being who acts personally, but in contrast to *deism accepts God's continuous active presence in the world. (The concept of theism was formed in the seventeenth century in the hope of formulating a view of God common to all the different religions so as to hinder the spread of atheism.) Theism's view of God is in general accepted by Catholic teaching about God but comes in for stronger ciriticism from Protestant theology. The basic question that needs to be put to theism is whether it sees itself as the result of some form of "natural theology" and thus is to be classified as a kind of philosophical foundation for theology without taking God's revelation into consideration, or whether it is meant to provide a philosophical (methodical, critical) reflection on and interpretation of *revelation. A philosophical theology which remains independent of revelation does succeed in reaching the ground and basis of everything (*proof of the existence of God) but only as a distant horizon that remains ever beyond our grasp. For this kind of metaphysical knowledge of God, God remains the essentially unknown; the human concept of the absolutely absolute remains "empty". Theist metaphysics, because it does not attain to God's being, can therefore not make any positive statements about the characteristics of God's being. This provides the basis for criticizing the naïve kind of theism that thinks it is able to draw conclusions about God's relationship to the world from the concepts of his qualities that have been obtained in the abstract (omnipotence, omniscience, etc.) and of his providence and on this basis asserts God's physical intervention in the course of the history of the world and of mankind. This critique applies all the more strongly to an ideological theism maintained to preserve the stability of existing patterns of social domination—something the existence of which cannot be disputed. A philosophical reflection on and interpretation of revelation, on the other hand, is something that can already often be perceived in Scripture: it does not involve trying to reduce God to a mere object or thing, as man in his hubris would attempt to do, but rather treats God as an object to the extent to which he himself has made himself an object in his word of revelation. God's characteristic qualities in his relation to the world can be read off from his sympathetic solidarity with mankind: the qualities that have been formulated as dogmas are expressions of the fundamental difference between God and the world, and what they express is that in himself God is independent of the world and infinitely superior to it—but what they do not say is in what sense and to what extent God has made himself dependent on the world and on man. Considerations of the *analogia entis* and the view of the ever greater God as a *mystery are inevitable attempts at self-correction by theological theism.

THEODICY

From the Greek θεός, God, and δίκη or δίκαια, justice; roughly, "justification of God's ways to man". Theodicy originally signifies the (at least negative) demonstration by philosophical or Christian reasoning that *evil in the world (suffering, misfortune, death, sin) in the biological and human spheres does not preclude philosophical or religious belief in the existence of a holy God who is infinitely perfect and good. It is helpful, towards this end, to bring out the distinction between the finite creature and the infinite God (against all forms of *pantheism), to emphasize the relative character of our judgment on the good and evil in an event (a thing may be good in a higher context which seems absurd to me on a lower level), the fact that the world is still on its way towards perfection and is capable of real improvement at man's hands by changing the conditions that cause suffering, the point of freedom even if it is capable of doing evil, the danger of an anthropomorphic interpretation of purely biological pain and death, and the fact that given man's *immortality perfect happiness cannot be demanded for man in the limited dimension of his earthly life. Accepting theodicy is ultimately a matter of a fundamental creaturely option (the finite creature is only well disposed if he allows the infinite God to be incomprehensible *mystery in this respect too), of hope and faith, of allowing God to try one and patiently awaiting the disclosure of the meaning of the world. This hope, which rests on the Incarnation of God and the resurrection of Jesus, is a hope that battles daily against the pessimism induced by experience and the evil in the world. It helps to avoid the question of evil and of meaningless suffering being robbed of its sting and being "solved" by not being taken seriously by philosophy; it makes it clear that evil can only be seen rightly from the point of view of its having been overcome. The question of theodicy, which has always to be kept alive, does not extend to a contestation of the existence of God; denial of God leads to the in fact insoluble questions of an anthropodicy. Rejecting theodicy does not solve the riddle of existence: this solution proclaims that the real meaning of life is that it is wholly meaningless. But man in his openness experiences too much light for us to be able to conclude that the real, ultimate sense of his life is utter darkness.

Theodicy is now often taken to mean natural philosophical knowledge of God's existence and nature in general (*God).

THEOLOGIANS

The unanimous teaching of theologians, as distinct from the *Fathers of the Church, in medieval and modern times, insofar as it exists, constitutes (like that of the Fathers) a norm for the individual modern theologian, just so far as in this teaching the authentic faith of the Church and its development become tangible. This is possible because orthodox theologians who are not repudiated by the Church but are at least tacitly acknowledged, work under the guidance and supervision of the Church's *magisterium, to which on the whole their teaching conforms, and therefore they cannot as a body and over a considerable period teach that a given doctrine is revealed and must be believed if in fact it is not, for otherwise the magisterium itself would be responsible for the error. In the case of other doctrines, of course, an error (ultimately concerning some non-religious matter) derived from ideas prevalent at the period may be general and may long persist. Honest and respectful appraisal of the common teaching of theologians constantly forces the conscience and personal intuitions of the individual believer—it may be with a painful effort—to enter into the larger consciousness of the universal Church, which is thus enriched by the creative individuality of new thinkers and changing times.—See also *Schools of Theology.*

THEOLOGOUMENON

This term may be used to designate a theological doctrine that is not directly taught by the Church's magisterium and thus does not authoritatively demand our assent, but is of such a nature that it sheds light on the connexion among many other explicit doctrines of the Church and for this reason is commendable.

THEOLOGY

From the Greek $\theta \epsilon o \lambda o \gamma \acute{\iota} \alpha$, an account of the gods or God, especially legendary or philosophical. In the strict sense (as distinct from philosophy, metaphysics, mythology, and natural knowledge of God) it is essentially the conscious effort of the Christian to hearken to the actual verbal revelation which God has promulgated in history, to acquire a knowledge of it by the methods of scholarship and to reflect upon its implications. Thus it does not produce verbal revelation but presupposes it, and yet theology cannot be sharply distinguished against *revelation, because this *revelation itself already includes an aspect of scientific scholarship of a conceptual and propositional kind which, as such an aspect of faith and of responsible proclamation directed at others, impels towards further development, reflection and confrontation with other fields of study and knowledge and from its own resources makes reflection possible. Again, just as is the case with pre-scientific and scientific knowledge in general, there is no sharp

497

distinction to be drawn between pre-scientific and scientific methodological intelligence of the faith.

Real theology has as its basis an undistorted hearing of God's word
with a view to salvation, ultimately in the service of salvation itself.
Thus it is tied to the revealed *word of God as permanently present
in the Church, which preserves the revelation it has received by its
living *magisterium (*Tradition) and interprets it with constant reference to *Holy Scripture. Consequently theology is a science which
presupposes *faith (grace of faith) and the *Church (magisterium,
Scripture, Tradition). Insofar as theology is concretely concerned
with Christian revelation, its subject-matter is *God who by his salvific dealings with men in *Jesus Christ reveals himself (*Trinity) in
his own glory—otherwise necessarily hidden from man (*mystery)—
and communicates himself in *grace. The act and content of Christian
faith (and the faith of the Church) form the object of theology, an
object that is investigated by means of methodical reflection. The fact
that this reflection is undertaken as an aspect of believing does not
remove its scientific or scholarly character, since absolute commitment can perfectly well co-exist with a critical attitude that does not
a priori exclude anything from the ambit of its critical investigation.
As an aspect of the Church's life theology possesses a critical function
vis-à-vis the Church and its life of faith. A broader and deeper knowledge of theology presupposes certain "natural" qualifications (which
from the point of view of theology always remain the result of grace):
these are not to be found everywhere in the Church nor necessarily
in all who occupy leading positions in its ministry. To this extent the
gift (*charism) of theology is not be be found in all ministers and can
also be found outside the ministry. The scholarly and scientific reflection involved in theology today demands so many technical qualifications that it has necessarily to be carried out by "experts".

This methodical effort to acquire knowledge of a complete, internally unified subject must be called a science, even though the way in
which its object first presents itself for study, its primary principles,
and to some extent its methods of investigation, are different from
those of the profane sciences (it is however evident that scholarship
or scientific study is not restricted to fields of study involving the
investigation of data susceptible of experimental verification). Since
revelation is meant to be heard and understood by a man already
shaped in definite ways, pre-scientific and scientific investigation of
revelation must always make full use of secular knowledge and methods: logic, philosophy, the contemporary world-picture. Thus theology inevitably bears the mark of its time, though this does not mean

that it becomes subject to man's earthly knowledge or becomes a "system" in the historical and relativistic sense (*Schools of theology). Since the word of God to which theology listens is the word which engages the whole man, judging and redeeming him, theology can never be a purely "theoretical" science, one that is existentially uninvolved. To be worthy of its "object" and thus become scientific, theology must be meditative and *kerygmatic theology. It is an essential part of the business of theology to confront contemporary man's understanding of the world with the message of the Gospel, because theology is always an effort to hear and understand on the part of a man who has a secular historical experience and because this experience must embody itself in the act of theology if he is to hear God's word at all. By reason of its reference to faith itself, theology is a *practical* science in the sense that it is oriented to the realization of hope and love in which an aspect of knowledge is provided that is not possible elsewhere. Orthodoxy and orthopractice (appropriate faith and appropriate practice) are reciprocally conditioned in a unique totality. Theology is not directed merely to the private salvation and inwardness of the individual, but has to consider in all its material aspects the social relevance of its pronouncements (see *Political theology*). In no other science is there such a gulf between the statement and what is stated, between what is expressed and what is implied, between what we lay hold on and the mystery which lays hold on us; and therefore it is not only the right but the duty of theology to allow this gulf to be sensed ever more keenly, to refer men from the apparent clarity of its conceptions to the blinding brilliance of mystery which seems to us to be darkness. Since the subject-matter of theology can never be expressed in reflex propositions otherwise than it was in the word of revelation, it is an essential part of systematic theology to revert to the history of this expression (history of revelation, history of *dogma, *development of dogma), that is to say, to its own history. (By reason of this permanent reference to unique, historical salvific events, theology is an *historical science* with an essential relevance to the future, for the historical aspect of theology is essentially one of promise). But this reversion must help us to understand the revealed reality itself, and must not become idle historical curiosity.

In the present state of the historical development of our one theology into various disciplines, we might divide these into historical and systematic disciplines, corresponding to the first hearing and the deeper understanding of the word. The former deal with either the historical event of revelation itself, up to the point where it reaches its

THEOLOGY

eschatological climax in Jesus Christ and the establishment of the Church, that is the history of revelation (together with *exegesis and other biblical sciences, *biblical theology), or the abiding presence of this now definitive salvation, namely *Church history (including *Patrology, the history of *dogma, hagiography). The systematic disciplines deal with the God of salvation and his work: *dogmatic theology; with man as an individual as he lives in view of this encounter with God: *moral theology with *ascetical and *mystical theology; and man in the fellowship of the Church: *canon law, liturgiology, *pastoral theology. And all theology presupposes reflection as to why and how such a thing as theology exists at all: *fundamental theology (apologetics).

HISTORY OF CATHOLIC THEOLOGY
In the time of the *Fathers of the Church theology consists primarily (second and third centuries) of a simple handing down of the traditional teaching, and the defence of it against Jews, pagans and heretics (through apologists like Aristides, St Justin, etc.) and against various gnostic attempts (*Gnosis) to systematize Christianity in the sense of a mystical rationalism and to identify it with the dualistic and mythological sentiments prevalent at that period (leading theologians: St Irenaeus, Tertullian, Clement of Alexandria). But a contrast is provided by the (essentially orthodox) attempt of Origen to work out the first Christian synthesis. In the fourth and fifth centuries, with the struggles against *Arianism, *Nestorianism and *Monophysitism, theology at once uses and dethrones contemporary philosophy (*Neoplatonism), formulating Trinitarian and Christological dogma in terms that have remained classic ever since: the repudiation of all cosmic demigods clearly distinguishes the world from God, yet takes it up into God's own life through the mystery of the *hypostatic union (*hypostasis) (St Athanasius, St Basil, St Gregory of Nazianzus, St Gregory of Nyssa, St Hilary). At the same time St Augustine in the West, in the course of his struggle with *Pelagianism, was working out a Christian *anthropology which sees man as open to God's free grace. The centuries transitional between antiquity and the Middle Ages are devoted to collecting, sifting and preserving the patristic inheritance; they are not characterized by creativity or new departures.

The eleventh century sees the beginning of a new age, the Scholastic period. Treatises are methodically elaborated on subjects which had received little systematic attention in patristic times (the theology of the sacraments, many aspects of anthropology); (Aristotelian)

500

philosophy is systematically applied to the analysis of dogma; relatively balanced syntheses appear (commentaries on the *Sentences,* the *Summae).*

The Council of Trent in the sixteenth century inaugurates a new period characterized by opposition to the teaching of the Reformers, and the spirit of the new age (baroque) is on the whole constructively embodied in post-Tridentine Scholasticism. Spanish theology—Dominican (Vitoria, Melchior Cano, Bañez, etc.) and Jesuit (Suarez, Vazquez, Molina)—is especially prominent. It sees the development of the tractates on the ecclesiastical magisterium and the Church as an external society, apologetics, and *controversial theology (Bellarmine), the beginnings of historical theology and the history of *dogma (Petavius, etc.), systematic presentations of dogmatic theology in the form of commentaries on St Thomas' *Summa Theologiae,* explicit treatment of the problem of *grace and *freedom (controversies on grace), and the emergence of *moral theology as a separate discipline.

Theology stagnates during the eighteenth century: development is almost exclusively confined to the historical disciplines (Church history).

In the nineteenth century efforts are made to relate theology directly to the radically altered intellectual situation (Kant, German Idealism); they either go astray (A. Günther, G. Hermes) or have little immediate influence on Catholic theology as a whole (*Tübingen school, John Henry Newman). The science is largely dominated by Neo-Scholasticism (Kleutgen, Scheeben, etc.), which sought (as was certainly necessary) to renew the contact that had almost been lost by the end of the eighteenth century with the genuine tradition of scholasticism (in systematic form, and especially by historical research into medieval Scholasticism). Thus the distance between the actual state of Catholic theology and the religious needs of the age remains greater than it should be, despite all our (especially historical) learning. Progress in overcoming this situation is slow and has been hindered by blunders (*Modernism, etc.).

Earlier *philosophy enjoyed the monopoly of mediating to theology the scientific findings resulting from man's growing understanding of himself. Today theology has to grapple with a great number of sciences and disciplines besides philosophy that are important for our understanding of man (*linguistics, *philosophy of science). As far as many scholars in these fields are concerned theology is open to the suspicion of being an *ideology. Theology as a human activity is always under suspicion of ideology and is guilty of this to the extent that it commits itself to serving the ideologies of particular historical periods and ruling classes. But the actual word of God that finds expression and is reflected on in theology is not only no ideology but provides its most radical critique. Christian theology as the theology of the God who is always greater than we can imagine, who is the unique and absolute future, who infinitely transcends all structures and systems to be found within the world, and who yet is really present for us as this God in grace and hope, and as the theology of death freely accepted as the starting-point of the absolute future, is the contradiction of all ideologies.

THEOLOGY OF THE PRIMITIVE CHRISTIAN COMMUNITY *(GEMEINDETHEOLOGIE)*

A term which has been devised to indicate the process of collecting and editing ("forming") the words of Jesus and the events of his life—with the Christological and soteriological definition and interpretation this involves—which went on after the "experience of Easter" and in its light, the reduction to writing (Gospels) being in part governed by the religious and cultic needs of the post-Resurrection "community" (which as such cannot be strictly defined, in terms either of space or of time); historical exegesis can provide evidence of this process even today. But this community activity can only be regarded as the unfolding of Jesus' message about himself and his work, not as the creation of something new which would serve as the foundation of New Testament theology (*Gospel, *Tradition).

THEORY AND PRACTICE

To the extent that dealing with questions of theory and practice also means tackling the relationship between thought and action, statement and fact, consciousness and object, what in general is involved here is the basic subject-matter of epistemology and the critique of scientific knowledge. For Christian theology these questions take on an explosive potential that is not to be overcome simply by a division of labour between the various disciplines: this reflects on the one hand the mediation made necessary by the passage of time between the original message and the present-day practice of faith, and on the other the contradiction that has to be overcome between theological reflection and practical proclamation. Neither the old interpretation of the relation between theory and practice as that of purely contemplative perception and moral behaviour, nor the more recent technological interpretation as the application of a system of methodically formed propositions to objectified processes and actions (according to the principles of fitness for purpose and functionality), is sufficient to comprehend the complex mutual interaction between thinking and living on the basis of faith and the theoretical and practical reason, nor to point the way to a salutary union of theory and practice. Traditional distinctions between inward contemplation and external action, between salvation history and secular history, are less able to help the more it is recognized that under the complex conditions of production and communication of modern social systems the immediacy of theory cannot be obtained without mediation through practice and that practical experiences are always impregnated with theory. Even the central forms of the Church's act of faith do not merely bear in themselves the traces of the history of past intellectual conflicts, as even the simplest statement of faith has to be accomplished in practice in order to be clear and to be verified, but both in addition reflect the historical development and past social conditions. In keeping with this Christianity has never been able to develop its own institutional forms and norms of behaviour and to make them more precise without having recourse to secular models and taking historical data into consideration. An attempt to interpret the statements of belief that depends purely on the humanities is as deficient as a descriptively empirical analysis of the existing data, since in neither is the historical and social mediation of theory and practice sufficiently reflected. A hermeneutics of faith with practical aims and based on the critique of society would therefore belong to a suitable sub-discipline of a critical theology (*Political theology).

THOMISM

The teaching of the Doctor of the Church, St Thomas Aquinas (about 1225-1274), and his school, which interprets his teaching in various ways and seeks to keep it alive. The Church recommends St Thomas as the "Common Doctor" for all Catholic schools of thought (D 3665f.; CIC can. 1366 § 2), though this does not apply where his doctrine is not also the explicit doctrine of the Church. Where weightier doctrines are concerned that are properly theological in the strict sense, the broad doctrine of Thomism—so receptive to new truth—has so widely established itself since the thirteenth century that it can hardly be called the doctrine of a particular school any longer. But the case is different with particular theological questions (such as the doctrine on *grace, *Banezianism), different especially where Aristotelian philosophy is concerned, which St Thomas uses as his intellectual instrument in interpreting the data of revelation. As to this latter point, an observer who is capable of a real appreciation of St Thomas' place in intellectual history will perceive that he was not the prisoner of this historically conditioned, pre-Christian, pre-personalist, cosmocentric philosophy, but can be seen as a creative philosopher and theologian in his own right who stands, facing the future, at the transition between (pre-Christian and Christian) antiquity and that (in the good sense) anthropocentric, personalist philosophy which (where it does not misconceive itself) comes from Christianity and therefore is perfectly appropriate for use in theology—more appropriate, indeed, than any philosophy of antiquity untransformed. Though with the passage of time St Thomas' position naturally becomes more and more that of a Father of the Church, he is still rightly considered the "Common" Doctor—in his respect for tradition, his bold intellectual clarity, his architectonic sense which reduces all particular problems to first principles, distinguishing and uniting faith and reason, nature and grace, the world and the Church, in his intellectual integrity and his humble adoration of the incomprehensible God.

TIME, TEMPORALITY

If we wish to acquire a genuine understanding of time we must not first think of the time told by the clock, for this is an external measure of physical processes which is extrinsic to temporal things in their temporality and their intrinsic time. Furthermore, it would conceal the fact that the measure can only be used by an intelligent being who knows by his own interior activity of growth what time is, and who can draw comparisons. Time is primarily the mode of becoming of finite freedom: coming from a *beginning beyond one's control, personally and selectively realizing the potentiality of one's own being, attaining the unique, irrevocable completion of its institution. The unity and differentiation of these elements is the time being—which does not mean that they form a mere succession of one different thing after another (in which case they would not be phases of a single occurrence), for in fact they form a single temporal complex. The experienced "succession" of these elements, cannot be "explained", that is synthetically constructed out of other more intelligible elements, since the being and experience of these other elements would still be temporal. Given this inescapable involvement in time, which is experienced but not overcome, a true notion of *eternity can neither be had by imagining time "indefinitely" continued (which would still be mere time) nor yet by denying time (in which case it would not be clear whether the idea of "something existing, minus time" would mean anything at all), but by reflection on that conclusiveness which is sought as the fruit of time in freedom and which this desire experiences even in time. Insofar as these elements are disjoined and the *beginning is not simply in free possession of the *end but "conceives" it while bringing itself to birth, temporality is a hallmark of creatureliness. Insofar as it is not the concluded but the conclusive which comes about with time, time is the positive means by which creatures participate in God's *eternity. Thus in this perspective the temporality of the individual biological being and the temporality that is proper to the world as a whole (*Creation, *End of the world) are seen to be diminished modes of the interior time characteristic of the history of free personal beings (*End, *Eschatology, *Judgment, *Hell, *Heaven).

TOLEDO

Certain local synods held in this Spanish city (the third, 589; the eleventh, 675; the fifteenth, 688; the sixteenth, 693) are of doctrinal importance, especially because the creeds they promulgated contain full expositions of the doctrine of the Trinity and the Incarnation (D 525–541, 566, 573).

TOLERANCE

Rightly understood and practised, tolerance does not arise from sceptical indifference to truth in general, or an opinion that all Christian religions are objectively of equal validity, but from Christian love, reverence for the conscience of others, and the realization that the act of true faith can never be extorted, that it would be immoral to attempt such a thing or to compel people to make false outward profession of any religion. Man has a natural right to an area of freedom within which he can carry out his free interior decisions. Since in actuality truth is never something possessed statically, but is always to be formed in historical processes, when the Church views such an area of freedom as legitimate, she never offends the truth (itself never static) entrusted to her. This area is limited by the same right in others. The existence and the limitations of this area of freedom therefore raise problems with which neither totalitarian coercion nor unrestrained liberalism can cope. Their solution is subject to historical change (so that caution is necessary in judging earlier forms of tolerance and intolerance) and is only possible in the concrete through patience, courage and magnanimity. Since the *State is a natural and earthly society which of itself has no duty to promote the interests of supernatural revelation and thus to offer the Church positive assistance in her task (though it may not hinder her), there is nothing in Catholic principles to prevent a civil equality for all Christian bodies today. This is the expression of tolerance that is appropriate today (and doubtless always will be) and which the Christian owes every other human being (see Vat. II, Church/world, 28, 43, 73, 75; Miss., 11; Rel. Free., 14). Many cases may arise, however, where the State must protect the norms of the natural moral law in public life even against the beliefs of individuals, for here the State is only defending the area of freedom to which all are entitled against attack by individuals. A system of this kind can prevail in Church and State which is withdrawn from public control and at the same time allows (ineffectual) criticism. But this kind of merely formal tolerance is ultimately a tool of repression.

TONSURE

See *Clergy.*

TORAH

See *Law.*

TRADITION

In a general, pre-theological sense, the sum of all the processes whereby insights and skills that have been acquired and institutions that have been established are handed down from generation to generation; and then the sum of all that has been thus handed down. Tradition ensures the continuance of what has been once begun, and through the wisdom and experience of one's ancestors gives one a perspective in which to classify and evaluate new experiences. On the other hand tradition is always liable to lose its receptivity to new experience and become a torpid conservatism.

The Second Vatican Council stated that the formation of Sacred Scripture was itself an event that formed part of tradition (Rev., 7); that the process of tradition continues in the *apostolic succession *(Successio apostolica)* with the assistance of the Holy Spirit; that tradition provides awareness of the canon of Scripture and brings Scripture to life *(ibid.,* 8); that Scripture and Tradition form a single unity because they have a single origin—God's unique revelation—and mutually condition each other *(ibid.,* 9–10). From this one can conclude that Tradition occurs always and everywhere in hearkening to Scripture, subject to Scripture as the critical norm which is always and everywhere necessary in order to distinguish "divine" Tradition as the handing on of God's revelation of himself in Jesus Christ from human traditions. The alternative—the idea that the propositions of Scripture "materially" contain Christian revelation in its fullness or that beyond this certain propositions have been handed down by ("oral") tradition "alone" so as to give "two" materially different "sources" for Christian Tradition—rests on a false understanding. On the one hand Tradition, which in the post-apostolic age presents itself as having taken on the form of Scripture, is in its original nature not a compendium of propositions but the lasting presence of God's revelation, the knowledge and experience of Jesus Christ with the inexhaustible stimulus these provide for thought and reflection, the mystery that can never be comprehended of God's revelation of himself. On the other hand this Tradition continues inasmuch as, understood in this way, it is the bearer of Scripture. Scripture for its part is the event in which the Church makes concrete and recognizes once again her *kerygma, her faith, and subjects herself to this objective criterion to provide a critique of what in the way of opinions, tendencies, etc, otherwise exists in her in the course of history, and thus maintains in its purity what is specific about her faith, which she has while she expresses it in Scripture.

Tradition for Catholic theology is the process whereby revealed truth (*Dogma), ultimately derived by oral preaching from the original bearers of Christian *revelation (particularly *Jesus Christ and the *Apostles) is transmitted by the Church, with the assistance of the Holy Spirit, and thereby developed; and the truth thus transmitted. Even when the original Tradition has been committed to writing in *Holy Scripture in the first Christian generation, the mind of the believing Church, passed on in Tradition and authoritatively proclaimed by the magisterium, as to the scope (*Canon) and meaning of Scripture still remains (as "Tradition") formal norm for the interpretation of Scripture, so that in this sense there are two "sources" of revelation: Scripture *and* Tradition (D 1501 and *passim)*. Indeed Tradition logically takes precedence over Scripture. But since the believing mind of the later Church, and therefore "Tradition", is always bound as regards its content to the preaching (tradition) of the apostolic age, of which Scripture contains at least the substance, and since it is not possible at least for us to prove with certainty that explicit matters of faith (apart from the scope of the canon) were held in apostolic times which have not been recorded in Scripture, Scripture alone remains for all practical purposes the sole material source of the faith drawn upon by later Tradition. This does not mean, of course—quite the contrary—that the further history of the Church's believing mind may not see considerable developments and constant new actualizations of these scriptural truths (History of *dogma); and the only ultimate guarantee of the soundness of this development on the permanent basis of Scripture is the assistance of the Holy Spirit, who is promised to the Church and her magisterium (*Deposit of faith). We must distinguish Tradition in the strict sense from doctrine and discipline that are traditional in the broad sense but cannot claim the direct authority of God revealing himself and always making himself heard through the Church (see *Consent*).

TRADITIONALISM

The doctrine of nineteenth-century Catholic philosophers and theologians like de Bonald, Bautain, and Bonnetty (as an escape from rationalism and scepticism) that metaphysical, religious, and moral truth cannot be ascertained by individual reason but can be certainly known only through a revelation (*Primitive revelation) that authoritatively attests itself in language, national spirit, tradition, Church, general common sense, etc. This doctrine, which the Church has condemned (D 2751ff., 2811ff., 3015, 3026; *Proofs of the existence of God), puts a one-sided emphasis on the inevitable historicity of human knowledge, makes *revelation the only source of knowledge, thus depriving it of its free historical character, and overlooks the fact that historical tradition and revelation necessarily address themselves to human *reason, which by a responsible judgment (that is, one based on intrinsic principles) can accept the historical word.

TRANSCENDENCE

Those predicates are called "transcendentals" in the logical sense which do not apply to a limited sphere of being but are necessarily valid for all real or possible being—such as *being, unity, intelligibility (*Truth), desirability (goodness, *good), etc. These predicates are genuinely transcendental—metaphysical—because they are (implicitly) affirmed of every conceivable being even when their application to that being is questioned or denied. We call transcendental that form of knowledge and enquiry which ascertains the metaphysical (apodictic) necessity of a proposition and its content (as contrasted with a proposition which merely affirms a factual situation that could very well not exist) by showing that the denial of this proposition implicitly contradicts itself. Man's power to know and love, assent and consent, grasps particular being against the background of *being in general; thus all its particularized knowledge is implicitly based on the unthematic awareness it also has of Being *simpliciter,* which includes an awareness—however inarticulate—of *God, *spirit, and *freedom and thus of the *mystery above us and within us. Consequently the transcendentality of the human spirit is the essential foundation of the *person, of responsibility, of religious *experience (including *mysticism), and of the possibility of God's self-communication in *grace and *revelation.

The objections that have been raised in recent (and especially Protestant) theology against the concept of transcendence are justified to the extent that God's relationship to man and the world is not one that ignores history and the here-and-now. But if transcendence is seen as the pre-condition for the mystery revealing itself in history to man, then it is possible to reconcile with the concept of transcendence the dimensions whose absence is complained of ("depth of being", the purpose of human solidarity, the answer to the question of meaning, the absolute future). The application of the concept of transcendence to an infinite transcending or self-surpassing of the individual human being and of mankind in its history is legitimate if included in this consideration is the foundation that makes such transcending possible (cf. the concept of self-transcendence with regard to the *creation of man, etc.).

TRANSMIGRATION OF SOULS

See *Pre-Existentianism.*

TRANSUBSTANTIATION

Neo-Latin, in the language of Catholic theology meaning "essential change": at the consecration in the *Mass, the changing of the substance of bread and wine, by the power of God, into the substance of Jesus Christ's Body and Blood, which thereby become present while the empirical realities as phenomena (*Species) of bread and wine remain. The defined doctrine of transubstantiation (D 1652) does not attempt to give an explanation of just how Jesus becomes present but simply to state in alternative terms that cannot be watered down that on the one hand what Jesus gives us is, as he says, his Body and nothing else, and that on the other hand the empirical reality available to our sense may and must be recognized as that of bread. The sense of "substance" and "species" in the context of the definition as such must therefore ultimately be sought in this theological datum and not in the maxims of philosophy. "Substance" means that which, taken in its ultimate being and significance, makes the offering bread (and nothing more) or the Body of Jesus Christ; "species" means that which in the world of ordinary human experience is accessible to us. By declaring that the species of bread and wine remain after the consecration, the doctrine of transubstantiation also expressly (and rightly) teaches us that empirical procedures cannot detect any physical change in the offering.—See also *Consubstantiation,* the view of Luther. A difficulty with regard to the doctrine of transubstantiation that does not affect the dogma itself concerns the non-personal concepts applied to the nonorganic realm. If while maintaining the transformation of the context of being stronger emphasis is placed on the fact that bread and wine have been set in a new context of meaning, then one can talk of transignification (or of transfinalization, with reference to the new end or purpose bestowed on this food). In this it should be observed that substance, being, essence, meaning, significance and end can here be completely identical.

TREASURY OF THE CHURCH

This term came into use in the 14th century in connexion with the theology of *indulgences (D 1025ff., 1447ff., 1467 and *passim),* but the reality referred to is independent of this occasion. Indeed the term itself only expresses by a different image what has always been made quite clear without its help; that God desires every aspect of the salvation of every individual by way of Christ, his infinite *satisfaction

510

and the "merits" he won on the cross (D 1528f., 3670, 3891 and *passim)*, and by way of the whole *Body of Christ, which draws from and in him the strength required for its own activity and causes this to redound to the benefit of every member (see 1 Cor 12:25f. and *passim)*. This total saving reality of Jesus Christ and his body is called the treasury of the Church insofar as it effects the obliteration of the temporal *penalties due to sin, in particular by means of indulgences. As to the manner in which we should conceive this to happen, see *Indulgences.*

TRENT

The Nineteenth Ecumenical Council was held here from December 13th, 1545 to December 4th, 1563 (under Popes Paul III, Julius II, and Pius IV). Besides initiating ecclesiastical reforms, it dealt with the problems raised by the doctrine of the sixteenth-century Reformers: the scope of the *canon of Scripture, the normative role of *Tradition, the doctrine of *original sin and *concupiscence; the doctrine of *grace, *justification, *merit, *certainty of salvation, *perseverance; the doctrine of the seven sacraments in general, in particular *baptism, *confirmation, the *Eucharist (*Transubstantiation), the *Mass, the sacrament of *penance, *anointing of the sick, holy *orders, and *marriage; the doctrine of *purgatory, the *veneration of saints, and *indulgences. The teaching of the Council of Trent is the most comprehensive of any Council before Vatican II (D 1500–1816, 1820–1825, 1830, 1835, 1847–1850). Though this teaching is wholly traditional and couched in largely medieval terms, it is nevertheless based on biblical theology, does not accuse its adversaries of particular opinions (the Reformers are never mentioned by name), and offers sufficient opportunity for the full integration into Catholicism of the real religious aims and aspirations of the Reformation.

TRIBULATION

A NT concept which must not be lacking in the unvarnished Christian version of man's Christian life (*Temptation, *World, *Death): man is constantly exposed to tribulation and trial in his experience of finitude, toil, and mortality, and as a Christian so much the more (Jn 17:14). He must not flinch from this situation but endure the little time we have to live (Jn 16:16ff.) in the strength of the Spirit (1 Thess

1:6), with confidence in God's grace in Christ (Jn 16:33), sharing the fate of Christ in hope and constancy.

TRICHOTOMISM

The false doctrine, which nevertheless frequently recurs in the history of Western thought, that the nature of man is composed of three elements: body, soul, and spirit, all of which are really distinct (*Distinction). Though such is often not its intention, this doctrine—which the Church condemns: D 301ff., 502, 657f., 900ff., 1440f., 2826— divorces man's spirit (and so his person, his free spiritual history) from his material, bodily being. It cannot really see this bodily history as a history of the spirit and therefore cannot accept that our supernatural redemption was wrought in human flesh. The spirit becomes the adversary of the soul, finds itself not merely in historical or personal terms, but in essential and therefore irreconcilable contradiction with earthly history and the body (*Soul, *Form, *Spirit). The "trichotomism" in Scripture means by "spirit" a particular—personal— aspect of the one soul, or man's supernatural grace, the Holy Ghost, who is not a component of human nature but is man's God-given salvation (*Pneuma).

TRINITARIAN MYSTICISM

This is the mystical experience, comparable with *Christ-mysticism, in which man's gratuitous relationship to the three Persons in God is explicitly realized. In the history of mysticism it has not had the prominence one might expect in view of the importance of the mystery in saving history. The reason for this fact may be that union with the absolute, simple, "modeless" God (in the empty silence of the Godhead) has until modern times remained the basic theoretical pattern of *mysticism.

TRINITARIAN THEOLOGY

Its task is to enable men to believe in this supreme *mystery of Christian revelation as readily and as intelligently as possible. It reviews the history of the revelation of this mystery in OT and NT, the history of its theological formulation and of opposition to it (*Tritheism, *Sabellianism, *Unitarianism), explains the terms used in expounding this doctrine (unity, *person, *nature, *essence, *relation, *perichoresis), and seeks itself to state the doctrine in terms as clear and intelligible as may be. Today in particular, Trinitarian theology has the further duty of explaining the religious significance of this doctrine of the Trinity "immanent" in God; the absolute self-communication of God as of him who, being "unoriginate" is subject to no norm ("Father"), necessarily occurs in two modes of communication: the living historical presence in the world of God's self-utterance (*Logos, "Son"), and the sanctifying gift-in-communication which effects its own acceptance in the depth of man's being ("Holy Spirit"). But these modes of communication must be conceived so entirely as modes of God's *self*-communication that no creature can account for the difference between them (for otherwise it would cease to be *self*-communication), but that these modes must be attributed to God "in himself". They must be the gracious, homogeneous diffusion of a twofold communication within the Godhead which constitutes a threefold relational distinction in God, bringing out the living plenitude of the one divine identity. That is, choosing either as its starting-point or destination the axiom that the "immanent" Trinity and the "economic" Trinity revealed for our salvation are the same, so that we may neither deny the one by a sort of Sabellianism nor reduce the other to mere *appropriations, Trinitarian theology must show that to confess that we have been blessed with God's grace in Christ and his Spirit is already to confess our faith in the Blessed Trinity, difficult as the subtle formulation of this mystery in classical theology may sometimes seem to us to assimilate religiously and existentially.

TRINITY

The name of the fundamental mystery of *Christianity, that of the one Nature and the three Persons (Father, Son and Holy Spirit) in *God.

TEACHING OF SCRIPTURE. (1) The Trinity looms in outline in the OT as a mystery ready for disclosure. God is the absolute *mystery, yet deals historically with the fathers; it is above all through the "Word", in which he is actively present, and in the "Spirit", which enables one to understand the Word, that God reveals and offers himself to man, but as long as the self-communication of God in Jesus Christ and in the Spirit had not yet occurred in an historically unrepeatable way, the revelation of the Trinity would have described a reality that did not exist within man's historical experience. (2) The NT, which by "God" always means the God at work in the OT, the father of Jesus, witnesses to the divinity of *Jesus Christ (the Son): in him is the fullness of the Spirit (Lk 4:18), forgiveness (Mk 2:1–12 and parallels), dominion over the law God gave in the OT (Mk 2:23–28 and parallels), incomparable intimacy with God (Mt 11:25ff.; Jn 10:30), the "I am" (Jn 8:58; 10; 11:25 and *passim;* *Yahweh). Similarly the NT is aware of the divinity of the *Holy Spirit, who being God's Spirit is simply the plenitude of his salvation (Lk 4:18; Tit 3:5f.). Yet *as* the very presence of God the Son and the Spirit are not simply the One whom they reveal: they stand in relation to him, are sent by him, each has his own special "relationship" to the Father (Jn 1:1, 18; 15:26). Thus, whilst firmly adhering to the uniqueness of God, the NT recognizes just here a triplicity: Father, Son and Holy Spirit, distinguished from each other by their different salvific operations and yet so equal among themselves that the Son and the Spirit cannot be thought of as mere "forces" (at a lower power) of God's work in the world. (See the many "Trinitarian" tests, such as Mt 28:19; 2 Cor 13:13; etc.). Though in the NT the "three" are not distinguished in a way proper to modern conceptions of personality, that does not mean that the NT does not make the distinction asserted in the Dogma of the Church. The language of the NT declares that the concrete Jesus is for us the very Being of God among us, and yet is not the Father, and this distinction is not merely due to the human reality of Jesus. The Spirit is experienced as the self-giving of God, but in such a way that the Spirit allows us to experience the illimitability of the increate God (the Father).

TEACHING OF THE MAGISTERIUM. The Trinity is a mystery *(mysterium absolutum)* in the strict sence (D 3015), which could not be known without revelation, and even after revelation cannot become wholly intelligible. Its import is as follows: (1) The one God exists in three "Persons" (Subsistences) which are the one divine Nature (the one divine essence, the divine substance) (see D 73, 112, 800 and *passim)* and therefore are equally eternal and almighty (D 44, 188, 526ff., 1330f. and *passim).* (2) These three Persons are (really) distinct from one another (D 75, 531f., 1330ff., 2828): the Father is in original possession of the necessary divine essence (D 188, 75, 800, 1330f.); the Son subsists through the eternal communication of the divine essence ("generation", uttering of the "Logos") by the Father alone (D 44, 188f., 804ff., 1330f. and *passim);* the Holy Spirit is not begotten, but proceeds both from the Father and the Son (as from one principle)

TRINITY

by a single "breathing" *(spiratio)* (D 75, 112, 850, 1300ff., 1331 and *passim)*. (3) Through these two relationships of origination, therefore, there exist relations (D 408, 528, 531f., 573, 1330; *Relation) and properties (D 531f., 573, 800) in God (really) distinct from each other (D 528, 573, 1330), but these in their turn are not really distinct from God's nature (D 803f., 1330). Each Person is the one God, everything is common to them without distinction except where there is relative opposition (D 1330). Each divine Person is wholly in each of the others (*Perichoresis; D 1331), each is the one true God (D 529, 680, 790, 851). *Ad extra* (with respect to creatures) they are a single operative principle (D 800, 1330 and *passim)*.

HISTORY OF THE DOGMA OF THE TRINITY. The dogmatic history of this mystery reduces itself to the one strenuous effort to preserve the affirmations of the NT and to defend them by an ever subtler terminology (mobilizing and developing the whole of Western thought: *Nature, *Person, *Essence) against ever subtler attempts to resolve the biblical mystery. The basic heresies which appeared (and were by the nature of the case to be expected) were: *Modalism (the Trinity is only the aspect of God "for us"); *Tritheism (Father, Son and Holy Ghost are simply three Gods; their "unity" is only a conceptual one); and *Subordinationism (in various forms: the Son and the Holy Ghost are "creatures" of the Father; forces of the one God at a lower power.

"IMMANENT" AND "ECONOMIC" TRINITY. From the actual development of faith in the Trinity and from systematic theology today it is clearly necessary to hold that God's *self-communication to his creature has been absolute so that the "immanent" Trinity (existing in God himself) is the "economic" (that which deals with men and brings about their salvation; *Indwelling of God). Conversely, the Trinity of God's dealings with us is already the reality of God as he is in himself: tri-"personality". From that experience of our faith which the Word of God himself (Jesus-Scripture) gives, we can therefore say that God's absolute self-communication to the world, *as a* mystery that has approached us, is in its ultimate originality called Father; *as* itself a principle acting in history, Son; *as* a gift bestowed on us and accepted, Holy Ghost. This "as", which is ordered to us, is really the self-communication of God "in himself"; the triplicity affirmed is thus a triplicity of God in himself. But since the communication of God is concerned in both cases (and not two effects that differ as creatures do), in both cases the "same" God is concerned.

TRINITY

PARTICULAR CONSIDERATIONS REGARDING THE THEOLOGY OF THE TRINITY. (1) According to revelation, activity in God, as the principle of immanent, substantial and necessary vital functions, does not flow from a faculty *(processio operationis)*, rather that which has been communicated flows from the pure actuality of the agent *(processio operati):* it does not flow from any need to come into being but is absolute, complete communication of God's own uncreated being in *two* processions *(processiones),* corresponding to the nature of the eternal God as knowledge and love. The Father, knowing himself in one act of infinite knowledge, and in himself everything that can be known, thereby utters his own essence (notional act) and so realizes the concept of "generation": one who is alive originating from another who is alive by the communication of the latter's aliveness, the bringing forth of an equal (biblically: only begotten Son of God, Logos). Father and Son (in Greek theology, substantially equivalent, "the Father *through* the Son") being, as a single operative principle, a loving consent to themselves, there occurs a procession (Jn 15:26) which is a communication of the divine essence as an assimilative reaching out of the lover towards the beloved ("breathing"), or as a loving embrace of the divine reality communicated: the Holy Ghost.

(2) These two processions are to be thought of as purely *relational* realities, for they are identical, in their reality, with the absolute being of the divine essence, and yet, being distinct processions, they cannot be nothing (*Relation). Thus they resolve themselves into *four* relations: begetting, begottenness, breathing, "being breathed"; the processions and relations are not really but conceptually (virtually) distinct from the divine essence.

(3) The one divine reality, then, exists in a threefold, "hypostatizing" (because as relation it is in each case incommutable), relational manner of being: in the manner of the uncommunicated Communicator, as begetting and uttering; in the manner of that which has been communicated, as begotten and uttered; in the manner of that which has been communicated, the breathed, loving reaching-out (or embrace) of the lovers: the one God exists in the singleness of his essence as three *Persons* in the triplicity of the hypostatizing relations, that is in the manner of a trebly opposed relatedness of the one spiritually conscious (essential) self-possession. If in using the expression "three Persons" we instinctively and thoughtlessly base our consideration on the modern formal concept of the *person we shall automatically visualize three different spiritual active centres which have relations among themselves. But then we have not only taken as our basis an idea that is alien to the ancient doctrine of three *Hypostases of the

one God, we have not only falsely conceived the *human,* psychological active centre in Christ to be divine and then as well falsely set this divine centre over against that of the Father, but in effect we have adopted *Tritheism, which is a serious danger today in view of the inadequate understanding our people have of the Catholic doctrine of the Trinity. The one God is the Father because he is the sourceless *source* (as the One who communicates himself); the one God is the Son and the Word, because by the fact that the Father utters himself (and thus is the Father) this utteredness as a relative opposition really exists in God and as a relational reality of the *one* God it constitutes a real distinction and therefore a relational incommutability in God; the one God is the Spirit because an analogous relational differentiation is set up with the second vital procession within God, that of yearning (and welcoming) love.

TRITHEISM

A third century heresy which attracted no adherents of any importance. It conceived the *Trinity in such a way that the absolutely single divine essence was divided into three Gods (D 112). In the twelfth century tritheism re-appeared as the consequence of a confused Trinitarian theology and was condemned in 1215 by the Fourth Lateran Council (D 804ff.; see D 2826).

TRUTH

In ordinary parlance, truth is the conformity of a statement with the fact it attempts to convey. But this conception varies greatly to the type of knowledge, the knower, and the thing known. If we are concerned, for example with the primordial knowledge a knower has of himself, then truth is merely self-presence, the inner luminosity of a being for itself. This fontal luminosity (which the intellect cannot grasp in objective concepts but which is involved in every act of cognition, whatever its thematic object) also entails, as a necessary condition of its own existence, an experience (primarily unthematic) of the *spirit's own *transcendence; so that this one truth, which, being contained in all other truths—not one truth among many—is the single comprehensive truth, also implies an orientation to *God, an inarticulate, unthematic awareness of the abyss of *mystery that is the ground of all being. When man does not repress this one truth of his, does not hate it, does not close himself against it, but freely and innocently accepts it and surrenders himself to it, he grasps truth as his own, is in the truth that embraces him and makes him true, that is, delivered up to the incomprehensible truth and thus freed from himself. For by such an act, in the concrete order, man has not only freely accepted his own transcendence, but—since this is "elevated" by God's universal, supernatural salvific will—also his own ordination to the God of eternal life, disclosing himself in self-communication: to truth absolutely (Jn 14:6), which is the absolutely luminous and loving possession from within of the infinite fullness of being, which bestows itself as gift in the *beatific vision.

TÜBINGEN SCHOOL

(1) The (more recent) Tübingen school is a trend in nineteenth-century Protestant theology, whose leading representatives (like F. C. Baur, D. F. Strauss, E. von Zeller) were chiefly associated with the University of Tübingen. It reflected in various ways the characteristic spirit of the nineteenth century—a penchant for speculative systems in the manner of German Idealism, and historical criticism.

(2) The Catholic Tübingen school (Drey, Hirscher, Möhler, Kuhn, Hefele, Staudenmaier, etc.), on a wholly Catholic basis, put an end to the rationalism of the eighteenth-century Enlightenment. Unlike Neo-Scholasticism, it used the intellectual tools of German Idealism and had a keen appreciation of historical development in religion and dogma and of the historical method in theology.

TUTIORISM

See *Moral System.*

TYPE

Persons or events in the divinely guided history of the Old Covenant are called "types" in the NT if they are typical of the free dispositions and attitudes characterizing the whole of God's salvific activity and therefore necessarily have their counterparts and fulfilments in the New Covenant, where they have been foreseen and forewilled by God. Thus, for example, Moses is a type of Jesus Christ; the forty years which the children of Israel spent in the wildnerness are a type of the Christian's pilgrimage to the promised land of eternal life. We can recognize these types most easily (but not only) if the parallel is drawn by the NT or the Fathers. Used with tact and circumspection, they can help us in our task of constantly actualizing the OT anew.

U

UBIQUITY, DOCTRINE OF

A momentary attempt by Luther to explain the presence of Jesus Christ's Body and Blood in the Eucharist by the communication to Jesus Christ's humanity of God's omnipresence. Here Luther overlooked the fact that the hypostatic union involves no divinization of Jesus Christ's finite human nature, and therefore cannot impart omnipresence to it, especially as such a thing would destroy the special character of Jesus Christ's presence in the Sacrament.

UNITARIANISM

The teaching of certain sects (Servetus, Fausto Sozzini) which arose from the Reformation of the sixteenth century. They denied the doctrine of the *Trinity, seeing in it a departure from strict monotheism. Unitarianism has had considerable influence in modern liberal Protestantism, especially in America.—See also *Socinianism*.

UNITY OF MANKIND

(1) A fact that emerges from the multitude of ways in which all men are bound to, and depend on, each other. (2) A task: on the one hand an historical goal to be realized to some extent in this world as a condition of the Church's unity and catholicity, and on the other hand an eschatological work of God.

The unity of mankind is based on: (a) the earthly, biological cohesion of the race in space and time, in human history (*Monogenism); (b) a common nature (*Spirit) which, despite the variety by which

520

God wills it to be characterized, admits of and requires a positive intercommunication; (c) the redemptive history of loss and gain based on these unities, and presupposing them, which reveals itself in the universal salvific will of God and its historical realizations (*Old Testament, *New Testament, *Original sin). This salvific will of God seeks the restoration of the lost unity of mankind (Jn 11:52; 17:11), a purpose vouched for by the Church's unity, and universality, and its sacramental dynamism orientated to the world. Thus the unity of mankind is at once a task for this world and a graciously eschatological one, in that man's initial unity has been lost through sin but cannot be recovered in this world without the gracious, salvific activity of God.

UNITY OF THE CHURCH

THE SCRIPTURAL NOTION. The NT considers the unity of the Church, denoted by the most various expressions (*Church [Gr. ἐκκλησία], seed of Abraham, God's field, temple of God, building, house of God) to be based above all on the fact that the Church has been established by the operation of the *one* God (1 Cor 8:6), by the *one* revelation in the *one* Jesus Christ (the crucified, risen, exalted) (Rom 14:7ff.), in the operation of the *one* Spirit (of God and Jesus Christ) (Eph 2:18). Finally, this unity is inaugurated (disclosed) in the *one* *Gospel, the *one* *baptism, and the one *office which is given to Peter and the Twelve. The essential and concrete unity of the Church is expressed particularly by the figure of the "body" in St Paul; this body is constituted by baptism and actualized by the Lord's Supper (1 Cor 10:17). This unity of the Church is sharply defined *vis-à-vis* the "outside world" by the treatment of the sinner (*Penance, sacrament of). Accordingly the NT always conceives Church unity as something given from the first, a thing present, concrete and historical (and not a mere general ideal), with which the one people of God are endowed by God's one and universal act of love towards the one human race in setting one Head over them (Second *Adam); this unity of the Church is entrusted to her to be preserved in history as a sign of her divine origin.

THEOLOGICAL NOTION. To theology, the unity of the Church means that the Church is both unique and one. Both these aspects are fixed in the Church's self-consciousness very early and are constantly upheld by the magisterium (the Creeds; D 802, 870ff., 3050ff., 3302ff.,

3802). Unity of faith, of the sacraments, of worship and of government are the external elements of Church unity, and flow from the internal principle of this unity—the operation of Jesus Christ and his Spirit; as such and at the same time they form the historical tangibility of God's one and unique will to save all men, which is to be displayed through and in the Church. Reflection on the really primary criteria of Church unity becomes increasingly necessary with the inevitable growth of the feeling that the present divisions of Christendom are a sinful perversion (*Ecumenical movement; *Ministries, recognition of). The restoration of Church unity cannot await the end of time, since the Church *in* her unity should and must be a sign of grace in time.

UNIVOCITY

See *Analogy.*

V

VALUE

See *Ethics, Good.*

VATICAN COUNCIL, FIRST

The Twentieth Ecumenical Council was held from December 8th, 1869 to July 18th, 1870, under Pius IX. Apart from matters of Church discipline, it concerned itself chiefly with the repudiation of *pantheism and *materialism, with God's infinite distinction from the world, his free act of creation, his verbal revelation, the nature of *faith and its relation to natural reason, with the universal jurisdictional primacy of the *Pope and his *infallibility when he pronounces solemn dogmatic definitions (D 3000 –3005; Church, 3). There was no time to define other doctrinal matters relating to *ecclesiology, as the Council was prematurely broken off for political reasons.

VATICAN COUNCIL, SECOND

Vatican II, accounted as the Twenty-first Ecumenical Council, met from October 11th, 1962, to December 8th, 1965, under the Popes John XXIII and Paul VI. What it had to say is contained in sixteen documents (constitutions, decrees and declarations) and can be classified as follows: (1) the *Church's fundamental theological understanding of itself (dogmatic constitution on the Church, *Lumen gentium);* (2) the Church's internal life—its liturgy (constitution on the liturgy, *Sacrosanctum concilium),* its administration and leadership (decree on bishops, *Christus dominus,* and decree on the Eastern

523

Catholic Churches, *Orientalium ecclesiarum),* its teaching authority (dogmatic constitution on revelation, *Dei verbum,* and declaration on Christian education, *Gravissimum educationis),* its structures (decree on the priesthood, *Presbyterorum ordinis,* that on priestly formation, *Optatam totius,* that on the renewal of the religious life, *Perfectae caritatis,* and that on the lay apostolate, *Apostolicam actuositatem);* (3) the Church's mission beyond its own membership—the Church's relations with non-Catholic Christendom (decree on ecumenism, *Unitatis redintegratio,* and in part that on the Eastern Catholic Churches, *Orientalium ecclesiarum),* with non-Christian religions and especially with Judaism (declaration on non-Christian religions, *Nostra aetate,* and decree on the Church's missionary activity, *Ad gentes),* with the world as such (pastoral constitution on the Church in the modern world, *Gaudium et spes,* and decree on the mass media, *Inter mirifica),* its attitude towards the ideological pluralism of today (declaration on religious freedom, *Dignitatis humanae).* The Council did not intend to formulate any new dogmatic definitions. Instead it wanted to make the Church's life and teaching come alive and to bring them up to date.

VENERATION OF IMAGES

This veneration is essentially directed to the person represented (to whom alone "absolute worship" may be due). It is therefore a "relative" *cult, in no way implying that the image itself deserves to be worshipped. True *adoration is due to God alone (D 600ff.); an image deserves only veneration. But the Church's tradition or the history of the image itself (its origin, its real connexion with the person represented; *Cross) may lend such veneration special weight and significance (icons, images associated with pilgrimage).

VENERATION OF SAINTS

The magisterium speaks of the significance of the saints when describing the *Church as a sign among the nations and basing her credibility squarely on her holiness (D 3013f.). The veneration of saints is licit and useful (D 1823 and *passim)* but the Church does not teach that it is a duty for the individual. The veneration of saints is scriptural because *holiness in the members of Holy Church is not only a moral requirement but above all is historical, eschatological, triumphant *grace itself, which is to be praised (see, for instance, Eph 1:6, 12, 14); the veneration of the "cloud of witnesses" (Heb 12:1) and the invocation of the saints according to their various gifts and *charismata are part of this praise of the grace of God itself. Catholic theology may not speak of a mere *possibility* of becoming holy; the doctrine of the Church's real sanctity does not apply simply to her objective institutions (for example, the sacraments) or to the primitive Church. This sanctity must be displayed to the world and it has a history: canonized saints are the creative models of sanctity who have set a concrete example, each for his own particular age, of a new way to be Christian and so have shown others how to accept Christianity creatively and with new understanding. The image of these models may fade with the passage of time or emerge with new clarity, as is shown by the fact that certain saints cease to be venerated or even disappear from the catalogue of the saints. This implies nothing about the eternal destiny of such saints since the Church is infallible when she officially beatifies and canonizes: this is the means by which she becomes officially aware of the modes of her self-realization in history. When a saint is recognized as a model and receives homage as such we speak of veneration or the *cult of "*dulia*"; it is sharply distinguished from *adoration (the cult of "*latria*"), which is due to God alone. To venerate the saints is always to praise and glorify God, since the quality of the saint which is recognized as worthy of imitation was the gift of God's grace. The "intercession" of the saints on our behalf is not to be considered a new historical initiative independent of their historical life, rather it is simply the enduring validity of their life for the world before God's countenance. The religious person easily feels misgivings about the veneration of saints because it is directed to a reality that is not the Absolute. But one should reflect that the religious *act, if it is really perfect, can also discover creatures *in* God, since the validity of creatures does not diminish but grows as one draws nearer to God. Popular piety, it is true, often regards God as no more than one reality among others and in many cases does not accept the saints as concrete models (always a kind of judgment on those who revere them) but yields to unbridled sentimentality and is impressed by religious trash; but such phenomena in Catholicism should not be thought any objection to a sensible veneration of the saints.

VICE

A technical term in theology for the sort of *habitus (operativus)* which regularly produces morally evil acts. The scholastic theology of the *habitus* teaches that vice develops through constant repetition. Thus vice is the opposite of *virtue. Depth psychology should frequently be used in judging diminished responsibility due to a weakening of the will by bad habits, for underlying vice there is also a *disposition that is not necessarily formed by guilty acts. As with the Aristotelian *cardinal virtues, there is a catalogue of capital sins whose influence, through Stoic popular philosophy, on the NT catalogue of vices is unmistakable, though the names of these latter derive from genuine Jewish tradition (for example, fornication or idol worship as metaphors for "heathen behaviour"). St Paul concludes many such catalogues with the phrase that those who (freely and deliberately, of course) do such things will not inherit the *basileia*. Here is the scriptural basis for the distinction between venial and mortal sin. This condemnation must be seen in the context of the Christian doctrine of *contrition and the conviction of the Church since her earliest days that the repentant sinner can always hope for forgiveness.

VIENNE

The Fifteenth Ecumenical Council, held in this town of southern France from October 16th, 1311, to May 6th, 1312, under Clement V, is of theological importance because it defined the passibility of Christ (declaring that the Church came from the wound in his side, D 900f.), defined the *soul as the *forma corporis* (D 902), defended *infant baptism (D 903f.) against Peter John Olivi, and repudiated the opinion of the Béguines and Beghards that man can attain supreme beatitude and the *beatific vision through his own natural powers (D 891–899).

VIOLENCE

In an initially still very "speculative" sense, violence or force is the subjective use of freedom to bring about a change in the freedom of another person without his or her free consent. Seen in these terms the use of violence cannot always and in every instance be considered as immoral, since it is indissolubly linked to the realization of freedom which seeks fulfilment and cannot always be dependent on the agreement of all. But such violence very often exists in immoral actions which reduce the scope of freedom of others and cannot therefore be seen as the personally or factually justified exercise of one's own freedom. The exact dividing line between the legitimate use of force and its immoral application is very often difficult to establish; human egotism deceives one all too frequently on this point. However, we can distinguish between the "sinful" violence of this world and the force which emanates from "almighty" God in which man may freely and responsibly participate. The history of all human civilizations and societies is replete with an enormous variety of different forms of force in the traditional sense as the use of immoral means to subjugate the will of another to achieve given aims by coercion: punishments, maltreatment, torture, murder, imprisonment, police force, kidnapping, assault and war. Each of these forms of violence (e.g., war) in turn consists of a further gruesome combination of different acts of violence (imprisonment, rape, torture, death) directed equally towards people or things. The demand for unconditional love made by Christ in the *Sermon on the Mount also calls for the renunciation of violence which destroys the existence, freedom, dignity and happiness of our fellow beings. Precisely because a Christian is exhorted to break the pernicious chain of violence and counter-violence he or she often finds himself or herself in a theoretically insoluble conflict, given that one has to function in a world where values are largely determined by force and which consequently combats any attempt to overcome it with a decisive counter-force. The almost inconceivable perfection of the means and methods of violence in the technological age and the increasing number of powers glorifying force, exploiting it commercially and politically, or rapidly and thoughtlessly treating it as inevitable renders largely invalid the traditional (abstract, not unjustified) distinction between bloody and unbloody, legal and illegal, appropriate and inappropriate uses of violence as means of ethical orientation. This is compounded by the fact that these means of force can at any moment become independent and are in a position to embroil even those who use them and to corrupt them. The fundamental problem of violence is not solved even when a Christian makes a decisive stand against glorification or self-justification of force and upholds as totally reasonable those tendencies which reject the use of force in politics and everyday life, seeking peaceful methods of bringing about political change (leaving aside the problem of self-defence and justifiable defence). According to Marx, the systematic use of violence throughout the history of mankind is itself a lamentable consequence of the existence of class antagonisms, and thus in the final analysis is caused by the stage of development of the forces and conditions of production, and is not merely due to moral recalcitrance on the part of

527

individuals. Structural antagonism postulates a primary violence which repeatedly leads to the use of instrumental violence, since no ruling (thus always "sinful") class ever voluntarily renounces the implementation of its power. The revolutionary counter-force thus compelled into existence (as is indeed the case) is consequently in a totally different category because it is based on the moral intentions of the individual. Any theological judgment of violence must take account of this distinction if it wishes to deal with the problem adequately, not limiting it to the free moral choice of the individual. When a Christian exercising revolutionary counter-violence feels himself or herself entangled in the "sins of the world", this force can, seen objectively, be considered to have been imposed on him or her, demanded of him or her by love for one's fellow beings and by one's responsibility in the face of history. But precisely through this awareness of inevitable involvement in this "sin", a Christian should be able to perceive a decisive task as the bad conscience of the revolution and help prevent it being distorted into the terrorist abuse of force.

VIRGIN BIRTH

A technical term in comparative religion for the birth of a human being as a result of union between a god and a woman; not for the appearance of a foetus in a female without the co-operation of a male (parthenogenesis: science has yet to demonstrate that this has ever occurred in a human being). The account of the birth of *Jesus Christ of the Virgin *Mary is fundamentally different from Greek mythology. Originally the fact was known only to a few people (see the opinion that Joseph was Jesus' father in Mt 13:55 and Lk 3:23). It is contained in the infancy narratives (Mt 1:18–25; Lk 1:26 –38), which are not dependent on each other and were composed with different ends in view, one to show the fulfilment of Jewish messianic hopes (Luke) and the other the Davidic descent of Jesus (Matthew). A comparison of the sources reveals that the Virgin Birth must not be regarded as an isolated biographical detail or a private miracle. Rather what is primarily recorded is Jesus' dignity as the Son of David, the Messiah, the Son of God, of which the Virgin Birth is a consequence (*Virginity, *Mary). The Virgin Birth does not mean that Jesus was half God and half man. The Virgin Birth teaches us in real terms that in Jesus the history of the world (not of ideas merely) recommences absolutely anew at the same time as the past is redemptively taken up. The Virgin Birth is already professed in the Apostles' Creed (D 11, 30).

VIRGINITY

As here used, virginity means neither the lack of sexual experience (a person having at no time in his life voluntarily actualized his power of generation) nor yet the unmarried state as such, but the practice of the resolution to observe permanent sexual abstinence "for the sake of the *basileia*" (Mt 19:10ff.). Virginity in the Church is an *evangelical counsel and a special manner of life derived from that counsel. The properly Christian character of this type of virginity cannot be explained by purely natural ethics. Sexual abstinence in itself is not a moral value; nor can it ultimately be justified as actively combatting *concupiscence. It did not exist before Jesus Christ. Rather the NT clearly derives it from the new economy of salvation brought about by the appearance of Christ. The ultimate meaning and validity of virginity must be sought in love, since this renunciation is a virtuous attitude adopted in view of Christian perfection and deriving its essential character from love. Consequently the renunciation of positive values and possessions, as represented by married life, must bear the hallmark of love. This happens when the very form of self-denial practised serves to represent love reaching out in hope. Only a positive call from God (*Vocation) makes virginity intelligible as signifying the displacement of a person's existence from this world; whence the connexion of virginity with *death in general and with the death of the Lord in particular is at once apparent. But also apparent is God's will that the *Church shall tangibly manifest the eschatological transcendence of the love which constitutes her interior life. This is done sacramentally in the *sacraments, existentially in renunciation. The evangelical counsels are an inalienable constituent of the form of the Church, tangibly representing and manifesting her intimate life: the love of God which eschatologically transcends the world (hence the Catholic doctrine on virginity: D 1810, 3911f.). But it also follows that the life of virginity must be given concrete form such that it can in fact clearly bear its witness in each concrete historical situation. The Latin Church imposes the celibate life on her priests and very exceptionally frees them from this obligation. This makes it necessary that the outward sign be inwardly fulfilled, lest its witness be perverted by ambition, lust for power, prudery, and resentment against life, and it requires the Church to play its part in finding adequate numbers of priests.

VIRTUE

In the broad sense any fully developed capacity of the human will or intellect (for example, in the sphere of knowledge, wisdom or science); in the strict sense, the power (competence) to accomplish moral good, especially to do so gladly and with constancy, even against opposition without and within and even at considerable sacrifice. Antonym: *vice. According to their origin, nature and goal, virtues are either natural or supernatural. Natural virtues are rooted in the psychosomatic *nature of man and are developed by constant exercise (acquired virtues; *habitus). They perfect one's natural character and are one's necessary defence against *concupiscence and domination by *instinct. The most important (basic and comprehensive) natural virtues are called the *cardinal virtues: *prudence, *justice, *fortitude, and *temperance. Since supernatural *grace (as God's *self-communication) radically orders the whole being of the human person in knowledge and *freedom to the triune God of eternal life, thus enabling him to tend towards this goal—through acts that have been elevated by grace—by accepting this self-communication, we speak of supernatural ("infused") virtues, that is, virtues bestowed by God in *justification as the dynamism of *sanctifying grace. They order man's moral and religious acts to direct participation in the life of the triune God. Scripture (1 Cor 13:13) and Tradition (D 1530f.) single out three such supernatural virtues as "theological"—divine—because they are directly ordered to God as he is in himself: *faith, *hope and *love. In and through them God in his self-communication effects both the capacity for and actual participation in the life of God himself, so freeing human *transcendence in its loving and obedient acceptance of revelation, so suffusing it with divine meaning, that it is no longer the mere preconditon for intellectual knowledge of finite being but is able as such to find its own fulfilment in the possession and *beatific vision of God in himself.

VOCATION

The recognition by an individual that a particular career (mode of life) corresponds to God's permissive or jussive will for him and is the life's work in which he can gain his eternal salvation. To this extent any career, even one that is disliked, can be a vocation, since one may have a duty to do what one finds difficult. A vocation means in particular, but not exclusively, a call to the priesthood or the religious life. This is presumed where a person has the intellectual and moral qualities appropriate to such a state of life and has chosen it for the right (disinterested and religious) motives, and the Church is prepared to accept the services he would offer in her and for her in this state. The further discussion of vocation merges into that of the knowledge of particular obligations, as distinguished from knowledge of the general norms that limit the field of what is right in particular cases but cannot clearly define it. It is the problem of "individual ethics" (*Existential ethics).

VOTUM

Theology speaks of a desire for the Church, baptism (D 1524) or some other sacrament (for example, penance: D 1542f.) in order to explain how a person can be justified, live in God's grace, and gain eternal life without visibly belonging to the Church, in the case of the unbaptized, or receiving a sacrament which of itself is necessary for salvation. A serious and steadfast desire for the Church and the sacrament, aroused and sustained by grace, takes the place of membership of the Church (as the *primordial sacrament) or of reception of the sacrament. This desire may be only implicit in the general readiness to whatever God wills according to the voice of conscience, and therefore does not necessarily require an explicit knowledge of the Church and the sacraments (D 3870ff.). This possibility of pre-sacramental (pre-ecclesiological) salvation does not mean that justification and salvation are obtained in two independent ways. The grace at work in the *votum* is Christ's grace, "incarnational" grace; it too seeks to embody itself in concrete, spatio-temporal, social form in *membership of the Church and in the *sacraments, though being the cause of the latter it precedes them. We are dealing with two phases of a single process of salvation. Even though the first phase can save a man if through no fault of his own he goes no further in this life, yet it imposes on him the objective duty of leaving it behind, to enter the concrete, ecclesial phase. Were he consciously and culpably to neglect this duty, he would destroy the first phase itself.—See also *Necessity for Salvation, Baptism of Desire.*

VULGATE

See *Holy Scripture.*

W

WAY

Since man is a being subject to growth, the Christian's ability and duty to develop religiously, by the *grace of God, until he reaches his final perfection in the *beatific vision (*Heaven, *Beatitude) can be described under the image of a Way (Acts 9:2); the necessity, growth, direction of the Christian way of life—the manner in which we "walk" —are so described. Insofar as any set manner of life can be thought of as a "way" or "course" of life, we may speak of two "ways", the good and the evil, the narrow and the broad (Mt 7:13f.). Since Jesus Christ is the foundation, strength and goal of the Christian's life, which consists in the *following of Christ, he is the Way absolutely (Jn 14:6).

WILL

Will belongs to the primordial data of the experience whereby man possesses himself, and it therefore can only be "defined" by oblique descriptive reference to this experience. Man is not simply "present to himself", accepting this experience in pure passivity. He actively goes forth to meet it and thus experiences cognition itself as activity. Always and necessarily he experiences cognition as will too, and thus will as the drive of cognition to realize itself, its active moment. At the same time the object of cognition, being thus willed, is experienced as a value (*Good), so that cognition is experienced as the clarity of will, its luminous moment. This shows that cognition and will, despite their reciprocal interplay, cannot be regarded as simply two moments of one and the same basic actualization of the finite spiritual person. Neither one of these two basic actualizations can be reduced to the

532

other, and only together do they form the self-actualization of the spirit, as there are likewise two "processions" in the Blessed Trinity; cognition is not simply the light of love and will is not simply the impulse to knowledge—it is love. Thus in its own way the spiritual will has the same *transcendence as the mind (*Spirit) and its knowledge; as love it is ordered to good as such, unbounded by the intrinsic finitude of its own horizon, and therefore it is *freedom: transcendence to absolute good which lovingly apprehends a finite good, or one presented in finite guise, as one that is not necessary, and so does not compel the will.

WILL OF GOD

Since every being, by a transcendental necessity, possesses as an intrinsic element of itself what we experience in the most various ways and degrees as the will to existence, self-assertion, ordination to good, love, etc., we must by *analogy predicate will of the absolute (yet personal) Being whom we call God. Given the simplicity of God, this will is identical with himself—absolute, infinite, eternal, an infinite plenitude of being (D 3002) and therefore of good. Its primary object (in the processions of the life of the Trinity) is God's infinite being, and therefore it is independent of any being that is not God, and in affirming this holy being of God is itself holy. With respect to the creation of finite being, different from itself, it is free (D 3025). Its supreme operation *ad extra* is the divine self-communication to creatures, which shows this will to be absolute *love and thus embraces all the ordinations of God's will which we do not understand. See *Fate, Prayer of Petition.* As to how God's will can be known, see *Revelation, Existential Ethics.*

WISDOM

In the religious sense, apart from the application of the name to the *Logos, or in Gnosticism to a hypostatized cosmic power under God, wisdom means, not a comparatively more analytical knowledge of particular beings as such but a basic ordering of man's morally ratified knowledge whereby he sees all that he knows within the larger whole of God's creation, as deriving from God and ordered to him, thus accepting the necessary transcendence of his spirit by a moral decision as well and giving ever more effect to it in his particular knowledge.

WORD

Insofar as this is an effect of justifying grace and one's knowledge is ordered to the God of eternal life and his self-communication, wisdom also counts as one of the seven "gifts of the Holy Ghost".

WORD

Primarily the phonetic "utterance" of an intellectual concept (as distinct from mere animal noises) or of some piece of knowledge, and secondarily this intellectual and imaginative knowledge itself, the "interior word". Since the *transcendence of the mind and our ability to acquire an analogical knowledge of being by systematic negation make it possible for us to understand and express in words things that have no immediate objective presence in our external or internal experience, it is above all through the "word" that God makes himself objectively (though "analogically") present to us in himself and in his sovereign decrees—as distinct, for example, from a mere mood, music, etc. Christian *revelation and *theology, as the objective and communicable enunciation of God's being and free purposes, neither of which can be manifestly registered by the world, come into being and exist historically in words, especially in view of their social character. *Sacraments too are formally constituted by words.

WORD OF GOD

This expression, in its primordial sense so far as the reality is concerned and in its most derivative sense so far as we are concerned, means the *Logos, the second divine Person of the *Trinity. The Logos is the reason why and the supreme, unique, absolute proof that being can be expressed, be made other yet retained, as its own "assertion", "image", "word", the fruit of its intellectual self-possession, and is not imprisoned in a dull identity. The "verbal" character (intelligibility, luminosity, self-transparence) for itself and others of every being therefore, always according to the analogically diverse degree at which the being concerned exists, derives from the Word of God. And it is the divine Word which ultimately enables God to give utterance to himself (*Self-communication of God, *Grace, *Beatific vision, *Revelation). When this utterance of God is given in human words, we have what is called the "word of God" simply speaking: the message of the *prophets, of *Jesus, the *Apostles, the *Church, the word of God in *Holy Scripture. The nature of the human word

534

is such that it has the *potentia obedientialis* to be the word of God—without in any way diminishing the word of God or reducing it to an essentially human word—while remaining subject to the *a priori* conditions of human knowledge. God makes it his word, and uses it as such, in three ways: (1) By his charismatic influence in the prophet he so shapes the word that it expresses everything God wishes to say to man (at least analogically), because the *analogy of being means that the human word, being the word of the mind, is subject to no intrinsic limitations, such as would place certain realities forever beyond its horizon. (2) The human word is attended by *grace, so that the act of hearing it in faith, being sustained by grace, that is, ultimately by God himself, does not imprison this objective word within the purely human *a priori* scope of knowledge, does not make it a merely human word. (3) Consequently it is an "exhibitive", efficacious word (most radically so in the *sacraments), because in the grace that attends it the very thing signified becomes present and is communicated.

WORK

All actions and achievements, both physical and mental, executed by man to ensure the practical needs of physical existence and the required conditions for its continuation. Theologians began very early on to contrast work as a creative activity desired by God by which man appropriated the world to provide his livelihood (Gen 1:28) with the concept of work as something joyless, compulsory and distressing (Gen 3:17–18). The obstinacy of human *Nature towards applying itself purposefully to this task (on both a mental and a practical level) is attributed to man's disturbed relationship to the God who created him (*Original sin). Despite the stark contrast drawn between the idea of work as something pleasurable and the tedious reality of carrying it out, the Judaeo-Christian tradition departed radically from the concept of the ancient world according to which physical labour was seen as something shameful. On the contrary, work was classified as man's basic communal duty (2 Thess 3:10). However, the danger was also foreseen that if man is too much absorbed by his work he will become alienated from himself and from God. Thus work is always seen as relative to man's need for self-realization, which is why it is granted such a limited value in the Bible (Ex 20:10; Mt 6:23).

In the face of the ever more apparent contradiction between paid labour and capital, theology must give thought to the difference between alienated and non-alienated work under such conditions. It should criticize this situation as repugnant to God, and demand the abolition of any factor which prevents the true image of the Creator being reflected in working people.

WORKS

Given man's bodily, earthly, and dialogical nature, he must always embody the free acts by which he directs and conducts his life, in "objectifications". It is only in these that the "mentality" of the person, his basic attitude, on which of course everything ultimately depends, can be properly realized. In the light of the transcendental structures of existence, we see that a basic attitude only comes into being when it realizes itself in something else as its real *symbol, in some "work"; and again, because only in this way can man "get outside himself ", which is the only way he has of truly finding himself. Any such objectification or work is of course dangerous: it is not identical with the person's basic attitude (a Christian one, say, of loving faith), though necessary to the latter, and so man can do even these works without their being the expression and exercise of his real and complete faith (that is of the unconditional surrender of man to God: Jas 2:17). Indeed works may be the means whereby man seeks to justify himself before God (Mt 23:1ff.): works are done so that the heart can be refused, works are done but not accepted as the gift of God's grace which they are. This is the false justice of works. All this applies to man's own self-realization insofar as he is ordered by grace to a supernatural end. Keeping God's *commandments, whose imperatives are the objective expression of man's own nature and his supernatural *existential, is the quintessence of the "works" of a Christian when they are performed by God's grace in faith, hope and love (Mt 5:16; Rom 2:6f.; 2 Cor 9:8; Col 1:10; 2 Thess 2:17; 1 Pet 1:17 and *passim)*. What we have said is especially true of *love of our neighbour; if it is genuine and inspired by God's grace, God himself at least implicitly is truly loved. For the rest, what has been said of *merit is also applicable to "works".

WORLD

Theology uses this term firstly in a neutral sense to mean the unity of all *creation, in the common origin, fate and goal of creatures, their

536

common structures, their mutual dependence, either including man or distinguished from him as his "environment", as the antecedent situation God has chosen for man's saving history. In this sense "world" means the same thing as "heaven and earth"; it is a *revelation of God, it glorifies him, it is good, meaningful, and beautiful, it is the recipient of God's self-communication which he has freely and lovingly created (Jn 3:16f.; D 800, 3025; Church). It does not separate man from God but mediates between God and man, as is most clearly brought out in the Incarnation. But secondly, since sin in the domain of the *angels and the sin of man from the beginning (*Original sin) and all the subsequent history of damnation have deeply marked man's world even materially with animosity towards God and its own basic structures, the world (what Scripture calls "this" world, "this" *aeon)* means all those *principalities and powers that are hostile to God, the tangible embodiment of sin in the world and everything in the world that incites to further sin. It is in this sense that the Christian is not to be "of the world" (Jn 18:36 and *passim),* though he cannot help being "in" it (Jn 17:11). But even this sinful world is an object of God's love, needs redemption yet is redeemable, is already embraced by God's grace despite and in its sin, and its history will end in the *basileia.* Hence the Christian must come to grips with it, notwithstanding its opposition to God, must uphold such true order as remains in the world in the strength of divine grace, must encourage the capacities within the world for sound development, carefully distinguishing these from its baser solicitations, and endure in *patience the burden and darkness of the world which will only cease when the end comes. This world has a history, which has entered its eschatological phase through the Incarnation, Cross and Resurrection of the eternal Word of God; that is, the issue of this history as a whole has already been decided by Jesus Christ in the heart of reality, even though that issue be still hidden from our eyes, visible only to faith. Consequently, the world (*Aeon) "to be" is already here and at work in the world that is still "present". Thus Christianity knows only a dualism of saving history which is already in process of resolution, no radical, irreconcilable *dualism between God and the world.

CHURCH AND WORLD. The new experience of the world as something that is not simply a pre-existing datum but as something planned and created by man himself which is of interest to people as people in its own empirically perceptible significance—this new awareness appears clearly in the documents of the Second Vatican Council (especially the pastoral constitution on the Church in the world of today, Church/

world). The Church is (very slowly) gaining a new and positive relationship towards the world and towards all its different aspects: towards the unity and variety of the many different Churches, towards the autonomy of the secular sciences and fields of study, towards the emergence of democracy (*democratization) and the growth and development of social structures and relationships, towards sexuality, etc. This change rests on the intellectual developments of recent times: the shift towards a more humanly-centred view of things, the exorcism of the world so as to strip it of its magical and demonic attributes and make it the raw material of human activity, the shift towards rationality and technology, reflection on man's own historical contingency, a critical attitude towards the past and towards tradition. This development derives ultimately from the spirit of Christianity even if it often rightly or wrongly attacks the Church as it is. Hence the history of the relationship of Church and world is the history of a growing self-discovery on the part of the Church accompanied by a growing willingness to let the world be in its secularity.

There are two fundamental heresies when it comes to defining the relationship between Church and world: integralism, which sees the world merely as the raw material for the Church's activity and for its presentation of itself, which aims at integrating the world into the Church, and which believes in the possibility of an adequate synthesis of the Christian and the secular under the guidance of the official Church; and an esotericism in which the secular is deemed indifferent for Christianity and for life directed towards salvation and thus for life directed towards God's absolute future—a dualism which regards *flight from the world as the genuinely Christian response.

The basis for the Church's relationship to the world is that God's acceptance of the world means its being set free in autonomy, deriving its meaning and power from itself; the world's closeness to God and its independence grow proportionately to each other and do not vary inversely. Since the acceptance of the world by God has its history (of salvation), this liberation of the world into its secularity can grow and become manifest. At the same time, under the power of *grace, this process of the world becoming secular under the mark of *sin, of *concupiscence, in unintegrated pluralism, is not a simple evolutionary process. What is Christian finds its realization in the secularity of the world; but for the Christian the secularity of the world is as immediately secularly experienced not what is Christian in such a manner that a Christian could begin to flourish freely, responsibly and with respect for the realities of history in this world experienced in this way. A Christian has to accept the world in the dimension of

538

profundity that has been established in it by God's grace and must accept its secularity as something accepted by God in Jesus Christ. The earthly task and the "heavenly" vocation thus stand to one another in a relationship of differentiation that does not abolish their unity (as against esotericism) and at the same time are one without becoming identical (as against integralism). The Church is the sacrament, i.e., the effective manifestation and sign in terms of the history of salvation and of eschatology that the *kingdom of God is being established in the unity, activity, and humanization of the world, so that here too the sign and what is signified should neither be separated nor identified with each other (cf. Church, 9, and elsewhere).

WORLD, RESPONSIBILITY FOR

Since all God's creation (*World), and therefore also the material world of nature and history, is to share in ultimate salvation (*Resurrection of the flesh, *Body), since bodily man can only really love his fellowman in the concrete, bodily world, since this is the necessary "material" for the obedience of faith to God in respect of the actual structure of all the beings that disclose its nature (*Natural moral law), man's relationship with the world cannot be confined to *flight from the world, but also involves a duty (for man in general and for the individual according to his circumstances and abilities) to help the world of nature and the world of the mind so far as possible to develop the powers within them, so that to shirk this responsibility must be considered sinful; always bearing in mind, of course, that the world's final perfection will be the work of God's grace, that all development which remains immanent is endless, that the world will never find peace and happiness within itself, and that whatever advances man may make his all-pervading mortality constantly faces him with the question of faith. How responsibility for the world and flight from the world are related in the concrete can never be finally and normatively determined. In Christianity itself this question has had a chequered history.—See also the absence or emergence of a theology of the *layman.

WORLD-VIEW

In a formal and neutral sense, any metaphysical, religious or ethical, and therefore theoretical and existential, general attitude (or the cul-

539

pable lack of one, in scepticism and positivism) towards total reality (including God). In this sense even the message of revelation and its acceptance in faith would be a world-view. But since there is an absolute, qualitative distinction between *faith, based on God's revelation and grace on the one hand, and a purely human doctrine of the world and life on the other, it is well to confine the term world-view to the latter. The question then arises how faith and world-view are related. For besides his faith the believer too has a world-view: the sum of his historically conditioned, empirical and philosophical views, explicit or unthematic, of the world, which reflect his capacity for transcendental knowledge, the effect on him of his creatureliness and historicity, his historical assumptions, his sinfulness, the fact that he is embraced by the grace of God, all in a unity that can never be wholly brought to resolution. We can only make a few very general observations about this relation, which constantly poses new tasks for man in the course of history. When one's world-view is adequate (and not ideology), it sees man as that being who is open, in his joint *transcendence and *historicity, to any ultimate divine ordination, and therefore to *revelation. And revelation obediently heard has a permanent critical function with regard to world-views. But revelation is always heard and expressed by means of a world-view. The pluralism of world-view (singular or plural) and faith—a pluralism which arises simply because of the pluralism of mutually irreducible sources of knowledge—must be patiently endured and each must remain open to the other. This pluralism can never be displaced by one absolutely monolithic system. Christian faith itself claims no such monopoly.

WORSHIP

The service of praise, *adoration, thanksgiving and petition expressly directed to God in sacred signs and inward attitude. See *Cult.*

The Church fulfils its mission not only through worship rituals, but also through the practice of a humane, Christian way of life based on memory and positive hope. The OT prophets' criticism of ritual is equally relevant to the NT concept of worship (*Liturgy).

Y

YAHWEH

In etymological or exegetical terms Yahweh is neither a proper name in the sense that it denotes an object (nominative) nor a description of a quality or relation (predicate). Rather it denotes and acknowledges with thankful praise the known source of an act of salvation whose literary explanation is undertaken in the oldest exodus story in the Bible.

The expression "I am who I am" (Exod 3:14), which one may well call a name, amounts to a brief declaration of God's salvific act towards his people and the guarantee of his unassignable presence, which is nevertheless always ready and close at hand. This phrase must be interpreted in a narrative sense, not ontologically: the episode recounted is an explication of the historically constant identity of the being it stands for and who vouches for its truth. It therefore continues to provide the basis by which, under different experiential conditions, the God of exodus is also seen from his actions to be the Liberator.